THE
SECOND ISAIAH

A NEW INTERPRETATION

BY

CHARLES CUTLER TORREY

PROFESSOR OF SEMITIC LANGUAGES
IN YALE UNIVERSITY

NEW YORK
CHARLES SCRIBNER'S SONS
1928

To
THEODOR NÖLDEKE
IN GRATITUDE AND AFFECTION

PREFACE

The discovery, or recovery, of one of the great writers of antiquity is likely to bring to light much more than the man and his work. These few who tower above the field, looking like isolated landmarks, are in fact widely and deeply connected. Each is in some true sense the characteristic product of his place and time and an index of the progress made by his people. Even that special creation, a great poet, arises where the way has been prepared for him; and he also—no less than the others, perhaps even more distinctly than they—marks the beginning of a new era. As the immediate achievement of such an individual is more clearly seen and understood, the wider influence exerted by his writings becomes gradually apparent. We revise some estimates of racial or national culture and of the origin and meaning of certain significant modes of thought. Chapters of history, hitherto obscure, may be illumined.

The fifth century B. C. saw great progress, in the lands of the eastern Mediterranean, and Palestine shared in the intellectual awakening; far more, probably, than we have been wont to suppose. The people of Jerusalem and Judea were at that time the principal custodians of a religious tradition unparalleled in ancient history. Several factors had combined to give them this share of the inheritance: foreign deportation and colonization in Northern and Central Palestine; extensive Hebrew emigration, especially from the seventh century onward; and the great prestige of the southern capital, soon restored after its partial demolition by the armies of Nebuchadrezzar.

In this Judean environment, in the days of the Persian and Seleucid rule, were produced not a few masterpieces of religious literature, and one of the earlier of these far surpassed its fellows. A Hebrew poet wrote of the Coming Age, of the plan of the One God in the unfolding of human history, and of the divine fatherly care embracing not merely a chosen people but a brotherhood of all the tribes of the earth. We see here, for the first time in the world's literature, a highly developed religious philosophy filled with the warmth of a universal sympathy; a new and profound creation made possible by the close contact of many races and modes of thought, but most of all by the steady advance and enrichment of the Hebrew faith.

In this instance, notably, the prophet was not without honor in his own country. No Hebrew writer made a deeper and more lasting impression on the literature and life of his people. Yet it was by the hand of one (or a consensus) of his compatriots that his work was later given a false interpretation, mischievous from the first and utterly mislead'ng to modern readers.

Habent sua fata libelli. History can show no more tragic illustration of this dictum than the one here demonstrated. The "captus lectoris" was not the mere harmless notion of a reader, but the ground of a significant alteration of the Hebrew text. In the interest of a theory, and in defense of Jewish prerogatives which were challenged and in danger, the little volume of great poems was marked as a work of 'the Babylonian exile.' This was done very simply, by inserting two words (the same two) in three different contexts, and by retouching one conspicuous passage, the promise of a great captain and deliverer, in such a way as to make it unmistakably a prediction of Cyrus. This insuring of the interpretation was doubtless made in good faith, perhaps with official sanction. It had two inevitable results: to transform the sublime poetry of a seer into a somewhat bizarre fantasia on current events; and to disintegrate the book for careful readers, for only a small part of it could be forced into the historical framework created by the interpolations. Thus it came to pass that the meaning and caliber of the work and the genius of its author were obscured, in ever-increasing degree, from the middle of the third century B. C. to the present day.

When the series of twenty-seven poems is seen in its true character, and the details are studied, new light is thrown on many important matters. The relation of the garbled prophecy to the fiction of a 'Return from the Babylonian Exile' is relatively of very small consequence; the weightiest questions of Jewish religious history are bound up with the problem of this little book. Facts and relations which could not have been established, nor even suspected, from study of the heterogeneous fragments hitherto recognized are rendered certain when the unity of the work is seen. By good fortune the literary evidence is singularly clear, many-sided, and conclusive. It is set forth in sufficient detail, though by no means exhaustively, in Chapter XI. There is no longer any possibility of maintaining a theory of composite authorship of the poems which constitute chapters 34, 35, 40–66 of the Book of Isaiah.

The work thus restored gives the Bible a new aspect. The

splendid progress of the religion of Israel in its golden age—the Persian period—is now revealed. We see its catholicity at the hands of its best exponents, and at the same time the widening sympathy of the masses of the Jewish people with their foreign neighbors and the growing popular interest, easily carried too far, in their rites and beliefs. We have for the first time the true key to the interpretation of the Later Prophets. The meaning of figures of speech and modes of expression which had been ambiguous is now apparent. Our nameless prophet is the central force in Hebrew thought from his day onward, and the influence of his work is plainly marked in all directions. In the writings of one and another of his great successors we recognize expressions to which he had given currency, and ideas which we know him to have originated; for instance, the glowing Messianic predictions in Is. 9 and 11 were certainly inspired by him, and direct dependence appears in one of the two passages.

In general, when full account has been taken of the literary relations, in either direction, of this central work, we shall find ourselves to have made great gain toward the shaping of a literary history which had been well-nigh shapeless. Of capital importance in particular are the questions concerning the direct and indirect influence of this 'prophecy' on the founder of Christianity and on the conceptions cherished and proclaimed by his first disciples. There is here opportunity for fresh study, and for the revision of opinions now generally held, both as to the history of the fully developed Messianic doctrine and also as to its traditional content, which was religious, not political.

Still another gain is in a truer estimate of the range and quality of Hebrew poetry. In the one consummate example can be seen the ideals of the art. Turning to the Psalter, there is now new light not only on the religious content, the breadth of view, and the pervasive Messianic element, but also on the purely lyric, idealistic quality of these noble hymns. They are as distinctly raised in our estimation as are the utterances of the prophets, through their reference to the standards set for us by the one masterpiece whose excellencies are supreme and transparent. No description or analysis, indeed, can do justice to the latter. In the soundness and scope of its religious philosophy it stands alone in the literature of the ancient world, while in the wealth of its formal beauties it is unapproached by any other Hebrew writing. Sweeping comparisons are generally of little value, when the attempt is made to put side by side literary compositions of very diverse nature and extent; nevertheless there is good ground for pronouncing this suite of twenty-seven lyrics the greatest single poetical work of any age.

There are famous utopias in the world's literature, and they have played their important part in arousing and inspiring men. The work of our poet-prophet belongs only partially in this class, for it deals mainly with the preliminaries, the end of the old order and the dawn of the new. Always present, however, whether in the dim background or brought forward in bright colors, is the picture of a better world; with a gloriously renovated Zion, worship of One God throughout the earth, peace and kindliness among men, and everywhere the just rule inaugurated by the Anointed of the Lord. The prophet does not concern himself with the restoration of the Hebrew kingdom, appears not to think at all of a Jewish state. He has neither political nor social program to recommend, no form of worship to prescribe as essential. There is nothing to indicate that he has attempted to visualize the actual régime of the Messiah. He writes as a fervently loyal Israelite and in the traditional formulas, it is needless to say, but his doctrine is not limited, nor his humanity. What he heralds is the triumph of pure religion, meaning just those few things which the prophet Micah and the apostle James declare to be the essentials. He knew well that only this, nothing more nor less, could make common ground for all men. The 'saved remnants of the nations,' led by a repentant and purified Israel, *must* come together here.

In Plato's *Republic*, at the close of the ninth book, Glaucon looks back over the magnificent picture of a political and social order which has been unfolded, and refers, a little wistfully, to "this city of which we are the founders and which exists in idea only." His master replies in these noble words (Jowett's translation): "In heaven there is laid up a pattern of it, methinks, which he who desires may behold, and beholding, may set his house in order. But whether such an one exists, or ever will exist in fact, is no matter; for he will live after the manner of that city, having nothing to do with any other." The Hebrew sage could not thus have rested in the ideal, his utopia must be realized. The God who had cleft the Red Sea and led his people through the desert has now declared himself the Father of all mankind, and promises a rescue reaching to the ends of the earth. Sin and unbelief hold back the hour, but it is sure to come. "I, the Lord, will hasten it in its time."

CONTENTS

xi

CONTENTS

THE SECOND ISAIAH

PART I

LITERARY AND CRITICAL ESSAYS

CHAPTER I

THE ECLIPSE OF A GREAT PROPHET*

1. *The Former View of 'the Second Isaiah'*

It is not easy to say, at present, what the term 'Second Isaiah' means. Fifty years ago the question would have been answered with little hesitation. The Book of Isaiah was then generally recognized as consisting of two distinct parts: the first, including the first thirty-nine chapters, written chiefly by Isaiah the son of Amoz; and the second, consisting of chapters 40–66, an appended prophecy of much later date, whose author was conveniently termed 'the Second Isaiah.' †

This second division was recognized as homogeneous. The more elaborate treatises and text-books of the past generation contained lists of words, phrases, and recurrent ideas which seemed to make it evident that one author wrote the whole block of twenty-seven chapters. The argument from style and subject-matter, in fact, seemed unusually strong in this case, and few doubted its validity. Thus the excellent *Einleitung in die Bücher des A. T.* of De Wette-Schrader (1869) declares it to be unmistakably (unverkennbar) the case, that the whole second part is the work of a single author, exhibiting everywhere the same spirit, leading ideas, and literary style (p. 414). He adds a concise list of the most striking items of evidence. In Driver's *Introduction to the Literature of the Old Testament*, second edition, 1892, space is given in pp. 225–228 to peculiarities of diction and style, and other literary features of the 'exilic' prophecy, collected chiefly with the purpose of distinguishing "the author of chapters 40–66" from Isaiah the son of Amoz, but also testifying to the literary unity of these chapters. Many other scholars might be quoted to the same effect; but it will suffice to refer, for evidence of the *literary* homogeneity of chapters 40–66, to the astonishing list of peculiarities of grammar, diction,

* This chapter and Chapter III, in abridged form, were read before the Society of Biblical Literature and Exegesis in New York City, December 28, 1901.

† This term is to be preferred to the prevalent 'Deutero-Isaiah,' inasmuch as the prophecy belongs to the man in the street quite as truly as to the scholar in his study. The greater public will derive no advantage from the strange and cumbersome Greek word, and the learned man can dispense with it.

3

and phraseology presented in pp. 255–270 of Cheyne's *Introduction to the Book of Isaiah;* a partial collection of the evidence which in former years had convinced scholars that they had before them the work of a single writer, but more recently has been accounted for in another way, as will presently appear.

The date, scene, and immediate occasion of this prophecy, moreover, were given with a definiteness which left nothing to be desired. The Persian king, Cyrus, is twice mentioned by name, in two adjoining verses, 44 : 28 and 45 : 1, and seems to be described as beginning, or about to begin, his career. There is repeated prediction, all the way from chapter 40 to chapter 66, that Jewish 'exiles' and 'captives' will be set free, and that there will be a glorious restoration of Jerusalem and the holy land. Accordingly, the scene of the prophecy was recognized as Babylonia, and the date as about 540 B. C. The prophet's mission was to comfort and inspire the Jews of the Babylonian exile, and to predict their release by Cyrus, and the 'restoration' of Judea and Jerusalem, which had been unoccupied since the sack of the city and the destruction of Solomon's temple by the armies of Nebuchadrezzar.

The general estimate of the 'book,' in the day of this simple theory, was high; it was called the Great Prophecy of Comfort, and was regarded as a fine specimen of Hebrew literature and a unique product of imaginative prediction, though distinctly inferior, after all, to the work of 'the genuine Isaiah'; see, for example, De Wette-Schrader (cited above), p. 425. During recent years, however, it has been subjected to a more thorough scrutiny, and—what is even more important—the contemporary history has been critically studied; in particular, the Chronicler's history of Israel, with its central representation of the depopulation of Judea and the restoration from Babylonia, has been estimated more nearly at its true value. The result has been to make a great change, in successive stages, in the critical view of the Second Isaiah, affecting the extent and form, and therefore of necessity the general estimate, of the prophecy. In the hands of those scholars who now hold the foremost place in the interpretation of Isaiah, the series of chapters beginning with 40 and ending with 66 has become an indescribable chaos. The once great 'Prophet of the Exile' has dwindled to a very small figure, and is all but buried in a mass of jumbled fragments. The valuation of his prophecy has fallen accordingly; partly because a brief outburst, with a narrow range of themes, can never make a like impression with a sustained effort covering a variety of subjects; and partly because the same considerations which governed the analysis of the book have necessitated a lower estimate of each of its parts.

2. *The Disintegration of the Prophecy*

The theory of the exilic origin of Is. 40–66, which is one of the oldest theories in the history of Biblical criticism,* began to receive important modification before the end of the eighteenth century, namely in the qualification that *not all of the prophecy was written in Babylonia;* and this significant revision of the older theory received the support of a steadily increasing number of scholars.† It is indeed plain to see that numerous passages, especially in the latter part of the book, point to Palestine as the land of their authorship. The chapters thus marked by Biblical experts as Palestinian include, first or last, the whole series 49–66.‡

There were various small beginnings. It was recognized at an early date that chapters 65 and 66 bear marks of a Palestinian origin. This was not at first felt, however, to imply diversity of authorship, nor even a wide interval of time; it merely was supposed that the prophet had continued to deliver his message after the migration from Babylonia to Judea. As late as 1889, Cheyne (*Prophecies of Isaiah*, II, 114) held chapters 65 f. to be Palestinian, while regarding 64 as Babylonian and the work of the same hand. A few, like Bredenkamp (see G. A. Smith's *Book of Isaiah*, 1893, II, 457, note), were so strongly influenced by the current theory of 'the post-exilic community' that they assigned these two chapters to a pre-exilic writer, in spite of all the evidence seeming to give them close connection with the preceding prophecies. Chapters 63–66 were oftenest named (by Ewald, Bleek, and many later scholars) as constituting a Palestinian stratum, the fruit of Second Isaiah's ministration in the homeland; others joined to these a part or all of chapters 54–62. More recently a considerable number of influential scholars, among them Cornill (*Einleitung*, 1891) and Wildeboer (*Letterkunde*, 1893), held that all the book from chapter 49 on must have been composed in Judea, though the pre-

---

* See Cheyne's *Introduction*, p. 239.

† Cheyne, *ibid.*, pp. 284 ff.; Driver, *Introd.*⁶, pp. 244 f.

‡ It is not possible to give here any extended account of the process of disintegration, or to mention a tithe of the names of those who have had an important part in this work of historical and literary criticism. The most of those whose names are cited, moreover, held different opinions at different times, as their publications show. I can only indicate some of the principal steps in the process.

vailing opinion was that it was written (mostly or wholly) by the
same hand which had written 40–48 in Babylonia.

The next step was inevitable. The fact began to be appreciated
that certain of these 'Palestinian' portions of the prophecy cannot
even have been written in the same generation with the return
from the Babylonian captivity. Both the circumstances indicated
and the tone of the utterances are removed by a wide interval
from those of any 'prophet of the exile.' That is, the hypothesis of
two or more authors became necessary. Stade, in his *Geschichte des
Volkes Israel* (1887), and Kuenen, in his *Godsdienst van Israël*
(Part II, 1889), were the principal leaders in giving the discussion
this ominous turn. The former found the work of later hands in
chapters 59 (possibly) and 63–66*; the latter designated as Palestinian chapters 50, 51, and 54–66, and regarded the greater part
of this as the work of writers who belonged to the generation following the Second Isaiah; writers who formed a 'school' founded
by that prophet, and wrote in imitation of him.

Stade was immediately followed by some of the foremost Old
Testament scholars, among them Cornill and Wildeboer (in the
works above mentioned). Thus it soon became an accepted feature of the advanced critical treatment of Second Isaiah to mark
at least a portion of the last few chapters of the book, and especially the greater part of chapters 65 and 66, as the addition of a
later hand. Cornill's conclusion, pp. 151 f., is fairly representative
of the stage of criticism reached at that time: It seems impossible
to discover either essential unity or definite historical background
in chapters 63–66; there are indeed many and important points of
contact with 40–62, nevertheless the excision must be made; "es
wird bei dem Ausspruche Stade's sein Bewenden haben müssen,
dass 63–66 'wenigstens in seiner jetzigen Gestalt nicht vom Verfasser dieser hergeleitet werden' kann."

This decision required not a little courage; for these chapters
are by no means and in no respect out of keeping with their surroundings, but merely out of keeping with the current theory as
to those surroundings. Diction, style, characteristic figures of
speech, the modes of thought and the underlying conceptions of
things human and divine—all these are just the same in 65 and
66 as in the immediately preceding chapters, just the same in
63 : 7–64 : 11 as in 61 : 1–63 : 6. But the manifest remoteness from
a generation of 'returned Babylonian exiles' weighed more heavily
than all the considerations of style and diction, and the consensus

* *Geschichte*, p. 70, note; p. 81, note.

of the best Biblical scholarship saw no way of avoiding the step. The undisputed 'Second Isaiah' now consisted of twenty-three chapters, 40–62.

Only a short time after this first curtailment of Second Isaiah, a much larger piece was cut off. Duhm's Commentary, *Das Buch Jesaia* (1892), assigned to the 'Unknown Prophet of the Exile' only chapters 40–55, thus reducing his book from twenty-three to sixteen chapters. Duhm argued, more forcibly and consistently than Kuenen, that the situation in 56–66 is not at all the exile, nor the 'exilic' period in general. Wherever these chapters may have been written, they certainly were not written in Babylonia. More than this, they date from a time when the temple at Jerusalem had long been built and the worship well established, when the Jews had for generations been in possession of their land. To the collection of writings contained in 56–66 and appended to the prophecies of 'Deutero-Isaiah' he gave the name 'Trito-Isaiah,' a designation which found speedy acceptance among scholars, and was ultimately adopted by the great majority of those who dealt in a thoroughgoing manner with the problems of the book.

There is certainly excellent reason why even conservative scholars, such as George Adam Smith (in the article 'Isaiah' in the Hastings *Dictionary of the Bible*), should feel compelled to pronounce Duhm's main argument conclusive. It is indeed quite plain that no sound exegesis can maintain that chapters 56–66 were written in Babylonia, or that they were addressed either to exiles in that land or to a generation which had experienced a 'restoration.' Whether a sound exegesis could maintain these things in regard to chapters 40–55, or to any portion of them, is a question that will be discussed presently.

If the first drastic application of the knife, by Stade, had required courage, this second excision, by Duhm, required far more. The basis of comparison afforded by two or three chapters is much less satisfactory than that given by eleven. In the present case, the result of the comparison of the excised half with the remainder (the two portions being of almost equal extent) is sufficiently interesting. It may fairly be illustrated in the following way. Take, from the works of any ancient or modern writer, whether poet, philosopher, or essayist, a section of about the extent of Is. 40–55; and then, from the same writer, another section of the extent of Is. 56–66. Making due allowance for changes in subject-matter, I venture to assert that in no case will the signs of unity of authorship be more plainly marked, or more evenly distributed, than is the case when 'Deutero-Isaiah' and 'Trito-Isaiah' are compared. The two sections are pieces out of the very same homogeneous block. Taking into account the difference in subject-matter, there is no kind or degree of literary resemblance closer than what we have here.

The salient features of this close resemblance of the one 'book' to the other could be neither denied nor ignored. As was remarked by De Wette-Schrader (quoted above), the evidence of literary unity is "unmistakable." Every one sees it. But if chapters 40–55 were written in Babylonia in the sixth century, it is impossible to suppose unity of authorship of the whole 'book' (40–66), seeing that chapters 56–66 were certainly written in Palestine at a considerably later date. It seemed necessary to adjust the facts in some way to the current theory, since the latter seemed unassailable. Accordingly, the resemblance was pronounced superficial; and, indeed, on the supposition that the Second Isaiah was a prophet of the restoration under Cyrus, the deeper and more vital unity of these two adjoining portions of the book could not have been seen. There appeared to be but one possible explanation of the literary phenomena, namely, that *Trito-Isaiah' was composed in imitation of 'Deutero-Isaiah';* and this is the theory with which exegetes and investigators of the advanced school have satisfied themselves.

Observe that the incongruity lies only in the historical situation demanded for chapters 40 ff.; demanded, that is, by the single verse 44 : 28* and the word *lĕ-Kōresh*,† "to Cyrus," in 45 : 1; for, aside from this one spot in the prophecy, there is nowhere anything to indicate a historical background different from that which is required for chapters 56 ff. The prophet presents, in the same forms of speech and in the same spirit, the identical themes in 56–66 which constituted his message in 40–55, as will be shown in a subsequent chapter.

It is to be remarked, moreover, that the grounds on which 56–66 are now separated from Second Isaiah are essentially the same as those on which chapters 63–66 were formerly set apart. At first incompatibility with the theory of the 'exilic prophecy' was strongly felt only in these few concluding chapters; then it was seen that the same incompatibility existed in the case of the eight or nine chapters preceding.

* The greater part of this verse is commonly recognized at present as interpolated; see below.

† This word is metrically superfluous and disturbing to the verse, as will presently be shown.

The theory of one or more *imitators* (some would prefer to speak of a 'school' of imitators) has therefore been adopted. There was an attempt, we are told—an attempt not altogether unsuccessful in its superficial features—to compose discourses patterned after the poems of the Second Isaiah. Men of a later generation, deficient in originality and with various minor messages, added their compositions to the work of the older writer, either as appendages or as insertions. According to Duhm, who is followed by Marti and numerous other scholars, chapters 56–66 are substantially the work of a single author. Steuernagel (*Einleitung in das A. T.*, 525–531) gives a list of the principal investigators of 'Trito-Isaiah,' remarking that the most of them do not follow Duhm in his recognition of a literary unit, but rather regard these chapters as containing a collection of compositions—or fragments—from different hands: "Tritojesaja gilt ihnen nur als eine Kollektivbezeichnung für eine Sammlung verwandter Stücke aus annähernd gleicher Zeit, nämlich dem ersten Jahrhundert nach dem Exil."* Duhm himself, as we shall see, regards the so-called 'Servant poems,' which he and others have thought it possible to discover in chapters 40–55, as imitated from Second Isaiah. In any case, then, Isaiah 40–66 is believed by the leading exponents of the modern critical school to consist, in more than half of its extent, of the work of imitators.

This intrinsically improbable theory has some very suspicious features. Foremost among them is the necessity of supposing that these 'imitators' were men of such splendid genius. The chapters 'they' have written, if only they are given the broad instead of the narrow interpretation, if they are understood as composed in the spirit of 42 : 1–9; 43 : 23 ff.; 45 : 14–17, 22–25; 48 : 3–11, are as fine as anything commonly ascribed to the Second Isaiah himself. The poem 56 : 9–57 : 21 is one of the boldest and most vigorous pieces of writing in all Hebrew prophecy. Only a great man—and

---

* See, for example, the extended discussion of this matter by Rudolf Abramowski, in an article entitled "Zum literarischen Problem des Tritojesaja," in the *Theol. Studien und Kritiken*, 1925, pp. 90–143. He concludes (p. 137): "Tiefgehende Differenzen in Stil und Situation machten es von vornherein unwahrscheinlich, dass die Duhmsche Hypothese aufrecht erhalten werden könne. Auch hat sich die Annahme mehrerer Verfasser durchaus bewährt." In like manner Jacques Marty, *Les Chapitres 56–66 du Livre d'Esaïe* (1924), presents an array of evidence to show that these chapters must be assigned to several different authors and dates. Moses Buttenwieser, at the end of his interesting article on the home of Deutero-Isaiah, in the *J. B. L.*, vol. 38 (1919), pp. 94–112, insists on the assured fact "that chaps. 56–66 are a composite work, comprising the products of various authors and even of different times."

one consciously great—could have produced it. The five chapters 60–64 are a series of cut gems, equal to any five chapters in the earlier part of the book. No grander poetry than 63:1–64:11 was ever written, in any language. 66:1–24 is a characteristic outburst of the widest-hearted seer of the Old Testament, one who was conscious of his own power but still more of the power of God; who had a sympathetic and hopeful outlook upon the nations of the world; whose heart was full of tender affection when he thought of Jerusalem, or of the tragedy of downtrodden Israel, but full of scorching indignation when he turned his eyes toward the multitude of the 'chosen people' all about him, in their unbelief, moral turpitude, and apostate adoption of heathen cults. In like manner the people had been scored for their idolatry in chapters 40 ff., called 'stubborn of heart and far from righteousness' in 46:12, told in 48:2 that they had no right to call themselves sons of Jacob, and in 50:11 that they were travelling straight toward the fire of Gehenna! Neither in denunciation, nor in promise, nor in logical grasp, nor in flight of poetic imagination does the work of the supposed 'Third Isaiah' fall below that of his supposed predecessor. The qualities, striking and well defined, which make chapters 56–66 great, are the very same qualities—precisely those and no other—which constitute the greatness of the Second Isaiah.

The presence here of great poetry is of course unrecognized, however, by those who find themselves compelled to postulate a Trito-Isaianic group of compositions, with their minor local and temporary interests and their pervasive lack of originality. Men do not gather figs from thistles. It is strange, nevertheless, that the evidence of *one* strongly marked personality—peculiar in literary craftsmanship and unique in depth of thought—should not have forced scholars, even in the face of strong prepossessions, to turn their critical attention to the other end of the 'book,' examining afresh the foundation of the traditional view of chapters 40 ff.

But even the sixteen chapters assigned by Duhm and the modern school to Second Isaiah are by many pronounced composite, and in part the work of other hands. There are a number of striking passages, within the limits of chapters 40–55, in which the writer speaks of a 'Servant of Yahwè,' the instrument of God's will and the mouthpiece of his word, whose work will usher in the age of righteousness and peace. These passages, which are among the finest in the book, have been for some time past quite generally assigned to another writer than Second Isaiah. They are not in any external way separate from the rest of the prophecy, it is true; it would not be possible to speak of 'lines of cleavage' here. Each 'Servant chapter' is woven out of the self-same material as the rest of the book, and even the pattern suggests Second Isaiah with every line and figure. Each briefer 'Servant passage' is part and parcel of the chapter in which it stands; scholars cannot always even agree as to where it begins and ends. But the troublesome factor, inevitably suggesting the hypothesis of diverse authorship, is this: the 'genuine Second Isaiah' himself also speaks of a great conqueror and deliverer, the instrument of God's will and the mouthpiece of his word, whose work will usher in the age of right-eousness and peace; and *at one point in the prophecy*, where the description is most vivid, the interpretation is twice expressly added: *This Coming One is Cyrus*. Indeed, the burden of the dis-tinctive message of Second Isaiah is universally supposed to be the prediction of the everlasting restoration of Israel by Cyrus, who is Yahwè's Anointed One (*měšīchō*, 45:1). Now it is a most significant fact that Second Isaiah's description of the career and work of his great hero very closely resembles the description of the Servant of Yahwè found in some of the so-called 'Servant passages.' And in general, the fact of a close literary relationship is altogether beyond question; either Second Isaiah and the author of the Servant passages are identical, or else the one wrote in con-scious imitation of the other. To many of those who have studied the evidence most thoroughly it has seemed incredible that any writer should thus have undone and obscured his own prophecy, making the whole scheme of salvation turn on Cyrus in one set of passages, and then, in the same terms, assigning the very same work in other passages to the Servant of Yahwè, who is plainly an altogether different personage. Accordingly, Ewald, Duhm, Smend, Wellhausen, Cheyne, Schian, Kosters, Kittel, Sellin, Ber-tholet, Stärk, and many others have excised the 'Servant pas-sages' (including more or less of chapters 42, 49, 50, 52, and 53) from the writings of the 'Prophet of the Exile.' Whether the author of the 'Servant passages' imitated Second Isaiah, or was imitated by him, has been an unsettled question. Now the one, and now the other, of the two has been held to have incorporated and ex-panded the work of his fellow. In either case, the result to the book of Second Isaiah is the loss of a series of magnificent pas-sages, which had been regarded as among its most characteristic portions, but are now found to be out of keeping with the message of this prophet as it is currently interpreted.*

The pruning-knife has found still other work to do. In the comparatively few chapters, or parts of chapters, which are now commonly assigned to II Isaiah, numerous sections of considerable length have been pronounced spurious by many scholars (Duhm, Cheyne, Marti, and most of the representatives of the prevailing school) and removed from the 'original prophecy' as later additions. These sections belong mainly to two classes, utterances against idolatry, and utterances in which Israel is severely blamed; and since both motives have a prominent place in the book, this further curtailment is not a slight one.

Again, in Cheyne's latest criticism of the book, represented especially by his 'Polychrome' Isaiah (1899), the conclusion is reached that everything from chapter 49 onward belongs not only to a later stratum, but to another author; the work of the 'Prophet of the Exile' is to be looked for only within the limits of chapters 40–48. This view had previously been held and defended by Kosters, in the *Theol. Tijdschrift*, 1896, 580 ff. See Cheyne's statement, *op. cit.*, 126, especially lines 25–35. He remarks that "the phraseological argument for the disintegration of chapters 40–55 is a slight one, but must be taken in connection with the extremely important evidence *based on the implied situation of affairs*" (the italics are mine). From these nine chapters, 40–48, there are also to be removed the numerous and extensive accretions to which allusion has just been made: 'Servant' passages, polemics against idolatry, and rebuke of Israel. Thus the final result is reached, that in the latest critical edition of the text of the book, instead of twenty-seven chapters we see only the equivalent of about *seven* assigned to II Isaiah—truly a *she'ērīth ū-felēṭāh!* And even this 'escaped remnant' is far from safe. It still contains numerous passages to which the hypothesis of a Babylonian and 'exilic' origin can be adjusted only with the greatest difficulty. It happens again and again, within the compass of the few unassailed chapters, that the words of the prophet unexpectedly contradict the thing he is supposed to be saying, or give an unhappy turn to the line of thought which he is believed to be following. As Cheyne, for example, exclaims in his note on 43 : 3 (*Polychrome Trans.*): "Again one must

---

* Only a thorough misunderstanding of the message and the literary art of the Second Isaiah could have brought forth the mischievous idea of 'Servant songs.' As well attempt to separate 'Wisdom songs' from the Proverbs of Ben Sira, or 'Father Anchises poems' from Vergil's Æneid.

lament the inconsistencies of the Second Isaiah!" It is, indeed, provoking. Just as we have discovered the prophet he eludes us. We have made a most elaborate theory, and have cut out from the book everything that seemed capable of interfering with it; at considerable cost, it has been made easy for II Isaiah to follow the prescribed ¸way—but he refuses to walk in it for even one whole chapter.

All this time, through the successive stages and with the help of many hands, we have been brought nearer and nearer to the true source of all the critical perplexity and contradiction. It seems possible to foresee the day when the genuine writings of the 'Great Unknown of the Exile' will be reduced by this same utterly logical process of criticism to the two verses 44 : 28 and 45 : 1 (the two which contain the name of Cyrus), with or without their immediate context.

Doubtless Professor Cheyne's analysis of the book is an extreme illustration; yet I cannot but regard it as a necessary fruit of the accepted modern theory of II Isaiah. He simply carried out, with his usual thoroughness and fearlessness of consequences, the processes initiated by others. The aspect of Isaiah 40–66 in the *Polychrome Bible* is only a little more mournful than it is in nearly every modern text-book and treatise. Instead of a comprehensive unit, the best scholarship of the present day offers us here only an incomprehensible scrap-heap. The necessity of making the division into "Deutero-Isaiah" (chapters 40–55) and "Trito-Isaiah" (56–66), with all that it involves, would of itself be a sufficiently great misfortune. That it is not possible to take this step without going still farther, the recent history of exegesis has clearly shown. The subsequent dissection of "III Isaiah" is a certainty, while that of the curtailed II Isaiah is not likely to be long delayed. We have here a good example of that which has happened not a few times, in the history of literary criticism, where scholars have felt obliged to pare down a writing to make it fit a mistaken theory. The paring process, begun with a penknife, is continued with a hatchet, until the book has been chopped into hopeless chunks.

3. *The Present Low Estimate of the 'Book'*

A generation or two ago, when the theory of a 'Second Isaiah' was still young, interpreters of the Old Testament were able to derive much more satisfaction from the book than their successors of the present day can find in it. Exegesis was far more easy-going and untrammelled. There was less of the strict inquiry of a historical investigation, and more of the warmth of a religious exercise. The old conception of a transcendent 'prophecy,' which was to be used mainly for purposes of edification and in the nature of the case was more or less incomprehensible, still exercised its influence. The prophet was allowed to contradict himself if he chose. Phrases or descriptions which were seen to be applied in one chapter or passage to a personage of history, or to a definite occurrence, could without difficulty be taken figuratively a little farther on. Second Isaiah could, and according to not a few good scholars did, predict in like terms *both* Cyrus and the Messiah. He could take as his supposed motto "Comfort ye my people," and assert that Jerusalem (supposed to mean the exiled Jews in Babylonia!) had paid double for all her transgressions, and yet repeatedly denounce guilty Israel with the utmost vehemence, naming such sins as no 'yearning exile' would be likely to commit. He was the great exponent of monotheism, and waged effective warfare against the idolatry which (somehow!) threatened the religion of Yahwè. The glorious future which he predicted did, it was believed, find its starting-point in the 'Restoration' in 538 B. C.; but the real mission of the prophet was nevertheless held to be to foretell and describe the Messianic age. Thus the book still enjoyed some of its ancient preeminence as religious literature of universal application, and was read with awe.

At the present day this attitude, among scholars, is impossible. The rights of exegesis are recognized, even if they are not always respected, and in the case of every Biblical book it is held to be the first duty of the interpreter to find out just what its author meant, with the assumption that he wrote under the same laws which govern modern writers. We wish to have a true estimate, not a merely conventional view. What, now, is the true value of Second Isaiah? We wish to know what it has to tell us of the history of its time and of the religious condition of the Jewish people; more than this, we would inquire into the depth and solidity of reasoning, and the moral earnestness of its author or authors. Now that it has been critically examined, with what rank, as Hebrew prophecy, does it emerge? Less urgent, but also important, is the question as to the literary qualities; the just rating of these long-admired poems, whether regarded simply as Hebrew poetry or from a still wider basis of comparison.

Whoever examines any recent commentary on Is. 40–66 can see

for himself the spectacle of dissection, rearrangement, and excision which has just been described; and also, in lesser details, the constant alteration of the text to suit the present theory of the book, and the condemnation of numerous passages as unintelligible— that is, under the present theory. It may be doubted, however, whether very many of those who accept without question the modern view realize the full extent of the depreciation which has taken place, not merely in the critical appraisal but also in the estimate of every thoughtful student.

The necessity of placing a low valuation on '*III Isaiah*' is perhaps sufficiently obvious. The qualities which can be recognized in any spoken word are already very largely determined if there is a preconception of the caliber of the speaker. Interpretation in detail is inevitably determined by theories of authorship and historical setting. In the work, or works, supposed to be contained in chapters 56–66, is there any profound treatment of a great theme, on broad lines, or merely a rhetorical flurry about loosely related subjects? The question is answered by any theory of a 'Trito-Isaiah.' Great problems, such as were faced by Jewish theologians of the Persian period, could not be adequately dealt with in small compass, least of all by men deficient in originality. In what spirit was the 'prophecy' composed? What was the writer's outlook upon human history, his idea of true religion, his understanding of the mission of his people, his conception of the attitude of the One God toward his creatures, the inhabitants of the wide world? A passage lies before the exegete. If it is believed to be the utterance of a great soul, a profound thinker, the author of an extensive and mighty work, it means one thing; if it comes from one who is thought to be the bearer of a minor message, one of a degenerate school of writers ('epigones' is a favorite term in the commentary on these chapters), it inevitably means something else. A small prophet can only produce a small prophecy. The detected imitator, however glib he may be, cannot deceive us by the use of high-sounding phrases, especially when these are already known to belong to another setting. If we see on every page language suited to lofty flights, we know that it is borrowed finery, covering commonplace themes and a narrow spirit; so we are informed by all the leading critics of the book. "Religious writers have begun, feebly enough, to copy the phraseology of chapters 40–55." These would-be teachers of the community take refuge in a "loud, imperious manner," and seek to hide the poverty of their thought under constant "exaggeration of language"; a reproach which is frequent in the principal commentaries. We are shown a picture of intolerance variously manifested, a narrow view of religion, a prevailing interest in external conditions and incidents rather than a passion for spiritual renovation. 'The temple, the sacrifice, the law, the sabbath, etc., are regarded as the things of highest importance' (Duhm). Where the writer might seem to be rebuking the faithless and wicked of his own people, or setting forth a lofty conception of the nature of true worship, we find that what he really had in mind was—a polemic against the Samaritans! The writer of chapters 61 and 62 displays "a colossal spiritual arrogance towards men," even though "side by side with this we notice a humility towards God." * Again and again the writer is said to breathe "hatred"; not of sin nor even of sinners as such, but of parties, sects, and peoples. He is represented as hoping for the ultimate extermination of the Gentile nations, with the exception of such survivors as would be the vassals and servants of the Jews. The passage 63:1-6 displays "elaborate ferocity" (Cheyne; similar characterizations in Smend, Duhm, G. A. Smith, Delitzsch, and many others).

The low estimate of the religious content of these chapters is fully paralleled by the judgment pronounced on their literary form. Here, again, the preconceived theory determines the verdict. The commentators have found it possible to persuade themselves that whereas Second Isaiah (ordinarily) wrote true poetry, the output of Third Isaiah should rather be spoken of as 'poetry' (versifizierte Prosa, Duhm) with an ironical accent on the word. While much of it is respectable doggerel, the reader is far too often wearied by its "artificiality," "poverty of style," "laboured use of phrases," and "unrhythmical quality." The figures of speech are unsparingly ridiculed, especially by Duhm in many passages. In truth, it is of little use to look for inspired poetry in the mutterings of a mean brood. If we are dealing with writers of "morbid and conflicting thoughts" against which "the moral sense of the reader protests" (Cheyne, 338, 364), then there is good reason for a depreciatory estimate at all points, even if not full justification for the profound contempt which is so freely bestowed.

The once 'great Prophet of the Exile' fares little better than his supposed satellites. The curtailment of his book is not the most serious misfortune that has befallen it. Since he is recognized as the prophet of an occasion, his work has not only been more or less

---

* Cheyne, *Introduction to the Book of Isaiah*, p. 343; where a foot-note remarks that Duhm would depreciate this "humility."

rigorously pared down and adjusted to the supposed historical situation, but also has been measured according to the relative importance of the events which are said to have called it forth. Formerly, under the influence of the Chronicler's history of Israel, it was believed that there was a 'restoration,' a fundamentally important turning-point, in 538 B. C.; at the present day it is well understood that neither the Babylonian exile, nor 'the return' from it, had any profound significance for the Jewish people.* The glowing predictions of the poet, seeming to include nothing less than a renovated world, and yet supposedly based on the advent of a heathen conqueror, certainly were not fulfilled under the Persian régime. The Second Isaiah was an enthusiast, a dreamer, we are told; the predictions were the product of his temperament and essentially hyperbolic; yet it is evident that he was credulous enough to believe in them. He has certain literary gifts; exuberant imagination, a rich lyric vein, much rhetorical power ("honeyed rhetoric," Cheyne, p. 320); but his language is generally more lofty than his theme. He has the merit of emphasizing monotheism, and yet his conception of the worship of the foreign peoples and of their 'idols' is too superficial to be just. His reasoning is not sound. According to the commentators, he believes, and more than once declares with impressive emphasis, that in the partiality of Yahwè for Israel, evidenced by the (expected) favor shown to the Jews by Cyrus, he can present an 'unanswerable argument' to the Gentiles. The latter, however, were not acquainted with the Hebrew records, nor, when told what they contained, could they well share the Jewish interpretation of them. They could readily believe that the Israelites had a god who was capable of helping his people, without admitting for a moment that he was the creator and ruler of other peoples, or superior to their deities. "Deuterojesaia sieht das alles gar nicht, auch er berührt den Boden nicht mit seinen Füssen" (Duhm, on 41:4). The poet's faith is magnificent, in spite of its feverish quality; he is certainly a man to be praised—and patronized (all the commentators patronize the Second Isaiah), but not to be followed.

It is a familiar fact, in the field of Biblical science, that traditional estimates and designations are sometimes retained long after they have ceased to be applicable. Not a few modern writers continue to speak of the 'great prophet' in terms resembling those which were employed in the days before the Cyrus-restoration poems had been critically examined. Even interpreters of the

* See now especially G. F. Moore, *Judaism*, I, 16 f., 23.

Bible should be just before they are generous. It is refreshing
to see the acknowledged leaders of the modern school expressing
themselves plainly and consistently. Duhm, in his introduction to
chapters 40 ff., says of their author: 'His flight is far above the
earth; he deprives us almost entirely of the advantage we might
have derived from information as to the real religious conditions
of his time.' 'He has no message directly addressed to his people,
calling on them to do or to cease from doing.' 'He frequently
(nicht selten) crosses the boundary which separates the prophet
from the mere poet.' Marti expresses the same things in other
words. Cheyne (*Introd.*, p. 248) says: "The writer of chapters 40–
55 is not, so far as the evidence goes, a prophet in the old style at
all. His word is not 'like a hammer that breaketh the rock in
pieces' (Jer. 23 : 29), with a declaration of impending judgment
and a stern call to repentance, but like 'wine and milk without
money and without price' (55 : 1)." Smend, *A. T. Religionsgeschichte*, 354, is more concise: "Er redet in derselben Form wie
die Propheten, . . . aber er ist kein Prophet mehr und will auch
nicht dafür gelten." What, indeed, had this enthusiastic preacher
to say concerning sin and righteousness? To our dismay we find,
when we turn to the text-books and commentaries of the present
day, that he had no ethical message at all. He shows a lamentable
lack of moral sense (see Duhm on 43 : 15). His work contains
"keine Busspredigt" (Stade). "Righteousness," *ṣedeq*, is even used
by him to mean political triumph and material prosperity; see the
comms. on 41 : 2 and similar passages. There are, to be sure, very
many and conspicuous utterances, all through chapters 40–66, in
which there is stern rebuke of wickedness, unbelief, idolatry, insin-
cere worship, and many other forms of sin; but these are all expunged, removed by emendation, explained away, and assigned to
other writers, partly because they do not at all suit the situation
of the return under Cyrus, partly because of the still prevailing
curious, utterly unhistorical theory of 'the exilic community,' and
partly because of the preposterous exegesis of 40 : 2.

If the 'prophet of the exile' were indeed the spineless and morally deficient sky-gazer which the prevailing critical view makes of
him, he would deserve all the disparagement which has been put
upon him. The notion of an upright, God-fearing Israel, needing
no censure, but only comfort, is utterly false, whether we speak of
the 'remnant' in Palestine or of the colonies in Babylonia, Egypt,
and elsewhere. At whatever time in the history of the Jews, or
of any other people, its religious leaders did not upbraid and warn,

preaching repentance and calling to better ways of life, those leaders were unworthy of their office, and are unworthy of our respect.
They were men who merited the stern sarcasm with which the
Second Isaiah himself denounced certain of his own contemporaries (56:10):

> Blind are his watchmen all, | all unperceiving; ||
> Dumb dogs, every one, | unable to bark! ||

CHAPTER II

THE SUPPOSED 'PROPHECY OF THE RETURN'

Our understanding of the Second Isaiah and consequent estimate of each and every member of the group of twenty-seven
poems, from 34 to 66, depend primarily on the interpretation of
chapters 41–48. It is here that modern exegetes have supposed
themselves to find in complete form the prophet's rhapsodies over
the career of Cyrus and his predictions relating to the capture of
Babylon by the Persian king, the edict restoring the Jewish exiles
to Palestine, and the subsequent Return, of which the author of
the Book of Chronicles furnishes the account. It is the fundamental question of these Cyrus-Babylonian allusions that must first of
all be discussed.* Reference to the supposed Return is also seen
here and there in chapters 49–55; but since there is to be found in
these seven chapters no direct or indirect allusion to Cyrus, nor
to any particular land of exile, they may be left out of account for
the present.

Few conclusions reached by modern Biblical scholarship would
receive more general assent than the following in regard to chapters 41–48. They were written in Babylonia, in the sixth century
B. C., near the close of the so-called 'Babylonian exile'; they have
for their principal themes the glorification of Cyrus, and the Return of the Jews from Babylonia to Jerusalem.

From the unanimity with which these propositions have been
held, one would expect them to be strongly supported by the internal evidence of the book; this, however, is far from being the
true state of the case. There is not a word in II Isaiah which
could be said to point plainly to Babylonia as the place of its
composition. A few scholars, in recent years, have thought of
locating the author in Phœnicia, or Egypt.† As for the sixth cen-

* It is customary, in speaking of the group of chapters which are considered
to reflect definitely the time of Cyrus, to include 40 with 41–48. In 40, however, there is nothing to suggest Cyrus, Babylonian exiles, or a return from
Babylonia to Jerusalem.

† Dr. William H. Cobb, to whom I had submitted the argument here presented, together with my commentary on chapters 34–53, was led thereby to
defend the Palestinian origin of these poems, in the *Journal of Biblical Literature*, vol. 27 (1908), pp. 48–64.

tury B. C., and a return of the Babylonian *Golah*, the entire unequivocal evidence consists of the mention of Cyrus twice by
name, and the presence of the names 'Babylon' and 'Chaldæa' in
three other passages which speak of a 'flight' from a land of bondage. These proper names are all palpable interpolations, as will
be demonstrated in the following chapter. Drop them from the
text in the five passages mentioned, and there is not a word or
phrase anywhere, as I shall show, to indicate that the prophet had
ever heard of Jewish exiles in Babylonia. This is a striking fact,
to say the least, when one remembers what the mission of the
Second Isaiah is supposed to be!

Professor Cheyne puts in concise form the modern theory of the
genesis of this prophecy. In the notes accompanying his translation (Polychrome Bible, *Isaiah*, p. 175, lines 20 ff.) he speaks of
the excitement in the East caused by the career of Cyrus, leading
the Jews in Babylonia to expect a political change, and adds: "To
this, combined with an intense belief in prophecy (Jer. 29 : 10), we
owe the splendid composition of the Second Isaiah." That is, the
prophetic impulse which produced these eight (nine? sixteen?)
poems had its rise in two concrete facts: the one, a childlike, almost
superstitious trust in a single written prediction; the other, a mere
guess at the future—and, as the event proved, a mistaken guess—
derived from the popular forecast.

It is singular that no trace of the second of these two 'moving
causes' should be found in the poems. There is no allusion whatever to the fulfilment of prophecy, no reference to an accomplished
period of time or to a definite turn of fortune which had been expected by the Jewish people. The 'intensity' of the prophet's belief in the prediction of Jer. 29 : 10 (or 25 : 12)—supposing him
ever to have heard of it—might therefore seem questionable, to
say the least. And did he not have an equally intense belief in
arithmetic? As the 'Prophet of the Restoration' he would be expected to date the seventy years of desolation from the beginning
of the Babylonian exile, as the period is actually reckoned in
II Chron. 36 : 20 and Jer. 29 : 4–14. Even if we take the year 597
(and not 586!) as the beginning, the interval amounts to only
fifty-eight years. It was in reality forty-seven years, however.
Bear in mind that this was mostly in his own generation. His
father, or his uncle, or almost any one of his older neighbors, could
have told him exactly how many years had elapsed since the burning of the temple and the cessation of the formal worship of Yahwè
in Jerusalem. There is therefore good ground for the suspicion

that the influence of this vaticination is to be found only in the
imagination of the commentators, fed by II Chron. 36:20 and
the tales thereupon told by this supposed historian, the Chronicler,
and his supposed sources. On *his* probable computation of the '70
years of exile,' at a time (three centuries later!) when the chronology of the late Babylonian and Persian periods was hopelessly
lost (*cf.* George F. Moore, in the *Harvard Theological Review*, 1924,
pp. 309–311), see my *Ezra Studies*, pp. 135 ff.

With the other 'moving cause' the case is quite different. Cyrus
stands before our eyes in the Hebrew text, not merely mentioned
by name twice over, but lauded in such extravagant terms as to
suggest a superhuman being. His triumph, which is represented
as near at hand, is made the subject of astonishing prediction, for
it will bring to every part of the inhabited earth, 'from east to
west,' the knowledge of the one true God. The claim that the
prophet was profoundly moved by the career of the Persian conqueror would seem to be quite beyond dispute, if the tradition of
the Hebrew text is to be trusted. It is necessary, indeed, to say
much more than this. The poems of the Second Isaiah have the
characteristic of returning again and again to certain themes, with
the repeated use of striking phrases and figures of speech. The
portion of the prophecy in which the name of Cyrus occurs has
several unmistakable parallels, so widely distributed in the
poems of the group as to exclude the supposition of a merely momentary burst of enthusiasm—as one might be thrilled by an item
in the morning paper. If the prophet wrote 44:28, and 45:1 as
it now reads, we have not only the historical background of his
prophecy but also the main source of the profound stirring of soul
which brought forth at least the eight poems, 41–48. The evident
connection of the prophecy, as thus interpreted, with the supposedly authentic account of the 'return from the exile' provided
by the Jewish Chronicler, gives an apparently firm basis for the
current view. The Second Isaiah, we are therefore told, predicts
the impending advance of Cyrus on Babylon, and its success; the
policy of the conqueror; and the results for Jerusalem and Judea.
Far more important than this, he promises the dawn of a truly
Messianic age, a spiritual renovation of the whole world in immediate connection with the 'triumph' which he heralds.

According to the ancient and wide-spread view, prevalent also
in modern times, the Hebrew prophet foretold coming events. By
virtue of the divine gift, each of the Major and Minor Prophets
made his definite prediction of this or that portion of future his-

tory. Little by little, the recognition of this superhuman clairvoyance in Hebrew prophecy has disappeared from modern scholarly treatises. At present, one remarkable example remains. The Second Isaiah is believed to foretell even such details as the co-operation of the Persian king in the building of Jerusalem and the temple, and the returning of the vessels carried off by Nebuchadrezzar.

Few of our Old Testament scholars, it would seem, have found difficulty in assuming that the people on the lower Euphrates in general, and the Jewish colonists of that region in particular, were able in 540 B. C. to predict with confidence the taking of Babylon by Cyrus and the subsequent policy of that monarch. We know, however, of no especial activity on his part, during the time immediately preceding the date just given, from which they could have drawn their conclusions. His conquests in Asia Minor, of which we have some account, took place seven years before this. We should suppose that the Babylonian Jews would have ceased to talk or think about these events, at least, long before 539 B. C. Of the movements of Cyrus during these seven years we know nothing. He may have been near Babylonia, or far away. When the stroke finally came, the progress of events seems to have been both rapid and unexpected. The Persian army appeared at Opis, on the Tigris, a hundred miles north of Babylon; defeated the forces of King Nabunaid; marched into Sippar; and then, two days later, into Babylon itself. It is one thing to know and describe what actually happened, and quite another thing to foretell the turning-points of history. Cheyne, *Book of the Prophet Isaiah* (trans.), p. 175, says that "the *large designs* attributed to Cyrus by Herodotus naturally produced a wide-spread excitement in the East, in which the Jews participated." This appears to be a sort of corollary: those who were able to foretell the events of the years 540 and 539 B. C. could foresee the conjectures of a Greek historian.

It is quite likely that Cyrus was hailed by a considerable party of the Babylonians as a deliverer. It is not easy to believe, on the other hand, that there was any general expectation of greatly improved conditions following the inauguration of his rule. Such a change of masters was too familiar a fact in that part of the world, where one 'deliverer' succeeded another. There certainly should have been no doubt in the mind of any one that the newcomer had in view solely his own interests when he captured Babylonia. Those who were far-sighted enough to look even a short distance into the future could have predicted in a general way this much of

what actually followed: conditions hardly bettered in the land;
more wars for the glory of Cyrus; after his death, the increasing
burden of his dynasty. As for the Jewish colonists, they were not
more credulous than their neighbors, and presumably had even
less reason to expect betterment for themselves as the result of a
political change. There were among them men of experience and
good judgment, who would have replied to any enthusiastic forecast in the words of the Psalmist (118:9): "It is better to trust
in the Lord than to put confidence in princes."

How did it happen, ask the commentators on II Isaiah, that
the prophet was so misled in regard to Cyrus? He pictures him
not simply as the instrument of the divine will, but very significantly as one who stood in a peculiarly intimate relation to the
God of Israel. Cyrus is Yahwè's "shepherd," his "anointed," who
is to carry out the eternal purposes of the creator of the world.
He is the one whom Yahwè "loves" (48:14); "the man of his
counsel," that is, of course, the one who shares his counsel, whom
he takes into his confidence. Nothing in the character or the
career of the Persian king satisfies any part of this characterization. "He came, calling on my name," the prophet makes Yahwè
say. On the contrary, the king himself tells us in his inscription
that he called on Marduk and Nabu on that occasion. Did Cyrus
confess Yahwè? There is not even the smallest likelihood that he
did, yet the commentators are obliged to admit that the prophet
asserts it; see Duhm and Marti on 41:25. It is also clearly implied
elsewhere, in a most exalted passage, that Yahwè grants a special
revelation of himself to this favored being, who previously 'had
not known' him; see the commentators on 45:4 f. How is it that
the prophet can assert this of *Cyrus?* Yahwè 'foretold him from
the beginning,' and that plainly, so that all Israel knew it. How
can this extravagant statement be justified? 'No one of the
heathen deities ever made a like prediction.' As Duhm remarks
(on 41:26), the prophet was, of course, ignorant of the Pythian
oracle in regard to Crœsus, to say nothing of other instances. The
gods of the Gentiles were constantly 'announcing' just such things
as this.

Perhaps the most surprising example of misguided exaggeration
—if the prophet is really speaking of Cyrus—is to be found in the
passages which tell how the Gentiles are to be confounded and
convinced by the advent of the great deliverer, Yahwè's 'anointed.'
It seems to be said that the conquests of Cyrus and his favor
shown to the Jews will make known to all the world that the God

of Israel is the God of all peoples, the omnipotent One, the only true God. This is put forth not merely as a joyful expectation, but rather as the presentation of evidence which cannot be gainsaid. As such it is triumphantly produced again and again; see 41 : 1–4, 21–26; 43 : 9; 44 : 7; 45 : 1–7, especially vs. 6; 48 : 14 f.* Now this is amazing folly, nothing less. The ridicule which Duhm (on 41 : 21–26) heaps upon this 'argument' is only too well deserved. The conquests of Cyrus neither did nor could demonstrate anything of the sort. Not even the edict permitting Jews to return to Judea (but this edict, according to the current belief, had not yet been promulgated) could prove any special power of Yahwè, seeing that other deported peoples were given the same privilege when the Persians took possession of Babylonia. Any one of the nations whose former worship was restored by Cyrus could claim that its god or gods had 'chosen him' for this purpose. Other gods had done such things, over and over again. The prophet's irrefutable evidence, to which he points in every part of chapters 41–48 as the means of silencing and winning the peoples of the earth, is really no evidence at all, for them. They could only laugh at it. What is the caliber of a 'seer' who could see no farther than this? Enthusiasm in a good cause is always attractive, but no amount of it can atone for the lack of common sense.

It is notorious that the transformation which he seems to predict did not, in fact, come to pass. The Jews did not triumph over their adversaries. Jerusalem was not forthwith glorified in the eyes of the world. No era of peace and prosperity followed the victories of Cyrus. The religion of Yahwè was not made known to the heathen nations. If the contemporaries of the prophet understood him to promise these things as the fruit of the Persian occupation of Babylonia, and allowed themselves to be influenced by him, they soon were sadly disillusioned. 'The Great Disappointment' is a prominent feature of every recent discussion of Second Isaiah.

Increasing emphasis is laid, at the present day, on the evidence that the prophet himself saw and regretted his mistake. Why did he drop Cyrus as suddenly as he had taken him up? After chapter 48 there is not the slightest trace of the great Persian benefactor, the savior of Israel, the foreign 'Messiah' whom Yahwè had announced from the beginning. In the seven chapters 49–55 (conventionally regarded as constituting the remainder of Second

---

* It appears once more in 57 : 11–13, where the massoretic text must be very slightly emended; see the translation and commentary.

Isaiah) the underlying conditions are precisely the same as in the
preceding chapters; the expected rescue has not yet come—consider, for instance, 51 : 5 and the whole of 52 !—but is immediately
impending. There is the same outlook into the future as before,
with the same absorbing ideas: the present distress, the approaching triumph, the return to 'Zion.' A great leader, destined to restore Israel, is indeed present and very prominent in these seven
poems, but he is now expressly designated as 'the Servant of
Yahwè' and defined as the product of Israel's own life.* In spite
of the prophet's habit of repeating himself, which is as conspicuous
here as before, there is no allusion to the Persian conqueror or to
any achievement of his, past, present, or future. What has happened? How did the prophet manage to forget the one who
'stood in the centre of his view of the world'?†

A solution of this puzzle is offered by Max Haller, "Die Kyros-
Lieder Deuterojesajas," in the *Festschrift für Hermann Gunkel*
(1923), 261 ff., as follows. The 'Cyrus-poems,' which include portions of each of the chapters 41–48, with exception of 43 and 47
(see p. 270), constituted an oracle which was not only formally
addressed to Cyrus, as in 45 : 1 ff., but was written to be presented
to him personally (274). It is not unlikely that he himself asked
to have it composed and delivered to him, since kings on the eve
of a great test of arms naturally wish to have as many indications
of divine support as possible (275). We may certainly suppose
that the Hebrew prophet had direct access to the Persian king
(*ibid.*), and it may be that he actually held a position in the royal
entourage something like that of Nehemiah at the court of Artaxerxes (277). This would account for the 'exact knowledge of
Cyrus, his deeds and campaigns' (270), and for the confidence with
which he forecasts the purposes and policy of the conqueror.
These Cyrus-poems have a distinct literary form of their own,
moreover, for they employ the characteristic formulas of Baby-
lonian-Persian court documents (269 f., 274).‡ When the prophet

* I have recently heard the view advocated that the Servant of Yahwè in
II Isaiah is|a designation of Cyrus! Certainly a desperate attempt to avoid
some of the difficulties of the current theory.

† Quoted from Budde, in Kautzsch's *Heilige Schrift des A. T.*, 4th ed., p. 654.
The same thing is said by many other scholars.

‡ The observation that the 'Cyrus-poems' are in their manner so distinctly
separated from the remainder of II Isaiah, the recognition of the 'Hofstil' in
44 : 24–28 and 45 : 1–8 especially, and the previous discovery by Kittel (*Zeitschrift für die alttestamentliche Wissenschaft*, 1898, p. 149) that the language and
style of 44 : 28–45 : 4 are closely paralleled in the Cyrus-cylinder, afford striking illustration of the possibility, under favorable circumstances, of hearing the
grass grow.

was granted his interview, and presented what he had written, he was given a bitter disappointment. The king refused to do more for the Jews than for other vassal peoples. He would permit their exiles in Babylonia to go to Judea if they wished, but had no intention of building Jerusalem or restoring the temple; to say nothing of confessing Yahwè, accepting the appointment as his emissary, and proclaiming him to the peoples of the earth (276). This, after the prophet had declared again and again, *speaking in Yahwè's name*, that Cyrus had been 'foretold from the beginning' in well-understood terms (267) as the coming deliverer of Israel and revealer of truth to the world, the *berīth 'am* of 42 : 6 (265, 276), the one who should do the very things which he now flatly refused! The crestfallen seer could do nothing but go back to his place and compose further oracles, chapters 49–55 (no longer in the 'Hofstil' of the Persian court), in which the place of Cyrus is taken by the Servant of Yahwè—which title must be understood as designating the prophet himself (261, 273). We may even see in the mortal distress of the Servant in chapter 53 a reflection of the disillusionment which 'Deutero-Isaiah' suffered on this occasion (276).

This explanation (which Judæus Apella may turn over at his leisure) at least takes full account of a fundamental incongruity in the current theory which others glide over much too easily, and is a truly ingenious attempt to avoid it. It is worth presenting here in summary because it shows in unusually clear light some of the absurdities of the Cyro-centric exegesis of II Isaiah. The 'prophet' who is pictured in this episode is a pitiable figure, though hardly more pitiable than he appears in the usual representations.

The Second Isaiah of our modern text-books and treatises is a man who had never thought anything through. He blundered about Cyrus, blundered about the return from the exile, failed to see that his people were sinful and in need of forgiveness, unduly magnified the importance of the Jewish ritual, was unable to see below the surface of the heathen forms of worship, was indifferent, or worse than indifferent, to the fate of the foreign nations, claimed a divine authority which he did not have; and, in general, is likely to contradict in any given poem what he had said in its predecessor. 'The writer's emotion and his delight in orating easily deceive him as to the meagre content (Inhaltsleere) of his utterances' (Duhm, on 41 : 12 ff.). 'Any one who believed the contrary could have refuted him, . . . but for our prophet the mere utterance of his

convictions is sufficient proof of their validity; he had not even
the smallest grain of self-criticism' (*Idem*, on 41 : 22 ff.). Even
those commentators who prefer not to express themselves thus
bluntly nevertheless fully justify Duhm's estimate by their exegesis.

If there were any truth in the traditional account of the depopulation of Jerusalem and Judea, the status of the Jewish exiles in
Babylonia, and the return under Cyrus, there would be good excuse for a certain portion of the extravagant utterances ascribed
to the prophet. But the account is not true. The fanciful story
of the 'Restoration,' all but incredible in each of its essential details, would hardly have been taken seriously by modern scholars
if it had not been for the support seemingly given by II Isaiah.
This wonderful confirmation by a contemporary Hebrew author
has had the effect of maintaining trust in the Chronicler and an
easy-going criticism of the Ezra-Nehemiah narratives. The prose
version is thought to derive some of its material from the prophecy.
Thus Duhm on 44 : 28 says: "Der Chroniker benutzt unsere Stelle
Esra 1 : 1; 6 : 1 ff." The process was the reverse, however, as will
appear.

We have no credible record of the return of any considerable
company from the Babylonian exile. No writer prior to the third
century B. C. shows any knowledge of such an event, whether
under Cyrus or at any other time. Numerous passages in writings
dating from the Persian period are—and are now generally acknowledged to be—clearly incompatible with the account for
which the Chronicler and his contemporaries* are our only authority. There is, moreover, not the slightest evidence either in the
known history of Palestine or in the development of Judaism that
would tend to make such a return seem plausible. Every indication speaks strongly to the contrary. The deportation in 586 was
a small affair in point of numbers (Jer. 52 : 28). It included the
royal family, however, and the kingdom was at an end. In all
probability (and we have nothing more than probability to guide
us) Jerusalem was abandoned only during the brief interval while

---

* Some scholars, among them Theodor Nöldeke (*Deutsche Literaturzeitung*,
Supplement, Oct. 4, 1924, col. 1852), believe the Aramaic section Ezra 4 : 8–
6 : 14 to be the work of the Chronicler, as well as 7 : 12–26. This puts upon the
Chronicler the entire responsibility for the story of the return under Cyrus.
I admit that there are strong arguments for this view, but am still inclined to
hold to my former opinion (*Ezra Studies*, 158 f., 161), that a contemporary of
his had prepared the way for him.

the Chaldean army remained in the vicinity.* If any of the villages and cities of Judea were much depopulated, it was certainly for a short time only. Would-be occupants of the land were pressing in from the south, especially, during all this time (see Chapter IV), and could never have missed such an opportunity as this to take possession.† The fact that the repopulation turned out so prevailingly Jewish seems good evidence that it was speedily accomplished. Jews who had taken temporary refuge in Ammon, Moab, Edom, and other neighboring regions (cf. Jer. 40 : 11 f.), as well as the large body that fled to Egypt (with the expressed intention of returning, Jer. 44 : 14), must have constituted the majority, in and near Jerusalem. This was the actual 'restoration.' Foreigners also poured in, as was inevitable.

The reason why the Chronicler insists, and is obliged to insist, on a complete and enduring depopulation of Jerusalem and the cities of Judea, and a restoration by Babylonian Jews only, I have set forth in the *Ezra Studies*, pp. 153–155, 208 ff., 235–239, 262 f., 321–333. A thorough literary-historical investigation here demonstrates for the first time the motive underlying every part of his great undertaking and the origin of the 'tradition' which hitherto had remained unexplained and therefore continued to be given some credence even after strong suspicion had been cast upon it by several scholars. The Chronicler was not a man of petty aims, but the doughty champion of 'the true Israel' and the Hebrew institutions at Jerusalem in opposition to the very dangerous pretensions of the community at Shechem and the temple on Mount Gerizim. There is some evidence (see the foot-note, above) that he himself did not originate the theory of a legitimacy derived from the Babylonian exile, but rather elaborated it on a great scale and with very characteristic creation of detail,‡ beginning

* The probable course of the history of Jerusalem and Judea during the century following the destruction of the city by Nebuchadrezzar is set forth, with references to the sources which we have, in my *Ezra Studies*, 285–307.

† It is easy for an oriental writer, in picturesque exaggeration of the calamity befalling a city or land, to speak of absolute and long-continued desertion and desolation. Thus the Arab historians of Egypt assert that after a certain conquest by foreigners the Egyptians were driven from their land, and that thereafter for forty years all Egypt was uninhabited, neither man nor beast passing through it; a tradition ultimately derived from Ezek. 29 : 10 ff. See especially Makrizi (Bulak ed.), I, 143, 14 f.; 39, 14 ff. The exaggeration in II Kings 24 : 14–16 and 25 : 9–12, 25 f. had unfortunate consequences.

‡ The Chronicler's attention to important details—in spite of the general impression of carelessness—is nowhere so well illustrated as in the management of his Great List, on which depended the success of his whole undertaking. This list, entirely his own composition, which gave to the Hebrew clans

with the all-important early genealogies and ending with the generation (Neh. 12 : 11, 22) which witnessed the Samaritan schism. The literary evidence shows with certainty that he composed long and circumstantial episodes in the history of the kingdoms, all contributing directly to his main purpose, as well as the entire story of Ezra and the greater part of the Book of Nehemiah.* He did his work so skilfully, moreover, that his curious 'history of Israel' in the Persian period, though discredited at first,† was eventually accepted as authentic, and in modern times has dominated the interpretation of a large portion of the Old Testament.

The main question for us at present, however, is not whether the Babylonian exile was unimportant for the history of Israel, but rather how important it seemed to the poet and prophet who was the author of Is. 40–55. His chief purpose is supposed to be to encourage these particular exiles, and, especially, to urge them to leave their Babylonian homes and migrate to Judea. How clearly is this purpose manifested in these chapters?

The prophet in several passages makes mention of Jewish 'exiles' sojourning in strange lands. They are in the west, the north, the south, and the east (the east mentioned in 43 : 5 but not in 49 : 12). They are "trapped in holes and hidden away in dungeons"

and families occupying Judea in the third century their legitimation, expressly excluding by name certain other clans and families, and denying to all outside it any share in the pure blood and unsullied tradition of Israel, is *repeated* in two widely differing contexts. No one knew better than the Chronicler how the authenticity and accuracy of such tables are always under suspicion; how easily they may be fabricated and how inevitably the names become changed or lost through the ordinary accidents of transmission, unless some special precaution is taken. He therefore presents his catalogue first as an item in the account of the return under Cyrus; and then, when he represents Nehemiah as compiling, many years later, an authoritative census of 'Israel,' the priests, Levites, singers, etc., in chapters 7, 11, 12, *the same list* is discovered, and reproduced without change. The all-important catalogue is thus authenticated at both ends of the period, and at the same time the danger of loss from the text is greatly lessened. (That Neh. 7 : 70–8 : 18 originally followed directly upon Ezra 8 : 36, I have shown elsewhere. See G. F. Moore, *Judaism*, I, 6, notes 2 and 3.) Very similar—whether the work of the Chronicler or of a predecessor —is the confirmation of the decree of Cyrus through its discovery by Darius, Ezra 6 : 1 ff.

* As I demonstrated in 1896, *Composition and Historical Value of Ezra-Nehemiah.* I am glad to see now added to the number of those who have published their approval of this demonstration the names of Hölscher (in Kautzsch's *Heilige Schrift des A. T.*⁴), Nöldeke (see the reference above, p. 28, foot-note), and G. F. Moore (*Harvard Theol. Rev.*, 1924, pp. 316 f.; *Judaism*, I, 23).

† As is shown, for example, by the total absence of reference to any feature of it in Jewish scriptures prior to the Book of Tobit and the interpolations in II Isaiah (older than the Greek translation of the book), by the Syriac Old Testament canon, and by the ignoring of Ezra by Ben Sira.

(42 : 22), a picturesque exaggeration which means merely this, that the Jews are everywhere a vassal people and liable to harsh treatment (see Duhm and Marti on the passage). Nothing is said about the condition of exiles in Babylonia, nor is there any allusion to the deportation thither or to a period of sojourn there. No word of the prophet gives the impression that he is dwelling among exiles, or near them. Now and then there is more than a suspicion that the readers addressed are not sojourners in a foreign land. Professor Marti, on 43 : 22 ff., wonders—as very many others have wondered—that the prophet should take his hearers severely to task for not offering elaborate and costly sacrifices: "Dabei lässt der Prophet ganz unbeachtet, dass die Israeliten im Exil gar nicht opfern konnten."* It is indeed astonishing that the prophet should not have known this much about exiles.† Is it not singular also that in chapter 47, which is devoted wholly to Babylon, there should be no mention of deportation, captivity, or return? And that in the centrally important 'Cyrus oracles' (41 : 1-5, 21-28; 42 : 5-9; 44 : 24-28; 45 : 1-8; 46 : 1-13; 48 : 12-16) not a word is said about exiles, or hope for them? How does it happen that the author of 51 : 19 f., 52 : 4, and 54 : 1-3 seems to know nothing of deportation and captivity as among the evils that have befallen the Jerusalem he is addressing?

There are three passages in which the poet appears to look forward to an exodus of Israelites from Babylonia. These are 43 : 14, 48 : 20, and 52 : 11. In the latter two cases there is a direct address in the imperative, "Go forth, flee!" etc., with such similarity of context as would seem to leave no doubt that the same exodus is referred to in both passages. In recent years, however, some commentators have seen—in spite of the delusion of 'the exile'— that in 52 : 11 f. the reference is to *the flight from Egypt*. There are, indeed, in these two verses five distinct reminiscences of the account in Ex. 12 f.; see the commentary on the passage. That is, the poet is using figurative language. He predicts a great homecoming 'from the east, the west, the north, and the south' (43 : 5 f.), and takes as the inspiring type the wonderful deliverance from

---

* The current understanding of the passage is mistaken (see the translation and commentary), but no interpretation of it can be made to fit the theory of an 'exilic' background.

† Such considerations as this may well have influenced Duhm in reaching his hypothesis that the Second Isaiah lived and wrote in Phœnicia, though addressing himself to Jewish captives in Babylonia; which is something like imagining a religious teacher in Berlin as habitually addressing his various productions to an audience in China or Central Africa. Though perfectly possible, it is unlikely.

Egyptian bondage. The Hebrew writers generally, from Amos and Hosea onward, point to this unique instance of Yahwè's intervention in the sight of the foreigner. Contrast with this the fact that no Hebrew prophet or psalmist, even in the latest strata of the Old Testament, ever reminds his hearers of a deliverance from a *Babylonian* captivity.*

In 48 : 20 the reference to the exodus from Egypt would be unmistakable (see vs. 21!) if it were not for the two words *mib-Bābel* and *mikKasdīm* ("from Babylonia" and "from Chaldea"). The command "Flee!" suits only the flight from Egypt (see Ex. 14 : 5), not at all the triumphant procession under royal patronage. The two Hebrew words just quoted stand outside the meter of the verse and are interpolated, as I shall show presently. In 43 : 14 the subject is the *great* home-coming, the same which is predicted in 49 : 18, 22. The poet touches upon the most picturesque feature of it, the return from 'the west,' with the procession of ships (*cf.* 60 : 8 f.). Here again the word "fugitives" and the allusions in vss. 16 f. make it plain that the exodus from Egypt is in his mind as the typical scene of deliverance and return, as in the other two instances. And finally, it is not just a strange coincidence that in this passage also the words "to Babylonia" and "to Chaldea" destroy the meter of the verse, which is perfectly restored when they are removed.

If these three passages are merely a poet's pictures, designed to say to his people, in characteristic manner (*cf.* 62 : 10 f.), 'Our long term of bond-service is nearly over; remember Egypt!' then where, in chapters 40–55, can Babylonian exiles or a return from Babylonia to Judea be found? The subject of the (few, very slight, and palpably external) Cyrus-Babylon additions to the original text will be treated in the next chapter. If the historical background of 540–538 B. C. were clearly indicated in a single chapter or poem, or even in one continuous paragraph, of this remarkably homogeneous work, there would be good reason for attempting to read it into other paragraphs and poems. But no such example can be found.

---

* The 'captivity' of which these writers so often speak is the Hebrew Dispersion, as is made especially plain in Deut. 30 : 3. See also *Ezra Studies*, 296 f., 308 ff., and Chapter IV in this volume. This is the case in all such passages as Hos. 6 : 11, Am. 9 : 14, Jer. 30 : 3, Ps. 14 : 7, 126 : 1, and (as already remarked) Is. 42 : 22. The prediction of a "second time," in the late passage Is. 11 : 11, tells a plain story. The only 'home-bringing' known to this writer was that from Egypt. The *second* return will be from the four quarters of the earth. *Cf.* also such passages as Ps. 106 : 40–47.

We may now come back once more to Cyrus. What part in the prophet's argument, or exhortation, does this 'great central figure' play? We have already seen some evidence tending to show that the chief passages commonly supposed to refer to Babylonian exiles have in reality quite another intent. It is now time to consider the question whether the dominating importance of the Persian king, according to the current exegesis, is not merely another detail of the same mistaken interpretation.

It has already been remarked, in connection with Haller's theory, that the rôle supposedly played by Cyrus in chapters 41–48 is taken up by the Servant of Yahwè in 49–55. This is certainly a very striking fact; what can it signify? To Haller it means that the Second Isaiah, finding himself obliged to drop Cyrus, brought in the Servant as a substitute, to do what the king would not undertake. To other scholars, it means simply that the prophet's ideas were confused. There is another fact to be noted here, however. One of Haller's 'Cyrus-oracles' is 42:5–9; that is, apparently, the second half of a paragraph dealing with the Servant; cf. vss. 6 f. with 49:6. Does 42:1–4 refer to Cyrus? The idea is most unpalatable; I will not call it ridiculous (though it inevitably makes the author of the passage ridiculous), for a few reputable scholars have felt themselves forced to this extremity. For my own part, I can see no valid reason for refusing vss. 1–4 to Cyrus if vss. 5–7 are made to apply to him. Conversely, it has been the belief of the great majority of scholars that the whole passage, vss. 1–7, refers to the Servant and his task. It appears, then, that *not only in 49–55* but at least at one point in 41–48 the outline of the Servant is blurred with that of Cyrus. Do not other portions of these chapters show a similar blurring?

In chapter 41 the prophet presents for the first time a partial outline of his Great Argument; mainly an appeal to history, but to history as it is to be explained to the world by the consummation which is rapidly approaching. It is to the foreign peoples that the argument is chiefly addressed, as both beginning and ending of the poem declare. What God has shown his omniscience and his control of the whole earth by bringing to completion a plan for all mankind which he had announced from the beginning? Verse 2: Yahwè aroused from the east (Ur of the Chaldees) righteous Abraham,* who came in his service (*lĕ-raglō*), calling on his name. Yahwè promised him that his race should ultimately

* Observe that the ancient interpretation, both Jewish and Christian, recognized only Abraham here, not Cyrus.

lead and bless all the peoples of the earth. In the person of one of
his offspring, the last great protagonist of his line, "he shall subdue nations; kings he shall trample under foot. He will make them
as dust with his sword, as driven stubble with his bow." No other
such plan was ever made and announced. 'Israel, my Servant,
whom I brought from the ends of the earth, whom I hold by the
right hand' (vss. 8–13), will execute the great commission. And
again: Jacob the Servant, who is now a mere worm trodden under
foot, will in the last days, in the person of the same great protagonist (without whom no conquest would be conceivable), "thresh
mountains, make the hills as chaff scattered by the wind" (vs. 15).
This triumph, with its accompaniments, will bring to all the world
the knowledge of the One God Yahwè (vs. 20). The *beginnings*
are already here, behold them: I raised up one from the north
(Harran) and the east (Ur). And the *end* is now in sight: the
voice of the herald is heard in Jerusalem (vs. 27).

In chapter 42 the great protagonist himself is introduced, the
Servant for whose beneficent rule the 'isles' are waiting.* The
phrases of chapter 41 are repeated: Yahwè holds him by the right
hand; his advent and triumph will open the eyes of the Gentiles
to the knowledge of the One God; the 'former things' are accomplished, and 'new things' are at hand. Another feature of the
argument is now presented, the reason why Jacob is ever trodden
under foot (41 : 14). Wherefore the delay in bringing the triumph
to pass? The answer: Israel has been from the first, and still is,
a *blind* Servant, never comprehending its Maker. Sin and unbelief are its offering to him; suffering and disgrace, therefore, its
lot. The Anointed One himself is slow to understand Yahwè and
his purpose (49 : 4; 45 : 4 f.). The children of Abraham have been
scattered throughout the world; now discouraged, now indifferent, now trusting in the gods of the Gentiles. But the promises
are sure, and faith can be aroused—is already aroused. Jacob
must now repent (44 : 22) and turn to his God. This will bring at
once the long-expected rescue, the second 'return from Egypt.'
The wicked will be destroyed, the exiles will return, and the nations will acknowledge and serve Yahwè.

This is all clear, strictly logical, and consistent. The record of
the past is open to all ("Ye are my witnesses," says Yahwè to
Israel); the final outcome is guaranteed by the Creator of the
universe, who has made definite promises; the relation of the pres-

* The old Jewish interpretation, represented by the Targum, "the Messiah,"
is the only one that fully meets the requirement of the passage.

ent distress to the eternal plan is now made manifest. The coming conquests of the one chosen of Yahwè, the beloved Servant, the great protagonist, will complete the demonstration.

In the latter part of chapter 44 and the beginning of 45 there is a return to the main ideas of chapter 41. Both the language and the connection of thought recall the former poem. Verses 24 ff.:* "Thus saith Yahwè, thy redeemer, who formed thee from the womb, . . . who confirms the word of his Servant and perfects the counsel of his Messenger [*i. e.*, Israel], who says to Jerusalem, Be peopled; and to the cities of Judah, Be built up;† . . . thus saith Yahwè to his Anointed, to him whose right hand I hold, to trample nations before him, and loosen the loins of kings; to open for him the portals, and the gates shall not be closed: I myself will go before thee" (*cf.* 41 : 10), . . . "I will give thee the treasures long hidden" (*cf.* 48 : 6). He concludes all this by saying: "This is that they may know, from the east unto the west, that there is none beside me."

The conclusion is as irresistible as the sword of the Servant. If the purpose of God shown in the choice and guidance of Israel is further proved by *the ultimate triumph* of the 'Messenger,' the peculiar people, the Righteous One who is to stand as its representative, then all mankind must acknowledge that Yahwè is the only God. And this is the only proof that could satisfy any part of the Gentile world.

But in the last verse of 44 and the first verse of 45 the prophet's words have been given a strange interpretation, which now, at least, forms a part of our Hebrew text. "Thus saith Yahwè to his Anointed, *to Cyrus*, whose right hand I hold," etc. And in 44 : 28, where the prophet has been speaking, in a most exalted strain, of God's eternal purpose in creating heaven and earth, choosing a people, and effecting the wonderful deliverance from Egypt, it suddenly transpires that this plan culminated in the 'calling' of a foreign potentate and the rebuilding of a temple! To one who comes to these passages from a careful reading of chapters 40–43, these two interpretative hints are a slap in the face rather than a light to the eyes. Like the sparks and stars which one sees when he receives a blow on the head, they are not really illuminating, and leave an unpleasant impression. We had supposed that God's "anointed," the one whose right hand he holds, the weak one who

* The new poem begins at 44 : 24, not 45 : 1; as commentators now recognize.
† *Cf.* 43 : 28 (as emended). Jerusalem and the cities of Judah, sadly weakened by the Dispersion, will be repopulated by the returning 'exiles.'

should at last thresh mountains, the righteous one destined to
trample on kings, bring the exiles home, restore the glory of Jerusalem, and give to the nations the knowledge of Yahwè, was always some representative of Israel. But no, it is Cyrus; and thus
the prophet's whole splendid argument falls to the ground. Nothing that the foreign invader had done or could do could prove anything, for any Gentile.

More than this, we are at once plunged in confusion. Given the
concrete allusions here and there is no escape from them in the
many similar passages, even where the wider context seems to
forbid the interpretation. It is the very same portrait that is
given now one name, now another. *Whom* did Yahwè bring from
the ends of the earth, *love,* and assure of triumph? In 41:8 f. it is
Abraham; in 43:4 it is Jacob; in 48:14 f. precisely these three
things are said (according to the modern interpretation)* of Cyrus.
The confusion, both here and elsewhere, is intolerable. We are
faced with an alternative. God's chosen instrument, the centre of
this whole prophecy, is either Cyrus or Israel; it cannot possibly
be both. If it is the former—indeed, if the Persian king is present
at all—there follows with absolute certainty the disintegration of
the book into inexplicable fragments, and the great depreciation
of 'the Second Isaiah' (wherever he is to be found). If it was
Israel whom God raised up to fulfil his eternal purpose for the
world, then the excision of the allusions to Cyrus is a necessity.

Even ancient interpreters were sometimes mistaken. In I Esdras
4:13, introducing the third and successful disputant at the court
of Darius, when we read, "This was Zerubbabel," we merely
smile; for we know that the words are a later addition to the text,
and that the hero of the original narrative was not Zerubbabel at
all. Remove the mistaken label, and no trace of him remains. We
have already seen how very slender, in general, is the evidence
tending to support the current theory of this much-discussed
'exilic prophecy,' II Isaiah. The lack of any substantial basis is
truly amazing. When we undertake seriously to question the accepted conclusions, and come to chapters 41–48 looking for indications of sixth-century Babylonia and a community of pining
captives and the career of Cyrus, but determined to read nothing
into the text, we soon have the feeling of one who finds himself at
a Barmecide feast. The disappointment goes even beyond this,
for the guests of honor, as well as the viands, are missing. We

* But not the ancient interpretation. The Targum is not led astray, but
labels the portrait "Abraham, your father."

were invited to meet Cyrus, but find him not present. His name was announced at the door, but by mistake. We were promised sight of the Babylonian exiles, but they have failed to put in an appearance. It turns out that the banquet was an afterthought, not authorized. See the next chapter.

Second Isaiah is indeed a prophecy of release from bondage and a triumphant return of 'exiles' to Jerusalem by sea and land; but the prophet is looking to the ends of the earth, not to Babylonia. There is indeed prediction, definite and many times repeated, of the speedy advent of a great conqueror and deliverer, the restorer of Israel and benefactor of the world; but the prophet is speaking of the Anointed Servant of the Lord, the Son of David, not the son of Cambyses.

CHAPTER III

THE CYRUS–BABYLON INTERPOLATIONS

It has been shown in the preceding chapters that the attempt to explain Second Isaiah as a prophecy addressed to the deported Jews in Babylonia breaks down completely and ends in chaos. The occurrence of the names "Cyrus, Babylon, Chaldea" in passages of obviously central significance claims for the poems a very definite situation and intention. In each instance, however, the claim is belied by the immediate context (a startling fact), while the effort to maintain it throughout even one of the chapters concerned is found fruitless, necessitating excisions and emendations of a well-attested text. There is hardly a single poem in the postulated literary unit 40–55 which can be forced into the required historical situation, and even after the scissors have been courageously applied our commentators must "lament the inconsistencies" of the prophet. He persistently loses sight of the thing he is supposed to be saying; while employing the same phrases which had seemed to mark him as 'the Prophet of the Exile' he deals with ideas quite incongruous with the situation in Babylonia and the year 540; in every single instance where he has seemed to be indulging in extravagant utterances regarding the Persian king there is more than a suspicion that he has in mind a greater and more enduring factor in the history of mankind. It is clear that he believes himself to be uttering things of great importance, not for Israel only but for all the world; our commentators easily show this to be a delusion.

There is something wrong here, and it will presently be seen that the trouble is not deep-seated, but purely an external matter. By a few slight touches here and there in well-chosen places it is possible to disguise any human face. By a similar process new and misleading features have been added to many ancient documents, since the time when interpreters first began to demand (and achieve) certainty in place of ambiguity, and propagandists to seek documentary authority for their views.

We have here before us what is doubtless the most important example of such disguise in all the history of literature. With the half-dozen slight but potent touches removed, we see one of the

38

greatest men of antiquity, and an unsurpassed creation of religious philosophy and poetry, without blemish or ambiguity. While the transforming touches remain, the 'prophet' is a forlorn figure, and his work is *tohu* and *bohu*. Confusion and incoherence are substituted for order and logical consistency, very extensive interpolation and editorial adjustment must be supposed, and the whole work is largely emptied of ethical value. Its second half (a succession of magnificent poems!) is of necessity ascribed to an inferior imitator, or to a school of imitators, no one of whom clearly understood either his own message or that of the predecessors whose phrases and figures of speech he copied.*

It is now in place to examine the Hebrew text of the passages which contain mention of the foreign king by name and evident reference to Babylonia as the land to be conquered by him and thereupon to be abandoned by Jewish exiles returning to Jerusalem. The ancient versions support the Hebrew; no argument against the traditional reading can be derived from any one of them, in any of the passages to be considered. If the original text has suffered alteration or received addition, the 'improvement' was made before the time when the work of translation into Greek was undertaken. There is, however, other and most important evidence, quite aside from the general literary considerations. The *meter* of the poems affords a criterion of which the value is universally recognized.

Emendation on the basis of metric form is now a commonplace of textual criticism, and wherever meter and internal evidence plainly support each other against the traditional reading the argument is justly regarded as conclusive. There is need of great caution here (see Chapter X), but valid evidence is to be had. Very many passages in the poetical portions of the Hebrew Bible have thus been restored to their original form, with the approval of all competent scholars. The Hebrew text of II Isaiah is generally well preserved, a fact which is of great assistance in an investigation of this nature. The present problem, moreover, is in fact simpler than appears at first sight. It can easily be shown that the whole question of the interpolation of Babylonian-exilic allusions hangs upon the single word *lĕ-Kōresh*, "to Cyrus," in 45:1. On this depends also the decision as to the meaning and value of the prophecy of the Second Isaiah. If the prophet himself wrote here

---

* If the reader supposes this to be an exaggerated statement, it is only necessary to refer him to any one of the modern standard commentaries. See also the concluding section of Chapter I in this volume.

the name of the Persian king, then the low estimate of the man and the utter confusion wrought in the book, as set forth in Chapter I, are inevitable. If he did not write it, then the whole modern theory of his book, with the tissue of contradictions and the chimera of a 'Trito-Isaiah,' is gone in a twinkling. It will be seen, when the passages are examined, that the 'Cyrus-exile' element is present only in a few small and purely superficial spots, dabbed on, as it were, in an easy-going way by some one who felt that he could render a useful service by making plain what was obscure. When the spots are removed—and they come off very easily, leaving no mark—*the meter of each passage is for the first time in order*, and there remains in the whole prophecy no suggestion either of Jews in Babylonia or of a foreign potentate.

1. *The "Cyrus" Interpolations in* 45 : 1 *and* 44 : 28

It has already been shown, in Chapter II, how terms definitely applied by the prophet *to Israel*, as God's 'elect,' the one who was 'called from the ends of the earth,' 'whose right hand God holds,' who is to 'perform all his pleasure,' who is to 'thresh mountains, and make the hills as chaff,' scattering all foes like a whirlwind, are in 45 : 1 ff. applied *to Cyrus;* and if in this passage, then presumably in others—with confusion as the result. Logically, all these passages should refer to the same chosen instrument of God's purpose; in fact, they cannot possibly all be made to refer to Cyrus, and the attempt to fit them to him necessitates in every case some slight alteration of the text. Do they not, then, all refer to Israel, or Israel's representative? Has the mention of Cyrus by name a place in the Hebrew text which is above suspicion?

There are probably not many who realize how strong is the merely textual evidence against the word *lĕ-Kōresh*, "*to Cyrus*," in 45 : 1. The fact is, it is metrically superfluous, and so distinctly so, that this one fact is sufficient of itself to mark it as a probable interpolation. The metric verse originally read as follows:

kōh āmár Yahwĕ limĕšīchŏ, | *ăšér hechĕzáqtī bīmīnŏ.*

To one who glances at Professor Cheyne's edition of the Hebrew, where the text is printed in metric lines, the length of this particular line, with the name added, cannot fail to attract attention. There is nothing else like it on the whole page; all the other lines are of about the same length, but the one word *lĕ-Kōresh* projects beyond the margin, and stares the reader in the face. When the attempt is made to scan the passage, the superfluous name is even more troublesome. As poetry, the line is ruined by the presence of this word; the fact is beyond question. In Kittel's *Biblia Hebraica*, it is relegated to the second half of the verse, but with no improvement in the result. Neither in the first half-verse nor in the second half can the word find a place.

The conclusion, supported by such evidence, internal and external, ought to be no longer in doubt; the word is *an explanatory addition to the text*, by a later hand; its office being to interpret the word *limĕšichō*, "to his anointed one."

Some one, it seems, saw in our poet's frequent songs of exultation promising "deliverance to captives," predictions of the return from the Babylonian exile, and wished to make them more definite. This was in every way most natural. More than half of the book is taken up with assurances of speedy help and release for downtrodden Israel. The 'exiled' children of Zion are to return. The former glory of Jerusalem, the holy city, now desolate, shall speedily be restored. The wasted cities of Judah shall be built up, and the faithful people of God shall again possess them. Strangers and enemies are to have the upper hand no longer in the sacred territory. God has been cherishing his great purpose, and will now show the nations his power. He is on the point of raising up a great deliverer, who shall trample upon the heathen nations, and bring release to the chosen people. He shall "raise up the tribes of Jacob, and restore Israel."

The prophet also predicts in a very striking manner the downfall and destruction of Babylon. In the fine poem which constitutes chapter 47 he rebukes at length (for the only time) the arrogant wickedness of a portion of the Gentile world, so mighty and prosperous, in contrast with Israel, and of course admired and envied by very many of the prophet's fellow countrymen. Babylon had long been for the Hebrew people of Palestine the symbol of worldly power, luxury, and pride. As such a symbol the great metropolis and former capital is presented and denounced in this poem. Nothing is said, indeed, of her present *power;* the picture is rather of pampered selfishness and of a contemptuous reliance on her own deities and enchanters—on her own 'wisdom.' She is soon to be brought to the dust, says the prophet, and her sages and sorcerers will feel the fire of hell. The worthlessness of her 'great gods' will be patent to the world. In all the poem there is not even a hint at any 'Babylonian captivity' of Jews, nor of any benefit which Israel is to receive from the fall of the city; and yet the place of the poem among its fellows, and especially the argument of the immediately preceding poem, chapter 46, make it plain that the doom of Babylon is contemporary with the restoration of Israel—whatever that may mean.

As is here shown, the poet's beautiful prophecies of a return home are the product of poetic imagination and religious fervor. His confidence springs from his faith in God, rather than from any change in the political situation. The return is repeatedly declared by him to be from the four quarters of the earth, and the impending catastrophe to be one which involves all the nations and races of the inhabited world. But to a Jewish reader who was familiar with the theory of a complete 'restoration' under Cyrus which is set forth *in the Chronicler's history of Israel*, the apparent literal fulfilment of a considerable part of the prediction in the 'return of the Babylonian exiles' could not fail to suggest itself.

The tendency to find a definite historical setting for Psalm or predictive Prophecy is universal and very strong. A superficial reader thought himself to find a remarkably suitable background here, with all the seemingly plain allusion to the Babylonian captors, to Cyrus, and to the expedition under Zerubbabel and Jeshua. He proceeded to put the matter beyond doubt by making a few slight additions to the Hebrew text, designed to assist the popular understanding of the book and to render unmistakable the meaning of certain striking passages.

Explanatory interpolations, interpreting supposed historical allusions, are frequently met with in the traditional text of the Hebrew prophets. It is noteworthy that such inserted explanations are usually mistaken. Thus, in Is. 7:17, 20 and in 8:7, "the king of Assyria" is an unfortunate addition to the original text. In 8:6, "Rezin and the son of Remaliah" is an erroneous gloss (see Gray's *Commentary*). In 29:10 "the prophets" and "the seers" are mistaken insertions. In Ezek. 26:7 "Nebuchadrezzar, king of Babylon," is a marginal gloss inserted in the wrong place, as the context shows. Thus also Nah. 3:18, "the king of Assyria" (so Arnold, Marti, Powis Smith, and almost all recent commentators); and Hos. 13:7, "Asshur," probably. In Neh. 8:9 and 10:2, the name "Nehemiah" is a misleading insertion; so also in I Esdr. 5:40, Neh. (Greek) 7:70; 8:9. In I Esdr. 4:13, the false interpolation, "this was Zerubbabel" (!), had very far-reaching consequences. The same name was interpolated also in 6:17, 26, 28. In I Kings 22:28 the last clause (not in LXX) was inserted in order to make the false identification of Micaiah the son of

Imlah with the prophet Micah (see Mic. 1:2). Similarly, in the Greek of Mal. 1:1 the words θέσθε δὴ ἐπὶ τὰς καρδίας ὑμῶν were added with the purpose of identifying this prophet with Haggai (see the Greek in Hag. 1:13; 2:15, 18). Finally—to return to Isaiah, in 42:1 the Greek translator has introduced the names "Jacob" and "Israel"; a harmless addition, as it happens. In 45:13, where in the original Hebrew the Servant of Yahwè was intended, the Greek has inserted the word βασιλέα, with Cyrus in view. These instances may serve for illustration of a well-known tendency.

Now that it has been shown that the name of Cyrus is out of place and a very disturbing element, not only logically but also metrically, in the text of 45:1, and that its insertion by a later hand is easily explained, it remains to investigate the only other passage in the book in which this king is mentioned; namely, 44:28. As this verse immediately precedes 45:1, the probability is at once suggested that another interpolation (or, rather, another portion of the same one) is to be recognized here.

In the great poem which begins at 44:24 and continues to the end of chapter 45, the prophet introduces again the theme first presented in 41:2 f., 15, *the triumph of Israel, under the divinely appointed Leader, in the Coming Age.* The argument follows the same general course as in chapters 41, 42, and 43. In vss. 24 f. the omnipotence of Yahwè is set forth. Vs. 26 promises the return of the dispersed of Israel, and the future glory of the holy land, under the ministration of the Servant (*cf.* 41:18 f.; 42:7; 43:5 ff.). Yahwè's *'ebed* and *mal'ak,* who was declared in 42:19 to be (temporarily) blind and deaf, is now presented, with the same titles, as counsellor and commander. In vs. 27 there is the usual reference to the deliverance from Egypt: "Who saith to the deep, Be dry, and thy rivers I make dry ground."

Vs. 28 then proceeds: "*Who saith of Cyrus, He is my shepherd, and all my pleasure he shall fulfil; and saying of Jerusalem, She shall be built; and the temple, Thy foundation shall be laid.*" Duhm, Klostermann, Cheyne, Marti, and others pronounce the second half of this verse a later addition, and expunge it. It is out of place after vs. 26b, they observe, besides being awkwardly expressed. This is true; but it is also the case that the *first* half of the verse is out of place after vs. 26a (where *mal'akō*, parallel with *'abdō*, is the true reading, as 42:19a shows conclusively).* The

* Some copyist or editor, knowing that the "angels" are the "counsellors" of Yahwè, made the foolish change to the plural number.

whole of vs. 28, in short, is a weak and mistaken replica of vs. 26, very badly out of harmony with its preceding context. It has a significant connection, however, with the following verse, 45:1! Unquestionably, it was inserted here in order to prepare the way for the *lĕ-Kōresh* in the latter passage; the hand which interpolated the single word there interpolated also the preceding verse. The corroboration of this conclusion obtained from the commentators just mentioned is very welcome. Now that they have pointed out the secondary character of the greater part of the verse, no one need hesitate to recognize the remainder as a part of the same addition.

The evidence afforded by this second, more extended interpolation is important. It shows that the insertion of the name in 45:1 was not a mere accident, such as the incorporation of a stray marginal gloss. On the contrary, the original text has received deliberate additions *in the interest of a theory.* We may therefore be on the lookout for other additions having the same purpose; *ab uno disce omnes.* There is, in fact, one other interpolation of this class, in some respects even more interesting, which has been made in three different places, as we shall see.

2. *The "Babylon-Chaldea" Interpolation*

The two passages in which the Persian king Cyrus is introduced into the text of II Isaiah do not stand alone. The same hand has interpolated, in three separate contexts, the parallel names "Babylon" (or "Babylonia") and "Chaldea," the one immediately echoing the other. The object of the interpolation is to assist the reader by definite allusions to the "land of exile" and the return under Cyrus. This is accomplished very simply, by inserting *Bābel* in the first half of a verse, or of a double clause, and balancing it with *Kasdīm* in the second half. The confusion (of meaning, or meter, or both) thus introduced into the text is in every case noticeable. The examples of this twofold insertion are 43:14; 48:14; and 48:20. That is, within the compass of a few chapters the same alteration has been made in three widely differing contexts, into no one of which can the addition be made to fit.

There are few, if any, examples of interpolation in the Hebrew Old Testament more interesting and instructive than these; nor, it may safely be asserted, are there any which from internal indi-

---

* The question is, simply, whether or not the glossator intended his gloss to become a part of the text of the book.

cations alone, unaided by the testimony of parallel passages or
versions, can be more certainly demonstrated.

For the sake of clearness, the evidence may be set forth concisely at the outset. Two of the three passages picture a journey
home to the holy land. In both cases, 43 : 14 ff. and 48 : 20 f., it
is the return of the great Dispersion that is imagined; in each, also,
the scene of the Flight from Egypt is reproduced, as the familiar
and indisputable evidence of Yahwè's long-standing purpose for
his chosen people. This interpretation is rendered certain by the
following facts especially: the express announcement of the return
from the Dispersion in 43 : 5 f.; the prediction of the journey *in
ships* in 43 : 14; the unquestionable allusions to the *escape* and
flight from Egypt in both passages; and, finally, the fact that the
omission, in either case, of the disturbing "Babylon" and "Chaldea" restores the original meter. In the remaining instance, 48 : 14,
both context and meter are decisive. Vs. 16 says explicitly that
Yahwè reminds his people (and in vs. 14 the foreign nations also
are reminded) of a lesson that has been before them "*clearly, from
the beginning*"; and here again the meter, rendered impossible by
the same "Babylon" and "Chaldea," is perfectly restored by their
omission. Aside from all this, an examination of the prophet's
argument, as embodied in these chapters and those adjoining,
shows that he is dealing with the early history of Israel and the
coming 'Messianic' triumph, not with any minor episode. This
will now be shown in more detail.

The first of the three instances of the twofold interpolation,
43 : 14, has long been a *crux* for the commentators. This much,
at least, is plain as to the general meaning of the verse, that it
has to do with God's rescue of his people; he speaks as Israel's
"redeemer" (vs. *a*), and the second half-verse begins with the
corresponding words, "for your sake I send." Moreover, it is
plain that the "sending" is for the sake of home-coming children
of Israel who are "escaping" (*bārīchīm*) from regions where they
have been held in durance; that the sea, and "ships," are to play
a part; and that there are to be "shouts of rejoicing." The connection of all this with the preceding passages 42 : 22 and 43 : 5 f.
(!) ought to be quite unmistakable—and would be at once if it
were not for the interpolation which has turned order into chaos.
From the context and the very striking parallels we should suppose that the prophet must have intended in 43 : 14 to predict
that the scattered people would return joyfully in ships from far-
off lands, in the glorious time to come. This conclusion is rendered

doubly sure by vs. 16, which continues: "Thus saith Yahwè, *who makes a way in the seas, and a path in the mighty waters,*" etc.

However, our present Hebrew text reads (vs. *b*): *lĕma'ankem shillachtī* Bābelah *wĕhōradtī bārīchīm kullām* wĕ-Kasdīm *bo'ŏnīyōth rinnāthām;* and as long as it remains in this condition there is nothing to do but either to follow Duhm, Cheyne, Marti, and others, who give it up as hopeless, and fill out their lines with asterisks, or else to rewrite it entirely, as Klostermann has done. In the Lexicon of Ges.-Buhl, *s. v. Bārīǎch,* the text of the passage is said to be "*nicht mehr verständlich.*" But the simple solution of the difficulty is certainly this, that *Bābelah* and *Kasdīm* are insertions by a later hand. (Observe that the latter is the name of the country, "Chaldea," as in the two other passages discussed below, and that, like *Bābelah,* it is in the accusative case as the limit of motion.) As soon as they are removed, everything is in order; the verse reads smoothly from beginning to end, and fits its context exactly: "For your sake I will send and bring* all the fugitives, exulting, in their ships."† *Cf.* 43:5 f.; 49:12, 22; 60:4, 9; 66:19! Of course 'Babylon' and 'Chaldea' are the last names we should expect to see coupled with mention of ships in which exiles are to return to Judea. Just how would the prophet have expected the people to make their sea-voyage from Babylonia to Palestine? The Suez Canal was not then constructed. But the interpolator evidently did not feel this difficulty strongly. Nor did the fact that the expanded verse reads awkwardly lead him to make any attempt at smoothing over the rough places. In the other two cases also, as we shall see, he makes his interpolation as simple as possible, without troubling himself about the difficulties of the resulting text. The comparison of these passages will be found to bring strong confirmation of the conclusion reached in the case of the verse just considered.

The second example is 48:14, a passage in which, fortunately, the progress of the prophet's thought is rendered quite certain by a considerable number of close parallels. Its theme is the one introduced for the first time in chapter 41, and repeated again and again in the succeeding chapters: Yahwè's omnipotence, and the right of his claim to be the only God, shown to the world by his dealing with his chosen people, from the very beginning on to the coming day of triumph.

Yahwè addresses the Israelites (vs. 12*a*), the contemporaries of

---

* *Hōrīdh,* because of the ships; *cf.* 42:10, etc.
† Literally, "in the ships of their rejoicing."

the prophet, and summons them to stand forth and listen (14*a*); they, of all the peoples of the earth, are his competent witnesses (43 : 19; 44 : 8, etc.). He then puts the familiar questions: What one of all the heathen 'gods' has given evidence of any such power to form an eternal purpose, and to fulfil it? What one of them has been able to foretell the wonderful triumph of an obscure people? The form of the question in this verse, *mī bāhem higgīd zōth*,* is exactly the same as in 43 : 9; *cf.* also 41 : 21, 26; 45 : 21, etc. He then declares the proof of his own supreme power. From all the parallel passages we should expect this to be the calling of Abraham, the preparing of a people, and *the final triumph of despised Israel*. See especially 41 : 8–19, and notice the conclusion in vs. 20; 42 : 1–8; 45 : 9–25; 49 : 7.† So in vs. 15 Yahwè continues, after his hearers have listened in silence to the evidence:

It was I who declared it, I who called him; | I brought him, and
　　prospered his way.
Draw near to me, hear ye this; | not in secret have I told it,‡ from
　　the first.

That is, Yahwè reminds his hearers that when he called Abraham and Israel he made them definite promises, telling them plainly the end from the beginning (the prophet's favorite phrase); from the first, he himself was with his people (vs. 16*a*). In the parallel passage, 45 : 9–25, almost the same words occur in vs. 19: "I did not speak in secret, in a dark place; I did not say to the seed of Jacob, Seek me for nothing!" §

We now turn to the second half of vs. 14, the all-important clause in which must be stated, even though very briefly, *the facts* of Yahwè's dealing with Israel; those facts which he had foretold, and which the nations of the world would be compelled to recognize. The Hebrew reads: ‖

hā'ēl Yahwè ăhēbō, ya'ăseh chephṣō bĕBābel ūzĕrō'ō Kasdīm.

This would be exactly what is required, if it were not for the two words *Bābel* and *Kasdīm*. That Yahwè's formally announced dem-

───────────

* On the Hebrew text of the verse, which is not quite in its original form even when the interpolation has been removed, see below.

† For a discussion of the passages supposed to refer to Cyrus, see above, pp. 33 ff.

‡ *Dibbartī;* same verb, same subject, and same meaning as in the preceding verse.

§ Observe how in the Greek text of 48 : 16 MSS. ℵ and A insert the words of 45 : 19.

‖ On the Hebrew text at this point, see the commentary on the passage.

onstration to the world of his sole right to be God should base
itself on a promise of vengeance on Babylonia (!) would be too
pitiful an anticlimax to be credible, even if the whole array of
parallel passages did not show conclusively that, to this prophet,
the great facts of the demonstration centred in *Israel*, not in this
or that outside incident, and covered the whole range of history
from the call of Abraham to the glorious future which God had
promised. Moreover, the triumph of the Jews over Babylonia
would be no 'demonstration' at all. Any heathen god, it could be
claimed, might do, and had done, just such things as these. As regards the form of the verse, moreover, it is to be noticed how the
word *Kasdīm* hangs loosely and awkwardly in its context, exactly
as is the case in the passage 43 : 14, considered above. It is obvious that we have here a second example of the *Bābel-Kasdīm* interpolation. These words being removed, there is no more dif-
ficulty: "The (One) God, Yahwè, has loved him; | he (Israel)*
will execute his pleasure and his might."† This is precisely the
convincing argument presented in the passages most closely parallel. *Cf.* at the beginning of the demonstration in 41 : 8 ff. the phrase
"seed of Abraham my beloved," and the general promise of Israel's
triumph in the sequel; in 43 : 1–13 the declaration "I have loved
thee" (vs. 4)‡—*cf.* vss. 1–3—and the splendid promise in vss. 5–6;
in 44 : 1–8 the words of affection in vss. 1, 2, and the promise in
vss. 3–5. The emendation thus receives strong support from without.

The third example is 48 : 20, where the prophet suddenly breaks
forth into one of the short songs of exultation which are so characteristic of him. His theme is: 'Go forth, and carry to the ends of
the earth the wonderful tidings of Israel's redemption!' The
original form of the opening lines was as follows:

Go forth, fly, with a shout of joy; | proclaim this, make it known;
Carry it forth to the ends of the earth; | Yahwè redeems his servant
    Jacob!

This has been ruined, both in rhythm and still more in meaning, by the very same interpolation which we have found in 43 : 14
and 48 : 14. Here, again, the disturbance introduced by the in-

---

* According to the interpolator, the subject here was Cyrus.
† The subject of the verb in the last clause might be either Israel or Yahwè
(46 : 10, etc.), but it is more probably Israel the Servant; *cf.* 41 : 2 f., 12–16.
On the meaning of *zĕrō'a* here, *cf.* especially 51 : 5 and 53 : 1.
‡ *Cf.* also 63 : 9.

tolerable "Babylon" and "Chaldea" is sufficiently obvious. The opening verse-member has become: *ṣĕ'ū* mibBābel *birchū* mikKasdim *bĕqōl rinnā*, "Go forth *from Babylon,* flee *from Chaldea,* with a shout of joy," etc.*

This reading is disturbing, and indeed quite unacceptable, for several reasons. In the first place, it is obviously an instance of 'great cry and little wool.' The incident of a portion of the Jewish colonists in Babylonia migrating to join their fellow countrymen in Judea would not impress "the ends of the earth" in the least. As has already been shown (see the preceding chapter), the argument, truly valid, which the prophet repeatedly presents, is based on something more substantial: the call of Abraham from a distant land, and the promises made to him; the escape from Egypt and the journey to the Promised Land; the mission of the Servant, now plainly appearing; the certain accomplishment, in the future, of the One God's eternal plan. The parallel between vss. 14 f. and vss. 20 f. is obvious, and hence the interpolator treated the two neighboring passages alike.

Again, the verb *birchū*, "flee," is clearly out of place in speaking of the joyful procession from Babylonia by edict of Cyrus and under his patronage. In the *Handwörterbuch* of Ges.-Buhl a special meaning of the verb, "eilig weggehen," is assumed for this one passage, but the assumption is purely arbitrary and mistaken; the verb, which is much used, invariably means "flee." In speaking of *the flight from Egypt,* to which, as we have seen, the prophet continually appeals, the verb would be quite in place; it is the one actually employed at the beginning of the account in Exodus (14:5). Vs. 21 shows, as plainly as words can show anything, that the prophet is in fact reviewing here, as also in 52:11 f., the story of the great deliverance from bondage.

Furthermore, the prophet's words in vss. 18 and 22 (to say nothing of vss. 1–11!) say, in effect, that although Israel was chosen in the beginning, and rescued once by divine power and with miraculous provision and guidance, and can therefore look forward with certainty to ultimate triumph, *yet the great day is still in the indefinite future. The "chosen" people are not yet prepared, either in faith or in conduct, for the promised restoration.* Our modern commentators have sought to avoid this by cutting out vss. 17–19 and 22 (and a considerable part of the first half of the

* That the words *bĕqōl rinnā* should be connected with the verb *ṣĕ'ū*, not with *haggīdū*, is of course the natural construction in view of the meaning of the word *rinnā*; cf. also the use with *bō'* in 35:10; 51:11.

chapter) as secondary; thus destroying the great teacher's argument, and removing all the ethical value of this most impressive poem.

Finally, verse 20, *as it stands*, is metrically anomalous, hopelessly out of keeping with the remainder of the poem. The despair to which it has reduced our critics of the metrical form can best be seen in the handful of minute and unmusical fragments into which this verse and the following have been chopped, in the texts of Duhm, Cheyne, Marti, and Kittel's *Biblia Hebraica*. As soon, however, as the two interpolated proper names are removed, the same result appears as in the other cases, 43:14 and 48:14; the three-beat meter, which would naturally be expected, is perfectly restored and everything is in order, as shown above.

The interpolation of the words "Babylon" and "Chaldea" in the three passages is thus sufficiently demonstrated. Some interpreter, we now know, wished to make it plain to all future readers of these poems that their author (supposedly Isaiah the son of Amoz) predicted the return of the Babylonian exiles under Cyrus, as narrated by the Chronicler in the first chapters of Ezra.

It may be well to summarize here the evidence thus far presented. The contention that the Cyrus-Babylonia patches are secondary, not a part of the original Hebrew text, is supported by (1) the meter, (2) the immediate context in each case, (3) the parallel passages, (4) the well-known fact of many similar interpretative additions to texts of the Old Testament, (5) the presence of an obvious motive for making these interpolations, (6) the acknowledged fact that the historical background which they demand can rarely be made to fit an entire poem, (7) the very remarkable uniformity of purely literary characteristics (including language, style, and mental habit) tending to show that a single author composed all of the twenty-seven poems, not merely a part of them, (8) the fact that by the removal of these palpable glosses, without further change, we obtain a glorious prophecy, clear and consistent from beginning to end, and the greatest of the Hebrew prophets; in place of bewildering contradictions, disarranged fragments, and very inferior writers. If there is anywhere else in the Old Testament any such array of evidence supporting a critical procedure, I do not know where it is to be found.

The question will doubtless be raised, whether 45:13 may not be another interpretative addition of the same sort:

I have raised him up in righteousness, | and all his ways I make
    straight;

He shall build up my city, | and my captives he shall set free;
Not for price nor for hire, | proclaims the Lord of Hosts.

On a first reading, this might, indeed, seem to be secondary, and
to be classed with the additions just considered; but I myself feel
sure that it is a part of the original prophecy; see the commentary
on the passage. The Righteous Servant, it must be remembered,
was destined to build up Jerusalem, and to bring home the 'exiles'
(*i. e.*, Jewish colonists) from all the regions of the earth; *cf.* 42 : 7;
43 : 5 f.; 49 : 5 f., 12, 17; 61 : 1, 4. They were sold into bondage
for nought (50 : 1; 52 : 3); and they are to be freed with honor and
escorted home in triumph by their erstwhile oppressors, not ransomed after the manner of captives; see 49 : 22; 52 : 3; 60 : 3 ff., 9,
14; 66 : 19 f. If I am right in regarding 45 : 13 as original, it is
quite likely that this verse, especially, suggested Cyrus and the
return from Babylon to the interpolator.

Whoever admits the presence of these five (or rather these two)
interpolations—the two containing the name of Cyrus, and the
thrice occurring *Bābel, Kasdīm*—will hardly doubt that they were
all the work of one and the same hand. They are worthy of praise
as the skilful achievement of a definite purpose. Few and simple
as they are, the ingeniously effective manner of their distribution
has made them a most powerful group. As for the date of the interpolation, this only can be said, that it was between the time
when the theory of the great return of "all Israel" from Babylonia
under Cyrus arose (before the middle of the third century) and
the time when the Greek translation of Isaiah was made.*

Aside from these few explanatory additions which I have mentioned, there is no further trace of Cyrus or of the Babylonian
exiles, either by direct mention or by indirect allusion, in the
whole book. There also remains no ground whatever for pronouncing the book the fragmentary work of a succession of imitators,
as must necessarily be the case when Cyrus and the 'Babylonian
captivity' are dragged in.

What is more than this, it is hardly too much to say that the

---

* It is an interesting coincidence that the two known examples of *athbash*
in the Old Testament, the substitution of *Šēšak* for *Bābel* (Babylon) in Jer.
25 : 26 and 51 : 41, and of *Lēbqāmai* for *Kasdīm* (Chaldea) in Jer. 51 : 1, play
upon the two names which we see to have been studiously inserted in II Isaiah,
and were also accomplished at an early date—perhaps even earlier than the
versions show, since the meaning of the cipher must have been generally
known. It would seem that some Jewish scholar or scholars in the last centuries
B. C., who tampered with the Hebrew text of the prophets, had an uncanny
interest in these two proper names.

now prevalent (or rather universal) theory, carried out with candor and adequate scholarship to its legitimate conclusions, must result in a *reductio ad absurdum*. This, I think, is clearly shown in the present treatise. It may be left to the judgment of scholars whether the current theory, with these inevitable consequences, is to be preferred to one according to which the book is a unit, the work of one author, with its parts in their original order and the text well preserved; consistent and transparent in its thought, from beginning to end; and beyond question the greatest and most original specimen of Hebrew poetry, or of Hebrew prophecy, that has come down to us. The theory which results in ascribing to any given composition coherency and textual soundness should certainly be preferred to one which necessitates the opposite verdict. With those who refuse, on principle, to recognize in the Old Testament any interpolation in the interest of a theory, or for the purpose of interpretation, I can of course have no argument; nor, on the other hand, with those (if there be such) who prefer to believe, in the case of any Old Testament book, that it is now in a confused and fragmentary condition, and was originally the work of an inferior class of writers.*

* As regards interpolations in the text, the choice is between these few and a multitude; as regards interpretation, the choice is between one overwhelming creation and a confused mass of occasional preachments.

CHAPTER IV

A NEW VIEW OF THE PROPHECY

1. *General Features*

Chapters 34–66 of the Book of Isaiah (with the exception of 36–39, which have a different origin) form a homogeneous group and are the work of a single hand. The evidence of unity of authorship is manifold and clear. The twenty-seven poems which constitute the group were composed and written down in the order in which we now find them. Their author wrote in Palestine, presumably in Jerusalem, near the end of the fifth century B. C. The people whom he addresses are in their own land, and there is in his words no hint that they, or any portion of them, have ever been anywhere else. The Second Temple has long been in existence. There is not only the constant implication that Jerusalem is still the actual centre of Israel's worship, the 'holy city' in fact as well as in name, or in imagination, and that the people can and do maintain the ancient forms of their cult, however unworthily and half-heartedly (thus 40:16 ff.; 48:1 f.; 54:2), but the very important passage 43:23 f. says plainly that they are, and have been, offering sacrifices and performing the prescribed rites.

Hast thou not brought me thy sheep for burnt offerings? | With thy
    sacrifices hast thou not honored me?
Nay, I have not made thee serve with offerings, | nor labor for me
    with incense!
Hast thou not bought me the fragrant reed with thy money? | With
    the fat of thy sacrifices hast thou not sated me?
Nay, rather, thou hast burdened me with thy sins, | hast wearied me
    with thine iniquities! *

With all the diversity of subject-matter and writer's mood in these twenty-seven poems, there is one main theme which is always present, usually in the foreground, sometimes in the background; it is *The Hope of Israel, the People Chosen of God to Save*

* See the discussion of this passage in the Commentary.

53

the World. The theme is old in Hebrew literature, it is true; but
it is here conceived and elaborated with such breadth of view,
profundity of thought, and logical grasp of the great problem in
all its bearings, as make it altogether new.

The condition of the Jewish people addressed by the prophet is
typical of the time, the latter half of the Persian period. The population of Jerusalem and its sister cities and towns has been deci-
mated by the long-continued stream of emigration to the Jewish
colonies in all parts of the world, and the fateful process is ever
going on. The 'holy land' has seemingly no religious future of
consequence. The vassal province is a miserable remnant. Out
of these conditions a new evil has arisen; new, that is, in its prev-
alence: the worship of foreign gods. The prophet's aim is to
arouse his people to new faith, by showing them the true meaning
of the past and the present in their history, and especially by
painting a soul-stirring picture of the future glory which is certain to come and may be near at hand. His book has often been
called the 'Prophecy of Comfort,' chiefly, no doubt, because of
the mistaken supposition that 40:1 is its beginning, but the title
is unsuitable. 'Prophecy of Rebuke' would be at least as applicable, for the prophet censures his contemporaries oftener than
he reassures them. There is, indeed, comfort for Israel, the downtrodden race; comfort for poor Jerusalem, the beloved, who has
"paid double for all her sins"; but when the seer turns his eyes
to the Jewish people of his personal knowledge, we are certain to
hear a deep note of indignation and a trumpet-call of warning.
They are faithless, blind, unworthy; those who still 'follow after
righteousness,' whether courageous or faint-hearted (35:3 f.;
48:10; 51:1, 7; 65:8 f.; 66:5) are a handful in comparison.

The prophet saw no immediate promise in the present situation.
His confidence rested on three supports: Yahwè's omnipotence,
the choice of Israel the 'Servant,' and his own vision of the possibility, through divine help, of arousing the Jewish people, and
through them all mankind, to a living faith and a better life. There
was nothing hopeful in the present attitude of his people, certainly
nothing in the political situation, to which indeed he pays no
attention beyond including it in his general picture of Israel's distress. In the conditions resulting from the Dispersion he saw
promise, as will appear. There was endless hope in the record of
the past, and he again and again reminds his hearers of the call
of Abraham and Jacob, and of the exodus, the Red Sea, and the
miraculously guided homeward march through the desert. The

Second Isaiah knew of no recent 'restoration,' or indeed of any restoration at all except the one from Egypt. At the time when these poems were written the theory of a 'Babylonian exile,' involving a complete depopulation of Jerusalem and Judea, such as we see pictured in Chronicles-Ezra-Nehemiah, had not yet arisen. The ground of his faith in the *speedy* coming of deliverance was in no human fact or condition, but in his own conception of the love of God for his people and for the world.

To one filled with this conviction the very hopelessness (to human eyes) of the present situation could give a vivid hope, as the blackest hour of the night foretells the dawn. The God of Israel *must* intervene, and that speedily; he must act, for his own sake. This is said, in impassioned language, more than once. First of all there is the dramatic passage 42 : 14 ff., with its daring picture of the God of Israel speaking in his own person in a state resembling desperation, unable to endure longer the torment of seeing his plan thwarted, his people persecuted, his honor doubted. He gasps for breath, utters a cry, then comes forth single-handed to the rescue:

For a long time I have held my peace, | restraining myself in silence; ||
I will cry out like a woman in travail, | panting and gasping at once. ||

There is no human helper, no other occasion for action than his own feeling of necessity. Other passages reiterate this. 43 : 25, "It is I, I only, blotting out thy transgressions for my own sake." 48 : 9, 11, "For my own sake will I do it, for how should my name be dishonored?" 52 : 5 is similar. 59 : 17 is the counterpart of 42 : 13; and 63 : 1–4 and 66 : 6, 9 reproduce the same scene in different language and with various figures of speech. It is especially to be noticed that in each one of the places in which the poet thus portrays Yahwè as the incensed Warrior, going forth alone to battle for right and justice in the world and for the true religion, there is added, very significantly, some statement of the fact that the men of Israel themselves are still faithless and undeserving; it is not because of any past or present merit of theirs that the change is to be expected.

Thus, immediately after the passage in chapter 42 just referred to, in vss. 18 ff., Israel—the Israel *of the present*, and not merely of the past—is sternly rebuked as blind, deaf, and disobedient. So in the similar context in chapter 43: Israel is 'weary of Yahwè' (vs. 22). It is plain that in the mind of the prophet the main evils of the present condition which make it a crisis necessitating divine

action are *two* in number: first, and obvious to all, the misery of
the scattered and despised people; second, what is much more distressing to Yahwè, the wide-spread unbelief and unfaithfulness of
the chosen race. In 48 : 1–11, where it is said, twice over, that the
situation is so desperate that Yahwè *must* act, this second cause,
the present sin of Israel, is asserted with vehemence.

Hearken to this, O house of Jacob !— | these who are called by Israel's
    name, | who sprung from the seed of Judah;
Who swear by the name of Yahwè, | and invoke the God of Israel;
Not in truth, nor by right, | do they name themselves from the holy
    city,
And 'rest themselves on the God of Israel,' | Yahwè of Hosts is his
    name !

The former things I declared of old, | from my mouth they issued, and
    I made them known; | then suddenly I wrought, and they came
    to pass;
Because I know thou art stubborn, | thy neck is a band of iron, | thy
    forehead is brass.
Yea, I told them to thee from the first, | before they appeared I an-
    nounced them,
Lest thou shouldst say, My idol wrought them, | my graven and
    molten image ordained them. . . .

Thou hast never heard, hast never known, | of old thine ear has not
    been open.
Yea, I know indeed that thou playest false, | transgressor from birth
    thou art rightly called !
For my name's sake I restrain my wrath, | for the sake of my praise I
    bridle it for thee, | not willing to cut thee off.

This is unsparing denunciation, in spite of the assurance that
Yahwè will not, even now, utterly abandon Israel. Again, in
59 : 16, in immediate connection with the passage cited above and
after a thrilling confession of sin and wretchedness, the prophet
declares that the God of Israel finds the situation hopeless without
his own intervention. As was said also in 42 : 18–23 and 48 : 1–11,
there is no one who hears and heeds, no human help to be had.

He saw that there was no man, | wondered that there was none to
    interpose;
Therefore his own arm wrought salvation, | his own righteousness was
    his support.

In 63 : 3, 5 there is the same scene, described in almost identical words:

I trod the winepress alone, | of the peoples there was no one with me.*
When I looked, there was none to help, | I wondered that there was
    no supporter;
Therefore my own arm wrought salvation, | my own wrath upheld me.

It is perhaps needless to say that in all this we have before us the work of an artist, not merely the utterance of a preacher, and that the picture is painted on a mighty scale with broad strokes. There were God-fearing men, faithful worshippers, among the people, though the prophet's message is rarely so conceived as to take them into account. In 66 : 5, immediately before the passage cited above (vss. 6–9), in which Yahwè's unaided work of deliverance is described and immediately after the unqualified accusation, "When I called, none answered; when I spoke, they did not hearken," we see express mention of the faithful few, men who already 'revere the word of the Lord' and therefore are scorned by their brethren. One poem of the collection, 51 : 1–16, is actually addressed to this loyal group, but it is the only instance of the kind. It is plain in nearly every chapter that the outlook on Israel as a whole was most distressing to the prophet, and that the cause of his distress lay in what he saw of the moral and religious condition of his people, far more than in any external circumstances.

The majority of those among whom the Second Isaiah lived, and whose daily activities he saw, were at best lukewarm in their faith. The ritual of the temple, carried on in a perfunctory way as far as the people in general were concerned, was of little value. Many had abandoned altogether the religion of their fathers and were experimenting with foreign gods and rites. Were the sacred land and the once-favored people doomed to still more bitter punishment than they had yet suffered? The soul of the prophet was too great to harbor despair; moreover, as his whole triumphant prophecy demonstrates, he saw more clearly than his fellows the possibilities of good even in the conditions out of which these present evils had sprung. He voices in one brief sentence his own anguish mingled with hope in the vehement cry which he puts into the

---

* Has Yahwè totally forgotten Cyrus, 'his anointed'? It would be singular ingratitude not to remember this great deliverer, whose right hand he held, who came from the east calling on his name, the 'man of his counsel.' Or had 'Trito-Isaiah' not read 'Deutero-Isaiah'?

mouth of Yahwè himself (44 : 21): *"O Israel, thou must not forget me!"* *

There is good evidence, as will be shown, that the twenty-seven poems of the collection were composed and written down in close succession, so that a comparatively brief period of time is covered by them. As far as it is possible to guess at the circumstances under which their author wrote, there is no clear indication of change in this regard between the limits of chapters 34 and 66. There is remarkable uniformity in the subjects presented and in the manner of their treatment. The poems are the product of diverse moods, as of course was to be expected, but numerous characteristic motives run straight through the whole, like the warp of a textile. Among the prominent themes, major or minor, the following may be selected for illustration. Others have already been mentioned or will receive notice in subsequent chapters.

The omnipotent Creator of heavens and earth, 40 : 22, 26, 28; 44 : 24; 45 : 12, 18; 48 : 13; 51 : 16; 66 : 1 f.; *cf.* 65 : 17; 66 : 22. The futility of rites and observances, if they are not performed in sincere contrition and devotion, 43 : 22 ff.; 58 : 3 ff.; 66 : 1 ff. Accusation of faithlessness, 40 : 27 ff.; 42 : 18–25; 43 : 22 ff.; 46 : 8, 12; 48 : 1–11, 18 f.; 50 : 1 f., 10 f.; 56 : 9–57 : 13; 59 : 1–8, 13 ff.; 63 : 17; 64 : 6 f.; 65 : 1–14; 66 : 3–5, 24. The specific charge of idolatry, 40 : 19–26; 42 : 17; 44 : 9–21; 45 : 20; 46 : 5–8; 48 : 5; 57 : 5 ff., 13; 65 : 2 f., 7, 11; 66 : 17. The day of wrath, at the end of the present age, 34 : 1 ff.; 51 : 6; 59 : 18; 63 : 1 ff.; 66 : 15 f. The destruction of the unfaithful Israelites, 50 : 11; 57 : 13; 65 : 6 f., 12; 66 : 17. Those who repent will be saved, 44 : 22; 48 : 9; 55 : 6; 59 : 20; 65 : 8. The incorrigible enemies of Yahwè, Gentiles and Jews alike, designated by the term "Edom," 34 : 5 ff.; 63 : 1 ff. The Servant of Yahwè, his call and his mission, 41 : 1–3, 8–16, 25; 42 : 1–7, 18–20; 44 : 1 f., 24–26; 45 : 1–5, 13; 46 : 11; 49 : 1–9; 50 : 4–11; 52 : 13–53 : 12; 55 : 4 f.; 61 : 1–3, 10 f.; 62 : 1–9; 63 : 7. The might of Israel under divine leadership, 41 : 15, 25; 45 : 1 f.; 54 : 15 ff.; 66 : 16. The herald of good tidings, 35 : 4; 40 : 2 f., 9; 41 : 27; 52 : 7 f.; 61 : 1 f.; 62 : 6. The highway through the desert, 35 : 8 ff.; 40 : 3 f.; 41 : 17 f.; 42 : 16; 43 : 19 f.; 48 : 21; 49 : 9–11; 51 : 10 f.; 55 : 12; 57 : 14; 62 : 10; 63 : 13; similar, 66 : 20. The return of the Jewish 'exiles' (*i. e.*, colonists), a long succession of similar passages, from chapter 35 to chapter

---

* The massoretic text here combines two variant readings, as in many hundreds of other cases. As between *tinšēnī* and *tinnāšeh* there can be no question what the prophet wrote; the former reading is the original, the latter the subsequent improvement.

66; expressly said to come from the four quarters of the earth, 43 : 5 f.; 49 : 12; 60 : 8 f.; 66 : 19 f. Salvation for the Gentiles, 42 : 6 f.; 45 : 14 f., 22; 49 : 6, 22 f.; 51 : 4 f.; 52 : 15–53 : 12; 55 : 5; 56 : 7 f.; 60 : 6–14; 61 : 1 f.; 66 : 20 f. Foreign kings shall pay joyful homage, 45 : 14; 49 : 7, 23; 52 : 15; 60 : 10, 16. The new Jerusalem, 35 : 10; 49 : 17–21; 51 : 11; 52 : 1 f., 8 f.; 54 : 11–14; 60 : 1–22; 62 : 1–12; 65 : 18 f.; 66 : 10–13.

This partial list of subjects which recur at intervals throughout the collection of poems gives striking evidence of unity of authorship, especially when the several passages are examined in their context with attention to the progress of the writer's thought, in the light of the interpretation offered in the following pages. The acknowledged homogeneity in vocabulary and phraseology has already been remarked upon, in the preceding Chapters. Some very striking peculiarities of literary conception and treatment, found in all parts of the collection and pointing plainly to a single author, will receive notice in Chapter XI.

2. *The Prophet of the Dispersion*

The great calamity, which had brought dismay to every loyal Israelite, and by reason of which so many were abandoning the faith of their fathers, was the breaking up of the nation. Not the cessation of the kingdom, for the hopeless inferiority of the Israelite states had long been manifest, and they were accustomed to vassalage; not the forcible deportation of a few thousands from Jerusalem and Judea to Babylonia, for this could only be a minor incident, however distressing; but the fact that the chosen people were being scattered to the four winds, emigrating to regions from which, in the present age, they would never return. The homeland and the temple at Jerusalem, however sincerely reverenced, had no longer any practical significance for the growing Jewish colonies. The possibility of a glorious 'kingdom of David' in Judea, with the world constituted as at present, was vanishing rapidly, or indeed had vanished already, as any thoughtful man could see.

The outflow from Palestine into foreign countries, which as early as the seventh century had begun to be important, was given impetus by the successive catastrophes wrought in the land by foreign armies. After nearly thirty thousand had been deported at one time from the Northern Kingdom in 722, and their place filled with natives of various northern and eastern regions, the old

Israelite tradition in this section of the country seems to have lost ground steadily. Samaria eventually became more heathen than Hebrew; the charming and fertile region about the Sea of Galilee was henceforth the 'District of the Gentiles.' The blow was felt in the south hardly less than in the north. Even in the time of the rival kingdoms there had been a strong feeling of unity, and the good hope of a time when the tribes of Jacob should again stand together, as in the days of David and Solomon. Now, however, the prospect of any such restoration was fast disappearing.

The Kingdom of Judah indeed had possession of the stronghold of Israel's faith. While the holy city and the temple were standing, the surviving tribes and families had their rallying-point and a nucleus for the long-desired union. The deportation to Babylonia in 597 and the greater catastrophe in 586 dealt a staggering blow to the hope of Israel. With the temple destroyed, and a part of the city* in ashes, it is no wonder that many were ready to turn away in despair, saying (Jer. 42 : 14): "We will go into the land of Egypt, where we shall see no more war, nor hear the sound of the trumpet, nor hunger for bread; and there will we dwell." Jerusalem was temporarily abandoned. Undoubtedly a considerable part of the old Hebrew population of the Southern Kingdom left the land at this time, to return no more. Another and probably a very large portion took refuge in the neighboring districts, in the hope of coming back to their fields, houses, and other possessions after the withdrawal of the Babylonians from the land. See Jer. 40 : 11 f., 43 : 5. Even those who had collected at Mizpah, who fled to Egypt with Johanan ben Kareah, intended to return to Judea (Jer. 44 : 14).† The Jews were a courageous people, and almost uniquely tenacious of their traditions. The religious motive, moreover, has tremendous power. It is not recorded, nor is it in the least probable, that Nebuchadrezzar's captains left a garrison in Judea or took other measures to prevent the restoration of the land. Whatever the progress of events and the interval of time which elapsed, the city and the temple were ultimately rebuilt, and Jerusalem restored to its primacy as the centre of the worship of Yahwè. Such

---

* II Kings 25 : 9 says that Nebuchadrezzar's army burned "the temple, the palace, and every great house"; the words "and all the houses of Jerusalem" are manifestly a later addition to the verse.

† According to Jer. 43 : 5, this company at Mizpah included "all the remnant of Judah" who thus far had returned from the regions whither they had fled. Even so, it can only have been a portion of the greater 'remnant'—both Jews and Gentiles—waiting to reoccupy the ruined city and the portion of the land which had been abandoned.

reverses as these, however crushing at the time, were only temporary. As early as the latter part of the sixth century there was an
appearance of prosperity. The citizens of Jerusalem could be re-
proached for living comfortably in their "ceiled houses" while
satisfied to leave the temple still inadequately built and equipped
(Hag. 1:4). After the completion of the building under the leadership of Zerubbabel, the restored service could keep pace with the
restored city.

There was a far more potent reason for the distress of the faithful in Israel. For the *dispersion* there was neither check nor rem-
edy. It was not chiefly because conditions in Palestine had become
less favorable than formerly that the Israelite inhabitants of the
land became restless, left their ancient home and sought their fortunes elsewhere; it was rather because they were learning to know
the wider world, and saw its doors thrown open to them. In this
awakening to the consciousness of a new era they merely shared
the experience of the peoples round about them. We know from
many sources that while the kingdoms of Israel and Judah were
still standing a breath of new enterprise had begun to stir all the
nations and races of Western Asia. In the eighth century B. C.
the great colonizing movement of the Phœnicians was in full
swing. By the end of the century all the countries around the
eastern end of the Mediterranean were in a ferment, and migra-
tory currents were flowing in all directions as perhaps never before.
The great cities of Asia Minor and the marts along the trade routes
from the east and south were already doing business on a new
scale. The Greek peoples, now beginning their marvellous renas-
cence, were flocking to the Ionian coast, as well as to other shores.
Then, as the next step, the doors of Egypt were opened wide to
foreign colonists, Psametik I (663–609) adopting this new and very
significant policy. Both Greek and Asiatic traders and emigrants
poured in. "Phœnician galleys filled the Nile mouths, and Semitic
merchants, forerunners of the Aramæans so numerous in Persian
times, thronged the Delta" (Breasted, *History of the Ancient Egyptians*, 1908, p. 398).

The Hebrews for the first time became fully aware of countries
incomparably richer and more prosperous than Palestine, culture
far superior to their own, opportunities of every sort such as they
had never dreamed of in their land of small farms, quiet villages,
and diminutive cities. Always alert and enterprising, they were
not slow to respond when they realized their own less favored position and saw the open road to prosperity. The 'big business' of

the world, the scenes of greatest material achievement of every sort, were inviting them. They went forth eagerly, in a small but unceasing stream of emigration, to the emporia bordering the Nile, the Euphrates and Tigris, the shores of the Mediterranean, and the trade routes of Syria and Asia Minor. Under similar economic conditions many portions of the civilized world have seen such currents set in motion and continued.

This history of temporary depopulation had, as usual, its reverse side in a gradual influx of strangers. Representatives of less highly civilized races, men of physical energy and simple requirements, were ready to take up the abandoned lands and sites when they learned of their existence. Border clans becoming restless or pushed out from their habitation by economic pressure or tribal movement, found in these depleted districts opportunity of betterment which they were not slow to take. Just as in our own generation Kurds, Circassians, Armenians, semi-nomadic Arab tribes, and other roving or transplanted peoples have sifted into Syria, Palestine, and Transjordania, finding room prepared for them, so from the seventh century B. C. onward Syrian and Mesopotamian emigrants from the north, and later Edomites and Nabateans from the south, Moabites and Ammonites from the east, pressed in to share the Israelite territory; coming in troops after each of the deportations, in an incessant trickle at other times, the influx in some measure corresponding to the outflow. Not only the farm lands but even more the cities were thus replenished. Jerusalem, which even in the time of David and Solomon had its considerable foreign element, became in increasing proportion a city of strangers, as more and more of the Hebrew population moved out and found business abroad. After the Chaldean invasion the portions of the city which were left vacant or thinned out by deportation, conflagration, and the exodus due to fear or discouragement were eventually reoccupied not only by Jews but also by companies of foreign immigrants. This was doubtless true also of the Judean villages which had been wholly or partially abandoned.*

In the time of the Second Isaiah the 'exiles,' i. e., Jewish emi-

---

* In the missing portion of the first chapter of Ezra which is now preserved only in 'First Esdras' the Chronicler represents Cyrus as including in his edict for the returning Jews the provision "that the Edomites should give up the villages which they had taken from the Jews" (4 : 50). This gives evidence that in his day at least there was a strong Edomite element in Judea. (In the First Esdras fragment the name 'Darius' has been substituted here for 'Cyrus' in order to make the account fit the interpolated Story of the Three Guardsmen.)

grants from the homeland, were in every quarter of the known world; see 43 : 5 f., 49 : 12, 60 : 4–9. They were at "the ends of the earth" (43 : 6); "ships of Tarshish" would be needed to bring them home (60 : 9, 66 : 19). Other Hebrew prophets make frequent mention of these widely scattered 'exiles,' and it is plain that they, like all the devout leaders of the people, are distressed by the incessant outflow with its incalculable consequences. Jer. 29 : 14, "I will turn again your captivity, and will gather you from all the nations, and from all the places whither I have driven you." 31 : 8, "I will bring them from the north country, and gather them from the uttermost parts of the earth." Cf. also 10 : 21; 23 : 1, 3, 8; 32 : 37; Is. 11 : 11; Zech. 2 : 6, "I have spread you abroad as the four winds of heaven"; 8 : 7 f. Joel 4 : 17 looks forward to the time when the holy city shall be freed from foreigners: "Then shall Jerusalem be holy, and there shall no strangers pass through her any more."

It was no mere loss of cherished tradition which was lamented; it was more even than the apparent certainty of deterioration which many of the people saw foreshadowed in the steady reduction of the ancient territory and the emptying and refilling of Jerusalem; it was the threatened dissolution of Israel. The inherited beliefs and formulas of their religion looked for a united people. All the promises, from the beginning, were attached to the holy land. Who could imagine a triumphant nation, showing to the world the might of Israel's God, and the service worthy of him and his elect, with only small and scattered bodies of worshippers and with no considerable extent of territory that they could claim as belonging to Yahwè? They had sinned and been punished, this they knew. Was it not possible that they had been cast off altogether? Some of the former prophets had seemed to threaten this. It was possible to see in the holy land with its Hebrew tribes and kingdoms, now apparently gone forever, the scene of a preliminary training which had been accomplished. The world was certainly wider and more enlightened than Abraham and Jacob and even David had supposed. There were other gods, other modes of worship. In Babylonia, Persia, Egypt, Greece, and Asia Minor there were great sanctuaries and a magnificence of ritual beside which the best that Jerusalem had ever seen was insignificant. Any inquiring Israelite living in the homeland at the close of the fifth century could visit the imposing Sidonian temple of Eshmūn on the height overlooking the Bostrenus River, only a few hours from the Palestinian border. These Gentile nations were mighty and prosperous, the world's traffic and culture were in their hands. A large proportion of Israelites had already thrown in their lot with them; even if they held fast to their faith—as they generally did—could they claim for it undoubted superiority to the Gentile faiths?

In the inspired utterances of the prophet we can see plainly mirrored the varied effect on his contemporaries of this uprooting of beliefs, an effect which included such extremes of loyalty and apostasy as were depicted by the historians of the Maccabean time under very similar conditions. The rank and file of the people were not 'disheartened,' as they are usually depicted in our treatises; it would be nearer the truth to say that they were somewhat apathetic as to the religious situation, while as energetic and open-eyed as ever in making the most of their circumstances. So far, indeed, as they reflected on the changing horizon and the new ideas which they received from their foreign neighbors, they were made uneasy, or sceptical; and the more thoughtful could not fail to be distressed by the present position of Israel in the world. Their religion was practical rather than speculative, however, and they were occupied with social and economic problems rather than with theology. The subsequent history shows that they were ready to be guided, and that their previous experience of faith and service had not been in vain. The religious leaders of the people were not discouraged; at best they were perplexed (51:18), and at the worst they were indifferent (56:10 f.; the shepherds unheeding, the watch-dogs either asleep or greedily filling themselves). Moreover, it may be remarked here that in all the surviving Hebrew literature of the long period of time during which these same untoward conditions persisted we are given no glimpse of a dispirited people or disheartened leaders. We see often deep distress, but always faith and hope.

The Second Isaiah deserves to be called the Prophet of the Dispersion. It was the fact of the 'desolate' city and land that gave his prophecy its most characteristic theme, his reflection on this ominous change in the fortunes of Israel that led him to work out and formulate his profound conception of God's dealing with the Jewish people and the Gentile world. The children of Abraham, scattered to the four winds, even in their punishment were intrusted with a mission. They were exiles in lands whose surviving inhabitants would in the end turn to Yahwè as their God. The influx of foreigners into Palestine and Jerusalem gave the prophet no great concern, for he saw it as an essential part of the divine purpose. His outlook upon the 'strangers,' whether conceived in the mass or as individuals, is invariably just and large-hearted, and he never leaves them out of account in his scheme of the renovated world.

It has already been observed that Jerusalem had its nucleus of earnest and open-minded seekers after truth, men on whom the prophet could rely; those who 'revered the word of the Lord' (66:5), who 'carried his law in their hearts' and 'pursued righteousness' (51:1, 7). It must have been plain to these that the old order was gone, in religious philosophy as well as in external affairs. The old formulas could no longer give the satisfaction which they had once given. The civilization of Babylonia, Egypt, and Phœnicia, including their art and to some extent their literature, had been exercising their quiet influence for generations past. Even the unthinking among the Jews could recognize some of the good in the Gentile religions; ethical elements, true religious feeling, ideas and rites which so often resembled their own. This was one reason why so many were inclined to make trial of foreign cults. It may well be that not a few would have approved the prophet Malachi's broad assertion (Mal. 1:11) that all sincere worship offered by the heathen to their gods is accepted by Yahwè as offered to him, though never entertaining the idea that the blessings of the chosen people could really be shared by others. Many, doubtless, could see that the hands of the clock were not to be turned backward, yet who could correlate the new ideas with the old dogmas? From the prophet's invectives (see especially chapters 46, 48, 59) it seems plain that a large and influential element of the people had cast off respect for religion and for the moral law as well, while still 'calling themselves by Israel's name.' To them one god was as good as another. For those who merely clung to tradition the danger was that they would withdraw into an inherited shell of forms and doctrines, maintaining a faith characterized by increasing rigidity and decreasing adaptability to the surrounding life. There were such in Israel at that time. Among them were earnest and faithful souls, undoubtedly referred to in 66:5; others were mere formalists—see 43:23 ff. (as interpreted above), 58, and 66:1 ff. The masses of the people lagged far behind, as usual, threatening to lapse into utter indifference.

The Jerusalem of the fifth century B. C. is at the present day commonly pictured as filled with zealous worshippers of Yahwè, who obeyed their religious leaders and magnified the Hebrew ritual. So the Chronicler wished to have it, and attempted to por-

tray it in his books of Ezra and Nehemiah. Trustworthy witnesses
give us unequivocal testimony to the contrary. It is made perfectly plain in Mal. 3 : 16, 20 f., and especially in Is. 66 : 5, that
those who 'feared the Lord' were a minority. Many of the Psalms
give the same impression, too clearly to be explained away. Was
the temple itself used only for the worship of Yahwè? See the
eighth chapter of Ezekiel—in spite of the exaggeration evidently
intended in the picture.* As Kraetzschmar remarks (*Das Buch
Ezechiel*, on 9 : 10): "Die Einwirkung der Politik auf die Religion
war in Israel nicht minder stark als bei anderen Völkern des Alter-
tums." The ridiculous designation "temple-community," "Tem-
pelgemeinde," for the Jewish inhabitants of Jerusalem and Judea
under Persian and Greek rule is now extensively used. It would
be equally suitable if applied to the population of the modern city
of Rome.

If the call of the new era was a test of the faith of individuals,
it was even more a test of the Jewish religion itself. If it was to
keep its hold on the people at home and abroad, claiming supremacy in some true sense, a new interpretation was imperative. If it
had anything to contribute to the wider world, now was the time
to show it. It would have been a sad condemnation of the faith
shaped by the great prophets of Israel and Judah if it had not
contained the principles of growth and adaptability which would
fit it to embrace the opportunity of the new age. With the national existence seemingly gone forever, and the humiliation of
'the chosen people' daily increasing, what was the meaning of the
promises to Abraham, the deliverance from Egypt, and the throne
of David? If these things had but a local and temporary significance, then the religion of Yahwè had had its day, it was time for
something greater.

There was need of a teacher who could correlate the old with
the new, and awaken the national consciousness, and the time
brought forth the man who was equal to the task. The Second
Isaiah, poet and patriot, saw how the hoarded property of a small
people was intended to become the property of the world; how
the time had come to show that the religion proclaimed by Amos,
Isaiah, Jeremiah, and their fellows included in its range every
clime and race. It was he who first comprehended and set forth
in an altogether new light the meaning of Hebrew history from
Abraham down to his own day. It had been plain even to the

* According to my own view of the Book of Ezekiel, this gives us an idea
of conditions in Jerusalem in the latter part of the third century B. C.

Gentiles that Israel was 'punished, smitten of God and afflicted' in
this age of light and enterprise more than at any other time; even
in this bitter chastisement the prophet saw hope. He has the
mission of announcing 'new things, things kept in store, not hitherto known' (48 : 6 f., 42 : 9). His message culminates in divine
announcements: to Israel, triumph and restoration in the Coming
Age, which he pictures as close at hand; to the Gentile world, light
and life, obtained through Israel; to both, a Messianic leader and
benefactor.*

3. *The Prophet's Argument from History*

The prophet was filled with the conviction that there is but One
God. There are indeed angelic beings, to whom certain powers and
offices have been given, but they were created by him, and obey
him (40 : 26; 48 : 13). They are not gods at all. There is no comparison of them with their creator.

The One God Yahwè, who made heaven and earth and all things,
the God of Israel, is equally the God of all races and nations on
earth. He has pity and affection for them all, and will bring them
home at last (chapter 35†; 45 : 14 ff., 22 f.; 49 : 1–13; 53 : 5 f.;
55 : 4 f.; 56 : 7 f.; 60 : 3; 61 : 1 f.; 66 : 17–21). For his chosen people,
Israel, there are especial blessings to come.

The One God has no likeness, no visible representation. The
attempt to make pictures or images of him is worse than folly.
The idols of the foreign peoples represent no real deities; worship
of these 'gods' by Israelites is a grievous sin. The worship which
Yahwè requires is worship of the heart, spiritual approach. Definite rites were originally necessary, and have their permanent value
(52 : 11; 60 : 7; 66 : 21–23), but are not essential (40 : 16). Sacrifices, fasts, and other ritual observances are an abomination unless
the worshipper is morally and spiritually right before God (43 : 23
f.; 58 : 1–7; 66 : 3). The offering which Yahwè accepts is the humble and contrite heart (66 : 2; *cf.* 57 : 15; 41 : 17; 50 : 10; 61 : 1).‡

Yahwè has no dwelling-place. He is everywhere, in the heavens
and on earth. It is folly to think of him as inhabiting a temple.
See especially 40 : 22; 57 : 15; 66 : 1 f. He dwells in the hearts of

---

* See 41 : 27; 42 : 6–9; 43 : 19–21; 45 : 1, 4, 13, 22; 48 : 6 f., 14 f.; 49 : 5 ff.;
55 : 5; 56 : 8; 61 : 1 ff.; 65 : 17 f.; 66 : 21 f.

† Chapter 35, like its counterpart 34, has in view all the world, Gentiles and
Jews alike. See the introduction to each of these chapters.

‡ Ps. 51 : 18 f., which was written under the direct influence of II Isaiah, gives
correctly the substance of the prophet's teaching in this regard.

his worshippers, "with the humble and contrite" (57 : 15; 66 : 2).
The holy land, the holy city, and the temple in Jerusalem are preferred places because of their history, as Israel is a preferred people, but no place may be thought of as Yahwè's abode. The 'exiles'
return to Zion, the beloved city; the Gentiles make joyful pilgrim-
ages thither; but Yahwè is not represented as returning there, as
though he had been absent.*

What the One God desires of both Jew and Gentile is first faith,
then repentance, uprightness, good-will, and kindly dealing among
men. See, for typical passages among the many, 40 : 21; 42 : 18 ff.;
44 : 21; 46 : 8 f.; 45 : 6, 22 (the Gentiles called to faith in the One
God, cf. 49 : 6 f.; 53 : 1–8); 51 : 4 f.; 55 : 1, 3, 7 (faith and repentance
sought from Gentiles and Jews alike); 43 : 24b; 46 : 12; 48 : 22 and
57 : 21; 58 : 3–7; 59 : 1–15. The Second Isaiah would have accepted
whole-heartedly the statement in Mic. 6 : 8 as to the compass of
Yahwè's requirement: "What does Yahwè require of thee but to
do justly, and to love mercy, and to walk humbly with thy God?"
He nowhere says or implies that more than this is necessary.

Starting from such premises as these, the prophet sets himself
to arouse his people to new faith, by invective, promise, and reasoned appeal. Especially prominent is his *argument from history*,
which occupies a large part of chapters 41–48, and appears at least
in the background of nearly every subsequent chapter. His view
includes both the beginning and the end, from Yahwè's eternal
plan for mankind to the coming Messianic age. It is at the dawn
of the latter that he especially likes to take his stand, speaking as
one who sees the promised day actually dawning. The watchmen
on the towers are already shouting the glad tidings. The main
outline of his argument may be sketched as follows.

Yahwè's omnipotence is shown by his wondrous deeds, well
known to all his people, but especially by the evidence of an eternal plan, which he has thus far carried out. He alone "announced
the end from the beginning" (41 : 4, 26; 44 : 7, as emended; 48 : 3
ff.). No other being, no 'god' of the Gentiles, has made, or could
make, a plan for all mankind, plainly unfolded in history (41 : 1 ff.,
21–29; 43 : 9; 45 : 21; 48 : 14). The Hebrews have the record, from
the creation of heaven and earth (40 : 26, 28; 44 : 24; 48 : 13, etc.)
down to their own day. He gave men the breath of life (42 : 5),

---

* Even in the picturesque passage 52 : 8 this is not the case, though many
interpreters have rendered, "When the Lord returns to Zion." The LXX and
Vulg. translate according to the correct interpretation, "When the Lord restores Zion."

destroyed the wicked in the flood, and saved Noah (54 : 9). The children of Israel, with their written record, are Yahwè's "witnesses" (43 : 10; 44 : 8). The initial promises have been kept, even miraculously, in the face of opposition by mighty nations and their 'gods,' as evidenced especially by the deliverance from Egypt, with its succession of wonders. What parallel to this can be shown? (41 : 18; 43 : 16 f.; 48 : 21). He who did these things can and will fulfil his promises (45 : 19, 23, 25).

The prophet reminds his hearers of *the past*, in emphatic reiteration. God called Abraham from remote lands, from Ur in the east, and Haran in the north (41 : 2, 8, 25; 46 : 11; 48 : 14 f.). He promised to make him the special agent of his divine purpose; Israel is to be his 'Servant' to execute his plan (41 : 8; 43 : 10; 44 : 1 f.; 46 : 11, as emended; 49 : 3). He held him by the right hand (41 : 13; 45 : 1, emended); destined him to lead and command all peoples in the last days, subduing the powers of evil by the divine help, 'threshing mountains and making hills as chaff' (41 : 15 f.), trampling on princes, breaking through gates of bronze, wielding Yahwè's own power (41 : 2, 25; 45 : 1 f.; 48 : 14).

41:2   Who aroused from the east a righteous one, | summoning him to his service?

He will deliver up nations before him, | kings he shall tread under foot.

8   . . . Abraham, my friend,

Whom I plucked from the ends of the earth, | and called from its farthest corners; . . .

11   Confounded shall they be, and put to shame, | all thine opponents.||

25   I aroused one from the north, and he came; | from the east, calling on my name!

He shall trample on princes like mire, | as the potter treads upon clay.

46:11   Calling my servant* from the east, | from a far land the man of my counsel.

48:14   The One God, Yahwè, loved him; | he shall execute his pleasure and his might.

It was I who declared it, I who called him! | I brought him, and prospered his way.

This final triumph over all foes had been promised to Abraham in the beginning (Gen. 22 : 17). The choice of Israel was not made in secret, all his people had known it from the first (45 : 19).

* Certainly the original reading; see the note on the passage.

Can anything be more secure than the ground of Israel's faith? (46:8–13).

The man became a nation. The choice and guidance of Israel by the supreme God was shown to the world in the deliverance from Egypt (a favorite theme, introduced again and again, sometimes in a sudden poetic outburst: 48:20 f.; 52:11 f.). Moses was raised up, to give Israel the divine law and ordinances (the *Torah*, 42:21), and to be the leader out of bondage to the promised land (63:11 ff.). Yahwè made for them a path through the seas (43:16 f.) and a safe highway through the fearful desert (hence the favorite picture of the safe and smooth road for the 'exiles' soon to be delivered from the *present* 'Egyptian bondage': 35:6 ff.; 40:3; 41:17 f.; 43:19 f.; etc.; and the similar figure in 57:14 and 62:10). He gave them water from the rock (48:21). Restored to the land of their fathers, they became a great people, built the holy city and the 'glorious house' (64:11), and saw the throne of David established, with the promise that from his house "the leader and commander of the peoples" should one day be raised up (55:3 f.). But the chosen people sinned and were punished. They had been transgressors and rebels from the first (48:4, 8). Therefore the foreign armies destroyed the temple and laid waste the 'holy cities' of Judah (43:28; 64:9 f.).*

The prophet's view of *the present* is equally important in his argument. The main features of the picture which he draws have already been set forth in this Chapter. A grievously sinning people, lacking faith and "far from righteousness" (46:12). Israel scattered to the four winds, humiliated and oppressed. Yahwè's name made a mockery. A nucleus of loyal believers within reach of the prophet's voice; a relatively small body, however, and apparently having little influence with the great majority. These conditions already of long standing, and the evil increasing. What relation has all this to the call of Abraham, the passage through the Red Sea and the desert, and the promise of triumph under a leader from the house of David?

The prophet replies that even the present distress has its essential part to play in Yahwè's plan. The omnipotent One, lover of his people, himself dealt out this punishment.

* There is no allusion to the kingdoms of Israel and Judah, and the fact is not surprising, for the argument could gain nothing from reference to them. It is a little more noticeable that there is no mention of prophets, the words "prophet, prophesy," etc., not occurring at all. Here again it is to be remembered that the argument deals only with the fundamental facts of the religious history.

Who gave up Jacob to the spoiler, | and Israel to those who plundered?
Was it not Yahwè, against whom they had sinned, | in whose ways
    they refused to go, | to whose law they would not listen? (42 : 24).

It is chastisement richly deserved, for sin both past and present
(43 : 26; 48 : 4; 59 : 12 f.). If strict justice were done, the whole
unworthy race would be 'cut off,' in spite of the few faithful souls
(48 : 9; 65 : 8). Yahwè is holding the punishment within his own
limits. Though he delivered Israel into the hand of foreign rulers,
he can at any time reclaim his own. "To which of my creditors
have I sold you?" (50 : 1). He will show his power in behalf of his
people whenever faith and repentance make such action possible
(44 : 21 f.). His plan will stand, and is even now being carried out
(46 : 8–13).

The present forlorn condition of the chosen people is not merely
a punishment for sin. Yahwè now declares, through his prophet,
that *here is the scheme through which he is accomplishing his pur-*
pose for the Gentiles. He announces "new things" not known
hitherto (42 : 9), namely that the Gentiles are to be gathered in
(vss. 5–7). The 'prisoners' and 'exiles' to be set free are not only
Hebrews but also those of other races and climes, to all of whom
alike Yahwè gave the breath of life (42 : 7; 49 : 8 f.; 61 : 1 f.).
Whenever Israel is 'redeemed' the Gentiles are to be redeemed
also. They too are God's children and 'the work of his hands'
(45 : 11). Israel the 'Servant' has the mission of bringing light to
these foreign peoples. The Messianic leader who is to 'restore
Jacob' will also be the leader and commander of the saved remnant of the nations (45 : 4 ff.; 49 : 5 f.). *Hence the Dispersion;*
hence the present misery of those who had been assured of especial
favor.

Yahwè had known from the first (43 : 27; 48 : 8) that his chosen
representatives would be stubbornly disobedient, and had formed
his purpose accordingly. If they had shown themselves more
worthy, the plan would have been very different (48 : 18 f.). As
it is, no one may question it (45 : 9 ff.).

Ho, man that strives with his maker, | a potsherd with him who formed
    the earth!
Says the clay to him who fashions it, What doest thou? | or, Thy
    work has no value at all?
Ho, man saying to a father, What begettest thou? | or to a mother,
    With what dost thou travail?*

---

* Professor Duhm and his followers *cancel this most important verse* on the
ground that it yields no possible sense here. 'Yahwè's purpose to restore Israel

72   SECOND ISAIAH

Thus saith Yahwè, | the Holy One of Israel, and his maker:
Will ye question *me* about my children? | * Concerning the work of
   my hands will ye command me?
It was I who fashioned the earth, | and man upon it I created;
My own hand stretched the heavens, | and all their host I appointed.

It is most significant that in the numerous poems which announce Yahwè's purpose to rescue his people the foreign nations
are nearly always introduced, either by direct address to them or
by other mention; at least as interested onlookers who receive
knowledge of the true God, sometimes also as recipients of the
very same blessings which are promised to Israel. Thus 41:1, 20,
27 f.; 42:1–9, 10–17; 45:6, 9–12, 14–17, 21–26; 48:20; 49:1–12,
22 f.; 51:4 f.; 52:10 f.; chapters 55 and 60; 61:1 f., 9; 62:10 f.;
66:12, 19 ff. To Abraham, Isaac, and Jacob the promise had been
made: "In thy seed shall all the nations of the earth be blessed"
(Gen. 12:3; 22:18; 26:4; 28:14).† The prophet thinks primarily
of spiritual blessings, which even now may be brought within sight
of the Gentiles by means of Israel's testimony in word and deed.
The Dispersion gives the opportunity. But Israel is not doing its
duty. The 'messenger' to the peoples is deaf and blind (42:19).
"Seeing great things, but not heeding them!" (42:20). "Hearing
and seeing all this, canst thou not proclaim it?" (48:6). In this
way, the prophet implies, the ground may be prepared, indeed is
already prepared in some measure. Yahwè's 'witnesses,' at home
and abroad, must be aroused to new faith. They themselves have
yet very much to learn of the nature of God and of true religion.
What they are now suffering is designed to teach them (52:5 f.).

And now, what do I here, | saith the Lord, ||
That my people is taken for nought, | that their rulers mock, ||
And that all the day, without ceasing, | my name is despised? ||
Therefore my people shall know my name, | yea, therefore, on that
   day, || that I am he who proclaims it, behold me!

through the agency of the Persian King could not be characterized by the use
of this figure of the begetting father and the travailing mother.' (Certainly
not!) The conclusion is accordingly drawn that vs. 10 was originally a marginal quotation, foolishly put here by some one and perhaps given in corrupt
form. Similarly the words "about my children" in vs. 11 are cancelled by
Duhm, Cheyne, and Marti as "a false gloss." These commentators, totally
misconceiving the prophet's meaning and the caliber of his message, fail to
see that "the children" of these verses are *the Gentiles*, with whose conversion
the remainder of the chapter is chiefly concerned.
   * See the note on the Hebrew text of this passage.
   † The verb understood as passive (not reflexive), as in the old Jewish tradition generally.

Compare 42:23 ff., 43:26 ff. The prophet in his argument makes clear his belief that the present time is a time of discipline, of preparation, for both Jews and Gentiles. In 50:6 ff. the Servant of Yahwè (here the ideal, repentant Israel rather than the actual people)* is represented as now undergoing painful discipline to fit him for his greater task. *Cf.* 49:4, 7. His testimony has acquired new value. He has been given "a tongue for teaching" and can give help to those who are seeking it (50:4). The whole people has been made more fit for service by the bitter experience. "I have refined thee for myself like silver, I have tested thee in the furnace of affliction" (48:10). The sight of Israel's steadfastness, his acknowledgment of sin and patient endurance of punishment, will make its impression everywhere (53:7), preparing the way for future recognition of the One God.

This is not all. In the fulfilment of Yahwè's plan the afflicted people is made to perform a still more definite and effectual service for the Gentiles. The sufferings of Israel make atonement for the sin of the heathen world. The 'lamb led to the slaughter' is the sacrifice offered in behalf of the nations and races which now have no knowledge of Yahwè (53:4–12). They will at last see this clearly and make full acknowledgment.

The most impressive part of the prophet's argument, by far the most important part as regards the conversion of the Gentiles, is that derived from his look into *the future*. The proof needed to convince the onlookers of other nations must obviously be more complete than that which would suffice for thoughtful Jews. The latter might readily share the prophet's own conviction after hearing his interpretation of Israel's past history and his eloquent assurance of the purpose and power of Yahwè to fulfil his promises. For sceptics and foreigners something more would be necessary. Gentiles would laugh at the tales of Abraham and Moses, sceptical Jews would point to the present miserable condition of the 'chosen people,' and neither class would admit the supremacy of Yahwè. One more link in the chain of evidence was indispensable, namely the actual triumph of Israel as a visible fact. Hence the prophet, whenever he depicts the Gentiles as acknowledging the God of Israel, joins the future to the past, standing in imagination at the coming day when the worshippers of the One God, led by a repentant Israel, are beginning to sweep all before them. *Then*, not before, the truth will be apparent to multitudes in foreign lands, to all those who are fit to understand it.

* See the chapter dealing with the Servant and the Messiah.

Thus in 45 : 6, at the close of a passage depicting the first amazing triumphs of the anointed Leader, Yahwè gives in the following words the purpose of this feature of his plan: "*That all may know, from the east and from the west, that there is none beside me.*" *Cf.* 41 : 25 f.; 49 : 26; 59 : 18 f. Similarly in 41 : 2, 25, where the prophet is dealing with the proof that would convince the Gentiles, he announces in one breath, in each instance in a single sentence, *both* the call of Abraham and the final triumph of the Israelite faith, both "the beginning" and "the end," neither one to be understood without the other. This period of conflict and progressive victory is the time of the final test, the sifting of the good from the bad, in all parts of the earth. A multitude will see and acknowledge the supremacy of Yahwè and the fact of his eternal purpose for Israel and the world, and will serve him henceforth. In the passages 45 : 14 f.; 60 : 14; 66 : 18–23 the scene is pictured when representatives of the foreign nations at last come and tell how they have been convinced.

Even the most loyal Israelites, moreover, would wish to see the prophet's argument include not only the beginning (*rō'sh*) of the divine plan but also its end (*acharīth*). Doubtless Yahwè 'must act, for his own sake,' but *how?* The prophet answers with pictures and figures of speech. There are certain necessary features of the great renovation which is to come, and these he touches upon from time to time, always in the language of a poet. First of all must be repentance. Then the faithful, both at home and abroad, will "proclaim the truth, make it known" as never before. Yahwè will help his people, and they will throw off the yoke of their oppressors. The upright, the truth-seekers among the Gentiles will enter the conflict on the side of Israel in ever-increasing numbers. The wicked of both Gentiles and Jews will eventually be swept from the earth. The Anointed One, of the house of David, will lead the hosts of the Lord. In the New Age he will be teacher and benefactor, as previously he had been the helper of the distressed. Multitudes will flock to the holy land to rejoice in its new glory. Kings and princes will acknowledge and admire. Jerusalem will be the pride and joy of all mankind.

These great events are represented as immediately impending, the turning-point as close at hand. Whether the prophet actually expected the spiritual renewal of the world to be inaugurated soon, is a question that we cannot answer. As poet and herald he could only picture it in this vivid way. He may possibly have imagined a beginning of resistance to oppression something like that which took place in the Maccabean time. More probably he gave no thought to such external incidents. What we know with certainty is that he was thinking primarily of a spiritual revival. With that accomplished, all the rest would follow. We can see that whenever this thought comes to him his faith blazes forth. It *is* possible now, he feels, to give the people a new view of their history and their destiny and thereby to arouse them to new life. 'The Lord's hand is not shortened, that it cannot save; his ear is not dull, that it cannot hear.'

The Second Isaiah had faith in the efficacy of his own message. He wrote with the spirit and aim of a true evangelist, and with the expectation that his words would carry conviction to many, perhaps to the multitude. He knew that his argument was sound in every part. He saw clearly why and how Israel had been chosen, guided, and chastised; and he believed that his people could at least be awakened to a new consciousness of religious leadership of the nations of the earth. The subsequent history justified his confidence, though he could not alter human nature, nor greatly improve conditions in Jerusalem. The seed was sown, and it eventually bore fruit. From the time when these poems first became well known, they were seized and cherished as the noblest expression of the best thought which the religion of Israel had produced. The whole succession of Jewish and Christian scriptures, from that time onward, turned to them for inspiration.

We have already seen how by a series of singularly foolish 'explanatory' interpolations the meaning of the prophet's prediction has been distorted and obscured, at least for modern students. To what extent the ancient readers of these poems were led astray by the phantom 'Cyrus' is a question. The Targum, though compelled to celebrate the Persian king in 44:28 and 45:1 ff., straightway leaves him behind and out of account, not even interpreting 46:11 or 48:14 as referring to him. The Servant of Yahwè in 42:1 and 52:13—passages of central importance—is expressly defined by the Targumist as "the Messiah." The appearance of Cyrus on the scene is evidently regarded as only a minor incident. The ancient interpreters and commentators generally, Jewish and Christian alike, saw in 41:2 no allusion to the Persian king. The Targum explains the passage correctly as referring to Abraham.

In general and taken as a whole, these poems seem to have been rightly understood by the people for whom they were written, even if there were few, if any, who could rise to the full height of the prophet's conception in his greatest passages culminating in chapter 53. His idea of the One God, his sympathetic outlook on the Gentiles, and especially his eschatology, depicting the end of the present age and the dawn of the new and centring in the person and work of the divinely anointed Righteous One, profoundly influenced the subsequent theology of his people. The pictures which he had drawn were constantly before the eyes of Jewish teachers and writers, as many passages in Psalms and Prophets attest. In the New Testament the prophecies of the Second Isaiah are generally interpreted as they were intended by their author and in the spirit in which he conceived them, as truly 'Messianic' from beginning to end.

CHAPTER V

PROPHET AND POET

Jewish tradition designated certain books of the Old Testament as the 'poetical' books *par excellence*. The Psalms, Job, and Proverbs were chanted in a peculiar way in the public worship; and correspondingly, a special system of accents for these three books has been handed down by the Massorites. This did not mean, of course, that these three writings were regarded as the sole representatives of any particular class or rank of Hebrew poetry, as though there were anything in either the matter or the literary form which could entitle them to a place by themselves among the writings of the Old Testament. The third chapter of Habakkuk, for example, is a psalm which was used like the other psalms in the public worship, as the liturgical directions appended to it show. Ps. 18 appears also in II Sam. 22; the psalm of Hezekiah, in Is. 38, is another composition of the same character; the songs of the Children of Israel (Ex. 15), Moses (Deut. 32 and 33), Deborah (Judg. 5), David (II Sam. 1), and still others, are expressly designated in our Hebrew text as poems. Moreover, at least two entire books from the remainder of the Old Testament, Lamentations and the Song of Solomon, have manifestly every claim to be classed as 'poetical books' which could be urged in favor of the Psalms, the Proverbs, or Job. Nor has this fact been denied. In short, the line drawn by Jewish custom and massoretic tradition is an arbitrary one, and has always been recognized as such.

The question to what extent the Hebrew prophets wrote poetry, in the stricter sense, remained for many centuries without any serious consideration, and has not even yet been satisfactorily answered. It is only in recent years that the view has gained wide acceptance that the message of the prophet—at least when he is speaking in an exalted strain—is always in the dress of *poetry;* poetry which exactly resembles, in its structure, the versification of the books which are universally recognized as poetical in form, such as the Psalms, the Lamentations, and the Book of Job.

In the preface to our English Revised Version of the Old Testament, of 1884, the following words occur: "In the poetical portions, . . . the Revisers have adopted an arrangement in lines, so as to exhibit the parallelism which is characteristic of Hebrew poetry. But they have not extended this arrangement to the prophetical books, the language of which, although frequently marked by parallelism, is, except in purely lyrical passages, rather of the nature of lofty and impassioned prose." With regard to the main opinion here expressed, that the language of the prophecies is, generally speaking, prose and not poetry, it may be said that it has been, and probably is now, the prevailing opinion among readers of the Old Testament. Professor Driver, in his *Introduction*, says practically the same thing as the Revisers. Even in classroom work, if I am not mistaken, the Hebrew prophets are still quite commonly read as prose, and with comparatively little attention to questions of purely literary form.

The matter which led the English Revisers to an expression of their opinion was one of no small importance, namely this: What portions of our English translation of the Old Testament shall be printed *in lines*, as poetry is usually printed? This question, as every one knows who has thought about it, is much more than one of external arrangement; it carries with it the literary estimate, and eventually exegesis as well. We are influenced by the impression received from the eye as well as by that from the ear. Print any modern poem in a solid block, like prose, and it would be very difficult for the reader, however attentive, to gain from it its legitimate effect, even if he knew himself to be reading poetry. Or, again, suppose that certain poems in which rhyme is absent and rhythmical correspondence not always manifest, such as Matthew Arnold's *The Future*, or Browning's *A Death in the Desert*, were printed in unbroken pages. The reader who supposed himself to be reading elevated prose would inevitably fail to get into the true spirit of the composition, and might even be led to form an unjust estimate of the writer.

We might then have expected that the answer of the Revisers to the question, What shall we print as poetry? would be this: 'All that we can recognize as poetry.' But this was not quite what they did, judging from their own words. They say: "The language of the prophets is, *except in purely lyrical passages*, of the nature of lofty and impassioned prose." The exception is highly important. What are "purely lyrical passages," and how numerous are they in the prophets? As far as the printed page is concerned, our Revised Version recognizes poetry in *two places* in the Prophetical Books, the psalm which forms the third chapter of Habakkuk, and the prayer of Jonah inside the whale. But of

course these are not the only "purely lyrical passages" in the
prophets. Even if the Psalms are to be taken as the norm, and the
single fact of "parallelism" is to be given such decisive weight, a
number of quite undoubted examples of poetry at once suggest
themselves.

Thus, Is. 42 : 10 ff.:

> Sing unto the Lord a new song,
>> And his praise from the end of the earth;
> Let the sea roar, and all that is therein,
>> The isles, and the inhabitants thereof.
> Let the wilderness and its cities cry aloud,
>> The villages also which Kedar inhabits;
> Let the people of Sela' raise a glad cry,
>> Let them shout from the top of the mountains.
> Let them give glory to the Lord,
>> And proclaim his praise in the farthest countries.

Or 61 : 10 ff.:

> I will greatly rejoice in the Lord,
>> My soul shall be joyful in my God.
> For he has clothed me with the garments of salvation,
>> He has covered me with the robe of righteousness;
> As a bridegroom decks himself with a garland,
>> And as a bride adorns herself with her jewels.
> For as the earth brings forth her buds,
>> As the garden makes its plants to sprout,
> So the Lord will cause righteousness and praise
>> To spring forth before all the nations.

Or again, turning to the phrase used by the Revisers, what passages in all the Old Testament have more of the true lyrical quality
than Jer. 20, from vs. 7 on, or the middle section of Is. 50—to
take examples almost at random? It was such passages as these
that caused the exception to be made to the general statement
regarding the language of the prophets. If there is any such thing
as Hebrew poetry, these passages are surely among those which
have the first right to the name. Nevertheless, they were not
printed in broken lines in our Revised Old Testament; and its
editors probably took the wisest course in declining the responsibility of doing so. The time for drawing the line between prose
and poetry in these books, in the printed Bible, had not yet come.
The defect in the Version, however, is a very serious one indeed.
Still more recent examples of a similar editorial uncertainty are

afforded by the *Polychrome Bible*. The Book of Jeremiah was
edited by Cornill, in 1895; Ezekiel by Professor Toy, in 1899. In
each case the editor seems to have made some attempt to identify
the strictly poetical elements and give them a corresponding prominence on the printed page. Toy finds four small bits in Ezekiel;
Cornill five, equally brief, in Jeremiah. Even Jer. 20, which contains what is perhaps the most striking transition from prose to
poetry which is to be found anywhere in the Old Testament, is
printed exactly as if it were a part of Leviticus, or Chronicles.
Since the time when these editions were prepared, however, there
has been a great advance in the understanding of Hebrew poetic
forms.

A remark made by Driver, in his *Introduction*, 6th edition, p.
96, also calls for notice here. In speaking of the 'Song of Moses,'
Deut. 32 : 1–43, he says: "The Song shows great originality in
form, being a presentation of prophetical thoughts in a poetical
dress, *which is unique in the O. T.*" * This is a mistaken and misleading assertion. The 'form' which Driver regards as so original
and as 'unique' is precisely that in which most of the poetical
parts of the prophetical books are written. The only difference is
this, that an accident of literary tradition has led to the writing
and printing of this particular poem in regular stichoi, in our Hebrew manuscripts and printed editions of the Old Testament.
The incident illustrates anew how natural it is to be influenced,
in judging of the literary character of a composition, by the manner in which it happens to be disposed on the page. The next
English Bible will have this great advantage over its predecessors.

The prophetical book whose poetical features have thus far received the most attention is Second Isaiah. Budde, in his epoch-
making investigation of the 3 | 2 meter (see the Chapter on Metric
Forms) in the *Zeitschrift für die alttestamentliche Wissenschaft*,
1882, 1891, 1892, pointed out specimens of this rhythmic scheme
in Is. 40–66. Duhm, *Das Buch Jesaia*, 1892, took a very important
forward step, endeavoring to demonstrate true metric form in
nearly every part of the book, and shaping his translation accordingly. He also made the attempt to divide considerable portions
of the prophecies into strophes of equal length; an unsuccessful
attempt, as I shall endeavor to show. His conclusions were adopted in the main by Cheyne, Marti, and others, who thought of the
meter, as Duhm had done, chiefly as a means of criticising the
massoretic text, and made little or no attempt to study it in de-

* The italics are my own.

tail. Klostermann's *Deuterojesaia*, 1893, printed the Hebrew
text of chapters 40–66 in broken lines designed to show the parallelism in the structure, but nowhere in his preface or commentary
indicated a belief that the book, or any part of it, is poetry. In
Kautzsch's *Heilige Schrift des A. T.*, 1894, large portions of the
translation (by Ryssel) of II Isaiah were printed in a form which
distinguished them from prose, though there was no attempt to
divide them metrically. Since that time there has been ever-
increasing appreciation of the fact that the prophets of the Old
Testament gave their messages prevailingly in verse. Even at the
present day, however, it does not seem to be well understood that
Is. 40–66 is *all* written in strict metric form, to say nothing of any
adequate recognition of the essentially poetic character of the
writer's thought.

It is of course true here, as in other poetical works, that inspiration is not always at the same height. Failure to understand
the mood in which the poet is writing is also likely to affect the
reader's estimate of the literary form. Historico-critical theories
of composition sometimes have such weight as to prevent the eye
from seeing regularity of structure and the ear from appreciating
true musical quality. It has already been observed that the poems
in chapters 56–66, so far as they are recognized as poetry at all,
are quite generally condemned as inferior, 'Trito-Isaiah' being
pronounced an imitation at best, easily degenerating into frothy
prose. Considerable portions are printed as prose by Cheyne in
his critical edition of the Hebrew text (*Book of the Prophet Isaiah*,
1899). A striking example of the same nature in the earlier part
of the book is the passage 44: 9–20, the ironical description of the
manufacture of a god. Duhm in his commentary pronounced this
a late interpolation, remarking on the improbability that a passage of this nature would have been written by the tenderly emotional (dem pathetischen) Second Isaiah, and calling attention
especially to its lack of rhythm. Cheyne agrees, saying in a note
to his translation that "the description is cold and labored, and
scarcely rhythmical." Marti also assents, declaring that the description is "kalt und *mühsam*" and with "nichts von dem pathetischen Schwunge Dtjes's." Kittel's *Biblia Hebraica* (1906) accordingly printed the whole section as prose; the only portion of
chapters 40–55 to be thus printed. So also most recently J. A.
Bewer, *The Literature of the Old Testament* (1922), p. 212, pronounces this section a late addition by another hand, on the ground
that "it is entirely in prose."

It is quite true that emotional fervor is not to be found in
44 : 9–20, and also true that those who conceive a feverish and
essentially feminine 'prophet of the exile' writing always in the
same mood will see in this and many other passages the work of
other hands. The highly characteristic humor of the poet seems
to be totally unseen, both here and everywhere else, by the commentators cited. As for the metric form, it is precisely the same
in this section as in its immediate surroundings. The rhythm is
as regular, and the lines as musical throughout, as in any other
portion of the book. The text is not everywhere faultless, and the
original appearance of regularity has suffered accordingly, but the
necessary changes are very slight. The passage is thoroughly
poetic, in form and diction, and is indispensable to the poem of
which it forms so large a part.

It is perhaps too early to expect any adequate understanding
and appreciation of the literary art of the Hebrew poets. It is only
very recently that scholars have begun to pay attention to the
purely literary qualities and technique of Biblical writings, in
either Testament. Other matters, of more obvious importance,
have occupied the interpreters, whether Jewish or Christian. At
first, and predominantly always, these productions were studied
from the point of view of their religious teaching. In modern times
they have been conceived also as historical documents and examined with a microscope, with a view to finding in every poetic composition a reflection of current events, tendencies, or small party
controversies. Studied from either point of view, they have come
off rather badly—worse and worse, in fact—in the past half-cen-
tury, inasmuch as the great mass of Hebrew poetry has been
branded as 'post-exilic' and therefore pronounced inferior. Of
this, more presently. It must of course be remembered, as has
been said in the preceding pages, that the first principles of Hebrew metric form are not yet thoroughly understood, while the
study of the conventions which inevitably result from any strict
use of meter has hardly come above the horizon at all. The choice
and arrangement of words; rules governing the position of the
accent; the studied use of different rhythms in alternation; the
quality of the poet's imagination as shown in his employment of
figurative language; the proportion of attention paid, in any given
passage, to matter on the one hand and artistic effect on the other;
the principal varieties of embellishment, and the influence of individual characteristics; the various ways in which single poems are
constructed; these and similar subjects of investigation have yet
to receive due consideration.

Both psalms and 'prophecies' are still awaiting full recognition of the fact that they are *poetry*. In former times the standard commentaries often showed fine sympathetic insight without recognition of the strict poetic form; more recently, while the formal scheme of the Hebrew verse has been discovered and emphasized, the atmosphere has not seemed favorable to literary appreciation. Even the leading exponents of metric theory seem to look upon the poetical character of these compositions as something purely external, and to believe themselves to have done their whole duty when they have cut up every chapter and verse into little pieces of approximately the same length. In some of the most widely read and influential modern commentaries on Isaiah and the Psalms, in particular, the failure to take account of the figurative and idealistic character of the writings commented on is a defect that makes itself painfully felt on almost every page. The interpreter professes to believe that he is dealing with poetry, to be sure; the fact is stated at the outset, and repeated from time to time. The interpretation, however, is that of prose, the commentator himself exhibiting no imagination, and virtually denying its presence in the book before him. Figures of speech are treated as descriptions of actual fact, and are not seldom ridiculed accordingly; metaphors easily become grotesque when taken literally. High-sounding phrases and unusual words or constructions are likely to be 'emended.' One reason for the failure to recognize the fine qualities of these poems is unquestionably the current low estimate of the Hebrew literature and religion of the Persian and Greek periods. But whether the failure is due to a lack of capacity to appreciate poetry or of inability to believe Jewish writers capable of producing it, the result is the same.

Professor Duhm, in his commentary on Is. 53, expresses his conviction that poetic imagination is out of place. The language is not figurative. 'The whole presentation is so far from having any of that idealistic mist which people are so fond of spreading over it, that the best thing to do is to take it as simple history' (comm. on 53:3). The chapter as he conceives it describes the death and burial of an actual contemporary of the writer (comm. on vs. 12), a leper, of whom the prophet predicts that he will not only be raised from the dead but will afterward beget children (vs. 10). This attitude as regards poetic imagery is generally maintained by Duhm, as a few examples will show. In 40:9 Jerusalem, personified as a maiden, is pictured as mounting a lofty hill to proclaim good news to the sister cities of Judea. But how can a city get up on a mountain? That would be "ein groteskes Bild." The conclusion is drawn that actual watchmen, looking for an actual human messenger, are described.—42 : 5, God "created the heavens and stretched them out." He could not have created them before they were stretched out; a possible lacuna in the text is therefore conjectured.—43 : 20, when the last great 'Return to the Promised Land,' typified in the exodus from Egypt to Canaan, shall come to pass, God will again provide a way in the wilderness and streams of water for his people. The wild creatures of the desert (favorites of the poet) will see the wonder and give praise. On this the comment: The simple poet does not reflect that the jackals and ostriches would clear out of the wilderness as fast as they could, if any such procession went through it.—49 : 16, God declares to Zion, "I have graven thee on my palms, thy walls are continually before me." The conclusion is drawn, that the prophet did not know the Pentateuchal law which forbids tattooing.—51 : 14–16, "The bowed captive shall soon be released" (vs. 14); and thereafter, in direct address (vs. 16), "In the shadow of my hand I have concealed thee." But how can one who is sitting in a dungeon be at the same time concealed in Yahwè's hand? There is either a "schriftstellerisches Ungeschick" here, or an interpolation.—56 : 9 ff., the prophet's most powerful picture of the guilty people and their faithless leaders: the shepherds are blind, or asleep; the watch-dogs are dumb; the flock is unprotected. 'Now is your opportunity, wild beasts of the field and forest!' the prophet cries. He has in mind, we are told, real beasts, which are to overrun the land, devouring especially the Samaritans (after the manner of II Kings 17 : 25 f.).— 60 : 19. The prediction of the prophet is to be taken literally. He actually believed, we are assured, that the sun and moon would be done away with in the new age, and that Jerusalem would be lighted by the radiance from Yahwè's person. The comment on vs. 20 reiterates that there is no figurative language here, it is "wörtlich gemeint."—62 : 10, the great Return in the Messianic time. "Go through, go through the gates; prepare ye the way of the people; cast up, cast up the highway; gather out the stones; lift up an ensign over the nations!" A parallel passage, it is noted, suggests figurative language; nevertheless the commentator maintains that this may be, what it would naturally seem, an exhortation to the right-minded citizens of Jerusalem to go outside the city and work on the road which the pilgrims were to use. 'How the Jerusalemites can "lift up an ensign over the nations" is hard to see.'—63 : 12, "He who caused his glorious arm to go at the right hand of Moses." 'Again an unfortunate picture, since an arm cannot go.' And so on. Such examples could be given by the score, from all parts of the Book of Isaiah.

This is the interpretation of the Hebrew poets and prophets which has been hailed on all hands, for thirty years past, as the true understanding. The 'idealistic mist' has been cleared away at last, and we have before us the oracles as they were originally intended and understood; inflated prose, dealt out in metric jerks. Yes, it is easy to see why the men of Jerusalem stoned the prophets.

As for the current conception of Jewish religious history in the so-called 'post-exilic' period,* a conception which after all is chiefly responsible for this depreciation of prophecy and obliteration of poetry, I can only record here again my conviction that it is thoroughly mistaken. It is customary to speak of the period as an age of legalism, and of spiritual degeneration; whereas it certainly was neither, as far as the great mass of intelligent and God-fearing Israelites was concerned. The principal phases of this subject have already been touched upon in a preceding Chapter.

It has been and is still customary to speak of a 'prophetic period' in the religious history of Israel, and to prescribe its limits. It was a dogma of those who (in the last centuries B. C.) preserved and edited the writings comprised in our Old Testament, that the bulk of Hebrew prophecy was produced in the time of the Kingdom, and that none of it, excepting only the brief and belated outgiving of 'Malachi,' was of a date later than the sixth century. Modern critical study has shown this view to be mistaken. By far the greater part of this literature was produced after the extinction of the Hebrew kingdom, and we are gradually becoming aware of the fact that the time of greatest production was in the late Persian and early Greek periods. The old dogma persists, however. Thus Robertson Smith, *Old Testament in the Jewish Church* (1892), 158: "The Jews had a dim sort of consciousness after the time of Ezra that the age of revelation was past and that the age of tradition had begun." Similarly Smend, *A. T. Religionsgeschichte*, speaking of II Isaiah: "In der That war die Zeit der Prophetie vorüber." Whitehouse, in the article 'Hebrew Religion' in the *Encycl. Brit.*, 11th edition, 184–186, says of the 'exilic' Second Isaiah that he marks "the climax and close of Hebrew

---

* As I said in my *Ezra Studies*, p. 289, with detailed argument in support of the opinion, the terms "exilic," "pre-exilic," and "post-exilic" ought to be banished forever from usage, for they make a division which is purely imaginary, corresponding to nothing real in Hebrew literature and life.

prophetism, which is henceforth . . . a virtually arrested development."

What was Hebrew prophetism? Smend (*ibid.*) expresses a view
which has had wide currency, elaborated especially by Wellhausen
and his followers. According to this conception, the prophet of
the early period was an isolated figure, a preacher who in spirit
stood quite outside the Hebrew community, delivering a message
of woe, namely, prediction of 'the downfall of Israel' (meaning
the cessation of the kingdom, the temporary destruction of Jerusalem, and the burning of the temple). The religious attitude of
this prophet was in sharp contrast (den schärfsten Gegensatz)
with the theology of his time; a great gulf (eine ungeheure Kluft)
had opened between him and his people. After the events just
mentioned had taken place, the mainspring of this 'prophecy' was
gone, since its all-important prediction (!) had been fulfilled.
The sharp contrast between prophet and people was now removed
(aufgehoben). Henceforth the chief business of the teachers of
Israel was to comfort and encourage rather than to threaten.
There was no more 'individual inspiration,' no more consciousness of being the chosen mouthpiece of a divine message. At the
time when Is. 63:11 was written, the presence of the spirit of
Yahwè in Israel was no longer felt (war der Geist Jahves nicht
mehr in Israel zu spüren). Moreover, we hear that the genuine
prophet of the early period was prevailingly concerned with in-
ternational movements and crises; his utterances indeed were always induced by the political situation. This dogma is stated most
concisely by Cornill, *Einleitung* (1896), 193 middle, 197 above,
relying on Amos 3:3–8 (where, however, the seemingly important
vs. 7 is certainly a later insertion, as many scholars have seen).

This hopelessly artificial, wooden representation of Hebrew
prophecy rests chiefly on three misconceptions: an obsolete view
of the composition and dating of the several prophetical books;
a mistaken estimate of the Chronicler's imaginary picture of the
Persian period, which is treated as sober history and as truly representative of the whole people; and last, not least, the treatment
of Hebrew poetry as though it were prose.

The Hebrew prophet, of whatever era, was a religious teacher
aiming to benefit his people, and his motives and utterances were
like those of other religious teachers, ancient or modern. He was
doubtless in advance of his generation, but was not foreign to it.
There was no 'gulf' between him and his people; like every other
true prophet, he grew from a favorable soil. There was never lack

in Israel of men who were eager to hear and follow such leaders as Amos, Isaiah, and their fellows. Their writings were preserved because they were welcomed and appreciated, and because there was *no* 'sharp contrast' between them and the best representative theology of their time. Our knowledge of Hebrew religious history gains nothing from the attempted demarcation of a 'prophetic period.' Amos and Hosea were certainly not the first critics of the national life whose teachings were written down. The religion of Israel had seen a noble development long before their day, and literature had flourished. As for the supposed lower limit of the 'prophetism,' it is a mere phantom. Later than the late period which produced those greatest of masters, the Second Isaiah and the author of the Book of Job, even after the day when a collection of The Prophets had been made and set aside, the line of teachers continued. The noble utterances preserved in the Book of Wisdom, the Messianic prediction of the Psalms of Solomon, the didactic poetry of the latter part of Baruch—to mention no other examples—are as truly 'prophecy' as anything that had preceded; the flavor of a later and more advanced stage of thought cannot deprive them of the name, however we may rank them in intrinsic merit.

It is doubtless true that the Jewish people, or at least their leaders, in the last two or three centuries B. C. believed that prophetic inspiration was a thing of the past—though it was to be renewed at some future day. The author of I Maccabees, in speaking of the desperate conditions in the land after the death of Judas, says (9 : 27): "There was great tribulation in Israel, such as had not been since the time that no prophet appeared among them," that is, according to the traditional view, since the fifth century. See also 4 : 46 and 14 : 41, and *cf.* the similar words of the author of the Books of Chronicles (middle of the third century) in Ezra 2 : 63, Neh. 7 : 65. The older Hebrew writings which had been preserved and set aside as monuments of the national religion had come to be regarded as miraculously produced, and their authors as men who could foretell future events. It must have been true in increasing degree, as century succeeded century and the Jewish horizon widened, that the bearer of a divine message, the herald of new aspects of religious truth, was without honor *as a prophet* in his own generation. The popular spokesmen of the time could hardly be expected to recognize in one of their contemporaries that exalted figure, an inspired prophet, successor of Elijah, Isaiah, and Jeremiah. The true prophet must be clairvoyant

and an infallible oracle. These notions—and their modern per-
petuation—belong properly to the sphere of folk-lore, and the oft-
cited passages quoted above have no significance whatever for the
actual history of the great line of Israel's teachers.

The relation of formal 'prophecy' to *poetry*, when considered at
all, has been treated as a merely superficial matter, the adoption
of a convention. In most treatises on Hebrew prophecy, even
those of very recent date, the words "poem, poet, poetry" do not
occur. Professor Budde, in the article "Poetry (Hebrew)" in
Hastings' *Dictionary of the Bible*, IV, 12, writing as a recognized
authority in both Hebrew metrics and the religion of the Old
Testament, sets forth the view that the prophet composes verse
merely in conformity to traditional usage. If he happens to possess the poetic gift, it is so much to the good; otherwise, he is likely
to drop into prose or something worse. "The prophet may adopt
the poetical forms current in other social circles, and come forward
himself as a poet, thus playing a strange part." And again: "One
might have the full consciousness of a call to the prophetic office
and yet be no born poet. Then it might happen that at one time
the prophet would put on the unwonted poetic harness and go
earnestly to work for a while, only to relapse presently into heed-
lessness." It can hardly be doubted that there were in Israel
religious essayists of the sort here supposed, but it may be questioned whether any of their writings have been preserved.

There is no prescribed literary dress of Hebrew prophecy. Prose
and verse are both represented, and are equally legitimate. Wherever the utterance rises to eloquence, however, under the influence
of strong feeling or quickened imagination, the Hebrew writer inevitably follows the ancient literary tradition—as old as Hebrew
literature, employing both parallelism of structure and the metric
line. He does this not because it is conventional, but because it is
the only way of expressing what he feels. The Old Testament
writers whose utterances have stirred the hearts of all hearers,
from their own day to the present time, were prophets because
they were poets, not *vice versa*. They were men of letters, who had
behind them the traditions of a great literature and appreciated,
according to the measure of their genius, the exacting standards
of their art. For any profound and highly finished work they could
count on a multitude of hearers, and of readers as well, who recognized refinements of rhetoric, felt rhythmic beauty and choice
diction as certainly, and perhaps as keenly, as any other ancient
or modern audience, and took delight in the creations of a master.

In estimating Hebrew poesy and prophecy alike we are confronted with the modern doctrine of the degenerate 'post-exilic community' inferior in both religion and literature. What is the quality of the poetry which comes from that period of Israelite history? The question is of prime importance, inasmuch as a very large part—perhaps four-fifths—of all the old Hebrew poetry that we possess was produced in the fifth, fourth, and third centuries B. C. It would also seem to be answered in advance, since the poet, even more than the prophet, is the child of his age. A small-souled people cannot possibly produce a body of great poetry. Cheyne, in beginning his picture of *Jewish Religious Life after the Exile*, remarks complacently (p. 9) that the Jews at that time "were poor specimens of religious humanity." If this were true, it would settle the matter, and we could regard Professor Cheyne's estimate as sufficiently generous when he says of the Hebrew psalmists (p. 114) that "they are not altogether without some faint idea of the consolations of art." As one proceeds in the perusal of this distressing little volume (truly representative of the modern school of interpretation) it becomes increasingly evident that its author believed both psalmists and prophets to be writing versified prose (see, for example, pp. 113, 117, 124) and, accordingly, to be wrangling over small matters and berating their contemporaries instead of giving free play to poetic imagination; views which are maintained, consciously or unconsciously, in the principal modern commentaries on the Psalter.

The picture, however, is utterly untrue. As I have shown in the preceding Chapters, it is the result of mistaking fables for trustworthy historical narratives. The period was one of steady advance, not deterioration, in culture, literature, and religion, as all the trustworthy evidence combines to show. There is in all history no finer example of the indomitable spirit of an afflicted people. This was the golden age of the national poetry, as well as of prophecy. What justifies this characterization is not the relative output, though a vast amount must have been produced; not the development of artistic form, and the technical finish of the verse, though these were often of a very high order; but the universal and permanent quality of the religious experience and the conception of a divine government of the world which these ancient poems embody. We hear in them the voice of a people conscious of its greatness, well aware of its leadership among the nations, and sure of ultimate triumph in an age in which all the races of the earth shall acknowledge the One God and worship him in their own way. The heights reached by the imagination of these Hebrew writers have not been realized, nor the breadth and depth of their religious conceptions appreciated, in the present generation. The Second Isaiah is one of many, though the greatest of all. It is needless to say that inferior poets are also represented, and that poems were occasionally preserved because of some minor interest rather than because of their high literary quality and their universal appeal. A strong national feeling is, of course, often in the foreground (Isaac Watts in his *Psalms of David* [1719] substituted 'Britain' for 'Israel'), but the Hebrew writer's patriotism is an excellence rather than a blemish. The imagination of prophet or poet wrought in its own local atmosphere and employed the characteristic framework of literary tradition and present reality; but the pictures drawn, like the best productions of any great era of creative art, remain true for all peoples and all time.

It may be doubted whether the Second Isaiah ever thought of himself as a prophet, but it is beyond question that he knew himself to be a master poet. There is in the book no intimation that its author was conscious of a divine election other than that which any devout man of letters might claim. He keeps himself entirely out of sight, never once speaking in his own person or alluding to his own experience. The passages in which many interpreters have supposed the prophet to be introducing himself, namely 61 : 1, 10; 62 : 1, 6; 63 : 7, are all soliloquies of the Servant of Yahwè, perfectly parallel to 49 : 4, where the Servant speaks with a purely human voice, as the spokesman of Israel's long experience of faith triumphing over discouragement. In 40 : 6, where some have wished to alter the text and read the first person, the 'voice' is merely a poetic figure (as in vs. 3) and the echoing reply is also impersonal:

A voice says, Proclaim! | And the answer comes, What shall I proclaim?

The massoretic reading is correct, and in keeping with the writer's habit; the interpretation given by the Greek and Latin versions is inferior. But whether the mantle of a prophet was ever consciously worn by him or not, he certainly knew that he had the seer's vision of divine truth and the poet's unique power to make it stir the heart. He wrote because the fire was in his bones (as Jeremiah puts it), and because great pictures rose before his eyes.

He is always the religious philosopher and teacher, and yet some of the minor scenes which he portrays in detail are pure literary embellishment, elaborated under an impulse which is solely artistic. An example is to be seen in the passage mentioned above, 44 : 9–20, where the arts and crafts connected with god-manufacture are introduced with a display of technical terminology which goes far beyond the needs of the lesson to be conveyed. There is poetry in the foundry and the blacksmith's shop. Another characteristic instance is the romantic picture of wild creatures living their family life in the ruins of a great city, in 34 : 11–17. In like manner a fellow artist, the author of the Book of Job, turns momentarily aside from his religious philosophy to descriptions of nature or of human undertaking, as when he depicts the labors of the miner in 28 : 1–11, or the great beasts of the earth in chapters 39 ff. This is all done with a master's delight in his literary craftsmanship and for its own sake. It is not religious poetry in a secular dress, but secular poetry in a religious dress. The Second Isaiah could have made for himself a name in any branch of imaginative literature. He was a prophet and the chief of the prophets. He was also a born poet, and in his own sphere he is supreme and unrivalled among the great poets of the world.

CHAPTER VI

THE POET'S BOOK AND ITS FORTUNES

1. *The Literary Unit*

We may presume that the poems of the Second Isaiah were given out by the poet himself, to be copied and circulated in the usual manner according to the demand. It is fortunately possible to speak more definitely as to the literary proceeding. There is convincing evidence that the productions of this author which now are incorporated in the Book of Isaiah formed a single publication. They were issued at one time and in one volume, not as separate poems or groups of poems which were afterward collected. When these masterpieces were rescued and preserved for the world by being brought under the cover of Isaiah's great name, they were not sought out one by one and here and there, and then assembled in a more or less arbitrary editorial arrangement, like the diwans of the old Arab poets. They were still in circulation as a literary unit, in the same form in which they had been put forth by their author. The proof of this is given by the poems themselves, in the evidence which they afford that an original order has been preserved. They are pearls strung on a string (to use the favorite Arabian figure), and yet possessing such essential unity and standing so certainly in a calculated sequence as to render the figure inadequate without further explanation.

In subject-matter, as has already been said and fully demonstrated, the twenty-seven* poems are closely related to one another. One definite and characteristic chain of ideas holds together the entire group. They form a suite, and, in a general way, were planned as a whole. Nevertheless, the several poems are complete in themselves as far as literary form is concerned. Each is a unit, inasmuch as it is the deliberate and finished treatment of a single theme, or of allied themes which are interwoven. The prospect of demonstrating an originally designed sequence of these units does not seem at the outset very promising. They have the appearance of being loosely joined, and even an attentive reader might con-

---

* Regarding the possibility that the collection, as incorporated in the Book of Isaiah, included more than the twenty-seven poems, see below.

clude that methodical collocation is rarely to be seen here. There is of course no such distinct progress in thought, in the successive members of the series, as to fix approximately the relative position of each. We see, in a general glance, the treatment of related subjects in an order which is artistically effective but not logically essential. It is hardly ever the case that a poem takes formal account of its predecessor;* the standing-ground reached in the one is not necessarily assumed in those which follow. There is also to be added the fact that these songs, homilies, and dramatic scenes are the product of very diverse moods, rendering more difficult the articulation of each new composition with the one which had preceded.

In view of these facts, the evidence gained from a close study of the poems is almost as unexpected as it is welcome. It shows a true literary continuity, internal and not merely superficial, plainly intended by the author himself.

Many commentators have remarked on the evidently designed and very effective collocation of certain chapters. Thus 34 and 35, by all recognized as separate poems, present "a fine contrast" (Cheyne) which certainly is not accidental. Few, if any, would doubt that the one chapter was written with the other in mind. Equally striking is the juxtaposition of the deep gloom of 59 with the brightness and splendor of 60, or the manner in which the tone of stern rebuke which is heard through chapters 48 and 50 is relieved by the burst of tender affection in chapter 49. The fact that strong contrast, of one sort or another, is such a frequently occurring feature in the single poems of the collection is also to be taken into account here.

There are numerous other cases in which the preservation of the original order of the poems is more or less generally recognized by commentators. Marti, for instance, holds that 41 was written to follow 40; pronounces 42 : 1–44 : 22 a continuous section; and sees evidence of the original succession in 48/49/50, 52/53, 58/59, 61/62/63, and 65/66. It is clear in some instances that an idea merely touched upon in a given poem is made the subject of the one which immediately follows. Thus, the humbling of Babylon's pride is a theme suggested in the first two verses of 46, and developed at length in 47. I have shown in Chapter VII how the "new things" announced in 48 are set forth in 49—an especially strik-

---

* The first verse of chapter 65, unquestionably the beginning of a new poem, brings an answer to the question (64 : 12) with which the preceding poem closed; see the note on the passage.

ing example. Similarly, the picture of the "highway in the desert," built by divine agency for the return of the "ransomed," is first introduced in 35 : 8–10 and thereupon taken for granted and further elaborated in chapter 40, which originally was the immediate sequel of 35. In 58 : 10*b* the prophet suggests in a single sentence two contrasted pictures: a scene of darkness representing the present condition of guilt and despair, and the glorious sunrise which will follow repentance and right living. The two themes are then developed in detail in the next following poems, the darkness in 59 and the endless day in 60. See the introduction to chapter 59, and observe especially how the words of 58 : 10 are repeated in 59 : 9 f. This manner of making a close connection by carrying over some striking phrase (perhaps merely incidental in its use) from one poem to its successor is very characteristic and has frequent illustration. An example is the "redoubling strength" of 40 : 31, which is repeated (ironically and with a different application) in 41 : 1. In 51 : 16 there is plain allusion to certain themes which were prominent in 49 and 50. The use of the introductory formula, "Hear me !" is peculiar to the three poems, 46, 48, and 51 : 1–16. In the case of 59/60, already discussed, there is to be noticed not only the manner in which the last verses of the one prepare the way for the other, but also the significant allusion in 60 : 18 to the "violence . . . rapine, and ruin" of 59 : 6 f. In 61 : 3*b* the "planting of Yahwè" was taken over from 60 : 21. I have noted in the Commentary other instances which need not be presented here.

The evidence obtained in these several ways seems quite sufficient, and the conclusion certain. The poems comprised in chapters 34, 35, 40–66 were composed and written within a brief period of time and in the same order in which we now find them. They were put forth by their author in a single volume, which seems to have been taken over entire by the compilers of the great collection which was given the name of Isaiah.

2. *The Library of Israel's Prophets*

It was not simply because of their extraordinary literary and religious interest that the poems of the little collection were preserved. It happened that under the direction of some authoritative council or group of religious leaders in Jerusalem a small library of Hebrew sacred writings, narrative, didactic, and poetical, was formed and perpetuated. In this library was incorporated, in a manner presently to be described, the work of the Second Isaiah. The bulk of old Hebrew literature had been allowed to perish— the normal fate of ancient literatures generally, however worthy of preservation. Some very important monuments dating from the time of the kingdoms and even earlier had survived, however; not by mere accident, but in the normal progress of a marvellous development. The Pentateuch was already complete when the Second Isaiah wrote, and the motives and means of its preserva- tion were largely practical. To the completed Pentateuch had been appended, as the necessary continuation of its narrative, the history of the nation Israel, comprising Joshua, Judges, and the Books of the Kingdoms. This, also, was sacred scripture. Of the literature of other types, ordinarily doomed to perish in the course of a generation or two, a portion had escaped the common fate. The religious writings produced by the Hebrews were unique in the ancient world, and the same mighty impulse which brought them forth also wrought through various agencies to preserve a part. To this small but noble survival from earlier times was now added a considerable amount of more recent material. That which chiefly concerns us here is the material which entered into the composition of the so-called 'later' prophetical books, namely Isaiah, Jeremiah, Ezekiel, and the Twelve.

It is becoming more and more generally recognized that the Books of the Old Testament Prophets were put together and ar- ranged in order in a definitive collection in the third century B. C. The need was then felt, apparently for the first time, of assembling the writings of this class and investing them with a certain author- ity not shared by similar writings outside the group. There was available for this purpose some material which had survived, as has been said, from earlier times; but the literature of the later period, and even that which was contemporary, was more exten- sively drawn upon. It was necessary to select the best of this, retouching here and there, and to devise an effective arrangement of the whole. Anonymous writings were provided with names or attached to books already existing. The internal evidence is suffi- cient to establish the main facts. Amos and Hosea (excepting slight additions to each); minor portions of Isaiah and Jeremiah; Haggai and the first chapters of Zechariah, and Malachi are clearly older than the fourth century. It seems equally clear that the bulk of the remainder must have been produced either in this cen- tury or in the beginning of the next.

Allusions to contemporary events are of course not to be looked for in religious poetry. The historical background recognized in this or that psalm or didactic composition is usually the creation of the commentator's imagination. There are exceptions, however. The Book of Habakkuk is certainly a meditation on the conquests of Alexander the Great and his armies in Asia.* In Zech. 9:1–8 there is allusion, as many scholars have seen, to the capture of Tyre and Gaza in 332. Ezek. 26 describes the siege and destruction of the former city by the Greeks (in vs. 7 the words "Nebuchadrezzar king of Babylon" are an obvious insertion). This is also the background of Is. 23, a poem assigned by Duhm and [Marti to the fourth century. (In vs. 1 read הֻבַּית: "The house has been devastated, so that none may enter; from the land of Kittim it has been laid bare." In vs. 12: "Kittim, arise and pass on! Even there shalt thou have no rest." In vs. 13, "the land of Chaldea" and "Asshur" are shown by the meter to be insertions; also by the sense, which has baffled all commentators.) Again, the splendid poem Is. 14:4b–21 has for its subject, as I believe, the tragic death of the demigod Alexander, far from his home and the tombs of his ancestors (vss. 18 ff.). Finally, considerable portions of Jeremiah are acknowledged on all hands to be very late. In short, the completed 'books' of the O. T. Prophets were made up at least a generation after the time of Alexander the Great.†

It is a very remarkable fact that Books of Prophecies were thus put together and invested with especial authority in the first half of the Greek period. The obvious intention to treat the whole collection, Major and Minor Prophets, as completed and closed in the *Persian* period—the traditional view—is equally remarkable. I used, a moment ago, the word "retouching." This means particularly the making of very slight interpretative additions, or, much more rarely, alterations, designed to make clear the early origin of the writing, or at least to remove what would plainly mark it as a recent composition. There was some slight revision of this nature, made on principle, and now apparent in various parts of the great collection, and the reason for it was the decision

---

* The fact was first demonstrated by Duhm in 1906. It was recognized quite independently, somewhat later, by the present writer. For a brief discussion of the evidence of data obtained from Habakkuk and the other writings here mentioned I may refer to my article entitled "Alexander the Great in the Old Testament Prophecies," in the *Festschrift für Karl Marti* (1925), pp. 281–286.

† There is good evidence, as will be shown in the sequel, that the expanded Book of Isaiah was the first of the Prophetical Books to be formed, and also the first to be translated.

that every one of these divinely appointed spokesmen of the Hebrew faith *must* have delivered his message before the fourth century. As I wrote in the article mentioned in the preceding footnote, p. 282, "no writing which obviously had originated later than the Persian period would have been given a place here. If the words or phrases pointing to a late date could be removed, altered, or interpreted in another way, the writing could be regarded as the work of one of the prophets; otherwise, it must be rejected." The fact of such systematic retouching is especially evident in the case of Habakkuk (where two words are slightly but very significantly altered), but is demonstrable also in numerous other places. It is of course not necessary to suppose that all of it was done at the time when the writings were collected and arranged.

Why, now, were the Hebrew 'prophecies' assembled at this particular time, and why were they in part antedated? Neither religious feeling, nor pride of race, nor literary interest, nor indeed the combination of all three motives, would seem sufficient to account for the undertaking, nor for the effort to place *all* the writings earlier than the time of Alexander. It may seem going far afield to raise these questions here, but they have their bearing on the principal problems of the present investigation. We have the best of evidence that the third century B. C. was the time of all others when the defining and assuring of the true Hebrew tradition was a burning question in Jerusalem. Were there *two* great central sanctuaries of Israel? And if so, to which of the two should the priority be given? We know that the claim was made for Shechem, the home of the patriarchs, and that the rivalry was intense. "Our fathers," said the men of Gerizim, "worshipped in this mountain, and ye say that in Jerusalem is the place where men ought to worship" (John 4:20). Hence the Jews had no dealings with the Samaritans. At the beginning of the present era, to be sure, the Jews had nothing to fear; their enmity was rather the echo of past struggle and peril. There had been a time when the pretensions of Shechem, backed by foreign preferment, seemed in a fair way to prevail (*Ezra Studies*, 153–155, 209, 321–333). The Samaritans had the complete Pentateuch in its final form, and thus far were on a par with the Jews in the matter of authoritative scripture. In Jerusalem was now undertaken the task of showing who were in fact the trustees of the religion of Israel. For one thing there was the attempt (in the end completely successful) to gain general acceptance for the view that the true tradition was preserved only

by the Babylonian exiles (see Chapter II). Chronicles-Ezra-Nehemiah was the historical document composed in support of this
view. Ezekiel was its prophecy, written by a man of imagination
and religious insight who believed the legend of the Babylonian
sojourn and used that setting for his teachings. I would venture
the conjecture that *the forming of a sacred library* was another feature of this awakening in defense of the Jewish church. Here is a
motive, already known to us, which would fully account for the
undertaking.

The Jews were indeed the rightful heirs of the splendid inheritance, and Jerusalem was the unrivalled repository of a divine
literature. The men of Judea had at hand the means of demonstrating to the world that the revelation once given to Moses had
been continued in a succession of prophets, whose writings they
possessed. Hence also the dating of the great collection, that is,
the fixing of its lower limit. The Samaritan schism took place at
the time of Alexander the Great, as narrated by Josephus;* see
also *Ezra Studies*, 328–331. It is obvious that the Library of the
Prophets could take no account of this event, and must appear to
antedate it. The shaping of the Jewish tradition would thus be
given a complete explanation. This theory of the genesis of the
Hebrew 'prophetic' collections is only a conjecture, but, as already remarked, it is a conjecture with a firm basis.

3. *The Compiling of the Book of Isaiah*

The prophet Isaiah the son of Amoz, however much he may
have written and published during his lifetime, certainly left behind him very few compositions that were preserved under his
name and generally known as his. The same was true of Jeremiah. When, at a much later day, search was made for the recorded utterances of the inspired teachers of Israel, there was a
very natural desire that the two great prophets of Jerusalem should
be represented by written oracles of an extent proportionate to

---

* The date and historical setting of *this* event could not possibly have been
forgotten in Jerusalem. We are without other definite information, however,
with one important exception. We have the good fortune to know that in the
year 408, the date of the letter from Elephantine, the schism had *not* taken
place; at that time there was no open hostility between Shechem and Jerusalem. In the letter there is mention of a Sanballat, who (as I have argued
elsewhere) was presumably the grandfather of the Sanballat named by Josephus. As I showed in 1896, *Composition of Ezra-Neh.*, p. 48, the story told by
the Chronicler in Neh. 13 : 28 f. is not an account of the schism, though it is
unquestionably a slap at the Samaritans.

their authors' reputation. It was certain that they had given forth more than the small amount attributed to them, and diligent search must bring other prophecies to light. The two most important collections in our Hebrew Bible, the Books of Isaiah and Jeremiah, thus came into being, put together from somewhat heterogeneous materials, as any careful scrutiny shows. The amount that could on good grounds be credited to the reputed author is in either case very small. How and by whom the work of collecting was accomplished, and on what ground the writings thus brought together were now assigned, or had already been ascribed, to the one or the other of the two prophets, are questions that we cannot answer. We can only say that it is fortunate for the world that the compilers proceeded as they did.

In the Book of Jeremiah a collection of late prophecies of various origin was authenticated for the prophet by incorporating with it a considerable section of narrative from the Second Book of Kings, dealing with the time of his activity and the fulfilment of his predictions; namely II Kings 24 : 18–25 : 30, with certain omissions and considerable additions. This borrowed and embellished narrative now forms a part of chapters 39–43 in Jeremiah and the whole of chapter 52. The collected writings attributed to Isaiah were similarly made secure for him, as a single collection, by the insertion of an extensive historical passage relating directly to his work as prophet. The major part of II Kings 18–20 is reproduced, with little change, in chapters 36–39 of the Book of Isaiah. There was an excellent reason for the choice of this particular place for making the insertion, as I shall try to show.

The largest single element in the compilation which was henceforth to be known as the Book of Isaiah, constituting its second half, was a group of twenty-seven poems (in modern times divided and numbered as twenty-nine chapters) whose authorship appears to have been unknown to the compilers. The poems referred to are those which are here designated as Second Isaiah. Seen in a single block, in any surroundings, they stand out distinctly as an indivisible whole, making on any reader the impression of being the work of one writer possessed of striking individual characteristics. The high-sounding exordium of chapter 34 formed the obvious beginning. The two poems which serve to introduce the brilliant prophecy are plainly of one piece with those which stand at the end of the group: the "great slaughter in the land of Edom" pictured in 34 has its companion picture in 63 : 1 ff.; the return of "the redeemed" to Zion, first described in 35, is given its final

199317

description in 66, after having received either brief mention or fuller treatment in many of the intervening poems. The language and style are unmistakably the same throughout; characteristic phrases and pictures are repeated; both the substance and the very words of 34: 2-5 reappear in 66: 16; the address to the nations of the earth with which 34 begins is seen again in 41: 1; the beautiful verse 35: 10 is characteristically repeated in 51: 11. In what way could so obvious a literary unit, familiar to many readers, be claimed for Isaiah the son of Amoz and firmly attached to his book?

It has long been the current critical theory that chapters 1-35 constituted the first main 'Isaianic' compilation. To this, it is asserted, the four historical chapters 36-39 were appended. Later, perhaps much later, chapters 40-66 were added. Quite recently has arisen the curious supplementary theory that chapters 40-66 formed a collection or book which in the time of the Chronicler (third century B. C.) was attributed to *Jeremiah*. This theory, formulated by Duhm, has been adopted by some other scholars, including Buchanan Gray. It is most completely stated in the latter's *Commentary*, pp. xxxvii ff. The argument rests on the assumption that II Chron. 36: 22 f. (= Ezra 1: 1-3) cites Is. 44: 28 and attributes the prophecy to Jeremiah. The assumption is mistaken, as I have shown. At the time of the Chronicler there was no mention of Cyrus in chapters 44 and 45; and as for the citation of Jeremiah, it refers to the prophecy of the "seventy years," as verse 21 shows, and as has long been taken for granted by students of the Chronicler's history. Moreover, there never was a time at which chapters 40-66 formed a separate 'book.' *No collection beginning with chapter 40 ever had separate existence except in modern critical theories.*

As for chapters 1-33, we have no reason to believe, but very good reason to doubt, that this portion of the present Book of Isaiah ever circulated by itself. It was remarked above that chapter 23 was composed in the fourth century, after the Greek invasion; and the following chapters, to the end of 33, consist in the main of late material, as is generally recognized. In all the principal treatises on Isaiah numerous late elements are recognized also in the preceding chapters of the book. The probability is that *all* these productions of the early Greek period which were used in making up the prophet's expanded book were brought together for the purpose at one time, namely at the same time when the poems of Second Isaiah were incorporated in the great collection.

The supposition of any other time, or times, of forming a *corpus Isaianum* either early in the third century or later merely creates improbabilities.

I am of course well aware that some commentators have proposed to date certain portions of the collection in the second century. On examining the grounds given for such dating, however, I have found no evidence tending to support the contention. There are, on the other hand, strong reasons for believing that the book existed in its final form at least as early as the middle of the third century. Sirach 48 f. shows that the "Library of the Prophets" (as I have termed it) had been assembled considerably earlier than 180 B. C. In the time of the Palestinian sage it was already a definite quantity, familiar in form and extent, and recognized by all his people as the authoritative booking of the Hebrew prophetic tradition. It included Ezekiel (which I suppose to have been written c. 230 B. C.) and the Book of the Twelve; and the passage Ecclus. 48 : 24 f. shows, as all agree, that its Book of Isaiah included chapters 40–66. If the reason which I have conjectured for the formation of the Library of the Prophets is recognized as valid, it would seem especially likely that the great edition was made at a comparatively early date, and that once made, and treated as authoritative, it was kept intact.

There is another important consideration. The Greek version of Isaiah is distinctly an early translation. This is still wanting complete demonstration, to be sure, besides being indefinite. We know very little in regard to the genesis of the earliest renderings of the Biblical books into Greek. The Pentateuch was translated before the middle of the third century; the historical books, Joshua–Kings, doubtless immediately after;* and Chronicles-Ezra-Nehemiah before (perhaps long before) the middle of the second century.† The prologue to the Greek Sirach (132 B. C.) plainly implies that Greek versions of "the Law and the Prophets and the rest of the books" were in circulation and well known. H. St. John Thackeray has argued forcibly that Isaiah was the first of the Prophets to be thus translated; see the references to his publications given in Gray's *Commentary*, xl–xlii, and also Thackeray's

---

*Considerable portions of the earliest version (or versions) of *these* books were revised, supplemented, or replaced at a later day. This was partly because the Greek had suffered corruption, and partly because it had been derived from Hebrew texts which differed from that which ultimately was selected for the authoritative tradition.

† Long ago demonstrated by Freudenthal. See *Ezra Studies*, 82 f., where the facts on which the conclusion is based are set forth.

Grammar of the O. T. in Greek, ix. He draws his conclusion from
the character of the Greek, the nature of the rendering, and affini-
ties with certain renderings in the Pentateuch.* I do not believe,
however, that even Thackeray has done justice to the antiquity of
these earliest versions of the Hebrew Prophet. He finds himself
compelled (*Grammar,* p. ix) to cast away the testimony of the
Sirach prologue; while to me, at least, it is quite incredible that
the Siracide should have appealed to the evidence of these
Greek renderings of "the Prophets and the rest of the books" if
they had not been in existence. Thackeray's date for the Greek
Isaiah is "near the beginning of the second century" (a date in
the third century would seem to me much more probable), and
he shows it to be the work of a single translator throughout. The
Hebrew book was certainly complete and in its present form at
the time when the version was made.

When the roll of twenty-seven poems was claimed for Isaiah,
it was not simply appended to a book which had previously been
completed and circulated, but was taken along with a considerable
assemblage of poems, mostly of recent date, which were collected
and shaped with the purpose of supplementing the comparatively
few extant compositions of the great prophet of the days of Hezekiah. The reason why the roll of the twenty-seven was put at
the end of the compilation was by no means because it was the
last to be chosen, but because of its character. It could not have
been put elsewhere. It was the unique prophecy of the World to
Come, such as no other Hebrew writer had even approached. As
Sirach 48 : 24 f. expresses it, the prophet Isaiah

> Saw in the spirit the last things,
> And comforted the mourners in Zion;
> Showing what should be to the end of time,
> And the hidden things before they came to pass.

These unsurpassed poems, which (as was usually the case) had
circulated anonymously from their first appearance, brought the
first volume of the new 'Library of the Prophets' to a most impressive close. The work of compiling and editing, thus inaugurated, was soon continued in the making of a corresponding Book
of Jeremiah, the assembling of the Twelve, and the addition of
Ezekiel.

* Gray's attempt, *ibid.*, to discount Thackeray's argument from the free
style of the rendering, by a reference to the later Targums, is beside the mark.
These are not primarily translations, but homiletic expansions and paraphrases,
to be classed with running commentaries.

It is now possible to see a valid reason for the position of the four historical chapters, between the two originally consecutive poems 35 and 40. It is not the result of accident, nor of the simple wish to provide the reading public with an Isaiah-chrestomathy. What was purposed in introducing the long transcript from II Kings was not, primarily, to authenticate the whole collection. That which stood in need of authentication, and of a locking device by which it might be securely attached to the book which had been built up, was the block of twenty-seven poems. There certainly were many, especially in Jerusalem, who were familiar with this literary unit, so homogeneous, peculiar in style, language, and religious content, and clearly distinct from the kaleidoscopic assemblage of poems to which it now was joined. If it were simply appended, it very possibly would be marked, in the literary tradition, as an unauthentic increment. By simply pulling it apart at the beginning, that is, at the end of chapter 35,* and inserting the chapters which recount the work of Isaiah, a satisfactory joint was provided.† It was well known that chapters 34 and 35 belonged to chapters 40–66, with which they had been in circulation; and with the great book once completed in this manner and put forth as the restored original, no one would be likely to question the authority of the compilers and to undertake a literary analysis and redistribution after the manner of modern criticism. Incidentally, the fact that this device was employed gives evidence that the poems 34–66 had *not* previously been attributed to Isaiah. As has already been said, they doubtless had circulated anony-

---

* It is of course obvious that 34 and 35 could not be separated.

† 'Locking devices' of this sort were of course familiar in Jerusalem. They are sure to be employed wherever intelligent editors are undertaking to effect the permanent external union of heterogeneous compositions. When the Chronicler incorporates the Aramaic Document in his Book of Ezra, he introduces it with a verse (4 : 6) which in language belongs to the preceding, in subject-matter to the following context. When the end of the document is reached, he continues with several verses *in Aramaic of his own composition* (6 : 15–18), and then—keeping the same subject—passes over into Hebrew. The interpolator of the Story of the Three Guardsmen in First Esdras pulls apart the Chronicler's narrative, at a short distance from the point of juncture of the two documents, and inserts two harmonistic patches. This dovetailing was so effective that at a later day, when the whole disturbing tale was officially excised, to form our present Book of Ezra, there went with it eighteen verses of the original history (*Ezra Studies*, 57–59; *A. J. S. L.*, xxxvii, 1921, p. 91). This closely parallels the case of Isaiah. The author of the second half of Daniel welded his Hebrew apocalypses to the Aramaic folk-tales by writing his first chapter, 7, in Aramaic and then translating chapter 1 from Aramaic into Hebrew; a most effective expedient (*Transactions Conn. Acad.*, XV, 1909, 241–251).

mously, a supposition probable on general grounds, and agreeing well with the self-effacement which is so characteristic of their author.

It is a legitimate question (though, as it now seems to me, the inquiry is hardly likely to be fruitful) whether still other poems of this author may not have been incorporated in the Book of Isaiah; and again, whether his work may not be recognized in other poetical portions of the Old Testament. It is of course hardly conceivable that the publication of such a literary genius, such a spokesman of Israel, should have been limited to the one roll of twenty-seven poems. It is not difficult to suppose that the rest of his output perished along with the mass of such literature; yet it is quite conceivable that in the course of time this or that utterance in Psalm or Prophecy may be recognized as his. I was at one time inclined to see his handiwork in the first chapter of Isaiah, "the Great Arraignment," and in the seemingly characteristic continuation in 2: 1-4. There is here indeed much to remind us of the great preacher, stern censor, and inspired evangelist; but the resemblances in language are scarcely sufficient to render the theory plausible. Deut. 32 is in style and diction singularly reminiscent of Second Isaiah. It is withal a very fine poem, the work of no ordinary writer. Here again, however, the assignment to our author, though certainly possible, seems too precarious. It is probably best, for the present, to be satisfied with what is assured.

4. *The Date of Second Isaiah*

An approximate dating of the poems is not difficult to obtain. As has already been shown, they were all written within a short time; there is here no question of successive dates. On the one hand, the lower limit is certain, unquestionably fixed by the passages in which the Babylonian power, *i. e.*, the Persian Kingdom (Ezra 5: 13, Neh. 13: 6), is spoken of as still standing. This is especially plain in chapter 47, vss. 8 and 9. If this had been a *vaticinium post eventum*, the prophet must have expressed himself very differently. Vss. 11 and 14 show that the doom here announced is the awful catastrophe which is to end the present age, precisely the same which is described in 34: 7-10 and again announced in 66: 15 f.; not the 'benevolent assimilation' by a foreign power which took place in 539, nor even the slaughter and conquest by the Greeks two centuries later. At the time when the prophet wrote, Babylon was certainly 'dwelling secure,' not threatened from without. Alexander and his armies had not yet appeared.

On the other hand, the work is relatively late. Recent commentators have generally agreed that 'Trito-Isaiah' cannot have been written earlier than the middle of the fifth century, and a still later date is commonly assigned to chapters 34 and 35. When the fact is recognized that in the poems 34–66 we are dealing with a single publication, the several lines of evidence all seem to converge in the latter part of the Persian period as the time of composition. Some details bearing upon this question were presented and discussed in Chapter IV.

We see settled conditions in Jerusalem and a considerable degree of material prosperity. (The prophet is little concerned, to be sure, with worldly standards of success. Even in 54 : 2, where he exhorts Jerusalem to add to her boundaries and increase in welfare, he is thinking mainly of spiritual resources.) There is no hint of any great calamity recently endured. In 51 : 19 and 60 : 18 we have only poetical and standing phrases; in 64 : 9 f. the allusion is to events long past but permanent in their effect and ever fresh in memory, the ruin and complete humiliation wrought by the armies of Nebuchadrezzar. Nor, on the other hand, is there reference to any recent sign of God's favor. The temple has long been built, and an elaborate ritual (43 : 23 f.) is a matter of course. The Jewish Dispersion is very far advanced, as many passages show. The people whom the prophet addresses call themselves *Yĕhūdîm*, "Jews" (48 : 1), a designation which we first meet in the latter half of the Persian period. Idolatry is prevalent, and foreign cults flourish even in Jerusalem. The little information which we possess concerning the Syrian deities mentioned in 65 : 11 comes chiefly from the Greek period. In general, we receive the impression of a people whose horizon is wide, and among whom the feeling is already strong—as we know it to have been in the Maccabean period—that the old faith has been outgrown.

From the theology of the book we gain an even stronger impression of late date; see the discussion of some aspects of this subject in Chapter IV. An important item not emphasized heretofore is the eschatology. Duhm (p. xxii) points with good reason to this feature of the bipartite picture drawn in 34 and 35, "das wegen seines theologischen Charakters sehr jung sein muss." We see precisely the same eschatology in 66, both the punishment by eternal fire and the portrayal of 'Zion's glorious future.' So also in chapters 47 and 50. The very same fire which is promised to

'Edom' in 34 is that to which Chaldea is doomed in 47 : 11, 14; and the Gehenna of 66 : 23 f. is prepared for the obdurate sinners who are addressed in 50 : 11. In this, as in every other particular, the theology of the poet-prophet is the same throughout the twenty-seven poems.

Both the number and the manner of the allusions to various passages in the Torah, from the first verses of Genesis to the Book of Deuteronomy, give evidence that the Pentateuch had received its final redaction before the time when these poems were written, and that it was already looked upon, not only by the priests but also by the Jewish people generally, as sacred scripture. In the first poem of the collection (34 : 11) we find the *tohu* and *bohu* of Gen. 1 : 2. The former (rare) word is employed also in 40 (twice), 41, 44, 45 (twice), 49, and 59. In 40 there is plain allusion to the first chapter of Genesis, and especially to the creation of the heavenly bodies; the prophet in his argument appeals here, as so often elsewhere, to holy writ. In 54 : 9 he appeals to Gen. 9 : 8–17, which also is a passage *in the 'Priestly' Document.** Allusions to passages in the Documents J and E (*e.g.*, to Num. 11 : 25 ff. in 63 : 10) are also frequent, and it is plain that these three separate elements have long been combined. In 43 : 17, where the destruction of the Egyptians in the Red Sea is described, the word *khail*, "army" (which Duhm finds noticeable), is simply reminiscent of the P Document, which repeats it several times (in Ex. 14). The influence of Deuteronomy is also obvious. Duhm is quite right in pointing to it in 42 : 21 ff., and it is equally plain in other passages. The *rakkā wa'anuggā*, "tender and delicate one," of 47 : 1 is a sure quotation from Deut. 28 : 56; observe how the latter verse proceeds! In 48 : 4 there seems to be a reminiscence of Deut. 9 : 6. The argument and the precise words of 50 : 1 refer directly to Deut. 24 : 1.

In all these and the other similar cases, the writer is not making mere literary references, displaying his knowledge of the Hebrew classics; he is evidently staying himself on the book which all his hearers recognize as having divine origin and authority. There is here no great gain, to be sure, for the dating of Second Isaiah, for we have no definite and trustworthy information as to the time when the Pentateuch was completed. What evidence there is appears to indicate the fifth century, but more than this can hardly be said.

* It is only by shutting the eyes to what is obvious that a commentator could persuade himself that the allusion is to Gen. 8 : 20–22.

From the recognizable literary relations of II Isaiah to other writings of the Old Testament there is something more to be learned as to the date, namely, that it cannot be placed much later than the beginning of the fourth century. Our poet is not one to borrow from other writers either phrases, ideas, or figures of speech. Aside from the Pentateuch, the only document of our Old Testament with which he shows acquaintance is II Samuel. In 55 : 3 f. there is plain allusion to II Sam. 7 : 13–16, including the quotation of several of the most significant words, as has generally been observed.* As for the quotation of II Isaiah by other writers, the instances are numerous, and the gain from them is important.

Among the writings which show acquaintance with our poet and prophet are several of those which were used in making up the Book of Isaiah. The Messianic passages in chapters 9 and 11 are of this number. These are generally recognized as the work of a single hand, and it is the prevailing opinion of scholars at the present day that they are a late element in the collection (so Stade, Hackmann, Cheyne, Volz, Marti, Kennett, Gray, Hölscher, and others). 9 : 5 is the result of reflection on 66 : 7, and develops magnificently what was given there in briefest compass. See the introduction to chapter 66. The passage 11 : 7–9 is very plainly an expansion of 65 : 25. Observe how the first part of this verse is repeated in vs. 7, and the concluding portion in vs. 9, while the intervening mention of "the serpent" is played upon at some length in vs. 8! In the last-mentioned particular there is indisputable evidence that the passage in chapter 11 is the later. There is nothing in 11 : 8 to suggest even remotely the "serpent" of Gen. 3 : 14 and the diet of dust. Vss. 10–16 of this chapter also contain numerous reminiscences of II Isaiah. The passage 13 : 20–22 is one of many in the O. T. Prophets which imitate or quote 34 : 11–15. There are manifest allusions to II Isaiah in chapter 14 (in the later framework of the great poem), and in other portions of the book, including chapters 29–33.

In the Book of Jeremiah an especially striking instance is 12 : 7–12. Here the main feature is a direct borrowing, in vs. 9b,

---

* This evidently shows that the *Biblia Sacra* to which our author appeals included not only the Law but also the sacred history attached to it; namely, both Joshua, which was manifestly inseparable from the preceding narrative, and also the subsequent records in Judges, Samuel, and Kings, all of which had undergone the same 'priestly' redaction as the Law, and perhaps at the same time. See the article "Historical Literature," by G. F. Moore, in the *Encyclopædia Biblica*, II, col. 2082 f.

from Is. 56 : 9, the "shepherds" also appearing in vs. 10. The last
clause of vs. 11 proceeds with a quotation from Is. 57 : 1—to make
the borrowing absolutely certain. Moreover, vs. 12, with its "on
all the bare heights," and the "sword of Yahwè" descending on
all flesh, reminds of Is. 49 : 9 and 34 : 6. There are numerous other
instances, such as 30 : 10 f. and 46 : 27 f., which imitate Is. 41 and
43; and 48 : 18, which is a paraphrase of Is. 47 : 1.

Ezekiel, who is much given to quoting from other writers, or
paraphrasing them, shows in many places the influence of Second
Isaiah. Chapter 34—very characteristic of Ezekiel throughout—
is a homily based on Is. 56 : 9–11, one of the most striking and powerful pictures drawn by the great poet: the shepherds who are not
only neglectful *but also greedy :* the wild beasts coming to devour
the flock. In the same chapter, vss. 4 and 16, the phrase *khābash
lannishbereth* is borrowed from Is. 61 : 1; note that the verb is
construed thus only in these three passages. Again, vss. 24 f.
show the influence of Is. 55: 3 f., a passage which is once more
expanded in Ezek. 37 : 24, 26. The latter half of chapter 39 is
full of like reminiscences. Observe the address to the birds of
prey and wild beasts in vs. 17 (Is. 56 : 9); the great slaughter on
the mountains, pictured as a sacrifice of lambs, goats, and rams
(obviously repeated from Is. 34 : 3, 6 f.); the glory shown to the
nations, whence the scattered Israelites return home, vss. 21, 27
(Is. 66 : 18 f.). In Ezek. 20 : 9, 14, 24 the words of Is. 48 : 9, 11
are repeated; the figurative 'desert' mentioned in vss. 34 f. is the
same which the Second Isaiah has made so familiar. In 22 : 30 f.
is expanded the very striking and original utterance, Is. 59 : 15 f.;
63 : 5.

These instances may suffice to show that II Isaiah was extensively quoted and paraphrased in the literature of the fourth century B. C. and thereafter. The quotations and allusions in various parts of *the Book of Isaiah* show also that the twenty-seven
poems of II Isaiah must have circulated as a separate publication
for some time.

All the evidence thus far presented seems to point to the end of
the fifth century, or the beginning of the fourth, as the most probable time of composition of these poems. This conclusion is supported by the evidence obtained from the language of the book,
with its very considerable list of Aramaic and late Hebrew words
and idioms.

It is possible to go still farther than this, in the attempt to reach
an approximate date. There is in the twenty-seven poems *one*

allusion to a recent historical event. In 57 : 9 f. the prophet reminds his hearers, in a sternly ironical passage, of the time, evidently fresh in memory, when they had thought to gain a place of
greater influence in the world by means of a new political alliance.*

Power thou sawest; didst send thy gift | of oil to the king; ||
Didst multiply thine unguents, and dispatch | thine ambassadors
 afar || —and thou wast brought down to the Pit!
By the length of the way thou wast wearied, | yet saidst not, 'Tis
 hopeless! ||
The reviving of thy *power* thou hadst seen, | therefore didst not lan-
 guish. ||

In the Commentary, in the note on this passage and especially
in the introduction to the poem 56 : 9–57 : 21, I have shown: (1)
that the allusion is to a political move; (2) that the king of Egypt
is intended; *cf.* Hos. 12 : 2 for the present of oil, and Is. 30 : 6 for
the long journey through the Negeb; and (3) that the one time of
all others when the Jewish province seemed to have an opportunity of advancement was when Egypt threw off the Persian yoke
in 407 B. C. The agreement of this date with the result obtained
from the lines of evidence considered above is so striking that I
cannot believe it accidental. I think we may conclude, with some
confidence, that the Second Isaiah composed these poems not
long after the year 407; we may take for convenience the round
number 400.

It may be that the ironical passage at the beginning of chapter
46, depicting the impotence of Bel and Nebo, was suggested by
the collapse which the Persian power and prestige suffered at this
time, not only in Egypt but throughout Western Asia. And
again, with the supposition of this date for the poems, one item
of the terrible indictment in chapter 59 would have been the murder of Jeshua in the temple by his brother Johanan, the High
Priest; an event which occurred at about this time, and probably
several years before the Second Isaiah wrote. See *Ezra Studies*,
318–320. There is no need, however, to look for specific instances
of the wickedness which so distressed and aroused the prophet.

Was II Isaiah written *before* Nehemiah repaired the wall of Jerusalem? The "walls" of the city are mentioned in 49 : 16, 60 : 10,
and 62 : 6. According to Duhm, Cheyne, Marti, and others, the
three passages are to be interpreted as follows: 49 : 16 speaks

---

* The passage begins with the last two words of vs. 8, the traditional division of the verses here being manifestly incorrect.

of the walls of the ideal city of the future; in 62 : 6 the watchmen stand on the few remaining battlements and ruined towers, imploring Yahwè to restore the city; in 60 : 10 it is clearly shown that the walls are in ruins and have yet to be rebuilt. These are all poetic pictures, to be sure, and for this reason even 60 : 10 should perhaps not be pronounced conclusive; yet the interpretation of the commentators just quoted seems the most probable. I myself have been coming more and more decidedly to the conclusion that the old Jewish (and massoretic) tradition is right in placing Nehemiah under Artaxerxes II Mnemon, thus making 384 B. C. the date of building the wall. This supposition agrees best with the documentary evidence and with the historical conditions known to us. The matter is discussed fully in the note on 62 : 6.

CHAPTER VII

THE ATTITUDE TOWARD THE FOREIGN PEOPLES

When a religion is held up to our view with the claim that it is the one true faith, we would know its animating principle and the scale on which it is built. We look first of all for a warm and deep sympathy of man for man, with a range as wide as humanity. This, at all events, must be present. We have seen faiths propagated by the sword; other admirable creeds or cults which from their very nature could embrace only the minority of human beings; the dogma "extra ecclesiam nulla salus" interpreted in a narrow way, through many centuries, even by men of broad humanity and deep religious feeling. This or that 'ecumenical' religion may show us a worthy idea of God, ardent devotion, a pure morality; but unless the heart of all mankind beats through it we cannot admit its claim.

In both Old Testament and New we hear the true universal ring; but in the former case it is sometimes uncertain to what extent the writer has in mind the wider world and to what extent the chosen people; and even the utterances which clearly are all-embracing are rarely expanded sufficiently to show satisfactorily the attitude of their author. We are perhaps hardly prepared to find, even on the soil planted by the Hebrew prophets, and even in view of such passages as Am. 5:24, Mic. 6:8, Mal. 1:11, Ps. 145:14–18, and many others, a Jewish writer of the fifth century B. C. seeing clearly the outlines of a universal faith and developing the idea with enthusiasm in a series of poems.

In every part of the ancient world, religion and nationalism seemed inseparable. The Second Isaiah certainly professes to deal with something greater than this mixture. He is loyal—intensely loyal—to his own people, but is able to see beyond them. There is a greater brotherhood, and a simpler worship of Yahwè, in which men of every heathen nation can participate with full acceptance. We hear of a coming régime for which "the isles" (the remotest inhabited lands) have been waiting (42:4; 51:5). Certain passages seem to proclaim a 'rescue' from bondage and an outpouring of mercy designed for all peoples alike. We would know whether these utterances are the product of momentary enthusiasm or of deep thought. If the latter, we shall expect to hear that the ground of the participation of the Gentiles in the blessings of the coming day is that they are the creatures of the One God, the Father of all men, who has pity and affection for his children. We shall hope to hear the prophet say that the God of Israel will accept all those who shall "do justly, and love mercy, and walk humbly before him," and that beyond this there are privileges, but not requirements, of cult and creed.

The end of the fifth century B. C. saw more than one intellectual prodigy. Greece was then producing the man who even now stands foremost among the masters of philosophic truth. Another people, farther eastward, had specialized in religious thought; and there were giants in Israel as well as in Hellas.

1. *The New Message*

There is a saying which occurs several times in these poems, in varying form, and in a setting which gives it emphasis. The prophet has something 'new' to announce. The first instance* is in one of the opening paragraphs of chapter 42. Vss. 1–4 introduce the Servant of Yahwè and give the most significant details of his character. He is not a king like other kings of the earth, not a ruler appearing in worldly splendor and wielding despotic power, but a quiet, patient, magnanimous benefactor of mankind. Vss. 5–9 then proceed to describe his work; and vs. 9, which forms the conclusion of this main division of the poem, declares the significance of what has just preceded.

The former things have come to pass, | *things which are new I now foretell,* | before they spring forth I proclaim them to you.

The "former things," namely the beginning of Israelite history and especially the choice and call of Abraham, were set forth in the preceding poem, chapter 41. The "new things" are here announced, in vss. 5–7:

Thus saith the One God, Yahwè,
Who created the heavens and spread them out, | who established the earth with all its offspring;

* It is legitimate to speak of it as the first occurrence, in view of the accumulated evidence that the poems were composed and published in the order in which we now find them.

Who gives breath to the people upon it, | and life to those who walk
  therein:
I, Yahwè, called thee in truth, | I took thee by the hand and kept
  thee safe; | *I have made thee my pledge to the peoples, the light of
  the nations ;*
To open the sightless eyes, | to bring out the captives from the prison, |
  from the dungeon those who sit in darkness.

In this instance, unquestionably, the prophet's new message,
the gospel not before proclaimed, is the announcement of salvation for the Gentiles, through the ministration of the Servant.
The God of Israel is the God of all the earth. He is accordingly
represented as saying, in vs. 8, that he will not share his praise
with any other. In him only is the hope of all races and peoples.

It is therefore not by mere chance that the lyric interlude,
which constitutes the next division of the poem, begins with the
words:

Sing unto the Lord a *new* song, his praise *from the end of the earth!*

and then tells of a sound of joy which is heard in the remotest
corners of the inhabited world: among the sailors in their ships;
on the far-off shores and isles of the sea; in the tents of the Bedouin;
on the cliffs of Edom, and in all the mountain habitations, wherever men dwell. Wherefore all this rejoicing, in the edges and
corners of the earth? If it were not for our commentators, it would
hardly be necessary to ask the question. The universal joy is because of the definite promise, just given, of universal help and
healing. A new age is at hand. The multitudes who had been
fatherless, "strangers from the covenants of the promise, having
no hope and without God in the world" (Eph. 2 : 12), hear the
proclamation that they are children of him who created heaven
and earth, joint heirs with the chosen people Israel.

The second passage, or series of passages, dealing with this
great announcement is in chapter 45, in a poem which has for its
subject the Messiah and the Messianic time. A mighty leader and
conqueror is coming, whose advent will bring to light new things:
"I will give thee the treasures of darkness, the hoards long hidden
in secret" (vs. 3). Yahwè girds him for action, and declares his
purpose: "That all may know, from the east and from the west,
that none is beside me; I am Yahwè, there is no other" (vs. 6).
The parallel with the beginning of chapter 42 is obvious.

There follow some remarkable lines, vss. 9–12, in which we see

indicated the incredulity and displeasure which the new announcement arouses in a certain class of hearers. As the laborers in the
vineyard who had borne the burden and heat of the day are ill
pleased that their fellows of the eleventh hour should be equally
well paid (Matt. 20 : 12); as the elder son in the Parable of the
Prodigal feels himself unjustly treated (Luke 15 : 28 ff.); so the
long-suffering children of Israel find it hard to be told that they
are only a part of God's great family. But as the owner of the
vineyard replies to the objectors, Do I not give you what was
promised? May I not do what I will with mine own? and as the
father says to the elder son, Thou art ever with me, and all that
I have is thine; so the Father of Israel answers: "Says the clay
to him who fashions it, What doest thou? Will ye question me
about my children; concerning the work of my hands will ye
command me?" * He adds, exactly as in chapter 42, in the similar context, that he, the creator of the heavens, also made the
earth and all the human beings who people it.

Finally, in the latter part of the chapter, vss. 22 f., the foreign
peoples themselves are directly addressed.

Turn ye to me, and be saved, | all ye ends of the earth! ||
For I am God, there is no other. | By myself I swear it, ||
The truth is gone forth from my mouth, | my word shall not turn
    back, ||
That to me every knee shall bow, | every tongue swear allegiance. ||

In chapter 48, vs. 6 proclaims again (as in 42 : 9 and in almost
the same words) the fact of a new truth just coming to light and
marking the beginning of a new era. The "former things," the
prophet says, are known to all Israel. The past history of the
chosen people, up to the present day, was clearly predicted. The
God of Israel had declared from the beginning this portion of his
eternal plan, so that all might know that he himself foresaw and
wrought it. But even these former things, though plainly to be
seen, were neither heeded at home nor published abroad. Yahwè
says to Israel:

Thou hast heard and seen all this, | and couldst thou not have pro-
    claimed it?
I make thee henceforth to hear new things, | things kept in store,
    which thou hast not known.†

* See Chapter IV, where the whole passage is quoted, with some comment
as to the current misinterpretation of its meaning.
† The resemblance of this to 45 : 3, in which the meaning is precisely the
same, must not be overlooked.

They are now created, not from of old, | before to-day thou hast
never heard them!

The prophet does not declare in this poem, however, what the
"new things" are. We are indeed led to expect him to repeat his
former announcement, but he leaves us, temporarily, in that expectation. The subject of the poem which constitutes chapter 48
is the *failure* of Israel; the failure to heed the truth already known
and to act upon it. Here, as in chapter 41, the "former things"
are in the foreground, and the call of Abraham is the central fact.
The poet is reserving his great announcement for a poem of the
coming age; a picture in which joy shall be unclouded by rebuke.
And the poem immediately follows.

The first half of chapter 49 consists mainly of the poetic development of two themes which had been stated in chapters 42 and
45: the Servant charged with a universal mission; and Yahwè
the father of all mankind. We certainly receive the impression
of an utterance for which its author has been preparing the way
and holding his best in reserve. Viewed as imaginative poetry,
it is a great masterpiece; seen as a declaration of religious truth,
put forth centuries before the Christian era and out of an atmosphere which is commonly supposed to be nationalistic and exclusive, it is overpowering.

(The Servant speaks)

1 Hear me, ye distant shores, | and hearken, ye nations, from far!
Yahwè called me from the womb, | from the bowels of my mother
he declared my name. . . .
3 He said to me, Thou art my Servant; | Israel, in whom I will glorify
myself.
4 But I said, I have toiled in vain, | I have spent my strength for
nothing at all;
Nevertheless my right is with the Lord, | and my recompense rests
with my God.
5 But now Yahwè saith: . . .
6 It is too light a thing that thou shouldst be my Servant, | to lift up
the tribes of Jacob, | to restore the residue of Israel;
I will make thee the light of the nations, | that my rescue may
reach to the end of the earth. . . .
8 I make thee the peoples' pledge, to uplift the world, | to apportion
anew the desolate inheritances;
9 Saying to the prisoners, Come forth! | and to those who are in
darkness, Appear!

Then follows, in vss. 9*b*–12, the description of the journey of
these rescued 'prisoners' to their home. A highway is built for
them; they neither hunger nor thirst; 'He who has pity on them'
is their guide. It all closes with a cry of joy (vs. 13):

Shout, ye heavens, and exult, O earth! | Let the mountains break
   forth into song!
For Yahwè has compassion on his people, | shows mercy to his
   afflicted ones.

Who are 'his people'? The question might seem to be superfluous, seeing that the prophet himself has just been telling us,
with impressive emphasis and in unequivocal terms, that God's
children from every race and region on earth are intended. But
no; our commentators, one and all, refuse to take the prophet at
his word. They insist (in spite of 42 : 7; 61 : 1, and the whole context here) that the 'prisoners' are the exiles in Babylonia. Announcement was indeed made, in vs. 6, of a rescue extending to
the end of the earth; but what is actually described, they assert,
is the return of a company of Jews to Palestine. "Observe," says
Cheyne (*Book of the Prophet Isaiah*, Translation, p. 183), "that
the sermon has a far narrower range than the text." Not so, if
the prophet is permitted to interpret himself! And has no attention been paid to the immediate continuation of the poem?
   It is most unfortunate that the modulation at vs. 14 should
have been misunderstood from the Targum down to the present
day. We are here standing before one of the finest things in all
literature, as well as in the history of religion. The word of the
Lord has just gone forth that the 'rescue,' the restoration, the
endless divine favor of the coming age, for which faithful Israel
has been waiting and longing through bitter centuries, will be
given to all peoples alike. Had not all the hope of the downtrodden Hebrew race rested in the repeated promise: The Lord hath
chosen thee to be a peculiar people unto himself, out of all peoples
that are upon the face of the earth? Was the dogma, 'Yahwè, the
God of Israel,' cherished for a thousand years, an empty form of
words? No wonder that Zion cried out: "Yahwè has forsaken
me, my Lord has forgotten me!"
   The current (and traditional) misinterpretation of this wonderful composition appears nowhere more clearly than in the assumption of modern critics and commentators that a new poem begins
at vs. 14 (in spite of the *wattōmer!*). It is indeed obvious that if

vss. 9–12 describe a Jewish restoration, vss. 14 ff. are completely
unsuited to be the sequel. No one, it would seem—at least since
the age in which the prophet himself lived—has ever recognized
the fact that the transition at this point is from the rejoicing of
the great Gentile world to the momentary disappointment of
Israel. The range of the sermon (in vss. 9–12) is *not* 'narrower
than that of the text,' but equally wide. In vss. 14 ff. we have
the most natural and powerful conclusion that could be imagined.*
The prophet has made his great announcement, that the love of
God is universal, not limited to any one race or quarter of the
earth. He has pictured the joyful home-coming of the multitudes
who had heretofore been accounted hopeless outsiders, if not enemies. He now assures Israel, precisely as he had done in chapter
45, and as St. Paul does in his Epistle to the Romans,† that there
is nevertheless a glory of the chosen people which no other can
share.

There is one other noteworthy passage in which the *novelty* of
the prophet's announcement seems to be emphasized. It is in
chapter 55, which begins with the words: "Ho, *every one* who
thirsts, come ye to the waters!" Vs. 3 proceeds:

Incline your ear, and come unto me; | hear, that your soul may live;
I will make an eternal compact with you, | the favor assured to David.

The meaning of the allusion is certain. The "favor assured," long
ago, to David and to the Hebrew people was the coming of a
divinely guided prince and leader from this royal house. What,
then, is the new compact, and with whom is it made? Thus far
the poem has been addressed to all mankind; now, with one of
those dramatic turns of which this poet is so fond, Yahwè speaks
to the anointed one who is to come:

Behold, I make thee the witness of the peoples, | the leader and com-
    mander of the peoples.
Thou shalt call nations that thou knowest not, | nations that know
    thee not shall run unto thee.

That is, the Messiah of David's line is to be the leader and savior
not only of Israel but of other peoples and races as well. The
prophet has said this of the Servant of Yahwè in previous poems.
It is a great gain to be definitely assured that his brilliant per-

* See, further, the introduction to chapter 49, where the general plan and
principal features of the poem are discussed.
† Especially in chapters 9–11; see also 3 : 1 f.

sonification, as it is applied to the coming deliverer, takes the form of the divinely appointed 'king' of the popular expectation.

We now know with certainty who is intended in the soliloquy with which the poem opens in chapter 61:

The spirit of Yahwè, my Lord, is upon me, | forasmuch as the Lord
   has anointed me,
Has sent me to bring glad tidings to the lowly, | to give healing to
   the broken-hearted;
To proclaim to the captives freedom, | to the blind the recovery of
   sight;*
To announce the year of Yahwè's favor, | the day of requital for our
   God; | to comfort all the distressed.

The poet's meaning is precisely that of the evangelist in the fourth chapter of Luke. For the further details of his development of this theme, the participation of the Gentiles in the blessings of the Messianic age, see especially the introduction to chapter 60.

The passages thus far cited show plainly that the Second Isaiah felt his own peculiar message, his new truth, to be this: the inclusion of the whole Gentile world, side by side with Israel, in the family of the One God. Many other passages in his book of poems bear out this conclusion, and nothing that he has written is inconsistent with it.

Here, then, is a great landmark in the history of the world's religious thought. In Judea, centuries before the Christian era, we are told of the love of God the Father for his children of whatever race, and of the destined co-operation of all good men in his service, in their many lands and various forms of worship, in the happy time to come. We have good reason to believe that no such announcement was ever made before. No former prophet of the Hebrews, to whom alone we could look for such a conception, had risen to this height. The Second Isaiah declares his message to be new. If it had already been uttered, he would have been the one most likely to know it.

Other prophets and poets followed, now that the way had been shown. An especially striking passage is Is. 25 : 7 f., from one of the later portions of this very composite book:

> Yahwè will destroy in this mountain
> The veil which is over all the peoples,
> The screen which covers all the nations.

* See the note on the Hebrew text.

> Death shall be done away forever;
> And the Lord will wipe the tears from all faces,
> Will remove from all the earth the reproach of his people.

Gray, *The Book of Isaiah*, rightly calls this "one of the most catholic passages in the entire Old Testament"; he did not know, in its true character, the mighty creation which had preceded. There are many such utterances in the latest prophetical books and especially in the Psalter; indeed, the most of this literature is essentially wide-hearted. The fact is obscured, for modern readers, by the ambiguity of the terms used (the "people of God" and the "enemies of Israel" not defined; old phrases and allusions necessarily employed, with only now and then a chance indication that new meaning had been given them), and by the customary mistaken estimate of these writings as descriptive rather than imaginative poetry. We have seen how in 49 : 8 the phrase "to apportion anew the desolate inheritances," traditionally applying to the Jewish people, signifies the restoration of the world. Similarly in the latter chapters of Jeremiah the long-cherished phrase "turn the captivity" is employed in promises to Moab (48 : 47), Ammon (49 : 6), and Elam (49 : 39). For the idea of the present "desolation" of the Gentile world because of sin against Yahwè, see especially Is. 24 : 5 f. We should also compare here the fine passage 2 : 2 ff., in which, after mention of the (ideal) House of God on a lofty mountain top, and the prediction that "all the nations shall flow towards it," the poem proceeds:

> And mighty peoples will go and say,
> Come, let us go up to the mount of Yahwè, | to the house of the God of Jacob;
> That he may teach us his ways, | and that we may walk in his paths;
> For out of Zion shall go forth the law, | and the word of God from Jerusalem.

The next following lines tell how the nations will live together in harmony, no longer in enmity and warfare. This poem, if not by the Second Isaiah himself (see the Chapter on the Poet's Book), is at least the work of a kindred soul.

2. *Interpolations in the Narrower Spirit*

It is not surprising that some readers of these poems should have failed to enter fully into the spirit in which they were writ-

ten. The prophet's large-hearted view of the Gentile world, giving the heathen an equal share with the chosen people in the
blessings of the Coming Age, and reserving for the elder brother,
Israel, only the added glory and privilege of the leader and benefactor, was not only "new" (as it is repeatedly declared to be)
but it also must have been unacceptable to many of those who
held fast to inherited notions. The ideal Israel of the future could
"be satisfied with knowing himself vindicated" in the eyes of the
world and preferred in the sight of God (53:11); but those who
interpreted the promised restoration in terms of the present worldly
standards of superiority would look for an adequate material return for the long-endured suffering and reproach. To have a portion with the great and divide the spoil with the strong was
hardly enough; there must be such exaltation above the former
oppressors as to make it clear that the relative positions have
been reversed.

This feeling finds expression in certain insertions in the text,
made at an early date. They are few in number and very brief in
extent, but stand in such sharp contrast with their surroundings
as to be easily recognizable. The most striking instance is 60:12,
already pronounced 'a prosaic gloss' by Duhm, Cheyne, and
Marti: *For the nation or kingdom that will not serve thee shall perish;
yea, those nations shall be utterly destroyed.* This is so completely
out of keeping with the spirit of the prophet, and with his express
declarations, as to require no further comment.

Very similar to this is 61:5, a verse which is equally 'prosaic,'
and is seen to be disturbing to its context not only in substance
but also in grammatical connection. *Strangers shall come and pasture your flocks, and aliens shall be your plowmen and vine-dressers.*
This repeats in effect what had been said in 60:12, and presumably comes from the same hand. The difficulty which commentators have encountered in trying to make the verse metrical may
be seen in Duhm's remarks on the passage. The grammatical disturbance lies in this, that a passage in the second person has been
inserted in a third-person context without making complete adjustment to the original text, with the result that a sentence beginning in the one person ends in the other. This fact of itself has
seemed to some scholars sufficient reason for supposing interpolation; see the *Wörterbuch* of Siegfried-Stade, s. v. רנן. The explanation is obvious. In order to make the desired contrast between Jews and Gentiles it was necessary to insert וְאַתֶּם, "But
ye," at the beginning of vs. 6. This made unavoidable the change

to the second person in the verbs and suffixes immediately following; see the note on the text.

Another interpretative addition, made in the same spirit,* consists of a single word. In 45 : 14, where the poet is drawing one of his favorite pictures of the future glory, a scene in which a great procession of foreign peoples is passing through the holy city, the word *bazziqqīm,* "*in fetters,*" destroys the meter and spoils the picture. There is neither room for the word nor place for the idea. The Gentiles come to Jerusalem joyfully and of their own free will; see especially chapters 60 and 66. In this instance they are represented as making the pilgrimage in order to bear testimony to the true religion. But the interpolator cannot let them off so easily, and must have them shackled.

The insertion of vs. 6 in chapter 47 (see the note on the text) had its origin in a similar feeling. Yahwè will destroy Babylon because of the harsh treatment of his favorite people by this "mistress of kingdoms." Compare again 60 : 12, also 52 : 4.

Somewhat similar to the foregoing in their general character are the two closely related interpolations 56 : 2–6 and 58 : 13, 14, plainly the work of a single hand. Their attitude toward the Gentiles is like that of the 'Judaizers' against whom the apostle Paul contends. Where the Second Isaiah calls for repentance and faith, the supplementing editor thinks of the Gentiles only as proselytes to Judaism, and promises especial favor with God as the reward of a strict observance of the Jewish Sabbath. See the note on 58 : 13 and the introduction to chapter 55.

3. *The Dies Iræ*

Thus far we have heard only of sympathy and magnanimity in the prophet's own utterances regarding the Gentiles. There is in these same poems, however, another and very different way of speaking of the peoples of the earth. Are they not represented as objects of wrath, doomed to destruction? There are two consecutive poems in which the Second Isaiah takes account of Babylon. The opening lines of chapter 46, severely ironical, declare the worthlessness of Bel and Nebo, doubtless with the Babylonian power in mind. Chapter 47 follows with a stern invective in the

---

* The most that can fairly be said against these interpretations is that they misrepresent the prophet, reflecting a view of the 'salvation of the Gentiles' which is decidedly narrower than his. We cannot even say that they embody hostility to these outsiders. Retributive justice in material conditions is what they call for, and this point of view, however inferior, is very natural.

same strain of irony, predicting, in figurative language, the utter
ruin of the exalted city. Cheyne, *Trans.*, entitles both passages
"songs of derision," and in his *Prophecies of Isaiah* (1889), chapter
47 was characterized as a "taunt-song." Others term chapter 47
"a poem of revenge," and it is customary to see foretold in it the
annihilation of the people of Babylonia. Taunts, derision, and
thirst for revenge, while human and excusable, are out of keeping
with the picture just drawn. A great religious teacher would not
write thus nor feel thus.

There are also several passages which have seemed to predict
the ultimate destruction of all the foreign peoples, in contrast with
the Jews. While differing considerably in form and extent, these
utterances are plainly expressive of the same underlying conception, and so they have been regarded.

Take, by way of introduction, vs. 16 of chapter 66:

For with fire will Yahwè execute judgment, | with his sword he will
   judge all flesh; | and the slain of the Lord will be many.

This, to be sure, is quite indefinite. Chapter 34, vs. 2, seems at
first sight to be more specific:

The Lord has anger in store for all the nations, | and wrath for all
   their host; | he has doomed them, appointed them for slaughter.

Chapters 34 and 35 are companion pictures: the one of doom, the
other of salvation. It has been quite common to see in chapter 34
the wholesale slaughter of the Gentiles, and in 35 the wholesale
salvation of the Jews. This very simple interpretation will not
stand, however, if the two poems are given the connection which
they seem to have with the other poems of the collection. It is
made sufficiently plain in numerous passages that the Gentiles
are not all to be exterminated, nor the Jews all to be saved.

Moreover, a particular nation, Edom, is introduced in a somewhat mystifying way, both in chapter 34 and in the similar passage at the beginning of chapter 63. It is on this 'Edom' that
vengeance especially falls, and (if only we suppose ourselves to
be reading prose instead of poetry) we seem to see the burning
dwellings of Bozrah, and the ground soaked with the blood of
Edomite citizens.

In the opening verses of chapter 63 we see pictured a majestic
figure approaching from Bozrah, showing in his bearing the
strength of a giant. The dialogue follows:

Who is this that comes?
It is I, announcing vindication; mighty to save my people.
Wherefore is thy clothing red?
I have trodden the winepress alone, from the peoples there was no
one with me. I trod them out in my anger, trampled them in my
wrath; their blood was sprinkled on my garments.

Here, obviously, is a close parallel to chapter 34. Both are commonly treated by modern commentators as utterances of a narrow and revengeful spirit. Professor Cheyne, speaking of the passage in chapter 63 (*Introd.*, p. 347), denies that it can be the
work of the Second Isaiah. "The latter," he says, "may not indeed always have been consistent with himself, . . . but could
not, as Smend truly remarks, have displayed such elaborate ferocity
as we find here." George Adam Smith—ordinarily so sympathetic
an interpreter!—uses the same term to characterize the prophet's
attitude (*Hastings B. D.*, "Isaiah," p. 494); others speak of his
"bloodthirstiness." Duhm (on 66 : 16) speaks of the author of chapter 34 as one who took delight in the thought of massacre. The
late Professor Friedrich Delitzsch asks emphatically,* after quoting
the dialogue at the beginning of chapter 63: "Are we to accept
such passages, full of hate as they are for surrounding peoples,
as proofs of the ethical content of the prophetic books? Are these
outpourings of the political jealousies of the time to serve the
children of the twentieth century as books of morals and religion?"
The children of the twentieth century, however, may still read
these poems without danger to their morals, when they—and their
parents—have a better understanding of their character.
The prophet was not bloodthirsty, he was only a poet. It is
abundantly evident, all through the book and even in these same
chapters, that he was a man of the tenderest heart and the broadest human sympathy. He had no personal hatred of the Babylonians, nor could he have imagined the slaughter of his Edomite
neighbors without feelings of horror and compassion. But the
logic of God's own program called for a final judgment and the
meting out of justice. There was no escape from this. As I have
shown in the introduction to chapter 34, and as numerous scholars
have seen and said, "Edom" is the symbolical designation of a
class: the enemies of Yahwè, the incorrigibly wicked. The way in
which the term is used interchangeably with "all nations," in both
chapters, might prove this sufficiently, even without other evidence.

* *Zweiter Vortrag über Babel und Bibel*, 1903, p. 44.

It is the class characterized in 66:24 by the phrase "those who in wickedness oppose me"; and, as the same chapter declares, Jews and Gentiles alike are included. The line of separation is essentially the same which is drawn so often in the New Testament.

Pictures of carnage and devastation are always terrible, but not always the product of a vindictive spirit. Is Matt. 25:41 ferocious? Is the woe pronounced upon Chorazin, Bethsaida, and Capernaum a derisive taunt, the utterance of hatred and the desire of revenge? Jesus of Nazareth predicted doom as well as deliverance; endless torment for the foes of righteousness, the utter downfall of unrepentant arrogance. The invective of our prophet has the same meaning. Just as "Edom" is merely symbolic, so "Babylon" stands for a type, representing worldly power and pride without justice and mercy. No commentator would attribute 'ferocity' to the Nazarene, for the sum of his words is sufficient proof of his feeling toward men. And all that we need ask for the Second Isaiah is that he be allowed to interpret himself. When a great book is cut up into a basketful of little authors, the possibility of any self-explanation is correspondingly limited.

The Second Isaiah was not a universalist. He did not believe that a blessed future was in store for the wicked. His conviction, resembling that of the most of the great teachers, Jewish and Christian, who followed him, was that the incorrigible enemies of God should at last be destroyed. He drew his mighty picture of carnage and conflagration in chapter 34, not because he gloated over bloodshed and the devastation of war, but as one who felt that the time had come for him to portray the day of wrath of God. It is a terrible theme, but a legitimate one, as many of the world's great painters and poets have agreed. We should laugh at the critic who attacked Michel Angelo for his "Last Judgment" in the Sistine Chapel, or Luca Signorelli for his treatment of the same subject in the cathedral at Orvieto, on the ground that their work showed ferocity, and that their choice of subject indicated low ethical ideals. It is only a great man, indeed, who can deal with this theme in a manner both adequate and artistic. Our poet-prophet meets the test in both particulars. He is not one to deal timidly with his material; those who wish to hear only mild words should not come to the Second Isaiah.

In the opening stanzas of the chapter, after the announcement of doom for all the peoples of the earth, vs. 3 proceeds:

Their slain shall be cast out, | and the stench of their corpses shall
    rise, | the mountains shall flow with their blood.

This is realism to cause a shudder; we should say the same of many passages in Dante's *Inferno*.* Even the last clause of the verse shows, however, by its evident exaggeration, that the poet is aiming to give an impression rather than to paint an actual scene. The next following lines confirm this:

All the host of heaven shall dissolve, | and the skies shall be rolled like a scroll;
All their starry host shall wither; | as the foliage wilts from the vine, | as the leaves which fall from the fig-tree.

After the one strong touch of horror, the effect is softened by the use of symbolical imagery. From this time on the human element in the picture is kept in the background. The prophet was too tender-hearted a man to depict human suffering at length, and too great an artist to spoil his poem by making it needlessly shocking. The "sword of Yahwè" is not bathed in the blood of men, but in "the blood of lambs and goats"; it is not of the slaughter and the anguish of men that we read; this is veiled under the symbol of a great sacrifice of rams and bullocks. And finally, it is to be observed how the unfailing kindliness of the poet asserts itself in the latter part of the chapter. He finishes this whole picture by dwelling for a moment, with evident satisfaction, on the happy, undisturbed life of the fowls of the air and the beasts of the field, who have found a peaceful habitation in the ruins where the wicked among men once dwelt.

There the little-owl shall nest and lay, | shall hatch and brood in its† shadow;
There, too, the kites shall gather, | each one seeking its mate;
From the book of Yahwè their names shall be read, | not one of them shall be missing, | none shall seek in vain for its mate.

These creatures of the desert have not sinned against God, and he cares for them. He himself reads off their names from his book, and they answer in turn. "He has cast the lot for them, and his hand has divided it unto them by line; they shall possess it forever." Their little family life is secure, they bring up their young

---

* Canto XXIX, 50 f.:
    ". . . tal puzzo n' usciva,
        Qual suole uscir delle marcite membre."
XII, 47 f.:
        "La riviera del sangue, in la qual bolle
        Qual che per violenza in altrui noccia."
† The pronoun referring to the city whose ruins have just been described.

in peace. "Not one sparrow falls to the ground without your Father's notice." And this is our bloodthirsty writer.

The picture of the Day of Wrath has its companion, the Day of Mercy, bringing in the era of peace and good-will. Both the treatment of the new theme and the manner of the transition from the one to the other are highly artistic; see the introduction to the two chapters. As has already been demonstrated, from the prophet's own words, the blessings of the new age are for the servants of Yahwè, elect from every nation. The determining factor is religion, not race nor region. That which is merely implied in chapter 35, by its evident relation to its predecessor, is made explicit in chapters 45, 49, 55, 60, and 66. "Turn ye to me, and be saved, all ye ends of the earth! For I am God, there is no other. By myself I swear it, the truth is gone forth from my mouth, my word shall not turn back, that to me every knee shall bow, every tongue swear allegiance."

4. Jew and Gentile

"What advantage hath the Jew?" Paul asks in Rom. 3 : 1. The apostle insists, in reply to his own query, that the history of the Jews, as the people originally chosen of God and the mediators of salvation to the world, assures them a certain distinction, a superiority of their own. They must indeed accept the new faith on the same terms as the Gentiles. This done, they retain their own rites and their unique position assured to them many times over by divine promise. The apostles in conclave at Jerusalem were called upon to answer the same question (Acts 15), and gave the same reply. *In the essentials of the new faith* there is to be no distinction whatever between Jew and Gentile; they are on equal footing. In addition to the mere confession of faith by the Gentiles, however, there is an obvious requirement of good conduct, that the adherents of the new doctrine may not appear to be without restraint of public morals and thus imperil the good name of the nascent Christian body. They are not bidden to perform any new rite, or to adopt any custom specifically Jewish, but merely to abstain from certain things generally recognized (Acts 15 : 21)*

---

* The fact that the writer supposes the universal abhorrence of these things to have been taught to the ancient world by the Hebrews is merely an interesting detail. The laws of Moses included many matters agreed upon by all civilized peoples in those times. The important fact here is the testimony that the things named were viewed alike by Jews and Gentiles. See, further, on this subject, the *Am. Journal of Theology*, vol. XXIII (1919), pp. 76 f.

as abhorrent to the religious feeling of that age and that quarter
of the globe. The Jews, on the other hand, as a matter of course,
continue in their ancient customs, not by requirement but as a
privilege. That which to them would be only a badge of distinction would be to the Gentiles a useless burden.

The great theologian of the fifth century B. C. has the same
clear perception of what constitutes true religion, acceptable to
the creator of the world. He takes his stand on the ground afterward occupied by Paul, James, and Peter. Confronted with the
same problem, he solves it in the same way; the only solution
which we can recognize as profound, the one for which the world
had hitherto been waiting. Faith, repentance, justice, a kind
heart and a helping hand are the requisites; there are no others.
There must, of course, be some forms of worship, the external apparatus of the service of Yahwè. For the Jews, the ancient Hebrew
cultus still has its place and presumably its permanence (45 : 14–
17; 56 : 7; 60 : 7; 66 : 21). Other peoples have, and may have,
their own rites. The distinction between Jew and Gentile is
not to disappear; this is made plain enough in chapters 45 and
49, to say nothing of other poems of the collection*; and it is only
in traditional rites and customs that the distinction can be preserved. With Jewish proselytes, in the usual sense of the term,
the prophet's vision is not concerned. Gentiles at Jerusalem will
be free to employ the Jewish ritual (56 : 7; 60 : 7); some of them
will even serve as priests and Levites (66 : 21); but these cases, as
the latter passage implies, are exceptional. The prophet's conviction, several times clearly expressed, that the ceremonial is unessential, even for Israelites, has been discussed sufficiently in the
preceding pages.

The polemic against idolatry has often been misunderstood,
interpreted as the result of a merely superficial and unsympathetic
view. Its author was unable, we are repeatedly told, to appreciate
the fact that the image is a mere symbol, and that sincere and
worthy worship may be offered with the apparatus of foreign cults
and in the name of strange gods. Duhm (on 40 : 22) imagines a
conversation between the Second Isaiah and Phidias or Plato, in
the course of which he thinks that the prophet "might perhaps
have learned that the ideas underlying the sculptor's art are more

* That Israel is an enduring entity, not merely an incidental unit of mankind brought forth to play a temporary part in the eternal plan, is often said
or implied, *e. g.*, in such passages as 46 : 4; 45 : 17; 51 : 17; 54 : 8, 10; 59 : 21;
60 : 21.

profound than he had supposed." The prophet was not, however, so destitute of ordinary human wisdom. Every educated man of his day understood the significance of these cultic symbols. It was precisely because he and his fellow countrymen knew that there was genuine worship beneath the idolatry that he so feared the growing encroachment of foreign rites and deities. His ridicule, with its obvious exaggeration, was not designed to convince the Gentiles, but to remind and rebuke the Jews. He had seen his people worshipping numerous deities, each represented by its own image corresponding in some way to the character and particular interests of the god. He knew the inevitable influence of the visible and tangible symbol. Yahwè himself was pictured, whether by Jews or not, at least by their next-door neighbors. There is a unique silver coin, preserved in the British Museum, which gives food for thought. It was struck at Gaza, presumably near the middle of the fourth century B. C. Our prophet may possibly have seen this very coinage; beyond doubt he had seen something like it. The design is well executed, but could hardly serve to illustrate the Old Testament. The god appears as a decrepit-looking bearded man crouched in an uncomfortable attitude above a cart-wheel and labelled *Yahū*, the shorter form of the name Yahwè.*

The main reason, however, why the Second Isaiah attacks so often, with argument and ridicule, the depiction of 'gods' in bodily form, and why again and again, in various contexts, he returns to his assertion of the one universal deity who created heaven and earth and all human beings, is to be found in his consciousness of bearing a universal message. The religion, the hope, which he announces is for all men alike. Jew and Gentile must turn to the one and only divine being, whose utterly incomparable nature he sets himself to proclaim.

He was familiar with the carved likenesses of gods and men, doubtless even more familiar than Duhm (on 40 : 17) supposes. The works of Egyptian sculptors and the productions of the eclectic Phœnician art had for many centuries been displayed in the cities of Palestine. It is quite possible that Hellenic sculpture was already known and admired there. At about this time there was considerable intercourse between Greece and the Syrian coast; exchange of commodities, migration to and fro, a strong Phœnician colony at the Piræus, diplomatic relations between Athens and

* A. B. Cook, *Zeus*, I, pp. 232 f., sees in this design the influence of conventional representations of the Greek god and his chariot.

Sidon. The author of Is. 34–66 was a man of the keenest æsthetic sense, an idealist who inevitably would have felt the thrill produced by the sight of a chiselled face of unearthly beauty, the conception surpassing any actual human model.* Nor was he exceptional in this, since the men of the ancient world were like those of modern times. But in the great scheme of things divine and human which he was meditating there was no place for iconic aids to worship; the thought of them was intolerable.

The Hebrews had their fair share of racial pride and prejudice. With them, as with every nation of the ancient world—to say nothing of modern times—the foreigner was the typical foe. Devout Israelites had long been accustomed to think of themselves as the allies of Yahwè in conflict with the armies of other faiths. Traditional phrases, especially in the language of religious poetry, had given this feeling conventional expression. In the old Hebrew literature which we possess, especially in the Psalter but also in the Prophets, there are many sweeping expressions of hostility which a sound exegesis can only regard as lyric exaggeration, using merely stereotyped language. Of course there may now and again be reasonable doubt as to the foes really intended, or as to the content of actual feeling. In Joel 4: 17b, for instance, we read the prediction that "Jerusalem shall be holy, and there shall no strangers pass through her any more." In view of other passages in the same chapter it is not unreasonable to suppose that the term 'strangers' is here truly ethnic and not merely theological. Other writers, using similar terms, have in mind only the enemies of Yahwè. The Psalmist voices his 'hatred' of imaginary foes in his religious fervor, and invokes destruction on 'nations' and 'peoples' which are simply a literary property.

In view of the influence of old literary tradition, especially in poetry, it is remarkable that the Second Isaiah, with his burning zeal, should hold himself so free from expressions which had their root in antipathy to foreigners. In a single passage, the passionate outburst of 52:1, he uses a phrase like the one quoted from Joel:

Put on thy glorious garments, Jerusalem, holy city!
For there shall no more enter thee the uncircumcised, the unclean.

Again and again, however, especially in chapters 45 and 60, he expresses his delight in the thought of foreigners coming in throngs

* Plato, *Republic*, V, 472 D.

to visit the holy city. 'The gates shall not be shut by day nor by night.' We can be quite certain that by 'circumcision' is here meant spiritual and moral fitness (as in Lev. 26 : 41; Jer. 9 : 25, end; Acts 7 : 51, etc.), not the Jewish rite. The prophet is using a stock phrase and a long-familiar figure of speech. In 63 : 18 he mourns over the profanation and destruction of Solomon's glorious temple by the foreign armies; in 62 : 8 he promises that his people shall themselves enjoy the fruit of the lands which they till, instead of surrendering it to oppressing strangers; but these utterly mild passages are the only ones that could be cited. Of aversion to foreigners as such his poems show not a trace. The occasional outbursts of wrath at actual and contemporary foes are directed against his own compatriots, never against outsiders. Israel, like all the weaker nations, had indeed suffered under the yoke of mighty and merciless neighbors; there was abundant reason for resentment. But, as we have already seen, when our prophet predicts the discomfiture and destruction of Gentile 'oppressors'— whom, be it noted, he never directly addresses as such—he has in mind something far different from chastisement on the ground of racial or national hostility, far greater than retaliation for present material injuries.

As far as can be learned from the poetic and conventional phrases employed, he conceives the existing distinctions of race and nation as preserved in the new world. Troops of foreigners present themselves in the new Jerusalem, led by their 'kings' and 'princes.' He may have thought that one or another of these now flourishing peoples would utterly disappear from the earth, though he does not say so. What he appears to say is that a 'remnant' will be saved even from the worst of them. The survivors of former opponents and persecutors are among those who confess their sin and acknowledge their debt to Israel in chapter 53, among those who bring home the exiles in 49, 60, and 66.

Least of all was the distinction between Jew and Gentile to be lost. The Second Isaiah, like the apostle Paul, was a Hebrew of the Hebrews, and the flame of patriotism burned high in his heart. The promise of peculiar blessing was 'forever,' and he would claim it to the full. The first-born has his especial right of inheritance, which the younger brothers cannot share. Nevertheless, the prophet felt himself held by a tie more potent than those of race or country. The feeling finds words in the deeply conceived prayer which forms the latter half of the great poem, chapters 63 and 64. In 63 : 16 he cries:

> Refrain not, for thou art our father—
> Though Abraham know us no longer,
> Though Israel acknowledge us not—
> Thou, Yahwè, art our father!*

He says here in express terms what he had said before in effect, that he is conscious of belonging to a truer brotherhood, a more essential community of interests, than the Israel of his affection. The love of God, which, as the prophet has repeatedly said or implied, extends to all the 'children' of his creation, is the most potent fact in the world. It is a wonderful utterance.

There is yet another mutual relation of Israelite and foreigner, profoundly significant for the theology of these poems. The passages dealing with it give the supreme testimony to their author's grasp of the whole great problem. The prophet sees a religious solidarity of mankind based not only on the love of God for his children but also on mutual sympathy, of Jew for Gentile and Gentile for Jew, the result of service and sacrifice. Israel 'intercedes' for the *goyim*, through mortal suffering 'makes atonement' for them, submitting voluntarily to the plan devised by Yahwè. They on their part at last understand and acknowledge. See the introduction to the poem 52:13–53:12, and also Chapters IV and VIII. The portion with the great, the division of spoil with the strong, is for him who cast in his lot with those who had been his enemies. The good-will among men which is to enter every part of the 'foreign' world will have in it the consciousness of a tie of kinship with him through whose stripes the healing came to all. Gentile looking toward the Jews, Jew looking toward the Gentiles, must say, with the author of the Epistle to the Hebrews, 'God so provided, that apart from us they should not be perfected.' Races and peoples will continue to hold their several places, no longer in enmity, nor merely now in friendly intercourse, but with the deeper feeling of those who through mutual help have survived the same great catastrophe.

We have no need to give any word of the prophet a forced interpretation, nor is it easy to exaggerate in summing up. His nova doctrina in potestate is a marvellous thing, but so also is the history of Israel. The religion of the earlier Hebrew prophets, adjusting itself to the changed conditions and new ideas of a world thrown wide open, might well produce such a teacher and such teaching. Because of misconception of quasi-historical documents

---

* Compare the words of Jesus in Mark 3:33–35.

and the consequent misinterpretation of imaginative poetry, first by ancient readers, then by modern scholars, both the man and the message have been lost to sight and the unfolding of Judaism has been misjudged. Professor Richard G. Moulton, in the admirable introduction to the volume "Isaiah" in his *Modern Readers' Bible*, p. xviii, is of course obliged to take what the experts in Hebrew literature and history have delivered to him. He declares that "In actual history, the men of the Return were distinguished by a spirit of violent exclusiveness," and speaks of "their literary production, *The Chronicles*," as representative of their view of the world. *Their literary production!* Did ever any other pseudo-historian work such dire mischief as this too zealous Jewish patriot of the Greek period? Professor Duhm's Commentary may also be cited in illustration of the now conventional estimate of the religion of 'post-exilic' Israel. We find only wholesale condemnation, on the ground that the community depicted in Chronicles-Ezra-Nehemiah could neither have produced nor tolerated a theology with truly universal application, a religion reaching beyond the little circle of Judaism. See, among many other passages, pp. xx, 389 ff., 396, 451.* We are told that the Hebrew prophets of the Persian period were utterly indifferent to the fate of foreigners, to whom they hardly gave the value of human beings (keinen vollen Menschenwert, 404, 146 f., 295, 309, 328, 456), and that the religion which they represented had greatly degenerated from the teaching of the earlier prophets (295, 328, 340, 451, 456). 'Deutero-Isaiah,' for instance, was—like all his fellows—lacking in moral sense, and 'without the clear consciousness which the earlier prophets possessed of that which advances a people and all mankind' (268 f., 147). 'Trito-Isaiah' had no true conception of religion (456); and this is also to be said of the author of the 'Servant poems,' who, like the others, sees only the form and not the inner meaning. As the climax to all this we read (394) that 'Judaism lagged far behind most religions.' If Professor Duhm's premises were true, his conclusions might seem defensible, in spite of the unsympathetic exegesis. In each and all of these instances, however, the true state of the case is the opposite of that which he supposes.

It is strange, even with the profound influence exerted by the Chronicler's writings, that the idea should not have suggested itself to the leaders of the modern school of Old Testament criticism that the reason why 'the earlier prophets' reprove the attitude of

---

* The references are to the pages of the third edition.

trust in traditional rites and ceremonies more sharply, on the whole, than their later fellows, is that the people of that day especially needed the rebuke. In the Persian period, with its wider outlook and more tolerant spirit, there was less need to inveigh against an orthodox formalism. As we learn especially from the Second Isaiah, but also from Malachi, Ezekiel, and others, the liberality of the later day went too far, in its neglect of the worship of Yahwè, its espousal of foreign gods (Mal. 2 : 11–16; Ezek. 8 : 10–17, etc.), and its blindness to the eternal plan and purpose of the One God in human history.

It would be a sad mistake to set the Second Isaiah over against his people as though in contrast with them. Aside from mere considerations of probability (see above, the chapter on Prophet and Poet), there is abundant illustration, even in the small portion of Hebrew religious literature preserved in our Old Testament, of the same broad view of human life and true conception of religious freedom.* There is indeed illustration also of the narrow view, and of every intermediate gradation; but the broader spirit greatly predominates, in any fair interpretation. In William Temple's little volume entitled *Plato and Christianity* (London, Macmillan, 1916) the author's final estimate of the great pagan philosopher, so nearly contemporaneous with the Hebrew prophet, contains a sentence which deserves to be quoted here, in concluding our brief attempt to do justice to the world-sympathy—the supreme test of any religion—manifested in these wonderful poems brought forth by one of the minor Semitic peoples. Page 101: "The Greek nation has been the source of nearly all that is alive in thought or civilization as distinct from pure religion, and Plato is the culmination of the Greek genius. It has, indeed, been said that Plato is not a typical Greek; that is true, but only because he is more Greek than all the other Greeks together." The dictum has significance for our own appraisal. That which the Hellenic genius, with all its glorious achievement, could not contribute to the world was being perfected in another atmosphere. The phrase applied to the incomparable Greek may with equal right be turned to characterize the master of divine truth, for in the same sense the Second Isaiah is more Hebrew than all the other Hebrews together.

The importance of realizing the *humanity* of this greatest of all prophets and of understanding the relation of his teaching to pre-

* See, for further illustration, *Ezra Studies*, 310 ff., and especially 314, where numerous passages are cited.

vious Hebrew tradition, on the one hand, and to the later Jewish and early Christian scriptures, on the other, and of appreciating its position as a landmark in the history of human thought, can hardly be overestimated. We have here a thing surpassingly great, unapproached in the literature of the ancient world prior to the four Gospels. Paul Elmer More, in his profound and sympathetic treatment of *The Religion of Plato* (1921), justly insists (Preface, p. vi) on the "straight line" of Greek tradition, both philosophic and religious, from Plato to the council of Chalcedon. On the other hand, when the discussion reaches the consideration of "pure religion before our God and Father" (James 1:27), he notes and emphasizes the contrast. Referring to the apostle's definition "to visit the fatherless and widows in their affliction, and to keep himself unspotted from the world," he remarks (p. 295) that the requirement of the second clause is prominent in Plato's teaching, but that "in the other clause of the precept there is a tenderness, a beauty of devotion, which cannot be found in Platonism." William Temple, *op. cit.*, has of course the same reservation to make. Plato's idea of justice, he notes, includes the unselfish rendering of service, but of deeper feeling there is a significant lack. The great philosopher teaches that pity is a weakness, and excludes sacrifice (pp. 89 f.). More's statement (p. vii) that "Christianity, notwithstanding its importation of a powerful foreign element into the tradition, . . . was the true heir and developer of Platonism," may stand, for the development which he has in mind. The "foreign element" has yet to be evaluated, however. It lies much closer to the heart of the Christian religion than anything derived from Greece. There is another "straight line" to be taken into account. The four Gospels are built solidly on the foundation laid by the Second Isaiah as interpreted in these essays, far more than upon any other basis. The latest writings of the Old Testament contain, in addition to the passages revealing a universal range of sympathy, a definitely Messianic element, cautiously expressed, sometimes obscured by a later, anti-Christian interpretation, and generally unrecognized at the present day. These all have their chief source in the writings of the prophet who proclaimed the New Message and depicted the Servant of the Lord.

CHAPTER VIII

THE 'SERVANT' AND THE MESSIAH

1. *The Figure of the Servant*

There is a figure of speech frequently employed by the Second Isaiah which embodies his most striking and original contribution to Hebrew religious thought. It is a personification, nobly conceived and handled in the poet's own characteristic manner, with a play of imagination which follows no beaten track and knows no limit. The underlying idea of the personification is that of *service*, in the performance of a great task which is variously but consistently outlined. The God of Israel, maker of heaven and earth, creator and father of all mankind, has at his right hand a 'Servant' whom he has chosen to share his counsel and execute his eternal purpose. The purpose is for the world, and the plan of its execution covers the whole course of human history, from the beginning to the Messianic age.

This idea of an emissary charged with a great work is a fundamental element of the prophet's theology. It recurs in various forms, and is also frequently implied where it is not definitely expressed. The term generally employed is *'ebed*, 'servant,' made definite either by the appended name of God, 'servant of Yahwè,' or by a suffix referring to him, 'his servant,' 'my servant.' The emissary is distinctly named in numerous passages, and is in effect always the same; namely, the personified nation Israel, or Israel's personal representative. In parallelism with the term 'servant' occur several other terms expressing related ideas: *mal'āk*, 'messenger, emissary,' 42 : 19; 44 : 26*; *bachīr*, 'chosen,' 42 : 1; 43 : 20; 45 : 4; and *cf.* the use of the verb *bāchar* in 41 : 8, 9; 43 : 10; 44 : 1, 2; 49 : 7; 'chosen,' that is, as the context shows in each instance, *to execute a commission;* *'īsh 'ăṣathō*, 'man of his counsel,' 46 : 11,†

---

* In the latter passage the present Hebrew text has the foolish reading "his angels" instead of the original reading "his messenger." See the comment on the passage.

† The true reading in this verse is *'abdī*, 'my servant,' instead of *'aiṭ*, a 'bird of prey.' See the critical note.

cf. 44 : 26; *'ēd,* 'witness,' 43 : 10; and *māšiăch,* 'anointed,' 45 : 1, 61 : 1 (where the verb is used instead of the noun). In each and all of these passages the prophet is speaking of Yahwè's eternal purpose, and of the agent Israel, specially appointed to carry it out.

This gives to the idea of "the chosen people" a content which is active rather than merely passive. Israel is a steward under orders; promised a splendid reward, it is true, but on conditions and not as a mere favorite. He must show himself a *profitable* servant (*lĕ-hō'îl,* 48 : 17). The divine commands must be obeyed, and the task faithfully performed; it is even conceivable that the chosen agent should be cast off (48 : 9, 19). The God of Israel is the God of the world. and will extend his 'salvation' to all mankind.

The 'Servant' as Israel's representative is sometimes presented in the person of one of the founders of the race. Thus in 41 : 8, the call of Abraham from Ur of the Chaldees: "Who aroused from the east a righteous one,* summoning him for his service?" Again in vs. 25, with reference to Haran as well as to Ur: "I aroused him from the north, and he came; from the east, calling on my name." Similarly in 46 : 11: "Summoning from the east my Servant; from a distant land the man of my counsel." It is Abraham the 'friend' (*'ōhēb*) of God in 41 : 8 and 48 : 14, passages dealing with the Servant's mission. Frequently it is Jacob who is named, as in 41 : 8 f.; "Thou, Israel, my Servant; Jacob, whom I have chosen; . . . whom I laid hold of from the ends of the earth, . . . saying to thee, Thou art my Servant; I have chosen thee, and have not rejected thee." Closely similar passages are 43 : 1; 44 : 1 f., 21; 49 : 3. The prophet saw clearly that the present condition of his people could be understood only by referring to the past and by looking into the promised future.

Elsewhere, again, there is a personification, more or less clearly indicated, of the present Jewish nation, or a part of it. In 43 : 10 Yahwè declares: "Ye are my Servant, whom I have chosen." In 42 : 18 f. the same thing is said in another tone: the blind, deaf, disobedient Israelites of the past and the present are nevertheless "the Servant of Yahwè" and his 'messenger.' When the poet introduces the Servant in 52 : 13 he coins for him the name *Yaskīl* (a fanciful and significant variation of *Yisra'ēl,* Israel), and in the following poem pictures the afflicted nation and shows how God's purpose is to be accomplished through its present distress. The

* See the note on the Hebrew text.

poet's figure of speech is varied, sometimes even suddenly changed, according to the play of a restless imagination. Always and everywhere the various designations of the Servant are in contexts which sound plainly the note of affection, even in 42:18-20. In the idealized conception of a leader of Israel in the more remote future the personification reaches its greatest height, as will appear.

2. The 'Servant Passages' and Their Context

The passages in which the figure of the Servant is made prominent have long held the foremost place of interest in the study and interpretation of Second Isaiah; in recent years they have formed the subject of numerous extended monographs. As has already been said, it is misleading to speak of 'Songs of the Servant,' 'Ebed-Yahwè Lieder,' as is now generally done. It is true that in certain passages this great figure, the Servant, stands out in an especially strong light, and that therefore some (though not all) of them are easily thought of as forming a group by themselves. Very many Old Testament scholars of the present day, holding different views as to the authorship and meaning of the Servant passages, regard them as detachable from their immediate surroundings. They are looked upon as lyrical pieces embedded in an extended 'prophecy.' Many suppose them to have formed originally a group by themselves existing as a separate work, or even to have been composed by another author. Thus for example Cheyne, *Introd. to Is.*, p. 305, "A fuller study of the Servant-passages reveals the striking fact that they form a connected cycle of poetical meditations," and the designation 'cycle of poems' has frequently been employed. But this view of the passages in question, as separate or separable, is utterly mistaken. They are not in any sense complete in themselves, nor even possessed of characteristics not shared by the rest of the book of which they form a part. To make separate 'poems' of them is like selecting certain details of a great landscape-painter's masterpiece and styling each a 'picture.' These paragraphs—and even the complete poem 52:13-53:12—can be considered by themselves only in the sense in which a single feature of a beautiful face could be studied separately. It is possible to admire them thus, but not to understand them.

The portions of the prophecy which are ordinarily set apart as 'Servant songs' are 42:1-4; 49:1-6; 50:4-9; and 52:13-53:12;

that is, the few passages which are generally recognized as containing either a distinct personification under the title of Servant or else allusion to a real person. We miss in this list the beautiful passage 61 : 1 ff., which is plainly indicated by its language and contents as of one piece with the others named, but is excluded by the theory that II Isaiah consists only of chapters 40–55. The brevity of these disconnected scraps is very remarkable. In at least two cases out of the four, moreover, there is evidence that the proposed separation from II Isaiah has been made in the wrong place. The literary analysis which stops short at 42 : 4 without including vss. 6 f., and at 49 : 6 without making vs. 8 an essential part of the same portrayal, merits profound suspicion.

The 'Servant' of the four passages is not always the same. In chapter 53 he is the personification of the whole nation Israel, as the great majority of scholars agree. In 49 : 5, on the contrary, he is the coming leader who is destined 'to restore Jacob and gather Israel.' We already know that the Second Isaiah variously employed the term *'ebed* as indicating God's chosen agent. It is at least striking that within the limits of this diminutive 'cycle of poems' the same thing is done. It should be added, that the precise intent of the personification or allusion is sometimes obscure, whether in the above-named Servant paragraphs or in the surrounding poems. There exists every gradation between such passages as 41 : 8–10; 43 : 10; 44 : 1–5, 21, etc., in which the Jewish people are designated as the *'ebed*, and the vivid creations in chapters 42, 53, 61, etc., where the dramatic imagination is absolute and an unnamed person stands before us.

It has already been remarked that the supposed interpolations are made out of the very same material as the contexts in which they are now embedded. Their language, style, and mode of thought all belong distinctly to II Isaiah. This is so generally admitted, even by those who hold a theory of interpolation, that it requires no argument. A quotation from Cheyne's *Introd.*, which also embodies one from Duhm, may suffice. Page 309: "That they [the Servant passages] come from the school of II Isaiah is clear, nor is it, I think, at all impossible that they may be the work of II Isaiah himself.* I admit that this makes that great writer extremely inconsistent, but I do not see that this objection is decisive. As Duhm frankly states, the passages 'have very close

* Cheyne subsequently abandoned this view, following Duhm in regarding these 'poems' as the work of another writer. See his *Book of Isaiah*, Hebrew text, 1899.

points of contact, both in word and in thought, with II Isaiah.'"
The homogeneity is, in fact, of the most striking character. The
metrical structure of the Servant lines has in it no peculiarity
whatever; the literary art is through and through that of Second
Isaiah; the rhetorical devices, the play of the imagination, the
picturesque phrases, the peculiarities of grammar and style, the
vocabulary, are all precisely those of the author of chapters 40,
41, 45, etc.

It is, moreover, quite unjustifiable to hold a few of the most
striking of these passages apart from the rest of the prophecy, as
though they were built upon *ideas* characteristically their own, or
stood for a peculiar point of view. Nothing could be farther from
the fact. It is quite true that there is a strong disagreement between their plain intent and the motives and interests now
commonly supposed to be those of II Isaiah. Hence Professor
Cheyne, in the passage just quoted, speaks of the 'extreme inconsistency' of the one with the other; and Duhm, in his commentary
on chapter 42 (p. 284), says that the idea of a Servant of God
"ist auch dem Dtjes. nicht fremd, wird aber von ihm ganz anders
behandelt." And again, on 49 : 1 ff. (p. 339), he remarks, as many
others have, that the lofty idea of Israel's future contained in
vss. 1–6 (supposed to be a 'Servant poem') is in contrast with
'the distinctly lower idea' found in the following verses (supposed
to belong to II Isaiah). The ground of the criticism is obvious; it is the belief that the 'prophet of the exile' was a man of
narrow sympathy and short vision. I confess that if I held the
prevailing view of the prophet, I should find it easier to hold,
with Duhm, the theory of interpolated Servant fragments than to
accept the hypothesis of a single author, with Cheyne (formerly),
G. A. Smith, Cornill, Steuernagel, Marti, and very many other
scholars. It is difficult to believe that a writer can be both narrow and broad, both vindictive and magnanimous, in dealing with
the same subjects. But it has already been sufficiently shown, I
trust, that the prevailing view of the Second Isaiah is thoroughly
mistaken. He was not a narrow nationalist, nor the prophet of an
occasion, but a poet of the broadest philosophy and of world-wide
sympathies. The Servant idea, given its best interpretation, is
his characteristic property.

It is not necessary to demonstrate here in detail that the four
passages under discussion are indispensable to their context and
are themselves comprehensible only in their present surroundings.
Abundant argument to this effect will be found in other parts of

the present treatise.   See especially the introduction to the Notes
on 52 : 13–53 : 12, and the discussion of the attitude of the Second
Isaiah toward the foreign peoples.

Sufficient attention has hardly been paid to the evidence that
the poet has the figure of the Servant before his eyes in some
places where he neither uses the title nor makes any definite allusion to the person or personification. The best example is chapter
62, consisting mainly of the words of encouragement and affection
spoken by the Messiah to the city Jerusalem.   In chapter 61 the
Anointed Leader is the speaker in the three opening verses and
the two closing verses of the poem; in 62 the same speaker takes
the word at the outset and holds it to the end.   It is natural to
suppose his presence also in 63 : 7 ff., for several reasons: the
proximity of the passages just mentioned; the close resemblance
to 62 : 10 f. and 42 : 10–13, both of which seem to be spoken by
the Servant; and the fact that the Second Isaiah keeps himself so
persistently out of sight, making it unlikely that he speaks here in
his own person. See the chapter on "Poet and Prophet." In 45 : 1
ff., 13, constituting one of the most important of all the Messianic
passages, the intent of the poet has been completely lost because
of the unfortunate interpolation of the name 'Cyrus,' and the
passage has therefore not been considered at all as belonging to
this group.

3. *The Shifting Aspects of the 'Servant' Idea*

As has already been observed, the figure of the *'Ebed Yahwè* is
pliable, not fixed in any one form.   It seems characteristic of the
poet that he should delight to use it in different ways; see the chapter on the "Literary Features." The Servant of the Lord is indeed
always Israel, or Israel's representative, and always one charged
with a task. But when the term has once been defined thus far, it
must be added that the prophet's use of it ranges back and forth
through all the possible variations of these fundamental ideas.
There are three basal conceptions, which may be compared to the
three typical colors of the modern pictorial process. There is,
first of all, the term 'servant' in its traditional and varied use, constantly necessary. Then there is the new and original application
which every one has recognized; certainly a *collective* designation
in chapters 50 and 53 and such single passages as 42 : 19 f. Lastly,
there is an *individual* portrait, once or twice so sharply outlined
as to be startling, and so clearly seen by the poet himself that the
personal leader is expressly distinguished from the group.   It was

quite inevitable that these varying conceptions should alternate and combine. The language which he uses flashes before us now one aspect of the idea, now another; and often within the compass of a very few verses two different pictures are brought close together, though never in such a way as to blur the outlines of either one.

Now it is an undefined personification, as in 42 : 1 ff. and 50 : 4 ff. Again, it is Abraham, the friend of God, who called him from the ends of the earth and holds his right hand; or Jacob, to whom also definite promises were given. It is the primitive children of Israel, miraculously delivered and conducted; more often it is the chosen race in its whole history, without limit of time. It is the Jewish people of the prophet's own day; now the brightest spot of hope on earth, with eternal glory in full view; now the saddest example of perversity and punishment—deaf and blind, and yet the Servant! Often it is the restored Israel, the nation as it has never been but is one day to be, gathered from the four corners of the earth, the erstwhile emigrants returning in triumph from every land, purified and strengthened. This is the Servant who is to sweep away his foes, subdue kingdoms and 'thresh mountains.' In 50 : 4–9 the Servant seems to be Israel's better self, the *repentant* nation as it should be and might be, listening to Yahwè's instruction, teaching and 'giving to the fainting a word of help.' If the portrayal were not so purely imaginative, and the relation to chapter 53 so evident, it might be possible to suppose allusion to the faithful minority mentioned in 51 : 1 ff. and 66 : 5. But the language is evidently figurative, and the picture would be spoiled by making it refer to any definite group or division of the people. In vss. 10 f. there is the characteristic dramatic transition from the ideal to the real!

Finally, out of this personification of the ideal Israel of the future there emerges the figure of a great leader, the Anointed One. Such a teacher and champion there must be, the future is unthinkable without him. The scattered sheep must have a shepherd. No one who had passed beyond the years of childhood and early youth could have believed that Israel would command the great nations of the world and execute upon them the will of Yahwè *without a leader*, a human figure about whom the hosts of the Lord could rally, whose rod the stubborn should feel, and for whose law the 'far countries' should eagerly reach their hands (42 : 4). "*He* shall build my city, and set free my exiles, not for price nor for hire" (45 : 13).

The passages in which this individual, Yahwè's human repre-

sentative on earth, is intended form a considerable group. In 61 : 1
and 45 : 1 (with the interpolation removed) the person is defined
by the use of the verb "anoint," and in the latter passage (45 : 4)
he is also expressly distinguished from the people whom he is to
lead. The same distinction is made in the very similar passage
49 : 1 ff. (see vs. 5), showing that there also the Anointed One is
the subject of the picture. The soliloquy in chapter 62 is plainly
the counterpart of that in 61; notice especially vss. 6 f.! It has
already been conjectured, above, that 63 : 7 ff. is still another soliloquy by the same speaker. In 55 : 3–5 the Messianic leader is
still more clearly designated by the allusion to the promised Son
of David (see below). The description of the Servant's work given
in 42 : 1–9 suggests an individual lawgiver and guide rather than
a people, and especially the very close resemblance of the passage
to 49 : 1–8 and 61 : 1 ff. renders probable the conclusion that the
opening verses of chapter 42 give us the prophet's conception of
the Messiah.

It is because the aspects of the Servant's work are many and
closely interwoven—though the task is always essentially the same
—that the rôle sometimes passes so suddenly from one to another
in the poet's imagery, the conception appearing and reappearing
in these shifting forms. It was remarked, above, that one Servant-
idea may be replaced by another not only within the limits of a
single poem, but even within those of a single paragraph. Examples may now be given. In 41 : 2 f., 25, it is Abraham who accepts
the task and also completes it; in vss. 8 ff. it is the seed of Abraham, the chosen people who are yet to be strengthened and made
fit for the work. In 42 : 1 ff. it is the Leader of the Messianic age
(as also in 61 : 1 ff.); in 42 : 18–20 it is the still unfaithful children,
in their present wretched condition. In 49 : 3 the Servant is introduced as Israel;* then, in a breath, as the vision opens, the Servant is the coming leader who is *to restore Israel* and "lift up the
tribes of Jacob" (vss. 5 f.). In 45 : 1 ff., where the same two
actors, the nation and its leader, are presented, the prophet re-
serves the term 'Servant' for the former, giving the title "Anointed" (*māšīăch*, Messiah) to the latter, the coming champion, already "called" in Yahwè's eternal plan and given this title of
honor ('*ăkanněkā*) even before he became conscious of his great
mission (vs. 4).

---

* The labored attempt of Duhm to expunge the word "Israel" from this
verse is a striking example of perverse exegesis. Even Marti, who generally
follows Duhm without question, sees that the attempt is futile.

Nothing could be more natural than that the poet should give his many-colored figure of speech these kaleidoscopic turns; nothing is more certain than that he did so. The shifting application is by no means a mere literary feature, however, and there could be no greater mistake, in the attempt to understand the prophet's use of the figure, than to consider it from this point of view only. His individuality is indeed to be seen in the manner of the changes which are sometimes effected, but the true reason for the sometimes perplexing use of the term 'servant' lies in the fundamental idea and purpose of the personification. The coming leader must perfectly represent his people; so perfectly, that he is as it were the embodiment of their essential qualities. For this reason the prophet is careful to keep the picture of the Messiah close to that of personified Israel.

There doubtless will be room for different interpretations here and there. The poet's imagination is not to be put in a straitjacket, nor may we require of a brilliant succession of pictures the strict consequence of a formal theological treatise. We have no ground for conjecture as to the chronological development of his conception of the Servant. It is plain that every variation of the idea was already present in his mind before he wrote the poems which we have.

4. The Servant's Task

The mission of the Servant has indeed many aspects, but in its presentation there are two outstanding features. It is first of all a mission for Israel: to restore the holy land, awakening the slumbering faith, bringing back the wanderers, presenting to Yahwè a repentant and purified nation. Equally essential is the second feature, to restore the desolate world (*lĕhāqīm 'ereṣ*, 49 : 8, see the commentary), to sweep away the wickedness and misery of mankind, and to unite all nations, with Israel as the leader, in a régime of righteousness and peace, in the service of the One God.

The prominence of the missionary idea in these poems is a fact of profound significance. Through the instrumentality of Israel the sorrow and suffering of all mankind will be relieved, and the wide world will be brought at last to the true faith. This idea is most plainly stated in two of the 'Servant' passages, 42 : 6 f. and 49 : 6. The latter passage reads:

It is too light a thing that thou shouldst be my Servant, | to lift up
   the tribes of Jacob, | to restore the residue of Israel;

I will make thee the light of the nations, | that my rescue may reach
to the end of the earth.

In 42 : 6 the same phrase, "the light of the nations," is employed,
and the next verse then carries out the figure, showing what this
"light" is to mean to the world.

To open the sightless eyes, | to bring out the captives from the
prison, | and from the dungeon those who sit in darkness.

Or again in 61 : 1, where the Servant himself is the speaker:

He hath sent me to preach glad tidings to the oppressed, | to bind up
the broken-hearted,
To proclaim freedom to the captives, | the restoring of sight to the
blind.

It is a splendid program. We have here in effect the same promise which is made (by another writer) in 25 : 7, 8: "Yahwè will
destroy . . . the veil which is over all the peoples, and . . . will
wipe away the tears from all faces."
How, then, was Israel to play its part in this great work? These
typical blessings are primarily spiritual, it is plain. Knowing the
writer with whom we are dealing, we are sure that he is not predicting the restoration of sight to veritable blind men, nor even
the opening of actual prison doors. The "rescue" which shall
reach "to the end of the earth" is the same which is promised to
the chosen people in the coming Messianic age. Through what
instrumentality could this illumination of the world, this renovation of the peoples of the earth be effected? Should not the Jews
send out missionaries, to preach the faith of their people? Should
not the scattered colonists, the 'exiles,' in all the corners of the
earth, begin a concerted work with the aim of making proselytes,
holding up their religion to plain view, and insisting on its superiority? These questions had already been asked, long ago, and these
plans put to the test, and the outcome had been unmistakable.
The Jewish colonists had held up their lamps, and the apologists
had lifted up their voices; the answer which the Gentiles gave
was the one quoted from them in Is. 53:

He has no form nor charm, that we should look upon him; | no
beauty, that we should admire him. . . .
We have accounted him punished, | smitten of God, and afflicted.

The great nations of the earth had their own religions, to which they were attached. Why should they think that their salvation rested in the faith of this prostrate people, this "root out of barren ground"?

Our poet-prophet had no idea of convincing the Gentiles by argument. His own elaborate and masterful trains of reasoning were not designed for foreigners, but for Jews. He knew perfectly well—and says, in effect, over and over again—that the only thing that ever would or could open the eyes of the nations would be the crack of doom. When he predicts, in inspired figures of speech, the redemption of these erstwhile foes or indifferent onlookers, it is only in the eschatological setting, in the great day of Yahwè, that he sees the conversion brought to pass. When blind and deaf Israel, restored to faith, shall make possible the divine leadership to victory, when the weak one shall at last triumph, *then*—but not before—the heathen will acknowledge that the God of Israel, Yahwè, alone had "seen the end from the beginning."

Nevertheless, the Servant has a present work to do. When the end comes, and the day of "the new heaven and the new earth" at last dawns, there will be found even then a multitude of the "friends of Yahwè" among the Gentiles. And there must be a continuous preparatory work, bringing this about. The prophet believed in standing up for the faith of the fathers, and commending it to the world. In 48 : 6 he represents the God of Israel as rebuking most severely the failure of his people to bear witness, proclaiming to all mankind the great things which they have seen and heard. Whatever it was possible to do in this way must be done; but the result was bound to be small at best, a mere drop in the bucket. This cannot represent the full measure of the Servant's work. Israel had been appointed as the *mediator* between Yahwè and the Gentiles—a mighty task. There must be in it something deeper and more significant than the winning of a small proportion of proselytes. Each of the foreign religions had indeed its element of truth; whoever looked beneath the surface could see a spirit of worship, a looking for divine help, that could not be called worthless. But their 'gods' were no gods at all. Yahwè could indeed look on them with compassion, and take to himself such of their worship as was offered in a worthy spirit; nevertheless they stood afar off, and were filling the world with every form of violence and corruption. They must all at last turn to Yahwè and accept him and be accepted by him. Was there to be no penance? Could he simply receive them to favor and permit them to share the blessings of the Messianic age without atonement? They have been allowed to trample Israel under foot without mercy; the 'chosen race' has been a mockery. Yahwè is all-powerful, and in his eternal plan even the unexampled distress of Israel must have been included. Is not the deeper meaning of the appointed task to be found here?

It is by following this line of thought that the Second Isaiah comes to his great conception of the suffering Servant. In the poem 52 : 13–53 : 12 he sets forth in a single unsurpassed picture his thought of the relation which the long-continued distress of Israel bears to his mission. The Servant suffers the penalty of the sin of the world, and through his woes makes atonement to God for the heathen nations. It is a profound solution of the hardest problem in Jewish theology.

5. *The Messiah*

In the background of both pictures of the future work of the Servant, the restoring of Israel and the bringing of light to the Gentiles, stands the figure of the Anointed One. Generally obscured, perhaps intentionally, by the personification of the Jewish people, the outline of an ideal person, the predicted leader, can nevertheless be made out with certainty. The prophet's faith in God and his logical interpretation of the divine plan could not have failed to provide this essential feature. The words of the apostle Paul in his letter to the Philippians (1 : 6), "Being confident of this very thing, that he who began a good work in you will perfect it until the day of Jesus Christ," might be taken as a strikingly apt expression of the conviction producing and underlying every part of the Second Isaiah's prophecy, if only in place of "Jesus Christ" there is substituted "his righteous Servant." The genius of the Hebrew prophet gave definite and final shape to ancient expectations which had lacked coherence and a spiritual content. His Servant-idea is given a wide range, as we have seen, but now and again the lines of the depiction converge to an individual, so that the main features of a single portrait stand before the reader, as they stood even more clearly before the writer. This brilliant individualizing of the conception, not only where the personal Messiah is in view, but also in the personification of the Israelite nation, has struck every careful reader of the book. Successive commentators have found it difficult to believe that the imagination of a Hebrew poet was capable of such a flight as this, depicting an ideal personage in such vivid language, and accordingly have made search for an actual historical personage who could satisfy the requirements of the portrayal. Some have thought of Zerubbabel, others of Job. Still others, among them George Adam Smith, have been persuaded that it is Jeremiah whom the prophet has in mind. But this and all the similar attempts to explain the individual Servant fall far short of satisfying. A greater than Jeremiah is here.

The Messianic leader, who stands at Yahwè's right hand, "will execute his pleasure and his might" (48:14, as emended). He will shatter the gates of bronze, break the bars of iron, and rescue the faithful of his people. No hostile king or army can stand before him; "he will make them as dust with his sword, as driven stubble with his bow." The holy city and land will be freed from foreign enemies, under his leadership, and in their place multitudes of the Gentiles, acknowledging the One God, will be led to Jerusalem to offer worship and to do joyful homage to the chosen people. He will also on the spiritual side be the fit representative of a purified race, the worthy instrument of an eternal purpose for mankind. "Hidden treasures" of wisdom will be opened to him (45:3, 48:6; cf. Deut. 32:34, 33:19, Jer. 33:3). He must conquer and rule the world not only by his might, but also by his character. He must be the "righteous Servant," endowed with God's own spirit (42:1, 61:1); an example of gentleness and humility (42:2, 50:4 ff., 61:1); ὁ δίκαιος of Acts 7:52. He will be the magnanimous one, sparing the bruised reed and the dimly burning wick, and bringing justice, peace, and a beneficent law to the Gentiles. He will be the champion of the weak and the oppressed, the helper of the needy and suffering, the world over; preaching good tidings and opening all prison doors. It is this picture, unexampled and unapproached, that we have especially in the opening passages of chapters 42, 49, and 61.

As was remarked above, the Messiah is the index of his people, in both character and experience. Even as the person fully individualized in the imagination of the prophet, the Anointed Deliverer must pass through his period of discipline. He is not from the first fully equipped for his task. It is only by degrees that he comprehends it, and is made to understand the character and purpose of the God who appointed him and holds him by the hand. In this again he is truly representative of his people. "Thou dost not yet know me" is the meaning of 45:4 f. Until *the people* come to this comprehension their great representative cannot stand forth from their ranks and lead them to victory.

The anointed leader and ruler is, of course, a scion of the royal house of David. No promises were more familiar, none more eagerly cherished, than those which definitely centred in the Davidic line; and no Hebrew prophet who was 'looking for the consolation of Israel' (προσδεχόμενος παράκλησιν τοῦ Ἰσραήλ, Luke 2:25) could have thought of any other origin. The long-traditional expectation for the Messianic time was that which is expressed in Hos. 3:5 and Jer. 30:9: "They shall serve the Lord their God, and David their king, whom I will raise up for them." That which had been promised in II Sam. 7:12-16 was claimed again and again by seers and psalmists, sometimes indirectly, sometimes very expressly, as in Ps. 89 (see especially vss. 34-38).

It is hardly accidental that the term *melek*, "king," does not occur in these poems as a designation of the Messiah. It is not in this character, but in other aspects, that he is pictured here. The rule of a *king* in Jerusalem—even a king endowed with more than human graces—was never in the foreground of the prophet's thought. It is needless to say, however, that for him also the coming captain, lawgiver, and friend of the lowly was to be the promised Son of David. In one striking passage this idea is plainly expressed—plainly, that is, for Jewish readers. The Second Isaiah mentions David once only, but then in a most significant manner. In 55:3 the great promise centres in the phrase "*the sure mercies of David*" (referring, as all commentators agree, to II Sam. 7:8-16), and in the two following verses the meaning of the phrase is briefly set forth in a characteristic way by a direct address to the anointed leader himself, with the dramatic turn of which the poet is so fond:

Behold, I make thee the witness of the peoples, | the leader and commander of the peoples.
Thou shalt call nations that thou knowest not, | nations that know thee not shall run unto thee;
Because of Yahwè thy God, | and for the Holy One of Israel, who has glorified thee.

Both verses refer to the future. The verb in *nĕthattīkā*, "I have appointed thee," is used precisely as in 42:1, 45:3, 46:13, 49:6, etc., and as *hinnē samtīkā*, "Behold, I have made thee," in 41:15. The twice-repeated *hēn* witnesses to the same effect.* The testi-

* The interpretation of these two verses by Duhm, Marti, and their fellows is forbidden by several considerations. It misses the significance of the special promise to David; he, moreover, was never a 'witness' or a 'leader' for the nations; the use of the second person singular masculine in vs. 5 is also decisive.

mony brought to the nations, the leadership and command of the peoples, are familiar and oft-repeated predictions. The whole passage closely resembles Ps. 2 : 6-8, is indeed the very same picture, in which the Messianic king is similarly addressed:

Ask of me, and I will make the nations thine inheritance, | the uttermost parts of the earth thy possession.

The Second Isaiah was too great an artist to bring unessential details into his picture. He resists the temptation to include conjecture as to the person or the destined activities of the great leader. He gives only the little which he sees to be perfectly assured, just those outlines and shadings which make the most effective contribution to the harmony—and the mystery—of the whole.

To what extent, and in what spirit, the character of the Messiah may have been depicted by predecessors of the Second Isaiah, we have no means of knowing. Certain it is that in the literature which has come down to us his portrayal stands alone in its originality and power. Whoever studies it carefully in the light of the whole series of poems will hardly doubt that it is essentially his own creation. The various motives entering into the conception had been at hand for some time; it was only necessary that some prophet greater than his fellows should comprehend and combine them. When the Second Isaiah had finished his work, he had set before the eyes of his people a picture which remained essentially the same through the succeeding centuries. It is the ideal figure sketched by him that we find partially reproduced in some of the latest Hebrew prophecies, in many poems of the Psalter, in the 17th and 18th of the Psalms of Solomon, and in the poems contained in the first two chapters of Luke's Gospel.

Whether 'Messiah' (Heb.-Aram. *mašīăch*) as the special designation of the expected Jewish leader was first given general currency by the prophecy of the Second Isaiah, is a question that can be answered with strong probability in the affirmative. It is beyond question that these poems are the principal source of the definitely Messianic pictures which appear in subsequent Jewish writings. The *mĕšīchō*, "his anointed," of 45 : 1 and "the Lord hath anointed me," of 61 : 1, standing at the head of two of the most striking and personally conceived passages, provided the title which was henceforth adopted. The later interpolation of the name "Cyrus" (which evidently was illuminating to some of the readers of its time!) did damage only to the immediate context;

see, for instance, the Targum to such passages as 41 : 2 and 46 : 11, in which no allusion to Cyrus is seen. It could not affect, in those days, the interpretation of the remainder, nor the already accepted title of the Coming One. The bulk of the prophecy, with its look into the future, continued to be for its readers, as it had been in the intention of its author, a picture of the Messianic time.

CHAPTER IX

METRIC FORMS AND DETAILS

The purpose of this chapter is twofold: to provide the general reader with a concise and untechnical description of those forms of Hebrew verse to which allusion is constantly made in these pages, and to give reason for my own proceeding where I have felt constrained to differ from the current view.*

The whole subject of Hebrew metrics is in its infancy, and any present treatment of it is necessarily crude and imperfect. The principal rules and conventions of Hebrew prosody are doubtless as old as the literary language, and are determined to some extent by details of vocalization, word-accent, elision, and the like, which are more or less obscured in the system of cantillation represented by our massoretic pointing. The poets, masters of their art, were provided with long-familiar rules of rhetoric and composition—to say nothing of musical setting—of which the modern student is as yet unaware, though long-continued study will doubtless bring many of them to light. The technique of a national poetry, developed by a literary people, is never simple, however ancient it may be. Some conclusions which seem to us highly probable may well be mistaken, and we must constantly bear this in mind in presuming to criticise either verbal details or principles of structure.

On the other hand, the traditions of versification are more persistent than those of prose composition. Poems are readily learned by heart, and are handed on from generation to generation in a form sufficiently unchanged to be recognized, in its main features, with certainty. The compulsion of rhythm is a safeguard, a means of preserving what might otherwise have been lost. This fact comes to our aid in the attempt to deal with Hebrew metrics. While we may be greatly in doubt as to the pronunciation of classical Hebrew *prose*, and may even feel certain that the massoretic punctuation is in important respects far from representing the actual spoken language of any period, yet in the metrical

---

* The greater part of the material of this chapter, in substantially its present form, was given as a lecture at the summer session of the Divinity School of Harvard University in July, 1905.

compositions we are at once on firmer ground. The prolonged, singsong vocalization, which is purely artificial in the traditional recitation of the prose writings of the Old Testament, is in place and very near to the original form of utterance in the chanting of the poetry—from which it seems to have been derived. In a considerable portion of such metrical lines as those of Second Isaiah, we are able to determine the relative prolongation of each syllable, the position of the main stress in each word, and thus the rhythm of the verse as its author conceived it. In other lines, while the metrical swing is obvious enough, there is plainly more than one way of producing it, and the precise verbal stress must remain for the present a matter of uncertainty. It is quite unsafe now, and in all probability it never will be safe, to cut loose from the massoretic system of vocalization in studying Hebrew metrics.

1. *General Features*

Hebrew verse is accentual, not quantitative, nor syllabic. Each line contains a definite number of well-marked beats, or accents; but the number of syllables is not constant, nor is there any ratio between the length of the stressed syllables and that of the unstressed.

The typical *line*, or verse-member, on which all Hebrew poetry is primarily built, is the line of three beats. For example:

40 : 1, *Nachămŭ nachămŭ 'ammí.*
41 : 4, *Mí fā'ál wă-'āsá.*
42 : 25, *Wattĕlahătĕhŭ missāvív wĕ-lō yādhá'.*
51 : 6, *Wĕ-habbítŭ el-hā'áreṣ mittáchath.*

It is plain that a poem consisting entirely of such lines as these, read in such a way as to make the stressed syllables unmistakably prominent, would be truly 'metrical,' the triad units which compose it being both distinct and regular. On the other hand, it is no less plain that the uniformity of the lines is merely relative. The number of beats is constant, and their distribution is approximately even, but within these limits there is considerable freedom.

The *measure*, or *foot*, which is the unit of the line, consists of a stressed syllable and (ordinarily) one or more unstressed syllables. The position of the accent in the measure varies. The opening syllable of the line may or may not be accented, and the same is true of the final syllable. Thus:

51: 9, *'Ûrī kîmē qédhem.*
51 : 14, *Wĕ-lô yechsár lachmô.*

The number of unaccented syllables in the measure is subject to considerable variation, the only restriction being that imposed by the inherent character of verse as opposed to prose. The structural principle is simply this: each stressed syllable is accompanied by a varying number of unstressed syllables; enough, on the one hand, to render the line musical, and on the other hand, nowhere so accumulated as to obscure the rhythm. The character of the unaccented syllables is also disregarded, as in accentual meters generally; they may be closed or open, long or short.

2. *The* 3 | 3 *Meter*

The true unit of Hebrew poetry is not the single line, but the *verse*, which is most commonly a double line. In the typical and simplest metrical mode, for example, the line of three beats has another similar line as its complement, each of the two forming half of a truly organic whole, which may conveniently be called the verse. The 'verse' of two three-beat lines, which is perhaps best designated by the sign 3 | 3, lies at the foundation of all Hebrew poetry. The term 'hexameter' is sometimes employed in speaking of this meter, but the designation is not quite suitable. Each separate member of the verse has a certain individuality to which the term does not do justice; and moreover, there is a frequently employed 3 | 3 | 3 verse, as will appear.

The two halves of the 3 | 3 verse are normally defined by a rhetorical pause; that is, if the text were punctuated in the manner of modern literary compositions, the first tripody would ordinarily be followed by at least a comma. Each member has thus a certain logical distinctness, the structure of the sentence setting it apart as a recognizable unit. It is this fact especially which makes the designation 'hexameter' less desirable. The division is such a necessary and permanent characteristic, touching the sense as well as the metric form, that it must be emphasized; moreover, the pervasive parallelism, soon to be noticed, gives the twofold structure a peculiar and very striking quality. It sometimes happens, indeed, that the sentence moves on without any necessary halt in the sense at the half-verse. Such cases merely illustrate a natural freedom. The metrical form being both fixed and obvious, the cæsural pause will be made in the conventional place, even when there is no rhetorical division. This subject will receive some further mention in the sequel.

The logical relation which exists between the two parts of the 3 | 3 verse is subject to no law, but may be of any character. Most common, however, and truly typical, is the relation of parallelism, the second member repeating in modified form more or less of what had been said in the first member. A fine example is 34 : 10*b*–13:

From age to age her land shall be waste, | for ever and ever none shall pass through it;
But the screech-owl and the hedgehog shall possess it, | the great owl and the raven shall dwell therein.
Over her shall be stretched the line of chaos, | and over* her nobles the plummet of desolation;
Her name shall be called NO KINGDOM THERE, | and all her princes shall be nothing.
Thorns shall grow over her palaces, | nettle and thistle in her fortresses;
She shall be the abode of jackals, | a fixed habitation for ostriches.

Since the complete sentence very frequently comprises two or more 3 | 3 lines, there is opportunity for considerable variety in the distribution of the parallelism. The entire line of two members may be the pattern for its successor; or the single members of adjoining lines may respond to one another in any order or arrangement which the poet's taste may prefer. The various modes and methods have been set forth in detail so often that there is no need to describe or illustrate them here.

The 3 | 3 verse, with its easy swing and steady march, has a wide range and is suitable for the treatment of any subject. The vast majority of the poems in the Old Testament, of whatever nature—didactic, lyric, gnomic, elegiac, etc.—consist in the main of a succession of such verses. It is truly the national meter, predominant in all periods of the classical literature, from the earliest times to the very latest.

The Second Isaiah, like the other Hebrew poets, very frequently employed the verse of *three members*, or tristich. Thus 40 : 12:

Who has measured the waters in the palm of his hand, | marked off the heavens with the span, | and enclosed in a measure the dust of the earth?

* The massoretic division of the verses is unusually faulty in this passage. A new verse should begin at 10*b*, also at 11*b*. The first word in vs. 12 belongs to the preceding verse.

And again in vs. 15:

The nations are a drop from the bucket, | they are counted as the
dust on the balance; | he lifts the islands like grains of sand.

Such verses are sporadic, and yet any 3 | 3 poem is likely to
contain examples, perhaps in considerable number. Such lines
may indeed be employed exclusively; it is not unlikely that in
Ps. 93 we have an instance of a poem originally made up of tristichs
only. Many such poems may have been composed; but they would
always be exceptional. The 3 | 3 | 3 verses are ordinarily intro-
duced for the sake of their contribution to the *variety* which is
such a pleasing feature of the old Hebrew poetry. Their number
and distribution seem to have been determined merely by the
taste and convenience of the poet. The poem may contain none
at all (though I find no such example in II Isaiah), or they may be
massed here and there; see, for example, 34 : 2–5. Very noticeable
is the frequency with which the 3 | 3 | 3 verse is employed by
Hebrew writers to end a poem, or to mark the close of a subject
or section. Examples in II Isaiah are, for the poem: 43 : 7; 49 : 26;
59 : 21; 60 : 22; 61 : 11; 66 : 24; and for the section: 41 : 24; 42 : 9;
43 : 13, 28; 44 : 20; 45 : 7; 46 : 2; 48 : 11, 16, 19; 54 : 10; 56 : 8;
63 : 6. The rhetorical effect of the verse thus weighted is obvious.
Chapters 48 and 57 also end virtually with a tristich, followed by
the sententious phrase, "No peace, saith Yahwè, for the wicked!"
as a sort of coda. The cases are also to be noticed in which the
poem, or section, closes with a tristich followed by a distich; thus
35 : 10; 40 : 7; 41 : 28 f.; 44 : 26 f.; 51 : 6, 11; 65 : 25.
   Failure to recognize the 3 | 3 | 3 verse as a legitimate unit in
the structure of Hebrew poetry has led to very considerable mutilation of the text by those who have sought to criticise it on the
ground of metric requirement. Examples could be given from all
the poetical parts of the Hebrew Bible and from almost any chapter in II Isaiah. It may suffice for illustration to point to three
instances, taken from Duhm's commentary, in chapter 43. On
vs. 7 he comments: "Der Relativsatz . . . würde in den drei
tautologischen Verben am Schluss einen unerträglichen Rede-
schwall loslassen, wenn man nicht annehmen dürfte, dass es sich
nur um drei Varianten handelt; welches von den drei Verben
ursprünglich ist, kann man nicht wissen, es ist auch gleichgültig."
He accordingly achieves his postulated 'stanza' by omitting two
of the offending verbs. With the last words of vs. 12, which origi-

nally formed the beginning of vs. 13,* he would make a three-beat
line by adding the word *mē'ōlām*, claiming (without right, see my
note on the passage) the support of the Greek version. In commenting on vs. 28 he remarks, "Das erste Distichon scheint in
der Mitte ein grosses Loch zu haben," and he proceeds to fill this
imaginary 'gap' with some Hebrew of his own. The havoc which
is wrought in the Psalter by such criticism can hardly be realized
without actual examination of the commentaries.

3. *The* 3 | 2 *Meter*

The other well-known variety of Hebrew meter, in which the
typical line consists of a 'major member' of three beats followed
by a 'minor member' of two beats, is much employed in II Isaiah.
This 3 | 2 meter is obviously a development from the 3 | 3. There
are two ways in which such development might take place. The
two-beat member might be thought of as an abbreviated form,
produced by curtailing the second line of three beats; or, the line
of 3 + 2 beats might be conceived rather as an expansion, each
three-beat line receiving an appendage of its own. The latter
seems to be the true theory. While the logical relation existing
between the two members of the 3 | 2 verse is in general of the
same nature as that in 3 | 3 and capable of the same variety, it is
unmistakably the case that it is a closer relation. The dipody is
normally attached to the tripody as its subordinate, having not
quite the same independence as the second member in a 3 | 3 unit.
It thus appears as a mere echo or re-enforcement of the preceding
member more often than is the case in 3 | 3.

66:6 A thunderous voice from the city, | a voice from the temple! ||
45:19 I did not declare it in secret, | in a region of darkness. ||

Where the division between the two parts of the verse is distinct,
the major member usually carries the main idea, the minor member appearing more or less plainly as an appendage.

66:9 Shall I bring to birth and yet restrain? | saith Yahwè; || Shall I
   beget, but close the womb? | saith thy God. ||
52:2 Shake off the dust, stand erect, | captive Jerusalem; || Free the
   bonds from thy neck, | captive daughter of Zion! ||

Even in the multitude of cases in which the relation is not logically subordinate, in the manifold development and wide use of

* I believe that the division of the verses which Duhm makes here is correct.

this metric form, the verse-member of two beats maintains its original character as the complement of the three-beat member and inseparable from it. It is thus in its origin and use analogous to the so-called dactylic 'pentameter' in the elegiac distich of the classical poets. This was created merely as a *response* to the hexameter, and is never used alone.

The essentially closer union of the two parts of the 3 | 2 verse, as compared with 3 | 3, is shown also in the treatment of the pause. It is far oftener the case in this meter than in the other that the cæsura cuts a phrase in two: separating, for instance, the subject from the predicate, the verb from its object, or intervening between two words which stand in the 'construct state' (equivalent to a compound word). In such cases it frequently happens that the parallelism maintains clearly the metrical division.

40:3 A voice proclaims in the desert: | Prepare the way of Yahwè; ||
    Make straight in the wilderness | a highway for our God! ||

51:17 Thou hast drunk from the hand of Yahwè | the cup of his wrath; ||
    The bowl that causes staggering | thou hast drained to the dregs. ||

57:7f. On a high, outstanding hill | thou hast placed thy bed; ||
    Behind the door and the post | thou hast put thy symbol. ||

57:9 *Power* thou sawest, didst send | to the King with thine oil; ||
    Didst multiply thine unguents, and dispatch | thine ambassadors afar; || —and thou wast brought down to Sheol!

From what has been said thus far it is evident that the structural unit of the poem in this meter is not the single 3 | 2 line, but the combination of *two* such lines. The scheme of the complete 'verse' is thus 3 | 2 || 3 | 2. There is in general the same correspondence between the two compound lines in this meter which exists between the two simple lines in the 3 | 3 meter; while the fact that there are now four distinct verse-members, instead of two, doubles the possible variety of logical response. There is often complete parallelism, the two major members corresponding and the two minor members likewise. Thus, 47 : 1:

Get thee down, sit in the dust, | virgin Babylon! || Sit on the ground, no throne for thee, | daughter of Chaldea! ||

The opposite arrangement in 52 : 10:

Yahwè has bared his holy arm | before all the nations; || And all the ends of the earth shall behold | the salvation of our God. ||

It is hardly necessary to remark that the 3 | 2 lines occur not only in pairs but also in triads. Chapter 47, for instance, is constructed largely of such triads, see vss. 1, 8, 9, 10, 11, 13, 14.

It is a fact deserving of especial notice (though overlooked, if I am not mistaken, by those who have treated this meter) that the 3 | 2 line not infrequently receives the addition of a three-beat member, thus becoming 3 | 3 | 2 or 3 | 2 | 3. If the occurrences were few in number, or in passages presenting textual or metrical difficulty, we might without misgiving conclude that they are in every case the result of accidental omission or editorial expansion. Such omissions and expansions must of course be reckoned with. The instances are a multitude, however, and are widely distributed in the Old Testament, in passages where we have no reason to suspect the text. It is usually true that the rhythm of the added line is as distinct and musical as that of any other, and that its contribution to the sense of the verse is obvious. There is ordinarily nothing in the context, or in the testimony of ancient versions, to suggest that the supernumerary tripody ever had, or would naturally be expected to have, a two-beat appendage of its own. What is still more important, both the fact and the manner of its use are perfectly in accord with what we already know of the art of the Hebrew poets. There can therefore be no question that the 'extra' line of three accents in the 3 | 2 poem is to be accepted as a standard feature.

The supernumerary line may occupy any place in the complete verse. In 51:23, 45:20, and 66:7, for instance, the verse is 3 | 3 | 2. In 42:16, 47:12, 50:5, and 62:10 it is 3 | 2 || 3. Similar examples are to be found in all parts of the other Hebrew poetical books. The occasional use of the weighted verse to end a paragraph (as so often the 3 | 3 | 3 verse, see above) is to be noticed; for example 50:5, 52:6. Sometimes the extra member has the nature of a parenthesis, or of a remark interjected as though by afterthought. It checks the flow of the verse for a moment, with an obvious rhetorical effect. An example is 57:9, quoted above in translation. See also Chapter XI.

The 3 | 2 verse has a quality of its own which is more easily perceived than characterized. It is the verse of emotion, of whatever variety, and the personal element is properly inherent in it. The peculiar movement of the rhythm, with its broken lines and short responses, has a suggestion of agitation, and thus lends itself easily to the expression of any strong feeling. Joy and grief are alike represented, the mood of meditation and the outburst of excitement. It is perhaps best designated as the 'lyric' verse (see below), but no single term is sufficient to characterize it.

When this meter was first identified and described, by Budde, it was given the name *Qīna* ("dirge ") because the principal specimens of poetry in which it had at that time been recognized are distinctly elegiac in character (chapters 1–4 of the Book of Lamentations; the elegy on the death of the Mighty Tyrant, Is. 14: 4–21, etc.), and because the little dirge-couplet in Amos 5 : 2, expressly styled a *qīna*, is in this meter. The name thus had its temporary justification, but the continued use of it by scholars at the present day is to be deplored. Now that the various uses of the 3 | 2 verse have received further study, it is evident that the proposed name is unsuitable, since the employment of the meter for the dirge is merely one of its adopted and less common applications.*

If a name derived from the actual and traditional use rather than from the metric form of the verse were to be adopted, it would be called *lyric;* for it is, generally speaking, the meter of Hebrew lyric poetry. In whatever type of composition it is employed, the subjective quality is always present and normally conspicuous. The Second Isaiah's handling of this meter shows an interesting variety; in fact, there is no other Hebrew poet whose work affords a like opportunity of studying its typical uses. On page after page, where the 3 | 2 line reappears, we see the tinge of the poet's own emotion: the excitement of 42 : 14 ff., or 51 : 9 f.; the joy of 52 : 7 ff.; the yearning meditation of 63 : 7 ff.; the stern sarcasm of 47 : 1–15 and 56 : 10–12; tender feeling flashing out in a single verse, as in 54 : 6 and 60 : 14. When the meter is employed in invective, as in 47 *passim*, 50 : 11, and 57 : 3 f., there is possible a pungency of expression which is quite beyond the reach of the 3 | 3 mode. If the tone is ironical, the brief metric response in each line can produce a peculiarly epigrammatic effect. For the potent expression of such emotions as these, no language is better equipped than the classical Hebrew with its 3 | 2 verse.

4. *Combination and Variation of Metric Forms*

It might be presumed that Hebrew poetry, because of the omnipresent line of three accents and the almost incessant parallelism,

---

* Observe that the two ancient specimens of Hebrew elegy preserved in II Sam. 1 : 19–27 and 3 : 33 f. are not in 3 | 2 meter, though described as *qīnōth*. On the other hand, see I Macc. 9 : 21, where the 3 | 2 meter is apparent even in the Greek translation.

would have an inherent tendency toward monotony. This is not the case, however. The parallelism is not repetition, but logical development according to a scheme simple in outline but endlessly varied in detail, and the metric requirement is sufficiently elastic. There are well-recognized and effective means of obtaining that freedom of poetic form which is among the excellences of Hebrew verse. In both the metric scheme of the poem and the fashion of the single line there is to be seen a variety which is deliberate, not accidental, and governed by considerations which we can partially understand. The essential elements of the verse—metric units and parallelism—are few and comparatively simple, but the possibilities of effective combination are a multitude.

A most important device is that of combining the two meters, 3 | 3 and 3 | 2, in a poem; or more particularly the transition from the one to the other in accordance with change of mood or theme, in order to produce a designed effect.

It is strange that it has been so generally taken for granted by those who have dealt with Hebrew poetry that there is but one meter for each single composition. The poems of the Second Isaiah have suffered especially from this false theory, for the assumption that change of meter indicates the beginning of a new poem, or 'fragment,' if not the appearance of another author, means the complete dismemberment of many of these masterpieces, the finest productions of Hebrew literature. The misguided dissection undertaken in accordance with this supposed criterion has had very frequent illustration.

As has been shown in the preceding pages, the two standard metric forms differ from each other in character. The change from the one to the other is a change of tone, not merely of rhythm. The Hebrew poets take advantage of this fact in compositions containing contrasted themes or representing different moods. The art of this metric transition deserves close study. Its value is everywhere apparent, and some very striking effects are produced.

A typical instance of the change of meter is to be seen in chapter 50, a poem whose general plan is obvious; see the introduction in the Commentary. The beginning, hortatory and argumentative, is in the 3 | 3 form. With verse 4 the second subject enters, a theme with an intimately personal tone, the soliloquy of the Servant of the Lord:

Yahwè my Lord has given to me | a tongue for teaching. ||

The meter is now 3 | 2, and this continues to the end of the poem. The total effect of unity along with strong contrast could not have been produced in any other way.

The triumphant poem 44 : 24–45 : 25 is divided in the middle by the change of meter, the two halves being held firmly together by the principal theme of the poem, the salvation of the Gentiles. There is an obvious change of scene and atmosphere at the point of transition, though the tone of triumph persists. The first half is majestic, beginning and ending (45 : 13) with a Messianic announcement. The stirring picture of Israel's advancing protagonist, first seen in 41 : 2 ff., now appears again. There is also a passage of stern admonition, in very general terms, but evidently addressed to Israel. The second half of the poem, which is the logical continuation of the first half, is in another key. It touches human hope and experience more directly and is in a milder mood. The change of meter adds considerably to the effect.

The poet's affectionate apostrophe to the holy city, Jerusalem, is likely to be conceived in the lyric verse. Chapter 40 begins in this strain. The poem as a whole is one of changing moods, and the two metric forms alternate in a charming manner. The rebuke, exhortation, and argument which make up the major part of the composition are in the 3 | 3 mode, as would be expected. Chapter 62, a psalm of Zion throughout, makes its entrance indeed in a major key, with a declaration of firm purpose; but the feeling soon grows more intense, and the 3 | 2 meter comes in. The passionate outburst of pity, encouragement, and exultation, 51 : 17–52 : 12, is all in this meter until the brief closing passage, or coda, 52 : 11 f., where the scene suddenly shifts, in characteristic manner, to the exodus from Egypt, and the cry of warning and encouragement is heard:

Turn ye, turn ye, go out thence; | touch no unclean thing!
Forth from the midst of her, purify yourselves, | ye bearers of Yahwè's
    utensils.

Any sudden dramatic turn, like the one just exemplified, bringing in a new scene or a new speaker, is likely to be accompanied by a metric transition of this nature. Thus, for instance, the interjected scene 66 : 6–9, in which the speaker hears in distant Jerusalem the roar of battle, the shout of triumph, announcing the restoration of the world under the rule of the Messiah. There is a particularly fine example in chapter 51 at vs. 9. The poem begins

in a quiet, didactic vein. Yahwè speaks, with reassuring words
which soon end in a sort of refrain, twice repeated, in vss. 7 and 8:

But my rescue shall abide forever, | and my salvation from age to age.

Then, like a bolt from a clear sky, comes the cry for help, couched
in the language of old Hebrew mythology and addressed to the
God of Sinai and the Red Sea:

Awake, awake, put on strength, | arm of the Lord ! ||
Awake, as in days of old, | the time long past ! ||
Art not thou he that cleft Rahab, | that pierced the Dragon ? ||

The effect is very striking, the more so because the original meter
of the poem is resumed as soon as this brief apostrophe is ended.
A similar case is 42 : 14–17, where Yahwè is suddenly introduced
as the speaker in a passage of great dramatic power; and here
again the effect is considerably heightened by the change of meter.
   The use of this poetic device is thoroughly embedded in the
national literature. There is a beautiful instance in the New Testament, in the opening portion of Luke's Gospel, the story of the
birth and childhood of Jesus, written in classical Hebrew by an
artist of the first rank. The Benedictus, spoken by Zacharias, is in
3 | 3 meter from the beginning, 1 : 68, to vs. 75. At vs. 76 the
speaker turns and addresses the infant John, *and the meter changes
to* 3 | 2:*

And thou, child, shalt be called | the prophet of the Highest, ||
For thou shalt go before the face of the Lord, | to prepare his ways. ||

   This meter is continued to the end of the poem, through vs. 79.
   As has already been said, the meter of lyric meditation in a
mood of deep feeling is preferably 3 | 2. The passage 50 : 4–12
has been cited in illustration, and there are many other examples,
one of the best of which is the meditation of the Servant of Yahwè
in 63 : 7–14 (see the introduction to the poem). An outstanding
illustration from the Psalter is the long alphabetic Psalm 119. A
more striking instance in the Prophetic literature is the opening
passage of the Book of Habakkuk, 1 : 2 f., where the poet-prophet,
before coming to the subject of his poem, speaks from a full heart
to the omnipotent God of a downtrodden people:

   * So I have demonstrated to my classes for many years past, attempting
also to restore the Hebrew. The question of the precise form of the original
is of minor importance, however, for no careful retroversion can fail to show
the change of meter.

How long, O Lord, shall I cry, | and thou not hear; ||
Complain to thee of violence, | and thou not save! ||
Why dost thou show me iniquity, | and make me see trouble? ||
For ruin and violence are before me, | there are strife and contention. ||

Thereupon vs. 4, with change of meter, introduces the 'burden' (*massā*) of his prophecy.*

It is easy to see how a lively imagination, of the dramatic quality, might occasionally interrupt the steady swing of the 3 | 3 meter with momentary lapses into the more intimate and emotional verse-form. Because of the essential character of the latter, as a mere expansion of the older form (see the preceding section), we should not expect to see *a single* 3 | 2 *line* inserted among 3 | 3 verses. A 3 | 2 *couplet* might well stand thus in metric isolation, in the expression of suddenly heightened emotion or to introduce a dramatic change, and such cases are hardly rare. The most striking examples in II Isaiah are 54 : 6, 60 : 14, and 66 : 11. See also 44 : 25, 48 : 12 f., and 65 : 13. It is such examples as these, precisely, that show the writer's temperament and the perfection of his art.

5. *Various Details*

The Question of Other Meters.—The reader of Hebrew poetry often meets with lines which seem too long for three stresses; it is more natural to read them with four. Such instances are not uncommon in II Isaiah. Thus in 40 : 8 it is easy to accent as follows:

ūdĕbár ĕlōhḗnū yaqúm lĕʿōlám.

Or at the end of 49 : 6:

lihyóth yĕšūathí ʿad qĕṣḗ hā'áreṣ

In both cases, however, the presence of the construct state strongly favors the division of the line into *three* measures. So also in 53 : 10 (end), 60 : 13 (beginning), 61 : 3 (fourth clause), and numerous other passages. More noticeable are a few instances such as the following:

49 : 4,   *wa'ăní amárti lĕríq yagáʿtí,*
    lĕthóhū wĕhébel kōchí killéthí.
53 : 10, *wĕYahwĕ́ chāphḗṣ dakkĕ'ó hechŏlí.*

* The fact of this transition is editorially recognized, if I am not mistaken, by the word *yissā*, which now stands at the end of vs. 3, but was originally in the margin as a gloss.

58 : 12, *ūbanú mimmĕká chārĕbŏ́th 'ōlám.*
60 : 1,　*qúmī ŏ́rī kī bắ ōrĕ́k.*
64 : 7,　*ănáchnū hachómer wĕ'attắ yōṣĕrĕ́nū.*

The extra beat seems especially in place when, as not infrequently happens, the line consists of two approximately equal parts with a logical division between. In such cases the natural way of reading, no technical rule hindering, is with four rhythmic accents. For example:

41 : 26, *aph ĕ́n maggíd, aph ĕ́n mašmí̆'.*

The first clause of 40 : 24 has almost exactly the same form, and very similar are the initial clauses of 40 : 21 and 28:

　　　　hălŏ́ yadá'tā im lŏ́ šamá'tā.
51 : 19, *haššŏ́d wĕhaššéber, wĕhāra'ắb wĕhachéreb.*
59 : 18, *chemắ lĕṣāráu, gĕmúl lĕ'ōyĕbáu.*
65 : 21, *wĕnaṭĕ'ú̆ kĕramím, wĕ'akĕlú̆ piryắm.*
66 : 12, *kĕnahắr šalĕ́m, ūkĕnáchal šŏ́ṭĕph.*

Other excellent examples are 48 : 8 (first clause) and 51 : 5, with or without the proposed emendation. It is to be observed that instances of the kind occur not only in a 3 | 3 context but also in poems or passages where the meter is 3 | 2. An example is 51 : 19 (quoted above); another is 50 : 8 (*cf.* 51 : 5):

　　　　qarŏ́b maṣdīqí, mī yaríb ittí.

　The question arises, how these occasional longer lines are to be considered. Do they represent another metric form? It is quite usual to treat them in this way, and on their occurrence is based the theory of a meter the scheme of which would be 4 | 4. It is indeed not uncommon to find in Hebrew poetry, of whatever date or literary character, a succession of lines, perhaps only two or three, perhaps a larger number, which *could* be read with four accents. There are a few such cases in the poems now before us; see for example the two lines in 49 : 4, quoted above.

　The hypothesis of a *meter* containing lines of four stressed syllables will be found in general to give only doubtful help; and in the case of Second Isaiah, at least, it is certainly to be rejected. The number of unaccented syllables in the lines which plainly suggest four beats is not larger than it is in some lines which certainly had only three beats. This matter will be treated further, and illustrated, in the sequel. Moreover, there is no regularity in the occurrence of these longer lines; they simply appear here and there among their three-beat fellows, the latter being as a rule only very slightly shorter. The evidence of a plan is lacking. The three-beat line is a definite and constant unit; the compound line of five (3–2) beats is also a fixed quantity, with its own characteristics and seemingly always deliberately employed. If the Second Isaiah, with his evident fondness for changes of poetic form, had recognized and used a four-beat meter, we could hardly fail to find some instance of a sustained use of it. But there is no such instance to be found. Nowhere in the whole collection of twenty-seven poems is there a 4 | 4 *passage*, not even of the extent of two or three double lines.

It is evident that the slightly longer lines described and exemplified above are merely incidental to the scheme of three accents. They afford another illustration of the freedom of metric form which characterizes Hebrew verse. This is perhaps most strikingly shown by their occurrence in a 3 | 2 context. To the examples given above might be added many others: *e. g.*, Lam. 3 : 23, Ps. 119 : 78, Is. 14 : 5. There is certainly no 4 | 2 meter. Some of the verse-members of this nature were presumably read, or recited, in four measures; the line in 51 : 19, cited above, is an example. Whether any of them were ever *technically conceived* in this way, however, is quite another question. The evidence at hand seems to show clearly that this was not the case. It is not merely that the lines under consideration occur where three-beat lines are demanded by the scheme; it is also true that in every such instance, whether in 3 | 3 or in 3 | 2 verse, they can be read in *three* measures according to demonstrable rules governing the structure of Hebrew verse, as will presently be shown.

The existence of a 2 | 2 meter in these poems has also been postulated. The outstanding example is 48 : 20 f., where nearly all those who have dealt with the meter would divide the text into lines of two stresses. See, for example, the commentaries of Duhm and Marti, the text edited by Cheyne in the *Polychrome Bible*, and Kittel's *Biblia Hebraica*. The supposed meter owes its existence, however, merely to an interpolated text, as I have shown elsewhere. See the critical note on the passage, and especially the discussion of it in Chapter III. There is no 2 | 2 meter in II Isaiah.

The Limits of the Measure.—The measure, the unit of all accentual meter, has in general in Hebrew poetry the same properties as in the verse of other languages. It ordinarily, but not always, coincides with a logical unit. As for the number of syllables comprised in it, it varies from one to a number whose range it is important to determine, if possible. The reduced (*shĕvā*) vowels may of course be disregarded. As was remarked above, the measure must not be so overweighted as to make the line unmusical. Is there a recognized limit? A well-known authority on the German folk-song, Professor Max Friedländer, has remarked that in some of these popular productions a single note may carry "a whole handful of words," with a corresponding loss of rhythm. Something similar may be seen in the popular verse of other languages, as for example in the modern Arabic; see especially Dalman's *Palästinischer Diwan*, p. xxiii. In these cases, however, aside from the melody there is the important aid of rhyme. This line-marking feature, with its accompanying psychological factor of expectation, the waiting for the recurrence of this predetermined and indispensable assonance, is wanting in the Hebrew verse. Moreover, we are not here dealing with the easy-going productions of unlettered men.

The question of especial interest relates to the number of suspended syllables permitted in a single measure *before* the accented syllable; and here, indeed, there is good evidence of a fixed rule. There are abundant examples to show that *three full syllables may be slurred immediately before the stressed syllable*. The verse 55 : 9 contains two such instances:

> *kēn gabĕhú dĕrakái middarkēkém*
> *ūmachšĕbōthái mimmáchšĕbōthēkém.*

See also the first clause of vs. 8. An example in the middle measure of a verse is 51 : 2:

> *habbítū el Abrahám ăbīkém.*

See further 43 : 9, *kol haggōyím;* 54 : 6, *wa'așūbath rúach;* 58 : 11, *ūkĕmōṣā máyim;* 61 : 7, *lākēn bĕ'arṣắm;* 63 : 16 (as emended), *al tith'appáq.* These are merely a few specimens out of very many. Observe also that such a measure is likely to occur in the minor member of a 3 | 2 verse; for example: 50 : 4, *lišmōʻ kallimmūdím;* 63 : 7, *lĕbēth Yisra'él;* 66 : 8, *im yūlad gói;* Ps. 119 : 90, *kōnantā éreṣ.*

In all such cases the sense, like the meter, can permit no pause. If two or more words are included in the measure, the connection between them must be immediate, so that the phrase would naturally be uttered like a single word. I have illustrated chiefly from II Isaiah for the sake of convenience, but in all the poetry of the

Old Testament these principles hold. The 'long' lines which occur sporadically in 3 | 3 verse, even those which may actually have been read or recited with four stresses, were technically conceived as three-beat lines, as was said above.

There is here intended no denial of the existence of a genuine 4 | 4 meter in the Old Testament. This meter, as a development from the 3 | 3 form, would be very natural indeed; and there are numerous passages—though far less in number than is commonly supposed—in which the evidence of a succession of four-beat verses is strong. Since, however, there is no such instance in II Isaiah, the subject need not be treated here.

The Place of the Stress.—The stress in the measure ordinarily coincides with the principal massoretic accent of a word. As was remarked above, the tradition, as far as the reading of poetry is concerned, is generally sound. As a matter of course, it is often the secondary accent of the word that receives the stress. It also very frequently happens that a single word of several syllables is divided between two measures and receives two stresses. An example from 55:9 was given above. Any one of the separate particles may receive the stress, and so also may the syllable formed by the inseparable particles at the beginning of a word. It is frequently the case that the conjunction *waw* is thus accented: 34:9, *wá'ăpharăh lĕgophríth;* 60:2, *wá'ăraphĕl lĕ'ummîm;* 41:2, *ŭmĕlakîm yarád;* 62:3, *úṣeníph mĕlūkă,* and many others.

The immediate juxtaposition of two stresses was of course generally avoided, and I know of no absolutely certain instance of the kind in II Isaiah. There is nothing to prohibit the occasional use of this arrangement, however, and it might sometimes be very effective. The most interesting passage to illustrate this is 41:28, *wâ'ēre wĕ'ēn ĭš,* repeated with very slight variation in 59:16, *wayyar kĭ ēn ĭš.* It would be possible to read *wâ'ēré* (compare *wáyyĕrá* in Ezek. 19:11), and even to vocalize and read *wáyyēré* in 59:16. If these lines are recited in the slow and impressive way which certainly was intended by their author, the stresses will be hardly noticeable; still, the effect is unquestionably more striking when the line ends with the two emphasized monosyllables *én ĭš.* It is also worthy of notice that the particle *ēn* is stressed in both 51:18 and 63:5, which are closely parallel to the passages under discussion. Another instance, hardly doubtful, is 42:13*b.* Others, if our text is correct, are 44:19 (end) and 60:15 (end). 40:4*a* may perhaps be added.

As is well known, the word-accent may vary according to the

requirement of the meter. A very familiar example is 51 : 9,
where '*ūrī* is stressed in two different ways. The word which begins vs. 17 in this chapter was probably read *hith'órĕrī*, though in
its second occurrence accented on the final syllable. The pronoun
of the first person is sometimes accented *anókī* (*e. g.*, 43 : 25); the
pronoun of the second person masculine may accent either syllable (44 : 21). The demonstrative *ēlle* is stressed on the final syllable in 40 : 26; 44 : 21*a*; 49 : 21*b* (twice); and in 66 : 2 on the *second*
occurrence; and there are other examples of the kind. The chief
accent of verb forms is frequently shifted; even the massoretic
punctuation notes such cases, *e. g.*, 44 : 3 (*éṣṣoq*) and 15 (*yísgod*),
40 : 7 (*nášĕbā*), etc. The *niph'al* imperfect is sometimes accented
on the second syllable. Unquestionable instances may be seen in
Ezek. 26 : 13 f., *ló yiššáma' 'ód* and *ló tibbáne 'ōd;* and numerous
lines in II Isaiah are best read with this accentuation. Whether
segholate nouns might be stressed on the final syllable is perhaps
questionable. The regular pronunciation in Aramaic would make
this natural enough, to be sure, and there are other parallels; for
example, Burckhardt, *Travels in Arabia* (1829), vol. II, 411, notes
that *laḥm* was pronounced *lăḥém* in Mekka. In such instances as
Prov. 23 : 2 and 3 the line certainly sounds better when the stress
is thus applied. The name *Yahwè* is sometimes stressed on the
penult; 40 : 7 gives one example, 59 : 19 another, and more could
be added. 63 : 16 is best read:

> *kī Ábrahām ló yĕda'ánū*
> *wĕYísra'ēl ló hikkiránū.*

In Zech. 9 : 5 we read *Ašqĕlón* (the name of the city) at the beginning of the verse, and *Ášqĕlōn* at the end. There are other similar
instances.

Long and Short Lines.—In Hebrew poetry the typical measure,
or 'foot,' contains two or three full syllables, with the stress upon
the last. Since this corresponds to the average length and normal
accentuation of the various forms of noun, adjective, verb, and
the longer adverbs and prepositions, it follows that the rhythmic
movement of Hebrew verse is given an inevitable regularity and
distinctness, at once by the customary word-stress and by the
grammatical disposition of the clause, to a degree hardly equalled
in the accentual verse of other languages. Along with the full syllables there is generally a sufficiency of reduced vowels to lighten
the line and render it musical. One rhythmic foot is especially
characteristic: namely, a short syllable followed by two long syl-

lables, of which the final one receives the accent. The three-beat line containing one or more such measures represents especially well both the normal length of the line and the swing of the meter. Thus, for example, 45 : 2:

> *dalĕthóth nĕchūšā́ ăšabbḗr,*
> *ūbĕrīchḗ barzél ăgaddḗ'.*

Or the line in 51 : 6:

> *wĕyōšĕbéhā kĕmō kĕ́n yĕmūthûn.*

The pretonic long syllable produces a more stately effect than the short syllable of the anapest; the line has a gravity like that given by the second foot of the Alcaic meter, or of the Tawīl in Arabic. There is considerable variation from this typical length, however. In a passage the tone of which is didactic or argumentative the line is likely to move slowly, either with accumulation of syllables, or else in the very briefest compass; in either case with a somewhat prosaic effect. An example of the former kind, 54 : 9:

> *kīmē Nóḥ zōth lî ăšer nišbá'tī*
> *mē'ăbór mē Nōḥ 'ṓd 'al hā'áreṣ.*

Compare also such lines as 41 : 7 (end), 49 : 7, third clause (see the note), 55 : 10 (end).

For examples of the short line, see 41 : 21, *qărĕbū rîbēkḗm;* 44 : 12, *ūphắ'al báppechăm;* 45 : 18, *bṓrē háššamáyim;* and the sharply vigorous lines (41 : 24), *hĕ́n attĕm mē'áyin | ūphó'olkĕm mē'éphes!*

It is hardly necessary to say that in passages in which the excitement of the poet runs high, from whatever emotion, the movement of the verse is especially unimpeded and regular, often approaching syllabic meter. There are examples on almost every page; such passages as 34 : 11–17, 41 : 2 ff., 45 : 1–5, 53 : 1–8, 63 : 1–6 may be mentioned as typical.

Because of the elasticity of the measure it frequently happens that the minor member of a 3 | 2 line appears longer than the major member, and in another context might be read with three stresses. Thus, 47 : 11*a*, 49 : 21*a*, 57 : 5*a*, etc. The clause at the end of 40 : 10 forms a three-beat line, while at the end of 62 : 11, in precisely the same form, it is given *two* beats.

The question occasionally arises, whether a single word, twice stressed, might constitute the minor member of a 3 | 2 line. In English verse of the comic-newspaper variety, for instance, the word 'impecuniosity' might figure as a line of four beats. Examination shows that this device was regarded as inelegant in Hebrew, as in other languages. I find no example in II Isaiah.

Certain words and phrases have generally been recognized as standing outside the metric scheme. Such are *wayyōmer* in 49 : 6, *wĕ'amar* in 57 : 14, an occasional 'Thus saith Yahwè' (50 : 1, 65 : 8), etc. See the indication of these in the Translation. There is sometimes room for difference of opinion as to such an introductory formula, when it would be possible to include it in the verse.

The Cæsura.—The metric division of the verse may cut through any construction. The close sequence of subject and predicate is interrupted, for instance, in 44 : 10:

mî yaṣar êl, ūphésel | nasák, lĕbíltî hō'íl.

Compare 49 : 14, 57 : 18, and 59 : 2*b*. The two elements of a 'construct' unit are divided in such verses as 35 : 2:

hĕmmā yir'ú kĕbód | Yahwê, hădár ĕlōhĕnŭ.

Compare 41 : 14, 66 : 24*a*, and Deut. 32 : 24. In the majority of the examples here given we should naturally recite the verse according to the scheme 2 | 2 | 2. This possibility is only occasional, however, and in all such cases the verses are certainly to be regarded as 3 | 3. We do not know, to be sure, the manner in which this poetry was recited. The rate of utterance, the intonation, the prominence given to the stressed syllables are significant details. In the modern Orient we are accustomed to a deliberate, singsong recital, with a decided protraction of the long or accented syllable. Whether the tradition of ancient Palestine resembled this, or was more in the manner of our Western reading of poetry, we have no sure means of determining.

In the 3 | 2 line the same division of grammatical constructions is common; perhaps even more so than in the 3 | 3 verse, as might be expected from the inherent character of this compound line, as previously described. See for illustration 47 : 9*b*:

bĕrób kĕšapháik, bĕ'oṣmáth | chăbaráik mĕ'ód ||.

Compare also Ps. 40 : 5*a*, 119 : 18 and 19, Lam. 2 : 14*b*, 3 : 20, etc. In such cases as these, again, the scheme of the meter remains unchanged; it is a mistake to speak of a 2 | 3 line.

On the basis of the frequent usage in quantitative meters (in Greek or Arabic poetry, for instance) we should expect that in occasional instances in Hebrew verse the cæsura might bisect a single word. See Goodell, *Chapters on Greek Metric*, p. 199. A virtual example occurs even in Horace, Od. 4, viii, 17. I have recognized no such instance in II Isaiah, unless 66 : 23b should be treated in this way.

Poetic Forms.—There is considerable difficulty here; for, although some forms are well known, there are others of which the explanation is doubtful, and we still know very imperfectly the extent to which they were used and the varieties which were permissible. Some instances are doubtless obscured by the massoretic vocalization.

Especially familiar is the use of the indefinite *mō* (originally *mā*) combined with particles, as in *běmō, kěmō, lěmō* (or *lǎmō,* which may represent either *lām* or *lō*), etc., merely for the sake of the meter. Also *minnī* (46 : 3) for *min, aphsī* (47 : 8, 10) for *ephes.* Possibly the *pěqach-qōch* in 61 : 1 originated in poetic license. A noun in the singular number is frequently used where the plural, required by the sense, would overload the meter. Thus *'am* in 42 : 6 and 49 : 8, *yām* in 60 : 5, *ĭš* in 52 : 14, etc. In 49 : 7 (see the critical note) *bězōh* seems to replace *bāzūi* by poetic license, while *měthō'ab gōi* (so to be read) certainly means "abhorred of nations."

In the forms of the verb, aside from the imperfect plural ending in *-ūn,* there is the very frequent slurring of the vowel of *waw* conversive, where the 'consecutive' imperfect is demanded by the context. In many cases, such as 44 : 17, it seems probable that the vocalization was original, the purpose being to render the line more musical. There are other cases, however, which seem to require the explanation now given by many scholars, that the Massorites, in their capacity as exegetes and with homiletic purpose, saw predictions where past tenses had been intended (*e. g.,* 63 : 3).

There are many examples of bold ellipsis, obviously in the sole interest of meter. Attention is generally called to these in the Notes. See for illustration 34 : 11 (with the first word of vs. 12, which belongs to the preceding context); 41 : 20 and 25; 42 : 1; the omission of *qōl* in vss. 2 and 11; 48 : 9, 21; 51 : 1; 53 : 3; 57 : 17; 59 : 10; 62 : 5b. Several of these examples are still unrecognized by commentators, who would needlessly suspect or alter the text.

A final caution against the attempt to make use of the massoretic accentual system, as though it stood in some direct relation to the original meter, will not be out of place. It is quite usual to see the main components of this superimposed and often very unsuitable notation appealed to as having authority, by those who are dealing with the technical form of the original verse. The student of Hebrew metrics, however, is better off without any of this baggage. Even the *maqqēph,* which is so commonly treated as a sort of hyphen belonging to the consonant text (and is even printed in some unpointed texts!), is merely one of the marks belonging to the mediæval scheme of cantillation, and has no other value. We need every help that is available, in our difficult and often baffling study; but attention to the details of this obsolete and irrecoverable musical setting will hinder oftener than it will aid our quest.

CHAPTER X

RECONSTRUCTION BY METER AND 'STROPHE'

The importance of metric form as an aid to the criticism of the Hebrew text, in the poetical portions of the Old Testament, is now well understood. In the translation and critical notes which here follow considerable attention is paid to this criterion, as will be seen. In many instances the slight changes suggested, involving the alteration, omission, or addition of a word, will commend themselves as probable, often because the same changes have already been shown by other investigation to be necessary or desirable. In other cases it may be that the critical proceeding will be questioned, with good reason, as arbitrary and precarious. There is great need of caution, in the present imperfect state of our knowledge of the Hebrew poetic art.

All the most recent commentators on the Hebrew poetical books have made great use of the metric line, the couplet, and the 'strophe' in criticising the traditional text; and with hardly any exception have undertaken a far-reaching reconstruction, involving almost constant emendation of the verbal form and involving the recognition of extensive loss, corruption, transposition, and interpolation.

The poems of the Second Isaiah have received very drastic treatment of this sort, as will appear. The purpose of the present Chapter is to protest against the uncritical method of procedure which has been so generally adopted and with such unfortunate result; to emphasize once more the *danger* of 'reconstruction' without a careful preliminary search for the plan which the author may have had in mind, and the laws, very imperfectly known to us, which he may have been obeying.

No scholar can fail to see that these monuments of ancient poetic art, survivals of Arabian or Hebrew or other great literatures, have suffered to some extent, often considerably, in the long process of transmission. It is easy to appreciate this fact, but to proceed to reconstruct is nearly always to enter upon a desperate task. Profound study, aided by a literary insight which is both sober and sympathetic, can hope now and then to remove spurious verses or verse-members and restore well-understood forms on the basis of conjecture. An easy-going 'rectification' on an extensive scale

173

is the worst thing that can happen. There is a clear difference between occasional surgery and habitual butchery. Professor Cheyne's text of the Book of Isaiah, printed in the *Polychrome Bible*, is the work of a very learned and painstaking scholar, interested only in ascertaining the truth, but perhaps too inclined to adopt the conclusions of others. From the poems which I regard as the work of the Second Isaiah he has excised *88 three-beat lines* (an amount equivalent to about one chapter), the ground of the removal being in most cases the wish to restore a uniform pattern. This count does not include the few lines which I also, in common with Cheyne and others, regard as secondary; nor do I attempt to enumerate here the lines *added* by conjecture, the rows of asterisks indicating supposed gaps, the postulated fragments of lines left partially filled out, etc.—all called into being by a too generally accepted theory. All the poetical portions of the Old Testament have suffered in like manner. For abundant illustration, see the writings of Bickell, Budde, Duhm, Marti, Cheyne, Briggs, Rothstein, Cobb, Sievers, and others who have treated the subject of Hebrew metrics. The attempt, by scholars of note, to force our Hebrew text into a metrical strait-jacket which fits nowhere is a remarkable fact. Some one who had little feeling for poetry must have given the first impulse; others then followed without subjecting the theory to any thorough scientific test.

Matthew Arnold, in his little volume entitled *Isaiah of Jerusalem* (1883), p. 34, remarks on the "sense of security" which is so necessary to the enjoyment of a great work. To what extent can we be confident that we are studying the work of the prophet or psalmist himself, rather than that of his modern editors? In truth, the sense of security is hopelessly gone when we examine the grounds on which this extravagant reshaping of Hebrew poetry is undertaken. The proffered reasons, exegetical, stylistic, or derived from a loosely used critical apparatus, are usually trivial and sometimes so evidently artificial as to be amusing. The one source of real difficulty, generally speaking, is the commentator's own shibboleth. Take, for instance, Rothstein's treatment of Ps. 19 : 7 in his *Grundzüge des hebräischen Rhythmus*, p. 231. This happens to be one of the very many cases in which a 'weighted' verse is employed for rhetorical effect at the close of one of the main divisions of a poem.* The verse reads as follows:

* In this case the first half of the poem, vss. 1–7, is in the 3 | 3 meter finished off with a 3 | 3 | 3 verse; the second half, which is lyric and personal, is in the 3 | 2 meter, and is likewise ended with a 3 | 3 | 3 verse.

From the end of the heavens he goes forth, | and to the end proceeds
in his circuit, | nor is anything hid from his heat.

The current theory, however, recognizes only a bipartite metrical
division, and Rothstein is therefore obliged to suppose some accident to the text. A verse-member must be added or subtracted.
He comments: 'It is very difficult to see what is meant by "to
the end" ('ad qĕṣōth) in connection with "the end" (qĕṣē) mentioned at the beginning of the verse, especially as the circuit of
the sun is spoken of. Possibly some cosmic-mythologic conception
came into the mind of an interpolator. Nevertheless the phrase
remains obscure. I therefore regard the last clause of the verse,
which it would otherwise be necessary to omit, as having originally formed the second half-verse.' He therefore removes the
middle member of the verse as secondary.* The 'obscure mytho-
logical conception' is obviously simply this, that the heaven has
two "ends," one where the sun rises and another where it sets.
The most of the ancient and modern writers who have described
the sun's course have used similar words. A good example of a
parallel and likewise very familiar use is Matt. 24 : 31. The reason
for drastic revision given in the foregoing example is typical of
what can be seen on almost every page of recent commentaries on
the Hebrew Psalms or Prophets. Verses and strophes *must* be cut
to the supposed pattern, and some pretext must be found or manufactured. One is now and then tempted to mutter, with Horace's
impudent slave, *aut insanit homo aut versus facit.*

The question whether the Second Isaiah makes use of *strophic
forms* is one of especial interest and importance, particularly in
view of recent criticism of the text. It should be observed at the
outset that there is nothing in the history of Semitic poetry to
lead us, in advance, to expect strophes here. The classical Arabic
poetry knew no division into stanzas; Syriac poetry—except in so
far as some of it was intended to be chanted antiphonally, or with
musical accompaniment—was also free from this restriction. The
Babylonian and Assyrian epics, legends, oracles, and hymns were
not strophic, though written in symmetrically divided columns.

Turning to the Old Testament, the reader will perhaps be surprised to see how little evidence of any arrangement in stanzas of
equal length is to be found in Hebrew poetry. Even in the Psalms,

---

* Duhm, on the other hand, in his *Commentary on the Psalms*, cuts off the
third member on the ground that it "hinkt nach" and is evidently only a
prosaic fragment.

where we should look first of all for instances of this kind, it is remarkable how very few and insignificant the examples are. It is natural that an order-loving mind should treat successive ideas, in a metrical composition, in passages of the same length. The Semitic feeling for number and symmetry is a well-recognized characteristic of the race, and we might well expect that in such liturgical compositions as make up the Hebrew Psalter would be found, if anywhere, poetry in strophic forms. But on the contrary, it is in only a few cases—noteworthy exceptions—that strophes are to be seen; quatrain following quatrain in unbroken succession, or other divisions corresponding to one another in number of lines, or in other points of structure. The conclusion should be obvious, that the stanza of a given length was not one of the recognized features of Hebrew poetry in general.

Returning to II Isaiah, we are struck at once by the prominence given to the strophic arrangement in the modern criticism of the text. In Duhm's translation, nearly every chapter is divided off, wholly or in part, into verses of an equal number of lines. In his note on 54 : 3 Duhm remarks incidentally, as though stating a settled fact, that the poetry of II Isaiah is constructed in general in stanzas of four lines each ("denn auch hier haben wir wie in den meisten Gedichten Dtjes.s Vierzeiler").* Cheyne, in his reconstruction of the Hebrew text of the book, and Marti, in his *Commentary*, follow in the same path.

It must not be supposed, however, that these poems, as they stand in our Hebrew Bible, lend themselves readily to this process of grouping in stanzas. On the contrary, it is only on the supposition of a very corrupt text, hopeless of satisfactory reconstruction and therefore a true *corpus vile*, that any considerable results in this direction can be obtained. The amount of space given, in such an extended commentary as that of Marti, to the emendation of the text in the interests of 'meter' and 'strophe' is very considerable. The tinkering undertaken for the purpose of recovering the supposed original uniformity is not occasional, but constant. Or take, for example, any one of the pages in Cheyne's text where the division into strophes is attempted. All looks as regular as a pattern of wall-paper; but inspection shows that this regularity was not simply observed and pointed out; it was achieved. Pieces are cut out and lines refashioned, or a bit is added here and there. Rows of asterisks are frequent, and often two rows appear in a

---

*The early editions of the Commentary spoke of "vier Distichen," by an oversight which was corrected in the third edition.

single stanza; not because there is any evidence of the loss of lines
in these particular places, but simply because the number of lines
in our traditional text is greater, or less, than the wall-paper
theory demands. In short, these 'strophes' have been hewn and
hacked into shape, and the chips at the bottom of the page tell
part of the story.

Again, the division of the poem into equal stanzas, which our
authorities feel constrained to make and to accept from one another, is not always the logical division, and the effect is not infrequently unhappy. It would be easy to give copious illustration
of this, but it may suffice to cite an example or two—typical, and
not more striking than many others—from chapter 53, a poem in
which the greater part of the material does in fact happen to fall
into divisions of four lines each. In Cheyne's translation a stanza
is made to begin with the second half of 52 : 15 and end with 53 : 1;
thus:

> For that which had not been told them, do they see,
> And that which they had not heard, do they perceive.
> Who indeed can yet believe our revelation? *
> And the arm of Yahwè,—to whom has it disclosed itself?

Duhm and Marti see the necessity of beginning a stanza with 53 : 1,
but avoid one awkward result only to adopt another. Vs. 2, which
is an obvious unit, is ruthlessly cut in two by them; half is un-
happily mated with vs. 1, while the other half is made to form
a stanza with the second half of 52 : 14! An equally striking example of critical ruthlessness is the union of the close of vs. 11
with the beginning of vs. 12, which has been adopted by all three
of these commentators:†

> My righteous Servant shall justify many,
> For he shall bear their iniquities.
> Therefore shall he receive a portion with the great,
> And shall divide the spoil with the strong,
>
> Because he poured out his soul, etc.

The theory which so frequently convicts the Hebrew poet of lack
of literary taste needs very strong support. See also, for a few

---

* This is an impossible rendering; adopted, evidently, because of the conviction that this line *must* in some way be made the immediate sequel of the
preceding line.

† The renderings vary considerably, but no one of them justifies the arbitrary proceeding at this point.

examples out of many, 42 : 11 ff., 18–25; 51 : 12 ff., 17–20; 52 : 1 ff., 10 ff.; 59 : 14–16; 66 : 5.

It is easy to see that in Hebrew poetry the minor logical divisions of the subject-matter must very frequently occupy just four 'lines,' that is, two metric 'verses.' The Hebrew sentence, like the Semitic sentence in general, is normally short, and simply constructed. Because of the principle of parallelism, with its repetition, *one* double line is ordinarily not enough for the expression of an idea. We should be left with the impression of abruptness, of a thing half constructed and left unfinished. The triad 3 | 3 | 3 is also likely to be insufficient, besides lacking the balance which is such an essential feature. It may frequently be employed for the sake of variety, either alone or in a series of consecutive verses in which it temporarily creates a new symmetry;* but it must always be exceptional, even when its compass could be made to suffice. The quatrain, on the other hand, is naturally suited to embody the short sentences which are so numerous; and is likely to be employed again and again, quite involuntarily, in passages where the movement of the poem is rapid or the feeling especially strong. There is this amount of truth, but no more, in the postulate of 'Vierzeiler' poems which plays such an important part in the modern German treatment of Hebrew verse. The period consisting of two double lines is by far the most common logical division of any Hebrew poem. It becomes a vicious unit only when it is insisted upon.

As for the supposed strophes consisting of a number of lines greater than four, it is sufficient to observe that in poetry—and even in prose, though in less degree—the rhetorical instinct of the writer very frequently leads him to marshal his thought in symmetrical periods; naturally, and without conscious effort; here and there, sometimes in a considerable succession of sentences of nearly equivalent length, but without any sustained uniformity. It is this fact which has afforded the basis for the imaginary division of numerous Hebrew poems, including many of those of II Isaiah, into stanzas of five, six, seven, or more lines. The fixed limit is Procrustean bed in nearly every case, and mutilation, or a tasteless arrangement, is the assured result. A typical example, which may serve for illustration, is Duhm's attempt to force chapter 47 into stanzas of seven lines.

I have thought it interesting to apply the test of accidental uniformity to casually selected specimens of classical Arabic poetry,

* Ps. 93, for example, seems to consist entirely of triads.

where we know with certainty that no strophic division was recognized. Here, as in Hebrew poetry, short sentences are the rule, and the basis of construction is the line of two members. I turned the leaves of Nöldeke's *Delectus Veterum Carminum Arabicorum*, selecting at random, in various parts of the little volume, poems of sufficient length to yield a satisfactory result. The poem on pp. 1 f. consists of twenty-three lines. Aside from line 5 (numbered 7 on the page), which may either be regarded as standing alone or joined to the two preceding, the whole falls naturally into stanzas of four members each, as any one can see. The shorter poem on pp. 2 f., divided according to the subject-matter, consists of four distinct 'quatrains.' Page 19, a single introductory verse followed by four quatrains (the first two might be taken together as a stanza of eight members). Pages 19 f., three distinct quatrains make up the poem. Pages 44 f., a famous composition in sixteen lines, made up as follows: The introductory *nasib*, two lines (*i. e.*, four members, as in the cases above). The poet lies awake and observes the stars, two lines. Reflections on the death of his brother, two lines. The murder of Bujair, in revenge, three lines. Thus far, the poet has busied himself with his own thoughts and deeds; now he turns to the battle of the tribes. The slain warrior, dragged from his place by a huge vulture, two lines. The rush and clash of the battling forces, two lines. The weapons and steeds of the poet's own tribesmen, three lines. The fact that each of the two main divisions of the poem ends in a 'stanza' of three lines is, like the other instances of regularity, purely accidental. Pages 45 f., a poem made up of logical divisions of 2, 2, 3, and 3 lines. Pages 67 f., similar divisions of 4, 2, 2, and 2 lines. Pages 88 f., a poem of twelve lines, which could be made into quatrains as successfully as any poem of II Isaiah, though lines 7–10 really form a single unit.

It is plain to see that by occasionally adding or subtracting a line, and changing a word here and there, the old Arabian poems could very easily be reduced to a strophic pattern. They were not originally so constructed, however, nor was the bulk of the Hebrew poetry of the Prophets, the Psalms, and the Wisdom books. There are, indeed, as was said above, *occasional* strophic forms, especially in the Psalter; and such are of course necessary where there is alphabetic arrangement, and to be expected where there is a refrain.

It will perhaps be useful to attempt an illustration of prevalent methods of reconstructing Hebrew poetry by the use of a modern example. Here is an English poem of four stanzas which is evidently the work of a master, and in its original form must have been a model of its kind. It seems to have suffered considerably in the process of transmission, partly from editorial hands, partly through mere accident. The form in which it is now current is the following:

> Sunset and evening star,
> 　And one clear call for me!
> And may there be no moaning of the bar,
> 　When I put out to sea,
>
> But such a tide as moving seems asleep,
> 　Too full for sound and foam,
> When that which drew from out the boundless deep
> 　Turns again home.
>
> Twilight and evening bell,
> 　And after that the dark!
> And may there be no sadness of farewell,
> 　When I embark;
>
> For tho' from out our bourne of Time and Place
> 　The flood may bear me far,
> I hope to see my Pilot face to face
> 　When I have crost the bar.

A little study—a very little—makes it plain that the poem was composed in that favorite variety of meter in which the alternate lines have respectively four and three accents. The original lines can be restored by conjecture; not always with certainty, indeed, yet with a very high degree of probability.

First stanza: "Evening" was originally written twice, with an intervening comma. One of the two words then fell out, by a most common accident. In the third line, the words "of the" are metrically superfluous and weaken the phrase. They are certainly the careless addition of a copyist. *Second stanza:* The first line is too long by one rhythmic beat. The word "moving" is plainly secondary. That which is moving does *not* seem to be asleep; the author of the poem is made to say a foolish thing. The origin of the superfluous word was a reader's comment. Some impressionable person recorded in the margin of a copy his feeling that this is a *moving* stanza.* From the margin the word crept into the text, as

---

*This is "der fromme Leser," whose marginal "Stosseufzer" are so often detected, in the attempt to restore the original pattern. Thus in Is. 40:7; 48:11; 55:7; 63:16 (Marti), and numerous passages in the Psalter.

usual. In the third line, "boundless" is too commonplace, as well as metrically impossible. The poet himself would certainly have spared us this overworked adjective. The last line of the stanza is plainly defective. It is also grammatically open to question. The verb is intransitive, and a preposition is to be expected; we speak of "turning *toward*" a person or a place. It is likely, moreover, that the word "back" originally followed the verb. Where the text is manifestly corrupt, the restoration should not be half-hearted. *Third stanza:* Lines 1 and 3 have suffered alike, each is defective by just two syllables. The second line furnishes the clew; the correlated phrases "*at first*," "*after that*," and "*at last*" were in the original text. An editor removed two of them, probably because he felt them to be superfluous. But meter has its rights. In the third line, "sadness of farewell," instead of the more simple and touching "sad farewell," is an alteration of the same sort as that which was recognized in the third line of the first stanza. *Fourth stanza:* The superfluous word "bourne" must have slipped in from some other poem. In the third line, "face to face" may have originated in simple dittography; but it is more likely that we have here a mixture of two readings: "to see my Pilot's face" and "to meet my Pilot face to face." Which of the two is the original the meter decides infallibly.

We have now before us the poem as it left the hand of its author:

> Sunset and evening, evening star,
>   And one clear call for me!
> And may there be no moaning bar,
>   When I put out to sea,
>
> But such a tide as seems asleep,
>   Too full for sound and foam,
> When that which drew from out the deep
>   Turns back again toward home.
>
> Twilight at first, and evening bell,
>   And after that the dark!
> And may there be no sad farewell,
>   When I at last embark;
>
> For tho' from out our Time and Place
>   The flood may bear me far,
> I hope to see my Pilot's face
>   When I have crost the bar.

Those who are not thoroughly familiar with the recent criticism of Hebrew poetry on the ground of metric theory will be likely to think the foregoing 'specimen' trivial or unfair. It is neither. There is no exaggeration here, every 'critical' proceeding in this pitiful reconstruction, including the 'grammatical improvement' in the last line of the second stanza, can be abundantly paralleled from the standard commentaries. Since it is not a matter of minor importance, how some of the greatest literary productions of antiquity are being handled by those who are generally looked upon, and followed, as the leading exponents of modern scholarship, there is no need of apology for this manner of presenting the challenge.

There is plenty of sound criticism of Hebrew poetry on the basis of metrical requirement. This consideration, unaided by any other, is sometimes a sure guide to the emendation of words and the restoration of damaged sentences, as in Is. 47 : 3b and 4a. It is very often possible to say with certainty that this or that single word is secondary, where the line is surely overloaded and there is some other cogent reason for suspecting interpolation. Similarly, where the line is too short, and the testimony of an ancient version is unequivocal, a word may be inserted with confidence. Textual criticism has thus profited greatly in the present generation, and every important commentary or technical treatise has made its contribution. These critical processes have been far too carelessly used, however, and with inadequate study of the details of Hebrew poetic art. In the demonstration of strophic forms, in particular, very little real progress has been made in modern times, and the critical operations by which such forms have been obtained are usually open to grave suspicion. It may be, indeed, that traces of strophic arrangement will eventually be pointed out in some poem or poems of the Second Isaiah; there is no impossibility in the supposition. I can only say, for my own part, that I have thus far been unable to discover anything of the sort; and that I feel quite certain that the Hebrew poet, if he could have foreseen the stanzas into which his verse is hacked and plastered by our modern school, would have shuddered—and then have smiled.

CHAPTER XI

CHARACTERISTIC LITERARY FEATURES

The poems of our nameless Prophet of the Messianic Age have a strongly marked character of their own. Certain literary habits, of which a few are both conspicuous and unusual, show themselves in every part of the book. Personal characteristics are also revealed, more or less distinctly, to such an extent that we can form some idea of the man himself in other aspects than those of gifted author or great Hebrew evangelist.

His notable reserve, the studious intent with which he keeps his own personality in the background, has often been remarked in the preceding pages. In spite of the lyric character of much of the poetry there is in it nothing resembling the *mē'ai mē'ai*, "My heart, my heart!"; "O Lord, thou hast allured me, and I was led astray"; "Cursed be the day in which I was born!" of Jeremiah (4:19; 20:7, 14), or even the quieter records of personal experience which are so important a feature of the prophecies of Isaiah, Amos, Hosea, and several others. The Second Isaiah never makes mention of himself.

His deep feeling, breaking forth now and again into passionate expression, has especially impressed and attracted the readers of his work. No Hebrew prophet, not even Hosea, shows so profound, so overwhelming a conviction of the love of God for his people. No other prophet manifests such intense loyalty to Israel, such affection for Jerusalem. In his constant portrayal of the contrast between the present sin and misery and the glorious future, always so vivid before his eyes, his emotion runs through the whole gamut from exultation to anguish of soul, revealing a heart that could never be lukewarm, but was always burning, when intent on great themes. In the current interpretation of Second Isaiah this emotion is held to be exaggerated. It is sometimes mildly ridiculed, as in Professor Duhm's commentary; others apologize for it, and attempt (without success) to excuse it; the supposed message of the 'exilic prophet' could not justify his extremes of language. But the historical situation and the prophet's main theme have been completely misapprehended. To one standing where he stood and seeing what he saw, exaggeration was hardly possible.

In his denunciation of the openly unfaithful of his people, the large and influential party of renegades, the devotees of miscellaneous gods, the prophet shows his capacity for other than tender emotions. When we hear his explosion of wrath in chapter 57, we could almost believe that he has momentarily lost control of himself; but the discord is immediately resolved, and with such art as to make the startling passage seem (as indeed it is) an essential element in the composition. Of this, more presently.

No personal quality of the prophet is more evident than his kindliness. Attention is frequently called to this in the Commentary, and also in the Chapter treating of "The Attitude toward the Foreign Peoples." All his utterances are characterized by a broad humanity, a sympathy with all mankind, showing both his inborn disposition and his long experience among men. "Experience engenders hope," as the Apostle to the Gentiles once declared (Rom. 5:4), and no man has felt this faith in human nature more strongly than the Second Isaiah. The vehemence of his denunciation is often relieved as it passes over into warning, expostulation, commiseration, tenderness. In every picture of gloom some brightening touch is sure to appear; there is hope of repentance.

He writes of the foreign oppressors with tolerance and a genuine solicitude, declaring them to be children of the One God, who will not suffer them all to perish. Every Gentile nation will have its share in the joys to come. In dealing with the fate of the unrelenting foes of Yahwè and Israel, in the catastrophe at the end of the present age, he will not dwell upon the scene of horror, nor paint it in detail. He would deserve no especial praise, to be sure, for abstaining from brutal realism, which was generally shunned in the earlier literature of the ancient world; Greek poetry shows few traces of it until long after the time of Second Isaiah. But his avoidance of the terms of human distress in making mention of the final clash is very noticeable, since the theme is one which must frequently recur, in the eschatology with which he is constantly occupied. He does not say to his people bluntly, 'You shall slay your enemies,' but rather, 'You shall seek them and not find them'; 'You shall be a threshing sledge shattering hills and mountains.' When he has occasion to speak of Yahwè's 'mighty slaughter,' in the great day, he turns immediately from the bloodshed of men to the figure of sacrificial beasts or of the pressed grapes of the vintage.

His kindly interest in dumb animals, the birds of the air and beasts of the field, is very frequently manifested. He introduces them again and again in his most striking pictures, even dwelling at length (in chapter 34) on their peaceful life, and representing them as under God's immediate protection (34 : 16 f.; 43 : 20; 63 : 13 f.). He looks with a friendly eye on all the objects of nature, the trees, the flowers of the wild, the running brooks, the desert plain, the heavenly bodies, and loves to include them in his pictures of the coming day.

No interpretation of the prophet is adequate which does not include the sense of humor to which his writings testify. This is perhaps the quality that we should least expect to see. It might seem in keeping neither with the subject-matter nor with the writer's deep and even passionate earnestness. There is no poem of the collection in which lightness of touch would be tolerable. But there is in fact no lapse from seriousness, nor the slightest evidence of a wish to be entertaining. The prophet's grim humor is less for his readers than for himself, and the way in which it sometimes comes to the surface in the most unlikely places gives evidence of a deep-rooted personal trait. See the Notes on 41 : 5–7; 44 : 9 f.; 47 : 14; 59 : 6; 65 : 25, and the Introduction to chapters 41 and 47. The man who wrote 41 : 5 ff. was accustomed to see the humorous side of any subject or situation. The passage stands at the beginning of the prophet's great argument from history. Yahwè issues his challenge, and the nations of the earth are summoned to appear as witnesses while their gods make reply. The picture is at once given a comical turn, and the writer heightens the effect by leaving it half finished, at the point where the patron deities are 'taking a firm stand'—with the help of nails securely driven.* The same tendency to imagine an amusing scene appears in 44 : 12–20, where the lively details testify to the spirit of the man who conceived them. Other examples are 46 : 1 ff., the gods who undertake to carry their worshippers out of danger, but themselves fall down, like jaded beasts, and are dragged away by the enemy; and 56 : 10, the watch-dogs unable to bark. These passages, with their testimony to the poet's quiet and not unkindly appreciation of the ludicrous, in themselves form a striking group. It is not here, however, that we receive the strongest impression of the writer's inveterate habit of mind, but rather from his manner of interjecting single sentences or phrases which give an unexpected turn to the train of thought, suggesting a more or less absurd contrast. The most conspicuous example is the brief

---

* The humor of the equivocal *lō yimmōt* repeated from 40 : 20 (compare also 46 : 7) is lost on some of our commentators, who propose to expunge the words.

'aside,' 47 : 14*b*. The poet threatens the evil counsellors of Babylon with the flames of hell, and then adds: This is not a fire for a
man to sit beside, to warm himself! Very similar in its manner is
the comment appended to 59 : 5*a*. This whimsical parenthesis,
comprising 5*b* and 6*a*, stands in the midst of a most unsparing
arraignment of the wicked in Israel, an eloquent passage, full of
deep feeling. There is of course nothing humorous here, but our
impression of the writer's mental habit is confirmed. Even more
characteristic is 65 : 25, with its allusion, *sotto voce*, to Gen. 3 : 14;
the joke is on the serpent. 57 : 9 is illustrative of the same tendency, though in a different way. Zion takes the royal road to
fortune, and finds herself at the mouth of the Pit. The last clause
of the verse is obviously parenthetical, and the effect of an aside
or an afterthought is heightened by the meter, in which the clause
constitutes an extra verse-member. (Observe that this is true also
of the similar clause in 65 : 25, just cited.) The following little
flashes of calculated absurdity may also be mentioned. 41 : 23:
'Prove your power,' says Yahwè to his supposed rivals, 'so that I
may be frightened and look about for help.' 44 : 8: 'Is there perhaps,' Yahwè asks, 'a God about whom I have not heard?' 60 : 11:
The foreign hosts will enter Jerusalem, in the coming age, 'with
their kings *led*' (not 'leading'). Compare, further, the irony of
40 : 19 f.; 43 : 23*a*, 24*a*; 58 : 2, 3*a*.

The boldness of some of these passages is paralleled or approached in 42 : 13 f.; 45 : 19; 50 : 1*a*, 11; 51 : 9 f.; 57 : 17; 59 : 16
and 63 : 5; 62 : 7; 63 : 15; 66 : 3, but hardly elsewhere in Hebrew
prophecy. The same free spirit is manifest in the play on the words
of holy writ in 34 : 12 and 47 : 1, in the coinage of the proper names
Yešūrūn (Jeshurun), Yaskīl, and Mešullam,* and in the creation
and varied use of the figure of the Servant. The man who wrote
thus felt his authority in the domain of letters as well as in that
of religion. He was conscious of creative power, and had also the
assurance which comes from long experience and acknowledged
leadership. He knew that he had received a divine appointment
and a unique vision of divine truth; but also that he was master
of the technique and resources of his art. He was not a young man.
The literary testimony to this effect agrees with the impression
which we receive from the deeply reasoned liberality of his utterances. He was one of the elders of Israel who had seen much of
the world, and who had already made his genius felt in the literature of his day.

* See the notes on 42 : 19; 44 : 2; and 52 : 13.

The richness and rapid play of the poet's imagination have always aroused wonder, and in the present study frequent attention is given to these properties. The suddenness with which the transition is sometimes made from one figure to another has perplexed those interpreters who have been inclined to look for matter-of-fact description rather than impressionistic art. In chapter 34, for instance, an imaginary 'Edom' is ablaze; its streams are pitch, its dust is brimstone, the smoke ascends forever. Thereupon, without a word of warning, follows an utterly different picture. The doomed land, however located in the poet's imagination, is a desert filled with great ruins; thorns and thistles grow over its palaces and fortresses; birds, beasts, and demons are in undisputed possession. How, demands one commentator, can these beasts maintain themselves on burning sulphur and brimstone? And another suggests that the solution is to be found in a change of authors at this point. The instance is by no means isolated; here and there in other poems a similar leap is taken, equally sudden, even if less striking. Characteristic examples are to be seen in chapters 41, 42, 61, and 63. In no case is there lack of congruity. Contrasting colors are laid on, side by side, in broad strokes, but the result is a calculated harmony. We see here an individual trait, and a corresponding literary procedure which has its own beauties. The personal characteristic is illustrated also, as above mentioned, in the employment of the figure of the 'Servant of Yahwè' in several different ways and even with sudden transition from one way to another (see the Chapter on "The 'Servant' and the Messiah"). There is to be seen here, in the shifting but never confusing application of the figure, something of the same restless energy, exuberant fancy, and refusal to be confined, which we see in the rapid succession of pictured scenes.

It is in the *dramatic* quality of this writer's imagination, however, that his individuality is most strikingly revealed; and this feature calls for special attention, for no other Hebrew author, whether prophet, psalmist, or religious philosopher, even approaches the Second Isaiah in this characteristic.

In poem after poem we can see the instinct of the dramatist, as the varied material is presented in the form of suggested scenes (often kept on the stage for a moment only) with action, dialogue, and soliloquy. A trial scene is several times imagined, the opposing parties being Yahwè and the gods of the nations, each with his own supporting witnesses; thus 41 : 1 ff., 21 ff.; 43 : 8 ff.; 44 : 11; 45 : 20 f.; 48 : 14–16. Yahwè pleads his cause, sometimes at con-

siderable length; his opponents are unable to reply, though their
action is described, and their spoken words are quoted, in 41 : 5–7.
The poem 42 : 1–43 : 7 shows a characteristic succession of scenes
and speakers. Yahwè, addressing the nations, first introduces the
Servant, to whom he then turns with a personal word in vss. 5–7.
The address to the nations is continued in 8 f. and 14–17; Israel
alone is addressed from vs. 18 onward; in 10–13 the Servant is
the speaker; in 14–17 Yahwè, represented as a warrior going out
to battle, utters a very dramatic soliloquy. The structure of this
poem, as I have shown elsewhere, is closely paralleled in 63 : 1–
64 : 11 (see the Introduction to the latter poem). Soliloquies of
the Servant are frequent. As such 49 : 1 ff. and 50 : 4–9 are universally recognized; to these are to be added 61 : 1–3, 10 f.; 62;
and 63 : 7–14. As has been shown, the poet frequently marks the
introduction of a new speaker, or a new scene, by a change of
meter. The poem which constitutes chapter 49 has a highly dramatic flavor; so also have 50, 56 : 9–57 : 21, 61, and 66.

The dialogue which introduces chapter 63 is the most impressive, as well as the most characteristic, of the passages of this
nature in II Isaiah. There are two dialogues of question and answer between Yahwè and his (professing) worshippers, 43 : 23 f.
and 58 : 3 f., the one passage very closely resembling the other;
and also several cases in which imagined sayings are indirectly
quoted, given only for substance, and then refuted. 'Have you
not "honored" me with your offerings, "sated" me with your
sacrifices? Nay, you have burdened me with your sins!' (43 : 23f.).
'These who "name themselves from the holy city," and "rest
themselves on the God of Israel"—not in truth nor by right!'
(48 : 1 f.). 'Yet they "seek me day by day," and "the knowledge
of my ways is their delight"—as though they had not forsaken
the law of their God!' (58 : 2). 'But (you say) "his people are
robbed and plundered, entrapped in holes and hidden in dungeons." Oh that one of you would listen! Who gave up Jacob to
the spoiler?' (42 : 22 ff.).

The repentant and rescued multitudes from the heathen nations are represented in several scenes as the benefactors and
beneficiaries of Israel, and in two remarkable passages they are
brought upon the stage as the speakers, 45 : 14–17 and 53 : 1–9.
In the latter passage there is a good illustration of the 'absolute'
quality of the poet's dramatic imagination. The foreign peoples,
whose address, or soliloquy, begins in the first person plural, of
course have their spokesmen; and when in vs. 8 we read "*my*

people," it is plain that the writer visualized the scene so clearly
that this most effective mode of expression came naturally from
his pen. Numerous other passages attest the vividness with which
he saw the actors and scenes which his fancy created.

The fondness for a dramatic setting, of some sort, is manifest
in every part of the book. Like the poet's humor, it is a personal
quality so deeply rooted that it is bound to appear. The scene or
action is often a mere touch, however, and is rarely sustained for
more than a few verses; the prophet was not writing dramatic
poetry. Very peculiar, and another manifestation of the same
tendency, is his way of interjecting a brief exclamatory passage,
in the form of an apostrophe, with a scenic setting not clearly suggested (or not at all suggested) by the preceding context. Thus,
in chapter 48, in a poem containing only argument and stern admonition, and as the sequel to a passage more quietly didactic than
the rest, we are suddenly transported to the scene of the flight from
Egypt:*

Go forth, flee, with a shout of joy! |
   Proclaim this, make it known;
Bring it forth to the end of the earth: |
   Yahwè redeems his servant Jacob!
They thirsted not, in the desert through which he led them; | water
   he made to flow for them from the crag; | he cleft the rock, and
   the water came pouring out.

So also in chapter 51, in the middle of a discourse uttered by
Yahwè to Israel, vs. 9 suddenly bursts forth:

Awake, awake, put on strength, | arm of Yahwè! ||
Awake as in the days of old, | the times long past. ||
Art not thou he that cleft Rahab, | that pierced the Dragon? |||
Was it not thou who didst dry up the sea, | the water of the abyss? ||

The words which immediately follow show that here, again, there
is allusion to the escape from Egypt and the journey through the
Red Sea and the desert ("a road for the ransomed to pass") to
the promised land. And vs. 11, by its repetition of 35:10, makes
it even more plain that the poet is treating the journey from Egypt
to Canaan as symbolical, the type and promise of a far greater
journey homeward.

* It is the interpolator, as has been shown, who would make this a flight
from Babylonia.

A third example, equally striking, is 52 : 11:

Depart, depart, go out thence; | touch no unclean thing!

It is Egypt again, even a third time, with allusion to the unleavened bread and the implements of sacrifice, and with the verbal
reference to Ex. 12 : 11. The prophet flashes before us his favorite
picture, the 'ransomed' people returning in triumph to Zion from
a land of bondage.

Next in the series comes 57 : 14, here again in the middle of a
discourse spoken by Yahwè, with the twice-repeated imperative
plural (and the preceding wĕ-amar, showing that the words are
not said by Yahwè) making the sudden transition as startling as
possible:

Build up, build up, prepare the way, | take stumbling-blocks from the
    way of my people!

It is the same picture of the great return home, and the same very
remarkable literary proceeding.

Once more, in 62 : 10, the now familiar sound is heard: the two
imperatives, undefined and unexpected, introducing a scene not
hitherto suggested in the poem, the joyful return to Jerusalem
along the 'highway' which was first mentioned in 35 : 8 and 40 : 3;
the deliverance from an 'Egypt' coextensive with the known
world and from a 'desert' which represented every obstacle in
Israel's all but endless path:

Pass through, pass through the gates, | prepare the way of the peo-
    ple! ||
Build up, build up the highway, | make it clear of stones; || lift up an
    ensign over the peoples!

The part which this brilliant fanfare plays in the structure of
the five poems in which it is introduced must not be overlooked.
In each case it is an essential feature of the whole composition,
designed and led up to from the beginning, the return of this
leading motive marking the transition to the principal key, while
also serving to link the poem to the other members of the cycle.

These are not the only instances in which the prophet shows his
liking for dynamic effects; the tendency is illustrated in many
other passages, of which 41 : 25; 52 : 1; 66 : 3 f.; and 66 : 6 may be
taken as typical. Moreover, this very characteristic way of mak-

ing the transition from one scene, or mood, to another, by means of a brief refrain of stereotyped character, has other illustration. No structural feature of these carefully planned compositions is more clearly the property of this author than what I have termed the 'lyric interlude,' appearing at the principal point of division in a poem. Sometimes it is only a momentary burst of song, as in 45 : 8 and 49 : 13; *cf.* 44 : 23 (at the end of a poem); at other times it is a more extended passage, as in 42 : 10–13; 63 : 7–14; and 66 : 10–14; *cf.* 61 : 10 f. (forming the close of its poem).

We have before us, in fact, not only finished works of art, each complete in itself, but also individual habits in their execution which can be traced all the way from chapter 34 to chapter 66. In the introductions to the several poems I have frequently pointed out the manner of their construction; a brief supplementary treatment of the subject here may therefore suffice.

In a few of the poems, namely, 34, 35, 47, 60, and 62, a single subject is developed. The usual mode of construction, however, combines two or more contrasted themes. The beginning of each poem is usually quite obvious even when, as frequently happens, the chapter-division is in the wrong place;* and as the poems have the property of moving to a climax, the ending is likewise unmistakable. As for the component themes, they are the simple motives which would be used by any earnest preacher; often stated, however, in forms characteristic of this author, as may be seen in the list which I have given in Chapter IV. They are combined in many different ways, with the utmost freedom, but now and again according to definite schemes which the reader can hardly fail to recognize.

One plan of construction is like the classical program of a serious musical composition in one of the standard forms. First an introduction, which announces the general subject; then comes the first theme (*a*), with its development; then the second theme (*b*), which in its working out is contrasted with the other; lastly a finale which combines the two. Chapter 40 is one example. Vss. 1 f. give out the subject, the assurance of coming relief, in spite of the present sin and misery. Thereupon *a*, the good tidings, vss. 3–11; *b*, the omnipotence of God, set over against the unbelief and idolatry of the people, vss. 12–26; and the conclusion, vss. 27–31, combining *a* and *b*. Another good example is chapter 58. Vs. 1: Proclaim to the house of Jacob their sins; and yet remember that

* As a matter of fact, *ten* of the twenty-seven poems are injured in this way, as they stand in our Bible.

they are *my people*. Then *a*, the transgression, and the false profession of service, vss. 2–5; *b*, the service which God requires of his people; the conclusion, with a repetition of the two themes, vss. 8–12. In chapter 41 each of the principal themes occurs twice in the body of the composition. Thus: Introduction, vs. 1; *a*, the conquering Servant, vss. 2–4 and 8–20; *b*, the discomfiture of the false gods, vss. 5–7 and 21–24; at the end, the recapitulation, vss. 27–31.

Another method of composition is well illustrated in chapter 53 (*i. e.*, 52 : 13–53 : 12). A brief introduction gives out a motive in a triumphant key, but immediately passes over into a strongly contrasted theme. The latter is then developed at length, as the true subject of the composition, until the finale is reached, when both motives are combined, with the emphasis put on the one which was first announced. Chapter 59 is another poem which follows this plan exactly.

In the introduction to chapter 50 I have described the tripartite plan of its composition: the word of Yahwè to the doubters; the soliloquy of the Servant; and the final word of Yahwè summing up the whole. Chapter 61, in the same form, is precisely the reverse: *a*, the opening soliloquy of the Servant, vss. 1–3; *b*, the word of Yahwè, vss. 4–9; and a final soliloquy of the Servant, giving the summary, vss. 10 f. The poem 55 f. combines two themes: a universal promise, and a call to repentance and righteousness; and these are recapitulated in the brief coda, 56 : 1, 7 f. Chapter 49 is a very finely constructed poem; see the introduction to it, and also the discussion of it in Chapter VII, § 1. It is perhaps the most striking example of the skill of the poet in dividing his material and leading up to his climax. This poem was announced by its predecessor, chapter 48, and every detail of its effective scheme must have been in the mind of its author before he began to write. The manner of employing the 'lyric interlude' is especially striking here; almost equally so in 45 and 57. I have called attention in more than one place to the exact correspondence, in plan, of the poem 42 : 1–43 : 7 with the equally elaborate composition 63 : 1–64 : 12, in its literary quality perhaps the greatest poem of the collection. Other poems interesting for their framework of recurring themes are 65, built upon two motives, and 66, built upon three.

One minor and incidental feature of composition, indicative of the intense earnestness of the prophet, may be mentioned here. There are *three* poems which in the vehemence of their denunciation surpass all the others; these are 48, 57 (including, of course, 56 : 9–12), and 66. In each of these the attack upon the faithless Israelites, occurring near the beginning of the poem, is truly startling. There is indeed a transition, as usual in such cases, to the vision of purification and future triumph; but the fire of indignation is still burning, and the prophet has no thought of taking back what he has said. The three poems end with the same note of warning, added, as though with the purpose of making the reminder ⸢doubly stern, after what seemed to be the formal close of the composition.

The manner of effecting a gradual transition from a picture of wrath and terror to scenes of peace, joy, and bright color is best illustrated in chapters 34 f. and 57. In the former instance the poem proceeds from the slaughter of the wicked among men to the figure of sacrificial beasts, then through successive pictures of conflagration, a deserted land, ruined palaces inhabited by demons and wild creatures, the happy life of beasts and birds under divine care, to the joyful homecoming of God's people. In 57, the blazing invective addressed in the second person plural passes over to the second person singular (the personified city); then, after stern accusation, comes milder reproach, the reminder of past and present failure and distress, expostulation, the assurance of mercy to the contrite, and the vision of a coming 'peace, peace to the near and the far.'

The Second Isaiah was keenly sensitive to the sound of words. It is easy to see how his choice of language was influenced by considerations of rhythm and assonance. His constant use of paronomasia, beginning with the *nāmássū—nāmáqqū* of 34 : 3 f. and ending with the *kĕnahar šālōm—kĕnachal šōṭēph* of 66 : 12, is perhaps too well known to need illustration. This variety of word-play is to be seen in nearly every poem of the collection, though it is everywhere used sparingly. Whether the *šeṣeph qeṣeph* of 54 : 8 and the *peqach-qoch* of 61 : 1 are to be regarded as his own property may well be doubted; the former locution was probably in use before his time, while the latter illustrates a secondary noun-formation which has its parallels elsewhere. Good examples of the habit may be seen in 34 : 6; 41 : 2; 43 : 24; 45 : 9; 48 : 19; 51 : 8; 53 : 10; 54 : 6, 10; 58 : 8; 60 : 5, 8; 61 : 3, 10; 63 : 1, 2; 66 : 10. There is a striking instance of alliteration in 62 : 10:

> *'ibrū 'ibrū baššĕ'arīm | pannū derek ha'ām ||*
> *sōllū sōllū hammesillā | saqqĕlū mē'eben ||*

where each verse has a consonant sound four times repeated. The phrase *sasōn wĕ-simcha* is found in 35 : 10; 51 : 3; and 51 : 11; *šōd wĕ-šeber* in 51 : 19; 59 : 7; and 60 : 18. Word-play of another variety will be illustrated presently.

There is some evidence, not quite satisfactory indeed, of a deliberate employment of rhyme. It is noticeable that the writers of antiquity generally saw little value in this feature of versification. The Greek and Latin poets did not feel the need of rhyme; the Arabs insisted upon it; the Hebrews shunned it. The Semitic mode of grammatical inflection, with its comparative monotony of endings and suffixes, rendered rhyming too cheap a device. In Babylonian, Assyrian, and Syriac prosody rhyme plays no part. In the Arabic poetry, with all the splendid skill in its employment and the beautiful effects which are obtained, its presence is very often an obvious burden and a blemish. And indeed in the case of any poetry, whoever is filled with the desire for the two main factors, musical rhythm and a corresponding flow of thought without impairment, is likely to rebel at the compulsion of a terminal assonance. Mozart, in a letter to his father written in 1781, frees his mind on this point. An opera is to be hoped for, he says, in which "the words are written simply to suit the music; not turned and twisted so as to ruin the composition for the sake of a miserable rhyme, which God knows does far more harm than good in a dramatic representation. Verse, indeed, is indispensable for music, but rhyme is bad in its very nature." Mozart, to be sure, was writing as one who had suffered unspeakable things at the hand of his librettists, but his words find an echo in every age. In the classical Hebrew poetry, with its parallelistic reiteration, persistent rhyme would soon become wearisome, if not intolerable. Our Hebrew poet would certainly have expressed himself in the manner of the great composer; and yet an occasional employment of the device would be almost inevitable in the verse of one who had as strong a feeling as he for cadence and the sound of the syllable.

The mere correspondence of final vowels, hardly to be called *rhyme* in a Semitic composition, need not be left altogether out of consideration. The repetition of the sound at the end of successive lines, ordinarily due to nothing more than the contingencies of grammar, could unquestionably heighten the musical effect in passages where the rhythm is especially distinct and regular. It is at any rate noticeable that cases of the kind occur where the enthusiasm of the poet runs high. Thus, in the first passage which describes the conquering career of the Messiah (41 : 2 f.): *yittḗn ke'aphắr charbố | kĕqáš niddắph qaštố | yirdĕphḗm ya'abốr šālốm | órach bĕ̆raglắu lō yabố*. It may be mere coincidence that in the next passage dealing with this subject the smooth and high-sounding verses are introduced by the words (45 : 1): *kō amár Yahwĕ̄ limĕšichố | ašér hechĕzáqtī bīminố*.

Such instances of genuine rhyme as 60 : 10, *kí beqiṣpí hikkūthík | ūbírĕṣōní richamtík*, can be given little weight, if any. The recurrence of the form was almost inevitable. In a few other passages, however, where the emotion of the writer is very plainly to be felt, it is difficult to resist the impression that the effect was designed. Thus 53 : 6: *kullánū kaṣṣốn ta'ínū | íš lĕdarkố panínū | wĕYáhwē híphgī'a bố | ēth 'awốn kullánú nĕgāsố*.* With this may be compared 64 : 5: *wannĕhí kaṭṭamḗ kullánū | ūkĕbéged 'iddím kolᵗ ṣidqōthḗnū | wannibbốl kĕ̆'āléh kullánū | wa'awōnénū kārúach yissa'ḗnū*. Here the rhymes alternate. Notice also the remarkable instances in 63 : 16 and 17, which need not be quoted here at length (see the note on vs. 16). Once more, there is the passage 65 : 1, in which the pronominal suffix at the end of the first clause must be restored (as is generally agreed), and where it is of course permissible to read *hinnĕ̆ní* instead of the pausal form *hinnḗnī*, though the resulting assonance in the second half-verse may be only accidental. The verse reads: *nidrắštī lĕlố ša'alúnī | nimṣḗthī lĕlố biqqešúnī | amártī hinnĕ̆ní hinnĕ̆ní | el gối lō qōrắ bišĕ̆mí*. The euphony of these passages is very evident, and they were written by one who had an ear for such effects. More than this cannot be said with certainty.

Side by side with the play upon sounds and syllables stands a closely allied habit, equally characteristic and very striking; namely, the repetition of words and phrases. In successive clauses, sometimes in a single clause, and very often in successive verses, a word is used twice or thrice where a synonym could easily have been employed. This peculiarity is illustrated uniformly throughout the poems in chapters 34–66, but has no parallel (though occasional instances are of course to be found) in the work of other Old Testament writers. For example, in 35 : 1 f. the verbs *tagḗl* and *tiphrach*, employed in the opening strain, immediately reappear in inverse order in the following couplet. (Repetition in inverted

repetita [margin note]

---

* For the correct reading and division of the verses at this point, see the note on the text.

† The possibility that this word is a later addition should perhaps be considered.

order occurs frequently elsewhere; for example, in 40 : 13 f.; 43 : 19 f.; 44 : 1 f.; 46 : 1 f.; 58 : 2 f.; 59 : 10, 16 f.; 63 : 7. See also 51 : 7*b*, 8*b*.) In 34 : 4 the root *nabal*, "wither," is employed three times; in 52 : 8 the noun *qōl*, "voice," occurs in two different constructions in a single line. Still other typical examples of this reiteration may be seen in 34 : 6; 44 : 13; 46 : 4, 13; 53 : 3, 4, 7; 57 : 15; 60 : 1 f.; 65 : 6 f.; 66 : 13.

In all such cases it is clear that the poet lingers on the *sound* of the word, and the habit belongs to the purely musical side of his art. No appreciative reader can fail to see this in such a verse as 59 : 18, or in 40 : 13 f. We find the same thing in the Greek melic poets; see, for instance, the index to Herbert Weir Smyth's edition (London, Macmillan, 1900), where some thirty examples are noted. If we possessed more than scattered fragments of the work of these writers, the list would doubtless be greatly increased. In the Second Isaiah's book the repeated word not infrequently stands at the end of successive metric lines, showing still more plainly the close relation of the habit to the feeling for rhyme. Among the best examples are 42 : 3 f.; 42 : 15; 44 : 9–11; 58 : 2 f.; 59 : 18.

Another practice of this author is of like character with the preceding. He frequently introduces in a poem which he is composing a metric line or verse which he has employed elsewhere. These melodies, once created, were ever sounding in his ear, and they occasionally flowed again, almost involuntarily, from his pen. Now and then such a verse is employed to end a poem or a paragraph, with something of the effect of a refrain; oftener it is a mere reminiscence, inserted in any suitable place. The principal examples form an interesting and very characteristic list. 40 : 10*b* is repeated exactly in 62 : 11*b*. The inspired utterance 42 : 6 f. appears again, with some amplification and change of form, but with the principal phrases verbally reproduced in 49 : 6, 8 f. The distich 49 : 2*a* recurs, slightly altered in its wording, in 51 : 16*a*. Chapter 60, the poem of the New Jerusalem, naturally contains a number of short passages, amounting in all to nine metric lines, which are reminiscent of former poems in the group. Verse 4 echoes 49 : 18*a*, 22*b*; vs. 9 contains 51 : 5*b* and 55 : 5*b*; vs. 13*a* is made up from lines in 35 : 2 and 41 : 19. The four lines of 63 : 5 are nearly identical with those in 59 : 16. The distich which ends chapter 52 (*i. e.*, 52 : 12) is recalled in 58 : 8*b*.

To these are to be added the repetitions which have something of the nature of a refrain. The couplet which forms the close of

51 : 6 is repeated at the end of vs. 8, preparing the way for the dramatic change in the following verse. There is a similar reiteration in 65 : 6b and 7b, and thereupon also a sudden transition ensues. The sententious warning at the end of 48, "No peace for the wicked!" is repeated at the end of 57. The most striking instance of all is the return of the beautiful verse 35 : 10 in 51 : 11. Our commentators, one and all, would expunge the latter passage as a later insertion, though this proceeding has about the effect which would be achieved by cutting out the nose or mouth of a successful portrait, seeing that the verse is essential to the structure of the poem. See the note on the passage, and the Introduction to chapter 51. Cheyne, *The Prophecies of Isaiah* (1884), remarks that the repetition would be "more congenial to a copyist than to a prophet." Similarly Marti, commenting on 49 : 8 f. (where he expunges the repetition from 42 : 6), exclaims that the prophet certainly "would not quote himself!" Perhaps not, if we were dealing with prose; but this is lyric poetry. And we must also consider the individual characteristic, as well as the type of literature. What would be the effect of a criticism of the Koran, for instance, which should excise all the verses or lesser passages which are verbally repeated?

In general, the minor literary habits discussed in the foregoing pages have been given either less or more weight than is due them. Our modern interpreters of the prophet usually make sad work of the assonances, word-plays, and repetitions. Some excuse them, others emend them, still others translate them; and it is hard to say which of the three modes of procedure is the most distressing. The imitation of these word-plays in a modern language gains nothing of the emotional effect which the original achieved, while introducing something repellent to the modern ear. It is more than a little surprising, too, to find interpreters of Second Isaiah disposed to censure the prophet for his attention to mere sound. The minor features of ancient rhetoric need for their appreciation the eye of the historian even more than the ear of the expert in modern literature; for literary taste did not originate in the nineteenth century. It is of course not permissible to cite the rules of elegant writing which prevail at the present day and then proceed to apply them to the compositions of antiquity. We can only inquire what did appeal to the cultivated readers of any given time; and the surest way of learning this is to study the usage of great representative writers.

There is no need to apologize for the studied repetitions (for they certainly are studied); they produced the effect which a master craftsman intended. It is therefore disconcerting to find them calling forth such comments as the following. From Cheyne's *Introduction*: 'poverty of invention'; 'the attempt to compensate for lack of ideas by multiplying words.' From Duhm's *Das Buch Jesaia*: 'überflüssige Textvermehrungen'; 'Gedankenarmut und sterile Phantasie'; 'leere Wiederholungen' (this phrase frequently used). In like manner the numerous examples of paronomasia, alliteration, etc., are visited with contempt as 'wohlfeiles Klangspiel.' And yet, what æsthetic delight such 'Klangspiel' has always afforded to oriental ears. It is only necessary to remember how the consensus of those scholars and literary critics whose native tongue is Arabic has awarded to Hariri and Mutanabbi the supreme place as exponents of the language in its classic elegance, mainly because of the purely verbal adornments, plays, tricks, and *tours de force* of which they were such consummate masters. Moreover, every student knows how honorable a place in the history of all great literature has been held by such operation with the sound of words. There is nothing in II Isaiah to equal the alliteration in the line of Sophocles (*Œdipus*, 371):

$$\tau\upsilon\phi\lambda\grave{o}\varsigma\ \tau\acute{a}\ \tau'\ \mathring{\omega}\tau\alpha\ \tau\acute{o}\nu\ \tau\epsilon\ \nu o\hat{\upsilon}\nu\ \tau\acute{a}\ \tau'\ \mathring{o}\mu\mu\alpha\tau'\ \epsilon\hat{\iota}$$

or the succession of sibilants in line 425 of the same tragedy. We think of the $\tau\acute{o}\xi o\nu\ \epsilon\mathring{\upsilon}\xi o o\nu\ \mathring{\iota}\xi\acute{a}\lambda o\upsilon\ \alpha\mathring{\iota}\gamma\acute{o}\varsigma$ of Homer, among many examples of the kind, and of the repeated syllable in Sappho's charming

$$\Pi\alpha\rho\theta\epsilon\nu\acute{\iota}\alpha,\ \pi\alpha\rho\theta\epsilon\nu\acute{\iota}\alpha,\ \pi o\hat{\iota}\ \mu\epsilon\ \lambda\acute{\iota}\pi o\iota\sigma'\ \mathring{a}\pi o\acute{\iota}\chi\eta;$$

Fastidious Cicero, moved to a smile by 'ista *vi*' thrice repeated in the line of Ennius, yet has no objection to this trick of rhetoric, but employs it more than once in his own poetry. Such examples could of course be greatly multiplied. In Is. 65:11 f., in the midst of a passionate invective, the prophet proclaims utter destruction to the apostates of his people who have forsaken the God of Israel and offered sacrifices to Gad and Meni, and in saying this he plays on the name of the latter deity. This is punning in a serious place. We may recall how Socrates, on trial for his life, is represented in the *Apology*, §§ 24, 25, as playing on the name of his chief accuser, Meletus. James Riddell, in his *Digest* of Platonic idioms, devotes a section to the examples of such paronomasia. It would be superfluous to illustrate this habit from the great writers of a later age, from Shakespeare, for instance.

It is to be noticed that the adverse comment on the stylistic features of the Hebrew poems here treated begins with the advent of 'Trito-Isaiah' in the criticism of the book. The explanation of this fact is provided in Chapter I of the present volume. Given the supposedly assured starting-point of an 'exilic' prophet writing in the time of Cyrus, the logical outcome is quite inevitable. The latter chapters of the book (it is now generally admitted) could not possibly have been written in Babylonia, nor in the generation which witnessed the career of Cyrus. On the other hand, they follow the pattern of the earlier chapters in subject-matter, structure, style, mannerisms, and a very individual phraseology, so exactly that the observant reader is forced to some theory of deliberate imitation—if he holds to the so-called 'exile' as the background of chapters 40 ff. Add to this the unfortunate dogma —long current and not yet outgrown—of a 'post-exilic period' in which both the literature and the religion of Israel had sadly degenerated, and it is plain that the wretched 'Trito-Isaiah' will be seen at the little end of the spy-glass. Hence it comes that especially in chapters 56–66 the repetitions, 'Klangspiele,' ellipses, etc., have been seen as blemishes and held up to scorn; though they are equally numerous, and of precisely the same character, in chapters 40–55.

There is yet another variety of play upon words, much more unusual in the Old Testament, and more plainly a personal habit, than any of those hitherto described. Although its presence in these poems is quite beyond question, and its recognition necessary for the correct interpretation of many passages, I believe that it has remained unnoticed by commentators and translators.

The Second Isaiah takes pleasure in the occasional use of a word capable of two different meanings, employing it first in the one signification, sufficiently indicated by the context, and then immediately repeating it in the other sense. These puns constitute a class by themselves; and they are distributed through all parts of the collection of poems, from chapter 34 to chapter 66. They are never dragged in, nor used in such a way as to disturb even slightly the flow of the writer's thought. It happens once or twice, as might be expected, that the use of the word in two distinct meanings is quite unmistakable (as in 56:1); ordinarily, however, the translators—and frequently the ancient interpreters as well as the modern—stick to one rendering through thick and thin.

A very good example is the word *limmūdīm* in 50:4, where it is twice employed. Its meaning at the end of the verse is necessarily "pupils," and so it is always rendered. In the first clause of the verse, however, this meaning is out of place; pupils have ears, not tongues, as their characteristic. The word in its first occurrence is the regularly formed abstract noun, "teaching"; the Greek rendering, παιδείας, is correct (the Syriac renders *both* times in this way). The teacher does need a tongue, and the Servant is both teacher and pupil.

Another excellent example is the double use of the word *neṣaḥ* in 63 : 3, 6. In the former verse, with its figure of the wine-press, *niṣcham* is "their juice," the juice of the trampled grapes. At the end of vs. 6, on the contrary, the same word has a very different signification (from another Hebrew root), the same which is found in I Chron. 29 : 11 and I Sam. 15 : 29, and the rendering must be: "I brought down their *glory* to the ground"; not "their *juice*" (!), as the modern translations would have it. In this instance all the ancient interpreters excepting the Greek and the Targum (which merely paraphrases) recognized the double use of the word and rendered accordingly in vs. 6: Lat. *virtutem*, Syr. "might," Aquila, Symmachus, and Theodotion νῖκος.

In 54 : 9 there is a 'glaring pun' (to use a favorite modern epithet) in the opening words, which might be read *kī mē Noach*, "for the waters of Noah," or *kīmē Noach*, "as in the days of Noah." The decision is apparently given in favor of the former alternative by the very next clause, which mentions the Flood as *mē Noach*, a designation found nowhere else. It is certainly the other alternative which was intended, however, as the sense of the whole passage shows, and as the majority of the ancient versions and the best modern translators have agreed.

In vs. 15 of this same chapter the verb *gūr* occurs in two utterly different meanings derived from roots originally distinct and otherwise well known. (When the vowel-pointing of one of the words of the Hebrew text is slightly altered, as is grammatically desirable, the play on sounds becomes even more striking.) The translation must be: The foe who *attacks* shall perish by my power; the stranger *sojourning* with thee shall join thee. See the note on the text.

In 34 : 5, 7 there is an obvious play on the word *riwwĕtha*. In vs. 7 the verb has its usual meaning, heightened by the use of the intensive stem. This meaning would not be at all suitable in vs. 5, however, where the modern renderings try in vain to make it fit; sometimes (as in Duhm, Cheyne, and Marti) by supposing that an explanatory word or phrase has accidentally been lost from the text. On the contrary, we must recognize here the usual *jeu de mots*. Whether we have before us two distinct Hebrew roots, or merely two idiomatic uses of the same verb, it may not be possible to say with certainty. See the critical note on vs. 5.

There are several excellent examples in chapters 40–43. In 40:12 the verb *tikkēn* has the meaning "measure, mark off"; in vs. 13 it means "direct, rectify, set in order," as often in the later Hebrew.—In vs. 19 the word *ṣōrēph* occurs twice; first as the noun "goldsmith," then immediately as the participle (apparently from a denominative use of the verb: "smithing"). This sudden shift led astray the Greek and Latin versions and even the Targum; only the Syriac translator saw through it.—The passage 42:3 f. contains a twofold play which is among the most interesting and characteristic of all. The prophet is foretelling the manner in which the Servant will deal with the weakness and sin of mankind. He will not break the *bruised* reed, nor extinguish the light which *burns low*. Then, in the next breath, he seems to employ the same two words, in reverse order, in describing the Servant himself. Not so; it is again the favorite device of this writer. Instead of the verb which means to be at the last flicker, on the point of going out altogether, he now uses one identical in form but altogether different in meaning, and probably from another Semitic root. So also with the second verb: instead of having the meaning "bruise" or "fracture," it is now used in a tropical sense well known elsewhere. The rendering in vs. 4 must be: "He will not *berate*, nor *deal harshly*"; both verbs, in the very forms employed here, being perfectly familiar.—The important passage 43:23 f. also plays upon a pair of words. In vs. 23*b* the two verbs mean: "I made thee serve" and "I caused thee to labor" (as in vs. 22). In 24*b*, on the contrary, the meaning is: "thou hast burdened me" and "thou hast wearied me." The verbal forms are identical throughout, but the progress of thought requires first the literal, then the tropical, use.

It happens once or twice that the play upon a particular word is repeated in a subsequent poem. Thus in 46:12 f. and again in 56:1 the word occurring first in the sense of personal "righteousness" is used immediately thereafter as a designation of the Messianic "vindication, triumph" of the true religion. Another instance is the double use of a verbal form which according to the context may mean either "fear" or "see." It is certainly used in both senses in 57:11; though the fact is recognized by no translator, ancient or modern. Duhm, Cheyne, and Marti would emend the text. There is the same double use in 59:19, in the form of

a zeugma, the word being employed but once, at the beginning
of the verse. As applied to the first clause it can only mean "fear,"
with the second clause only "see" (notice Duhm's comment on
the verse). This, to be sure, is a unique instance; I know of no
similar example of zeugma in the Hebrew Bible. It is however
exactly the sort of verbal conceit that we should expect to find
in this writer.

The preceding verse, 59:18, shows the prophet in the mood for
employing such devices. It contains *two* instances of the double
use, though for the reader of his day there could have been no
ambiguity whatever. The form *kĕʻal*, representing two utterly
different words, occurs twice in the same clause. The two meanings of *gemūl* (*gemūla*) are also employed in the verse; first "deeds,"
then "requital." See the note on the passage.—Equally daring is
the double use of *nephesh* in 58:10, where the word in the meaning "self" is immediately repeated (not even a single word intervening) in the signification "hunger, craving."

Other instances may be mentioned briefly. In 51:5 the same
word means first "arm," then "help."—The verb at the end of
51:6 has a different meaning at the end of vs. 7.—*Rabbīm* in
52:14 is "many," in 15 it is "mighty."—There is a double use of
nephesh in 55:2 f.—In 55:4 the word *lĕʼummīm* in its first occurrence is the simple plural of the noun *lĕʼōm;* in the second occurrence it is the combination of the preposition with the plural of
umma (see the note).—58:2 plays upon *mishpaṭ*, and 59:6 upon
maʻăseh.—The phrase *chēl gōyīm* in 60:11 has a very different
meaning from that which it had in vs. 5.—In 60:9 occurs a metric
line which had previously been used in 51:5; but the verb now
has another meaning, and indeed belongs to a different Hebrew
root.—In 66:20 the word *mincha* appears first in its original sense
of a "gift" presented, then in the strictly technical sense belonging to the Hebrew ritual.

The foregoing list, with its twenty-eight examples, has more
than ordinary interest for the student of II Isaiah. Though from
one point of view a literary feature of minor consequence, its value
as a link in the chain of evidence, and as an aid to our understanding of the personality of the prophet and poet, is not to be mini-
mized. The gain in the interpretation of single passages, though
very considerable, is a comparatively slight matter; what is of
prime importance is the recognition of *the mental habit*, revealed
here again by an indication so obviously consonant with those
which have already been discussed. We observe once more the
sensitiveness to sound, resulting in the tendency to linger on the

single word; the love of unexpected transitions; a certain delight in the momentary shock of a suggested incongruity.

In the face of the array of evidence presented in this chapter, so varied in character and yet so self-consistent, it would be superfluous to insist again that the twenty-seven poems are the work of a single hand; there is clearly no other possibility. The hypothesis of 'imitation' would be absurd. *Such* imitation as must be postulated, such exact duplication of personality (not merely of chosen themes, general treatment, and perhaps a few outstanding mannerisms), is not only without example in the literature of any age, but is also humanly impossible. It seems amazing that even the very effective Cyrus-Babylon interpolations should have been able to blind modern scholars to the truth. It is only fair, however, to reiterate here what has been said repeatedly in the preceding pages, that the now accepted theories of Jewish history and religion have not prepared the way for such recognition.

This chapter has in large part been occupied with lesser details of the writer's art. These contribute materially to our understanding of the prophet's mind, but their importance must not be exaggerated in the general estimate of his literary style. He was not one to let any sort of adornment impair the force of his message. We feel his command over the finer tones and typical rhythms of a great language, and at the same time cannot fail to see how completely the concern for these and other stylistic features is subordinated to his main purpose to arouse and persuade. The reader who appreciates the strong æsthetic tendencies of this Hebrew author is surprised to see how seldom it is obvious that the choice of a locution was determined by its sound. He draws music from the commonplaces of speech; partly by his arrangement, sometimes by the repetition which has been described. In his use of meter it never appears that he holds to a sonorous rhythm for its own sake. There is no passage in which the musical suggestion predominates. Where he is most brilliant as a poet he is even more effective as a preacher. There are not a few passages, moreover, in which smoothness of rhythm and regularity of meter are obviously sacrificed to homiletic force and directness. The balance between thought and emotion is everywhere preserved, and both are communicated without loss. The vocabulary is extensive, but the diction prevailingly simple; there is no fondness for unusual words or obscure grammatical constructions. Students of the Hebrew language find this part of the Book of Isaiah comparatively easy reading.

It has been shown that the twenty-seven poems of this publication stand in a fixed order. It is also evident that there is a comprehensive plan of the series, conceived at first as an open framework and then freely worked out in detail. All the way from the announcement to the world in 34 : 1 to the grim warning to the renegades of Israel in 66 : 23 f. (after all, the prophet's most earnest message) a certain logical progress is unmistakable. The artistic form and finish of the whole work are the more noticeable when we consider that its author is obeying the call to 'lift up his voice like a trumpet and declare to his people their transgressions.' With the weight of a new world on his shoulders and the full realization of a desperate surrounding condition that would have checked the enthusiasm of a lesser soul, he lays out the technical scheme, sometimes quite elaborate, of each of the successive compositions, and calculates his rhetorical effects, while from time to time little touches of a lighter humor reveal his own indomitable spirit.

The quality of these lyric-didactic masterpieces is not to be learned from the study of any single specimen or group of them. In the point of view indeed, in the situation of the writer in his surroundings, no change whatever is to be seen; but the mood is never twice the same, and new conceptions and modes of treatment are constantly appearing. There is profuse variety in perfect unity. Behind the lyric songs, the many dramatic turns and episodes, the sustained argument, the sharp rebuke, the pictures of future glory, we can see everywhere the same personality and the same firm hold on both matter and form.

In all this we are given, beyond doubt, a glimpse of the literary Jerusalem of the prophet's day such as we could obtain nowhere else. The writer has in mind his nearest readers. He hopes to make his voice reach to the outer edges of the Jewish Dispersion, coextensive with the civilized world, but the formal dress of his message is that of the cultivated circles in which his life has been passed. His work displays the consciousness of a scholarly and refined audience. Whatever the personal history of our nameless prophet may have been, he certainly wrote as one who lived in a cosmopolitan city in whose upper stratum there was a prevailing atmosphere of urbanity, æsthetic appreciation, and intellectual freedom. Whether the spiritual response was delayed or speedy, there were very many of that day who could take delight in these incomparable poems.

CHAPTER XII

THE CRITICAL APPARATUS AND THE PRESENT INTERPRETATION

The Hebrew text of II Isaiah has been unusually well preserved in the long process of transmission. The massoretic recension is generally correct as it stands, as is shown not only by the satisfactory sense which it yields, but also by the extent to which the meter has been kept intact. In nearly every case where the text is manifestly corrupt, the original reading can be restored with certainty or a good measure of probability. The trouble is nowhere deep-seated, and in nine cases out of ten the requirement of the context is a sufficient guide. Occasionally the ancient versions give help.

The inevitable minor errors introduced by the inadvertence of copyists are present in considerable number. In not a few passages the division of the consonant text into its separate words has been wrongly made; see especially 44:7, 11*a*; 49:19*a*; 63:18; 64:4; 65:14*b*, 15. The eventual disregard of the meter helped to bring about such changes. There are several instances of the careless repetition of a letter, and of the corresponding omission by haplography. The mistaken insertion of the conjunction *waw* has often wrought mischief, in cases where the connection of clauses might easily be misunderstood; and in one or two instances this has necessitated the insertion of a word to complete the supposed sense, as in 41:29. In 53:11 the accidental transposition of two almost identical words has caused great trouble. The verse-division is often wrongly made in the massoretic text, and the mistake is sometimes serious, as in 34:15 f.; 47:3 f.; 53:6 f.; 56:11 f.; 63:15 f. The vocalization is frequently erroneous. In some cases this is due to the later current interpretation, as when forms of the imperfect tense which were originally 'consecutive' are made over into predictions. The name 'Yahwè' is sometimes inserted, for the purpose of guiding the reader, where the metre shows it to be secondary. In cases where the original text mentioned the 'gods' or 'idols' of the Gentiles the Massorites have sometimes made a characteristic substitution, or else have omitted the offending word altogether; see, for example, the notes on 41:21; 48:5;

205

and 57 : 13. One striking instance of carelessness in copying is to
be seen in the passage 63 : 19–64 : 1; see the note on 63 : 19. Another is 66 : 17 f., the only extensively corrupt passage in the
whole book. A very interesting example of the insertion of a
marginal note (working havoc with the text!) is to be seen in
65 : 7; see the note.

We have no reason to suppose any material omission from the
original text of the poems. There is no place where the line of
thought is broken, suggesting a gap that needs to be filled. No
one of the ancient versions testifies to an older, more complete
text than the massoretic. The many 'editorial additions' postulated in recent commentaries and other treatises are, with very
few exceptions, merely incidental to a false theory of the book.
In general the absence of interpretative additions, whether mistaken or based on a true understanding, is remarkable. There are,
however, as has been sufficiently demonstrated in the preceding
Chapters, a few very disturbing interpolations of two distinct
classes. Those of the one series, treated in Chapter III, were designed to support the theory of 'the return from the Babylonian
exile' introduced by the Chronicler and his contemporaries, and
evidently date from the same period as his great revision of the
history of Israel. Those of the other series, described in Chapter
VII, § 2, were introduced by some overzealous patriot (or pa-
triots) who wished to have it plainly stated that the day of triumph is to belong to the Jews, not to the Gentiles.

There is one very important peculiarity of the traditional text,
as yet unrecognized by scholars, to which I have many times
called attention in the critical notes in this volume, as well as in
a number of earlier publications. I refer to the fact of an ancient
editorial revision extending through the whole Hebrew Bible, having for its aim the preservation of variant readings. Those learned
men of Israel who gave to the sacred text its present form deliber-
ately embodied in it a very interesting and useful critical apparatus. This means not merely qerē and kethîb, which on the contrary play but a small part in the undertaking; the main body of
this diaskeuasis is not intended to be apparent to the eye, nor
indeed to any but the initiated, the professional readers, for whose
benefit numerous subtle indications are provided. Different manuscripts and corresponding oral traditions frequently showed a
slight disagreement in the consonant text or the vocalization of
single words. Who could distinguish the primitive reading from
the secondary, when either made good sense? It was a genius of

no common order who first conceived the notion of preserving as much as possible of this variant material by means of internal combination; since it was obviously impossible to permit the use of varying texts or to give official sanction to the transmission of a marginal apparatus. Hence the system of *alternative readings*. Words differing slightly in appearance were fused together into a single word of manifestly impossible form, sometimes explained by the device of *kethīb* and *qerē*, but oftener not explained at all, or else called to the attention of the expert reader by some curious vowel-pointing. See, for instance, in II Isaiah the notes on 47 : 13; 48 : 6; 59 : 3; 63 : 3 (end); 64 : 5 (end), etc. Where two well-attested readings differed in respect to tense, number, person, and the like, the sentence was divided between the two constructions, half to the one and half to the other; see 42 : 20; 61 : 7; 63 : 16*a*; etc. The instances of such artful combination are a multitude. In the 'Later Prophets' and the 'Kethubim' there are comparatively few chapters whose text can be correctly understood throughout without this key. In the Pentateuch the instances are fewer, though numerous.

A host of seeming blunders and anomalous formations, either contravening rules of grammar or else mere monstrosities for which the Massora must prescribe intelligible readings, are therefore not, as they are commonly regarded, the result of carelessness or ignorance, but are the product of a well-executed plan. When once this fact is recognized and utilized by the experts in Biblical Hebrew, the dictionaries and grammars of the classical language will be freed of considerable collections of curious forms and constructions now erroneously supposed to have been in actual use. As I am reserving the fuller discussion of this matter for another publication, I will not attempt any general treatment here. Further characteristic illustration, in addition to what has already been given, may be seen in the notes on 35 : 2; 42 : 20; 44 : 21; 51 : 21; and 60 : 21*b*. I do not suppose myself to have recognized all the instances of the kind, in my study of the text.

Of the ancient versions, the LXX is of course the most important. The Greek Isaiah is certainly one of the oldest translations in the Bible; see the evidence presented in Chapter VI. In making use of it for criticism of the Hebrew text there are three preliminary questions that must be answered after careful study of the material at hand. What is the relative value of the Hebrew text rendered by the Greek? To what extent can the translator be relied upon to give an accurate rendering of the original? What

amount of corruption has the Greek text undergone in the process
of transmission? Up to the present time, no one of the three
questions has been answered satisfactorily, and I am unable to
discover that the second and third have even been raised by any
recent commentator or editor.

Duhm, *Jesaia*, p. viii, speaks of "die LXX, die älter ist als unser
hebräischer Text." This, if it has any significance, means that
the Hebrew rendered by the LXX is more primitive, nearer to
what the prophet himself wrote, than the text of our massoretic
Bible. That this is in fact the meaning is made plain by other
utterances and by the actual procedure in the attempt to determine the original readings; see also the more extended discussion
of this matter in the first edition of the commentary, p. vi. The
opinion is mistaken, however. Dillmann, *Der Prophet Jesaia*
(1890), was right in his conclusion (p. xxviii): "Der Text in seiner
massoretischen Gestaltung ist dem LXX Text fast durchaus vor-
zuziehen." In the case of Isaiah, as in that of the other books of
the Old Testament, the intending translator, in Egypt or elsewhere,
took the Hebrew text which he happened to have or was able to
procure. Careful comparison usually shows, as in the present instance, that the stray copy, or copies, picked up in the Diaspora
yielded a text decidedly inferior to that which was obtainable in
Palestine, where the Jewish authorities had both the opportunity
and the inclination to preserve and copy good manuscripts. Of
course the best were decidedly faulty, and so also was the edition
finally made and ratified in Jerusalem; though it will one day be
recognized that a large proportion of the supposed errors of transmission are merely products of the massoretic system of alternative
readings, described above. The relative excellence of MT is, I
think, sufficiently demonstrated here in the Translation and Commentary.

It is to be observed—and the fact is highly important—that
LXX and MT in Isaiah represent the same type of text, not two
different types. In almost every one of the places where the massoretic Hebrew is sufficiently corrupt to be troublesome the Greek
testifies to the same defect in its original. The following examples
will suffice for illustration. The confusion in 63:19 and the following verses, caused by carelessness in copying, is attested by
the LXX, which has also made its own contribution to the resulting chaos. The still worse corruption in 66:17 f. has the same
form in both texts. This is true also of a considerable number of
passages in which impossible readings have resulted from a false

division of words in the consonant text; see 44 : 7 (!), 11; 45 : 11;
63 : 18 (!); 64 : 4 (twice); 65 : 15 (!). Striking examples of false
reading combined with a wrong verse-division are 34 : 11 f., where
the Hebrew underlying the Greek had added its own further corruption; 47 : 3 f.; 57 : 12 f.; 63 : 15 (end); 65 : 15. See also the corrupt readings attested by both texts in 35 : 7b and 8b; 41 : 24, 29;
42 : 19, 25; 43 : 28; 44 : 12; 45 : 3, 9; 46 : 1; 48 : 10, 14; 49 : 19 (!);
50 : 4; 51 : 20; 53 : 11; 57 : 6; 59 : 10 : 61 : 3, 7a (evidently omitted in the Greek as quite impossible to translate), 8; 63 : 11;
64 : 3 f. (!); 66 : 5. Add to this the fact that all of the principal
interpolations, not only the Cyrus-Babylon group but also those
which have been recognized by all recent commentators, are present in the LXX text.

The Greek is not able to contribute even one clause to the
restoration of the original. The current examples of such insertion
in editions and translations "on the authority of the LXX" are
all mere blunders, due generally to mistaken theories of Hebrew
metrics added to misinterpretation of the Greek text. It is only
by a single word here and there, more often by a single letter, that
it enables us to emend the massoretic text; and in the majority of
these instances the correction is so obvious that it could have been
made by conjecture alone.

The significance of all this is apparent. When the anonymous
collection of twenty-seven poems was adopted as Isaianic by the
authorities in Jerusalem who undertook to make up the Book of
the Prophet Isaiah (see Chapter VI), the best text that they
could find had already undergone considerable corruption. With
this as the norm, and with an apparatus of variant readings
faithfully incorporated, a final edition was made. This was henceforth the standard text, and no trace of any other survived. In
Palestine, at least, it suffered little subsequent alteration. The
manuscript tradition in the Diaspora in Egypt was evidently
more free and easy, and the newly formed Hebrew Isaiah while
circulating there was somewhat carelessly handled. In the copy
which served as the basis of the Greek translation a new crop of
errors had been added to those previously existing. From these
general conclusions there is no escape.

The second question concerns the character of the translation
and the habits of the translator. This subject has received partial
treatment at the hands of more than one competent scholar. Doctor Anton Scholz, in his little pamphlet (Rectorsrede) entitled
Die alexandrinische Uebersetzung des Buches Jesaias, Würzburg,

1880, discussed the main features of the version and appended
lists (pp. 29–47) designed to illustrate the most striking characteristics. The lists are useful, though the explanations are often incorrect; some of the general conclusions drawn are also uncon-
vincing. Further material of considerable value is provided by
R. R. Ottley in the Introduction to his *Isaiah according to the
Septuagint*, Cambridge, 1904. Besides illustrating the variation
between LXX and MT with some such examples as were given
by Scholz, he classifies and describes the families of Greek MSS.,
and comments upon the peculiar readings found here and there.
He also discusses concisely, but with sound judgment, the nature
and value of this very peculiar and faulty translation. Much remains to be said as to the use—and abuse—of the Greek Isaiah
as a tool for repairing the Hebrew text. It has been handled in a
most unscientific way during the past few decades, apparently
without protest from any quarter. A thorough comparison of
LXX with MT will doubtless be made at some future time, and
will be useful in more than one way, though the gain might now
seem hardly worth the labor. It is of course not possible here to
do more than touch the surface of the subject, with bare mention
of the most important features, illustrated by a few typical examples.

When the author of the Greek translation of Isaiah knows what
his Hebrew means, he is likely to render with some freedom. He
does not feel himself bound to the wording of the original text.
It is ordinarily much the easiest course to follow it closely, but
sometimes he finds it more convenient to cut loose from it entirely. When, as very often happens, he does not know the meaning of his Hebrew, he is likely to render literally, without much
regard to sense, whatever words he recognizes, this proceeding re-
quiring the least labor. Sometimes, however, he guesses wildly,
or fills the gap with a passage from some other poem. It is of
course to be borne in mind that the distressing appearance of our
present Greek text is due in considerable part to the careless work
of transcribers.

The following examples are taken only from II Isaiah. *Free
renderings*. 35 : 5, 'shall hear,' instead of 'shall be opened.' 41 : 14,
where the Hebrew declares Jacob a 'worm' the Greek prefers to
call him 'diminutive, insignificant' (ὀλιγοστός). 42 : 4, instead of
'he will not be quenched' the rendering is 'he will shine forth.'
44 : 23, 'he has wrought it' becomes 'he has had mercy on Israel.'
45 : 15, 'Thou art a God who veils himself' is rendered 'Thou art

God and we did not know it.' 49 : 24, 'righteous' (the result of corruption of the text) is rendered by ἀδίκως in order to make good sense. 51 : 14, for the reading of the Hebrew, 'The bowed (captive) shall soon be released; he shall not go down to the pit of death, nor even want for bread,' the Greek substitutes 'For in rescuing thee he will neither halt nor delay' (!); probably from the very same Hebrew, perhaps from a slightly altered text. 56 : 8 (end), we should be very glad of a translation of the suffixed pronoun. The translator certainly had it before him, but renders merely 'assembly.' Chapter 57 is full of examples of miserably careless and irresponsible rendering. Vss. 2 and 14a may serve as specimens; the underlying Hebrew in the former case probably, in the latter case certainly, identical with ours. 60 : 7, 'they shall serve thee' (a somewhat difficult reading) is altered to 'they shall come to thee.' 65 : 1, the first word appears to mean 'I was sought,' which would not suit the context; hence the Greek substitutes 'I became manifest.'

Awkwardly literal or meaningless renderings. These are very numerous; it is hardly necessary to give examples. 34 : 15, "There the hedgehog nested, and the land (reading *biq'ā*) rescued her young with safety." 42 : 22, "For the snare is in the chambers (reading *khădārīm*) everywhere, and in houses together, where they hid themselves." 44 : 11, "And all who associated with them (emending the Greek; see note) withered, and (were) dumb from men." 45 : 9, "What have I made better as clay of the potter? Shall the plowman plow the land?" 45 : 16 f., "All his adversaries will be put to shame and confounded, and will proceed in shame. Renew yourselves to me, islands. Israel is saved by the Lord with an eternal salvation." The Hebrew text was slightly corrupt here. 59 : 11, "Like a bear and a dove they shall proceed together." See also 41 : 7; 42 : 21; 44 : 25a; 49 : 25a; 53 : 9; 57 : 8; 66 : 5.

Additions and omissions. These also are a large number. Scholz's lists (not always trustworthy) fill five pages. In almost every instance it is plain that the massoretic reading is superior, the Greek text showing a careless manner of translating. The insertion of a word or two, by way of interpretation or in order to complete the sense, may be seen on every page. Those critics of the Hebrew text who are inclined to 'follow the LXX' without any careful study of the version are likely to be led astray. A few typical examples follow. 40 : 2, the insertion of 'priests.' 42 : 10, 'glorify his name.' 43 : 26, the words τὰς ἀνομίας σου πρῶτος. 44 : 9,

ποιοῦντες. 45 : 13, the insertion of 'king.' 54 : 17, 'and they shall
be defeated (in the legal process) by you.' (Here the Greek reading—the true Hexaplar text—is corrupt. The sentence ends with
ἔσονται; ἐν must be omitted, and the following word read αὕτη.)
59 : 17, καὶ περιέθετο. 60 : 4, 'thy children.' 63 : 16 (end), thy
name 'is over us.' 64 : 2, 'the adversaries.' The words 'Lord' and
'God' are frequently inserted, and also occasionally proper names,
in order to make the interpretation sure. Thus 51 : 9, 'Jerusalem';
52 : 1, the first 'Zion.' In some cases of the kind it would seem
that the insertion had been made in a Hebrew text; thus in 60 : 1
(attested by the Vulgate), and very probably in 42 : 1.

The omissions are more numerous than the additions. In some
cases there is reason to believe that the Hebrew which was rendered had accidentally dropped the words or clauses which are
missing, but in the great majority of instances the defect is plainly
due to the translator's habit. Where a word is repeated in the
Hebrew, the Greek is likely to render it but once, as in 41 : 13 f.;
57 : 6a, 14; 59 : 18; 61 : 3; 62 : 10 (!). Where synonyms are employed in successive clauses, in the usual parallelism, the translator
sometimes omits one, as in 34 : 14; 40 : 3, 12a, 15, 17; 44 : 16;
46 : 13; 55 : 7. Synonymous clauses are omitted, evidently as unnecessary to the sense, in 35 : 4b; 40 : 14; 41 : 19; 59 : 18; 60 : 13,
14; 63 : 3; 65 : 18.

Loose renderings. In passages where the Hebrew is corrupt or difficult of interpretation the Greek translator sometimes goes his own
way. Now and then he helps himself by inserting a passage from
the neighboring context or from another poem. Thus 44 : 13 is en-
riched from 40 : 20 and 41 : 7; 44 : 16 from verse 15 (some codd. also
from vs. 19); 45 : 16a from 41 : 11, and the end of the verse from
41 : 1 (!). The rendering of 60 : 4 (end) is obtained from 49 : 22,
and that of 60 : 7 (end) from 56 : 7. Compare also 40 : 5 with
52 : 10. Occasional transposition of clauses *ad sensum* is of course
to be expected. A good example is to be seen in 57 : 8b, 9a, a passage which shows the Greek version at its worst. One entire clause
(five words) is omitted, and the clauses *hirchabt mishkabēk* and
ahabt mishkabām are transposed, making what would seem the
more natural order. The rendering of the former phrase, καί
ἐπλήθυνας τὴν πορνείαν σου μετ' αὐτῶν, has led astray a succession of scholars, beginning with Duhm and ending with Kittel's
Biblia Hebraica, who have not observed the transposition and
would insert four Hebrew words at this point. (The resemblance
to Ezek. 16 : 25 is purely accidental; there is no literary dependence

of the one passage on the other.*) Another example of a loose rendering misunderstood is in 34:11, where in place of the words *we'abnē bohu* the translator read or conjectured *we'iyyîm bāh*, and wrote καὶ ὀνοκένταυροι (οἰκήσουσιν) ἐν αὐτῇ. Here the authorities mentioned above, not seeing the origin of this Greek, would make another insertion 'according to the LXX.'

Again, as to the preservation of the Greek text. The Book of Isaiah has fared in this respect like the most of the books of the Greek Bible. Its text suffered a considerable amount of accidental corruption at so early a date that certain erroneous readings are attested by all the extant witnesses. There is need of a scholarly edition, and until something of the sort is provided the use of the version for critical purposes will be seriously hampered.† With the aid of the massoretic Hebrew many of the original readings can be conjecturally restored. A few examples may be given here.— The personal pronouns in 35:4 must originally have been second person, not first person.—The contrary is true in 41:22 and 44:7. —35:7, ὀρνέων was originally σειρήνων, as the parallel renderings show.—40:25, the second verb was probably ἰσωθήσομαι in the original rendering; see a similar copyist's variant in the MSS. of 35:4.—41:19, the word λεύκην should be πεύκην, as is shown by comparison with 60:13 (this conjecture already made by Schleusner).—41:27 (end), εἰς ὁδόν (the reading of the best MSS.) is a corruption from εἰ εἶδον, the original beginning of vs. 28; see the note on the passage.—41:29, εἰσίν is the corruption (in cursive script) of οὐδέν. This translator uses the latter to render *'ayin, ephes, hebel,* and *tohu.*—43:12, ὠνείδισα is the result of corruption in the Greek, not in the Hebrew. This translator occasionally renders 'hear' by the postclassical verb ἐνωτίζομαι (probably a 'translation-Greek' coinage); see especially the neighboring passage 44:8. Here in 43:12 it would seem that he used the *active voice*, writing ἠνώτισα. The customary careless transposition of syllables in copying produced the reading of our text.—43:14, δεθήσονται was originally δεηθήσονται, see the note on the passage. The proposal in Kittel's *Biblia Hebraica* (following Duhm) is an amazing bit of criticism.—43:24, instead of the impossible

---

* There are several instances of a literary relation between Ezekiel and Second Isaiah, and in each case of the kind it is apparent that Ezekiel is the borrower. See the evidence presented in Millar Burrows, *The Literary Relations of Ezekiel*, pp. 37 f., 73–79 (Philadelphia, Jewish Publication Society, 1925).

† For information as to the Greek MSS. of Isaiah, the student is referred to Ottley's book, mentioned above.

ἐπεθύμησα the translator wrote ἐμέθυσάς με. The standing equivalent of *rawā* in Isaiah is μεθύω; see 34: 5, 7; 55 : 10; 58 : 11. Here again Kittel's *Biblia* supposes a variant Hebrew reading.—44 : 8 (end), καὶ οὐκ ἦσαν τότε is the corruption of καὶ οὐκ ἦσάν ποτε, the beginning of vs. 9.—44 : 11, ὅθεν ἐγένοντο was probably οἱ συνεγένοντο, a fair rendering of the Hebrew, as noted above.— 53 : 2, ἀνηγγείλαμεν must have been originally ἀνέτειλεν.—54 : 10 (end), instead of the words γὰρ ἵλεώς σοι Κύριε the translator wrote ὁ ἐλεῶν σε Κύριος.—54 : 17, the correction of the Greek text was made above, under 'Additions.'—56 : 8, ὅτι was originally ἔτι, an easy corruption which is found in many places, *e. g.*, Qoheleth 12 : 9, Jer. 22 : 11 f. (MS. Q), and in the N. T., John 8 : 25.—63 : 12, κατίσχυσεν is a copyist's error for κατέσχισεν.

It is evident from all this that 'the LXX' of Isaiah is a version which must be used with great caution. It has not, in fact, been thus used in the past few decades, but with a carelessness which seems almost incredible. Some illustration has already been given; but since the treatment of the Hebrew text of this great work is a matter of high importance, the subject may be pursued a little farther. The extent to which the LXX virtually supports the massoretic recension has hardly been realized by any scholar of the present generation. In many passages where the Greek has been supposed to render a text different from ours more careful examination shows that there was no variation. In 41 : 27 f., for example, a passage which according to Duhm's commentary "sieht im griechischen Text sehr viel anders aus als im hebräischen," it is doubtless precisely the text of MT that is rendered in vs. 27, while in vs. 28 the only difference is the omission of the conjunction before the second *'ēn*. This is one instance of a great many. The freedom with which the traditional Hebrew is rejected, and something else substituted for it, on the basis of hasty guesses, is characteristic of the present stage of textual criticism in the Old Testament. A striking example of such 'emendation' is Duhm's operation on 44 : 26*b*, where the manifestly corrupt reading of a single Greek MS. is made the basis of a new Hebrew text. The case of 43 : 14 (end) is somewhat similar. See also the notes on 35 : 8*a*; 41 : 5; 42 : 16 f.; 43 : 10; 44 : 15; 45 : 16*a*; 49 : 15 f.; 60 : 14; 64 : 3. The fact that so many of the unfortunate conjectures made in these and numerous other passages have been adopted by the most influential modern scholars is the sufficient excuse for calling renewed attention to them here. The apparatus of Kittel's *Biblia Hebraica* contains very many readings erroneously supposed to be attested by the Greek version, readings gathered blindly from the commentaries, and the same is to be said of the *Handwörterbuch* of Gesenius-Buhl.*

This much in regard to the Greek translation of Isaiah. The other ancient versions need not be described here. The Vulgate, the Targum, and the Hexaplar Syriac show the same features as elsewhere. The Peshitta has been treated by Gustav Diettrich, *Ein Apparatus Criticus zur Pešitto zum Propheten Jesaia* (1905). This version alternates independent rendering of the Hebrew with timid dependence on the Greek. The Ethiopic, generally of no value, sometimes helps to determine a Greek reading. The 'Old Latin,' frequently cited in Kittel's apparatus, is worthless, since it is merely a mediæval rendering from the Greek. I have not often cited these versions in my Commentary, but I have consulted them at every point where it seemed possible that they could give help. I would record here with emphasis, however, my conviction that these ancient versions, including even the Greek, are useful chiefly for confirming rather than for emending. The all-important task is to understand and interpret the massoretic Hebrew; especially since we have such slight knowledge of the classical language, and of the procedure by which the authoritative recension was finally made.

My chief concern in the Translation has been accuracy. I have tried first of all to give the precise meaning of every Hebrew sentence and to reproduce each word by its English equivalent. The rendering is always clause for clause, without transposition or paraphrase. I have also wished to make the translation easily intelligible to all readers. For this reason I have studiously avoided the use of high-sounding words and poetical phrases of uncommon occurrence, even where their employment might seem to be invited by the diction of the original. The style of the Hebrew poet himself, as was remarked above, is prevailingly simple; and that which gave his writings their vast influence in the Jewish world and in incipient Christianity, and is of prime value to us now, is not the diction but the thought. It is true that no adequate idea of the quality of this poetry can be gained without reading the Hebrew, but even in the simple and often bald rendering which is here offered the beauty of the original is not altogether lost.

I have aimed to give some idea of the metric forms employed in the poems, indicating the metric lines by marks of division which

* I do not forget that the progress thus far made in every branch of Biblical science is due mainly to German scholars.

are intended to correspond exactly to the division of the Hebrew verse. I have not, however, undertaken to imitate the form of the original to the extent of preserving the precise number of rhythmic beats, except where this could easily be done without loss of accuracy. Experience has shown that the attempt to combine a closely faithful translation of Hebrew poetry with an exact imitation of the meter inevitably results in an unpleasant monotony, with a dangerous approach to mere doggerel. The present rendering of II Isaiah, with its many defects, will certainly be improved upon by others; but in the meantime I think it may fairly be claimed for it that it is the only translation, in any language, that can give the reader an approximately correct idea of the prophet and his work.

A few minor inconsistencies will perhaps be pardoned. The Tetragrammaton is ordinarily rendered by the proper name, Yahwè, but in some cases I have preferred "the Lord," either for the sake of euphony or in order to avoid repetition. The rendering is justified by the prophet's monotheism. In a few passages the translation reads "idols" or "false gods," where the Hebrew omits the offending word or the massoretic tradition has made a characteristic substitution. Every such proceeding is remarked in the foot-notes, which are intended to indicate all emendations or other deviations from the massoretic text. The poet's verbal conceits described in the preceding chapter, which were effective in the Hebrew verse but would not adorn a modern translation, are not imitated here. The choice between "shall" and "will" is often a matter of hair-splitting, where the intention of the original might equally well have been simple prediction or the execution of a divine decree.

The purpose of the Commentary which follows the Translation is first of all to give the prophet's work the true and consistent interpretation which has hitherto been wanting. It has therefore been found necessary in every chapter to controvert the views now universally accepted, showing their inadequacy and explaining the author's intention. It is of course in the earlier chapters of the book that space for argument of this nature is especially needed. With the prophet's point of view once established and shown to be the same throughout the whole series of poems, the later chapters can be given briefer treatment. The work was originally planned, moreover, on a somewhat larger scale than its present form. The commentary on chapters 34–53, which was finished in 1905, was found to be too extended for the plan finally adopted, and is given here with some abbreviation. For the same reason, the need of economizing space, the notes on chapters 54–66 omit or treat summarily many things which would be looked for in any full exegetical treatment, but are not essential to the purpose of the present work.

Since the poems are separate units, and not merely successive chapters in a connected work, I have in each case prefixed to the commentary a general introduction giving a brief statement of the contents and a characterization of the whole composition, whether as a work of art or as an essential part of its author's plan, with notice of any especially striking features. Following the introduction is a paragraph devoted to the metric scheme of the poem.

I have paid especial attention to the criticism of the Hebrew text and to the discussion of the meaning of single words, and in some chapters these features occupy a large part of the commentary. The reader will find my attitude toward the massoretic tradition decidedly more conservative than that of any other recent investigator, partly for reasons already given in speaking of the critical apparatus, and partly because the view of the book which is here maintained does not require alterations of reading and arrangement, aside from the removal of the few very important interpolations. The minor necessary changes in consonant text or vocalization are numerous, however, and the evidence in support of such change is given in each case. The textual emendations here adopted were, with few exceptions, made by me independently from the Hebrew and the versions, twenty-five to thirty years ago. In many of these conjectures I have been anticipated by other scholars, to whom I have intended to give due credit in the critical notes.

If I have seemed to give inadequate attention to various scholarly treatises on II Isaiah, especially to those which are concerned with the historical background of the several supposed divisions of the book, it is because there are so few points of contact between their basal assumptions and my own that argument in detail would be either futile or interminable. In the lack of common standing-ground it seemed the most fruitful proceeding to set forth as clearly as possible my own view, to be accepted or rejected *in toto*.

In my exegesis, which contains so much that is totally new, I have constantly been on my guard against giving to any poem or passage an unnatural interpretation. To foist fine sentiments upon a writer is no less reprehensible than to disparage him without warrant. In any case of real ambiguity, where the written words might suit either a high or a low plane of thought, without decisive evidence in either context or parallel passages, the writer is, of course, entitled to the benefit of the doubt. I know of no such instance, however, in II Isaiah. His thought is so perfectly consistent, from the first poem to the last, that the true intention is never hard to find, when once the unity of authorship is recognized and the poet is allowed to interpret himself. He is, moreover, so distinctly original, and consciously so, saying more than once with emphasis that he is bringing forth something new, hitherto unheard, that he is entitled to be considered by himself without prejudice derived from any estimate of his fellow authors, to say nothing of the bias which can see no possibility of any great creation arising in Palestine in the days of the second temple. In some of the modern comment on Old Testament writings, indeed, the reader can hardly escape the feeling that the interpretation is more or less colored by a still wider prejudice. Whether anti-Semitism is desirable or not as a social principle, it certainly is not a suitable point of view for interpreting the Hebrew scriptures. The commentator should feel at least some measure of sympathy with his author, and the value of the exegesis will be largely determined by this factor.

If the tone of controversy in the Commentary and in the foregoing essays should seem now and then unduly sharp, I can only say that (to my regret) sharpness is unavoidable in view of the matters that are at stake. A false theory is securely intrenched, in the view of the foremost experts the world over, as one of the 'assured' results of modern Biblical criticism. The greatest prophet of the ancient world is now almost hopelessly hidden from sight, and in his stead the supposed authors of his work, pictured as misguided enthusiasts, are treated with easy scorn. The true interpretation of II Isaiah carries with it also a new view of the history of Israel and of the progress of its religious thought in the most critical and influential period. A mistaken interpretation of the beginnings of Christianity as well as of the Hebrew prophets and psalmists is now practically undisputed. What sort of single-handed attack on this intrenchment can hope to succeed?

Many years ago the first critical analysis of the Book of Isaiah divided it into two parts. Each of the two divisions, as we are now aware, was thoroughly misunderstood. The materials necessary for a satisfactory analysis could be gained only by slow degrees, and even now are insufficient. The average layman, however, still knows only a bipartite book, 'Isaianic' and 'exilic,' and even among experts in Old Testament science some influence of this outgrown stage of criticism persists. When in the course of time the second division of the book was clearly shown to be not at all 'exilic' in its major portion, the consequences of this new advance were not realized. The prophet whose Messiah was Cyrus continued to be held in an uncritical esteem inherited from antiquity. At last the fallacy was exposed. A scholar of note, Doctor Bernhard Duhm, saw more clearly than any of his predecessors the implications of the view hitherto prevailing, and in his work of 1892 carried them to their logical outcome. He uncovered mercilessly the weaknesses and inconsistency of the supposed prophet, and showed the necessity of dissecting his supposed work; following sound reasoning in the main, though handling both Hebrew text and ancient versions in an unwarranted manner. The resulting picture, however distressing, could only be accepted, at least in its principal features, by those who recognized a 'prophet of the exile,' trusted the Chronicler's history of the Jews, and were willing to follow the argument without fear of consequences. In fact, this treatise of 1892, repeated in subsequent editions, has dominated all subsequent critical investigation. In particular, the commentaries and other influential writings of Cheyne in England and Marti in Switzerland adopted without reserve the conclusions of Duhm, including even the detail of his exegesis and treatment of the Hebrew text.

In this state of things it is important to call attention as pointedly as possible to the fact that the new theory takes full account of its predecessor and finds it utterly wrong and very widely misleading. The policy of ignoring the structure raised by these scholars and simply offering another in its place would be likely to gain few converts. Unless the contrast is set forth sharply, unless the fatal weaknesses of the now accepted theory and the faults of an unsound method are held up to view repeatedly and unsparingly, the reader may not realize that the antagonism between the two modes of dealing with this literary masterpiece exists at every point, from top to bottom. If a note of strong feeling sounds here and there, it is in the defense of a great cause and of a person who has long been misjudged.

PART II

TRANSLATION

WITH INDICATION OF METRIC FORM

1

Chapter 34

¹ Draw nigh, ye nations, to hear, | and hearken, ye peoples!
  Let the earth listen, and its habitants, | the world, and all its
  offspring.
² For Yahwè has anger in store for the nations, | and wrath for
  all their host; | he has doomed them, appointed them for
  slaughter.
³ Their slain shall be cast out, | and the stench of their corpses
  shall rise, | the mountains shall flow with their blood.
⁴ All the host of heaven shall dissolve, | and the skies be rolled
  like a scroll;
  All their starry host shall wither; | as the foliage wilts from the
  vine, | as the leaves which fall from the fig-tree.

⁵ For my sword is anointed in the heavens, | lo, it descends on
  Edom, | on the people I have doomed, for judgment.
⁶ A sword for Yahwè! 'tis sated with blood, | besmeared with
  fat;
  With the blood of lambs and he-goats, | with the fat of the kid-
  neys of rams.
  For Yahwè has a sacrifice in Bozrah, | a great slaughter in the
  land of Edom.
⁷ Wild oxen shall go down with them to death, | the young of
  the herd with the mighty bulls;
  Their land shall be sated with blood, | and their dust enriched
  with fat.
⁸ For a day of vengeance has Yahwè in store, | a year of requital
  has the Champion of Zion.

⁹ Then shall her* streams become pitch, | and her dust be turned
  into brimstone, | her land shall be burning pitch;
¹⁰ Night and day it shall not be quenched, | its smoke shall ascend
   forever.

¹¹ From age to age her land shall be waste, | for ever and ever
   none shall pass through it;

* The pronoun refers to the imaginary land previously called "Edom."

[¹¹] But the screech-owl and the hedgehog shall possess it, | the great-owl and the raven shall dwell therein.

¹² Over her shall be stretched the line of chaos, | and over [¹²] her nobles the plummet of desolation;
Her name shall be called NO KINGDOM THERE, | and all her princes shall be nothing.

¹³ Thorns shall grow over her palaces, | nettle and thistle in her fortresses;
She shall be the abode of jackals, | a fixed habitation for ostriches.

¹⁴ And demons of the desert shall meet there with goblins, | the satyr shall call to his fellow;
Yea, there the fiend of the storm shall house, | and find a secure retreat.

¹⁵ There the little-owl shall nest and lay, | shall hatch and brood in its* shadow;
There, too, the kites shall gather, | each one [¹⁶] seeking its mate;

¹⁶ From the book of Yahwè their names shall be read, | not one of them shall be missing, | none shall seek in vain for its mate.
For the mouth of Yahwè† has given command, | and his own spirit has gathered them;

¹⁷ He himself cast the lot for them, | his hand apportioned it‡ with the line;
It shall be their heritage forever, | for age upon age they shall dwell therein.

2

(CHAPTER 35)

¹ The desert and the barren shall rejoice, | the wilderness exult, and burst into bloom;
Like the crocus [²] it shall put forth blossoms, | and exult with a shout of gladness.

² The glory of Lebanon shall be given it, | the majesty of Carmel and Sharon;
These shall see the glory of Yahwè, | the majesty of our God.

---

* The pronoun referring to the city whose ruins have just been described.
† Heb. omits *of Yahwè*.   ‡ Heb. adds *for them*.

183

Pg 48 ←

Chap I
4

To: Carl Kleidman
Re: SA Finance Board

I would like to be considered
of the SA Finance Board. I a
Business Administration with a
interested in the allocation o
the courses I have taken will
fair distribution of these fun

Since
Ste

³ Strengthen the hands which are drooping, | the tottering knees make firm;

⁴ Say to those who are faint of heart, | Be strong, fear ye not! Behold, your God will avenge; | the recompense of God will come, | he himself will come to your rescue.

⁵ Then will the eyes of the blind be opened, | and the ears of the deaf unstopped;

⁶ Then will the cripple leap like a hart, | and the tongue of the dumb shout for joy. For waters shall burst forth in the desert, | and running brooks in the wilderness.

⁷ The scorching surface of the sand shall be a pool, | and the parched ground fountains of water; The pasture land shall become a marsh,* | in place of grass shall be reeds and rushes.

⁸ And there shall be there a causeway and a road, | and it shall be called The Holy Way; The unclean and the perverse will not pass over it, | the depraved will not lead astray him who treads it.†

⁹ There will be no lion there, | no ravenous beast will come up thither;‡ | but the redeemed shall walk therein.

¹⁰ And the ransomed of Yahwè shall return, | and come to Zion with singing, | and upon their heads shall be endless joy; Rejoicing and gladness shall be their portion, | sorrow and mourning shall flee away.

3

(CHAPTER 40)

¹ Comfort ye, comfort ye my people, | saith your God; ||
² Speak to Jerusalem kindly, | and to her proclaim ||
That her warfare is fully achieved, | her penance accepted; ||
For she has received from Yahwè two-fold | for all her sins. ||

³ A voice proclaims in the desert: | Prepare the way of Yahwè, ||
Make straight in the barren wild | a highway for our God! ||

---

* Heb., *In the haunt of jackals is her lair.*
† Heb., *The unclean will not pass over it and he is for them he who treads the way and fools will not err.*
‡ Heb. adds *nor be found there.*

⁴ Every valley shall be raised, every mountain | and hill shall
   sink down; ||
The heights shall become a plain, | the rough ridges a lowland. ||
⁵ And the glory of Yahwè shall appear, | and all flesh shall see it
   together, | for the mouth of the Lord has declared it.

⁶ A voice commands, cry aloud! | And the answer comes, What
   shall I cry?
All flesh is grass, | and all its beauty as the flower of the field.
⁷ The grass withers, the flower fades, | when the breath of the
   Lord blows upon it; | surely the people is grass.
⁸ The grass withers, the flower fades, | but the word of our God
   stands forever.

⁹ Get thee up to a lofty mountain, | O Zion, with good tidings; ||
Lift up thy voice with might, | evangelist Jerusalem! || Yea,
   lift it up, fear not;
Say to the cities of Judah, | Behold your God! ||
¹⁰ Lo, Yahwè* comes with might, | and his arm achieves his do-
   minion; ||
Behold, his recompense is with him, | his reward before him. ||
¹¹ Like a shepherd he will feed his flock, | gathering them with
   his arm; ||
The lambs he will carry in his bosom,† | those with young he
   will lead. ||

¹² Who has measured the waters in the hollow of his hand, | marked
   off the heavens with the span, | and enclosed in a measure
   the dust of the earth;
Weighed the mountains in scales, | and the hills in a balance?
¹³ Who has directed the spirit of the Lord, | or what man of his
   counsel may teach him?
¹⁴ What adviser has shown him the right, | and taught him the
   pathway of judgment;
Has given unto him instruction, | and shown him the way of
   discernment?
¹⁵ Even the nations are a drop from a bucket, | they are counted
   as the dust on a balance; | yea, he takes up the islands
   like grains of sand.

* Heb. adds *the Lord*.
† Heb., *He will gather the lambs in his arms and carry them in his bosom*.

¹⁶ Lebanon itself would not suffice for fuel, | nor its beasts for a burnt oblation.
¹⁷ All the nations are as nothing before him, | they are counted by him as naught whatever.*

¹⁸ To whom, then, will ye liken God, | or what semblance will ye devise for him?
¹⁹ An idol, the workman casts it, | the smith overlays it with gold, | fashions for it silver chains!
²⁰ He who is poor† in substance‡ | chooses a wood that will not decay;
Seeks out a skilful workman, | to set up an image that shall stand securely.

²¹ Will ye not understand? Will ye not hear? | Has it not been told you from the beginning? | Have ye not seen aright from the founding§ of the world?
²² It is he who sits on the circle of the earth, | and its inhabitants are as grasshoppers;
Who stretches out the heavens as a veil, | and spreads them like a tent to dwell in.
²³ It is he who brings princes to naught; | the rulers of the earth he makes as nothing.
²⁴ They are scarcely planted, they are scarcely sown, | their stem has hardly struck root in the ground,
When he breathes upon them, and they wither, | and the tempest bears them away like stubble.

²⁵ To whom, then, will ye liken me, as mine equal? | saith the Holy One. ||
²⁶ Lift up your eyes to the heavens, and see; | who created these? ||
He who brings out their host by number, | calling each by his name; ||
Of all their mightiest, excelling in strength, | not one is missing. ||

²⁷ Wherefore dost thou say, O Jacob, | and why declarest thou, Israel,
My way is hid from the Lord, | my right overlooked by my God?

* Heb., *as nothingness and vanity.*   † Lit., *reduced to poverty.*
‡ Heb., *oblation.*   § Heb., *have ye not seen the foundations.*

²⁸ Dost thou not know? Hast thou not heard? | Yahwè is the
    God everlasting, | creator of the ends of the earth.
  He tires not, grows not weary, | nor can his wisdom be fath-
    omed.
²⁹ He gives new strength to the fainting, | and vigor to those who
    are powerless.
³⁰ The young men, indeed, may flag and languish, | the strongest
    youth may fall exhausted;
³¹ But they who hope in Yahwè shall renew their might, | they
    shall mount on pinions like eagles,
  They shall run and not be weary, | ever proceeding they shall
    not faint.

4

(CHAPTER 41)

¹ Listen to me, ye distant lands; | and the nations, let them
    redouble their strength!
  Let them approach, and speak; | we will come together for
    judgment.

² Who aroused from the east a righteous one,* | summoning him
    to his service?
  He will deliver up nations before him, | kings he shall tread
    under foot;
  With his sword he shall make them as dust, | as driven stub-
    ble with his bow.
³ He shall pursue them, and pass on safely; | no path shall he
    tread with his feet.
⁴ Who has done and performed such things, | proclaiming from the
    first the ages to come?
  I, Yahwè, am the first, | and with the last I am also.

⁵ The far lands saw, and feared, | the ends of the earth were terri-
    fied; | they approached, and came near.
⁶ Each one aided his neighbor, | and said to his fellow, Take
    courage!
⁷ The craftsman encouraged the smith, | the smoother with the
    hammer him that smote on the anvil;
  Saying of the soldering, It is good. | And they fastened it with
    nails, that it should not be moved.

* Heb., *righteousness.*

⁸ But thou, Israel, my servant, | Jacob, whom I have chosen, | seed of Abraham, my friend;—

⁹ Thou whom I plucked from the ends of the earth, | and called from its farthest corners,
Saying to thee, Thou art my servant, | I have chosen thee, not despised thee;—

¹⁰ Fear not, for I am with thee; | look not anxiously about, for I am thy God;
I will strengthen thee and help thee, | I will stay thee with my true right hand.

¹¹ Confounded they shall be, and put to shame, | all thine opponents; ||
They shall become as naught, and perish, | those who assail thee. ||

¹² Thou shalt seek, but not find them, | these thine aggressors; ||
They shall be as nothing at all, | who contend against thee. ||

¹³ For I, Yahwè thy God, | hold thy right hand; ||
It is I who say to thee, Fear not, | I myself will help thee. ||

¹⁴ Fear not, thou worm Jacob, | thou feeble insect* Israel;
I myself aid thee, saith Yahwè, | thy redeemer is the Holy One of Israel.

¹⁵ I will make thee to be a threshing-sledge, | yea, a new sledge armed with teeth;
Thou shalt thresh mountains and shatter them, | hills thou shalt make as chaff.

¹⁶ Thou shalt winnow, and the wind shall carry them, | they shall be scattered by the tempest.
But thou shalt exult in Yahwè, | in the Holy One of Israel shalt thou glory.

¹⁷ The lowly ones and the needy | seek water, but find it not; | their tongue is parched with thirst.
I, Yahwè, will answer them, | the God of Israel will not forsake them.

¹⁸ I will open rivers in the hills, | and springs in the midst of the valleys;
I will make the desert a standing pool, | the arid land fountains of water.

* Heb., *ye men of Israel.*

¹⁹ I will plant in the desert the cedar, | the acacia, and myrtle, and olive;
I will put in the barren the cypress, | the plane and the pine tree at once.
²⁰ To the end that they may see and know, | may attend, and perceive together,
That the hand of Yahwè has wrought this thing, | the Holy One of Israel has brought it to pass.

²¹ Present your champions, | saith Yahwè; ||
Bring near your idols,* | saith the King of Jacob. ||
²² Let them approach,† and announce to us | the things which shall happen. ||
The beginnings, what are they? Tell us, | that we may take notice, ||
That we may know their conclusion; | or declare for us coming events. ||
²³ Foretell what shall come hereafter, | that we may know that ye are gods, ||
Who can benefit and harm; that we may look for help, | and be terrified together. ||
²⁴ Nay, indeed ye are nothing, | and naught can ye do. || Misguided is he who prefers you! ‡

²⁵ I aroused one from the north, and he came; | yea, from the east, calling on my name!
He shall trample§ on princes like mire, | as the potter treads upon clay.
²⁶ Who announced, from the first, that we might know? | from aforetime, that we might say, True!
There was none who announced, none proclaimed, | nor will any attend to your words.
²⁷ The beginnings of Zion, behold them! | and I give to Jerusalem a herald of joy.
²⁸ But when I looked,¶ there was no one; | nay, among these there** was no adviser, | none whom I might ask, and be answered.
²⁹ Lo, they are all of them naught whatever, | vapor and vanity all their works!††

* Heb., *strong ones* (fem.).
‡ Heb., *An abomination* (fem.), *he chooseth you.*
§ Heb., *shall come.*
¶ That is, to the gods of the heathen.
** Heb. prefixes *and.*
† Heb., *bring near.*
†† Heb. adds *their idols.*

5

(Chapters 42 : 1–43 : 7)

(*Yahwè addresses the peoples*)

1 Behold my Servant, whom I sustain; | my chosen, in whom my soul delights.

  I have caused my spirit to rest upon him; | he shall bring forth judgment for the nations.

2 He will not cry out, nor shout aloud, | nor make his voice heard in the street;

3 A bruised reed he will not break, | a dimly burning wick he will not quench.

4 He will bring forth justice faithfully; | [4] chiding not, nor dealing harshly,

  Till he have established judgment in the earth; | and for his law the far countries wait.

(*Yahwè addresses his Servant*)

5 Thus saith the One God, Yahwè,

Who created the heavens, and stretched them out, | who established the earth, with all its offspring,

Who gives breath to the people upon it, | and life to those who walk therein:

6 I, Yahwè, called thee in righteousness, | I took thee by the hand, and have kept thee, | I have made thee my pledge to the peoples, the light of the nations;

7 To open the sightless eyes, | to bring out the captives from the prison, | from the dungeon those who sit in darkness.

(*Again addressing the peoples*)

8 I am Yahwè, that is my name, | my glory I give to no other, | nor my praise to graven images.

9 The former things have come to pass; | things which are new I now foretell, | before they spring forth I proclaim them to you.

(*The Servant exults*)

10 Sing a new song unto Yahwè, | his praise from the end of the earth!

Let the sea roar,* with all that it holds, | the distant shores and their inhabitants.

* Heb., *Those who go down to the sea.*

¹¹ Let the desert and its cities lift up their voice, | the villages also
which Kedar inhabits;
Let the people of Sela raise a glad cry, | let them shout from
the top of the mountains.
¹² Let them give glory to Yahwè, | and proclaim his praise in the
farthest lands.
¹³ Yahwè goes forth like a mighty hero, | like a warrior he wakes
his ire;
He calls to battle, yea, shouts aloud, | shows himself mighty
against his foes!

(*Yahwè speaks*)

¹⁴ For a long time I have held my peace, | mute, restraining my-
self; ||
I will now cry out like a woman in travail, | panting and gasp-
ing at once. ||
¹⁵ I will dry up mountains and heights, | all their herbage I will
wither; ||
I will change the rivers into islands, | and make dry the pools. ||
¹⁶ And I will make the blind to walk | in a way they know not, ||
In paths which they have not tried | I will conduct them. ||
The darkness before them I will turn to light, | rough ways to
level ground. ||
These are the things which I have prepared, | nor have I re-
nounced them. ||
¹⁷ Turned back, utterly shamed shall they be, | who trust graven
idols, ||
Who say unto molten images, | Ye are our gods! ||

(*Yahwè addresses Israel*)

¹⁸ Hearken, ye who are deaf; | and ye who are blind, look and see!
¹⁹ Who is blind but my Servant, | or deaf like the Messenger I
send?
Who is as deaf* as my Perfected One,† | or as blind as the Ser-
vant of Yahwè?
²⁰ Seeing great things, but not keeping them in mind, | with ears
open, yet without hearkening!
²¹ Yahwè was pleased, for his righteousness' sake, | to magnify his
law and make it glorious.
²² 'But his people are robbed and plundered; | they are all en-
trapped in holes, | and hidden away in dungeons;

* Heb., *blind*. † Or *Meshullam* (proper name).

They are become a prey, with none to rescue; | a plunder, with
none to say, Restore it!'

23 O that one of you would hear this word, | would attend, and
proclaim* it for the future:

24 Who gave up Jacob to the spoiler, | and Israel to those who
plundered?
Was it not Yahwè, against whom they† had sinned; | in whose
ways they refused to go, | and to whose law they would
not listen?

25 So he poured out upon him the heat of his wrath, | and his
might like a flame;‡
It scorched him round about, but he understood not; | it burned
him, but he would not comprehend.

43 : 1 But now, thus saith Yahwè,— | he who created thee, Jacob, |
he who fashioned thee, Israel:—
Fear not, for I have redeemed thee, | I have called thee by
name, thou art mine.

2 When thou passest through the waters, I am with thee; | and
when through the rivers, they shall not overflow thee.
If thou pass through fire, thou shalt not be scorched; | and if
through flame, it shall not consume thee.

3 For I, Yahwè, am thy God; | the Holy One of Israel is thy
helper.
Egypt I give for thy ransom, | Ethiopia and Seba in return for
thee;

4 Because thou art precious in mine eyes, | honored art thou, and
I love thee.
I will give in thy stead far countries,§ | peoples in exchange for
thy life.

5 Fear not, for I am with thee;
I will bring thy seed from the east, | and from the west I will
gather thee;

6 I will say to the north, Give up! | and to the south, Withhold
not!
Bring my sons from afar, | and my daughters from the end of
the earth;

7 Every one who is called by my name, | whom for my glory I
created, | whom I fashioned, yea, I prepared.

* Heb., *hear*.   † Heb., *we*.
‡ Heb., *heat, his wrath, and the might of battle.*
§ Heb., *mankind.*

6

(CHAPTERS 43 : 8–44 : 5)

^{43 : 8} Bring forth* the people who are blind, though having eyes; |
     those who are deaf, yet having ears!
[⁹] Gather together, all ye nations, | and let the peoples assemble.

⁹ Who among them can declare this, | and show unto us the be-
     ginnings?
     Let them bring their witnesses to justify them, | to hear, and
     respond, It is true!
¹⁰ Ye are my witnesses, saith Yahwè, | and my Servant, whom I
     have chosen,
     That ye may know, and believe me, | may perceive that I am
     that One;
     Before me, no god was created, | nor shall there be any after me.
¹¹ I, I, am Yahwè, | no other than I can rescue;
¹² It was I who proclaimed it, and delivered; | I declared it, no
     stranger among you; | and ye are my witnesses, saith
     Yahwè.
¹³ I am God, [¹³] yea, from henceforth the same; | there is none
     who can snatch from my hand; | I perform, and who shall
     reverse it?

¹⁴ Thus saith Yahwè, | your redeemer, the Holy One of Israel:
     For your sake I will send,† | and cause all the fugitives to em-
     bark,‡ | with shouts of rejoicing, in their ships.§
¹⁵ I am Yahwè, your Holy One, | the creator of Israel, your King.
¹⁶ Thus saith Yahwè,— | who makes a way in the sea, | a path in
     the mighty waters;
¹⁷ Who makes an end of horse and chariot, | host and hero to-
     gether;
     They sink down, to rise no more, | they are quenched, gone out
     like a wick:—
¹⁸ Remember not the beginnings, | consider no more the former
     things;
¹⁹ Behold, I bring a new thing to pass, | even now it springs forth,
     will ye not perceive it?
     Even in the desert I make a road, | rivers in the arid plain.

---

* Heb., *He brought forth*.   † Heb. adds *to Babylon*.
‡ Heb. adds *and to Chaldea*.
§ Literally, *in the ships where they shout for joy*.

²⁰ The beasts of the wild will honor me, | the ostriches and the jackals;

For I give waters in the wilderness, | streams in the arid waste;
²¹ To give drink to my chosen people, | [²¹] those whom I fashioned for myself, | who shall set forth my praises.

²² Not thou didst call me, O Jacob, | that thou hast labored to retain me, O Israel!
²³ Hast thou not brought me thy sheep for burnt-offerings? | with thy sacrifices hast thou not honored me?

Nay, I have not made thee serve with offerings, | nor labor for me with incense.
²⁴ Hast thou not bought me the fragrant reed with thy money? | with the fat of thy sacrifices hast thou not sated me?

Nay, rather, thou hast burdened me with thy sins, | hast wearied me with thine iniquities!

²⁵ I it is, I, and no other! | For my sake I blot out thy wickedness, | thy sins I remember no more.
²⁶ Remind me of the past, and let us judge our cause; | set forth the matter, that thou mayest be justified.
²⁷ Thy first father transgressed, | and thy representatives sinned grievously against me.
²⁸ Therefore I let my holy cities* be profaned; | I put Jacob under the curse, | and gave up Israel to mockery.

^{44 : 1} But now hearken, Jacob, my Servant, | and Israel, whom I have chosen:
² Thus saith Yahwè, thy maker, | who formed thee from the womb, and will help thee;

Fear not, Jacob, my Servant, | Jeshurun, whom I have chosen.
³ For I will pour out water on the thirsty land, | running brooks on the arid ground;

I will pour out my spirit upon thy seed, | and my blessing upon thine offspring.
⁴ They shall spring up like grass amid waters,† | like willows by water-courses.
⁵ This one will say, I am of Yahwè, | another will call himself by Jacob's name;

And another will write on his hand, Yahwè's, | and will give himself the name of Israel.

* Heb., *the holy princes.*   † Heb., *They shall spring up in—among—grass.*

7

(Chapter 44 : 6–23)

44 : 6 Thus saith* the King of Israel | and his Redeemer, Yahwè of
　　Hosts:
　　I am the first and the last; | beside me there is no God.
7 Who, like me, could proclaim it, | could declare and set it forth
　　before me;
　　Announcing the future from of old,† | declaring unto us‡ the
　　things to come?
8 Be not in dread, nor affirighted; | have I not announced it from
　　the past, | and declared it, with you as my witnesses?
　　Is there a God beside me? | or§ a Rock, of whom I know not?

9 All they who make idols are inane, | and worthless their precious
　　productions;
　　False gods,¶ their 'witnesses' see not | and know not; that they
　　may be disgraced.
10 Who fashions a god, and casts | an image,—to profit him
　　nought?
11 Lo, all who hold to them shall be shamed; | they who make
　　them, confusion is their utmost !**
　　Let them all assemble, and stand forth; | affrighted they shall
　　be, confounded together !

12 The ironsmith cuts out the metal,†† | and fashions it over the
　　coals;
　　With hammers he gives it shape, | forges it with his mighty arm.
　　Yea, he hungers, and is wearied; | he has tasted no water, and
　　is faint.

13 The carpenter stretches a line, | and marks the shape with a
　　pencil;
　　He fashions it with the square, | describes its form with the
　　compass.
　　He makes it like a human figure, | like a comely man, to dwell
　　in a house.

---

* Heb. inserts *Yahwè*.
† Heb., *from my putting an eternal people, and the things to come.*
‡ Heb., *them.*　　　　　　　　　　　　　　　§ Heb., *and there is not.*
¶ This word is not in the Hebrew.
** Heb., *they who fashion, they are of mankind.*
†† Heb., *The ironsmith, an ax.*

¹⁴ One cuts down* cedar trees; | he chooses an ilex, or an oak,
And lets it grow with the trees of the wood; | he plants a fir for
the rains to nourish.
¹⁵ So it becomes fuel for the man; | he takes a portion and warms
himself, | he kindles a fire and bakes bread;
Yea, he makes a god, and worships, | he fashions an image and
bows before it.
¹⁶ The half he burns in the fire, | yea, over the half he makes his
meal, | he roasts meat, and is satisfied;
Yea, he warms himself, and cries, Aha! | I am warm, I have
seen the fire!
¹⁷ Then of the rest he makes a god, | an image, and bows before it;
He falls down prostrate and prays to it, | saying, Deliver me,
for thou art my god!

¹⁸ They know not, they have no discernment; | for besmeared are
their eyes, past seeing, | and their hearts, past right under-
standing.
¹⁹ They have not straitly considered; | theirs not the wisdom and
insight to say:
The half I burned in the fire, | bread I baked† on its embers, | I
roasted flesh, and did eat;
And now shall I make of the residue an idol,‡ | and bow down
to the product of a tree?
²⁰ Feeder on ashes! A misguided heart has led him astray, | nor
can he rescue himself; | nor does he say, Is there not in my
right hand a lie?

²¹ Remember these things, O Jacob; | O Israel, for thou art my
Servant;
As such I fashioned thee, mine art thou; | O Israel, thou mayest
not forget me!
²² I will sweep away thy sins like a cloud, | and thy transgressions
like mist; | return to me, for I have redeemed thee.

²³ Sing, ye heavens, for he§ has wrought it; | shout, ye depths of
the earth;
Break forth, ye mountains, into song; | forest, and every tree
therein!
For Yahwè has ransomed Jacob, | he glorifies himself in Israel.

* Heb., *To cut down.*   † Heb. adds *also.*
‡ Heb., *abomination.*   § Heb., *Yahwè.*

8

(CHAPTERS 44 : 24–45 : 25)

44 : 24 Thus saith Yahwè, thy redeemer, | he who formed thee
from the womb:
I am Yahwè, maker of all;
Stretching forth the heavens—I alone, | making firm the earth
—who beside me?

25 Who confounds the omens of babblers, | and mocks at di-
viners; ||
Who turns back the wise in confusion, | befooling their wis-
dom; ||

26 Who confirms the word of his Servant, | and perfects the coun-
sel of his Messenger;*
Who says to Jerusalem, Be peopled; | and to the cities of Judah,
Be builded, | yea, all its ruins I restore;

27 Who says to the deep, Be dry, | and thy rivers I make dry
ground:†

45 : 1 Thus saith Yahwè, to his Anointed,‡ | to him whose right
hand I hold,
To trample nations before him, | and loosen the loins of kings;
To open for him the portals, | and the gates shall not be closed:

2 I myself will go before thee, | and I will make straight the
ways;§
I will shatter the doors of bronze, | and sunder the bolts of iron;

3 I will give thee the treasures of darkness, | the hoards long
hidden in secret.

For¶ I am Yahwè, he who calls thee | by thy name, the God of
Israel;

4 For the sake of my servant Jacob, | and Israel mine elect,
I call** to thee by thy name, | I entitle thee, while thou knowest
me not.

5 I am Yahwè, there is no other, | beside me there is no god; | I
gird thee, while yet thou knowest me not;

---

* Heb., *messengers.*
† Heb. adds 28*Who says of Cyrus, He is my shepherd, and all my pleasure he
shall fulfil; and saying of Jerusalem, She shall be built; and the temple, Thy
foundation shall be laid.*

‡ Heb. adds *to Cyrus.*
¶ Heb., *That thou mayest know that.*

§ Heb., *heights* (?).
** Heb., *and I called.*

⁶ That all may know, from the east | and from the west, that
    none is beside me; | I am Yahwè, there is no other.
⁷ Maker of light and creator of darkness, | author of peace and
    creator of evil; | I, Yahwè, perform all this.

⁸ Shower, ye heavens, from above, | and let the clouds rain down
    righteousness;
Let the earth open, and rescue bloom forth,* | let righteousness
    spring up at once; | I, Yahwè, have brought it to pass.

⁹ Ho, man that strives with his maker, | a potsherd with him
    who formed† the earth!
Says the clay to him who fashions it, What doest thou? | or,
    Thy work has no value at all?
¹⁰ Ho, man saying to a father, What begettest thou? | or, to a
    mother, With what dost thou travail?
¹¹ Thus saith Yahwè; | the Holy One of Israel, and his maker:
Will ye question me‡ about my children? | command me con-
    cerning the work of my hands?
¹² It was I who fashioned the earth, | and man upon it I created;
My own hand stretched the heavens, | and all their host I ap-
    pointed.

¹³ I have raised him up in righteousness, | and all his ways I make
    straight;
He shall build up my city, | and my captives he shall set free,
Not for price nor for hire, | proclaims the Lord of Hosts.

¹⁴ Thus saith Yahwè:
The wealth of Egypt, and the merchandise of Cush, | and the
    Sabeans, men of stature, ||
They shall pass before thee, and be thine, | thee shall they fol-
    low; ||
Passing,§ they shall fall down before thee, | to thee make en-
    treaty: ||
Verily God is with thee, nor is there another, | a god beside
    him. ||
¹⁵ Yea, thou art a God who veils himself, | the God of Israel.¶ ||
¹⁶ Confounded, utterly put to shame, | are they all together; ||

* Heb., *and let them bring forth rescue.*   † Heb., *with potsherds of.*
‡ Heb., *Ask of me the things to come.*   § Heb. adds *in fetters.*
¶ Heb. adds *the saviour.*

Gone are they into disgrace, | the makers of idols.* ||
¹⁷ Israel is saved by Yahwè | with endless salvation; ||
Ye shall not be ashamed nor confounded | for ever and ever. ||

¹⁸ For thus saith Yahwè,
He who created the heavens— | he is God; ||
Maker and fashioner of the earth— | he established it; ||
Not a waste did he create it, | he made it for habitation: ||
I am Yahwè, there is no other.
¹⁹ Not in secret did I declare it, | in a place in a land of darkness; ||
I said not to the seed of Jacob, | Seek me for nought. ||
I, Yahwè, proclaim aright, | declare the truth. ||

²⁰ Assemble, now, and approach! | Present yourselves for judgment, | ye remnant of the nations! ||
No knowledge have they who carry about | their image of wood, ||
Who make supplication to a god | that cannot assist them. ||
²¹ Proclaim the trial, and produce your idols,† | yea, let them consult! ||
Who declared this from the first, | of old proclaimed it? ||
Did not I, Yahwè? Nor is there another, | a god beside me; ||
A god righteous and rescuing, | there is none but I. ||

²² Turn ye to me, and be saved, | all ye ends of the earth! ||
For I am God, there is no other; | [²³] by myself I swear it, ||
²³ The truth is gone forth from my mouth, | my word‡ shall not turn back: ||
That to me every knee shall bow, | every tongue shall swear. ||

²⁴ Yea, in Yahwè, men shall say,§ | are righteousness and strength; ||
Unto him shall come in abasement | all his opponents. ||
²⁵ In Yahwè shall be justified and in him shall exult | all the seed of Israel. ||

9

(Chapter 46)

¹ Bel sinks, Nebo breaks down! | They¶ have proved like the beasts and the cattle;

---

* Heb., *pangs.*
† Heb. simply, *proclaim and produce.*
‡ Heb., *a word and.*
§ Heb., *to me he said.*
¶ Heb. adds *their idols.*

The things which they* carried are heavily borne, | a load on a jaded beast.

2 They droop, they sink down together; | they are powerless to save their burden, | yea, themselves go into captivity.

3 Hearken to me, house of Jacob, | all who remain of Israel's house—
Borne since ye came from the womb, | carried from the day of your birth!—

4 Even to your old age I am the same, | until ye are white-haired I bear you.
It is I who made, and will carry; | I who bear, and will rescue.

5 To whom will ye liken me, and make me equal? | To whom compare me, that the likeness may appear?

6 They pour out gold from the purse, | and silver they weigh with the balance;
They hire a smith, and he makes it a god, | then they fall down and worship!

7 They lift it, and bear it on their shoulders; | they put it down; there it stands, | it cannot stir from its place.
Yea, to it they cry, but it answers not, | it cannot deliver them from their distress.

8 Consider these things, and be assured; | recall this to mind, ye evil doers! | [9] Remember the past, from the very beginning;

9 For I, and I only, am God; | there is none other like me:

10 Announcing the end from the first, | from aforetime things not yet performed;
Saying, My counsel shall stand, | and all my pleasure I will execute.

11 Calling my Servant† from the east, | from a far land the man of my counsel.
Yea, I announced it, and bring it to pass; | I shaped it, and I will perform it.

12 Hear me, ye stubborn of heart, | ye who are far from righteousness!
I bring near my triumph, it is not far off, | and my rescue will not delay.
I will put salvation in Zion, | bestow upon Israel my glory.

* Heb., *ye*.   † Heb., *Calling a bird of prey.*

10

(Chapter 47)

¹ Get thee down, sit in the dust, | virgin Babylon; ||
Sit on the ground, no throne for thee, | daughter of Chaldea! ||
For thou shalt no longer be called | the tender and dainty. ||
² Take the mill-stones and grind meal, | put off thy veil; ||
Lift up the train, uncover the leg, | pass through the streams.* ||
³ Vengeance I will take, nor will I be entreated, | saith our redeemer,† ||
⁴ Yahwè of Hosts is his name, | the Holy One of Israel. ||

⁵ Sit in silence and walk in darkness, | daughter of Chaldea; ||
For thou shalt no longer be named | the mistress of kingdoms.‡ ||
⁷ Thou saidst, I shall stand forever, | a queen for all time; ||
But of one thing thou tookest no account, | thou didst not heed the end! ||

⁸ Now hear this, thou lover of pleasure, | who dwellest secure, ||
Thou who sayest in thy heart, | There is none beside me, ||
I shall never be left a widow, | nor see myself childless: ||
⁹ These two shall indeed overtake thee, | of a sudden, at one blow; ||
Bereavement and widowhood, to the full, | they shall come upon thee; ||
Spite of thy host of sorceries, the might | of thine incantations. ||

¹⁰ Thou didst feel secure in thy wickedness, | thou saidst, No one sees me; ||
Thy wisdom and thine understanding | did lead thee astray; ||
And thou didst say in thy heart, | There is none beside me. ||
¹¹ But evil shall come upon thee | which no bribe can avert,§ ||
Upon thee disaster shall fall, | no escape canst thou purchase; ||
Yea, a storm shall break over thee suddenly, | of which thou hast no foreboding. ||

* Heb. adds *Thy nakedness shall be uncovered, and thy shame shall be seen.*
† Heb., *nor will I meet any man.* ⁴*Our redeemer, Yahwè of Hosts is his name.*
‡ Heb. adds ⁶*I was angry with my people, and let mine inheritance be profaned; I gave them into thine hand; thou didst show them no mercy, upon the aged thou didst make thy yoke exceeding heavy.*
§ Heb., *whose dawn thou knowest not.*

¹² Stand fast with thine incantations, | thy host of enchantments, ||
    the goods thou hast earned from thy youth!
Perchance thou mayest succeed, | mayest yet play the tyrant. ||
¹³ Thou art jaded with the host of thy counsels; | let them stand
    forth and save thee, ||
Those who partition the heavens, | who gaze at the stars, ||
Who by the new moons predict | what things* shall befall thee. ||

¹⁴ See, like stubble are they all, | the fire consumes them;
They cannot deliver themselves | from the grasp of the flame. ||
(No coals for warming are these, | not a fire to sit near! ||)
¹⁵ Thus have availed thee thy hard-earned allies, | thy partners
    from thy youth; ||
They flee in confusion, each one his own way; | there is none
    to save thee! ||

11
(Chapter 48)

¹ Hearken to this, O House of Jacob!—
These who are called by Israel's name, | who sprung from the
    seed of Judah;
Who swear by the name of Yahwè, | and invoke the God of
    Israel;—
² Not in truth, nor by right, | [²] do they name themselves from
    the holy city,
And rest themselves on the God of Israel, | Yahwè of Hosts is
    his name!

³ The former things I declared of old, | from my mouth they
    issued, and I made them known; | then suddenly I wrought,
    and they came to pass;
⁴ Because I knew thou art stubborn— | thy neck is a band of
    iron, | thy forehead is brass.
⁵ Yea, I told them to thee from the first, | before they appeared,
    I announced them;
Lest thou shouldst say, My idol† wrought them, | my graven
    and molten image ordained them.

⁶ Thou hast heard and seen all this, | and couldst thou not have
    proclaimed it?‡

* Heb., *from the things which.*   † Heb., *My pain.*
‡ Heb., *and ye, will ye not proclaim it?*

I make thee henceforth to hear new things, | things kept in store, which thou hast not known.

[7] They are now created, not of old, | before to-day* thou hast never heard them— | lest thou shouldst say, Behold, I knew them.

[8] Thou hast never heard, thou hast never known, | from of old thine ear has not been open.

Yea, I know indeed that thou playest false, | transgressor from birth thou art rightly called.

[9] For my name's sake I restrain my wrath, | for the sake of my praise I bridle it for thee, | not willing to cut thee off.

[10] I have refined thee for myself like silver,† | I have tested thee in the furnace of affliction.

[11] For my sake, mine own sake, I must act, | for how should my name‡ be profaned? | Nor give I my glory to another.

[12] Listen to me, O Jacob, | and Israel whom I called. ||
It is I, I myself am the first; | I am also the last. ||

[13] My hand established the earth, my right hand | stretched out the heavens; ||
Whenever I call to their host,§ | they stand forth at once. ||

[14] Assemble, all ye, and hear! | What one among them foretold this?
The One God,¶ Yahwè, loves him, | he will execute his pleasure and his might.**

[15] It was I who declared it, I who called him; | I brought him, and prospered his way.

[16] Draw near to me, hear ye this; | not in secret have I told it, from the first; | since the time it began, there am I!††

[17] Thus saith Yahwè, | thy redeemer, the Holy One of Israel,
I am Yahwè thy God, | who teaches thee to profit, | who leads thee in the way thou shouldst go.

[18] Hadst thou but hearkened to my bidding, | thy peace would have been like a river, | thy righteousness like waves of the sea.

---

* Heb. inserts *and*.   † Heb., *I have refined thee, but not with silver.*
‡ Heb. omits the noun.   § Literally, *to them.*
¶ Heb. otherwise.
** Heb., *his pleasure on Babylon, and his might on Chaldea.*
†† Heb. adds *And now my Lord Yahwè hath sent me, and his spirit.*

¹⁹ Thine offspring had numbered as the sand, | and the fruit of
thy loins as its grains; | they would never be cut off nor
destroyed* from before me.

²⁰ Go forth, flee,† with a shout of joy; | proclaim this, make it
known;
Bring it forth to the end of the earth: | Yahwè‡ redeems his ser-
vant Jacob!
²¹ They thirsted not, in the deserts through which he led them; |
water he made to flow for them from the crag; | he cleft
the rock, and the water came pouring out.
²² No peace, saith Yahwè, for the wicked.

12

(Chapter 49)

¹ Hear me, ye distant shores; | and hearken, ye nations, from
far.
Yahwè called me from the womb, | from the bowels of my
mother he named my name.
² He made my mouth like a keen sword, | in the shadow of his
hand he concealed me;
He made me a sharpened arrow, | in his quiver he hid me away.
³ And he said to me, Thou art my Servant; | Israel, in whom I
will glorify myself.

⁴ But I said, I have toiled in vain, | I have spent my strength for
nothing at all;§
Nevertheless my right is with Yahwè, | and my recompense
rests with my God.

⁵ But now Yahwè saith | (he who formed me from the womb to
be his Servant,
To bring back Jacob to him, | and to collect for him Israel;
For I was honored in Yahwè's eyes, | and my God became my
strength),
⁶ Yea, he saith:
It is too light a thing that thou shouldst be my Servant, | to
lift up the tribes of Jacob, | to restore the residue of Israel;

---

* Heb., *nor his name be destroyed.*
† Heb., *Go forth from Babylon, flee from Chaldea.*
‡ Heb. prefixes *say.*   § Heb., *for emptiness and vanity.*

I will make thee the light of the nations, | that my rescue may
reach to the end of the earth.

⁷ Thus saith Yahwè, | the redeemer of Israel, and his Holy One, |
to one self-despised, world-abhorred,* servant of rulers:
Kings shall see, and rise up; | princes, and shall prostrate them-
selves;
Because of Yahwè, who is faithful, | the Holy One of Israel,
who has chosen thee.

⁸ Thus saith Yahwè:
In a time of grace I have answered thee, | in a day of rescue
have helped thee;
I make thee† the peoples' pledge, to uplift the world, | to appor-
tion anew the desolate inheritances;
⁹ Saying to the prisoners, Come forth! | and to those who are in
darkness, Appear!
Along the ways they find pasture, | on all the bare heights shall
be grazing for them;
¹⁰ They shall not hunger nor thirst, | neither sun nor scorching
air shall smite them;
For He who has pity will lead them, | and to fountains of water
will guide them.
¹¹ And I will make all my mountains a way, | and my highways
shall be built up.
¹² Lo, these shall come from afar, | these from the north and the
west, | and these from the region of Syene.‡
¹³ Shout for joy, ye heavens, and exult, O earth! | Let the moun-
tains break forth into song.
For Yahwè has compassion on his people, | will show mercy to
his afflicted ones.

¹⁴ But Zion said, I am forsaken | of Yahwè, my Lord has forgotten
me.
¹⁵ Can a woman forget her babe, | with no pity for the child of
her womb?
Yea, these indeed may forget; | but I, I can not forget thee.
¹⁶ I have graven thee on my palms, | thy walls are continually
before me.

* Heb., *abhorring nations.*
† Heb., *I have kept thee and made thee.*
‡ Heb., *the land of Sinim.*

¹⁷ Thy builders outstrip thy destroyers,* | and those who lay thee
waste shall go forth from thee.
¹⁸ Lift up thine eyes round about, and see: | they all gather, they
come to thee.
Yea, as I live, saith Yahwè, | thou shalt be decked with them all
as with ornaments, | thou shalt fasten them on as a bride
her jewels.

¹⁹ True, I laid thee waste, made thee desolate, | razed thee even
to the ground;† ||
But now, thou shalt be too strait for thy people, | thy devourers
far removed. ||
²⁰ Yet will sound in thine ears these words | from the children
thou hadst lost: ||
The place is become too strait for me, | make me room to dwell
in! ||
²¹ And thou wilt say to thyself, | Who has borne these for me? ||
I was bereft and barren,‡ | but these, who has reared them? ||
Indeed I was left quite alone; | whence then do these come? ||

²² Thus saith Yahwè, my Lord:
Lo, I lift up my hand to the nations, | to the peoples I raise
my signal,
And they shall bring thy sons in their arms, | and thy daughters
shall be borne on their shoulders.
²³ Kings shall be thy guardians, | and their queens thy nursing-
mothers.
With their faces to the ground they shall fall down before thee, |
and lick the dust of thy feet.
Then thou wilt know that I am Yahwè, | and that those who
await me shall not be ashamed.
²⁴ Can booty be recovered from a giant? | or can the captives of
a tyrant§ be rescued?
²⁵ Yea, thus saith Yahwè:
Even the captives of the giant shall be taken, | and the prey of
the tyrant be delivered;
For I myself will espouse thy cause, | I myself will rescue thy
children.

* Heb., *Thy children hasten; those who tear thee down.*
† Heb., *Thy ruins and thy devastation and the land of thy ruined condition.*
‡ Heb. adds *exiled and imprisoned* (?).
§ Heb., *righteous man.*

²⁶ I will make thy tormentors to eat their own flesh, | to be drunk
   with their own blood as with new wine.
And it shall be known to all mankind | that I am Yahwè, thy
   saviour, | and thy redeemer, the Mighty One of Jacob.

13

(Chapter 50)

¹ Thus saith Yahwè:
Where is the bill of divorcement | with which I dismissed your
   mother?
Or to which one of my creditors | is it that I have sold you?
Nay, for your sins ye were sold, | for your crimes was your
   mother put away!
² Wherefore did I come and find no one; | call, but with none to
   answer?
Lack I aught of power to ransom? | Is there not in me strength
   to rescue?
Lo, by my rebuke I dry the sea; | rivers I make an arid plain;
Their fish are distressed for want of water, | perish for lack of
   moisture.
³ I clothe the heavens with darkness, | sackcloth I make their
   covering.

(The Servant of Yahwè speaks)

⁴ Yahwè my Lord has given to me | a tongue for teaching; ||
To give to the fainting a word of help* | he wakens me early, ||
Yea, early he quickens mine ear | to hear as a pupil; ||
⁵ Yahwè my Lord has opened mine ear, | and I was not wilful, ||
   I turned not back in rebellion.
⁶ I gave my back to the smiters, | my cheeks to those who plucked
   the beard, ||
My face I shielded not | from insult and spitting. ||
⁷ For Yahwè my Lord is my helper, | hence I was not con-
   founded; ||
Therefore I set my face like flint, | knowing that I should not
   be shamed. ||
⁸ My champion is near; who opposes me? | let us stand forth
   together. ||
Who is the adversary of my cause? | let him approach me. ||

* Heb., *To know, to help the fainting with a word.*

⁹ Nay, Yahwè my Lord is my helper, | who is he that can harm
    me? ||
  Lo, they all shall perish like a garment, | the moth shall con-
    sume them. ||

(*Yahwè speaks*)

¹⁰ Who among you fears Yahwè, | hearkens to his Servant, ||
  Him who walked in the darkness, | seeing no light, ||
  Trusting in the name of Yahwè, | leaning on his God? ||
¹¹ Nay, ye are all of you kindlers of fire, | lighters of brands! ||*
  Go, then, in the light of your flame, | in the brands ye have
    kindled. ||
  This ye shall have from my hand, | ye shall lie down in
    anguish. ||

14

(Chapter 51 : 1–16)

¹ Hear me, pursuers of righteousness, | ye who are seeking the
    Lord:
  Look to the rock from which ye were hewn, | to the hole of the
    pit from whence ye were quarried;
² Look to your father Abraham, | and to Sarah who gave you
    birth.
  For him alone did I call; | I blessed him, and gave him increase.
³ Yahwè will indeed have mercy on Zion, | mercy on all her ruins;
  Her wilderness he will make like Eden, | her desert like the
    garden of the Lord.
  Joy and gladness shall be in her, | praise, and the voice of sing-
    ing.

⁴ Hearken to me, my people; | my nation, give ear to my word!
  For from me the law shall go forth, | and my rule for the light
    of the peoples.
⁵ My triumph is at hand,† my rescue now begun, | and my arm
    shall govern the nations;
  For me the far countries hope, | for my support they are waiting.
⁶ Lift up your eyes to the heavens, | then look to the earth below !
  The heavens shall vanish like smoke, | and the earth wear out
    like a garment, | its people must likewise perish;

---

* Heb., *girding yourselves with brands*.   † Heb., *at hand, near*.

But my salvation abides for ever, | my triumph shall ne'er be
   ended.

⁷ Hear me, ye who know righteousness, | people in whose heart
   is my law:
Fear not the reproach of men, | nor be frighted by their blas-
   pheming.
⁸ For as a garment the moth shall devour them, | the worm shall
   consume them as wool;
But my triumph abides for ever, | my salvation through all the
   ages.

⁹ Awake, awake, put on strength, | arm of Yahwè! ||
Awake as in days of old, | the times long past. ||
Art not thou he that cleft Rahab, | that pierced the Dragon? ||
¹⁰ Was it not thou who didst dry up the sea, | the water of the
   abyss; ||
Who didst make the depths of the sea a road, | for the ransomed
   to pass? ||
¹¹ And the ransomed of Yahwè shall return, | and come to Zion
   with singing, | with endless joy on their heads;
Rejoicing and gladness shall be their portion, | sorrow and
   mourning shall flee away.

¹² I, I am he that comforts thee;* | how is it that thou fearest
   mortal man, | or the son of man, who is made as the grass;
¹³ That thou forgettest Yahwè, thy maker, | who spread the heav-
   ens and founded the earth,
And art continually filled with dread, | fearing the wrath of the
   oppressor, | when he sets himself to destroy?
And what is the wrath of the oppressor?
¹⁴ The bowed one shall soon be released; | he shall not go down to
   the pit of death, | nor even want for bread.
¹⁵ I, Yahwè, am thy God; | he who stirs up the sea, that its billows
   roar, | Yahwè of Hosts is his name.
¹⁶ I have put my word in thy mouth, | in the shadow of my hand
   have concealed thee;
Stretching† the heavens, founding the earth, | and saying to
   Zion, Thou art my people!

* Heb., *you*.   † Heb., *planting*.

15

(CHAPTER 51 : 17–52 : 12)

⁵¹ʼ¹⁷ Arouse thee, arouse thee; | stand up, Jerusalem ! ||
Who hast drunk from the hand of Yahwè | the cup of his
    wrath; ||
The bowl* that causeth staggering | thou hast drained to the
    dregs. ||
¹⁸ (There is not one to lead her, | of the sons she has borne; ||
None to take her by the hand, | of all those she has reared.) ||
¹⁹ These two ills are upon thee; | who shall console thee? ||
Rapine and ruin, famine and sword, | who can comfort thee? † ||
²⁰ Thy children are fallen down fainting,‡ | like an antelope en-
    trapped; ||
They are filled with the wrath of the Lord, | the rebuke of thy
    God. ||

²¹ Therefore hear this, thou afflicted one, | drunken, but not with
    wine; ||
²² Thus saith thy Lord, Yahwè, | and thy God, who strives for his
    people: ||
Behold, I take from thy hand | the cup of staggering, ||
The bowl§ of my wrath, not again | shalt thou drink it, ||
²³ And I put it in the hand of thy tormentors;
Those who did say unto thee: | Fall down, let us pass ! ||
Yea, thou didst make thy back like the ground, | like the
    street for them to traverse. ||

⁵²ʼ¹ Awake, awake, put on | thy strength, O Zion; ||
Put on thy glorious garments, | Jerusalem, holy city ! ||
For there shall no longer enter thee | the profane, the unclean. ||
² Shake off the dust, stand erect, | captive Jerusalem; ||
Free thy neck from its bonds, | captive daughter of Zion ! ||
³ For thus saith Yahwè: | Ye were sold for no price, || and with-
    out money shall ye be redeemed.¶

⁵ And now, what do I here, | saith the Lord, ||
That my people is taken for naught, | that their rulers mock,** ||

---

* Heb., *The bowl, the cup.*   † Heb., *How can I comfort thee?*
‡ Heb. adds *at the head of all the streets.*   § Heb., *The bowl, the cup.*
¶ Heb. adds ⁴ *For thus saith the Lord, Yahwè: My people went down to Egypt
at the first to sojourn there, and Assyria oppressed them for naught.*
** Heb., *Their rulers howl, saith Yahwè.*

And that all the day, without ceasing, | my name is despised? ||
⁶ Therefore my people shall know my name, | yea, therefore, on
    that day, || that I am he who proclaims it, behold me!

⁷ How welcome upon the mountains | the messenger's footsteps! ||
    The herald of peace, with good news, | proclaiming deliver-
    ance; || saying to Zion, thy God is king.
⁸ The voice of thy watchmen; they shout, | they exult together; ||
    For they shall see eye to eye, | when the Lord restores Zion. ||
⁹ Burst into song together, | ye ruins of Jerusalem! ||
    For Yahwè comforts his people, | Jerusalem he redeems. ||
¹⁰ Yahwè bares his holy arm | before all the nations, ||
    And all the ends of the earth shall see | the salvation of our
    God. ||

¹¹ Depart, depart, go out thence; | touch no unclean thing!
    Forth from the midst of her,* purify yourselves, | ye bearers of
    Yahwè's utensils.
¹² For not in flight shall ye go forth, | nor shall ye remove in haste;
    For Yahwè goes before you, | and the God of Israel is your rear-
    guard.

16

(Chapter 52 : 13–53 : 12)

(*Yahwè speaks*)

⁵²:¹³ Lo, the Wise One,† my Servant, shall be lifted up; | he shall
    be honored, and greatly exalted.
¹⁴ Forasmuch as many were dismayed at him,‡ | for§ his face was
    marred more than any other, | and his visage than the
    children of men,
¹⁵ So shall mighty ones be startled at him,¶ | kings shall be silent
    before him;
    For what had not been told them they shall see, | what they
    had not heard they shall understand.

(*The Gentiles speak*)

⁵³:¹ Who had believed what we report? | and to whom was Yahwè's
    arm revealed? ‵

---

* *I. e.*, Egypt.   † Or *Yaskil* (as a proper name).
‡ Heb., *at thee.*   § Heb., *so.*   ¶ Heb. is corrupt.

² For he grew up as a slender shoot before us,* | as a root out of
   arid ground;
   He had no form nor charm, that we should notice him; | no
   beauty, that we should admire him.
³ He was despised and forsaken of men, | a man of sorrows, ac-
   quainted with pain;
   As one from whom men hide their faces, | he was despised, we
   esteemed him not.

⁴ Yet it was our own woes that he bore, | our own sorrows that he
   carried;
   While we accounted him punished, | smitten of God, and
   afflicted.
⁵ But he was wounded for our transgressions, | bruised for our
   iniquities;
   On him fell the chastisement that made us whole, | and with
   his stripes we were healed.
⁶ All we like sheep had gone astray, | we had turned each one to
   his own way;
   And Yahwè laid on him the penalty, | charged upon him the
   guilt of us all.

⁷ He was afflicted,† but opened not his mouth;
   As a lamb led forth to the slaughter, | as a sheep before her
   shearers;
   He was dumb,‡ he opened not his mouth.

⁸ From dominion and rule he was plucked down, | and who could
   make account of his line?
   For he was cut off from the land of the living, | for our own
   sin§ was he smitten.
⁹ They appointed his grave with transgressors, | and with evil
   men,¶ when he should die;
   Although he had done no violence, | nor was any deceit in his
   mouth.

(Yahwè speaks)

¹⁰ But Yahwè saw fit to afflict him with suffering.
   When his life shall make atonement for sin, | he will see his

* Heb., *before him.*   † Heb., *He was distressed, and he was afflicted.*
‡ Heb., *she* (the sheep) *was dumb.*
§ Lit., *for the sin of my people* (said by each of the Gentile rulers).
¶ Heb., *with the rich.*

seed, will prolong his days, | and Yahwè's purpose will prosper in his hand.

[11] He will see the fruit of his mortal travail, | in knowing himself true will be satisfied;

My Servant will bring many to the right,* | for he will carry their sins.

[12] Therefore I give him a portion with the great, | and he shall divide the spoil with the strong,

Forasmuch as he poured out his life to the utmost, | and was counted among the transgressors;

Yea, he bore the misdeeds of many, | for the sinning he made intercession.

17

(CHAPTER 54)

[1] Shout, barren one, who hast not borne; | burst into raptured song, thou who hast not travailed;

For she who is desolate shall number more children | than any who is wedded, saith Yahwè.

[2] Enlarge the space of thy tent, | let the curtains of thy dwelling be extended;

Refrain not, lengthen thy tent-ropes, | and fasten thy stakes securely.

[3] For right and left thou shalt spread abroad; | thy seed shall be heir of nations, | shall people the desolate cities.

[4] Fear not, thou shalt not be confounded; | be not troubled, thou shalt not be put to shame;

The disgrace of thy youth thou shalt forget, | thy widowhood's reproach recall no more.

[5] For he who weds thee is thy maker, | the Lord of Hosts is his name;

Thy redeemer is the Holy One of Israel, | God of All the Earth is his title.

[6] For as a woman forsaken and distressed | Yahwè has called thee, ||

And, "Wife of youth—that she should be rejected!" | thy God hath said. ||

---

* Heb. untranslatable because of the accidental transposition of a word.

⁷ For a single moment I forsook thee, | but in mercy I restore thee. ||

⁸ In a burst of wrath I veiled | my face for a moment from thee, But with endless affection I will cherish thee, | saith thy redeemer, Yahwè.

⁹ 'Tis to me as the time of Noah,* when I swore | that the Flood should not again o'erflow the earth; | so I swear not to show thee anger, nor to rebuke thee.

¹⁰ For the mountains shall all be removed, | and the hills shall totter and fall;
But my favor shall not be removed from thee, | and my covenant of peace shall not be shaken, | saith Yahwè, who shows thee mercy.

¹¹ Thou afflicted and disquieted, not comforted!
See, I lay thy foundations† with beryl, | and ground thee with sapphires;

¹² I will make thy battlements of rubies, | and thy gates of carbuncle-stones, | wholly of gems thine enclosing wall.

¹³ Thy sons shall be pupils of Yahwè, | abundant the peace of thy children.

¹⁴ In righteousness shalt thou be established. | Away from oppression! thou needest not fear it; | and from terror, for it shall not approach thee.

¹⁵ The foe who attacks shall perish‡ by my power; | the stranger sojourning with thee shall join thee.

¹⁶ Behold, I created the smith, | who blows on the burning coals, Producing the tool for his work; | and I also created the destroyer.§

¹⁷ No weapon fashioned against thee shall prosper; | every tongue that contends with thee thou shalt confute.
This is the portion of Yahwè's servants, | and their triumph by my power, saith the Lord.

18

(CHAPTERS 55 : 1–56 : 8)

¹ Ho, everyone who thirsts, come ye to the waters, | yea, come, he who has no money;

* Heb., *For this is to me the waters of Noah.*   † Heb., *thy stones.*
‡ Heb., *it is not.*   § Heb. adds *to destroy.*

Buy and eat,* without money | and without price, both wine and milk.

² Why will ye spend money for that which is not bread, | and your labor for that which satisfies not?
Hearken unto me, and eat what is good; | let your soul delight in abundance.

³ Incline your ear, and come unto me; | hear, that your soul may live;
And I will make an eternal compact with you, | the favor assured to David.

(*Addressing the Messiah*)

⁴ Behold, I make thee† the witness of the peoples, | the leader and commander of the peoples.

⁵ Thou shalt call nations that thou knowest not, | nations that know thee not shall run unto thee;
For the sake of Yahwè, thy God; | for the Holy One of Israel, who has glorified thee.

⁶ Seek ye the Lord while he may be found, | call upon him while he is near.

⁷ Let the wicked forsake his way, | and the evil-doer his thoughts;
Let him turn to the Lord, and he will show him mercy, | and to our God, for he will abundantly pardon.

⁸ For my thoughts are not your thoughts, | nor are your ways my ways, saith Yahwè.

⁹ For as the heavens are higher than the earth, | so are my ways higher than your ways, | and my thoughts higher than your thoughts.

¹⁰ Like as the rain descends, | or as the snow comes down from the heavens,
And returns not thither, but waters | the earth, and makes it bring forth and sprout, | giving seed to the sower and bread to the eater,

¹¹ So shall be my word which goes forth from my mouth; | it shall not return to me void,
But shall have accomplished that which I purposed, | and have prospered that whereto I sent it.

---

* Heb. adds *and come, buy.*   † Heb., *I make him.*

¹² For with gladness ye shall go forth, | and in peace ye shall be brought home.
The mountains and the high hills | shall burst into song before you, | and all the trees of the field shall clap their hands.

¹³ Instead of the thorn shall grow the cypress, | instead of the brier the myrtle;
And it shall be for Yahwè a token, | an enduring sign, which shall not cease.

^{56 : 1} Thus saith Yahwè: | Observe justice, and deal uprightly;
For close at hand is my rescue, | and my triumph nigh to be revealed.*

⁷ And I will bring them to my holy mountain, | and give them joy in my house of prayer;
Their whole burnt-offerings and sacrifices | shall be offered†
with acceptance on my altar.
For my house a house of prayer | for all the peoples shall be called.

⁸ 'Tis the word of the Lord, Yahwè, | who gathers the scattered of Israel: | Yet others to him I will assemble, my own,‡ to be ingathered.

19

(Chapters 56 : 9–57 : 21)

^{56 : 9} All ye wild beasts, come hither! | to devour, ye beasts of the forest!

---

* A later hand inserts here:
^{56 : 2} *Blessed is the man who shall do this, | and the son of man who shall hold it fast;*
Keeping the sabbath, not profaning it, | and withholding his hand from evil doing.

³ *Let not the stranger say, | who has joined himself to Yahwè:*
Separated indeed am I, | by Yahwè, from his own people;
Nor be it said by the eunuch: | Lo, I am a withered tree.

⁴ *For thus saith Yahwè to the eunuchs: | To those who shall keep my sabbaths,*
Who shall choose that in which I take pleasure, | and lay fast hold of my covenant;

⁵ *I will give them within my house | and my walls a mark and a name, | better than sons and daughters;*
An endless name I will give them, | one which shall nowise perish.

⁶ *And the strangers who join themselves | to Yahwè, to do his bidding,*
To love the name of Yahwè, | and to prove themselves his servants;
All who keep the sabbath, not profaning it, | and who lay fast hold of my covenant:—

† Heb. omits *shall be offered.*   ‡ Heb., *his own.*

¹⁰ Blind are his watchmen all, | they cannot discern; ||
Dumb dogs, every one, | unable to bark! || Dreaming—nap-
ping—loving slumber.
¹¹ Yea, and the dogs are greedy, | they cannot be sated. *||
They are turned all to their own ways, | each man to his gain. ||
¹² As he wakens,†—[¹²] "Come! I fetch wine, | let us revel with
drink; ||
And thus shall be yet the morrow, | a great day, surpassing!" ||

^{57 : 1} Gone is the righteous man, | but no one cares; ||
The upright have vanished away, | there is none who heeds. ||
² The just man has fled the wickedness here, | [²] taking his leave. ||
They lie on their couches at ease; | he has gone his way. ||

³ But as for you, come ye hither, | sons of the sorceress! ||
Seed of the adulteress and the harlot,‡ | [⁴] whom are ye mock-
ing? ||
⁴ At whom do ye make wide mouths, | and thrust out the
tongue? ||
Are ye not the offspring of sin, | the seed of falsehood? ||
⁵ Ye who burn with lust at the terebinths, | under each green
tree; ||
Who slay your children in the valleys, | in§ the clefts of the
rocks. ||

⁶ In the smooth stones of the valley is thy¶ portion, | they, they
are thy lot! ||
Yea, to them thou hast poured a libation, | brought forward an
offering. **||
⁷ On a lofty, o'ertopping mount | thou hast placed thy couch, ||
thither hast gone up to offer sacrifice;
⁸ Behind the door and the post | thou hast set thy symbol. ||
Yea, deserting me thou hast gone up, | hast made wide thy
bed; ||
Thou hast taken thee a compact from them, | preferring their
couch. ||

⁹ Power thou sawest; [⁹] didst send thy gift | of oil to the king; ||

---

* Heb. adds *And they are shepherds who know not how to discern.*
† Heb., *All of it.*   ‡ Heb., *of the adulterer and she played the harlot.*
§ Heb., *under.*   ¶ The pronoun referring to the apostates of Israel.
** Heb. adds *Can I be appeased for these things?*

Thou didst multiply thine unguents, and dispatch | thine am-
bassadors afar— || and thou wast brought down to the pit!
¹⁰ By the length of thy journey thou wast wearied, | yet saidst not,
'Tis hopeless! ||
The reviving of thy power thou hadst seen, | therefore didst not
languish. ||

¹¹ Now whom hast thou dreaded and feared, | that thou hast
proved faithless; ||
That me thou rememberest not, | hast not held in thy
thought? ||
Is it not that I long have refrained, | while thou sawest me
not?* ||
¹² It is I who proclaim thy triumph, | I who will save thee!† ||
They will not avail, [¹³] when thou criest, | nor save thee, thine
idols! ||
¹³ All these the wind will take up, | a breath will take off; ||
But who trusts in me will possess the land, | will inherit my
holy mount. ||

¹⁴ Then the cry will be:
Build up, build up, prepare the way, | take stumbling-blocks
from the way of my people!
¹⁵ For thus saith One high and exalted, | abiding ever, holy is His
name:
On high and in sanctity I dwell, | and with the contrite and
lowly of spirit;
To revive the spirit of the humble, | to restore the courage of
the contrite.
¹⁶ For I will not contend for ever, | nor shall my wrath be endless;
For from me the breath of life proceeds, | and the souls of men
have I wrought.

¹⁷ Because of his guilt I was wroth for a moment,‡ | I smote him,
hiding my face in anger; | then he went astray in the way
of his will.
¹⁸ I saw his ways, and restored him, | I led him, and gave in full
measure | consolation to him and his mourners.
¹⁹ Making the lips utter:§ Peace; | peace to the far and the near.¶

* Heb., *and thou didst not fear me.*   † *Heb., thy triumph and thy deeds.*
‡ Heb., *Because of the guilt of his gain I was wroth.*
§ Lit., *Creating the fruit of the lips.*
¶ Heb. adds *Saith Yahwè, and I healed him.*

²⁰ But the wicked are like the tossing sea, | for it cannot be quiet, | and its waves cast up refuse and mire.
²¹ No peace, saith my God, for the wicked.

20

(Chapter 58)

¹ Cry with thy might,* refrain not! | Lift up thy voice like a trumpet;
  Proclaim to my people their wickedness, | to the house of Jacob their sins!

² Yet me day by day they 'seek,' | and 'the knowledge of my ways' is their pleasure—
  As though they were a nation that had dealt uprightly, | nor forsaken the law of its God!
³ They ask of me a just judgment, | would be brought with God face to face:
[³] *"Why did we fast, and thou not see it; | afflict ourselves, and thou not know it?"*

⁴ If, on the fast-day, ye seek your pleasure, | and exact in full your own profit;
[⁴] If with strife and quarrelling ye fast, | smiting with the fist of a villain;
  Then ye do no fasting, this day, | that can make your voice heard on high!

⁵ Or is this the fast I have chosen: | a day for a man to afflict himself,
  To bow his head like a bulrush, | to put on sackcloth and ashes?
  Is it this that ye will call 'fasting,' | and 'a day well pleasing to Yahwè'?

⁶ Is not this the fast that I desire:
  That ye loose unrighteous bonds, | and burst the bands of the yoke;
  That ye set the crushed at liberty, | and unbind every grievous burden†?

---

* Heb. literally, *with the throat.*   † Lit., *yoke.*

⁷ Is it not to share thy bread with the hungry, | bringing the poor
and oppressed to thy house?
When thou seest one naked, that thou clothe him, | and hide
not from thine own flesh!

⁸ Then thy light shall break as the dawn, | and thy healing spring
forth at once;
Thy triumph shall march before thee, | and the glory of Yahwè
shall follow thee.*
⁹ Then thou shalt call, and Yahwè will answer; | when thou
criest, he will say: Here am I!

¹⁰ If thou banish from thy midst false dealing,† | the pointing fin-
ger, and slander;
[¹⁰] If thou pour out thyself for the hungry, | and satisfy the crav-
ing of the afflicted;
Then thy light shall shine forth in the darkness, | thy gloom
shall become as the noonday;
¹¹ Then Yahwè will lead thee alway, | and will sate thy soul with
good things, | thy bones he will give new strength.
Thou shalt be a watered garden, a fountain | whose waters
break not their promise.
¹² Thine ancient ruins shall be builded, | thou shalt revive the
foundations of old;
They shall call thee Repairer of the Breach, | Restorer of Ruins
for habitation.‡

21

(Chapter 59)

¹ Lo, his hand§ lacks not power to rescue, | his ear is not dull of
hearing;

---

* Or *shall be thy rear-guard.*   † Our Heb. is pointed as though it were *yoke.*
‡ There follows an addition by a later hand:
¹³ *If thou turn back thy foot from the Sabbath, | from doing thy pleasure on my
holy day;
If thou call the Sabbath a delight, | the hallowed of Yahwè glorious;
If thou honor it, not going thine own way, | not seeking thy pleasure, nor talk-
ing idly;*
¹⁴ *Then in Yahwè shalt thou find thy delight, | and I will make thee to ride on the
heights of the earth;
I will feed thee with the heritage of Jacob thy father, | for the mouth of Yahwè
hath spoken it.*
§ Heb., *the hand of Yahwè.*

2 Nay, your own sins are barring you, | withholding you from
    your God;
  Your own transgressions have hidden | his face, that he hears
    you not.

3 For your hands are defiled with blood, | and your fingers with
    evil-doing;
  Your lips have spoken falsehood, | your tongue repeats iniquity.
4 No one cries out for righteousness, | no one gives truthful judg-
    ment.
  Trusting in vanity, speaking lies; | conceiving trouble, and
    bringing forth deceit!

5 They hatch the eggs of basilisks, | and weave the spider's web.
  (He who eats of their eggs will die, | from the one which is
    crushed a viper is hatched;
6 Their webs will make no garment, | they will not be clad with
    their handiwork!)
  Their works are works of mischief, | deeds of violence are in
    their hands.
7 Their feet run swift to evil, | haste to shed innocent blood;
  Their plans are plans of wickedness, | rapine and ruin are in
    their highways;
8 The road of peace they know not, | no rectitude is in their
    goings;
  Crooked have they made their path, | whoever treads it knows
    no peace.

9 Therefore is justice far from us, | uprightness cannot reach us;
  We wait for light, and lo, darkness; | for dawn, but we walk in
    gloom.
10 Like blind men we grope for the wall, | as though without eye-
    sight we strike against it;
  We stumble at noon as in twilight; | groping, reeling* like dying
    men.
11 We all groan like bears, | like doves we moan aloud.
  We look for justice, there is none; | for rescue, it is far removed.

12 For our wickedness is great in thy sight, | and our sins bear wit-
    ness against us;

* Heb. unintelligible.

Yea, our transgressions are before us, | and our iniquities, we
  know them:
¹³ Dealing wickedly, falsely with Yahwè, | turning back from fol-
  lowing our God;
Speaking deceit* and rebellion, | conceiving† in the heart lying
  words.
¹⁴ Justice is made to turn back, | righteousness stands afar off;
For truth has fallen in the street, | and rectitude cannot ap-
  proach.
[¹⁵] Verily truth is missing, | piety has fled because of evil.‡

¹⁵ Yahwè beheld, and it was grievous | in his eyes, that no right
  was there.
¹⁶ He saw that there was none to help,§ | was distressed that there
  was none to interpose;
So his arm wrought deliverance for him, | his righteousness gave
  him support.
¹⁷ He put on uprightness as a breastplate, | a helmet of salvation
  on his head;
Clothed himself with vengeance as a garment, | wrapped him-
  self in zeal as in a cloak.

¹⁸ According to their deeds even now he will repay, | wrath to his
  enemies, requital to his foes; | full recompense he gives to
  distant lands.
¹⁹ So from the west they shall reverence his name, | from the ris-
  ing of the sun see his glory;
For it shall come like a torrent,¶ | the breath of Yahwè driving
  it on.
²⁰ And a redeemer will come to Zion, | to those of Jacob who turn
  from sin.**

²¹ As for me, this is my covenant with them, | saith Yahwè: My
  spirit which is upon thee, | and my word which I put in thy
  mouth,
Shall not cease from thy mouth, nor from that of thy seed, | nor
  that of their offspring, saith the Lord, | from now onward,
  even forever.

---

* Heb., *oppression.*   † Heb., *conceiving and uttering.*
‡ Heb., *he who turns from evil is despoiled.*
§ Lit., *that there was no man.*
¶ Lit., *a river pent in.*   ** Heb. adds *saith Yahwè.*

22

(Chapter 60)

1 Arise, shine, for thy light is come, | and the glory of Yahwè
   has dawned upon thee!
2 Darkness indeed o'erspreads the earth, | and deepest gloom the
   peoples;
   But upon thee the Lord beams forth, | on thee his glory appears.

3 Nations shall come to thy light, | and kings to thy dawning ra-
   diance.
4 Lift thine eyes round about, and see! | They are gathered all,
   they approach thee.
   They are bringing thy sons* from far, | and thy daughters are
   borne on the side.

5 Then thou shalt see, and be lightened; | startled, thy vision
   shall widen;
   For the abundance of the seas shall be turned unto thee, | the
   wealth of the nations to thee shall come.
6 Trains of camels shall cover thee, | young camels of Midian and
   Ephah, | all those from Sheba shall come;
   Carrying gold and incense, | proclaiming the praise of Yahwè.
7 All the sheep of Kedar shall be gathered for thee, | the rams of
   Nebaioth be brought for thy service;
   They shall be offered with acceptance on my altar, | and my
   beauteous house I will glorify.

8 Who are these that fly as a cloud, | even as the doves to their
   cotes?
9 Verily for me the isles are gathering, | and the ships of Tarshish
   first,
   To bring thy children from far, | their silver and gold with them;
   For the name of Yahwè thy God, | and for the Holy One of
   Israel, who has glorified thee.

10 The sons of the stranger shall build thy walls, | and their kings
    shall minister to thee.
    For though in my wrath I smote thee, | yet in my favor I show
    thee mercy.

* Heb., *Thy sons are coming.*

¹¹ Thy gates shall stand open continually, | day and night they shall not be shut;
That the host of the nations may be brought to thee, | and their kings conducted in state.*

¹³ The glory of Lebanon shall come to thee, | the cypress, the plane, and the pine;†
To adorn the place of my sanctuary; | yea, the place which I tread I will glorify.
¹⁴ There shall come bowing down before thee | the sons of thy oppressors; ||
There shall prostrate themselves at thy feet | all those who despised thee; ||
And they shall call thee the City of Yahwè, | the Zion of the Holy One of Israel.

¹⁵ Whereas thou hast been forsaken | and hated, with none passing through,
I will make thee a pride everlasting, | a joy of many generations.
¹⁶ Thou shalt suck the milk of nations, | at the breast of kings thou shalt nurse;
And thou shalt know that I‡ am thy savior | and thy redeemer, the Mighty One of Jacob.

¹⁷ For bronze I will bring gold, | for iron I will bring silver;
Copper in place of wood, | iron in place of stones.
I will make thy officers peace, | and thy magistrates righteousness.
¹⁸ Violence shall no more be heard in thy land, | rapine and ruin in thy borders.
Thou shalt call thy walls Salvation, | and thy city gates Thanksgiving.

¹⁹ For thee shall be no longer | the sun to give light by day,
Nor shall the moon with its brightness | illumine thee by night;§
But Yahwè will be thy light forever, | thy God will be thy glory.
²⁰ Thy sun shall set no more, | thy moon shall not withdraw itself,

---

* Heb. adds ¹²*For the nation or the kingdom which will not serve thee shall perish, and those nations shall be utterly destroyed.*
† Heb. adds *together.*   ‡ Heb. adds *Yahwè.*
§ Heb. omits *by night.*

But Yahwè will be thy light forever, | ended shall be thy days
of mourning.

21 Thy people shall all be upright, | forever they shall possess the
land;
The sprout of my own planting, | the work of my hands, for
my glory.

22 The little one shall become a thousand, | the small one a mighty
nation; | I, the Lord, will speed it in its time.

23

(CHAPTER 61)

(*The Servant speaks*)

1 The spirit of Yahwè, my Lord, is upon me, | forasmuch as
Yahwè has anointed me,
Has sent me to bring glad tidings to the lowly, | to give aid*
to the broken-hearted;
To proclaim to the captives freedom, | the opening of eyes to
the blind;†

2 To announce the year of Yahwè's favor, | the day of requital
for our God.

3 To comfort all the distressed, | [3] to hearten‡ the mourners in
Zion;
Giving them adornment for ashes, | the oil of gladness for sor-
row, | a garment of praise for a sinking spirit.
They shall be called trees of righteousness, | the planting of the
Lord, for his glory.

(*Yahwè speaks*)

4 They shall build up the ruins of old, | the ancient wastes shall
be restored;
They shall renew the ruined cities, | desolate now for genera-
tions.§

6 And they¶ shall be called Priests of Yahwè; | entitled, Ministers
of our God.
The wealth of nations they shall eat, | and with their splendor
shall be glorified.

---

* Lit., *to bind up.*   † Heb., *prisoners.*   ‡ Heb., *to appoint for.*
§ Heb. adds 5 *And strangers shall come and pasture your flocks, and aliens
shall be your plowmen and your vinedressers.*
¶ Heb. has the second person plural throughout vs. 6.

⁷ Instead of their* twofold disgrace, | their portion insult and
     spitting,†
    Twofold in their land they shall inherit, | gladness unending
     shall be theirs.
⁸ For I, the Lord, love justice, | false dealing I hate from eter-
     nity;‡
    I will give them faithful recompense, | an eternal compact I
     will make with them.
⁹ Their seed shall be known among the nations, | their offspring
     in the midst of the peoples;
    All who see them shall acknowledge them | as a seed which
     Yahwè has blessed.

(*The Servant exults*)

¹⁰ I will greatly rejoice in the Lord, | my soul shall exult in my God;
    For he has clothed me with the robes of salvation, | wrapped
     me in the garment of uprightness;
    As the bridegroom decks himself with a garland, | as the bride
     puts on her jewels.
¹¹ For as the earth brings forth her tender plants, | as the garden
     makes its herbs to sprout,
    Even so will Yahwè, my Lord, | make righteousness and praise
     spring forth, | in the sight of all the nations.

24

(CHAPTER 62)

(*The Servant speaks*)

¹ For Zion's sake I will not keep silence, | for Jerusalem's sake I
     will not rest,
    Until her triumph comes forth as the dawn, | her rescue like a
     blazing torch!
² Nations shall behold thy triumph, | and all the kings thy glory;
    Unto thee a new name shall be given, | which the mouth of the
     Lord shall bestow.

³ Thou shalt be a beauteous garland | in the hand of the Lord; ||
    Yea, a diadem of royal state | in the hand of thy God. ||
⁴ No more shall they call thee Forsaken, | nor thy land,§ De-
     serted; ||

---

* Heb., *your.*   † Heb. is corrupt.   ‡ Heb., *in the burnt offering.*
§ Heb., *nor shall thy land again be called.*

But thou shalt be called, My Delight is in Her, | and thy land,
　　The Espoused. ||
For the Lord takes pleasure in thee, | and thy land shall be
　　wedded. ||
⁵ For as a youth weds a virgin, | thy Builder* will wed thee; ||
With a bridegroom's joy in a bride | thy God shall rejoice in
　　thee. ||

⁶ Upon thy walls, O Jerusalem, | I have stationed watchmen; ||
All the day and all the night | let them ne'er be silent. ||
Ye who put the Lord in mind, | no rest for you! ||
⁷ Yea, to him shall ye give no rest, | till he confirm it; ||
Till he shall have made Jerusalem | a praise on earth. ||

⁸ By his right hand has Yahwè sworn, | by his mighty arm: ||
No longer will I give thy grain | as food for thy foes; ||
Nor shall the stranger drink thy wine, | for which thou hast
　　labored; ||
⁹ But they who have gathered it shall eat it, | and praise the
　　Lord; ||
And they who have stored it shall drink it, | in my sacred
　　courts. ||

¹⁰ Pass through, pass through the gates, | prepare the way of the
　　people! ||
Build up, build up the highway, | make it clear of stones; ||
Lift up an ensign over the peoples!
¹¹ Behold, Yahwè proclaims, | to the end of the earth: ||
Say to the daughter of Zion, | Lo, thy rescue comes! ||
Behold, his recompense is with him, | his reward before him. ||
¹² And men shall call them The Holy People, | The Ransomed of
　　Yahwè; ||
And thou shalt be called Sought out, | City not Forsaken. ||

25

(CHAPTERS 63 : 1–64 : 11)

¹ Who is this who comes from Edom, | with crimsoned garments
　　from Bozrah?
This one in glorious apparel, | striding in the fulness of his
　　strength?

* Heb., *thy children.*

It is I, announcing vindication, | mighty to save my people.*

2 Wherefore is thy clothing red, | thy garments as one who treads the vat?

3 I have trodden the winepress alone, | from the peoples there was no one with me.
I trod them out in my anger, | trampled them in my wrath;
Their blood was sprinkled on my garments, | and all my apparel I stained.
4 For a day of requital is in my heart, | and the year of my redemption is come.

5 When I looked, there was no helper, | I marvelled that there was none to give support;
Therefore my arm wrought rescue for me, | yea, my own wrath upheld me.
6 I trampled the peoples in my anger, | I shattered them in my fury, | and brought down their glory to the ground.

(*The Servant meditates*)

7 I will tell of the lovingkindnesses of Yahwè, | the praises of the Lord; ||
According to all that he has done for us, | the great goodness to Israel; ||
Which he dealt them according to his mercy, | the abundance of his kindness. ||

8 He said, Surely they are my people, | children who will not deal falsely; ||
And he became a savior for them | [⁹] in all their distress. ||
9 Not a strange god, not an angel, | his own person saved them; ||
In his affection and his forbearance | he himself redeemed them; ||
And he lifted them up and carried them, | all the days of old. ||

10 But they rebelled and sorely distressed | his holy spirit, ||
And he was turned to be their foe, | himself opposed them. ||

11 Then one recalled the days of old, | the savior of his people;† ||

* Heb. omits *my people*.   † Heb., *Moses his people*.

Where is he who led up from the sea | the shepherds of his
   flock? ||
Where is he who put in their midst | his holy spirit? ||
12 Causing to go at Moses' right hand | his glorious arm, ||
Cleaving the waters before them, | to make his fame endless; ||
13 Making them walk in the deeps | as a horse in the desert;* ||
14 As the beast goes down through the valley, | led on by his
   spirit.† ||
Thus thou didst lead thy people, | to make thy name glorious.||

(*The Poet speaks*)

15 Look down from the heavens and behold, | from thy holy and
   glorious abode!
Where are thy zeal and thy might, | thy fervor of pity and
   mercy?
16 Refrain not,‡ [16] for thou art our father; | though Abraham
   know us no longer, | and Israel acknowledge us not!
Thou, Yahwè, art our father; | thy name, Our Redeemer of old.

17 Why dost thou let us err from thy ways, | and harden our heart,
   that we fear thee not?
Turn again for thy servants' sake, | the tribes of thine own
   heritage!
18 Wherefore did evil men desecrate thy shrine,§ | our enemies
   trample thy holy place?
19 We have long been as those not ruled by thee, | even as those
   not bearing thy name.

64 : 1 O that thou wouldst rend the heavens and come down,¶ |[64 : 1]
   like the kindling of fire in brushwood, | the thunder of boil-
   ing waters,**
To make thy name known to thy foes; | before thee nations
   would tremble!
2 When thou didst thy terrible deeds, | we had not to wait, thou
   descendedst; | before thee mountains dissolved.

---

* Heb. adds *They did not stumble.*
† Heb., *the spirit of Yahwè giving it rest.*
‡ Heb., *Unto me they refrained.*
§ Heb., *For a little they inherited thy holy people.*
¶ Heb., *thou didst come down,* and adds *before thee mountains dissolved* (see
vs. 2).
** Heb., *(like) water which fire boils.*

LXIII, 11—LXV, 2

³ They have never heard, nor attended: | There is no* God aside from thee, | doing well by those who await him.

[⁴] Thou bringest rejoicing to those who do right,† | who walk‡ in thy ways.

⁴ Thou indeed hast been wroth, but we have sinned, | dealing treacherously, wickedly of old.§

⁵ We have all become like an unclean thing; | like a garment polluted, all our virtues.

We all have faded like leaves, | and our sin, like the wind, is bearing us away.

⁶ There is none who calls on thy name, | who stirs to lay hold on thee.

Nay, thou hast hid thy face from us, | hast delivered us up to our sin.¶

⁷ Yet even now, Yahwè, thou art our father; | we are the clay and thou our potter, | the work of thy hand are we all.

⁸ Be not exceedingly angry, O Lord; | remember not our guilt forever. | Nay, look, we all are thy people!

⁹ Thy holy cities became a desert, | Zion was made a desolation, | Jerusalem an execration.**

¹⁰ Our holy and beautiful house, | in which our fathers had praised thee,

Was burned, consumed by fire, | and all our treasures were laid waste.

¹¹ Even after this wilt thou refrain, Yahwè? | wilt be silent, and afflict us to the utmost?

26

(CHAPTER 65)

¹ I sought invitation from those who asked not for me, | I would fain have been found by those who sought me not;

I said, Here am I, behold me! | to a nation not bearing my name.

² I spread forth my hands all the day | to a people unruly and rebellious,††

* Heb., *Eye has not seen.*
† Heb., *Thou hast met one who is rejoicing and does right.*
‡ Heb., *who remember thee.*
§ Heb., *in them—an age—and we shall be saved.*
¶ Heb., *thou hast fluctuated for us in the power of our sin.*
** Heb., *a desolation.*   †† Heb. omits *and rebellious.*

Walking in the untoward pathway, | following their own conceits.

¹² I will destine you to the sword, | ye all shall bow for the slaugh-
    ter;
For I called, and ye answered not; | I spoke, and ye did not hear.
Ye did what was evil in my eyes, | that which pleased me not
    ye chose.

¹³ Therefore thus saith Yahwè:*
Behold, my servants shall eat, | but ye shall hunger; ||
Behold, my servants shall drink, | but ye shall thirst; ||
Behold, my servants shall rejoice, | but ye shall be discomfited. ||

¹⁴ Lo, my servants shall sing from gladness of heart, | but ye shall
    cry out from distress of heart.
From anguish of spirit ye shall wail, | [¹⁵] and your name ye
    shall leave for a curse.
¹⁵ But my chosen I will hold fast, saith Yahwè,† | and my‡ ser-
    vants shall be given another name:
¹⁶ He who blesses himself in the land | shall bless by the God of
    the True,
And he who takes oath in the land | shall swear by the God of
    the True.
For the former distresses are forgotten, | yea, they are hid
    from my eyes.

¹⁷ For behold, I create new heavens | and a new earth. ||
The former things shall not be recalled, | shall not enter the
    mind. ||
¹⁸ But rejoice and be glad, ye eternal cities,§ | which I create! ||
For I create Jerusalem an exultation, | and her people a rejoic-
    ing. ||
¹⁹ And I will be glad in Jerusalem, | and joy in my people. ||
No more shall be heard in her the voice of weeping, | the sound
    of crying.¶ ||

²¹ They shall build houses and dwell therein, | shall plant vine-
    yards and eat their fruit.

* Heb., *the Lord, Yahwè.*
† Heb., *And ye shall leave your name for a curse to my chosen, and my Lord
Yahwè will slay thee.*
‡ Heb., *his.*   § Heb., *rejoice and be glad forever.*
¶Heb., ²⁰ *And there shall be there no more the infant that dies and the old man
who does not complete his days ; for the child shall die a hundred years old, and he
who fails to reach a hundred years of age shall be accursed.*

²² They shall not build, and another dwell; | they shall not plant,
and another eat.

For as the days of a tree shall be the days of my people, | and
the work of their hands shall they enjoy.

²³ My chosen, [²³] they shall not toil in vain, | nor bring forth
children in apprehension;

For the seed of the blessed of Yahwè are they, | and their off-
spring I will perfect.*

²⁴ It shall be that ere they call I will answer, | while they are yet
speaking I will hear.

²⁵ The wolf and the lamb shall feed together, | the lion shall eat
straw like the ox; | (the serpent, dust is his food!)

They shall neither harm nor destroy | in all my holy mount,
saith the Lord.

27

(Chapter 66)

¹ Thus saith Yahwè, The heaven is my throne, | and the earth
the footstool of my feet;

What manner of house will ye build for me, | and where is the
place of my abiding?

² All these my hand created, | these are all my own, saith the
Lord.

Upon this will I look, upon the lowly, | him of contrite spirit,
who trembles at my word.

³ He who slaughters an ox slays a man; | he who offers a lamb
kills a dog.

He brings an oblation—blood of swine! | offers incense—'tis
the worship of an idol!

Verily these have chosen their ways, | and in their abomina-
tions their soul delights.

⁴ I also will choose their torment, | I will bring their terror upon
them.

Because I called, and none answered; | I spoke, but they did
not hearken;

They did what was evil in my eyes, | that which pleased me not
they chose.

⁵ Hear ye the message of Yahwè, | ye who tremble at his word!

* Heb., *and their offspring with them.*

Your brethren say, who hate you, | who spurn you for my
    name's sake: | Let Yahwè be glorious, that we may behold.
But I will make you rejoice,* and they shall be confounded!

6 A thunderous voice from the city, | a cry from the temple! ||
    The voice of Yahwè, paying in full | the meed of his foes. ||
7 Before she travailed she brought forth; | before her pains came
    upon her | she bore a male child. ||
8 Who has heard of aught like this, | who has seen such things? ||
    Can a land be given birth in a day, | or a nation be born at
    once? ||
    For verily Zion in travail | brought forth her children! ||
9 Shall I bring to the birth and not complete it?† | saith the
    Lord; ||
    Shall I cause to bear and yet close the womb? | saith thy God. ||

10 Rejoice ye with Jerusalem, | and exult in her, all ye who love
    her.
    Be glad with her exceedingly, | all ye who mourn for her.
11 That ye may suck and be satisfied | from the breasts of her
    comfort; ||
    May nurse and be filled with delight | at the breasts of her
    glory. ||
12 For thus saith Yahwè, | Behold, I extend unto her,
    Like a river at the full,‡ like an overflowing stream, | the splen-
    dor of the nations, and ye shall suck;
    Ye shall be borne on the side, | and on the knees shall be dan-
    dled.
13 As one by his mother is comforted, | so will I comfort you; | and
    in Jerusalem ye shall have consolation.
14 Ye shall see, and your heart shall rejoice, | your limbs feel the
    vigor of springing herbage;
    And the power of the Lord for his servants shall be known, | and
    his wrath for his enemies.

15 For behold, Yahwè comes with fire, | and like a stormwind his
    chariots,
    To achieve his wrath with burning heat, | his threat with flames
    of fire.
16 For with fire will Yahwè execute judgment, | with his sword he
    will judge all flesh, | and the slain of the Lord will be many.

* Heb., *that we may behold your rejoicing.*
† Lit., *cause to bring forth.*   ‡ Heb., *Like a river, peace.*

¹⁷ As for me, I have reckoned their deeds;* | these who consecrate
themselves† for the gardens, | following One in the midst;
These who eat the flesh of swine, | and creeping things,‡ and
the mouse; | they shall perish all together, saith Yahwè.

¹⁸ For the time is at hand§ to assemble | all nations and tongues
together; | they shall come and behold my glory.
¹⁹ I will put my sign among them, | and will send from them a
remnant
To the nations, Tarshish, Pūt,¶ and Lūd, | Meshek,** Tūbal,
and Yāwān, | the lands which lie far away,
Which have heard no tidings of me, | nor have they beheld my
glory; | my glory shall be told to the Gentiles.
²⁰ And they shall bring all your brethren, | from all nations, as an
offering to me,
On horses, in chariots and litters, | on mules, and on drome-
daries, | to my holy mountain,†† saith Yahwè;
In like manner as the offering is brought‡‡ | in clean vessels to
Yahwè's house.
²¹ Also of them will I take for priests, | and for Levites, saith the
Lord.

²² For as the renovated heavens | and the new earth which I
create
Shall stand before me, saith Yahwè, | so shall stand your seed
and your name.
²³ And it shall be, from new moon to new moon, | and from one
Sabbath day to another,
That all flesh shall come to offer | their worship before me, saith
Yahwè.
²⁴ And as they go forth, they shall see the corpses | of those who
in wickedness opposed me;
For their worm shall never die, | their fire shall not be
quenched; | they shall be a horror to all mankind.

* Heb., *As for me, their deeds and their thoughts;* the clause found in Heb. at
the beginning of vs. 18; see note there.
† Heb. adds *and purify themselves.*   ‡ Heb., *abomination.*
§ Heb., *As for me, their deeds and their thoughts.* *It* (fem.) *has come,* etc.
¶ Heb., *Pul.*   ** Heb., *Those who draw the bow.*
†† Heb. adds *Jerusalem.*
‡‡ Heb., *as the children of Israel bring the offering.*

PART III

INTRODUCTIONS AND NOTES TO THE SEVERAL POEMS

These two chapters are inseparable. It is true that each is formally complete in itself, like the two sides of a coin; they are not to be regarded as constituting a single continuous poem. On the other hand, when taken together they form—and were certainly intended by their author to form—companion pictures, each supplementing and explaining the other. When 34:1 was written, the prophet must have had chapter 35 also in mind.

The picture is purely eschatological, having for its subject the time when Yahwè will make the final separation between his friends and his foes. The two poems might well be called a highly imaginative development of the theme given in Matt. 25:46: "These shall go away into everlasting punishment, but the righteous into life eternal." Chapter 34 depicts the doom of the wicked, chapter 35 the blessing in store for the true people of God. The closing verses of 34 were doubtless intended to effect (as they do) an easy transition from the dark side to the bright side of the picture; see below. Be that as it may, the two chapters were written at the same time, and were intended to stand side by side, in the same way and in the same order in which they stand in our Hebrew Bible. As has already been shown, the immediate sequel of chapter 35 in this collection of poems was chapter 40.

CHAPTER 34

The great day of retribution; the eternal desolation of the regions once inhabited by those whom God has marked for destruction. The all-important question is: What does the poet intend by "Edom"? It is plain at the outset that he does *not* mean the Edomites and their country. On the contrary, as Cheyne and others have rightly observed, "Edom" is here (just as in 63:1) the current symbolical designation of a class: the incorrigible enemies of Israel and of Yahwè. The prophet does not attempt here to define this class, he is dealing with familiar ideas. That the line which he draws is not the line between Jews and Gentiles is certain. It is true that not a few commentators have been willing to attribute to the author of chapter 34 this incredibly stupid and brutal eschatology; but their exegesis is not merely gratuitous, it

is indefensible. Obviously, such a designation as "Edom" could
not have been intended to stand for *all* the heathen nations.
When, in 63:1–6, Yahwè returns "from Edom, with dyed garments from Bozrah," he has been executing his judgment upon
"the peoples"; but this does not mean that he is returning from
a butchery of the whole Gentile world. When the term "peoples"
is used in 63:6, or "nations" in 34:2, or "all flesh" in 66:16,
the writer has in mind *the wicked* in all parts of the world. These,
and these only, are the object of Yahwè's wrath. Out of "all the
nations," even the most remote of the earth, he will single them
for punishment. So in 34:5, "those whom I have doomed," the
phrase used in parallelism with "Edom." In 66:24 this class is
more nearly described by the phrase "those men who in wickedness oppose me"; and *this* is the true line of separation between
"Edom," the doomed, and the saved of Yahwè. So also 59:18–20
declares distinctly.

Multitudes of the heathen are Yahwè's own people, and the
sheep of his pasture; see especially the notes on 42:7; 49:8–10.
And on the other hand, among the wicked, destined to perish, are
Jews as well as Gentiles; 50:11; 59:20; 65:13 ff., and similar
passages. Even if the author of chapter 34 were supposed to be
distinct from, and uninfluenced by, the writer or writers of the
other chapters just named, he should yet, in common fairness, be
assumed to take the broader view until the contrary is proved.
But when the fact is recognized that one and the same hand wrote
all these passages, they are seen to interpret one another admirably, and we know with certainty the splendid magnanimity
with which the prophet thought of the races and nations of the
earth, along with the stern sense of divine justice demanded by
his picture of the final judgment. In 66:16 he wrote that the
sword of Yahwè was to descend upon "all flesh," and that many
should be the "slain of Yahwè" (*cf.* 34:2, 3, 5). But a few verses
farther on he predicts that "all flesh" will come to worship before
Yahwè (66:23), and that he even "will take some of them (the
heathen) for priests" (66:21). Compare also 49:26, the doom of
the wicked, with 49:9–13, the home-gathering of the Gentiles (a
picture closely resembling the one portrayed in chapter 35).

It is "Edom-Bozrah" at the outset, but merely for the sake of
the picture, as in chapter 63. In the latter case the definite scene is
left behind after the first verse. So also in 34 it is confined to the
two verses 5 and 6. As the chapter proceeds, it becomes increasingly evident that its author had in mind no definite people or

part of the world. The land whose "streams shall be turned into pitch and its dust into brimstone" is an imaginary land. The description in verses 11–15 plainly has in mind rather the ruin of a great city than the desolation of a country; the suffix in בְּצִלָּהּ, "in her shadow," in verse 15, is especially to be noted. But it is no more likely that the prophet thought here of Babylon, or of any other real city, than that he had in mind the actual nation Edom in the earlier part of the chapter. On the contrary, his imagination, which was such as perhaps no other Hebrew writer could boast, is at work here. The land and the city pictured in this chapter are as purely literary creations as are the "desert" and the "highway" in chapter 35.

The manner in which the *dies iræ* is here depicted has been censured by those who have misunderstood the picture. See the examples given in Chapter VII, § 3. It is true that one and another of the details of the description are terrible to contemplate, but this is inevitable in view of the subject itself, provided the latter is treated in any adequate manner. Verse 3, in particular, is startling in its realism; a ghastly scene of horror is made to pass before our eyes for a moment. The day which is here portrayed represents, on its dark side, the climax of dread in the range of human imagination, and the extremity of mortal anguish, and in one powerful, unsparing verse this fact is brought to view. The touch is effective and artistic, because only a touch. From this point onward the details which are dwelt upon are not the terror and suffering of men, but far more impersonal and essentially picturesque elements.

In 63 also the scene of carnage is only momentarily present. In that poem the relief is brought, in characteristic manner, by a lyric song which has for its subject the mercy of God. In 34 the transition is gradual, effected by a succession of pictures, each less fearsome than its predecessor. Now, rivers of pitch and dust of brimstone; a blaze filling the horizon, and columns of smoke mounting to heaven. Then, with a complete change of scene, majestic ruins of a great city, gloomy and silent in the desert plain, an eternal lesson to mankind. Ruins, but not uninhabited. All the denizens of the wilderness, demons, strange creatures, the beasts and birds which shun the haunts of men, may live there undisturbed, among the broken columns and shattered walls. The prophet's kindliness and sympathetic interest in all living things, so often manifested, here come to the fore. The God who made these wild creatures has care for them; they are all present, each

one has its mate. But where are the men who once dwelt here?
The note of doom still sounds.

The poem which follows is a blaze of light, beauty, and bright
color, the other side of the picture. Taken together, the two chapters constitute one of the finest pieces of imaginative poetry in the
world's literature.

The metre is 3 | 3 throughout the two poems. Both are musical
from beginning to end, with notably regular and well-marked
rhythm. There are several excellent examples of an effective use
of the 3 | 3 | 3 verse. In several cases the massoretic verse-division
is wrong, and once or twice it is very misleading; see the notes on
34 : 11 f., 15 f.; 35 : 1 f. Duhm remarks: "Der Text zeigt merk-
würdig viel Lücken." I have been unable to find any of these
lacunæ.

---

34 : 1. This form of introduction is a favorite one with the
Second Isaiah. See 41 : 1; 49 : 1, and compare also 41 : 21 f.; 43 : 8
f.; 48 : 16. Here the prophet has risen above race-distinctions,
and is looking upon the world. He summons all the peoples of
the earth, Jew and Gentile alike, to hear a prediction of the impending day of judgment.

Duhm's comments on the first half-dozen verses of this Chapter are not pleasant reading, for they show that he has for this
'prophet' both contempt and dislike.

צאצאים. A word which the Second Isaiah is fond of using.
Here it is the practical equivalent of מלא, both meaning "inhabitants."

34 : 2. *Cf.* Rev. 6 : 17 (in a passage derived chiefly from Is.
34 f.): "The great day of [God's] wrath is come." Yahwè's sword
descends upon all nations of the earth (66 : 16, כל בשר), and the
wicked are slain (see the introduction to the chapter). On the
other hand, a multitude out of every nation (Rev. 7 : 9) will be
saved (Is. 35 = Rev. 7 : 9–17).

The first line of the verse is unusually long; the article in הגוים
may be secondary.

Observe the frequent and very effective use of triple lines in
this poem; thus, 34 : 2, 3, 4, 5, 9, 16a; 35 : 4b, 9, 10. See the Chapter on "Metric Forms."

34 : 3. A good example oı a verse, our estimate of which turns

altogether on our estimate of the man who wrote it. It is a grim
and powerful touch; the chapter would be poorer without it.

With "their slain" compare "the slain of the Lord" in 66 : 16.

34 : 4. נמקו was chosen for the sake of the paronomasia with
נמסו in the preceding verse.

The "abgeschmackter Gedanke" which Duhm censures is here
also, as in the many similar cases, his own property; our Hebrew
text does not suggest it.

The repetition of the words שמים and צבא is in accordance
with the habit of the poet. Thus, in this same poem, verses 4
(נבל), 6 (חלב), 9 (זפת), 35 : 1 (תפרח).

The latter part of the verse elaborates in a highly picturesque
manner an idea which had been stated in its simplest form at the
beginning of the verse.

34 : 5. With the whole verse compare especially 66 : 16.

The phrase רותה בשמים is difficult; the correctness of our
text should not be doubted, however. The verb רוה might mean
either "to be wet, bathed," or "to be sated" (*cf.* verse 7). The
latter meaning is altogether out of place here; the sword is "sated"
after it has descended upon the victims, not before. Nor could
the sword in heaven possibly be thought of as wet with blood.
The idea demanded by the context for this verb is something like
"make ready" or "dedicate." The translation "anointed" (literally, "bathed [with oil]") therefore suggests itself as the most
probable one. The verb *riwwā* is used in just this way in Jer.
Mo'ed Qaton iii, 82 (middle of col. 3): "Inasmuch as ye were
anointed (*nithrawwîthem*) with the anointing oil for seven days,
so observe the seven days [of mourning] for your brethren." There
is nothing difficult in the supposition that a similar use of the
word was current in the prophet's time, so that he could omit the
noun 'oil' without danger of being misunderstood. We could then
compare the Rabbinical phrase מְשׁוּחַ מלחמה, "anointed for
battle," and perhaps Is. 21 : 5.

Another possibility is that we have here not the pi'el of *rawā*,
as in verse 7, but an altogether different verb, namely, the pu'al
of *ra'ā:* "my sword appears (*videtur*) in the heavens." Observe
that this was the way in which the Targum (*tithgĕlî*) understood
the verb. There would be nothing remarkable in the form: first
ruwwĕthā for *ru'ătha* (the natural phonetic tendency; *cf. muruwwa*
for *murū'a, nubuwwa* for *nebū'ā*, etc., and see Wright, *Compar.
Gram.*, p. 46 f.); then *riwwethā*, with the regular dissimilation of
the vowel (Barth, *Nominalbildung*, p. xxix f.). If this was the verb

intended by the author, then it is certain that he chose it because of its identity in sound with the word which he uses just below, in verse 7; and we then have a capital example of the favorite literary device of this writer, who delights to repeat the same form in two more or less distinct significations. See the principal examples, pages 199–202.

There is nothing unusual or noteworthy in the change to the first person in this verse, Yahwè speaking in his own person instead of through his mouthpiece the prophet. That which has led Duhm and others to rewrite this verse is really their mistaken theory as to the meter. We have here an irreproachable triple-line.

Regarding "Edom," and "the people whom I have doomed," see the introduction to the chapter. With מִשְׁפָּט compare the נִשְׁפָּט of 66 : 16.

34 : 6. The חֶרֶב לַיהוה is probably a reminiscence of Judg. 7 : 20; this is the most natural way of explaining the לְ .

The word הָדְּשָׁנָה is twice accented; for other examples see Chapter IX. Is it not likely that this and the two other "hoth-pa'al" forms (Ges.-Kautzsch, § 54, h) had their origin in alternative readings, i. e., either hoph'al or hithpa'el? This word would then be a combination of the readings הָדְשְׁנָה and הִתְדַּשְּׁנָה. Observe that in no one of the three known cases does the ת of the reflexive stem appear, since it has been assimilated. The hoph'al would then be sure to arise as the most natural reading of the consonant text.

"Bozrah" exactly as in 63 : 1. The prophet has no particular city in mind.

34 : 7. The symbolical character of the whole picture appears more and more plainly.

The suffix in עִמָּם refers of course to the "lambs, goats, and rams" of the preceding verse.

There is no good reason for emending the word רֻוְתָה.

34 : 8. With יוֹם נָקָם compare 47 : 3; 61 : 2; 63 : 4. There is nothing fierce or bloodthirsty in the word נָקָם; the attitude of the prophet in all these passages is precisely that of Paul in Rom. 3 : 5 f.; 2 Thess. 1 : 8.

The word רִיב is here not the verbal noun "quarrel," which would be altogether out of place, but the verbal adjective (nomen agentis, intrans.) of the form qatīl; Barth, Nominalbildung, §§ 30, b; 127, c. It has the force of the active participle, "he who strives";

see 41 : 21, where it is again used in precisely the same sense as here. Compare further קִים, "adversary," Job 22 : 20 (too hastily emended by some scholars); צִיר, "messenger"; Aramaic עִיר, "watcher," etc.; also in Hebrew the qatîl forms לִן, "passing the night" (Neh. 13 : 21), לִיץ, "scoffer," etc. These are all perfectly regular derivatives from "hollow" verb-stems.* The word נִים, "fugitive," Jer. 48 : 44 (consonant text), is also to be included here. It is at least an old variant reading (whether the best reading or not), and is certainly to be preserved as a genuine form. It cannot easily be explained as the result of a scribal error; and the suggestion in Gesenius-Buhl that it was intended to be a hiphil (!) can hardly be taken seriously.

The minor divisions, or stanzas, of this poem are generally not very well marked. Here in verse 8, however, we have the plain indication of such a division. The part of the poem which depicts a scene of carnage is now finished; and this short verse, giving the reason for the carnage, is employed to bring it to a formal close. With verse 9 a new scene is introduced.

34 : 9. An excellent example of a triple-line.

The feminine suffixes, employed from this point on, show how far the poet was from thinking of the real Edom. See also the note on verse 15. It is hardly necessary to say that the prophet is not predicting in all this as though he were describing such things as should actually come to pass. But having undertaken the task of depicting the doom of the wicked, he draws rapidly a series of terrible pictures, made up, no doubt, partly from current eschatology and partly from his own imagination. Their variety is remarkable, and each one is more or less independent of the others. Thus, the picture of the 'burning land,' which ends with 10a, is really incompatible with the picture of the 'land of ruins,' which begins with 10b.

The massoretic verse-division between 9 and 10 is correct; the attempt of Bickell and others to connect בערה with the following is a mistake. The transfer of the word reduces verse 9 to an anticlimax, and seals the ultimate ruin of verse 10. The proposal to follow the Greek translation here is particularly unfortunate in view of the palpably confused and defective character of that version in the clauses which immediately follow.

34 : 10–12. The massoretic division of these verses is not the

---

* Even in Arabic, where this contraction is not the rule, we have such forms as zīr, "visitor" (of women), "ladies' man," from zūr.

right one. With the words "its smoke shall ascend forever" a
distinct feature of the description is brought to a close; while with
the next clause a new feature, or rather an entirely new picture,
is introduced. Instead of a land which is blazing with eternal fire,
the poet now paints for us a deserted land, or rather a deserted
city, filled with vast solitary ruins. Verse 11 should begin with
the word מדור and end with ישכנו בה; verse 12 should begin
with ונטה. These are the divisions which mark off the successive
stages in the description; and when the slight change is made, the
improvement is striking.

34 : 10. The Greek trans., which in this chapter is even more
unsatisfactory than usual, omits אין עבר בה, and apparently also
וירשוה, and then makes terrible work of the following.

34 : 11. Cf. 14 : 23 and Zeph. 2 : 14 (plainly derived from
II Isaiah; cf. verse 15, especially, with Is. 47 : 8).

קאת is hardly "pelican." In every one of the passages where
the word occurs, the context (so far as any inference can be drawn
from it) seems to exclude every sort of water-fowl. In Lev. 11 : 18
and Deut. 14 : 17, the קאת is mentioned among the birds of prey,
and before the water-fowl are reached; the attempt to arrange
according to a rough classification being obvious. In the present
passage and in Ps. 102 : 7, the bird is mentioned as an inhabitant
of "the desert"—a waterless desert, of course. From Zeph. 2 : 14
no inference can be drawn, especially since the words are merely
borrowed from Is. 34 : 11. The later Jewish exegesis, represented
by the versions and the Talmud, not knowing the meaning of the
word, gave it an etymological connection with קיא, "vomit," and
then identified it with קיק, קוק, "pelican." It is to be noticed
that in both Lev. 11 : 18 (= Deut. 14 : 17) and Ps. 102 : 7 the
קאת appears side by side with a species of owl. Moreover, the
sound of the word plainly suggests an onomatopoetic origin for
the name; and it is well known that the characteristic cries of several species of owl begin with a distinct K-sound. The owl is also
the typical bird-inhabitant of ancient ruins. Cf. Ibn Khallikān,
Slane's transl., III, 193 f. Tristram (Survey of Western Palestine,
Fauna and Flora, 1884, pp. 90 ff.) enumerates five species which
are now common in the land, besides several others which are less
frequently seen. The translation "screech-owl"—so also Wellhausen (Ps. 102 : 7) in the Polychrome Bible—is perhaps as convenient as any that can be found.

The meaning of קפד, on the other hand, ought not to be in
doubt. Against overwhelming testimony of tradition (all the old

versions) and philology (the same word, or its phonetic corre-
spondent, meaning "hedgehog" in Late Hebrew, Aramaic, Syriac,*
Arabic, and Ethiopic) only very strong counter-evidence can be
allowed a hearing. But there is no such evidence. In the present
passage, it is most natural that beast and bird should be put side
by side as the joint heirs of this solitude.† Paronomasia was also
an object sought: קאת and קפד here, like ציים and איים in
verse 14. In 14:23 the "hedgehog" could not fairly be objected
to even if the soundness of the text were undoubted; observe, however, that the Greek did not read ואגמי מים. As for Zeph. 2:14
(the sole remaining passage), aside from the fact that the phrase
in question is simply borrowed from Is. 34:11 (see the preceding
note), the context is altogether non-committal.

The word קפד is not Hebrew, but Aramaic in its origin, as is
shown conclusively by the Arabic *qunfudh*, supported by the
Ethiopic *quenfez*. The corresponding Hebrew word must have
been קפֹּוֹ; in fact, the very word which we have in verse 15,
below, with a different meaning. See the note there.

The verse should end with ישכנו בה; see the note on verses
10–12, above.

34:12. This verse, which should begin with the words
ונטה עליה, is a very fine one, weirdly picturesque in its conception, and expressed in a way that reveals the master conscious of
his power. This last fact can be appreciated only by those who
read the verse in the original Hebrew. Unfortunately, an accident
of transmission has wrought ruin in it. The Massorites, by dividing it in the wrong place, have stretched over it the line of תהו
and the plummet of בהו; it has become a terror of exegetes. The
second line of the verse should of course read, ואבני בהו חריה.
As for the construction of חריה: it is certainly not to be taken
as the subject of נטה; there could be no reason nor excuse for
making the nobles of the land (or city) the agents here. It is,
on the contrary, to be understood as = על חריה, parallel to עליה
in the preceding line; with ellipsis of the preposition, as in many
other places.

The whole verse, as thus restored, consists of two double-lines
which are completely parallel, member *a* corresponding to *c*, and
b to *d*:

---

* The use of *qupda* in *late* Syriac to mean "owl" (see Wright, *Kalilah and Dimnah*, Glossary, p. liii) seems to have had its origin in a misunderstanding of the O. T. passages in which the word occurs.

† Just as in verse 13 (jackal and ostrich); 43:20!

> Over her shall be stretched the line of chaos, | and over her
>   nobles the plummet of desolation;
> Her name shall be called, No Kingdom There, | and all her
>   princes shall be nothing.

The testimony of the versions, especially the Greek, has been
widely misunderstood. The emendations adopted by Bickell,
Duhm, Cheyne, and Marti, for instance, professedly based on
"the LXX," have in fact no such basis. For the first line of the
above stanza, the Greek translation has καὶ ἐπιβληθήσεται ἐπ'
αὐτὴν σπαρτίον γεωμετρίας ἐρήμου, that is, it exactly reproduces
ונטה עליה קו תהו. For the next line, ואבני בהו חריה, it has καὶ
ὀνοκένταυροι οἰκήσουσιν ἐν αὐτῇ. Οἱ ἄρχοντες αὐτῆς κ.τ.λ.; that is,
the translator had before him בה (so also the Syriac) instead of
בהו, and read or conjectured איים in place of אבני (where Syr.
read אין (?)). The next word was read אין instead of ואין. Aside
from these variations, there is nothing to indicate that the text
rendered by the Greek in this verse differed in any respect from
our massoretic version. When, in the face of these plain facts,
the three most recent and widely known discussions of the text
of Isaiah insert five words at this point *on the authority of the Greek*
(!), the reader can hardly believe his eyes.

As for the Syriac version, the important fact to notice is that
it divides the verse as I have done. Judging from its rendering,
the translator read ואין בה חדיה in place of ואבני בהו חריה.

That אבן means here "plummet" appears not only from the
parallelism, but also from 28 : 17 and II Kings 21 : 13, where
משקלת is its equivalent. Is the plural אבנים used here merely
for the sake of better rhythm? The best parallel to this passage,
showing how widely the figure of speech was used, is II Kings
21 : 13.

With יקראו (indefinite subject), לה should probably be understood. There is no need, however, to supply anything: "They
shall proclaim, No Kingdom There !"

34 : 13. "Thorns shall grow up over her palaces"; an old and
favorite picture in Hebrew poetry. The exact meaning of קמוש
(or קמוש) is unknown.

By תנים, jackals are probably meant, in all the passages where
the word occurs.* The testimony of the Peshitto to this effect is
valuable. The translation "wolves" (Cheyne, in Is. 13 : 22) can

---

* In Mal. 1 : 3, לתנות must be emended. The לת came from the preceding
word; the remainder is to be pointed וית, as in Zeph. 2 : 6 (not נאות; Stade and
others).

derive no support from the "Arabic *tīnān*." The latter word is to be found in the *Lisān el-'Arab*, s. v. *tyn*, and in the *Qāmūs* and its descendants (entered doubtfully under both roots *tnn* and *tyn*), and is said to have been used only by the poet El-Aḫṭal. See the *Lisān*, vol. XVI, pp. 224 f. If the word is an Arabic formation (and there is no reason to doubt that it is) it cannot be derived from a root *tnn;* neither the meaning of the root nor the grammatical form would allow this. It is either a *fi'lān* form derived from a hollow verb (Wright's *Grammar*, I, pp. 184 C, 242 D; compare, *e. g.*, *sirḥān*, "wolf"), notice the verb *twn* VI, "to hunt game by stalking it first from one side and then from the other"; or, what is much more likely, a *tif'āl* from the root *'anna*, "to moan, wail." Words of this form are intensive adjectives (Wright, *op. cit.*, I, p. 138 D), and *tīnān* (for *ti'nān*) would mean "the [beast] much given to wailing"—a not unnatural designation for this particular wolf, inasmuch as the very next words of the poet describe it as *howling with hunger*. The verse is in El-Aḫṭal's *dīvān*, ed. Salhani, Beyrout, 1891, p. 187, line 6 (where the St. Petersburg MS. gives the reading *tītān*).

For חָצִיר read of course חָצֵר; the י came in from 35 : 7, which verse has suffered more in its turn by contamination from this one.

34 : 14 ff. These verses are valuable both for the remarkably vivid imagination which they display and also for the testimony they give as to the kindly heart of the writer, and his interest in beasts and birds as well as in the flowers of the field (35 : 1, 2).

34 : 14. The צִיִּים are the jinn, the demons of the desert (צִיָה; *cf.* Matt. 12 : 43, etc., and see Schrader-Zimmern, *Keilinschriften und das A. T.*, p. 459, and note 2; Wellhausen, *Reste arabischen Heidentumes*, p. 136). The uncontracted form of the singular was therefore צִיִי, with the ending *î* of appurtenance. This rendering suits admirably in all the passages where the word occurs (in Ps. 72 : 9, read צָרִים). The Greek, Latin, and Syriac translators are right with their δαιμόνια, etc. Even if the אִיִּים should be regarded as animals of some sort, the fact could throw no light on the meaning of צִיִּים; the two words are coupled for the sake of the paronomasia, like קָאת and קִפֹּד in verse 11. As for Bochart's connection of צִי with Arabic *ḍaiwan*, "wild cat," adopted by Cheyne and others, this is absolutely forbidden by the fact that the *nun* belongs to the root.*

---

* Duhm translates here "Schreier," following Ewald, Barth, and others in deriving the word from a supposed root צוה, "to howl." Regarding this derivation, see the note on the following word.

The meaning of אִיִּים has been the subject of much conjecture. The word (always in the plural) occurs in two other passages: 13 : 22 and Jer. 50 : 39. From the context in the former of these two passages, nothing as to the nature of the אִיִּים can be inferred. There, as in the present case, they appear among the inhabitants of ruins in the desert; their companions are jinn (צִיִּים), owls (?), ostriches, satyrs, and jackals, all howling or dancing together in the good-fellowship which such beasts and demons were supposed to enjoy. In the place which the word in question occupies, at the beginning of verse 22, either beast or demon would feel quite at home.* As for the other passage, Jer. 50 : 39, it simply repeats this first clause of Is. 34 : 14 without adding anything that could aid us in interpreting it.

The rendering "jackals," which has recently come into vogue, and now stands almost unchallenged in the Hebrew dictionaries, is chiefly based on a false etymology. Since Ewald, *Lehrbuch der hebr. Sprache*, 1870, p. 383, note 1, it has been customary to connect אִיִּים with the Arabic *ibn 'āwā* (Modern Arabic *wāwī*), "jackal," by postulating a root אוה, "to howl," and pronouncing אִי a contracted form of the *nomen agentis*. But the Arabic name is of course purely onomatopoetic; there is no trace of any such Semitic root, or derived verb, as *'awā*, אוה, "howl"; nor, if there were, could such a form as אִי be obtained from it. The forms with which Barth (*Nominalbildung*, p. 188) attempts to associate the word, for example, are all derived from hollow roots; no such contraction takes place where the ו has consonant value. And finally, the meaning "jackals" is rendered very improbable, at least, by the juxtaposition with תנים in 13 : 22; the same creature can hardly be intended by both words.

The testimony of the ancient versions, so far as anything can be gained from it, favors the view that the אִיִּים were demons or goblins of some sort. The Greek renders by ὀνοκένταυροι (except in Jer. 50 : 39, ἐν ταῖς νήσοις); the Latin has *onocentauri* in the present passage, *ululae* in 13 : 22, and *fauni ficarii* in Jer. 50 : 39. The Syriac translator handled the word very gingerly. In 13 : 22 he translates it by "sirens"; in Jer. 50 : 39 this same word† is made to do duty for both צִיִּים and אִיִּים; and again, in the present

---

* Cf. Wellhausen, *Reste arabischen Heidentumes*, 136: "Es ist leicht zu verstehen, dass die Feldteufel den wilden Tieren ähnlich und mit ihnen zusammengehörig gedacht werden."

† In both of these passages, the choice of the word was evidently due to the proximity of σειρῆνες in the Greek version.

passage the word *rūḥē*, "demons," represents both of these nouns.
The Targum, finally, has חתולין, "cats," in all three passages.

Turning again to etymology, the way in which צײם and אײם
are always associated suggests that they are parallel noun-forma-
tions. And this is probably the case. As the צײם are inhabitants
of the unknown waste, so the אײם are the strange creatures of
the demon tribe which dwell especially in the 'remote regions of
the earth' (אײם). Thus in Tobit 8:3, the demon, when driven
out, flies to "the uttermost part of Egypt" (said by a man who
wrote in Babylonia). So, commonly, in popular mythologies, the
outer edges of the inhabited world are peopled, in part at least, by
fiends and fabulous beasts. *Cf.* Lane, *Thousand and One Nights*,
i, 20 f., in a description of the cosmography of the Arabs: "On the
west is a portion of the Circumambient Ocean, which surrounds
all the countries and seas already mentioned, as well as immense
unknown regions adjoining the former, and innumerable islands
interspersed in the latter. These *terrae incognitae* [which are exactly what Second Isaiah designates by the word אי] are . . .
mostly peopled with Jinn, or Genii." *Cf.* also Jastrow, *Religion of
Babylonia and Assyria*, pp. 260–265. We shall hardly go far
astray if we render אײם by "goblins." * The translations
ὀνοκένταυροι, *fauni*, etc., if mere guesses, were very good ones.

It may be remarked, finally, that this translation, "goblins," is
unquestionably the one which best satisfies the context in each
of the three passages: 34:14; 13:22 (certainly written in imitation of Second Isaiah); Jer. 50:39 (certainly derived from
Is. 34:14). In 34:14 the whole verse is given up to the demon
tribe: jinn—goblins—the satyr—Lilith. In 13:21, 22, on the
other hand, beasts and demons are grouped in pairs in 'happy
family' style—possibly by accident, but more probably by design:
the jinn have owls for their guests; the ostrich and the satyr dance
side by side; the goblins and jackals howl in friendly chorus. We
may be thankful for this bit of demonology in the Old Testament,
which usually has so little to say in regard to popular superstitions.

יקרא. This is not the verb קרה, "meet" (Duhm, Guthe,
Cheyne, Marti), but קרא, "call," as all the old versions understood it. It gives the picture another lively touch. For this use
of the preposition על, compare for example Targ. Micah 6:9,
על קרתא מכלן, "they cry to the city"; *ṣaraḥat 'alaihī*, "she

* The original (uncontracted) form of the singular was therefore אִי, with the
ending *î* of appurtenance.

called to him," 1001 N. (Macnaghten), i. 68, line 15; also 41, line
7; g'au 'alau^{hi} (Syr.), "they cried unto him," Num. 11 : 2. It would
be easy to multiply such examples. The suggestion to emend עַל
to אַל is not a happy one.

הרגיעה. This word and מָנוֹחַ are also coupled in Deut. 28 : 65.

לִילִית. Cheyne, *Introduction*, p. 206, appears to censure the
author of this poem for introducing "the ugly myth of Lilith."
How did Professor Cheyne know in what way this being was conceived in Palestine at this time? Judging from the Babylonian
parallel, which is our one valuable source of information, Lilith
was a demon of the storm (see Schrader-Zimmern, *Keilinschriften
und das A. T.*, p. 460, note 7). It is easy to see how, many centuries
later, popular etymology should have made of her first a "demon
of the *night*" (לַיְל), and then the figure which appears in the
Talmud.

34 : 15. The reading of the text, שָׁמָּה, is better than שָׁם, which
some have proposed to substitute.

The second word in the first line seems to have been accented
קִנְנָה.

קִפּוֹז. This word, found only in the present passage, is the
Hebrew equivalent of the Aramaic קְפַד; see the note on verse 11.
Its *original* meaning must therefore have been "hedgehog" (as
the old versions all render). But here, at least, it had a different
meaning; the verbs "build a nest," "hatch" (eggs), "brood" (over
the young) show plainly that a bird of some sort is designated by
the word. So commentators reasoned, quite correctly, until Bochart (*Hierozoicon*, 1663) introduced the ingenious but unfortunate theory of the "arrow-snake" (see below). The question,
what bird was designated by this term, is one which admits of a
very probable answer. The bird is one which houses in old ruins,
and *looks very much like a hedgehog;* that is, its characteristic appearance is that of a mere ball of feathers, of about the size and
color of the ball into which the hedgehog rolls himself. This can
hardly be anything else than some species of owl. As for the particular species intended, there are two which most naturally suggest themselves, being common in Palestine, of the color required,
and apparently not otherwise designated in Hebrew literature: (1)
the Tawny Owl, *Syrnium aluco* (in Palestine generally not tawny
but gray; Tristram, *Fauna and Flora of Palestine*, 1884, p. 92);
and (2) the small Scops Owl, *Scops giu* (Tristram, *ibid.*). This
latter species is strongly recommended by its small size, which
would both increase its resemblance to the hedgehog, and render

it especially liable to receive such a popular name as this one. Tristram describes it as "very common" in the land, especially in the old ruins, and himself also identifies it with the קִפּוֹז; for what reason, I do not know. I have chosen the rendering "Little Owl," since the size of this species is its characteristic feature among the Palestinian varieties.

The history of the word קִפּוֹז, then, would seem to have been this: originally meaning "hedgehog," it came to be applied popularly to the "little owl," and was finally usurped altogether for the latter use, the Aramaic word קֻפְדָּא being borrowed to designate the hedgehog.

As for the translation "arrow-snake," now almost universally adopted, it is based on the evidence which a certain Arabic word has been wrongly supposed to furnish. Modern scholars have been led astray by Bochart, who found the word qaffāz, "springer," used in Ibn Sīnā with the meaning [serpens] jaculus, and naturally supposed it to be a genuine native Arabic name. But it is, on the contrary, a word of early mediæval coinage, having come into use merely as a translation of the Greek ἀκοντίας, Latin jaculus, or of their Syriac rendering. These Greek and Latin terms, as is well known, were used to designate a certain fabulous reptile, believed to exist in those typical abodes of fabulous creatures, Ethiopia and Arabia. Diodorus and Strabo speak of such a "darting serpent"; Pliny mentions it in his Hist. Nat. (viii, § 35); Lucan writes of the "Arabum volucer serpens" (Phars. 6 : 677), and of the "jaculi volucres" (9 : 720, 822); Ælian (Hist., viii, 13) asserts that it could spring to a distance of twenty cubits. It can easily be imagined with what interest the Arabs, when they came to translate (as they did with such zeal and thoroughness) the Greek and Latin authorities on natural history, read and transmitted these accounts of the "springer," said to be a native of their own land. The chief words used by them to designate it seem to have been ṭaffār and qaffāz (see Ibn Sīnā, Roman ed., 1593, ii, p. 139), synonymous terms meaning "the springer," and thus parallel in their use to the Latin jaculus. By the time of Ibn Sīnā (1000 A. D.), these Arabic words had become true appellatives; a fact which is also attested for qaffāz by certain Syriac lexicographers of about this time (see Payne-Smith, Thesaurus, s. v. harmānā).* That they are merely artificial terms, however, belonging only to the vocabulary of late Arabic, is certain. *Neither of the two is to*

---

* A word used to designate the basilisk, the cerastes, and other fabulous or fearful serpents.

be found in any native lexicon, and the fact is decisive. Even if
there were any such creature as this "arrow-snake," or any reason
to suppose that the accounts of the fabulous reptile originated in
Semitic lands, there would be no justification for an appeal to the
Arabic. And aside from the (supposed) support of the Arabic,
the translation has nothing whatever to rest upon.

The line ובקעה ודגרה בצלה is right as it stands, and needs
no emendation. The verb דגר means "to brood," both here and
in Jer. 17:11, and could of course be used equally well for brood-
ing over either eggs or fledglings. Here, it is necessarily the
fledglings that are meant; thus also probably in Jer. 17:11.
The order of the verbs in the verse is the logical one: nest—lay—
hatch—brood. Duhm remarks: "Den Verben תמלט u. s. w.
fehlt das Object." But why should any one expect an object to
be expressed? There is none in Jer. 17:11; nor would there be
any, ordinarily, in such passages as these.

The suffix in בצלה is especially important as confirming the
observation made above (note on verses 10–12), that the picture
in the poet's mind changed with the words מדור לדור, etc.,
verse 10, from that of a land to that of a city. It is in the shadow
of the ruined walls that the owlets are hatched and brought up.

Here again, at the end of verse 15, the traditional division of
the text is wrong, and has wrought great mischief. The last line
should be אשה רעותה דָרֵשׁוּ, "each one seeks its mate." Verse
16 then begins with מֵעַל. Observe that the LXX divides the
verses in this way.

34:16. The current exegesis of the first part of this verse is at
least as "sonderbar" as the passage itself has been supposed to be.

For וקראו we must read נִקְרָאוּ: "From the book of Yahwè
they [*i. e.,* their names] are read off; not one of them is missing."
It was the accidental reading (here extremely easy) of ו for נ
that caused all the trouble. The preposition מֵעַל now comes to
its rights for the first time; we (like the Hebrews) "search" *in* a
book, but "read" *off from* it. As for this book, or register, kept
in heaven before Yahwè, it is the same poetical figure of speech
which we meet with in Ps. 56:8; 139:16, etc. We have a still
closer parallel, however, in the writings of the Second Isaiah himself. In 40:26 he describes how Yahwè musters the stars, the
"mighty ones" of heaven, to their places, and calls the roll: "He
brings out their host by number, and calls each one by his name;
. . . not one is missing (איש לא נעדר)."

In the latter part of the verse, it is plain that the word יהוה has fallen out between פי and הוא.

In the last clause, the gender of הוא (after רוחו) could be supported by numerous parallels, even if it were not secured by the masculine verb קבצן.

34:17. Only a true lover of nature could have written the concluding verses of this chapter.

Cheyne is probably right in omitting להם. The change in the gender of the suffix is suspicious, and the meter seems to be improved by the omission of the word. The fact that the Greek version contains nothing to correspond to it may therefore be allowed some weight. It may originally have been a marginal variant of להן.

CHAPTER 35

See, in general, the introduction to chapter 34. The poet now turns to the bright side of the picture, the "new earth," and the joy of the saved. As chapter 34 had closed with desolate tracts and solitary ruins, so the new strain begins with a blossoming desert. This is continued for only two verses, however; from verse 3 on to the end, the joys of restored mankind form the theme.

There is no one of the many other pictures of this nature which the Second Isaiah has drawn which can equal this one for beauty. It is a gem of the first water, cut and polished; we cannot imagine any way in which it could have been improved. From beginning to end it is filled with glad sights and sounds. The note of tender feeling which pervades it reveals the warm and wide heart of its author. It is no wonder that several of its verses have been especial favorites in the Christian world, for they have the true universal ring.

It remains to ask, who "the ransomed" are, whose blessings are described in verses 3–10. It is generally taken for granted, by commentators, that the Jews only are meant; but this interpretation is not well grounded. There is nothing in the wording here to point especially to the Jews. Even if this poem stood quite by itself, its author would be entitled to the broader interpretation, inasmuch as the broader view is elsewhere well attested. But when the relation of this chapter to chapter 34 is taken into account, the question is answered at once. As was shown in the introduction to 34, the line drawn between the doomed and the saved is not the line between Jews and Gentiles, but between the foes of Yahwè and his friends, between the wicked and the righteous. Yahwè's "rescue" truly reaches "to the end of the earth" (49 : 6), and the heathen nations share in the joy. This conclusion is borne out by the passages which are most nearly parallel. The dumb, the blind, the oppressed, who now hear the glad tidings of their release, are the same who are mentioned in almost the same words in 42 : 7; 49 : 9a; 61 : 1, 2; namely, the suffering *of all mankind*, not merely those in the one small nation. The ransomed of Yahwè, who return to Zion through the desert, are those—Gentiles as well as Jews—whose return is similarly described in 49 : 8–13. The prophet's promise here is on precisely the same plane with that in 25 : 7, 8: "Yahwè will destroy . . . the veil which is over all the peoples, and . . . will wipe away the tears from all faces."

For the meter of chapter 35, see the note at the beginning of chapter 34.

---

35 : 1. Marti, "Jede äussere Verbindung mit cap. 34 fehlt" (repeating Duhm, who makes a similar statement both here and also at the beginning of chapter 34). Why should any one expect such a 'connection,' and in what way could it seem desirable? Making allowance for the fact that the *subject-matter* of the one chapter is totally different from that of the other, there are no two poems in the book which more closely resemble each other in manner, style, and literary qualities than these two.

The מ in ישֻשׂום is probably the result of assimilation of a final *nun* in the verb-form to the initial *mem* of the following word, in the actual recitation of the poem. The phonetic change is a commonplace; only the *writing* of the new consonant is remarkable.

The massoretic division of verses 1 and 2 is incorrect; כחבצלת is to be connected with what follows, not with what precedes, and the same is true of ותגל (in verse 2). Verse 1 should end with the word ורנן.

Notice the favorite repetition of words in these two verses.

35 : 2. The particle אף is one which the Second Isaiah is fond of using, as commentators have observed. Its use by him is confined, however, to this chapter and chapters 40–48.

The anomalous vowel-pointing of גֵילַת is the result of an attempt to preserve two variant readings in the learned tradition.

One reading (the original) had this word in the form גִּילָה, but was otherwise like our M. T. The other made a full stop after וְתָגֵל, and then proceeded: אַף גִּילַת יַרְדֵן כְּבוֹד הַלְּבָנוֹן נִתַּן לֹה וגו',
"Also *the joy of the Jordan*, the glory of Lebanon, shall be given to it, the splendor of Carmel and Sharon." In the Hebrew text which lay before the Greek translator this גִּילַת had been altered to גְלִילַת, and he rendered the phrase (*cf.* Josh. 22 : 10 f.) by τὰ ἔρημα τοῦ 'Ιορδάνου.

The pronoun הֵמָּה is best understood as referring to the regions which are mentioned in the preceding verses.

35 : 3. The plural imperative is used here exactly as in 40 : 1. The poet has no particular class of hearers in mind, but addresses all who may hear his words.

35 : 4. With the phrase "faint-hearted" compare the very similar words in 32 : 4.

In the second half of the verse, it is obvious that נָקָם is incorrectly pointed, doubtless intentionally. It should be the participle, *i. e.*, either נֹקֵם or (better) נֹקֵם; *cf.* Nahum 1 : 2. With this word the line ends, and יָבוֹא (wrongly connected by the accent) begins the next line.

The vowel in the second syllable of יֶשַׁעֲכֶם is not shortened for metrical reasons. There is no need of shortening here, and the case would be without parallel. On the contrary, we see the usual indication of an alternative reading, namely: "He will come, and your salvation (*yiš'ăkem*)."

35 : 5 f. This is the exact counterpart of 42 : 7; 49 : 9; 61 : 1, 2; and here, as in those passages, the prophet has in mind *all* the afflicted servants of God, whether Jews or Gentiles, in all parts of the earth. That the blessings which he promises are primarily spiritual blessings is made sufficiently clear by the conjunction כִּי, "for," at the beginning of verse 6*b*. This is all figurative language. See also the note on 44 : 3.

35 : 6 f. Compare the similar promise, made to Israel especially, in 43 : 19-21, etc.; and see the note on 49 : 9. The "desert," מִדְבָּר, is of course purely imaginary, as it is in 40 : 3; 43 : 19 ff., and the other similar passages.

35 : 7. The שָׁרָב is here the scorching surface of the sand (and thus a very good parallel to צִמָּאוֹן); see the note on 49 : 10.

The traditional text of the third clause of this verse, בִּנְוֵה תַנִּים רִבְצָה, is of course impossible; neither the first nor the third of these words can be right as it stands. The meaning of the

verse is plain: Blessing (symbolized by the greatest of all blessings
in the Orient, *water*) will abound; what is now arid plain will be a
marsh, corresponding to the grass of to-day will be a luxuriant
growth of reeds and rushes. The presence of the preposition in
לקנה, showing that the construction והיה ל' has been carried
through the whole verse, makes one emendation absolutely certain: רבצה must be corrected to לבצה*. Upon this follows of
necessity the omission of the preposition ב before נוה; its insertion was probably accidental, due to the preceding מ. The clos-
ing couplet of the verse then reads: נוה תנים לבצה | חציר לקנה וגמא:
"The haunt of jackals will become a marsh; instead of grass
there will be reeds and rushes." Compare 55 : 13: "Instead of
the thorn will grow the fir-tree, and instead of the brier the
myrtle."

It may perhaps also be doubted whether תנים was the original
reading. It is true that "haunt of jackals" would be a not unlikely
paraphrase for "waste land"; but, on the other hand, from the
closeness of the parallelism here we should expect something more
nearly corresponding to חציר. The conjecture might then be
hazarded that the original reading was רעים, a word which is
graphically almost the exact equivalent of תנים. Both נוה
רעים ("pasture-land") and חציר ("grass") are good in their
place;† but the poet predicts that the rich vegetation of a swampy
soil will be as common in the future as these are now. As has already been observed, this verse has been contaminated from 34 : 13
(see the note there); the presence in both of the words נוה and
חצר first occasioned the trouble. After ב had been carelessly prefixed to נוה, the now impossible לבצה was altered to רבצה
under the influence of 34 : 13 and 13 : 21, while רעים (if the conjecture just proposed is correct) easily became תנים. חציר and
חצר were interchanged (see note on 34:13, and the Greek
ἐπαύλεις in the present passage), and the Syriac introduced still
another word (the verb corresponding to עלתה) from 34 : 13.‡

As for the further testimony of the versions here: the Latin
and Syriac translators seem to have rendered a text nearly or
quite identical with our massoretic Hebrew. The Syriac does not

---

* According to Cheyne, *S. B. O. T.*, Ruben has made this same conjecture.
† So, for example, the נוה רעים in Jer. 33 : 12.
‡ Some of our modern scholars are not even satisfied with all this contamination of the one passage from the other, but wish to transfer also the ציים
and the איים and the ostriches!

venture to translate רבצה (or לבצה). The Greek presents the
following characteristic monstrosity: ἐκεῖ εὐφροσύνη ὀρνέων,
ἐπαύλεις καλάμου καὶ ἕλη! Here, again, רבצה (or לבצה) seems
to have been avoided. Εὐφροσύνη, for נוה, shows that רנה was
read, the latter word often rendered by εὐφροσύνη in the Greek
of Isaiah. As for ὀρνέων, it certainly stands in the place of תנים,
but cannot possibly be regarded as a translation of it. It is probably the result of corruption in the Greek text, from σειρήνων,
which is the translation of תנים in 34 : 13 and the similar passages.
Finally, the word ἐπαύλεις has been interpreted in some texts
(אΓ Q Syr.-Hex., etc.) by the addition of ποιμνίων.

35 : 8. The following description of the "holy way," by which
the redeemed of Yahwè are to return home to Jerusalem, is a fine
bit of poetic imagery. Compare especially 49 : 9–13; 57 : 14; 62 :
10–12; 66 : 20–23.

The phrase מסלול ודרך, "a causeway and a road," is probably correct as it stands. The word מסלה, like "highway" in
English, is commonly used to mean simply "road," with a more
or less complete loss of its original signification. מסלול, on the
other hand, seems to have preserved the meaning of its root verb.
The poet looks, with the eye of imagination, out into the desert
with its sands and its marshes, and sees there a long line of em-
bankment (מסלול) stretching away into the distance, and upon
it the road (דרך) for which it was built.

The proposed reading מסלה טהרה (Cheyne, Marti), because
of the Greek ὁδὸς καθαρά, is feeble in comparison, and, what is
more, it is not at all likely that the Greek translator had these
Hebrew words before him. The rendering of סלו סלו פנו דרך,
57 : 14, by καθαρίσατε ἀπὸ προσώπου αὐτοῦ ὁδούς shows that this
translator found in the verb סלל the idea of "cleansing" [a road].
What he had before him in the present passage was undoubtedly
מסלול ודרך, nothing else.

For יעברנו read יעברנה. The word דרך is feminine throughout
this whole passage.

The four words והוא הלך למו דרך are quite hopeless as they
stand. So the old versions regarded them, and each met the
difficulty in a characteristic way. The Greek grasped at the single
word דרך, and guessed wildly at the rest of the clause: οὐδὲ
ἔσται ἐκεῖ ὁδὸς ἀκάθαρτος (!). The Syriac (as not infrequently
in such difficult passages) refused to take any responsibility, but
simply translated the Greek (omitting ἀκάθαρτος). Jerome, un-

willing to write nonsense, emended slightly and construed very
ingeniously: *et haec erit vobis directa via.*

Modern scholars have generally either abandoned the passage
as hopeless, or tried to be content with Weir's conjecture, לְעָמוֹ
for לְמוֹ. Such a clause as והוא לעמו הלך דרך might indeed be
possible, though a little awkward, in another connection; but here
it is absolutely impossible. The solution, finally, which would
accept this emendation and then pronounce the whole clause *a
gloss* (!) is certainly much worse than no solution at all.

We may perhaps read as follows: לֹא יַעַבְרֶנָה טמא וְנוֹאָל | וּמְהַלֵּךְ
דרך אוילים לא יִתְעוּ: "The unclean and the perverse will not pass
over it; fools will not mislead him who treads this road." For the
meaning of נוֹאָל (*niphal* participle of יָאַל), *cf.* Num. 12:11. The
meaning of the last clause (where the *hiphil*, יַתְעוּ, is to be read)
is that 'the wicked shall cease from troubling.' It is worthy of
notice that in the passage 19:11–13 the words אֱוִיל, נוֹאָל, and
התעה are all used. As for our massoretic text, it may be explained
as arising from an easy clerical error; the letters נוא were read
הוא, and the rest (only a very slight alteration) followed naturally.

The fact that אוילים seems to be represented in the Greek
by οἱ διεσπαρμένοι, "the dispersed" (!), has been the cause of
much conjecture. This is not, however, the rendering of any
Hebrew word. The translator merely writes here, as very often
elsewhere, what he deems to be suitable.

35:9. It may be that the clause לֹא תמצא שם, "none will
be found there," formed a part of the original text, but it seems
to me more likely that it is an old expansion of the original, or
possibly a variant reading for בל יעלנה. Either a masculine
or a feminine verb would be permissible after פריץ חיות, but
it is hardly probable that the author himself would have used
both genders in such close connection as this.

In the last clause of the verse, we should probably insert בָּהּ
after הלכו, for the sentence is really defective without it. To
claim the support of the Greek ἐκεῖ for this emendation (Duhm,
Cheyne) is hardly permissible, however.

There has been some difference of opinion as to the verse-
division here. In the first place, the Greek and Syriac versions
connect פדויי יהוה closely with the preceding, making it a
second subject of הלכו, and prefix the conjunction ו to ישבון;
thus: "But the redeemed and* the ransomed of Yahwè shall walk

* The Syriac omits the conjunction.

therein, and they shall return and come to Zion," etc. But this cannot have been the original reading. It fails to give sufficient emphasis to the idea of *returning* (ישבון). The verb is made to occupy a secondary position; the most natural way to understand the clause would then be: "they shall go and come"; but the context shows that this was not the meaning intended.

Duhm and Cheyne, while adopting the massoretic reading in other respects, put the verse-division after ישבון, and begin a new 'stanza' with ובאו. The effect is extremely weak, even more so than in the reading of the Greek and Syriac versions. This is, in fact, one of the worst examples of that amputating process to which the unfortunate theory of 'four-line stanzas' drives its devotees.

The words "*And the ransomed of Yahwè shall return*" are those for which the whole chapter (or rather, the whole poem, chapters 34 and 35) has been waiting. The only suitable place for them is the beginning of the stanza. This idea of the return with joy is a distinct advance over the idea expressed in the phrase "but the redeemed shall walk therein." The latter is properly the contrast to the negative statements in verses 8 and 9, and should be connected with them. At the same time, it prepares the way admirably for verse 10. The massoretic division of the verses is therefore the correct one.

35 : 10. It is no wonder that this beautiful verse should have been treasured in the memory of its author. He introduces it in a later poem with fine effect; see the note on 51 : 11. There is no valid reason for preferring the text here to that of 51 : 11, or *vice versa*. There is no reason why the poet may not have written the two passages with just the same few and insignificant divergences which they now present.

Chapter 40

This poem immediately followed chapter 35 in the collection of the poems by this author which was used in making up the 'Book of the Prophet Isaiah' (see Chapter VI, § 3).

It is a fine specimen of the poet's work. The prevailing tone is didactic, and the writer speaks with the voice of one conscious of authority. The structure of the poem is characteristic of his art: first a lyrical passage, occupying verses 1–11; then the argumentative portion, verses 12–26; and at the end a formal conclusion, verses 27–31, in which the thought of both of the preceding divisions is briefly summarized and blended. Compare, for example, chapter 50, where the structure is precisely similar, except that the argumentative passage precedes the lyrical or dramatic.

In the lyrical introduction, verses 1–11, the poet's imagination has free play. One picture succeeds another, and all are drawn with the same sure hand. The weary city, whose debt is more than paid; the 'way in the desert,' typifying the coming of the Messianic glory; the dialogue proclaiming the weakness of mankind; the city Zion announcing glad news to her sister cities; the great shepherd, Yahwè, caring for his flock; all these have one key-note, the absolute power of the God of Israel to fulfil his promises. The artistic effect of this part of the poem is considerably heightened by the alternating use of meters, the 3 | 2 meter being employed where there is either dramatic action or especially strong feeling.

In the argumentative portion, which comprises the most of the poem, the underlying idea is again the same: the absolute power of the God of Israel to fulfil his promises. The comparison of Yahwè, the creator, with the 'gods' of wood and metal is used effectively here, as in several other passages. From the frequency with which this argument is employed by Jewish religious writers of the last few centuries B. C., it is plain that it was really needed. The tone of the prophet here is less severe than in some of the parallel passages, e. g., the first half of chapter 48, or chapter 59; still, he rebukes his fellow countrymen emphatically for their short-sightedness.

The poem is complete in itself. We have here the original beginning, and the original close, and there is no evidence that anything has been lost or added. Some of those who have attempted to approach it from the metrical side, in recent years, have sadly mutilated it, especially in the first part.

This chapter has long been regarded as the beginning of a series; and that, too, not merely as the first of a number of separate poems, but as the formal commencement of a more or less connected 'prophecy.' Its opening words, "Comfort ye my people," have been taken as an announcement of the prophet's main theme, the proclaiming of which he regarded as his mission; and the interpretation of all the subsequent chapters assigned to this writer has been conformed (often with unfortunate results) to this assumption. Hence, for example, the dismemberment of such chapters as 44, 48 (!), and 50, by Duhm and his followers, and the emasculation of many characteristic passages.

But the underlying assumption is mistaken. In the first place, it is not true that this poem was placed by its author at the head of the collection; and again, there is nothing in its character to render it especially fit to occupy such a place. It is true that chapter 40 is given a close internal connection with some of the next following chapters through its polemic against idolatry (*cf.* chapters 41, 44, 46, 48); but this, after all, is only a subordinate feature of the prophet's main line of reasoning. It could be urged with more plausibility that chapter 41 formed a distinct starting-point; for in this chapter begins the prophet's great argument from history, to which he returns again and again in the immediately succeeding chapters. But chapter 40 is not so distinctly a beginning. Nor is there anything in the opening lyric, verses 1–11, which could be called especially representative of the message of this writer. The reflections contained in verses 6, 7, consonant though they are with all of the Second Isaiah's teaching, are nevertheless very far from characteristic of the tone and temper of his discourses. Some have thought to find in them the burden of his whole message! Like the generality of such lyrical utterances, they are the product of a mood, and cannot be carried beyond their immediate surroundings. The figure of the 'way through the desert,' continued from chapter 35 (the poem which immediately preceded), is quite as truly incidental. It may be expected to appear wherever and whenever this prophet is writing in an exalted strain, all the way from chapter 35 to chapter 66. But it is a mere illustrative picture.

And finally, it is a mistake to suppose that the prophet sums up his message in the word "Comfort," with which the chapter begins. The word is merely expressive of the poet's mood at the time when he began this poem, chapter 40. That he himself thought of it as the key-note of the whole poem which he was about to write is possible; though as a matter of fact it is given very little prominence in what follows. The joyful message, which the prophet had in mind, was that of the coming triumph of Israel, through God's help; first the uniting of its scattered forces, and then the fulfilment of its great mission. This message, which was generally uppermost in his thought and appears prominently in all parts of his book, he delivers here anew in the opening lines, as he had probably done in previous poems. As he began to write, on this occasion, the thought of Israel's long and hard struggle, and the suffering and degradation of Jerusalem, the chosen city of God, came to him with great force; therefore he begins with words of consolation, declaring that Jerusalem has already atoned twice over for all her sin; a poetical exaggeration which is no more to be regarded as expressing the writer's formal opinion than are the numerous utterances (likewise poetical) out of the exactly opposite mood, in which he asserts, in striking hyperbole, the utter unworthiness of the chosen people; *e. g.*, 42 : 18; 48 : 1 (last clause); 65 : 1 f., etc.

But this idea of comfort to one in distress did not maintain a prominent place in his thought—as far, at least, as we can judge from the chapter itself. From the beginning of verse 3 to the end of verse 31, there is nothing which might not have been said, in the same words, to people and cities in prosperous circumstances. So also in the following chapters generally; the thought of misfortune, present or past, though occasionally expressed with great force, is not especially prominent. To style the whole book, or even any single part of it, such as chapters 40–55, or 40–48, a "Prophecy of Comfort," is to magnify unduly what is in fact only secondary. The idea which predominates, wherever the writer is encouraging his people rather than rebuking them, is triumph rather than deliverance, revival rather than relief; not restoration to any former condition, nor consolation for any past misfortune, but the sure and speedy coming of a glorious time.

Both meters are employed. The manner in which they alternate in the first part, according to the nature of the subject-matter or the manner of its treatment, is especially instructive.

The first paragraph, verses 1–5, is in the 3 | 2 meter, with a closing 3 | 3 | 3 verse, as often elsewhere. Verses 6–8 are 3 | 3; 9–11 are 3 | 2. Verses 12–24, constituting the principal division of the poem, argumentative in character, are 3 | 3. Verses 25 and 26 are 3 | 2; 27–31 are 3 | 3.

---

40 : 1. נחמו, "Comfort ye." The plural is rhetorical and indefinite, just as in 42 : 10; 48 : 20 (emended); 57 : 14; 62 : 10; 66 : 10, etc. The writer, speaking in the name of Yahwè, is addressing no particular class of men, but all those who might hear his words. If he had been pressed to define those who are meant, he would have answered in the words of 66 : 10: "All those who love Zion."

יאמר. Imperfect tense as in verse 25, 41 : 21, etc.

40 : 2. The second כי is rightly excised by Duhm, Cheyne, and Marti. The passage sounds better without it, and the meter is

improved by its omission. The fact that the word is not translated in the Greek, Syriac, and Latin versions cannot fairly be
used as an argument, however.

In the last line of the verse, the cæsura must come after כפלים,
not before it.

This rhetorical exaggeration, 'to pay double,' is familiar elsewhere; thus, for example, in the Koran, Sur. 7 : 36; 34 : 36; 33 : 68.
The poet's affection for Jerusalem the city stands forth prominently in this passage, especially when it is compared with its
striking parallel, 51 : 17 ff. How truly a poetical exaggeration,
and the product of a mood, this saying is may be learned from
such passages as 43 : 25; 48 : 9, in which the prophet says emphatically that the coming blessing is not based on any merit of Israel,
or on any atonement which it has wrought, but solely on the free
grace of Yahwè. See also the passages referred to above, in the
introduction to the chapter.

40 : 3. The metrical division of the first line which makes the
cæsura follow במדבר is the correct one. This is also the division
which best suits the sense of the passage. The principle of parallelism is not omnipotent, and the cry of the herald would hardly
have begun with the word במדבר.

Both here and in verse 6 the "voice" is merely a poetical device, introduced for literary effect. The "desert," also, is a pure
abstraction. The prophet dwells frequently on his figure of the
desert for two chief reasons: first, it represented the hindrances
and difficulties in the way of the returning Jews of the Dispersion;
and again, it gave him the opportunity to depict, in a most striking way (as just before, in 35 : 8 ff.), God's loving care and guidance of his people, especially since the old traditions of the journey from Egypt to the promised land (cf. Deut. 2 : 7; 8 : 2-4, 15 f.;
Amos 3 : 1, 2; Hos. 13 : 5, etc.) were among the most precious religious possessions of Israel. This latter reason was the principal
one; notice especially his use of the return from Egypt in 43 : 16 f.;
48 : 21; 63 : 11 ff.; and see also the notes on 51 : 10 and 52 : 11 f.

40 : 5. The triple line used at the close of a section; see the
chapter on "Metric Forms."

40 : 6. Regarding the "voice," see the note on verse 3.

Until recently I had pointed וָאֹמַר, "and I said," in company
with the Greek, Syriac, and Latin versions and most modern scholars. But I have come to feel more and more doubtful about the
emendation. The indefinite third person, "and it is said [in reply],"
"the word comes back," sounds much more like the Second Isaiah

than the introduction of himself at this point. This is all as impersonal as possible. The very same use of וַאֹמַר is seen in 57 : 14; see the note there. *Cf.* also 53 : 9; 63 : 11; 65 : 8. The reading of the three old versions is very easily accounted for—the Latin makes the same mistake in 57 : 14—but the reading of our Hebrew text is not easily explained except on the supposition that it is really the original.

The 'emendation' of חסדו is altogether unjustified. The possibility of such a derived meaning of the word as "grace, loveliness" cannot be denied, nor is there anything unlikely in it; observe the parallel afforded by the English word "grace," for example. The fact that this use does not appear elsewhere in the O. T. is not of decisive importance, especially since the writer is the Second Isaiah. To doubt the word on the ground of the Greek δόξα is a singular proceeding. How should we expect this translator to render the word חסד here? By ἔλεος, or ἐλεημοσύνη, or some other word which would make nonsense? That is not his way of translating, where the author's meaning is as plain as it is here. On the contrary, he rendered according to the obvious intent of the original, and the word which he used was well chosen.

40 : 7. "Yea, indeed, mankind is grass." Why any one who is not influenced by a theory of Hebrew meter should object to this line, I am unable to see. To my own ear it improves the whole passage decidedly.

40 : 8. The second half of this verse can be read as a 3-beat line, though four beats may have been intended. See p. 163.

40 : 9. A beautiful figure, very similar to the one used in 52 : 1 f. Zion, personified, is commanded to assume the office of a herald, and proclaim to her sister cities the joyful news. The current mistranslation of this verse is a striking illustration of the baneful effects of the 'exile' theory. Our Revised Version, for example, renders: "O thou that tellest good tidings to Jerusalem." But this is impossible. That the construct מבשרת is used appositively (just like the construction תולעת יעקב in 41 : 14, *e. g.*) is proved conclusively (1) by the gender, which appears not only in both occurrences of this word, but also in the five verbs of the verse, and admits of no other explanation; (2) by the fact that the proclamation of the herald is to be addressed, not to Jerusalem, but "to the cities of Judah." It is hardly necessary to say that the similar but not parallel passages 41 : 27 and 52 : 7 ff. (in both of which מבשר, masc., is employed, and the message is spoken to Jerusalem) cannot be cited as evidence to the contrary.

The idea of a messenger of good news is one which this poet, of all others, might be expected to use, and does use, in a variety of ways.

Duhm has the following, which is a fair specimen of his way of interpreting imaginative poetry: "Die erstere Annahme, bei der מבשרת als Collectiv für מבשרים zu fassen ist, . . . passt besser zu der Aufforderung: steige auf einen hohen Berg, die, an die Stadt Zion gerichtet, ein groteskes Bild ergäbe."

40 : 10. The original text had only "Yahwè," as Duhm, Cheyne, and others have rightly observed. The same conflation has taken place in numerous other passages.

בְּחֹזֶק is an 'alternative' reading, combining בְּחֹזֶק and חָזָק. Compare the similar case in 35 : 4.

40 : 11. I have followed Budde and others in making a new division of clauses in the middle of the verse, and omitting the conjunction in ובחיקו.

40 : 12. The contrast which this verse introduces was planned by the poet, and is very effective: the gentle shepherd of Israel is the one who holds the heavens and the earth in his hand. Such rhetorical effects as this are eminently characteristic. The force of the passage is greatly weakened by the arbitrary transposition of verses which some modern scholars have attempted.

Observe how *mayim* and *shamayim* are put side by side for the sake of the sound, after the usual manner of this writer.

40 : 13. The meaning of the verb תכן is not the same here as in verse 12. There, it was "measure"; here, it is more like the "rectify" of Ps. 75 : 4. On this double use of the word, see Chapter XI.

40 : 14. The characteristic repetition of words.

40 : 15. A good example of a triple line.

40 : 19. The word צרף in its first occurrence is a noun, "smith," but at the end of the verse it is a participle, "casting," or "smithing"; used here as a substitute for the imperfect tense, and so to be rendered. An excellent example of the favorite device of this writer (see Chapter XI). On the syntax of this participle (the subject pronoun omitted) see *Gesen.-Kautzsch*, § 116, s. רתקות is direct object. The Greek translator was frightened by the strange Hebrew word, and (like many modern commentators) failed to understand the poet's double use of צרף; hence he omitted the clause.

40 : 20. The present text is evidently faulty, and the trouble lies in the first two words; תרומה is quite impossible. This much is plain: the image described in verse 20 is not the one described in verse 19. There, an idol of cast metal, overlaid with gold, and

provided with silver chains, is elaborately made; here, one is fashioned out of wood by a carpenter. Moreover, the clause "he seeks
for himself a skilful workman" shows that mention has been made
of the man for whom the 'god' is to be constructed. We should
expect him to be called a poor man, since the cheap idol is contrasted with the expensive one; a place in the text is thus assured
for the word הַמְסֻכָּן (however it may be pointed). There is, therefore, no gap in the text here; nothing more is needed than what
we have. The word which originally stood in the place of תְּרוּמָה
was certainly one of only secondary importance. It might have
been a verb, but was more probably a substantive qualifying or
further describing the word מְסֻכָּן. The *pual* participle, finally, has
a strong presumption in its favor; it is not a form which any editor
or punctuator would have been likely to originate. By reading
תְּמוּרָה instead of תְּרוּמָה, all difficulty is removed. The phrase "he
who has been reduced to poverty *in his trading*" or "to poverty
of substance" (תְּמוּרָה exactly as in Job 20 : 18) is just what the
context requires. The choice of this high-sounding phrase is probably due to the poet's sense of humor, which appears so often in
these descriptions of idolatry, and is also displayed in the sententious brevity of these two verses. The fantastic Jewish exegesis
of the (corrupted) passage, adopted by Jerome, who says that
amsuchan was a kind of 'wood that would not rot' (!), does not
deserve any serious attention. In regard to the tasteless proposal
to transfer 41 : 6 f. to this place, see the note there.

With לֹא יָמוֹט compare 41 : 7; 46 : 7; another example of the
poet's grim irony.

40 : 21.   These words, like those in 25 f., are addressed to the
people of Israel, who, as the prophet repeats with emphasis in so
many places, have been strangely slow to understand their God,
or to recognize his plan. *Cf.* with these passages the following,
observing the important part which this idea plays in the argument to which chapters 41–48 are mainly devoted: 42 : 18 ff., 25;
43 : 24*b*; 44 : 21 f.; 45 : 4 f., 9 ff.; 46 : 8, 12; 48 : 1, 4 ff., 8, 18.

מוֹסְדוֹת, "foundations," is impossible, and the emendation
מִיסוֹדוֹת (*cf.* also Ps. 87 : 1) quite certain.

The comments of Duhm and Marti on this verse express a very
low estimate of the intellectual equipment of the prophet, whom
they thoroughly misinterpret.

40 : 22.   A characteristic verse, with its unusual words and its
paronomasia.

Of course no conclusion whatever as to the cosmography of the writer can be drawn from these phrases. Any modern poet might use the same figures.

40:25 f. The 3 | 2 meter is introduced here not merely for the sake of variety, but because of the lively *dramatic* quality of these two verses. *Cf.* 51 : 9 f.

40:26. "He calls them all by name." So Ps. 147 : 4, Enoch 43 : 1, Bar. 3 : 35. *Cf.* also 48 : 13, and see the note there.

The adjectives רַב (so to be read instead of רֹב) and אַמִּיץ are collective, and refer to the "mighty ones" of the host of heaven, not to Yahwè. Ps. 103 : 20 is a striking parallel which should not be overlooked. The customary conception of the stars as *gibborim;* see Smend, *Alttest. Religionsgeschichte,* pp. 470 f. *Cf.* also such passages as Neh. 9 : 6.

The phrase "not one of them is missing" (when the roll is called) is closely paralleled in 34 : 16.

40 : 27. Here begins the forcible conclusion, in which the whole of the preceding is summed up.

With the complaint which the unbelieving people make, compare especially Mal. 2 : 17; 3 : 13 ff., where the prophet is confronted with the very same situation. See the *Journal of Biblical Literature,* 1898, pp. 11 ff.

40 : 28. The first part of the verse, "Dost thou not know? hast thou not heard?" is a single line of three beats. The beginning of verse 21 is precisely similar.

40 : 31. "They shall mount up *with wings.*" The verb is the *qal* stem of עלה; the noun אֵבֶר is adverbial accusative, of a variety (means or instrument) which has numerous examples in Hebrew poetry and is quite in keeping with the genius of Semitic speech, though developed farther at this point than in the sister languages. There are similar accusatives in the next following poem, see the note on 41 : 2.

The translation of the English Bible (both A. V. and R. V.) is thus the correct one. As for other translations which have been proposed: "They shall lift up wings" (Gesenius, Delitzsch, Reuss) is so manifestly unsuitable, though doing no violence to grammar or lexicon, that it has been quite generally abandoned. "They shall put forth pinion-feathers (or pinions)," the translation of Pusey, Ewald, Duhm, Cheyne, Gesenius-Buhl, and others, has even less to recommend it, for it not only substitutes the incidental for the essential, but also creates a new and intrinsically improbable Hebrew verb. The same may be said of Ryssel: "Sie verjüngen [ihr] Gefieder," in Kautzsch's *AT.*

The verb ילכו seems to have here the meaning "go on, continue" which its infin. absol. or participle so often has when in
close connection with another verb. So Cheyne rendered in his
Prophecies of Isaiah (1889). Understood in this way, it gives a
very effective close to the poem. The verb may be taken in its
most common meaning, "walk," however, with no resulting anticlimax. The high flight and the sharp sprint are only occasional
and of short duration. The ability to continue the slow, steady
gait, league after league and day after day, without tiring, is the
better test of endurance.

The proposal to omit the second half of this verse, as secondary,
might well be passed by without notice if it were not such a typical
case. Duhm writes: "Das letzte Distichon bringt ein anderes Bild
hinzu, das das vorhergehende Bild entschieden schädigt, weil es
statt an Adler an Strausse denken lässt" (!). This, including the
"ostrich" pleasantry, Marti solemnly repeats. Cheyne (Text) has
this note on 40 : 31*b*: "A late, prosaic insertion *outside of the poetical scheme of double distichs* (Duhm)." The italics are mine.

CHAPTER 41

The distinguishing feature of this fine chapter is that it introduces the prophet's great argument from history. The train of
reasoning appears in several forms, adapted to different ends, and
dominates his thought in a number of successive poems, which
were evidently written at about the same time. First of all may
be described the form in which it is presented to his fellow countrymen—though this is not the form which appears most prominently in the present chapter. Briefly stated, the argument is as
follows: (*a*) Yahwè called Abraham, and him alone. (*b*) Yahwè
is the one and only God. He alone has power (1) to form an eternal purpose, and (2) to fulfil it. (*c*) The conclusion: The triumph
of Israel is sure.

No other Old Testament writer has stated this argument with
such fulness and cogency. On its validity depended manifestly the
claim of Judaism to religious leadership. It is plain that the Second Isaiah felt that he could count upon many of his countrymen
to admit the two main premises of his syllogism. On the other
hand, the tone of these chapters shows that a considerable number
even of his well-disposed hearers had sore need to be reminded.
The truths which they still held in theory they set aside in practice.
Some had been led into the worship of the idols of the heathen;

many others, no doubt, had acquiesced in such worship; but there were few of them who would not have agreed, after hearing the prophet's plea, that Yahwè was the one supreme God, the creator and ruler of all.

Again, Israel's actual position among the nations was undeniably very inferior, and broader conceptions of the world and its races had taken the place of the older and narrower ideas. The cherished doctrine of a chosen people might therefore easily become obscured, or even be practically abandoned. But there were comparatively few of the Jews, we may suppose, who had any doubt of the fact that Yahwè once called the founder of the Hebrew nation from the far northeast, and made him great promises. It is this constant appeal to acknowledge facts which gives this chapter and the succeeding ones their power. The same argument, in one or another of its essential parts, is carried on with few interruptions through chapters 42–46, and 48, and appears again plainly stated in 51 : 1–8. After this, it is not again presented in the same form; though such subsequent chapters as 52, 53, 62–64 are very closely related to those just mentioned.

Hardly any one of the poems of our prophet has suffered more than this, which constitutes chapter 41, from the current false theory of the book. The unfortunate hypothesis of a prophecy of the return from the Babylonian exile has blinded the eyes of our best scholars, and turned exegesis upside down. The following synopsis of the poem may serve to make this plain.

With the first verse the poet introduces, as frequently elsewhere, one of the main themes of his composition, which is then reiterated and developed, in characteristic manner, throughout the whole chapter. 'Come, ye nations (says Yahwè), behold the evidence of my eternal purpose, which is now to be fulfilled, and show, if you can, that your own "gods" have any such power.' The next verse brings in a second theme, which is also fundamental to the whole composition. This is contained in verses 2 and 3, and reads as follows:

> Who aroused from the east a righteous one,* | summoning
>   him to follow?
> He will deliver up nations before him, | kings he shall tread
>   under foot.
> With his sword he shall make them as dust, | as driven stub-
>   ble with his bow;
> He shall pursue them, and pass on safely, | no path shall he
>   tread with his feet.

>   * See the critical note on the passage.

These words, as their context shows, describe the way in which Yahwè has proved, and will yet prove, his omnipotence. Who, then, is the all-important personage whom Yahwè chose "from the beginning" (מראש, verse 4), and whom he will in "the end" (אחרנים, verse 4) make to triumph over kings and nations? Certainly not Cyrus; this the whole chapter forbids. It is, on the contrary, Israel, as the several repetitions of the theme—verses 8 ff., 14 ff., 25 ff.—all say more or less distinctly. So, too, the old commentators, Jewish and Christian, agreed. The one who was called "from the east" (verse 2) and "from the north (verse 25) was Abraham, who came from Ur and Harran. He is expressly named in verse 8; cf. also especially 51 : 2. His call (again alluded to in verse 25) was the "beginning of Zion" referred to in verse 27; see the note there. Verse 2a finds its exact counterpart in verse 9; every single element of the former passage is paralleled in the latter. The one who was destined to "trample on kings" and "make them as dust with his sword" was the future Israel, or Israel's representative. This, again, is made as plain as possible by verses 11, 12, 15, 16. Other features of the description, which apply perfectly to Israel (or Abraham), could not be made to apply at all to Cyrus; thus: (1) He came, "calling on Yahwè's name." (2) He was "a righteous one." (3) He "shall tread no path with his feet" (compare, for Israel, the statement in 15b). (4) Yahwè had announced him "from the beginning." And finally, in verses 1, 4, 26 it is made as plain as words can make it that the prophet is presenting his unanswerable argument in verses 2 and 25, especially. That is, these two verses contain the whole 'line of proof' in a nutshell; it is proof, moreover, that could not fail to convince the Gentiles. This, again, is decisive. The career of Israel, ending with victory, would compel the acknowledgment sought; the career of Cyrus, on the contrary, could 'prove' nothing whatever.

Verses 8–19, then, are the elaboration of the theme provided in verses 2, 3. Verses 1, 4 are elaborated in 5–7 and 21–24. The formal conclusion, or summing up, which we find in so many of the poems of this writer, then follows in verses 25–29, the two principal themes being repeated and combined in the customary way. This *finale* is very effective rhetorically, and the poem closes with a brief and vigorous answer to the question with which it began.

That the whole is a unit is obvious; nor is anything missing. A characteristic feature is the caustic humor which appears especially in verses 5–7 and 23. We have no better example of this

quality in the Second Isaiah than the former of these two passages,
where the heathen nations are pictured as pulling themselves together, in nervous haste, and mustering all their resources for the
purpose of turning out the very best 'god' that skilled labor could
produce, in order to meet Yahwè's challenge. The dramatically
abrupt way in which this picture is introduced, and then as suddenly cast aside, with a smile of contempt, is worthy of especial
notice.

The meter of the poem is 3 | 3, except in verses 11–13 and 21–24,
where it is 3 | 2.

------

41 : 1.   With the opening words *cf.* 34 : 1; 49 : 1.

The change of person, from the second to the third, should occasion no difficulty. It takes place very naturally, even immediately
after the direct address; *cf.* Micah 1 : 2 (where כלם is *not* to be
altered to כלכם), Mal. 3 : 9, Is. 54 : 1, etc.

The phrase יחליפו כח, "let them redouble their strength," is
just what best suits the context. The writer is simply anticipating
the ironical passage verses 5–7, and his choice of these high-sounding words is itself ironical. Whether they were suggested to his
mind by 40 : 31, or not, is a question of very small importance. It
is probable, to be sure, that the two poems were originally written
in this order.

41 : 2.   For the interpretation of this and the following verses,
see the introduction to the chapter.

The massoretic division of the first half-verse is wrong. The
word צדק cannot possibly belong to the second clause, but must
be connected with the preceding words, as all the old versions
(Greek, Syriac, Jerome, Targum) rightly saw. A direct object of
the verb העיר is demanded;* preferably, of course, a word in the
same clause. To make צדק the subject of יקראהו is to construct a
phrase of the most awkward and artificial kind. The translation
adopted by Duhm and Cheyne, "dem Sieg begegnet auf Schritt
und Tritt," "him on whose steps attends victory," gives neither

------

* In verse 25 the case is different. There the phrase is simply a repetition, and
the object of the verb can be supplied with certainty. But here, *the first time*
that this all-important statement is introduced, clearness and completeness
are indispensable.

the noun nor the verb a defensible rendering. The meaning of the
verb, "call," is indicated both by a number of parallel passages
(see 46 : 11; 48 : 15; also 41 : 9; 42 : 6; 49 : 1, etc.), and also by the
evident parallelism in the two halves of this line.

The word צדק belongs to the first clause of the verse, and is the
direct object of העיר. The context shows that *a person* is here
described. We must therefore point צַדִּיק, as Jerome actually read
(rendering *justum*). This would be a most suitable adjective to
apply to Abraham; and it is to be noticed that the word is better
suited to the rhythm. Both halves of the line now read smoothly.
The reason why the Massorites pointed צֶדֶק and connected the
word with the following clause is to be seen in 42 : 6 and 45 : 13.

The question remains, whether the variation of the Greek version, which adds καὶ πορεύσεται to the second clause, is to be
given any weight. It seems to me most likely that it represents a
later addition to the text, perhaps derived from the ויאת of verse
25 (not rendered in the Greek).

With לרגלו compare לרגלה in I Sam. 25 : 42.

"He will deliver up nations before him," *i. e.*, will give them
into his hand; the same idiom in Deut. 2 : 31; 33; 7 : 23.

For the form יְרְדְּ, which cannot possibly be correct, we must
read יָרְד.* It is imperfect Qal of רדד, a verb found elsewhere with
this meaning only in Ps. 144 : 2 (רוֹדֵד) and Is. 45 : 1. That the
vowel of the second syllable was *a*, not *o*, is made probable by the
infinitive לְרַד in 45 : 1; see the note there.

It is probable that the subject changes at this point, so that,
whereas Yahwè was the subject of the preceding verbs, from this
point on (beginning with ירד) Abraham (*i. e.*, Israel) is the one
intended, as in verse 25. I have translated in this way. *Cf.* the
note on 48 : 14, at the end.

The clause יתן כעפר חרבו has seemed to present difficulty, since
the "sword" (the Hebrew word is feminine) cannot be either the
object or the subject of the verb. The old versions rendered a text
identical with ours. The nouns חרב and קשת here are examples of
the adverbial accusative, similar to the one in 40 : 31; see the note
there. We may compare, for example, Ps. 17 : 13 f., "Deliver my
soul from the wicked one *with* thy sword; from men, *by* thy hand,"

---

* The massoretic vocalization is probably an example of the artificial pointing designed to call attention to *a variant reading*. (Notice that either יְרְדֶּה or
ירד would make good sense here.)

where Duhm, *Die Psalmen*, recognizes an 'instrumental accusative' in both cases. The חרב in Is. 1 : 20 is another example, generally explained incorrectly. So also 43 : 23, "Hast thou not honored me *with* thy sacrifices?"; Micah 7 : 2, "They hunt their
brethren *with* a net"; Ps. 60 : 7 (108 : 7), "Save *with* thy right
hand"; Is. 10 : 30, "Cry out *with* thy voice"; Prov. 10 : 4, "He
who deals *with* a slack hand."* Compare the colloquial Arabic
ḍarabahu kaffan, "he struck him *with* the open hand" (examples
in Dozy, *Supplément*, and JAOS. xxiii, pp. 250, 252). Our Hebrew
grammars have been slow to recognize this construction, of which
there are numerous other examples in the Old Testament.

The direct object of יתן is understood, as in very many other
passages.

41 : 4. קרא הדרות מראש, "proclaiming the cycles [of history]
from the beginning"; that is, in calling Abraham and preparing
for the ultimate triumph of his seed.

קרא exactly as in 44 : 7. That this phrase refers to the events,
past and future, which are summarized in verse 2, is plain from
the context and also from the parallel passages. In a precisely
similar manner verse 25 (corresponding to verse 2) interprets verse
26 (corresponding to this phrase). In these and the other similar
passages, it is from the way in which beginning and end agree
together that the poet argues the foreseeing omnipotence of Yahwè.
The argument is entirely valid, for Gentiles as well as for Jews.
Duhm's note on this verse shows how far he is from understanding
the prophet.

The frequent challenge to the nations, 'Foretell the future!'
means simply: 'Acknowledge that you can show nothing to compare with this divine purpose, advancing steadily from Abraham
to the Messianic kingdom.' Compare verses 22, 23, 25 f., also
43 : 7, 9; 44 : 7 f.; 45 : 21; 46 : 10 f.; 48 : 3, 14; 57 : 12.

With the second half of the verse compare 44 : 6; 48 : 12, 16.
אני הוא might be translated, "I am *the same*"; compare with this
use of הוא 43 : 10, 13, 25; 46 : 4; and apparently also 52 : 6.

41 : 5–7. The way in which the fine humor of these verses has
been ignored by scholars is most remarkable; and the proposal to
transfer the passage verse 6 f. from its present position, where it
was planned with such skill, to 40 : 20, where it is altogether disturbing and out of place, is certainly one of the curiosities of mod-

* The grammar of Gesenius-Kautzsch, 144 *m*, explains these last examples
as nominative; but if the appeal is made to Semitic usage in general, there can
be no question that the accusative is indicated.

ern Biblical scholarship. See further the introduction to the chapter, at the end.

41 : 5. The pointing of וַיִּירָאוּ is perhaps not to be altered. Observe the usual paronomasia.

The irony of the poet appears also in his choice of words, and in the amusing pomp and circumstances of these three verses. קרבו וייאתיון is a fitting counterpart to יחליפו כה in verse 1.

By a misuse of the Greek translation, Duhm (followed by Cheyne and Marti) adds two words to the verse. The Greek read יחדו in place of יחרדו; cf. verse 1.

41 : 7. The words lō yimmōṭ (in which the irony of the passage culminates!) are certainly not to be expunged "for the sake of the meter." This concluding line of the verse is not unusually long.

41 : 8. "Israel, *my servant.*" Here the poet touches for the first time the theme which he afterward elaborates in such incomparable fashion: Israel chosen of Yahwè *to fulfil a mission.* Wherever he uses the word *'ebed* as a designation of the Hebrew people, or of the people's representative, it is with this underlying idea.

"Seed of Abraham, my beloved." *Cf.* 43 : 4 and (especially) 48 : 14. Abraham, Israel, Jacob are names used interchangeably to designate the chosen people.

41 : 9. This is not a promise, and thus parallel to 43 : 5 f.; 49 : 12, etc., but a reference to the call of Abraham, and thus parallel to verses 2a, 25a, 46 : 11.

Marti's mutilation of this verse in the interest of imaginary 'strophes' is a typical instance.

41 : 11–13. An example of the change of meter mainly for the sake of variety. The reader cannot fail to see, however, that the whole passage receives a new emphasis—is put in a stronger light, so to speak—by the use of the 3 | 2 meter.

41 : 11a. Nearly the same words appear again in 45 : 24. *Cf.* also 45 : 16.

41 : 12. With מצת (only here) *cf.* מצה in 58 : 4.

41 : 13. "Who takes hold of thy right hand." Compare the use of the same words—and in the same application—in 42 : 6; 45 : 1 (where the glossator has introduced Cyrus!).

41 : 14–16. Duhm (followed by Cheyne and Marti) endeavors to fit these verses also into the 3 | 2 scheme. The fact that *four* of the six short half-verses demanded by the theory have to be reduced to length by the arbitrary excision of a word in each, while one of the two remaining is noticeably long, should have deterred him from the attempt.

41 : 14. מתי is of course impossible here. Ewald's emendation רִמָּת is undoubtedly correct, and has been adopted by most modern commentators. Compare 14 : 11, where the same two words for "worm" are in juxtaposition. So also Bar Sira 10 : 11, and especially Job 25 : 6, אף כי אנוש רמה ובן אדם תולעה. Notice, moreover, in the present passage, the way in which the fem. sing. suffix is employed in the immediate sequel.

41 : 15. Those whom Israel is to "thresh" and "shatter" are not the heathen nations in general, nor any of the surrounding nations in particular, but *the wicked*, of all races and lands; the incorrigible enemies of Yahwè and the religion of righteousness. Before the Messianic reign can begin, they must be dealt with. See especially the introduction to chapter 34, and *cf.* such passages as Ps. 2 : 9 and 110 : 5 f.

חרוץ for לחרוץ, with ellipsis of the preposition, as in many other cases.

41 : 17. Spiritual blessings are here pictured in the usual and (for an oriental) most forcible way, by the figure of desert land turned into an oasis. The "thirst" is the same which is spoken of in 55 : 1. See 35 : 6 f.; 43 : 19 ff.; 44 : 3 (where מים is interpreted by רוחי); 49 : 10, etc.

41 : 19. The massoretic division of the first clause is wrong; the cæsura comes before שטה, not after it. So also in the second half-verse, the cæsura must follow בראש.
It is not certain just what trees are intended by the last two names; *cf.* 60 : 13.

41 : 20. Observe the ellipsis of the direct object in ישימו; the complete phrase occurs in verse 22. "They" means all mankind.

41 : 21–24. With this characteristic challenge compare especially 43 : 9 (where מי בהם = "what 'god' among them?"), 12; 44 : 7, 8; 45 : 21; 48 : 14. On the validity of the prophet's argument, which has been frequently misunderstood, and accordingly jeered at (see Duhm's note, for example), see the introduction to the chapter.
The use of the 3 | 2 meter in verses 21–24 serves to mark off the prelude, which is addressed to the nations, from the actual challenge to the false gods.

41 : 21. ריב in this passage is not the *nomen actionis*, "quarrel," but the *nomen agentis*, "champion." It must here be pointed רִיבֵיכֶם, *plural*. The word occurs also in 34 : 8, where it is used in just the same way; see the note there.
Duhm thinks that the Greek translator read האל after יהוה.

Compare, on the contrary, the Greek in verse 17; 42:6, 8, 13, 21; 43:1, 10, 12, 14, 15; 44:2; 45:1, 3, 5, 6, 7, 11. In all of these cases, the κύριος ὁ θεός is a mere embellishment in the Greek. The combination יהוה האל, moreover, is not found anywhere in the Old Testament.

It is plain that עצמותיכם is a mere scribal error for עֲצַבּוֹתֵיכֶם. The latter word does not, to be sure, mean "images," "false gods" (which the context demands), but "pains" or "woes"; it is thus one of those punning *substitutes* for "idol" which the Jewish scribes delighted to use. The prophet himself presumably wrote עֲצַבֵּיכֶם, "your idols." The very same substitution has been made in Ps. 16:14, and many have been led astray by it. In Is. 48:5 the same wit has substituted עֹצֶב for עֶצֶב, so that the text now reads "my misery" instead of "my idol." See the note there, for further examples. A precisely similar case is the use of צירים, "pains," for "idols" in 45:16. See also the note on יהילילו, 52:5.

41:22. For יגישו we must read יַגִּשׁוּ, with all the old versions and the evident meaning of the passage.

The challenge is: Show some evidence of an eternal plan! Show a definite *beginning* (like the call of Abraham), and its justification in a *final triumph* (like the glory of Israel, now just at hand).

41:23. With לאחור compare 42:23 (noting the emendation there).

In the first clause of the second half-verse the particle כי is omitted, as frequently happens. The two verbs תיטיבו and תרעו are dependent: "That we may know . . . *that* ye can help or harm." 48:8 furnishes a similar example. The customary treatment of these verbs, translating them like the imperatives which precede, is both ungrammatical and altogether unsuited to the sense of the passage.

The two verbs נשתעה and נִירָא (so to be read) have exactly the same meaning here which they have in verse 10, where they are also put side by side. 'Show that you have some power, so that we may be duly frightened!' The irony is characteristic.

41:24. The metrical brevity of the two lines which constitute the first half-verse is very effective here; they were pronounced with deliberate emphasis.

We must of course read מאפס, as in 40:17. Compare also verse 29, below.

תועבה יבחר בכם. Duhm, translating (in the way that is customary) "Ein Greuel, der euch erwählt!" thinks this "unlike

Second Isaiah," and accordingly pronounces the clause a gloss. Cheyne and Marti follow him. But even glossators were Jews, and familiar with the Hebrew tongue. תועבה is fem., not masc.,* and the suffix in בכם refers to the "gods," beyond any question (as do the pronouns and suffixes, second person plural, all through the preceding verse and in the first half of this one). Neither the prophet nor any glossator, moreover, would think of using תועבה for *the worshipper* of false gods. Nor is there any possible way of translating these three words, in the present context. On the contrary, the text is certainly corrupt. Judging from the evidence contained in בחר בכם, the meaning of the clause must have been: 'Those who choose you [as their gods] are badly deceived'; an idea which is exactly suited to the context (*cf.* 44 : 9 ff., 18, 20, etc.). Read therefore תּוֹעֶה הַבֹּחֵר בָּכֶם, "He who chooses you *goes astray.*" The verb תעה is often used in this way, and the accidental corruption of the text is easy to understand.

41 : 25. ויאת. This word is not "eingeschoben" (Duhm), but is quite as important a part of the sentence as is the preceding verb. The expression יקרא בשמי may be translated in more than one way, but is not in any case to be taken as the direct object of העירותי. The object of this latter verb could be left unexpressed, as it is made so evident by all that has preceded. This is a variety of ellipsis which is very common in these poems.

ויבא should of course be ויבוס, as many scholars have observed. The ס was accidentally dropped because of the ס beginning the next word; the rest followed of necessity.

Israel, called (in the person of Abraham) from the ends of the earth (so verse 9), is destined to trample upon kingdoms (so verse 15). This one verse sums up the positive side of the prophet's present argument.

41 : 26. "Who announced from the beginning [any similar thing]?" Here, again, the object of the verb is omitted. With this question compare especially 48 : 14.

With the threefold use of אף compare the similar case in 40 : 23.

It would be difficult for any exegete to explain how Yahwè had "announced from the beginning" the career *of Cyrus.* Supposing that מראש could mean here merely "beforehand" (though its true meaning is evident enough from 41 : 4; 45 : 19; 48 : 14, 16, etc.),

---

* The desperate expedient of making יבחר בכם the subject, and תועבה the predicate, of this sentence, is altogether contrary to Hebrew usage. The few examples given in Gesenius-Kautzsch, 155, *n*, are either the product of text corruption, or not really parallel to the present case.

the "foreknowledge" of Yahwè would then seem very commonplace, to say the least. According to the current theory, reiterated
in every commentary, it was not a difficult matter, at the time
when this was written, for an observing man (like our prophet) to
foresee the taking of Babylon, and even to predict the policy of
Cyrus.

41 : 27. The Hebrew translated by the versions was probably
identical with our massoretic text. The Greek omits הנה הנם, undoubtedly because the translator did not understand the verse.
The text is perhaps correct as it stands, and the meaning of the
verse is clear. The prophet is again presenting, in a nutshell, the
evidence afforded by the history of Israel, past and present (including the immediate future). He has just pointed to the heathen
gods, and asked: What 'beginnings' have they to show? What
great 'coming events' can they foretell? He now turns to Zion,
and cries out: Here are its beginnings (the call of Abraham, verse
25a, and the history of his children); and now, at last, has come the
great end predicted (cf. again verse 25b); the voice of the herald can
be heard (cf. 40 : 3 ff.; 52 : 7 ff.). ראשון is the equivalent of הראשנות,
verse 22, 42 : 9; cf. also 43 : 9, 18; 48 : 3. The use of ל in לציון
is the familiar substitute for the construct state, "the beginnings
of Zion." The expression הנה הנם can be defended. The repetition
sounds like this writer; the first time הנה is used it is a mere inter-
jection, as often (Gesenius-Kautzsch, 147, b); the second time, it
is given a suffix (masculine *in form*, of course!) which corresponds
to the plural idea in the preceding noun. *Cf.* the feminine plural
in verse 22, *e. g.* The poet wrote the noun in the singular simply
for the sake of the sonorous phrase, ראשון לציון; he did not use
the singular pronoun, however, because the idea was distinctly
plural, the successive preliminary stages of the history. If any
one prefers to emend the text, it is easy to do so by substituting
הֵנָּה (fem. plur. pronoun) for הנם, comparing verse 22. 'As for the
beginning of Zion, behold *these things!*' (those already referred to).
It should be noticed that the Syriac renders the verse correctly,
from beginning to end. The whole is exactly parallel to 42 : 9,
and the "beginnings" (especially the calling of the chosen people)
are similarly referred to in 43 : 9 f.—notice אתם עדי, etc., in verse
10—and 48 : 12–15.

The "herald," מבשר, is of course not the prophet himself. This
would be altogether contrary to his mode of thought and literary
habit. We must rather compare 52 : 7, etc.

41 : 28. וארא ואין איש. *Cf.* 59 : 16; 63 : 5. It was probably

through the influence of these two very similar passages (as well as the influence of the preceding clause here) that the conjunction ו was wrongly inserted before *the second* אין. It must be cancelled.

Duhm begins the verse: ואלה ואין איש. What that can mean, I have no idea. It certainly could not pass for Hebrew, in this context.

The strange εἰς ὁδόν, which appears in the Greek version (most manuscripts, also Syr.-Hex., Eth.) at the end of verse 27, is more interesting than appears at first sight. It is the result of ancient corruption from εἰ εἶδον, which was the translation of ואָרא, the first word in verse 28. The translator rendered the conjunction (correctly) by a conditional particle, both here and in the following clause (ואשאלם translated by ἐὰν ἐρωτήσω). ΕΙΕΙΔΟΝ became ΕΙΣΙΔΟΝ and then (naturally) ΕΙΣΟΔΟΝ. The Greek originally read: εἰ εἶδον, [ἀπὸ τῶν ἐθνῶν] ἰδοὺ οὐδείς, καὶ ἀπὸ [τῶν εἰδώλων] αὐτῶν οὐκ ἦν ὁ ἀναγγέλλων· καὶ ἐὰν ἐρωτήσω αὐτοὺς κ. τ. ἑ.; a translation which is excellent, aside from the exegetical expansions which I have bracketed.

The requirement of the metric line might seem to show that we should read וָאֵרֶא, with two accents; but see on the contrary the treatment of this line in the chapter on "Metric Forms."

41 : 29. It is plain that there is something wrong with the end of the verse. The suffix in the word נסכיהם is quite impossible here, for the third plural suffix has already been used twice in this verse to refer to the false gods themselves. Neither the Greek nor the Syriac read any such word; on the other hand, it is evident that the text before them was felt to be incomplete, and in either case the gap seems to have been filled by conjecture. The Syriac adds, after תהו, "their works" (simply repeating מעשיהם); the Greek adds, "those who lead you astray" (מתעיכם). The origin of the trouble is not difficult to find. The conjunction ו fell out by accident after און (an extremely easy accident, for more than one evident reason); the rest followed naturally. The verse read originally:

הן כלם און ואפס | מעשיהם רוח ותהו.

CHAPTERS 42 : 1–43 : 7

This poem might appropriately be entitled "The Great Contrast." The poet draws, with marvellous power, a picture of Israel in which the effect of strong light and deep shadow is both startling and moving. On the one side, the Israel of God's purpose, "the light of the nations"; on the other, the people as it actually stood before the world: "robbed and plundered, trapped in holes and hidden away in dungeons," the spoil and the sport of all mankind. Here the Servant of Yahwè, majestic and magnanimous, embodying the righteousness and the compassion of God, and establishing peace on earth and good-will among men; there, the faithless messenger, Jacob, stubborn and disobedient, forgetful of his mission, and even bowing down to the images of other gods. This contrast reaches its climax in the paradox of verse 19: "Who is as deaf as Meshullam, as blind as the Servant of Yahwè?"

The leading note in the whole composition, nevertheless, is one of hope. This appears at once in the opening words, *Behold my Servant, he shall bring forth judgment for the nations;* and in the jubilant verses at the close (43:1–7) every cloud is brushed aside. The highly dramatic passage, verses 14 ff., which forms the true centre of the poem, shows deliverance close at hand, and gives at the same time the reason for expecting it. It is not because of any merit on Israel's part; far from it; the nation is utterly undeserving, as the prophet constantly asserts. Nor is it because of any sign of hope in the circumstances of the time. On the contrary, no word of this prophet, here or elsewhere, gives evidence that he saw encouragement in the actual situation, or in the march of recent events. Such verses as 42:22; 64:11, etc., show rather that from the merely human point of view Israel had no promise of relief. But in the love of Yahwè for his own people, a love unchanging and unchangeable, the prophet saw the sure ground of hope. Indeed, in the very increase of suffering and humiliation was the assurance of speedier help. Hence the strikingly bold metaphor in verse 14, where Yahwè is pictured as one who has endured to the bursting point, but can now restrain himself no longer. With a gasp for breath, and an involuntary cry, he breaks his enforced silence and begins his work of deliverance. It was in a somewhat different mood, but with the same underlying thought, that the prophet wrote in 40:2 of Jerusalem as one who had "paid double for all her sins." There also it was to satisfy Yahwè, even more than Israel, that the announcement was made. His love for the city and the people of his choice, rather than any consideration of justice, was the deciding factor. He could wait no longer, but in an outburst of affection declared himself willing to accept what Zion had already suffered as full penance—nay, as double penance—for her iniquity.

This thought of the necessity of speedy deliverance, a necessity felt by Yahwè himself far more keenly than by any of his people, is prominent in many of the poems of this writer and gives splendid testimony to his faith. Not only Yahwè's affection for his children, but also his jealousy for his honor among the nations of the earth, will compel him soon to interpose. "For my own sake, for my own sake, I must act!" 48:11; 43:25; *cf.* such passages as 52:1–6.

On the Servant of Yahwè in this poem, see the chapter on "The Servant and the Messiah." Those features of the picture which were especially prominent in chapter 41, and which reappear in 45:1 ff., namely, the terrible might of the Servant, and his work as an avenger, are here entirely out of sight. This is a poem in which the maltreatment of Israel by its neighbors is strongly stated, and in which idolaters are warned of their folly; yet the Servant, with absolute power in his hands, is not pictured as "trampling on princes" (41:25; 45:1) and "dividing the spoil with the strong" (53:12). Even while still engaged in the endeavor to establish his law in the earth, he will show himself the friend and helper of these once tyrannous and idolatrous nations, and indeed of all those evil-doers who acknowledge their guilt and would fain do right. "He will not chide, nor deal harshly." This of course involves no contradiction with the warlike passages just cited, and such similar ones as 45:14; 60:11, etc., nor with the "vengeance" (נקם) of 34:8 and 63:4. No one of these details, moreover, could be spared from the great program.

This poem is similar, both in the material out of which it is composed and in the manner of its composition, to the one which constitutes chapter 50. The passage describing the Servant of Yahwè, verses 1–7, corresponds to 50:4–9; verses 15, 16 closely resemble 50:2b, 3; the argumentative passage, verses 18–25, is paralleled in 50:1, 2a; both poems contain a word of stern rebuke, enforced by the metaphor of a blazing fire; and there are still other minor points of correspondence. In both cases it is evident that the structure of the poem is carefully planned. In the present chapter, which is a fine example of variety in unity, the way in which the 3 | 2 meter is employed for dramatic effect, and the skill with which the transitions from paragraph to paragraph are effected, are points which deserve especial attention. See the notes below, and the introduction to chapter 50.

The question as to the extent of the poem cannot be settled without reference to the similar problem at the end of chapter 43. In both cases the conclusion seems certain that our present chapter-division is not the correct one. 43:27 f. could not possibly form the close of the poem to which it belongs; verses 25 and 26 show plainly, on the contrary, that just such a passage as 44 : 1–5 was still to come. The structure of the whole composition, too, presupposes this. At the end of chapter 42 the case is hardly less clear. Verse 25, powerful though it is, is not the logical ending of the prophet's composition; moreover, the following ועתה, 43 : 1, shows that he did not in fact drop the subject at this point, but added the characteristic and necessary conclusion, in 43 : 1–7. With 43 : 8 a new poem begins.

It might appear to be a legitimate hypothesis, starting from the ועתה of 43 : 1 and 44 : 1, that we have here three (or more) poems written not merely in close succession but also in logical sequence, each taking formal note of the preceding *and forming its continuation*. But, aside from the fact that no such continuation is to be found elsewhere in the book (except in chapters 34 and 35; see the introduction to chapter 34; and apparently in 65 | 66), any careful study of the poems themselves shows the hypothesis to be untenable. Taken as a whole, and viewed as to its material contents, 43 is in no sense the continuation of 42, nor is 44 that of 43. There is no progress of thought from the one to the other (leaving out of account, for the moment, the two paragraphs 43 : 1–7 and 44 : 1–5); they are altogether independent poems, and are intelligible only when they are so regarded. The reason for the present division of the chapters here (first made in the Latin Vulgate, in the thirteenth century) is probably to be found partly in the didactic instinct of Stephen Langton, or his possible predecessor, who wished to make the moral effect of the two passages 42 : 24 f. and 43 : 27 f. as pronounced as possible, and partly in the feeling that the word ועתה was the natural beginning of a new section.

The unity of the first part of chapter 42 has been denied by some scholars. Verses 1–4 have been cut from their connection with the following—a singularly blind proceeding. Verse 9 has been declared "the continuation of 41 : 29"; verse 18, the "continuation" of verse 9, and so on; assertions which could be made only with a thorough misunderstanding of the literary character of these "prophecies" and of the literary habits of this writer.

———

The meter of the poem as a whole is 3 | 3 (namely, verses 1–13; 18–25; 43 : 1–7). For the passage 14–17 the 3 | 2 meter is employed.

———

42 : 1. "Behold my Servant." The personification in the verses which follow is not more distinct than in some parts of chapter 41,

but the strain is loftier and the picture more impressive. The poems of the Second Isaiah which we have do not show us the chronological development of his idea of the Servant. Every one of the features which are successively developed—the great conqueror and avenger, the teacher, the suffering redeemer of mankind, the healer of broken hearts and the opener of prison doors —must have been distinctly outlined in his thought before any of these poems were written. He returns to the one or the other according to the mood in which he happens to be writing.

בחירי. Hence "the Elect One" of Luke 9 : 35; 23 : 35, etc., and the name of the Messiah in the Book of Enoch. For this collocation of עבדי and בחירי, *cf.* especially 41 : 8, 9; 43 : 10; 44 : 1, 2; in each of which passages the Servant and Elect One is expressly said to be Israel.

רצתה נפשי. Observe the ellipsis, so frequently seen in these poems.

"I have put my spirit upon him." So also in the very closely allied 'Servant' passage 61 : 1, 2.

42 : 2. For ישׂא, Reifmann, Cheyne, and others read ישׂאג. But it is worse than useless to 'emend' in this way. נשׂא for נשׂא קול is a well-known Hebrew idiom. It is found, for example, in Is. 3 : 7, where Cheyne himself translates: "On that day, he shall *cry aloud.*" *Cf.* also Num. 14 : 1; Job 21 : 12; also verse 11 of this same chapter. The Second Isaiah, of all writers, ought to be allowed this ellipsis. The Targ. יכלי should not be cited as evidence. The Aramaic כלא, אכלי, has quite as wide a range of meaning as Heb. קרא, and is used in the Targums to translate all kinds of words which contain the idea of 'crying aloud.' See Is. 22 : 12; Jer. 1 : 15; Mic. 6 : 9; Zeph. 2 : 15; I Kings 9 : 8; Ps. 29 : 3, etc.

The division of the verses is hardly correct. It would have been much better to extend verse 2 through יכבנה and then make only one verse of the remainder, to the end of verse 4.

42 : 3. For פשׂתה *cf.* 43 : 17, and for כהה 61 : 3. With לאמת a new verse should begin.

42 : 4. The words לא יכהה ולא ירוץ are generally rendered: "He shall not burn low (fail), nor be broken (discouraged)." This is the rendering of the Greek and Syriac versions, and is the one naturally suggested (*to us*, at least) by the use of the similar words in the preceding verse. It is certainly wrong, however. The clause, thus understood, is altogether out of keeping with its surroundings. In this preliminary sketch of the Servant, mighty but magnanimous, there is no place for any allusion to weakness or suffer-

ing on his part. Furthermore, if such an allusion is out of place
here on general grounds, it is much more so in this particular connection. "The bruised reed he will not break, and the dimly
burning wick he will not quench. *He* will not be a *dimly burning
wick*, nor a *broken reed*, until, etc." The effect is most unhappy,
and the force of the passage is sadly weakened. The poet who
wrote these chapters could never have made such a blunder.

It is true that we have here a play on words (after the favorite
manner of this writer), but it is not the one which tradition has
established. On the contrary, the verb כהה in verse 4 has a very
different meaning from the כהה of verse 3; it is the verb found (in
piel) in I Sam. 3 : 13, "to rebuke, chide"; allied with כאה, and
Syriac כאא. It was undoubtedly chosen because of the word-play
(see the many similar examples, Chapter XI). Whether it was
pronounced as *qal* or as *piel* can of course only be conjectured;
judging from the Syriac, the *qal* would be better. The massoretic
pointing is therefore to be retained. As for the word ירוץ, it also
has a meaning somewhat different from that which appears in the
preceding verse. It is the same verb רצץ, with the signification
which it usually has when used *tropically*, viz., "oppress, deal
harshly"; as in 58 : 6; I Sam. 12 : 3 f.; Am. 4 : 1; Deut. 28 : 33. It is
quite possible that the unusual (?) pronunciation ירוץ was chosen
here for the sake of the paronomasia with רצוץ; see, however, ארץ
(same verb) in Ps. 18 : 30, where scholars may well think twice
before emending.

42 : 4. "Till he shall have established judgment in the earth."
It is of course plain that ארץ is here not the land of Palestine, but
the whole inhabited world. See also the note on verse 7, below,
and *cf.* ארץ in 49 : 8.

With this whole verse compare 51 : 4, 5. The Servant is Yahwè's
true representative. With such ideas as the starting-point, the
speedy growth of a belief in a personal "Messiah" was a certainty.

42 : 5. האל יהוה is not "an impossible combination" (Cheyne),
nor even a difficult one. It is not at all likely that the Greek translator read יהוה האל (Duhm). Could any one who is familiar with
the Greek Old Testament expect the translator here to write
ὁ θεὸς κύριος ?

Failure to appreciate the difference between poetry and prose
has made the second and third clauses of the verse seem difficult
to some commentators.

42 : 6. The three imperfects in this verse are all 'consecutive'

imperfects, of course; it is a mistake, however, to change the
pointing of the conjunction to the prose form. This appears to be
a common poetic license.

The verb ואצרך is from נצר, and is to be connected with what
precedes, not with what follows, as the meter shows. The massoretic division of the verse is incorrect; the second 'half' should
begin with ואתנך, as the Greek and Syriac versions divide. *Cf.*
49 : 8, and see the critical note there. This writer uses the verb
יצר (as we should expect, from its use elsewhere) to express the
initial act by which God "brought into being, fashioned," his
people, or "prepared" them, at the very beginning, for himself.
It is thus used again and again in parallelism with ברא. A comparison of the passages 43 : 1, 7; 44 : 2, 24, *cf.* also 45 : 7, 18, etc.,
is sufficient to show how decidedly out of place this verb would
be in the present passage, *after the phrase,* "I took thee by the
hand." Marti argues for יצר by referring to 44 : 21; 49 : 5. But
the former passage proves nothing, and in the latter the word is
used precisely as in 44 : 2.

לברית עם. In the Prophets, ברית is frequently used to mean
not simply "covenant," but distinctly, "covenant *of grace,*" or
even "gracious promise," the idea of a counter-obligation resting
upon Israel being almost lost from sight. It is thus put in parallelism with חסד, 54 : 10; 55 : 3; Deut. 7 : 9, 12; Neh. 1 : 5; *cf.* Jer.
31 : 31 f.; 32 : 40. By the phrase here used, the prophet therefore
means to say, that *in Israel is embodied God's gracious provision
for the nations;* this chosen people is the manifest token, or pledge,
of his purpose for all mankind.

That עם is in the singular number should give no difficulty
to those who are familiar with Hebrew poetry. גוי (for גוים),
49 : 7, is a precisely similar case, and there are many others. *Cf.*
especially Ps. 22 : 7. Notice that this line is a long one, and that
abridged forms would therefore naturally be preferred.

Duhm, in commenting on this phrase, asserts that the parallel
clause in 49 : 8*b* is a gloss "later than the LXX." From what edition of the Greek version is this observation derived?

42 : 7. The way in which this verse is interpreted is a matter
of very considerable importance, especially because of its inseparable parallels, 49 : 9 ff. and 61 : 1 ff. The question is simply this,
whether the prophet is looking here at all mankind, as in verse 4
(משפט בארץ, איים) and as just announced in the last words of
verse 6 (אור גוים), or whether in this picture of rescue and healing
he is thinking of the Jews only. The answer ought not to be in

doubt, for the evidence in favor of the former alternative is overwhelming. In the first place, there is nothing in the wording of
the verse to point to Jews rather than Gentiles, and it is certainly
not difficult to believe that the prophet was large-hearted enough
to wish that the misery of all mankind—and not merely of the
Jews—might be alleviated. In what blessings would God's "rescue" (ישועה) for the Gentiles, which was to "reach to the ends of
the earth" (49 : 6), be likely to consist, if not in the release of captives and the healing of the diseased? More than this, the direct
connection between the emphatic closing words of verse 6, אור
גוים, and the specific blessings described in verse 7 is as obvious
as language can make it. How shall the Servant be "the light of
the nations"? By "opening the blind eyes," and by "bringing
out of dungeons those who sit in darkness"! This is quite conclusive. See also the notes on 49 : 8 f.

Marti, arguing that the subject of the infinitives in verse 7 is
Yahwè, makes this astonishing assertion: "To take Israel as the
subject . . . is grammatically possible, *ergiebt aber einen schlep-
penden Satz.*"

42 : 8. A capital example of a triple line. Verse 9 furnishes
another, equally good.

אני יהוה. How natural it was for the writer to continue in
this way, after verse 7, may be seen by comparing such passages
as 43 : 14, 15; 48 : 15, 16; 51 : 11, 12.

לפסילים. We may be very certain that the tendency to abandon Yahwè for the gods of Babylonia, Syria, Phœnicia, and Egypt
—or at least to put him on an equal footing with them—was wide-
spread at that time.

42 : 9. *Cf.* 41 : 27, and the note there.

42 : 10. This brief lyrical interlude is characteristic. *Cf.* 44 : 23;
45 : 8; 48 : 20 (emended); 49 : 13; 63 : 7.

The emendation of יורדי into ירעם (*cf.* Ps. 96 : 11; 98 : 7; I Chr.
16 : 32), proposed by Lowth, and adopted by Cheyne, Oort, Duhm,
and Marti, seems to me a desirable one. In each of the two following clauses the glad shout is raised (1) by a great division of the
earth and (2) by its inhabitants: "the isles and their peoples, . . .
the wilderness and its cities." We should expect here, "the sea
and all that inhabit it."

Notice that the writer has in mind especially the remote parts
of the earth in this passage. Observe, too, that the exultation is
because of *blessings coming to the whole world* (*cf.* verses 4, 6, 7),
not merely to the Jews.

42:11. יַשְׂאוּ. This word is much better suited to the context than יָשִׂישׂוּ (so emended by Klostermann, Cheyne, and others). The latter word means 'rejoice, be glad'; whereas in this passage a word signifying to 'shout, sing aloud' is to be expected. Our massoretic text meets this requirement perfectly; see on verse 2. If the Greek translator had before him יָשִׂישׂוּ (which is by no means certain), he had an inferior reading. The statement, frequently made, that the Targum supports the emendation, is not true.

42:12. Duhm's tasteless comment on this verse (echoed by Marti) plainly had its origin in the attempt to "restore" stanzas of four lines each. Cheyne (*SBOT.*) simply excises the verse without any remark.

42:13. It is not the intent of this verse to give the ground for the joyful cries of the distant peoples (which was given in verses 1–7); it was rather designed—and very skilfully designed—to effect the transition to the following passage.

42:14. Only a poet of the caliber of this one, and conscious of his mastery, could venture to depict the distress of Yahwè in such terms as these. The change of meter adds not a little to the dramatic effect.

With the first half of the verse (both the wording and the underlying idea) compare especially 57:11; 63:15 f. (emended); 64:11. The two imperfects אַחֲרִישׁ and אֶתְאַפָּק are circumstantial; subordinate to הֶחֱשֵׁיתִי, not co-ordinate with it, as they are generally translated.

42:15. This picture of Yanwè withering mountains and drying up streams is intended to show at once his indignation (see the verse just preceding) and his absolute power. 50:2*b*, 3, which is a very close parallel, should be compared; see the note there. The way in which the poet then passes on, from Yahwè's display of power to his help for the helpless of mankind, is characteristic of his art. Another fine example is 51:9–11, where the smiting of Rahab and the Dragon and the annihilation of the Great Abyss are made to pass over into the preparation of a safe road for the redeemed. Compare also 44:27.

The word אִיִּם, "islands," ought not to be questioned; the poet should be allowed to make his own picture. The pointing לָאִיִּם is a curiosity. Was there an alternative reading (possibly צִיִּים, adj., without the preposition)?

Notice the characteristic repetition of אוֹבִישׁ; the repetition of לֹא יָדְעוּ in the following verse is another example.

42 : 16. It may be that the last clause of the first half-verse is
an example of an extra 3-beat member in a 3 | 2 passage, but it
seems to me more probable that אני was accidentally omitted before אדריכם.

The way in which Marti and Duhm mutilate verses 16 and 17
is a striking example of the attempt to gain 'strophes of four
lines' at any cost. Observe the solemn fiction of following "the
LXX," and Duhm's grammatical objection (!) to the first words
of verse 17.

42 : 17. The progress of the writer's thought, from verse 16 to
verse 17, has a good parallel in the transition from verses 12–17
to 18 ff. in chapter 40. יבשו is decidedly preferable to ילבשו (Reifmann and others), both in meaning and on metrical grounds.

מסכה should not be changed to the plural. The אתם is not
difficult; cither פסל and מסכה are used here collectively—an easy
supposition, and probably the correct one—or else the writer, in
finishing his sentence, had in mind both nouns, as they are so
frequently used in juxtaposition.

42 : 19. The most powerful verse in the chapter, forming (with
verse 20) an exceedingly effective introduction to the passage
which follows. It contains two strongly contrasted ideas: *first*,
the splendid opportunities, and the splendid mission, of Israel
(repeated in verse 24*b*); *second*, the blindness and deafness of the
chosen people (repeated in verse 25*b*). See, for other examples of
this same contrast, especially 48 : 1–11 and 65 : 1 ff.

The whole passage, verses 18–25, is intended by the poet as the
striking counterpart of verses 1–9. To obscure this fact by 'emendations' or excisions is to ruin one of the finest and most thoroughly characteristic passages in the whole book.

In the clause מי עור כמשלם, we must substitute חֵרֵשׁ for עוּר. In
favor of this can be urged: (1) The literary form. The chiasmus
is more effective here than the repetition in the original order. As
the same person is described in all four clauses, it is not necessary
to use both adjectives with the name "Servant." The repetition
of the first clause of the verse at its close, in almost identical form,
may well have been designed by the poet to make the effect more
striking. (2) It is easier to explain our present Hebrew text on
this supposition than on any other. The copyist's eye wandered
to the מי just above. (3) The origin of the present text of the
Greek version is now obvious. The translator wrote: καὶ τίς
τυφλὸς ἀλλ᾽ ἢ οἱ παῖδές μου, καὶ κωφοὶ [ἀλλ᾽ ἢ οἱ ἄγγελοί μου,
οὓς ἀποστέλλω; τίνες κωφοὶ] ἀλλ᾽ ἢ οἱ κυριεύοντες αὐτῶν; κ. τ. ἑ.
The words which I have bracketed were omitted through a very

common scribal error. The omission probably took place in the
Greek text, rather than in the Hebrew from which it was translated.

מֻשְׁלם. It is dangerous to attempt to emend this word, strong
as the temptation is. The Greek conjectured מָשַׁל, but this is not
a conjecture that deserves serious attention. What is obviously
required is some title or descriptive epithet of Israel the Servant,
parallel to עבד ,מלאך ,בחיר ,משיח (45:1), איש עצה (46:11), אהב
(41:8), etc. The form מְשֻׁלָם (*pual* participle) looks original; it is
not such as a scribe or interpreter would be likely to devise. And
with the meaning "the perfected one"—decidedly the most natural translation, in view of common Semitic (including Hebrew)
usage*—it is excellently suited to this passage. We are not familiar with this as an epithet of Israel, it is true; but if we possessed more of the writings of the Second Isaiah—to say nothing
of the other writers of his time—we should very likely find that
it was not unfamiliar to his contemporaries. *Cf.* the (also unusual)
names יְשֻׁרוּן, 44:2, and יְשִׁפִיל, 52:13. It is hardly to be doubted
that one and the same writer—namely, our poet—coined these
three names. See the chapter on the "Literary Features."

42:20. רָאִית. Why prefer the second person singular here? It
is unlikely in itself, and by no means required by the context. It
is indeed attested *as a variant reading* by the consonant text. The
Massorites are right in pointing רָאוֹת; this not only improves decidedly the symmetry of the verse, and its stately swing, but also
gives a smoother connection with the preceding. Read ישמר (instead of emending ישמע, as must otherwise be done); the second
person was brought into this first clause by the false reading ראית.
The Greek trans. renders freely.

This use of the infinitive absolute followed by the imperfect
tense is very effective. *Cf.* the parallel passage 48:6 (see note
there), where the course of the prophet's thought is the same,
and the expression of it hardly less vigorous.

42:21. A difficult verse, because so much seems to be condensed in a few words (though such condensation is met frequently
in these poems), and because of the omission of any direct mention of the chosen people—see the next following words. The

* Note especially in Syriac the use of this participle (*pael* passive) to mean
"perfect." So also in Palestinian Syriac: "If thou wouldest be *perfect* (מְשַׁלַם),"
Matt. 19:21; "That they may be perfected (מְשַׁלְפִין)," John 17:23. In Hebrew, *cf.* Job 8:6.

general course of the prophet's thought is easy to see. "Thou
art a blind servant, Israel! (verses 18 f.). Thou hast seen wonderful things, but without observing (verse 20). The beginning and
the sum of these 'wonderful things' was this, that Yahwè saw fit
to glorify himself in a chosen people (verse 21). But (you say)
this 'chosen people' is in sore distress (verse 22). True; but do
you not understand (verse 23)? It is Yahwè himself who has
brought his people into distress, because they sinned against him
and rejected his *tōrah* (verses 21 and 24). Yahwè himself gave
them this severe lesson (verse 25a); yet they somehow fail to
understand and take it to heart (verse 25b)."

By the *tōrah* תורה (the text is certainly right) is meant, of course,
the "law" which is spoken of in verse 4, above, and in 51:4,
namely, *the true religion;* the principles underlying Yahwè's régime of righteousness (the משפט of verse 4); the "instruction"
which was to be "the light of the nations" (51:4). Of the Hebrew
Pentateuch, or any part of it, the poet can hardly have thought
here; though he doubtless knew it in nearly or quite the form in
which we now have it, and looked upon it as having divine
authority.

42:22. We should probably read בְּחוּרִים, and הֻפַּח (*hophal*), as
the context favors a verb in the passive. (Or should we suppose
that the infinitive absolute was used here also?)

The "captivity" is primarily *the Dispersion; cf.* especially
43:5, 6. If the prophet had ever heard of a 'Babylonian captivity,' he at all events gives no sign of the fact in any place. For
him, the exiles are in all the corners of the earth. Camel-trains
are to bring them from Arabia, and the ships of Tarshish from the
isles of the sea. The "captivity" means for him not only the wide
scattering of the Jews through the earth, and their political inferiority; it includes everything that holds them back from their
promised place at the head of a righteous and happy world. This
is also the usage in the later Hebrew writers generally. It is the
prophet's passionate feeling of the contrast between the promise
and the present reality that drives him to the strong exaggeration
of this verse.

There is the usual ellipsis of the preposition ל with משסה.

42:23-25. A passage of splendid power, drawing the moral
lesson from the contrast just painted, and preparing the way for
the concluding paragraph, 43:1-7.

42:23. Compare 48:6, 14; 50:10.

וישמע. The pointing וְיַשְׁמִיעַ is decidedly preferable to that of our M. T. *Cf.* 41:23, 26; 44:8; 45:21, etc. So the Targ., correctly, ויסבר. This writer, with his mastery of style, would not have thus employed three verbs of 'hearing' in the verse, ending with the weakest of the three.

42:24. The form מְשׁוֹסֶה, participle *poel* (Ges.-Kautzsch, 75, *z*), is correct. The massoretic text gives us the choice of alternative readings, as so often. There is nothing to justify the supposition that any part of this verse is a later addition. On the contrary, it is indispensable to the context. So far as rhythm and language are concerned, moreover, it is of one piece with its surroundings. The first half-verse should of course end with לבוזזים, as rhythm and sense require (so also Duhm, Cheyne). The first person plural חטאנו is a mere scribal blunder for חָטָאוּ. This is evident not only from the context but also from the rhythm. LXX, ἥμαρτοσαν.

The relative pronoun זו also in 43:21. Compare the extensive use of זי as relative pronoun in old Aramaic inscriptions, from the eighth century B. C. onward, and all the way from the Euphrates down into Arabia.

Of the construction of שמע with the preposition ב in this verse Duhm says that it "verrät geringes Sprachgefühl." This scathing criticism touches not only our poet, however, but also the Semitic race in general, for the construction is one which is well known and approved in all parts of the Semitic world. It is not only frequently used, with just this shade of meaning, by the Hebrew writers, including the best prose narrators (in the phrase שמע בקול יהוה, etc.), but is also quite classical in Arabic and Syriac. One would really like to hear what the prophet would have said in reply to this stricture of Professor Duhm.

42:25. The return to the third person singular (עליו) is both natural and effective, in view of 24*a*.

Read חֲמַת instead of חמה, with all the old versions.

ועזוז מלחמה can hardly be right. "Battle" is not what the parallelism would lead us to expect. Judging from other passages, moreover (*e. g.*, 51:19), *war* played a very small part in the woes which this poet had in mind. The following clauses are much more forcible when referred directly to the wrath of Yahwè, without any intervening allusion to "war." The following verb, להט, suggests (so also does the parallelism) that some word meaning "fire" or "flame" had preceded, and it is hardly a mere coincidence that the last four letters of מלחמה are almost the exact graphic equivalent of להבה, "flame"; *cf.* also 43:2. It is best to adopt Kloster-

mann's very ingenious emendation, and read וְעָזוּזוֹ כַּלֶּהָבָה. See
also Cheyne's note on the passage, in the *SBOT*. With the wording of the whole verse, *cf*. 66 : 15.

43 : 1. וְעַתָּה. *Cf*. 44 : 1, and see the introduction to this poem.

"I have called thee by thy name." Compare especially 45 : 3, 4,
and 49 : 1. The addition of the suffix to the verb (קְרָאתִיךָ), advocated by Klostermann, Budde, and others, does not by any means
improve the verse. The rhythm is better as it stands, and there
is no possibility of any misunderstanding. The same phrase, used
in the same way, occurs in 45 : 3. See also 44 : 5, and the note
there.

43 : 2. The form בְּמוֹ for בְּ simply for the sake of the meter.
So also in 44 : 16.

It is probably best to read וּנְהָרוֹת (without בְּ), with all the old
versions, supported by the seemingly parallel structure of the
second half-verse. Even then it seems probable that the preposition represents the correct interpretation, so that we should understand בְּ both with נְהָרוֹת and with לֶהָבָה. The ellipsis is a characteristic one.

43 : 3. The verse should end with מוֹשִׁיעֶךָ. A new subject is
introduced with the word נָתַתִּי.

"I give Egypt as thy ransom, . . . nations in thy stead." The
well-known figure of speech, meaning simply, "Ye are dearer to
me than the other peoples." This is a very common metaphor in
Arabic poetry: "I and my father's house are thy ransom"; "The
whole tribe is payment for thee," and so on. The way in which
the most recent exegesis has turned this into prose, and into an
utterance of the most narrow-minded and feeble-witted type, is
eminently characteristic. Cheyne comments (*SBOT*., *Eng. Trans.*,
p. 178): "Again one must lament the inconsistencies of the Second
Isaiah. The richest lands in the world he would see given up to
pillage as a ransom for Israel." And Duhm: "Cyrus wird Israel
freigeben und dafür mit der Eroberung Afrikas entschädigt werden. . . . In der Ueberlassung Afrikas an Cyrus zeigt sich eine
Gleichgültigkeit gegen den Wert der einzelnen Nationen," etc.
And this is "the great Prophet of the Exile"!

43 : 4. The massoretic punctuation wrongly connects בְּעֵינַי
with נִכְבַּדְתָּ.

אֲנִי אֲהַבְתִּיךָ. This great fact, the love of God for his people, held
the foremost place in the prophet's theology. On this, and on the
like certainty that God would carry out his eternal purpose, he
based all his hope.

Read אִיִּים in place of אָדָם. The word is used in parallelism with לְאֻמִּים, also in 41 : 1; 49 : 1.

"I give nations for thy life." In 53 we have the reverse side of this, and Israel is given for the life of the nations.

43 : 5 f. The return of the Dispersion. In the similar passage, 49 : 9–13, the Gentiles are included; see the notes there, and also the introduction to chapter 35. The idea of the home-gathering of the Jews in particular, which appears again and again in the sequel, is here introduced for the first time. As the poet had just spoken of Israel as the spoil and prey of all the nations, so now he promises that the corners of the earth shall be made to give up their booty.

43 : 7. Cheyne (following Duhm) omits בְּרָאתִיו, on the ground that "Second Isaiah does not link more than two verbs in the same hemistich." This criticism is the result of misunderstanding the division of the stanza, which consists of three lines, as so often at the end of a poem or of a chief section.

CHAPTERS 43 : 8–44 : 5

On the limits of this poem, see the introduction to the preceding. In both structure and subject-matter it closely resembles its predecessor, though approaching its theme from a different side, and generally treating it in an altogether different manner.

In the opening paragraph, verses 8–13, the poet returns to the themes of chapter 41 and the "great argument" addressed both to Israel and to the nations of the earth (see the introduction to chapter 41).

In verses 14–21 the promise of the home-gathering of Israel (43 : 5 ff.) is again introduced, in more elaborate form. The "exiles" are to be brought from the isles and far countries in ships (so 60 : 9; 66 : 19 f.), they are to be led in safety through the waterless desert (so 49 : 10), by Him whose power is supreme over both sea and land.

The following paragraph, verses 22–28, is the counterpart of 42 : 18–25; 48 : 8–11; compare also chapter 59. Israel has done nothing by reason of which it can claim Yahwè's favor; it has deserved nothing but punishment at his hands. But 'for his own sake' (verse 25; see the introduction to chapter 42, and *cf.* 48 : 11) he must and will blot out the sins of his own people. Similarly, in the opening paragraph of the poem, the poet had asserted the need of Yahwè for his people. They are his "witnesses," he could not cast them off. So also in 43 : 4, the ultimate ground of this necessity had been declared to be the divine love.

The poem closes in the same way as its predecessor, light succeeding shadow; the rebuke, which had constituted the most striking part of the poem, being followed by a promise of the spiritual restoration of Israel (44 : 1–5).

In the vigorous passage just referred to (43 : 22 ff.) the prophet touches a very interesting subject, and one on which we are especially glad to hear him express himself; namely, the efficacy and relative importance of the Hebrew ritual. Had not the Jews developed elaborate forms of worship, and been persistent in following them? Were they not spending large sums of money on the daily services and the solemn festivals? Whole burnt-offerings, sacrifices from the herd, incense, sweet cane—did not these give them a claim upon Yahwè? The prophet's reply is worthy of him, and worthy to be put beside the best of the similar utterances of his fellow teachers. Just as in chapter 58 he declares that fasting is in itself worthless, and that God has no pleasure in the outward observance, but rather in a pure heart and helpful hands, so here he insists with all emphasis that the sacrifices and offerings are of no consequence in themselves. "Ye did not choose me," he represents Yahwè as saying; "I chose you" (οὐχ ὑμεῖς με ἐξελέξασθε, ἀλλ' ἐγὼ ἐξελεξάμην ὑμᾶς, John 15 : 16). "Why should ye think that I am to be retained by such 'inducements'? I called you, in order to satisfy my own love, and to fulfil my own purpose. I burdened you with no ritual—that was your own invention—I only required righteousness of you; but ye have burdened me with your sins!"

This poem contains the first of the passages (43 : 14) in which the "Babylon . . . Chaldea" interpolation has been made; see the Chapter dealing with this subject. It has also suffered in an unusual degree from a false division into verses and paragraphs.

———

The meter is 3 | 3 throughout.

———

43 : 8. Read, of course, הוֹצֵא, imperative, with the Latin and (probably) Syriac versions (how can any one who appreciates the difference between poetry and prose find this imperative difficult?). The resemblance of the passage to 41 : 1 ff., 21 ff., is very close. This dramatic introduction of the discourse is eminently charac-

teristic of the writer's imagination, and also of his literary art.
"All the nations" and the "peoples" are summoned to assemble
and listen, and give answer if they can. They are not directly addressed, however; indeed, after verse 9 they are not again mentioned at all; from this time on Yahwè speaks only to his chosen
people. Whether the Gentile nations are to be thought of as listening to the whole discourse (which does indeed concern them
vitally; see chapter 49, for example), or whether they are summarily dismissed after their failure to respond to the challenge in
verse 9, it is perhaps useless to conjecture. Certain it is that the
poet has only momentary need of them, except for the fact that
their presence at the start gives his whole argument an impetus
which it otherwise would not have had. By "the blind, though
having eyes, the deaf, though having ears," the prophet means
his own people; *cf.* 42 : 18-20. They witness the discomfiture of
the heathen gods, and then receive their own admonition.

The massoretic tradition understood verse 8 in this way, but
made no stop after verse 7, interpreting what follows as immediately connected with the preceding and therefore pointing הוֹצֵא,
"*he brought forth*" (*i. e.*, Israel out of the land of Egypt); see the
Targum. The Greek translator read הוֹצֵא, but also connected it
with the preceding and took it as infinitive absolute.

43 : 9. The form נִקְבְּצוּ might possibly be regarded as an unusual *imperative nif'al* (*cf.* Joel 4 : 11), but the jussive probably
was written by the prophet himself. *Cf.* the sequence in 41 : 1.
The Massorites certainly preferred the ordinary understanding as
perfect tense; see the preceding note. Similarly, וְיֵאָסְפוּ might be
either jussive or consecutive imperfect. These two verbs may thus
be regarded as containing the characteristic *alternative* readings.

מִי בָהֶם, *i. e.*, what one of their gods? *Cf.* 41 : 22 f., 26, which is
very closely parallel to this passage. So also 48 : 14. By the "beginnings," רִאשֹׁנוֹת, exactly the same thing is meant here as in
41 : 22, 27; see the notes there, and *cf.* 48 : 3. Who, besides Yahwè,
can show that he has formed, and is executing, an eternal purpose?
Let them show their "first steps"—such as the calling of Abraham
and Jacob; or the purposed "end"—such as the triumph of Israel
and the true religion, which is just now coming to pass, and in
which the demonstration of Yahwè's plan is made complete. It
is to this demonstration in general, which was given in chapter 41,
and is now repeated here in verses 11-21, that the pronoun זֹאת
refers. The same words (after a slight emendation of the text) are
used in an exactly similar context in 48 : 14, where their meaning

is explained in the sentences which immediately follow. See the critical note.

With the latter half of the verse *cf.* 41 : 22 f., 26*a*. The subject of יתנו and יצדקו are the false gods; of the two following verbs their "witnesses," the heathen nations. The text needs no emendation; the pause between the hemistichs is sufficient preparation for the change of subject. See the very similar case in 44 : 9.

43 : 10. The reason why the prophet emphasizes אתם עדי by the addition of נאם יהוה (both here and in verse 12) is obvious to any one who understands his argument. In the words "ye are my witnesses" one of the most important facts in all this prophecy is stated. The Greek addition καὶ ἐγὼ μάρτυς renders וְאֲנִי עֵד, a foolish reading suggested by the similarly placed וְאֲנִי אֵל in verse 12. Some Greek MSS. then repeat in the latter verse the whole phrase καὶ ἐγὼ μάρτυς λέγει Κύριος, from verse 10. A good example of contamination in both directions.

The text-reading, עֲבְדִּי, singular, is far better than the plural. *Cf.* 41 : 8; 44 : 1, 2, etc.

"That ye may know, and believe me; may perceive that I am that One!" This was the end and aim of all the Second Isaiah's teaching. There is hardly a poem in his divan that does not reiterate the sorrowful truth that "Israel doth not know; my people do not understand."

With אני הוא compare 41 : 4, and the parallel passages.

43 : 11. This is the point at which Yahwè's plea begins.

43 : 12. "I proclaimed, and delivered; I declared it." The first verb refers to the announcements made to Abraham and the patriarchs; the second, to the rescue from Egypt (to which the prophet so often refers); the third, to the subsequent proclamations. *Cf.* 45 : 19*a*; 48 : 15, 16*a*.

זָר, "stranger," is for אֵל זָר, "strange god," as in Jer. 2 : 25, 3 : 13; Deut. 32 : 16. *Cf.* also Jer. 5 : 19; Deut. 32 : 12; Mal. 2 : 11; Ps. 44 : 21; 81 : 10.

The Greek has ὠνείδισα for והשמעתי. This does not mean, however, that it rendered another Hebrew verb (שסעתי, according to Duhm); on the contrary, the word is due to a scribal error in the Greek itself, which originally had here a form of the verb ἐνωτίζο-μαι; notice the translation of the same word in the same context in 44 : 8, השמעתיך = ἠνωτίσασθε.

The latter part of the verse is not right as it stands. The clause ואתם ... יהוה is a full three-beat line; the remaining phrase ואני

אל is not only metrically superfluous, but is also an extremely weak pendant to the verse. The Greek translation is untrustworthy, as usual; it furnishes the solution of the difficulty, however, in that it joins these two words *to the following verse* (so also the Hexaplar Syriac). That is, verse 12 must end with יהוה; the first line in verse 13 ran as follows: אני אל גם מיום אני הוא; a verse which is both satisfactory from the metrical point of view, and excellently suited to its context. Probably the conjunction in ואני should be omitted.

43 : 13. A triple line closing the section, as so often elsewhere. מיום, "from this time onward," as in Ezek. 48 : 35. It is the equivalent of מעתה, 48 : 6. יום is for היום, "to-day"; *cf.* the phrase לפני יום "before to-day," in 48 : 7. The Grk. and Lat. versions misunderstand the passage, and render מיום as though it were equivalent to מראש; *cf.* 40 : 21; 41 : 4, 26; 48 : 16.

43 : 14. This verse, in which בבלה and כשדים have been interpolated, has already been discussed; see the Chapter dealing with this subject. כשדים is not "Chaldeans" here, it is to be noted, but "Chaldea," the name of the country; so also in the other places where this interpolation has been made.

בריחים, "fugitives"; compare especially 48 : 20 (ברחו), and see the note there. The word is taken from Ex. 14 : 5. The prophet uses the word "flee" in speaking of the return of the Jewish Dispersion simply in order to carry out his much-used parallel with the deliverance from Egypt; see the verses which immediately follow. That no real flight was thought of is sufficiently evident from 48 : 20; 52 : 12; 60 : 9; 49 : 22; 66 : 20, etc. This is merely a literary touch.

In באניות, the noun is in the construct state; the preposition is the complement of the verb הורדתי (ירד ב') "embark in"); *cf.* Ps. 107 : 23, יורדי הים באניות; the Targum of Is. 23 : 1, נחתו ספיני ימא; etc. With the whole passage compare 60 : 9.

The versions render our massoretic text throughout, except that the Greek had העורתי in place of הורדתי. The reading κλοιοῖς, "pillories," for πλοίοις, in Cod. A, is of course the result of a conjecture—a very ingenious one—due to the following δεθήσονται, which is itself the result of a copyist's blunder. For רנתם the Greek had originally δεηθήσονται, "they shall cry for mercy"; compare Ps. 16 : 1, II Chr. 6 : 19, where רנה is translated by δέησις.

43 : 16. In this verse the writer makes his favorite transition from promise to past history. The God who will make a safe way for his returning people over the great waters is the God who

once made a path for them through the Red Sea. *Cf.* especially
51 : 10 f.

The long parenthesis here (verses 16, 17) is characteristic; *cf.*
49 : 5, 6.

43 : 17. המוציא could be understood literally, "he who brought
out" (from their land), *cf.* Ex. 14 : 4; but the meaning "destroy,
make an end of," suits the context better. *Cf.* the use of the *qal*
in Ezek. 26 : 18, צאתך "thy destruction" (*exitium*); and in Dan.
10 : 20, where יוצא is "finish." Also שיצי in the Targ. Onk. to
Num. 24 : 22.

The massoretic division of this verse is incorrect. The second
line of three beats obviously ends with the word יחדו.

43 : 18. Compare 41 : 27, and the numerous parallels.

43 : 19. The first half of this verse (*cf.* 48 : 6) is very far from
being a mere burst of rhetoric. The prophet is not dealing with
such passing trifles as the campaigns of a king, or changes of the
political horizon; he has before his eyes something immensely more
important, the spiritual awakening and salvation of his people.
In his fervor he sees them already 'turning to Yahwè' (44 : 22)
and receiving the promised blessing.

On the latter half of the verse Marti writes: "Dass hier an eine
wirkliche Bahnbereitung in der Wüste gedacht ist, kann man nicht
zweifeln" (!).

On the "rivers in the desert," see the note on 41 : 17.

43 : 20. Jackals and ostriches are mentioned as the typical inhabitants of the desert (just as in 34 : 13); the one representing the
beasts, and the other the birds. חית השדה "the wild creatures,"
includes both groups. We see here the same warm-hearted lover
of nature who showed his affection for beast and bird in such a
striking manner in 34 : 15 ff.

Duhm's attempt (repeated by Marti) to demonstrate the prophet's ignorance of natural history, or his carelessness, seems to me
to show in fact something quite different; the carelessness is not
on the part of the prophet. But we have no need to appeal to the
zoologist here, or to conjecture whether ostriches would continue
to live in a desert through which brooks flowed, for the words of
the poet have no bearing on such questions. The inhabitants of
the wild "glorify" Yahwè, not because of any benefit which they
themselves receive, but simply as the witnesses, in their desert
home, of the wonderful work which he performs *for his people*.
Their relative fondness for water has nothing whatever to do with
the matter.

Duhm's remarks elsewhere (*Comm.*², p. 81) on the Semites as generally unfriendly toward animals (!) reveal either a surprising lack of acquaintance with the Semitic world or else undue haste in writing this part of the commentary.

Notice how the words נהרות בישימון are repeated from verse 19, in the manner so common in these poems.

That the Massorites have made a false division of the verses here, is at once plain. Verse 20 ends with בישימון; the clause following is worse than useless as an isolated appendix to verse 20, but is sorely needed at the beginning of verse 21, where it restores the parallelism, and fills out the verse to its proper dimensions.

43 : 21. "To give drink to my people." *Cf.* 41 : 17 f.; 49 : 10, etc.

Regarding זו, see the note on 42 : 24.

"They shall set forth my praise." This is the indispensable counterpart of the praise rendered by the beasts of the desert. *Cf.* also 44 : 4, 5, where the same ideas are repeated, at the close of the poem.

43 : 22–24. This most important paragraph is the direct continuation of verse 21: "my chosen people, those whom I fashioned for myself, who shall set forth my praise." But it is a continuation in the form of one of those sharp contrasts in which this writer delights; the ideal is suddenly confronted with the actual. Do the children of Israel, in fact, "glorify" God and "set forth his praise"? On the contrary, the prophet sternly declares here, as on every other occasion, that they are faithless, disobedient, and altogether unworthy.

The general intent of these verses is placed beyond doubt, both by the context in which they stand, and by the spirit and motive of the whole prophecy. The comparison of verse 23*b* with 24*b*, especially, shows that the prophet is giving characteristically forcible expression to the truth, that what God wishes from his people is righteousness, not a ritual. His noble utterance in regard to fasting, 58 : 5–7, is a close and instructive parallel. See also the notes on 66 : 1–3. The Second Isaiah did not look upon the Hebrew ritual as efficacious in itself, nor, on the other hand, had he any objection to it; he merely appreciated it at its true value. What he insists is, that without a heart right in the sight of God it is worse than useless. In saying this, he is simply taking his stand with the most of the great Hebrew teachers; compare especially Amos 5 : 21–24; Hos. 6 : 6; Jer. 7 : 21–23; Mic. 6 : 6–8;

Zech. 7:5–10; Is. 8:10–17; Mal. 3:3–5; Ps. 40:6; 50:8–15; 51:16 f.

It was inevitable that some readers of a later day should misunderstand these verses (notice, for example, the Greek in verse 22). The passage has been totally misunderstood by most modern commentators. Viewed in any light, it would be altogether out of place in an "exilic" composition.

43:22. Yahwè called his people; they did not call him. They therefore had no need to propitiate him, to soothe him with sacrifices, and retain his favor by means of offerings. The decision as to what constituted "service" did not rest with them at all.

Omit the conjunction before לא. It came in by accident from the preceding word, and is out of place here. All the versions omit it.

The suffix in אתי is strongly emphatic. The verb קרא is used here as it is in the multitude of other passages in which Yahwè's calling of Israel is spoken of (קרא almost = בחר).

The following clause, כי יגעת בי, is comprehensible only when the whole passage is understood in the way just indicated.

43:23. The structure of the verse, exactly repeated in the one which follows, and with a play on words in the second half of verse 24 which makes the parallel all the more striking, is especially to be noticed. The first distich is an interrogation (without the interrogative particle, as so often elsewhere; Ges.-Kautzsch, § 150, a), to which the second distich brings an emphatic denial.

זבחיך is an adverbial accusative similar to those observed in 40:31; 41:2; see the notes on those passages. This is not a case of double object of the verb, like those classified in Ges.-Kautzsch, § 117, 5, b. In every one of those cases, the verb could govern either accusative separately as its direct object; not so in the present instance.

"Didst thou not bring . . . honor me?" Yahwè repeats the question which his easy-going people would be sure to ask, but answers it with an unexpected negative. Compare the quiet irony of Socrates, dealing with the same subject, in the latter part of Plato's Euthyphro.

Whether the *hiphil* forms העביד and הוגיע are simple causatives —"made thee *to serve*," "caused thee *to labor*" (from the יגע of verse 22)—or have the same (derived) meanings here which they have in verse 24, is a question which we are able to answer with some confidence, from our knowledge of the habit of this writer. In all probability we have here an example of the favorite device, the repetition of words with altered meaning. In verse 23 the verbs are much more forcible in the purely causative signification; in verse 24, on the contrary, they could not be thus rendered. The case is an interesting one, and the effect of the whole fully justifies the literary device, even to our modern ears.

מנחה and לבונה are intended to cover the whole range of sacrifices and offerings.

43 : 24. In קנית — קנה there is the paronomasia which we meet on every page of Second Isaiah.

The little word אך here carries tremendous emphasis.

העבדתני, "Thou hast burdened me"; with a different signification from that in verse 23, see the note there. הוגעתני, "thou hast wearied me," as in Mal. 2 : 17 (an excellent parallel). The play on the words of verse 23, with slightly altered meaning, is very characteristic.

43 : 25. אנכי הוא; cf. 41 : 4; 43 : 10, 13; 48 : 12, 16; 52 : 6.

למעני, "for my own sake"; strongly emphatic, as it is in 48 : 11. "Thy sins I will remember no more"; cf. 44 : 22, not overlooking the שובה אלי, "return to me!" in the second half-verse. Regarding the strangely blind assertion that this prophet makes little account of the ethical fitness of Israel for the promised restoration, see the fourth Chapter of this volume.

43 : 27. "Thy first father," Abraham or Jacob; "thy representatives," including all of the great figures of Hebrew history, who had been the spokesmen of the nation before God; lawgivers, priests, judges, kings. All, without exception, had sinned grievously. Whether he had also prophets in mind may be doubted, for he never alludes to prophets (see page 70). He would hardly have excepted them, however, convinced as he was that every human being is guilty in the sight of God.

43 : 28. Read ואחלל עָרֵי קָדְשִׁי, "Therefore I gave up my holy cities to be desecrated." The personal suffix (also read by LXX, τὰ ἅγιά μου) is a necessary emendation. That שׂרי is merely an easy blunder for ערי can hardly be doubted in view of 64 : 9. See also 61 : 4; 44 : 26; and cf. 40 : 9; Jer. 9 : 10; 33 : 13; 34 : 22; Zech. 1 : 12, etc.

The vowel-pointing of the conjunction with these two verbs probably means that the Massorites meant to leave open the possibility of reading the verse interrogatively, in the future tense. There is no compulsion of meter here.

גדופים. Cf. 51 : 7 and Zeph. 2 : 8.

344 SECOND ISAIAH

44:1. Regarding the false chapter-division here, see the introduction to 42.

"My Servant," and "whom I have chosen," exactly as in 42:1. "Servant" is the same title of honor here as in the preceding poem. *Cf.* also the phrases in verse 2 with those in 49:5, etc.

Another title of honor is certainly to be found in the name יְשֻׁרוּן; compare מְשֻׁלָּם, 42:19, and see the note there. Whatever its meaning (but it is undoubtedly to be connected with יָשַׁר, "upright") it originated in a play on the word יִשְׂרָאֵל, the form being further determined by the wish to gain the favorite metric foot, a short syllable followed by two long syllables. The only other occurrences of this name are in the poems of Deut. 32 and 33 (32:15; 33:5, 26), poems which remind us of the Second Isaiah in every line, and might well have been written by him.

44:3. Here the poet tells us exactly what he means by his favorite figure of "water in the desert," namely *spiritual blessings* for the chosen people. And his meaning in the use of this figure is always and everywhere the same.

44:4. Read כְּבֵין מַיִם, with the Greek version and many commentators.

44:5. Those referred to in this verse are (as the context shows) the children of Israel, not proselytes. *Cf.* especially 48:1, 2, where the prophet begins his invective against the faithless sons of Jacob by saying that they have no right to the names of Yahwè and Zion. Fundamental to the whole prophecy of Second Isaiah is the charge against Israel that it has cut loose from its past history and from its God.

יִקְרָא and יְכַנֶּה are correct as they stand. The omission of the object (for metrical reasons?) is altogether characteristic. See the note on 43:1, and *cf.* also 45:3. The verb כִּנָּה means simply "to name"; the signification "einen Ehrennamen geben" (Ges.-Buhl) does not necessarily belong to it.

CHAPTER 44:6–23

This poem is simply an elaborate development of the theme in 40:19 f. and 41:7; namely, the folly of idol-worship. That the prophet's rebuke was directed against his own countrymen, and was sorely needed, has already been remarked.

Yahwè is the speaker throughout. In the brief introduction, verses 6–8, he asserts his absolute supremacy, and gives the ground

of his claim to be the one and only God, employing phrases which
are already familiar from their use in chapters 41 and 43. Verses
9–20 constitute the main body of the poem. The kernel of this is
the ironical description of the manufacture of a god (verses 12–17),
one of the most characteristic bits of grim humor in all Second
Isaiah. The conclusion, verses 21–23, draws the lesson for Israel,
in a few vigorous words, and ends with a sudden burst of joy, in
which the prophet transfers himself to the future, as usual: Israel
has repented, Yahwè has therefore wrought his deliverance, and
the Messianic time has begun.

Judged from the literary point of view, this poem is fully up to
the standard of those which surround it. The description of the
making of the idol, in particular, is very spirited and picturesque.
If it were to be turned into prose (!), and interpreted without the
least appreciation of the writer's sense of humor, it would indeed
be a tiresome composition and worthy of the scorn which has been
dealt out to it in some of the most recent commentaries. Why
these same commentators should pronounce the section "less
rhythmical" than the surrounding passages is a question for the
psychologist. The metrical qualities are in fact precisely the same
here, in every respect, as they are in chapters 40–43 and 45 f.
The style and diction of the passage are those of the Second
Isaiah throughout. The assertion that verses 9–20 "break the
connection" (!) between 8 and 21 (Duhm, Cheyne, Marti) is
based on a misunderstanding of the character and structure of
these poems.

It is obvious that the poem ends with verse 23. With verse 24
a new subject is introduced, and the poet begins to write in quite
another mood.

The meter is 3 | 3 throughout.

44 : 6. Omit the first יהוה, which is wanting in the Greek, and
is metrically superfluous. It was very naturally inserted before
the words "king of Israel"; ὁ θεός is similarly inserted in the
Greek (best attested text).

"I am the first and the last"; cf. 41 : 4, and see the note there.

44 : 7. On this challenge, and the significance of the argument
which it introduces, see the notes on 41 : 4, 21–24.

יקרא, "proclaim," exactly as in 41 : 4, but here with the characteristic ellipsis of the direct object. The three verbs here are

good examples of the potential imperfect. The Greek prefixes the word στήτω, one of its customary interpretative additions, derived in this case from verse 11.

The phrase משומי עם עולם is improbable in itself, and out of place here. It is plain that both the words and the verse have been incorrectly divided. Read מַשְׁמִיעַ מֵעוֹלָם אתיות, "announcing from eternity the things to come"; cf. 41 : 4, 26; 48 : 3 ff., etc.

We should probably retain the plural יגידו. For למו we must either read לנו, cf. 41 : 22, or else omit it altogether, with the Syriac. Not only here, but also in 41 : 22, our present Greek text has ἀναγγειλάτωσαν ὑμῖν, though ἡμῖν was probably the original reading in both cases.

44 : 8. תרהו is pretty certainly wrong. There is no known Semitic root (רהה or ירה) which is of any use here. Since Gesenius' Commentary (1821) it has been customary to appeal to the Arabic verb wariha, "vor Furcht gelähmt sein," Ges.-Buhl, s. v. רהה; but in reality the Arabic verb has no such meaning, but rather signifies "to be stupid, foolish, thick-witted," etc. Gesenius apparently derived his prae metu attonitus fuit from Golius' Lexicon; I suspect that the ultimate origin of it was in a misunderstanding of the word warhā' in the oft-quoted verse of El-Find (Hamasa, ed. Freytag, i, 272 top). תִּרְאוּ (Ges.-Buhl, s. v. רהה; Marti) is unlikely. The use of this verb after פחד would be an anticlimax, and the corruption of the text would not be easy of explanation. Lagarde, Cheyne, and others propose תֵּרְהֲבוּ, "be alarmed, dismayed"; probably an Aramaic verb, though the root is also found in Arabic, and apparently in Assyrian (see especially Jensen's note in the Keilinschr. Bibliothek, vi, pp. 398 f.). The Syr. renders here by this very same verb, but it is not at all likely that the translator actually had it before him in the Hebrew. The old Greek version (nearly all MSS., Syr.-Hex., Ethiop.) omitted the word altogether. The μηδὲ πλανᾶσθε of Cod. B is taken from Theodotion's translation.

It seems the most probable conjecture that the original reading was אַל תִּדְּהוּ, hofal of נדח; cf. Is. 13 : 14 (see also the Grk.) and Deut. 13 : 14 (hifil). That is, the rendering might be either "led astray" or (better) "startled, affrighted."

With מאז cf. 48 : 5, and the frequently employed phrases מראש, מיום (see note on 43 : 13), מעתה, etc.

Read השמעתי (without the suffix), and notice that here, again, the direct object is omitted.

"Ye are my witnesses" (cf. 43 : 12); that is, all Israel knew, and
had known from the beginning, what Yahwè had "declared" and
"announced."

Klostermann's emendation, וְאִם for וְאֵין, while not absolutely
necessary, yet seems very desirable. The double question (as in
50 : 2a, for example) is most likely here.

For צוּר, "rock," as a synonym of "god," cf. not only 17 : 10,
etc., but especially Deut. 32 : 31, 37, where the word is applied to
the heathen deities, as here. The Greek translator omits the word
altogether, as he very frequently does when synonyms stand side
by side.

The phrase בל ידעתי is best understood as a relative clause, as I
have rendered it. In the boldness of its irony it is the striking
counterpart of 41 : 23b, and reveals the touch of the same master
hand. The proposal to "emend" it away is most unfortunate. In
all probability, the choice of the phrase was due in part to the
author's fondness for paronomasia.

The riddle offered by the Greek version at this point has not
hitherto been solved, as far as I know. The *textus receptus* (Rom.
ed., Swete) reads: καὶ οὐκ ἤκουσαν τότε, a monstrosity which
sounds truly characteristic of our Greek Isaiah. But ἤκουσαν is
the result of text-corruption (ουκ ησαν, ηκ ουσαν) from ησαν, the
reading which has far better manuscript attestation and was rendered by the Syr.-Hex., Ethiopic, and Armenian versions. Obviously, this was originally ᾔσαν, "they *knew*" (from οἶδα) and the
τότε is a corruption of ποτέ. Compare the variant reading in the
Greek of 41 : 7. The clause was connected by the translator with
verse 9; and the whole read thus: καὶ οὐκ ᾔσάν ποτε οἱ πλάσ-
σοντες, καὶ οἱ γλύφοντες πάντες μάταιοι: "Those who fashion
[idols] have never known [anything]; and those who carve [them]
are all foolish"; corresponding to a Hebrew text | בְּלִי דַעַת יֵצֶר
וּפֶסֶל כֻּלָּם תֹּהוּ. Whether this (very inferior) Hebrew text ever actually existed, or was only conjectured by the Greek translator, is a
question of no importance. We now see the origin of the ποτέ,
namely in the sweeping negation in בְּלִי.

44 : 9. The first half of this verse is a very close parallel to
41 : 24a. תֹּהוּ here is the exact equivalent of מֵאַיִן there, and of
אוֹן וְאֶפֶס in 41 : 29 (emended).

For the Second Isaiah's use of הוֹעִיל cf. vs. 10, 47 : 12, 48 : 17,
57 : 12.

In the Heb. text rendered by the Greek, five words had been

omitted through a common scribal error, the copyist's eye wan-
dering from בל יועלו to בל ידעו.

The word המה, with its marks of cancellation, must of course
be expunged.

The חֲמוּדִים are the idols, and "their witnesses" are their worshippers, as the passage 43 : 8–10 shows conclusively; see the notes
there. There is the same change of subject here as in 43 : 9b; in
חמודיהם the suffix refers to the worshippers, in עדיהם to the gods.

44 : 10. "What man does this?"; the usual rhetorical question, such as we may see on almost every page of this argument,
from chapter 40 to chapter 48; much better suited to the style of
this poetry than the prosaic "whoever does this." Verse 11 is
the conclusion; introduced by הֵן, like 40 : 15, etc. Duhm's proposal (repeated by Marti) to make the apodosis begin with ופסל
turns order into confusion.

44 : 11. The word חבר, "associate," is used exactly like the
Arabic ṣāḥib: "all those who have to do with" the false god.
Here, of course, those who manufacture the idol are especially intended; so the Syr. translates. The Greek has ὅθεν ἐγένοντο (!),
perhaps merely a corruption of οἳ συνεγένοντο [αὐτῷ].*

The text of the following clause is corrupt, as is generally recognized. The Greek and Syriac translators tried to mend matters
by reading חֲרָשִׁים, but this is obviously unsuitable. The source of
the trouble lies in the incorrect division of the words; the original
text must have been וְחָרָשָׁיו מְהֻמָּה מֵאָדָם, "and as for those who
fashion them, confusion is all that they can accomplish." חרשיו
parallel to חבריו; מהומה (a synonym of the writer's favorite תהו)
as in 22 : 5, etc.; מאד, "might," "utmost effort," used exactly as it
is in Deut. 6 : 5, II Kings 23 : 25. It may well be that the passage
in Deut. suggested the ironical use here.

The interpretation of the verse proposed by Duhm, and adopted
by others, taking חבר and חרש as synonyms meaning "incanta-
tion," has no probability. Incantations are quite out of place
here. יבשׁו suggests here only the men who make the idols, and
thus supports the massoretic pointing of the two nouns. So also
do the verbs in the next verse. As for the saying in regard to in-

---

* This would be a most natural translation. We may perhaps compare the
Greek ideas and usage alluded to in Dieterich, *Eine Mithrasliturgie*, 1903,
pp. 93 ff.: "Aller Mysterien Wesen ist es, dass der Myste irgendwie an eine
Gottheit gebunden wird, aller Mysterien Höhepunkt war . . . das συγγε-
νέσθαι τῷ δαιμονίῳ" (from Maximus of Tyre, cited in Diels, *Parmenides*,
1897, p. 17).

cantations that "they are of men," it is merely stupid. It would
be exactly similar to say of prayers that they cannot be efficacious
because "they are of men." Of course they are.

44 : 12 ff. Among the other excellences of this passage, the
highly finished poetic form deserves to be emphasized. Not only
is the rhythm of the separate lines very marked and regular, but
in verses 12 and 13 we have a good example of symmetrically built
stanzas, the labor of the carpenter (verse 13) being set over against
that of the smith (verse 12). In each stanza a double distich describing the work is followed by a single distich in which another
theme is introduced.

44 : 12. The word חרש is a noun, as verse 13 shows. It follows
of necessity that the text of this first clause is corrupt. מעצד, "ax,"
is quite out of the question. What the context demands at this
point is either a verb or a participle. The versions give us no help
at all. The repetition of יחד as a *verb* (ὤξυνεν, *leṭash*), in the Greek
and Syriac, represents merely the attempt (here quite unsuccessful)
to make sense out of nonsense. On the other hand, the proposal
to regard מעצד as *a gloss on* ברזל (!) is easier to make than to
defend. Why should glossators be denied intelligence, and a reasonable motive for their action? By simply reading מְעַצֵּב (*piel*
participle of עצב, used exactly as in Job 10 : 8) every difficulty is
removed. "The worker in iron cuts it out," etc. Verse 12 is
parallel to verse 13, and the progress of the smith's work is the
natural one: first, he fashions "it" roughly; then puts it in the
forge; then hammers it into its final shape. The direct object is
studiously omitted, both here and in the following verse. The fitness of the verb עצב to play a principal part in this detailed description of the making of a "graven image" (עצב) is obvious.

ופעל. This is not used absolutely (Ges.-Buhl), but with sup-
pression of the direct object, which is understood.

בפחם. The Greek does not translate this word. The noun is a
rare one; used by this writer also in 54 : 16.

For במקבות יצרהו the Greek had ἐν τερέτρῳ ἔτρησεν αὐτό,
"bored it with a gimlet," deriving the noun from נקב, "bore,
pierce." The verb was then in a few MSS. corrupted to ἔστησεν.
The massoretic division of the verse is wrong; the *athnachta* should
be under כחו.

The concluding distich is intended to give an idea both of the
eagerness of the workman and of the very considerable labor
which he undertakes. In spite of his "strong arm," he finds himself exhausted more than once before his god is finished.

44 : 13. This verse affords a good illustration of the relative excellence of our massoretic text and of the unreliability of the Greek translation. The Hebrew, with its three strange words, reminds us how little we know of the language of the arts and crafts in old Jerusalem. It does not appear that the text is corrupt; on the contrary, the smoothness of the metre, the perfect correspondence of the verse, in structure, with verse 12 (see the note there), and the fact that no one of the three troublesome words gives any ground for suspicion by its form, create a strong probability that the tradition is accurate. On the other hand, the Greek omits all three of the words (perhaps by accident, see below), only supplying the place of one of them by borrowing from a parallel passage in another chapter—a characteristic proceeding. The Syriac leans on the Greek, with the result described in II Kings 18 : 21.

"The carpenter"; plainly contrasted with the "ironsmith" of verse 12. The Greek inserts ἐκλεξάμενος, "choosing"; not because a verb בחר was made out of [ויע]ף חר[ש] (Duhm, Cheyne, and others),* but simply because of the necessity of supplying something in order to make a sentence. Neither here nor in verse 12 did the translator see that חרש is in the construct state. The phrase ἐκλεξάμενος τέκτων ξύλον was derived from the parallel passage 40 : 20, ξύλον ἐκλέγεται τέκτων. Similarly, the "glue," κόλλη, of this same verse, came from the דבק of the other parallel passage, 41 : 7 (very likely with intentional variation of the translation; observe how Aquila, Symmachus, and Theodotion render there by κόλλη, and the other old versions understood it in the same way).

נטה קו the Greek renders very suitably: "he measured it with the measuring-line," ἔστησεν αὐτὸ ἐν μέτρῳ. Μέτρον for קו, as in II Kings 21 : 13; Lam. 2 : 8; Zech. 1 : 16; Ezek. 47 : 3; and Is. 28 : 17 (Aquila, Theodotion). Whether the twofold vowel-pointing of יתארהו corresponds to any original difference in meaning, we shall probably never know. Certain it is that no writer would be more likely than this one to repeat the verb in slightly different form, or with slightly different meaning, if it could be done.

שרד is completely unknown; Aquila's παραγραφίς is the safest conjecture. The old Greek version seems to have simply omitted†

---

* The word ויעף was of course omitted in the translation because a synonym (καὶ ἀσθενήσει) had just been used. This is very commonly done by this translator.

† Possibly the omission was in its Hebrew original, the eye of a copyist having passed from one יעשהו to the other.

this and the two following nouns, introducing in their place the
דבק ("glue") of 41 : 7.

מקצעות and מחוגה are also otherwise unknown. Judging from
the allied nouns, מקצע "corner" and חוג "circle," they mean
"square" and "compasses," respectively. Here probably used
loosely (as the corresponding words might be used in English, for
example) as the typical instruments for exact measurements and
shapes—with which this whole verse is primarily concerned.

44 : 14. Read יכרת. The perfect כרת is also possible, but the
imperfect is to be preferred for every reason.

The idea which the poet introduces in this verse and carries
through to the end of verse 19 is one which he evidently wished
to make especially prominent. Notice how the same thing is said
three times over, in varied phraseology, in verses 15, 17, and 19.
The progress of the writer's thought is natural, and his expression
of it powerful, throughout the whole passage.

ויאמץ לו is quite unobjectionable. The direct object is omitted,
as usual. The treatment of this verse by some modern scholars
offers a good example of a thoroughly uncritical mode of procedure. A characteristic blunder of the Greek translator is adopted;
תרזה is removed because it occurs nowhere else (!), and because
"ז is a letter which often appears in a corrupt word" (Cheyne);
and so on.

Notice the manner of indicating the variant readings, "cedar"
and "fir."

44 : 15. By a singular misuse of the Greek translation, Klostermann "emends" ויקח to ויקדה. Cheyne and Marti follow him,
apparently without looking at the evidence of the Greek apparatus,
which gives no ground at all for any such alteration. Marti even
writes "nach LXX (!) καύσας." ישיק is not Hebrew, but Aramaic
(סלק). Forms written with ש are found also in Ezek. 39 : 9 and
Ps. 78 : 21.

סגד is another Aramaic word. Also in verses 17, 19, and 46 : 6.

That the suffix in למו is here that of the third person *singular*
admits of no reasonable doubt. The מו (indefinite relative מה) is
added to ל just as it is to כ, and ב, and על, by a usage which has
many Semitic analogies. *Cf.* במו (without suffix) in 43 : 2; 44 : 16;
למו (without suffix) in Job 27 : 14; 29 : 21; and עלמו (with suffix
of third person singular) in Job 20 : 23; 22 : 2; 27 : 23. In the last
case, as in the למו before us, the suffix pronoun is contracted with
the preceding syllable. Analogy, as well as metrical considerations,

may have influenced these forms, which in the Old Testament are used only in poetry. This writer employs לְמוֹ also in 53 : 8 (see the note there).

44 : 16 f. These two verses are the elaboration, in the usual manner, of the picture outlined in verse 15.

The regular structure of verses 15 and 16 should be noticed, especially as it is exactly repeated in verse 19, where the writer returns once more to this picture (from חֶצְיוֹ to the end of the verse). In all three cases we have a triad followed by a couplet.

בְּמוֹ. Also in 43 : 2; see the note on לְמוֹ, verse 15.

עַל חֶצְיוֹ. This is of course *the same* "half" which has just been mentioned; we have merely the usual repetition. "Half" of the wood is burned, serving to warm the man and to cook his food; "the rest" (*i. e.*, the other half) he makes into a god. חֶצְי and שְׁאֵרִית are the two halves, just as חֶצְי and יֶתֶר in verse 19. The old versions (except the Latin) wisely declined to translate the second חֶצְי in verse 16, for the result would certainly have been an absurdity (two halves plus a remainder), inasmuch as the conjunction ו had crept in by mistake before עַל! So the Greek has for [ו]עַל חֶצְיוֹ simply καὶ ἐπ’ αὐτοῦ, while the Syriac avoids all ambiguity by supplying the word "coals" from verse 19. In the best attested Greek text (codd. אAQΓ, and most cursives) the clause καὶ καύσαντες ἔπεψαν ἄρτους ἐπ’ αὐτῶν has been introduced from verse 15. Duhm and Marti change the text to עַל נֶּחָלִין, professing to follow the Greek translation; but codex B is not "the Septuagint."

The verbs יֹאכַל and יִצְלֶה are in their proper order. This is poetry, not prose, and the two clauses were intended to be parallel. The versions point to no other text. The Syriac, for example, could not have translated in any other way, after it had once introduced the "coals" in the preceding clause (see the note above).

Such passages as this closing couplet of the verse are extremely valuable for the light which they throw on the character and the art of this poet. He was a man of genuine humor, which keeps finding its way to the surface, even in unpromising places; and one who took an artist's delight in the details of his picture.

אוּר, "fire," is an unusual word. It is found also in 31 : 9; 47 : 14; 50 : 11; and Ezek. 5 : 2.

44 : 17. Read, of course, לְפֶסֶל וַיִּסְגָּד לוֹ. The emendation would be obvious even without verse 15, and the Greek and Syriac versions.

44 : 18. The form מטח should not be altered. It is grammatically unobjectionable, and is obviously better for the rhythm than מטחו would be. As for the signification of the verb, it is plainly intransitive here, like its Arabic equivalent ṭāḫ (middle i).

We should probably read ומהשכיל, adding the conjunction. All the versions express it, and its presence improves the rhythm.

44 : 19. השיב אל לב (so also 46 : 8, and Deut. 4 : 39; 30 : 1) is plainly more emphatic than שים אל לב.

Omit the word אף before אפיתי, as it is the result of dittography. It is superfluous both to the sense and to the meter, and no one of the versions (excepting the Targum) seems to have read it.

It is a legitimate question whether תועבה here is not a substitute for אלהים (as it is, for example, in II Kings 23 : 13, and other similar passages). Notice that Syr., Lat. (p'thakra, idolum) seem to have read, not תועבה, but some such word as פסל. The preposterous thing ridiculed by the prophet is not that a man should make an *abomination* out of a block of wood, but that he should make a *god* out of it. It is hardly likely that תועבה was already a current synonym for "god" (i. e., idol) in the time of the Second Isaiah.

בול, "product," occurs only here and in Job 40 : 20. The meaning is apparently not "that which a tree produces," but rather "that which is produced (by man's labor) from a tree." Is it not probable, however, that the reading here was originally ליבול? This improves the meter.

44 : 20. The phrase רעה אפר is exclamatory. אפר is either "dust" or "ashes," and the figure is apparently that of flocks pasturing in a grassless barren.

44 : 21. Here the prophet turns directly to his countrymen, just as he does in 40 : 21, 27, in a very similar context. He was arguing with his own people, not with the heathen. The demonstration that Yahwè was the one and only God, and not to be represented by any image or likeness, was as important a part of the one poem as of the other.

The Massorites have wrongly connected עבד with the words which follow it; it should be connected with יצרתיך, as the Greek and Syriac translators saw. With לי אתה compare 43 : 1.

The word תנשני embodies a double reading, in the manner which has so many illustrations in the O. T. One current reading was תנשה, "Israel, thou shalt not be forgotten"; the other, better suited to the present context, was תשני, "Israel, thou mayest not forget me." Compare both זכר אלה, at the beginning of the verse, and שׁוּבה אלי, verse 22. See also the similar passages 42 : 18 ff., 25; 46 : 8; 48 : 4–6, 8, 18.

Here, again, we have the same strong contrast: Who is as blind as the Servant of Yahwè?

44 : 22 f. The perfect tense here, as in the multitude of similar passages in Second Isaiah, represents a triumphant flight of faith rather than an accomplished theological fact. "Turn to me !" is the key-note of a large part of these poems, and the prophet would have been the very last to imagine that the sin of the people could be "wiped away" *until they had repented*. He loves to take his stand in the future, but is again and again called back to the present. Compare 43 : 25 f.

44 : 23. With this characteristic outburst compare especially 45 : 8; 49 : 13.

The word יהוה, near the beginning of this verse, must be omitted. The original text was as follows: רנו שמים כי עשה | הריעו תחתיות ארץ "Sing, ye heavens, for he has wrought [it]; shout, ye depths of the earth !" This is sufficiently explicit; both subject and object of עשה are placed beyond doubt by the context. It is not surprising, however, that the condensed poetical form of expression should have been variously expanded in the versions. The simplest form of the expansion was the addition of יהוה, as in our massoretic text and the Syriac. Another form included the interpretation of עשה; thus the Latin, *quoniam misericordiam fecit Dominus*. The Greek has both, though not reading יהוה; ὅτι ἠλέησεν ὁ θεὸς τὸν Ἰσραήλ.

CHAPTERS 44 : 24–45 : 25

Just as the preceding poem harks back to 40 : 19 f. and 41 : 7, so this one develops, as its characteristic feature, the theme given in 41 : 2 f., 15: The conquering Servant. This forms the subject of the two leading passages, 45 : 1–7 and 13–17, and the poet returns to it for a moment, after his customary manner, in his brief epilogue (verse 24). The Servant, as Israel's representative, will trample on the kings and nations of the earth. Yahwè, who "holds him by the hand," will guide and strengthen him; will break down all the barriers that stand in his way, and lead him to the "hidden treasures" of the glorious age which is now at hand. Israel, and especially Israel's religion, will triumph; all the peoples who now fight against Zion and oppress her will be utterly defeated and forced to submit; the obdurate, the incorrigibly wicked, will be destroyed, but the "residue of the nations" will acknowledge fully and freely that Yahwè is the only God, and will be accepted at last as his worshippers and his children.

This is a program, every feature of which is repeated in nearly or quite the same words in other poems of the collection. References to the principal passages will be given in the notes. The other elements of which the poem is made up are also familiar from their use elsewhere by this writer, especially in chapters 41–43 and 48.

The personification of the Servant is carried to the same degree here as in chapter 49; it has gone so far, in fact, that in both 45 : 4 and 49 : 5 he is no longer identified with the nation Israel, but is clearly distinguished from it. He is Israel's representative; the "Anointed One" (45 : 1) who is to restore the people, build up the holy city, and establish a reign of righteousness in the earth. On this whole subject see the Chapter dealing with the Messiah.

The opening paragraph of the poem, 44 : 24–27, is merely prefatory, preparing the way for the announcement in 45 : 1 ff. Yahwè is all-powerful, over men and over nature, and has long ago made known his good purpose for the chosen people and the holy city. He now announces his definite plan, about to be put into execution, namely *the mission of the Servant.* Compare, for example, 42 : 5–9.

The structure of the whole poem is like that of chapter 49 (see the introduction there); it consists of two parts, each made up of an introduction (44 : 24–27 corresponding to 45 : 9–12), a principal theme (45 : 1–5 corresponding to 13–17), and a conclusion (45 : 6 f. corresponding to 19–25). The momentary outburst of joy in 45 : 8 was designed to mark the close of the first half of the poem, exactly like verse 13 in chapter 49. In the second part, the themes are more fully and vividly set forth, and the conclusion sums up the teaching of the whole poem.

Yahwè is the speaker, and—as in chapter 42—his words are addressed now to Israel (44 : 24; 45 : 10 f.; 14 ff.), now to the Servant (45 : 2–5), and again to the nations (45 : 20–23).

This poem receives added interest from the fact that it contains the two "Cyrus" interpolations (44 : 28 and the word לכורש in 45 : 1), which have worked such far-reaching mischief. Regarding these, see the notes, and especially the general Introduction.

In 44 : 24–45 : 13 the meter is 3 | 3, except in 44 : 25, which consists of two 3 | 2 lines. From 45 : 14 to the end the 3 | 2 meter is employed.

---

44 : 24. It is better to read מי אתי, with the *kethîb* and the versions. A good example of "alternative" readings.

44 : 25.   The Hebrew word בַּד (root בדד) includes two quite separate substantives: (1) the verbal noun of the form *qatl*, meaning
"foolish talk," found in Is. 16 : 6; Jer. 48 : 30; Job 11 : 3; and line
6 of the Eshmunazar inscription;* (2) the adjective of the form
qatil,† meaning "babbler," found in this verse and in Jer. 50 : 36.
From both of these passages it would appear that this term of contempt was a current designation of foreign diviners. Neither the
derivation of the word, nor its form, nor this use of it, gives any
ground for suspecting it. The derivatives of the root בדא, "originate, devise," then "lie," must have been at first quite distinct
from those of בדד.

With יהולל *cf.* Job 12 : 17. The change of meter in this verse
seems to have no especial significance. See the note on the metrical features of chapter 54.

44 : 26.   Read מלאכו (singular), comparing especially 42 : 19.
The Servant of Yahwè is the one referred to, as is also the case in
the similar passage 46 : 11 (אִישׁ עֲצָתִי). *Cf.* 41 : 10; 42 : 6; 48 : 15;
50 : 7–9; 53 : 10–12. His "counsel" is his purpose for Israel and
the world. He is not a mere instrument in the hand of Yahwè,
but has his own program, which he carries out wisely and firmly,
with Yahwè's help. So 42 : 4: "He (the Servant) shall set judgment in the earth," shall establish "his law."

A feature of the Servant's work to which the prophet returns
with delight is the exaltation of Jerusalem and the cities of Judah,
which have fallen far below their former glory. Thus in 49 : 17, 19,
the rebuilding of the "ruins" of Jerusalem is promised; *cf.* verses
6 and 8. And in 61 : 4 (also a passage describing the work of the
Servant) similar phrases again occur: חרבות . . . יקוממו and עָרֵי
חרב; *cf.* also לחקים להקים in 49 : 8. With עָרֵי יהודה *cf.* 40 : 9; 43 : 28
(emended); 61 : 4; etc. Duhm adopts the reading 'Ιδουμαίας in
this verse, and thereupon alters the Hebrew text. But codex B
is not "the Septuagint," and the confusion of 'Ιδουμαία with
'Ιουδαία is a blunder that occurs on page after page of the Greek
O. T.

44 : 27.   צולה is the same as תהום רבה in 51 : 10, a verse which

* The word ברנם is not a mistake for ברברנם, as some have regarded it, for
it is written the same way in *both* copies of the inscription (a fact generally
overlooked). The original of this inscription would certainly have been looked
over very carefully before it was given to the stone-cutters; and there is no
other case in which the two copies make the same mistake. The signification
"prating" suits the context perfectly.

† Contracted in the usual manner; see Stade, *Lehrbuch der Hebr. Gramm.*,
202*a*, 193*a*; Barth, *Nominalbildung*, 10*a*, etc.

is the exact parallel of this one. *Cf.* also 42 : 15; 43 : 16 f.; 50 : 2, and see the notes on these verses. This is the proper conclusion of the introductory passage describing the power of Yahwè; we now expect the כה אמר יהוה (45 : 1).

44 : 28. This verse, as has already been shown (see Chapter III), is a later addition.

45 : 1. "Thus saith Yahwè"; the beginning of the promise for which the preceding verses have been the preparation.

"To his Anointed." The Second Isaiah seems to have been the first to use the term "Messiah" (משיח) as a designation of the ideal leader of Israel and vicegerent of God (*cf.* Ps. 2 : 2). Fortunately, we know from another passage whom the poet intended by the title, for in 61 : 1 the Servant introduces himself with the words, "the Lord hath *anointed* me." The grand picture of the Messiah which we see in the Psalms of Solomon 17 : 23–18 : 10 had been painted in all its details more than three centuries earlier, in the poems of Second Isaiah. But for the unfortunate Cyrus-glosses its effect would have been much greater.

לכורש. There is no more palpable gloss than this in all the Old Testament. Context, meter, and historical fact all exclude it. See, further, the introduction, Chapter III. For similar interpretative glosses in Isaiah, see 7 : 17, 20; 8 : 6 f.; also 29 : 10, where "the prophets" and "the seers" are plainly explanatory additions. Observe also how a similar addition (βασιλέα) has been made in the Greek in verse 13 of this same chapter.

"Whose right hand I hold"; *cf.* 41 : 13; 42 : 6.

There is no adequate reason for rejecting the massoretic pointing of the word לְרַד. For (1) the participle רודד occurs with exactly this meaning ("bring into subjection") in Ps. 144 : 2. (2) The *qal* infinitive of verbs of this class, both transitive and intransitive, occasionally exhibits the vowel *a*. Examples of transitive verbs are: בַּר, Eccles. 3 : 18; חֲנָן, Is. 30 : 18; גַּל (imperative), Ps. 119 : 22. (3) We have no other example of the *qal* infinitive or imperfect or imperative of this verb, with the exception of the ambiguous ירד in 41 : 2 (see the note there); nor have we any other means of criticising this form. Therefore, as the massoretic tradition is opposed neither by analogy nor by any direct evidence, the form in our text is to be retained. We should have expected לְרַד, to be sure.

The Greek ἐπακοῦσαι may originally have been ὑπακοῦσαι (Schleusner). But the translator perhaps wrote ἐμπατῆσαι.

Duhm, followed by Marti, inserts האל after יהוה, at the beginning of this verse, "on the authority of the Greek." But if Duhm
had read the Greek version of this part of Isaiah carefully, he
would have seen that Κύριος ὁ θεός is merely a habitual embellishment of the translator. See, for example, 41 : 17, 21; 42 : 6, 8, 13,
21; 43 : 1, 3, 10, 12, 14, 15; 44 : 2; 45 : 1, 3, 5, 6, 7, 11! In no one
of these cases is there the smallest likelihood that ὁ θεός is the
translation of a Hebrew word.

45 : 2. For והדורים we should probably read והדרכים; comparing especially verse 13, where this phrase is repeated. אושר is a
double reading, *pi'el* and *hif'il*.

The time-honored attempt to find some real "bronze doors"
which Cyrus broke through is the legitimate offspring of the prosaic exegesis which led to the interpolation in verse 1. Ps. 107 : 16
has the true interpretation.

45 : 3. The second half of this verse is metrically troublesome,
and all the versions seem to have had precisely our massoretic text
before them. It is probable that the source of the trouble is the
superfluous phrase למען תדע (so also Duhm). The force of the
passage is increased by its omission, and it is easy to see how it
might have been accidentally inserted.

The "hidden treasures," which the Servant and his people are
to possess, are of course the coming blessings—the blessings of the
Messianic age—which are now for the first time to be plainly announced. Compare especially 48 : 6; Deut. 32 : 34; Jer. 33 : 3 (reading נצרות); also Deut. 33 : 19.

"He who calls thee by thy name"; *cf.* 43 : 1 and 49 : 1.

45 : 4. *Cf.* 49 : 5, 6, where the Servant is distinguished from
Israel in precisely the same way as here. These passages are especially valuable as showing how far the writer sometimes carried
this personification, in his own thought; and also, how easily he
passes from one conception of the "servant of Yahwè" to another.
See Chapter VIII.

Omit the conjunction in ואקרא. Both of these verbs, like the
one in the next verse, are in the present tense. There is no essential difference in meaning between קרא and כנה, though the latter
strictly has the meaning '*designate*,' as in Phœnician (Lidzbarski,
Handbuch, 425, 4, line 5); *cf.* 44 : 5. Here, indeed, the כנוי is a
name of honor; the future leader of Israel receives the title "Anointed One."

It is not likely that the words "thou knowest me not" (also in verse 5) are intended to convey any reproach—the reproach, namely, of 42:19, etc. On the contrary, the prophet is speaking of the Servant's call to his new task. Yahwè chose him while he was still ignorant; he had everything to learn (50:4b, 5).

45:5. The way in which verses 4–6 are bound together by the two repeated phrases is characteristic. Observe the succession of 3 | 3 | 3 stanzas.

45:6. An important verse. The triumph of Israel's Messiah was not merely intended for the benefit of the chosen people, but also for the whole world. Compare verses 14 and 22 f.

45:8. The end of the first half of the poem; cf. 49:13.

With the wording of the first couplet compare Deut. 32:2. Instead of ויפרו we must read וְיִפְרַח, the verb used in 35:1, 2; 66:14. We must also point the following verb as qal, תִּצְמַח; cf. 42:9; 43:19. M. T. combines with this another reading containing וְיִפְרוּ and יַצְמִיחוּ, the subject being the clouds.

The blessings designated by the words צדק and ישע, here as everywhere else in Second Isaiah, are primarily spiritual blessings, which the following verses show to be intended also for the Gentiles.

45:9. Instead of חָרְשֵׁי read חָרַשׁ (construct of חָרָשׁ, "maker, fashioner"). The text as it stands cannot be right; את in the second line must have the same meaning as the את just preceding, and רב must be construed with it. That is, the יֹצֵר (Yahwè) is seemingly put in parallelism with "potsherds of the earth" (whatever that curious phrase may be supposed to mean). It is no wonder that the Greek makes such terrible work of this verse—and even returns to it in verse 10. The fact is, we have here one of those word-plays in which this author so delights, and which have so often perplexed his translators. חָרָשׁ is used here in the tropical sense; for an example of a still wider use, see Ezek. 21:36. It would be possible to point חֹרֵשׁ, participle; but the natural way of translating would then be, "[with] him who plows the ground" (cf. the Greek!), which would be decidedly inferior to the other reading.

In the last clause of the verse we must either suppose the use of an idiom, "it has no hands," meaning "it is useless"; or else transpose the two suffixes. I have preferred the former alternative.

45:11. It is obvious that the words האתיות תשאלוני are wrongly divided. As the context shows, the original must have been either הַאַתֶּם תשאלוני, "will ye [my own handiwork] question me?" or else הַאֹתִי תְשַׁאֲלוּן, "will ye question *me* [your maker]?" The latter seems more probable. The words עַל בָּנַי of course belong to this clause. *These "children" are the Gentiles;* see Chapter IV, § 3.

45:13. The transition from verse 12 may seem a little abrupt, but it is in fact a very characteristic one. The progress of the writer's thought is precisely the same in 42:5 f.; 48:13 f.; 51:15 f.; *cf.* also 50:3 f.

This verse may well have been largely, if not chiefly, responsible for the Cyrus interpolations in this poem. Failing to understand the prophet's picture of the Servant of Yahwè, conquering, delivering, building up the waste places, and restoring Israel and the Gentile world, the interpreter would inevitably think of the first chapter of Ezra.

With the first clause of the verse compare 41:2, 25; 48:15; with the "building of Jerusalem" *cf.* 49:8, 17, 19; 61:4; with the "freeing of captives" *cf.* 49:9; 61:1, etc.; and with the phrase "not for price nor for hire" *cf.* 52:3, which says (and means) exactly the same thing. The "free" grace of Yahwè is promised in this figure of speech. *Cf.* also 55:1 (end).

45:14. After the Servant has conquered the world for Yahwè, the chosen people will take its promised place at the head of the nations, and receive their admiring homage. Wealth and honor, instead of poverty and disgrace, will come to Jerusalem, the holy city. It is the very same picture which is given in 49:22 f.; 60:9, 11, 14; and 66:20, 23. See the note on 49:23 and the introduction to chapter 60. The incorrigibly wicked, the arch-enemies of Yahwè and Israel (those who are called "Edom" in 34:5 and 63:1), have now been swept from the earth; the remaining multitudes, from all parts of the world, will acknowledge the One God and worship him sincerely and acceptably (verse 23; 59:19; 66:18, 23, etc.). They do not become Jews, but acknowledge the Jews as their leaders and benefactors. Similar pictures, hardly less distinctly poetical and thoroughly Oriental, are familiar in the New Testament.

The word בַּזִּקִּים, "in fetters," I believe to be a later addition. It is out of keeping with the scene which the poet evidently intends to depict in this verse; this is not the triumphal procession on the return of the victorious Servant from the conquest, it is the voluntary thronging of the Gentiles to Jerusalem, as the parallel passages 49:22 f.; 60:9, 11; 66:20 prove conclusively. The word בַּזִּקִּים, moreover, is metrically superfluous; there does not seem to be any satisfactory way of dividing the verse while it remains in the text. As a later addition, it has its striking parallel in 60 : 12.

The *athnachta* should be under the word ילכו.

45 : 15. It is probable that these words (verses 15–17) are spoken by the Gentiles, rather than by the prophet.

The word מושיע, which is metrically superfluous, probably originated either in dittography of the following word, or else in the נושע (also following ישראל) just below.

45 : 16. The use of צירים, "pangs," in place of צורות, "images," is a characteristic bit of massoretic humor. A substitution of the same kind has been made in 48 : 5; see also the note on 41 : 21.

The massoretic division of the verse is incorrect; the *athnachta* should be under the word יחדו, as in the Syriac and (with a different reading, see below) the Greek. The colon הלכו בכלמה (three beats) is not unusually short. The Greek reading, πάντες οἱ ἀντικείμενοι αὐτῷ, has been strangely misused by some recent commentators. Duhm remarks, "Die LXX hat für כלם etwa כל קמיו gelesen," and 'emends' accordingly. Cheyne improves this to כל מתקוממו, which he prints in his Hebrew text. Marti, following as usual, without question, says that either Duhm or Cheyne must have the correct form. Kittel, in his *Biblia Hebraica*, proposes to read "with the Greek" כל מתקוממין. But surely not all will be able to follow this reasoning. Just why should a form of the verb קום be the thing to insert at this point; and what is the evidence that the text rendered by the Greek contained a word more than our massoretic text? In the first place, no part or derivative of the verb קום is ever rendered by ἀντίκειμαι in the O. T. Again, neither Duhm, nor Cheyne, nor Marti remarks that יחדו is not translated by the LXX, either at the end of this colon or at the beginning of the next. Moreover, the comparison of 41 : 11 gives at once the explanation of the Greek rendering. The latter passage reads, הן יבושו ויכלמו כל הנחרים בך; which the Greek renders, ἰδοὺ αἰσχυνθήσονται καὶ ἐντραπήσονται πάντες οἱ ἀντικείμενοί σοι. Put this side by side with 45 : 16, בושו וגם נכלמו כלם יחדו, translated, αἰσχυνθήσονται καὶ ἐντραπήσονται πάντες οἱ ἀντικείμενοι αὐτῷ, and it is perfectly plain that the Greek translator had before him in 45 : 16 simply our M. T.; only that he read ר for ד, and regarded יהרו as the same verb (חרה) which he had translated in 41 : 11.*

* It is perhaps worth noticing here that in verse 24, below, the word נחרים, in a clause almost identical with the one in 41 : 11, is rendered by the LXX διορίζοντες (or ἀφορίζοντες); *i. e.*, it is derived from חרם, *cf.* the rendering in Lev. 27 : 21.

45 : 18. The opening phrase, "For thus saith Yahwè," stands outside the 3 | 2 metrical scheme, as is often the case; so too at the beginning of verse 14. Similarly, at the end of the verse the phrase "I am Yahwè, there is no other," is an extra three-beat line; see page 158.

45 : 19. "I did not say it in secret"; cf. 48 : 16, where the argument is very similar; also 48 : 3, 5. When Yahwè called Abraham, he made him very definite promises; he announced himself as the one and only God; he chose Israel with a definite purpose, which he declared and will certainly fulfil. The people are his "witnesses"; these facts are all well known to them; so 41 : 9; 43 : 10; 46 : 8–10, etc.

במקום ארץ חשך. The double construct state was designed to give added indefiniteness to the expression: "some spot in some dark land!" It is not likely that the author intended anything more definite than this with his ארץ חשך.

תהו, "for nothing," is a good example of a common Semitic accusative.

45 : 20. The first two words of this verse form an isolated 3-beat member, inserted for dramatic effect. With פליטי הגוים compare 66 : 19.

45 : 21. "Bring near [your false gods]!" With the omission of this direct object cf. the similar omission in 44 : 12 f.

"Let them take counsel together," the usual irony; cf. 41 : 5–7, etc. For the parallels to the remainder of the verse, see the note on 41 : 4.

45 : 22 f. A grand utterance, repeated in 59 : 19; 66 : 18–23, and paralleled in many other places in these poems (e. g., 49 : 6–9, etc.). Was any other ancient writer able to equal this prophet's conception of the world's future? It was he, also, who wrote chapter 35, not for the Jews only, but for all mankind.

The verse-division is in the wrong place; it should come after נשבעתי.

45 : 23. With צדקה, "truth," cf. verse 19b. We must of course read דְּבָרִי לֹא in place of דבר ולא.

45 : 24. For אמר לי read יֵאָמֵר, and for יבוא read יָבוֹאוּ. The corruption of the text was due to a very natural misunderstanding of the verse, which is attested by both the Greek and the Syriac. The first clause was connected with the preceding: "Yea, [they shall swear] by Yahwè" (ביהוה); this led to the reading לאמר,

rendered by both Greek and Syriac. In our massoretic text *both* readings, לאמר and יאמר, are combined in the manner elsewhere familiar; *cf.* 44 : 21. As a further consequence, עדיו יבוא was joined to the preceding words, the verb being put in the singular number to guard against any mistake (see especially the Syriac). This phrase must, however, be connected with the following, as 19 : 22, Micah 7 : 12, Ps. 65 : 3 show conclusively.

CHAPTER 46

This poem is based on themes which are already familiar. Its subject-matter is the same as that of the passages 40 : 17–26; 41 : 21–29; 43 : 8–13; 44 : 6–23, but the argument is presented in a fresh and striking way. Still another close parallel—the last passage of the kind—is 48 : 3–19. The prophet is reiterating a part of his 'Great Argument': gods are to be judged by what they can do; and if Yahwè is truly the One God, then let the faithless Israelites take warning!

Cheyne (Trans., note 68) characterizes this chapter as "A fragment of a song of derision on the expected captivity of Babylon." But there is not a particle of evidence, either external or internal, that the poem is fragmentary. No chapter in the book has a better claim to being regarded as complete than this one.

Moreover, the characterization "song of derision" is ill suited to the poem. It is an earnest and forceful appeal, argumentative in tone, addressed (like so many of its fellows, wholly or in part) to the less worthy, the less loyal, of the people. The ridicule of the heathen gods is merely incidental, here as in the other passages just named; none the less incidental because the gods are introduced in the first verse of the chapter, and two of them happen to be mentioned by name. The prophet is dealing with ideas of the most general character. It is an enticing conjecture that he was thinking here of the ominous sinking of the Persian power near the close of the fifth century (see page 109); but it is quite as likely that he had in mind in this passage no more definite picture of possible happenings than he had in 42 : 17 or 45 : 16. See, further, the introduction to chapter 47.

It seems tolerably certain that the three poems which constitute chapters 46, 47, and 48 were composed and written down in this order and at about the same time. 46 : 1 seems to have suggested to its author the theme of 47; and 48, again, returns to 46 with its formula שמעו אלי, as commentators have remarked. The same formula recurs in 51; see the introduction there.

The meter is 3 | 3 throughout.

46 : 1. The difficulty which exegetes have found in this verse is due in part to text-corruption (though this is only slight), but still more to the unexpected vigor of the poet's language.

The word עצביהם is plainly secondary. Aside from the fact that it makes the meter impossible, the presence of the suffix הם (which could hardly refer to Bel and Nebo; "their idols") gives a sure hint at the origin of the word. It is an explanatory addition, designed for the common people, who could otherwise hardly have known (in the latter part of the Greek period) what "Bel" and "Nebo" meant. The suffix הם refers to the Gentiles, as usual; in this case, the Babylonians. A similar gloss is צלמיכם in Amos 5 : 26, explaining the names סכות and כיון.

The suffix in נשאתיכם (second person plural, by which the two gods themselves would be directly addressed) can hardly be right. The Syriac, whose text is an instructive study, seems not to have had this suffix in its original; and the Targum read the suffix of the third person plural. Correct, accordingly, to נשאתיהם, "the things which they carry." The feminine gender of נשאות represents the indefinite neuter, of course; the suffix הם would seem most naturally to refer to the gods Bel and Nebo, and the following verses show that it does, indeed, refer to them. The "jaded beast" (עיפה) can only be the false god, which "breaks down" and "cannot save its load" (verse 2; compare verse 4, last clause). "The things which they carry" are their worshippers. Cf. especially 57 : 12 f.

With regard to the general meaning of verse 1, the sequel is decisive. Heretofore, in these poems, the "gods" of the heathen have been described as mere lifeless images; now, for the sake of the caricature, they are called worn-out beasts of burden. In verse 2 they break down and sink to the ground; they are not only unable to rescue their "load" (i. e., the people who put their trust in them), but are themselves carried off as booty. In verses 3 and 4 the contrast is drawn; Yahwè says: 'I never tire; I can and will carry you, all the way from your childhood to your old age. You are my "load," and I can and will rescue you.'

Point בָּרַע, to correspond with קָרַס; the participle is more vivid than the perfect. In verse 1 the poet sees the beasts sinking down; in verse 2 he describes the result. The vowel-pointing of the Massorites is a capital example of their way of preserving two recognized modes of reading the text—giving half of each. It is quite likely that the suffix in נשאתיכם is the witness to still a third variant reading, the three verbs being taken as imperatives: קָרַס, בְּרַע, and הֱיוּ.

הָיוּ לחיה ולבהמה, "They have proved like (lit., have become) beasts and cattle." The idiom—a vigorous one—exactly as in I Sam. 4 : 9. The Targum (דְמוּת) understood the phrase correctly.

It seems preferable to give עֲמוּסוֹת here the meaning "borne heavily, with difficulty," which properly belongs to the root. So the Targum, whose interpretation throughout the verse is the correct one. It is not necessary, however, to make a distinction in meaning between נשא and עמס, for the important part of the phrase is that which follows these two words. In verse 3, where the two participles are repeated, they are of course synonymous. The Syriac rendering *adide* (incorrectly interpreted in Brockelmann's *Lexicon*) is merely a translation of the Greek καταδεδεμένα.

It is possible that in place of the preposition ל we should read עַל. The emendation is not necessary, however.

The Greek rendering of the last clause of verse 1 and the first clause of verse 2 (not always correctly understood by recent critics of the Hebrew text) is: ὡς φορτίον κοπιῶντι, πεινῶντι καὶ ἐκλελυμένῳ, οὐκ ἰσχύοντι ἅμα, κ. τ. λ. This is the order attested by the best MSS. and by the Ethiopic version. The word עֵיפה is twice translated, the verb πεινᾶν being ordinarily used to render עָיֵף and יָעֵף in Isaiah; *cf.* 5 : 27; 28 : 12; 40 : 28, 29, 30, 31. It seems pretty certain, moreover, from the rendering of the Syriac version that the Greek text which it consulted did not contain κοπιῶντι, but only πεινῶντι, as the equivalent of עֵיפה. Nowhere else in the Syriac O. T. is the word rendered in this way ("hungry"), while the standard translation is the equivalent of κοπιᾶν.

46 : 2. The order of the two verbs is changed purposely, for literary effect; *cf.* 51 : 6, 8, etc. With כרעו compare Ps. 20 : 9.

מלט משא must of course mean: to rescue the load which they themselves are carrying.

46 : 3. "Remnant," שארית, the term so often used by the poets and prophets, meaning either those who have survived the many calamities which have befallen Israel, or else the fraction of the

nation who still occupy the holy land, in contrast with the multi-tude of Jews (the "captives") dwelling in all the Gentile lands.

The use of מִנִּי (twice) for מִן in this verse is a good illustration of the wide difference between the diction of poetry and that of prose, in classical Hebrew. The use of the article, which would equally well have satisfied the metrical requirement, is avoided, and the lines are made of the necessary length by the employment of this dissyllabic form of the preposition.

46 : 4. "I am the same"; see the note on 41 : 4, and the parallel passages there enumerated.

The meaning of עָשָׂה here is just the same as in 44 : 2; 54 : 5, etc. "Israel is the work of my hands (cf. 45 : 11), and I will carry him; what is more, I can rescue my burden" (contrast verse 2).

46 : 5. "To whom will ye liken me?" Cf. 40 : 18, where the context is very similar.

46 : 6. הַזָּלִים should not be changed to הַסֹּלִים (Perles, Cheyne, Marti). Our traditional reading is certainly possible, and the pro-posed emendation would be a very precarious one. These terms taken from the language of the tradesman and the craftsman are just the ones in regard to which we are most ignorant; see the note on 44 : 13.

46 : 7. In the opening clause the pause comes after the first word; עַל כְּתֵף is to be connected with the following. So also in the second clause; we must read יַעֲמֹד (without וֹ), and connect תַּחְתָּיו with it. So the Greek. The וֹ came from the preceding word.

With לֹא יָמִישׁ compare 54 : 10; 59 : 21; also 40 : 20; 41 : 7.

46 : 8. "Remember this"; cf. 44 : 21, where the preceding con-text was just the same as it is here.

וְהִתְאֹשָׁשׁוּ. This seems to have been the reading which all the old versions, excepting possibly the Greek, had before them. The form has probably been correctly transmitted, and is an Aramaic loan-word, from the (denominative) verb אָשַׁשׁ, "to found," which appears for example in the Palestinian Syriac of Matt. 7 : 25, and occurs in several forms in Rabbinical Hebrew. "Put yourselves on a secure foundation!" is a warning suited to this place. This is the way in which the word was understood by both the Syriac and the Latin (fundamini; see Cheyne's note on the text).

46 : 11. Read עַבְדִּי in place of עַיִט, improving thereby both the sense and the meter. "Bird of prey" is not a suitable parallel to "man of my counsel." The one "called from the east" was Abraham (41 : 2); with "from a far-off land" compare especially

41 : 9. The Targum interprets here correctly. In the similar passage 44 : 26 עבד and עצה are also juxtaposed.

The reading עצתו could be explained without difficulty, in the present context (though it would necessitate an awkward transition to the following דברתי), if we had any reason to suppose that the original text contained it. That the ו is merely a late copyist's blunder is the testimony not only of the Massorites, but also of the whole Jewish tradition, including the LXX, the Syriac, and even the Latin and the Targum.

With דברתי compare 45 : 19, where the meaning is the same; see the note there. With יצרתי compare בראתיו in 45 : 8.

46 : 12. With אבירי לב, "stubborn of heart," cf. 48 : 4, Ezek. 3 : 7, and Mal. 3 : 13a. The reading אבדי לב, "ye who lose heart," presupposed by the Greek, is far inferior, for it is not only out of keeping with its surroundings ("far from righteousness," the parallel clause of this verse, and "evil-doers" in verse 8), but is also contrary to the habitual attitude of the prophet. He was not speaking to men who had lost courage. He, the man of God, felt keenly the disgrace of Israel's present condition, and mourned the unworthiness of the chosen people; but it does not appear from any word of his that any considerable proportion of his fellow countrymen shared his feeling. He speaks glowing words of comfort, it is true; but they are addressed to Zion, to the city Jerusalem, to the ideal "Israel" of his imagination, not to the men whom he saw day by day. In nearly every case where he directly addresses his fellow countrymen, those of his own time and place, it is with argument, warning, and stern rebuke; as a preacher of righteousness addressing those who are in sore need of his exhortation.

"Far from righteousness"; the meaning is the same here as in 59 : 14. At the beginning of verse 13, on the contrary, the word צדקה has a different meaning. This is a good example of the favorite literary device of this writer, the repetition of a word in two distinct uses.

CHAPTER 47

This is a fine specimen of the poet's work in the treatment of a theme which lies outside his chief interests. Woes pronounced against foreign cities and nations, so common in the later prophecies of the O. T., are not in the Second Isaiah's usual repertory.

In fact, the poem stands quite alone in the collection; nowhere else does the prophet concern himself with a definite city or country of the Gentile world. It is plain that Babylon was for the prophet and his fellow countrymen the typical embodiment of the worldly power and pride which he declares to be fleeting, and the moral corruption whose punishment he predicts.

The subject, very likely suggested to the poet by 46:1, which was before his eyes, is the certain doom of the proud city Babylon, because of her wickedness and her arrogance. It is not a *vaticinium ex eventu*, nor was it even written at a time when *the city* seemed to be threatened; on the contrary, it is made perfectly plain by verses 8, 9, 11 that she was at this time in the full enjoyment of prosperity and apparent security, and with no threatening cloud on the horizon. There is nothing to suggest that the writer had any personal acquaintance with Babylonia, or that he was especially well informed in regard to it.

Both in the circumstances of the prophecy and in the spirit in which it was uttered, it resembles the denunciation of the city Capernaum in the Gospels: "Art thou exalted to heaven? Thou shalt be brought down to the pit!" And here, also, as in the New Testament parallel, no hatred of the city is apparent, no exultation in her downfall, no spirit of revenge; but the stern assurance of the wrath of God, which must be executed at last, and will not tarry long.

The language is nearly always high-sounding and vigorous; see, for example, verses 11 ff. The sustained irony of some of the passages reminds us forcibly of 44:9–20 and especially 56:9–57:10, to which the literary resemblance is very close. There is hardly any witness to this writer's irrepressible humor more striking, or more characteristic, than the unexpected litotes—not in itself humorous, it is needless to say, but testifying to the writer's habit of mind—at the end of verse 14.

The structure of the poem is unusually simple, for it is based on a single theme. The text appears to have received one or two slight additions from a later hand. Verse 3a is probably secondary, and verse 6 is certainly a later insertion. See the notes on the two passages.

The poem is interesting metrically, as the only one in the collection which is written in the 3 | 2 meter from beginning to end. Judging from the other 3 | 2 poems in the group, it was the habit of this writer to begin or close with a passage in the 3 | 3 meter. Thus, in 50, verses 1–3 (eight metric lines) are 3 | 3; in 51:17–52 : 12 the closing verses (four metric lines) are 3 | 3. The poem 56 : 9–57 : 21 begins with a single 3 | 3 line and ends with ten lines in this meter (verses 14–21). In chapter 62 the first two verses consist of four 3 | 3 lines.

There is only one "extra" three-beat line in the poem, namely, the last clause of verse 12a. Verse 6, in which, after the first two phrases, there is no semblance of meter, is a later addition to the poem; see the note. In several places the massoretic division is incorrect, especially in verses 3 f., 7, 9.

---

47 : 1. The word בְּתוּלַת, "virgin," is used of Babylon for the same reason for which it is so often used of Jerusalem, to picture the city as in her full strength and beauty. It is by no means implied in the use of the word that the city has 'never been conquered in war' (Duhm, Cheyne).

"Tender and dainty"; the same two adjectives in Deut. 28 : 56.

47 : 2. The queen is to become a common slave. What is meant by "pass through the rivers" is not entirely clear. It probably refers to the journey into captivity; but we should expect to find this more clearly indicated.

47 : 3. That verse 3a is a later addition seems likely for several reasons. It is rhythmically anomalous, in a poem so regular in form as this one. It introduces an idea which is not only unnecessary, but also confuses the picture which the writer has drawn. A probable reason for the addition may be seen by comparing the Syriac: the phrase חֶשְׂפִּי שֹׁבֶל was misunderstood. Duhm, Cheyne, and Marti also regard this half-verse as secondary.

For the phrase "take vengeance" see, for example, Jer. 20 : 10; with the idea expressed cf. 34 : 8 and the note there.

The text at the end of the verse is corrupt. We must point אֶפְגַּע as passive voice, read אָמַר in place of אדם, and cancel the verse-division. As for the verb פָּגַע, it is used in the active voice with the meaning "entreat" in either the qal stem or the hif'il (53 : 12, Jer. 36 : 25). For the passive voice either nif'al or hof'al may therefore be supposed, neither being actually known to occur elsewhere in this sense. The latter form, אָפְגַּע, would suit the meter better than the nif'al, and I accordingly prefer it, since the choice is open. All the testimony of the versions points to these same consonants.

The attempt (Klostermann, Cheyne) to show that the Greek παραδῶ was originally παριδῶ, which translated אפרע, is quite fruitless; it is only necessary to point to the passages 53 : 6, 12. The original Greek translation of this verse, represented by the codices AQא (*sec. man.*), many cursives, the Syr. Hex. and Ethiopic versions, etc., rendered *both* אדם and אמר, and it is plain that the former word is a corrupt variation of the latter. With the phrase אמר גאלנו compare אמר מרחמך in 54 : 10.

47 : 6. The greater part of this verse, *i. e.*, all after נחלתי, is quite unmetrical; the attempt to cut it into verse-members is fruitless. The substance of the passage is even more objectionable than its form. The idea that Yahwè's anger against Babylon *was due to her treatment of Israel* is utterly out of place. There is no hint of it elsewhere in the poem, nor is there any other passage in Second Isaiah from which it would appear that the prophet thought of the Babylonians as the oppressors of the Jews. Duhm, in his comment on this verse, shows at length that the idea which it expresses is decidedly inferior, theologically, to the utterances of such prophets as Amos, Isaiah, and Jeremiah. It is, indeed. And could we credit to a poet of high rank the sentimental phrase: "Upon *the aged* thou didst make thy yoke very heavy"? The whole verse is an interpolation, very similar to 52 : 4; see the note there.

47 : 7. It is obvious at the first glance that the half-verse ends with the word עד.

The emphatic אלה is at once interpreted by אחתריתה.

47 : 8. Evidently Babylon at this time had no reason to apprehend danger from any foreign foe.

The middle portion of this verse has been borrowed by the writer of Zeph. 2 : 15.

The poetical form אפסי also in verse 10. The idea expressed in this clause is exactly paralleled in 14 : 13 f.

47 : 9. The reading כתמם is decidedly preferable to פתאם (Grk., Syr.). The latter reading came in through the influence of verse 11. The *athnachta* is in the wrong place; it should be under the word אחד. The arrogant queen must stand alone and undefended in the day of judgment.

47 : 10. This verse consists of three compound lines which are closely related in idea. It is an act of violence to connect the first of the three with the preceding verse (Duhm, Müller, Cheyne) for the sake of imaginary 'strophes.'

"Thy wisdom and thine understanding," ironically.

With שׁובבתך *cf.* 57 : 17.

47 : 11. This verse also consists of three compound lines. The longer member of the last one ends, of course, with the word פתאם. We should probably read שַׁחְדָּה (Krochmal) instead of שׁחרה. See Ges.-Buhl, s. v. שׁחר.

הוה, "disaster, doom." The corresponding Arabic form, *hāwiya*, is used by Mohammed in the Koran (Sur. 101 : 6) with this same meaning, the doom that comes upon the wicked at the last judgment.

If the poem had been written after the conquest of Babylonia by Alexander the Great, this verse would hardly have been couched in such general terms. It is not likely that the poet had in mind any definite picture of the doom that was to befall the city. In any case, he would have been more likely to think of such scenes as those depicted in chapter 34 than of an invasion by a hostile army.

47 : 12. With הועיל compare 44 : 10; 48 : 17; 57 : 12. The extra three-beat line in the middle of this verse illustrates a common feature of the poems written in the 3 | 2 meter.

47 : 13. The word עֲצָתִיךְ contains a double reading; *cf.* the note on 44 : 21. The two readings here combined are עֲצָתֵךְ and עֲצָתִיךְ. Either one would be satisfactory.

The second compound line in this verse has evidently suffered some slight change from its original form. The article is not necessary with הזים, but it is needed, for the sake of the meter, before שׁמים. (Notice that in the parallel clause, following, it is used with the noun, but not with the participle.) I suspect that it was omitted by accident, and then reinserted in the wrong place. Emend accordingly.

The text of the last clause of the verse is certainly not what the prophet wrote. It is too long for the meter, and admits of no satisfactory rendering. The מאשׁר is mere nonsense. Ewald's 'explanation,' with which some commentators have tried to be satisfied, is no explanation at all, and "von wo es kommt" is quite impossible as a translation. I was at first inclined to think, as others have thought, that the מ might be due to dittography; but this is too improbable, and the difficulty of the clause is not thereby cleared away. The plural יבאו is plainly wrong. Duhm says, "read יבא," but this is running away from the problem without attempting to solve it. The explanation of the plural verb—the only possible explanation, as it seems to me—lies in the word

חדשים, which obviously can be pointed and understood in more
than one way. Our text is conflate; one reading was: "Making
known the new (enemies) who shall come against thee" (לְחָדָשִׁים
אֲשֶׁר, etc.); the other was: "Making known by the new moons
what shall befall thee" (לְחֳדָשִׁים מַה יָבוֹא). The Massorites combined the two readings in a typical manner. The second of the
two is of course the original.

47 : 14. On the latter half of this verse, see the introduction to
the chapter. Duhm is possibly right in seeing here a grimly
humorous reminder of 44 : 16*b*; but he is certainly wrong in supposing it to be a later addition to the poem. No Hebrew writer
could be more likely than this one to insert such a parenthesis. *Cf.*
59 : 6. The "fire" is, of course, the standing feature of Second
Isaiah's eschatology which we also meet (in pictures characteristically varied) in 34 : 9 f.; 50 : 11; 66 : 16, 24.

In לחמם we have the pausal form of the infinitive חֲמֹם; an entirely unobjectionable form, corresponding to the imperfect יֵחַם.

47 : 15. This verse forms a powerful *coda* to the poem. The
first half sums up verses 8–11, and especially verse 10 f.; the second half verses 12–14.

No emendation is called for. סֹחֲרַיִךְ, "those with whom thou
hast dealt," is a much better reading than the proposed substitutes; the general term is more forcible than the designation of a
particular class. Both here and in verse 12 the verb יגע seems to
be used in the secondary sense 'to acquire' (by toil).

With לעברו compare especially Ezek. 1 : 9, and also Amos 4 : 3,
Jer. 49 : 5.

CHAPTER 48

This poem is in many respects the counterpart of chapter 43.
In it the prophet sums up for the last time his 'Great Argument,'
which has occupied so much of chapters 41–46. Like the other
poems of this group, it is addressed mainly to the doubters, the
backsliders of Israel. No new feature is introduced, we have
merely a vigorous recapitulation.

The most prominent note is that of rebuke. With this the poem
begins and ends. In all its parts it contains the emphatic declaration that Israel, although the chosen people, is unworthy. This
note is struck, it is true, and often with considerable emphasis, in

each one of the chapters 42–46; and farther on in the collection
there are several poems (chapters 57, 59, and 65, especially) in
which the prophet, speaking in a less ideal strain, denounces his
people most sternly for their faithlessness and their wickedness.
But the way in which the picture of Israel's apostasy is here given
the background of an exalted conception of his place in the world
is especially interesting. The prophet is looking at the whole
course of history, taking in past, present, and future at once.

The introductory passage, verses 1, 2, gives both sides: the
heritage of Israel and the forfeiture of its right. (The verse-
division is incorrect; see the note.) Verses 3–8, which contain the
charge of faithlessness, combine themes which are familiar from
42 : 20; 43 : 18 f., 24*b*; 44 : 6 f., etc. Yahwè has proved his foreknowledge and shown his eternal purpose. Israel, though deserv-
ing to be "cut off" (verse 9), must yet fulfil his mission. Yahwè
has tried the nation in the furnace of affliction, and is ready to
work its salvation (10 f.). Verse 12 accordingly begins the announcement, the same which has been made repeatedly in the
preceding chapters; the promise of the coming Messiah, the representative of Israel, the counterpart of Abraham of old. The order
of the writer's thought in these verses (12–16*a*) shows a striking
correspondence with the order in the parallel passages, 41 : 1–10;
42 : 5–9; 43 : 8–15; 44 : 24–45 : 7; 45 : 12 f., 18 f.; 46 : 9 ff. The way
in which the polemic against idolatry is joined to every one of
these passages (here, in verses 5, 13, 14) is worthy of especial
notice. Verses 17 ff. renew the reproach of unfaithfulness; and in
reminding the people of the blessing which they might have had,
the poet suddenly brings before them, in his picturesque manner,
the old story of the deliverance from Egypt, and the miracles in
the desert (verses 20 f.; *cf.* 43 : 16 f.). Verse 22 (*cf.* 46 : 12; 50 : 11;
57 : 20 f.; and 66 : 24) brings the chapter to a characteristic conclusion.

There is no reason to doubt the integrity of the poem. The passage verses 1–11, which has recently been "analyzed" by Duhm
and his school, is thoroughly homogeneous, and as characteristic
of the Second Isaiah as anything in the book. The attempt to dis-
sect it is due to a fundamental misconception of the message of
the prophet. The only secondary elements in the chapter are the
כשדים . . . בבל interpolation (twice; verses 14 and 20), and the
last clause of verse 16; see the note.

As has already been remarked, in the introduction to 46, there
seems to be good reason to believe that this poem was written

very soon after 46 and 47. The three cannot be said to form a group by themselves, however, for they are very intimately and obviously related to their predecessors, and the connection with the following poems is hardly less close; see the introduction to 51 : 1–16 and 51 : 17–52 : 12. The interval of time between 41 and 48 cannot have been a long one, and 49 ff. continued the series without any apparent halt.

The meter is 3 | 3, except in verses 12 and 13, in which the scheme is 3 | 2. There is a rhetorical reason for the change of meter in this passage; see p. 163. The number of 3 | 3 | 3 verses is noticeable; such are 3, 4, 7, 9, 11, 16a, 17b, 18, 19, and 21.

---

48 : 1. Cheyne's division of this verse from verse 2 is the correct one; the latter must begin with לא באמת. His translation is meaningless, however—whether we take the one in the *Polychrome Bible*, which is the same as that of the Revised Version, or the one in his *Introduction to Isaiah*, p. 54; where he renders: "without faithfulness and truth." With the new stanza *a new sentence* begins: "It is not in truth, nor by right, that (כי) they name themselves," etc.

They "came from the loins of Judah." That is, this was written at a time when the term יהודים, "Jews," was used (and had for some considerable time been used) to include all the children of Israel.

The correction מעי for מי is probable, in spite of the Assyrian parallel. Compare especially verse 19.

"Who call themselves by the name of Israel, and invoke the name of Yahwè"; cf. 44 : 5.

48 : 3. The verb ואשמיעם is of course consecutive imperfect, and to be translated as a past tense; but here, again, the pointing of the conjunction need not be emended. Compare the pointing in this word with that in the first word of verse 5, where the line is short and needs the full vowel.

For מאז, see the note on 44 : 8. With the whole passage compare 43 : 9, 12, etc.

48 : 4. With this verse compare 42 : 24; 43 : 24b, etc. It is to be connected with the preceding verse, rather than with the following.

48 : 5. An important verse, for its testimony as to the spread of foreign cults in Israel.

עֲצַבִּי. The original reading was unquestionably עֲצַבִּי, "my *idol*." The pointing עֹצֶב ('pain, misery') is the well-known mocking device of the Punctuators. We have the same thing in 41 : 21 (עֲצַבוֹת for עֲצַבִּים; see note there) and in 45 : 16; also in Ps. 16 : 4 and other passages. In Jer. 44 : 19 the impossible verb לְהַעֲצִבָה is the result of a similar witticism, being the substitute for an original לְהֵיטִיבָה, or its equivalent ("to make her miserable" instead of "to please, propitiate her").* *Cf.* also such passages as Ex. 8 : 22, II Kings 23 : 13 (four cases of such substitution), etc.

48 : 6. The word חזה must be pointed חָזֹה, infinitive absolute. The clause is thus the counterpart of 42 : 20 in form, as well as in meaning. This construction, finite verb followed by infin. absol., is often used by the poets and prophets, and is a favorite with the Second Isaiah, especially when he is speaking with emphasis. The peculiar vowel-pointing here probably indicated a variant reading חֲזֹת.

In the clause וְאַתֶּם הֲלֹא תַגִּידוּ, the plural is not permissible. Read וְאַתָּה הֲלֹא תַגִּיד. The existence of a variant reading אַתֶּם accounts for our present text. In any case, the imperfect is iterative, referring to past time. The כָּלָה is exactly parallel to the רַבּוֹת of 42 : 20.

מֵעַתָּה is contrasted with מֵאָז of the preceding verse.

With נְצֻרוֹת, "things kept in store," *cf.* Jer. 33 : 3 (emended), and see the note on 45 : 3.

48 : 7. "They are created"; *cf.* 45 : 8.

The conjunction in וְלֹא must of course be omitted. So Greek, Syr. Notice the idiom לִפְנֵי יוֹם, "before to-day," and *cf.* מִיּוֹם in 43 : 13.

48 : 8. With the first half-verse compare 40 : 24, which is very similar in form. "Thine ear has not been open"; the same accusation as in 42 : 19 f. The pointing פִּתְּחָה is correct, and not accidental. *Cf.* 60 : 11, Cant. 7 : 13, and see Gesenius-Buhl, s. v.

The כִּי is emphatic. "Thou playest false"; the same accusation which Malachi reiterates (Mal. 2 : 10 f., 14 ff.).

48 : 9. "For my name's sake"; compare verse 11 and 52 : 5. Before תְהִלָּתִי the governing word לְמַעַן must be understood.

* A similar substitution in the Talmud (Shabb. 137*b*), noticed by Levy, *Wörterbuch*, s. v. חָתַם.

376 SECOND ISAIAH

The reading אחטם is correct. All the old versions seem to have had this word before them; the Grk. and Syr. translated by guess, but Jerome renders correctly. This appears to be an Aramaic loan-word, denominative from חוטם "nose." The verb meant "to bridle," as the corresponding verb is used in Arabic, in both the literal and the tropical senses. The direct object ("it," referring to אפי) is here understood.

For the idea that Israel is to be the bearer of Yahwè's "praise" (תהלה) among the nations, compare not only 42:11, 12, and the many similar passages in Second Isaiah, but also Deut. 26:19, Jer. 13:11, 33:9, Zeph. 3:19, 20.

48:10. Instead of ולא בכסף, or ולא ככסף, either one of which is mere nonsense, read לי ככסף, which is what the context demands. The whole difficulty was caused by the accidental writing of לו instead of לי.* Compare the corruption of 63:9, and many similar cases.

48:11. "For my own sake I must act." Compare 43:25 and see the introduction to 42.

Our massoretic text, with the repetition of למעני, is decidedly to be preferred; both because of the emphasis required at the climax of this very powerful passage, and on metrical grounds. In the second line, after יחל, the word שמי has fallen out by accident. The text rendered by the Greek *probably* contained the word. Its presence in the verse is required, both by the verb and by the need of a parallel to כבודי. The reason for the accidental omission of the word is plainly to be seen in the close resemblance which the beginning of this verse bears to verse 9. The scribe thought that the word שמי had already been written. The Greek and Syriac versions omit one למעני (according to their frequent custom in such cases), but appear otherwise to translate a Hebrew text identical with ours. It is not at all likely that Syr. and Lat. had the form אחל before them.

48:12. "I am the first, and the last"; so also 41:4 and 44:6; and in each of those passages, as here, introducing an estimate of the false "gods" worshipped by so many men, even in Israel.

48:13. "My right hand stretched the heavens"; also in 40:22; 42:5; 44:24; 45:12, 18; 51:13.

This whole verse, moreover, is exactly parallel to 40:26 (see the

* It may be that the corrupted verse was intended thus, "I have purchased thee, but not with silver"; cf. 52:3, and the uses of צרף in late Hebrew and Arabic.

note there). Both verses have been quite generally misunderstood. The intention is not to represent Yahwè as speaking to "the heavens," but to *the heavenly host,* the angels (identified with the stars), the "mighty ones" who occupy the middle position between God and man. Yahwè "calls them by name" as their commander, who appoints them their work, and compels them to obey; Ps. 103 : 20 f.; 104 : 4; 82 : 1 ff., 6 f. ("Ye are gods!"); 58 : 1 f. (reading אֵלִים); *cf.* also such passages as Is. 24 : 21. These angels, represented by the heavenly bodies, were the objects of worship among the heathen nations, and Yahwè himself had given them a little brief authority there; Deut. 4 : 19, 32 : 8 (reading בְּנֵי אֱלֹהִים, with the Greek), Dan. 8 : 10, 11 (where Yahwè is called the שַׂר הַצָּבָא), Enoch 80 ff. See Moore in the *J. B. L.*, 1896, pp. 193 f.

48 : 14. "Assemble, all ye!" The address this time is to the nations, as the course of the argument demands, and comparison of all the parallel passages clearly shows. 43 : 9 alone would be sufficient demonstration of the fact.

"Which one of them foretold this?" *i. e.*, which one of your "gods," those just referred to in verse 13*b*. *Cf.* 41 : 22, 26; 43 : 9; 44 : 7; 45 : 21. The reading בָּהֶם is decidedly preferable to בָּכֶם.

This verse has suffered from the בָּבֶל . . . כַּשְׂדִים interpolation; see the Chapter dealing with this subject.

The text in the middle of the verse is also slightly corrupted. The אֵת is quite unexpected, as commentators have remarked (Duhm terms it "sonderbar"); and יְהוָה אֲהֵבוֹ is hardly a satisfactory three-beat line, even when we point the second word as participle. Comparison of the parallel passages suggests the solution of the difficulty; this is a standing phrase, "Who foretold *this?*" and the prophet always uses זֹאת; see 43 : 9; 45 : 21, and *cf.* 42 : 23, and verses 16, 20 in this chapter. אֵלֶּה was originally הָאֵל. This is just the place for the emphatic phrase, "The [One] God, Yahwè"; compare 42 : 5, where the phrase occurs in a very similar context.

The word אֲהֵבוֹ should certainly not be questioned; it is the most important word in the verse, precisely what is demanded at this point in the prophet's argument, in accord with all its surroundings, and supported by the parallel passages. Compare especially 41 : 8 f.

The subject of יַעֲשֶׂה might be Yahwè, though it is more probably the Servant himself, *cf.* 41 : 2 f., 12–16. With חֶפְצוֹ compare 46 : 10*b* and 53 : 10*b*; and with זְרֹעוֹ, 51 : 5 and 53 : 1. Verse *b* is a striking example of conciseness. It gives in the briefest possible compass the gist of the 'great argument.'

48 : 15. We must read either וָאֲצַלִיחַ or else הִצְלֵחַ, infinitive absolute. The massoretic text combines both readings.

With the whole verse compare 41 : 9 f., 13, 25; 42 : 6; 45 : 1 f., 13; 46 : 11; 49 : 8; 53 : 10, and especially 51 : 2. Observe how the Targum interprets it as describing the call of Abraham.

The verse is in its original form as far as the word אני. But the last clause is certainly a later addition, and must be omitted, with Oort and others. It is not only condemned on metrical grounds, but is plainly due to a careless misinterpretation of the verse at the end of which it stands. The origin of the misinterpretation, or, rather, the passage that suggested it, is evident from the אדני יהוה. It was 50 : 4 ff. The glossator wished to explain that the speaker in verse 16a is the same one who speaks (with the characteristic use of אדני יהוה) in 50 : 4–9 and 61 : 1. Whether he supposed this "servant of Yahwè" to be Cyrus, or not, is of course another question. רוחו is subject, not object, of the verb.

"I did not say it in secret"; the same words were used in 45 : 19, and with the same meaning. When Yahwè called Abraham and Israel, he made them definite promises, which were well known and will be fulfilled. מראש; the Assyrian ultu rēši is used in just the same way.

Since the very first, "there am I" (שם אני); a characteristically forcible way of expressing the idea; cf. 41 : 4.

48 : 17. לְהוֹעִיל; cf. 47 : 12, and the passages there referred to.

48 : 18. The particle לו written לוא, as in 63 : 19. Beyond all question, the apodosis begins at once with the words: "Then had thy peace been like a river." The consecutive imperfect here (the first וַיְהִי) is simply the syntactical equivalent of the perfect, the tense to be expected here. It is of course important to take account of the change of tense in 19b. The phrase "they would not be cut off," etc., implies nothing whatever as to the present condition of Israel; it is simply a stock expression, the same which we see in 55 : 13 and 56 : 5.

48 : 19. מֵעֶיךָ כִּמְעֹתָיו; a good example of this writer's fondness for paronomasia.

In the last clause the word שמו, which is in every way superfluous, is the result of dittography and should be cancelled.

48 : 20. The בבל ... כשדים interpolation again. See on verse 14. The metrical form of this stanza is for the most part quite

transparent. The first two lines, צאו בחתו בקול רנה | הגידו השמיעו
זאת, are distinctly marked; so, too, is the third, ending with הארץ.
But the fourth has perhaps a word too many. Either אמרו stands
outside the metric scheme; or יהוה is a later insertion, as often; or
else the article with the noun is secondary, the line ending with
imrū.

With the whole verse compare especially 43 : 14, where the
"escape" of the Jewish "exiles" from the remote islands of the
sea (*i. e.*, the return of the Diaspora) is predicted in a similar context. The reason why the poet uses the word "flee" (בריחים, בחתו)
in these passages is seen not only in the immediate context in both
cases, but also in the imagery, which is repeated on page after
page: the road through the wilderness; Yahwè going before his
people; the waters in the desert; the drying up of the sea. He takes
the word from Ex. 14 : 5. Throughout all his prediction of deliverance for Israel, he is constantly reminding his hearers of that
one supreme work of Yahwè in their past history, *the rescue from
Egypt*. In both of these passages, after speaking of the coming
"escape," he at once adds an unmistakable allusion to the Exodus
(43 : 16, 17, and 48 : 21). In the present passage it may be questioned whether the imaginary hearers whom he is addressing are
the Jews who are soon to be saved, or the Hebrews of the time of
Moses, about to fly from Egypt. The dramatic habit of the writer,
and the extraordinary vividness of his imagination, make the latter supposition quite possible.

See also the very similar verses 52 : 11 f., and the notes there,
and compare further the very late passages Jer. 50 : 8; 51 : 6, 45.

48 : 21. The conjunction in וְלֹא is explained by the preceding
note. The prophet takes it for granted that his hearers would be
reminded of the Exodus by verse 20.

The grammatical construction of the first part of this verse has
been generally misunderstood. It is the poet's favorite use of
ellipsis: "They did not thirst in the deserts [through which] he led
them." That which is to be supplied is probably a second direct
object; see 50 : 10 and the note there. The ellipsis would be no
less easy, to be sure, if a preposition were to be supplied; *cf.* 51 : 1,
"look to the rock [from which] ye were hewn."

48 : 22. This sententious phrase (also 57 : 21; see the note there,
and the introduction to that poem) sums up a large portion of the
preceding discourse. Like chapter 50, this poem ends with the
same note with which it began.

According to Marti, the tone of a considerable part of this chapter—namely, the part in which the people are censured, and summoned to repent—is "pessimistisch." But does any one suppose that the prophet painted his people any blacker than they were? or that he exaggerated the distance which lay between the fulfilment of the promises made to Abraham, Jacob, and David and the actual condition and prospects of the "chosen people" in the fifth century B. C.? Judged by such a standard as this, there is not an earnest appeal for righteousness or call to repentance in all the world's literature that could be saved from the charge of pessimism. Duhm (on verse 19) says that for the Second Isaiah "die Sünden des Volkes längst vergeben sind." If this were really true, then those who heard the prophet might well have prayed to be delivered from him and his kind: the preachers of soft things; those who proclaimed "Peace, peace," when there was no peace.

CHAPTER 49

This chapter may well occupy the central place in the book. It sets forth at some length the most characteristic ideas of this prophet regarding the future; ideas combined here as nowhere else so distinctly. It thus affords an excellent starting-point for the study of his ideas in regard to the Servant, the 'restoration,' the conversion of the heathen nations, and the final status of Jews and Gentiles in God's kingdom. It is the 'new message' which was promised in 48 : 6 b, 7, and for which the way was then prepared; see page 115.

It is a complete poem by itself, introduced (like chapters 34 and 41) by a formal summons to the nations of the earth, and brought to a fitting close by verse 26. The first half of the poem, verses 1–13, sets forth primarily the purpose of God for the Gentiles; the second half, verses 14–26, deals primarily with his purpose for Jerusalem and the Jews. This order is plainly not accidental. The prophet is here speaking as a patriot, and his heart is in a blaze. He is not now in the mood for the rebuke, argument, and exhortation which constitute so large a part of his message. We may well believe that he wrote this poem as a contrast to the preceding (chapter 48). There God had said: 'Ye are children unworthy of my name!' Here the prophet is moved to show that God's choice and his promise were no empty form of words. He does not argue, however, but writes in an unusually tender strain.

The construction throughout shows the hand of a master. In the first part, there is a steady increase of enthusiasm until the final outburst of joy in verse 13. Then there is a sudden change to a low key, and the second theme—Zion the beloved of Yahwè —is introduced, in a passage of singular pathos. During all this latter half of the poem, the feeling is more intense, and the expression more dramatic, than in the first half; the momentary change of meter, in verses 19–21, adds to the increasing effect; and finally, in the concluding promises, verses 22–26, expressed in words which show the poet's own excitement, a most powerful climax is reached.

The meter is 3 | 3 everywhere except in verses 19–21, where it is 3 | 2.

---

49 : 2. Compare 51 : 16, "In the shadow of my hand I concealed thee," which unmistakably shows that the downtrodden Israel of that passage is only another aspect of the 'Servant' who appears in 49 : 1 ff.; 50 : 4 ff.; and 61 : 1 ff. In the present passage the poet certainly has in mind an individual, the Messiah. Verse 5, especially, makes this plain. See Chapter VIII.

49 : 3. The attempt to remove the word ישראל from this verse by some commentators (Klostermann, Duhm, Schian, Cheyne) is inexcusable. Its presence in the original text is attested (1) by all the versions; (2) by numerous parallel passages (e. g., 41 : 8; 43 : 10; 44 : 1, 2, 21); (3) by the rhythm of the verse, which is sadly impaired by its omission.

49 : 4. With לריק יגעתי cf. 65 : 23.

With this use of אכן, "nevertheless," "nay rather," cf. 53 : 4.

49 : 5. In the fourth clause of the verse, which the Massora recognizes as corrupt, it is perhaps best to read וישראל אאסף. The subject of the verb is the Servant. This seems to have been the consonant text rendered by both Gr. and Syr. Our Hebrew combines two readings. For the change from the infinitive construction to the finite verb, cf. 45 : 1.

ואכבד. The verb is a consecutive imperfect, as the following היה and the context show.

This last line of the verse refers to the honor previously shown to the Servant, with which is contrasted the greater honor now announced.

49 : 6. The word ויאמר should not be excised. It repeats the

אמר of verse 5, now left quite a distance behind, and could no more be dispensed with here than it could in any similar modern composition. Metrically, it probably stands quite outside the line. This suspended construction, with a long parenthesis, is used in other places by the Second Isaiah; see, for example, 43 : 16–18.

The phrase נקל מהיותך לי עבד is neither "barbarous" (Duhm) nor even difficult. The verb נקל is used impersonally, in the manner so common in the Old Testament; see Gesenius-Kautzsch, 26th ed., § 144, b; and as for this use of מן with the infinitive, see the abundant parallels noted in the same grammar, § 133, c. The whole phrase is almost exactly paralleled, for example, in Ezek. 8 : 17; cf. also Ex. 9 : 28, I Kings 12 : 28, etc. This is an idiomatic Hebrew construction, in which there is neither awkwardness nor ambiguity. It is unfair to require that the prophet should confine himself to the use of the most familiar idioms.

The meaning of נצורי ישראל (so read), judging from Ezek. 6 : 12 (הנשאר והנצור), is nearly or quite "the remnant of Israel"; cf. שארית בית ישראל, 46 : 3, and פליטי הגוים, 45 : 20.

In the last line of the verse the words of 42 : 6, appointing the Servant, Israel, to be "the light of the nations," are not merely repeated, but are made more explicit. The "rescue" which had been promised to Israel, and which was the Servant's first mission (verses 5, 6), is to include the Gentiles as well; even the most remote nations are to be gathered in.

49 : 7. The line beginning with the words לבזה־נפש deserves especial attention from the metrical point of view. It would be possible to make it a double line, with a "feminine" cæsura; but if that had been intended we should doubtless have had the following text:

לבזוי נפשו | למתעב גוים | לעבד משלים

There are, on the contrary, plain indications that the poet intended this for a single line of three beats. Three instances of unusual abbreviation are to be noted: (1) גוי instead of גוים. In the other similar cases (e. g., עם in verse 9 and in 42 : 6), the singular is employed for the sake of the meter. (2) נפש for נפשו; "self-despised," "lightly esteemed in his own eyes." (3) בזה for בזוי. This is the only instance of the kind, to be sure; on the other hand, the reason for its appearance here is plain to see. As we do not know the extent to which such poetic modifications may have been used, and as this form, considered as such a modification, is just what we should expect (בזוי could hardly be shortened to anything else than בזה), we may well retain it as it is. *Cf.* Ps. 22:7, doubtless influenced by this passage. It would seem, then, that the poet (doubtless with a rhetorical purpose) condensed into this single line of three beats his powerful description of the low estate of Israel, each one of the three measures containing a separate item of the reproach; even in the translation the effect is not lost.

For מְתָעֵב read מְתַעֵב. It is altogether likely that our massoretic reading is the result of intentional change.

משלים here just as in 52:5.

This whole verse finds its exact parallel in 52:14, 15. *Cf.* also such passages as 60:14.

The verb וקמו corresponds very well to the ירגזו (emended) of 52:15. The kings "stand up" as a mark of reverence; *cf.* Job 29:8 (Duhm).

With שרים, the verb יראו is to be understood. There is also an ellipsis of למען before קדש ישראל.

49:8. As the text stands, the metrical division presents great difficulties. It is necessary either to regard ואצרך ואתנך as forming a complete line, or else to put the line-division between the two words, making the one the end of the third member of the stanza, and the other the beginning of the fourth. Neither one of these two alternatives is at all satisfactory. As for the latter one, the very close parallelism of the second and third lines of this stanza is obviously against it; בעת רצון עניתיך is so repeated, word by word, in ביום ישועה עזרתיך that the rhythmical beat of the former line must have been exactly reproduced in its successor; the addition of a word, which under other circumstances would be quite unobjectionable, is not to be thought of here. As for the proposal to regard ואצרך ואתנך as making up a complete line, the obvious reply is, that this line is both incomplete and weak; for, on the one hand, the separation of ואתנך from לברית עם cuts in two an organic unity, and, on the other hand, the two verbs which are thus brought together and made to form a whole, really belong, the one to what precedes, the other to what follows (see note on 42:6). With the words "I make thee a covenant of the peoples" an entirely new idea is introduced, which is then carried on, both in the remainder of the verse and in the one which follows.

In spite of all this, I should leave the text as it stands, if the external testimony gave us no ground for suspecting it. But as a matter of fact, the evidence against וְאֶצָּרְךָ—the one superfluous word here—is strong. Of the four uncials, אABQ, used by Swete, only one (B) contains the word, and it is lacking in a considerable proportion of the cursives. Additional evidence of the same nature is afforded by the Ethiopic version, which omits the word. When, in addition to these facts, it is observed that by cancelling וְאֶצָּרְךָ every difficulty is at once removed, the conclusion seems certain that the word came in (as might very easily have happened) from the parallel passage 42:6; at an early date, but later than the time when the Greek translation was made. The original line was, therefore:

$$\text{וְאֶתֶּנְךָ לִבְרִית עָם לְהָקִים אָרֶץ}$$

Observe that this corresponds exactly to the form of the verse in 42:6.

The phrase בְּרִית עָם has precisely the same meaning here as in 42:6. עָם is for עַמִּים, by poetic license, and means 'all the nations.'

Similarly, אָרֶץ means here just what it meant in 42:4; namely, 'the inhabited world,' ἡ οἰκουμένη. הָקִים is used here in the same way as קוֹמֵם in 44:26; 61:4. The necessity of interpreting אָרֶץ in correspondence with עָם is of course obvious; but there is a reason for taking them both in this broad way far stronger than the mere fact that they were so taken in chapter 42. The Second Isaiah must be allowed to interpret himself. He has said twice over, with emphasis (verses 6, 8), that Yahwè now promises to "rescue" not only the children of Israel, but the Gentiles with them. It is evident that he is leading the way to some description or picture of the glad time, such as he gave, for example, in 42:7 (see the note on that verse). *And the picture now comes*, in verses 9 ff. The Gentiles are gathered in, from every land under the sun (verse 12; cf. עַד קְצֵה הָאָרֶץ, verse 6). The prophet means what he says; and the home-gathering which had been promised only to the chosen people in 43:5, 6 is now sketched on a larger scale, giving all the peoples a share in it. See, further, on the interpretation of this verse and the following context, the chapter on the prophet's attitude toward the foreign peoples. There are many sheep of Yahwè's flock among the heathen nations, and they are all to be gathered into his fold (verses 9b, 10; 56:8).

49:9. "Saying to the prisoners, Come forth! to those who

are in darkness, Appear !" The subject of the infinitive לֵאמֹר, as
of those immediately preceding, is of course the Servant, not
Yahwè.

This passage is the counterpart of 42 : 7. There, however, the
promise stops with the release of the world's "prisoners" (prisoners of sin, suffering, and injustice) from their dark dungeons;
here there is also a description of their return home, to "Him who
has mercy on them." 61 : 1, 2 is a third closely similar passage;
there, also, the blessings promised are for all mankind.

It would be better to end the verse with הִגָּלוּ. What then follows, to the end of verse 10, is the development of a single idea.

The Greek seems to have read כל between עַל and דְּרָכִים. It is
questionable, however, whether that reading is to be preferred;
the word might easily have come in through conformation with
the following clause. That the meaning of the phrase would be
improved by inserting it, cannot be successfully maintained.

49 : 9b, 10.   The ingathering of the Gentiles, described in figures which are often applied to the restoration of the Jews in the
Messianic age. Cf., for example, 40 : 11; 41 : 18; 43 : 19–21; 48 : 21.
The picture of Yahwè leading the Gentile flock as their 'good
shepherd' is worthy to put beside 25 : 8, where he is represented as
'wiping the tears from their faces'; cf. also such passages as 2 : 2–4;
19 : 24 f.; 66 : 18, 21; Ps. 65 : 3; 145 : 14–18; 146 : 7, 8; and (perhaps
the most remarkable of all) Mal. 1 : 11.

49 : 10.   On the words וְלֹא יַכֵּם שָׁרָב, Duhm remarks that the
verb is not suited to the noun, and thinks that "lead astray"
might have been expected. But Hebrew usage is a sufficient answer to this. The word שָׁרָב does not anywhere mean mirage, Fata
Morgana, but "hot air," "scorching wind," "burning surface of
the desert sands," and the like, as in 35 : 7, and all the other (late
Hebrew) passages where it occurs. The Greek καύσων, which well
translates the word here, is also used to render it in Sir. 43 : 22.
Of course the transition to the secondary meaning seen in the
Arabic sarāb was an easy one.

49 : 11.   Cf. 40 : 3, 4, etc. In יְרֻמָּן we have a favorite Aramaic
construction, the indefinite third pers. plur. active used in place
of a passive; "and my highways shall be built up."

49 : 12.   The word סִינִים is probably the result of some scribal
error. The reading סְוֵנִים, "the people of Syene," proposed by
J. D. Michaelis, and recently favored by many scholars, is perhaps the most likely.

49:13. *Cf.* 44:23; 52:9. It is better to read יִפְצְחוּ, third person plural, following the consonant text, which is supported by the Greek. The M. T. combines two readings.

In both עַמּוֹ and עֲנִיָּו, again, the Gentiles are included. The, former word is used in the same way as in 25:8 (see pages 118 f.), and the latter term would be most suitable to apply to those whose wretched condition is described in verse 9*a*.

49:14. Here the second main division of the poem begins. From this point on to the end Israel is the central figure, and the foregoing description of Yahwè's tender care for the Gentiles is now surpassed by the picture of his affection for his own peculiar people. See the introduction to the notes on this chapter. The sudden change here from *forte* to *piano*, and from triumph to pathos, is characteristic.

49:16. "I have graven thee on the palms of my hands." The prophet is undoubtedly using here a long-familiar figure of speech, this and nothing more. The name Jerusalem—not "the walls" (Duhm), nor "das Städtebild" (Marti)—Yahwè will thus keep ever before him. The exegesis which turns poetry into prose is nowhere better exemplified than in the comments on this clause which would infer from it the Second Isaiah's attitude toward the Levitical law !

The "walls," as the commentators agree, are the walls of the ideal city. See the note on 62:6.

49:17. Read בָּנָיִךְ, with most of the versions and the best commentators, and—what is no less important—point מְהָרְסָיִךְ; "those who build thee up outstrip those who tear thee down." The *qal*, not the *piel*, is the usual stem of the verb הרס; and the verse is metrically hopeless until this slight change is made.

With this verse thus restored to its proper form, the metrical regularity and smoothness of the whole passage, verses 16–18, is as perfect as anything in Hebrew poetry. That Cheyne should print the whole passage as *prose*, and that Duhm (followed by Marti) should feel obliged to subject it to an extensive 'restoration' are remarkable facts.

Notice the change of meter at this point, and the apparent reason for it. Verses 19–21, which form an episode in a somewhat subdued strain, are in the 3 | 2 mode. The triumphant strain, verses 22 ff., where the original meter is resumed, is thus given still greater prominence.

It is sufficiently obvious that something is wrong with the text of the first half of this verse. See any good commentary. As the words are now pointed, we have what sounds like a mere fragment, part of which is obscure, to say the least. אֶרֶץ הֲרִסֻתֵךְ could not mean "thy destroyed land." The word הֲרִיסֻת (found only here) does not mean "destruction," but is the abstract noun formed from the verbal adjective הָרִים (with passive meaning) "torn down"; cf. Amos 9:11. It could thus only mean "thy condition of being torn down."

All the difficulties disappear at once, when a slight change is made in the vowel-pointing. Read שִׂמַּמְתִּיךְ, חָרַבְתִּיךְ, and הֲרַסְתִּיךְ, "I devastated thee, laid thee waste, razed thee to the ground." אֶרֶץ accusative, limit of motion, as in verse 23, Amos 9:9, Lam. 2:1, and many other passages. Compare with the verse thus emended, 47:6; 42:24; Jer. 12:7.

49:21. The words גוֹלָה וְסוּרָה are both metrically superfluous and otherwise objectionable, as they interrupt the thought of the verse and weaken the figure employed by the prophet. סוּרָה is probably for אֲסוּרָה, as it is regarded by the Latin Vulgate (captiva) and the Hexaplar Greek (ἐκκεκλεισμένη). The fact that the two words are wanting in the LXX makes it certain that they are a later addition. A glance shows that they were first suggested by a misreading of the word גלמודה.

49:22. With אָרִים נִסִּי cf. 62:10; and with the whole verse, 60:4 ff.; 66:12, 20. This is a picture in which the poet delights. and it is beautifully drawn by him.

49:23. Israel, the weakling, the "feeble worm" (42:14), is to be reared to strength and tenderly cared for by the nations, as a child is reared by its nurses or its foster-parents. They fall down before it in admiring homage, as would all the subjects of an Oriental ruler, even though he were a prince in the cradle. This is not the attitude of "the meanest slaves" (Duhm), but the common figurative way of describing the homage of all subjects, however high their rank, before their king, however mild and magnanimous he may be. The phrase עָפָר רַגְלַיִךְ יְלַחֵכוּ means no more (and no less) than the omnipresent "he kissed the ground before him," in the stories of the *Thousand and One Nights*, wherever king or caliph is approached by one of his subjects. Duhm comments on this verse as though he had forgotten all his knowledge of the Oriental mind, customs, and figures of speech. Even if the passage were prose, there would be in it nothing to object to; but this is not prose, it is poetry.

In 45:14; 60:11, 14 the same thing is said in the same pictur-

esque way. Israel is now trodden to the earth, suffering and despised; where are all the splendid promises of the Most High?
The prophet cries out that in Yahwè's great day faithful Israel
shall be the king of all the nations of the world! In all of these
passages he is writing in an impassioned strain, and it is certainly
not easy to imagine any more forcible way of painting the picture
—Israel enthroned, and all the nations at his feet—than this which
he has employed.

To the question whether the prophet is to be blamed for giving
the Jews this preference in the Messianic age, there can be but one
answer. As a patriot, and as a believer in the promises of God, he
could do no otherwise, nor could we wish to have him. This belief
was the heritage of ages, and was built on a most secure basis.
Common justice could demand no less; the nation which has
"poured out its soul unto death" must at last "divide the spoil
with the strong" (53 : 12); he who has led the way, faithful in
spite of suffering, must receive a proportionate reward. So, for
example, in the New Testament, Luke 22 : 28 ff.: "But ye are
they which have continued with me in my temptations, . . . and
ye shall sit on thrones judging the twelve tribes of Israel." Duhm
fails utterly to appreciate the spirit in which the Second Isaiah is
writing.

49 : 24. The scribal error, צדיק for עריץ, was an extremely easy
one. Our massoretic text, from here to the end of the chapter,
is otherwise quite unobjectionable.

49 : 25. The כי at the beginning of the verse, which some have
found troublesome, is exactly what it is in verse 19 (twice; but
especially 19b) and so often elsewhere, a strongly emphatic particle, "yea (or nay) verily; nevertheless; assuredly." It could not
be dispensed with here; nor could the whole clause כי כה אמר יהוה
be removed from the beginning of this verse (Dillmann, Duhm;
cf. Marti, who makes even greater havoc with the original) without considerably weakening its force.

49 : 26. This is the climax, and it can be understood only by
those who observe how the feeling of the poem has been steadily
increasing in intensity from verse 14 onward. But the poet would
have been horrified by the thought that any one could take his
words here as a literal prediction or wish.

CHAPTER 50

With 50 : 1 begins a new poem, quite distinct in character and
tone from the preceding, and by no means to be joined to it, as
some have done. This poem of eleven verses is, moreover, in spite
of its brevity, a fine representative specimen of its author's work.
It shows him in a characteristic mood, argumentative and denun-
ciatory, though with hope always kept in sight. It illustrates the
range of his thought, the vividness of his imagination, and his
mastery of metaphors. It contains both varieties of meter, combined with studied purpose. The artistic manner in which its
component elements are combined is especially to be noticed as
typical. It is dramatically conceived, from beginning to end, and
admirably proportioned, with nothing lacking and nothing superfluous.

It is unfortunate that the structure of the poem should have
been so frequently misunderstood, and its unity therefore questioned. So far from finding any 'difficulty' in the transition from
verse 3 to verse 4, whoever understands the art of the Second
Isaiah will see here one of his master strokes. There is no more
reason for objecting to abruptness here than there would be in case
of the introduction of a new character or scene in a play, or of the
'second theme' in an orchestral composition. The only question
is, whether these units are made into a consistent whole. The
third division of the poem, verses 10, 11, is the sufficient answer.
Verse 10 is the *résumé* of verses 4–9, and verse 11 of verses 1–3,
and there is certainly no obscurity in the mutual relation of these
two! It is not easy to see how this device could be improved upon.

This poem closely resembles the one which constitutes chapter
42 in the materials out of which it is made: The Servant passage;
God manifesting his ability to save by his power over nature; the
rebuke of the disobedient and faithless people, and so on. The
tone is noticeably different, however, as is also the manner in
which the Servant theme is employed.

The meter is 3 | 3 in verses 1–3; from verse 4 on it is 3 | 2.

---

50 : 1. The introductory כה אמר יהוה forms an isolated line of
three beats, as in numerous other places.

כריתות (Deut. 24 : 1). Observe the Aramaic ending, also in

קדרות, below. The preference of this form is a sure indication of late date.

הן for הנה; also in verses 2, 9 (twice), 11. So frequently in the last poems of the collection, 58 ff.

"For your sins ye were sold, for your crimes your mother was put away!" The verse is highly important, for the poet gives us here his view of present conditions. Israel was "sold," "put away" from the presence of Yahwè, and *had not yet been received back* into favor. Both Yahwè and the prophet must say to the people (as verses 10, 11 of this chapter do say, for example): 'Ye are still false and unworthy; unrighteous of life and destitute of faith. Why will ye not turn, so that the long-delayed deliverance may come?' And this is the attitude which the prophet consistently maintains, throughout the book. As for the figures employed here, it is important to notice that everything turns on the distinction drawn between a "divorce" or "sale" that is irrevocable, and one that can be recalled. Zion was given no formal writing of divorcement; she can therefore be taken back. The children of Israel were not sold to a creditor, *i. e.*, by one who was bankrupt; but by one who has full power to redeem them. *Cf.*, for the figure of selling, 52 : 3; also Judg. 2 : 14; 3 : 8, etc.; Deut. 32 : 30; for that of the rejected wife, 54 : 6–8; 62 : 4; and for the same idea in somewhat different form, 42 : 24; 63 : 10. The same technical terms in Jer. 3 : 8.

50 : 2. "Why did I come, but find no one; call, but hear no answer?" *Cf.* 59 : 16; 63 : 5, in both of which passages he brings in this same phrase, in characteristic manner. The first two verses of this chapter find a close parallel, moreover, in the first two verses of chapter 59. *Cf.* also 51 : 18.

The words "Lo, by my rebuke I dry the sea" introduce a new part of the argument, namely that in which the poet points to the absolute power of God over nature as giving proof of his power to help his people. No one of all the Old Testament writers puts this argument so forcibly, or gives it so prominent a place, as does the Second Isaiah. We have, moreover, a striking parallel to this present verse in 42 : 15. When, in the face of all this, Duhm pronounces verses 2b, 3 a later insertion in the chapter, we must admire his courage, but not his exegetical insight.

It is possible that the poet, in thus speaking of rivers and seas becoming dry ground at God's rebuke, had in mind the march through the Red Sea (Ex. 14 : 21 ff.) and the crossing of the Jordan (Josh. 3 : 14 ff.), for the story of the deliverance from Egypt

and the journey thence to Palestine is a theme to which he delights to return. But he may only be speaking in general terms.
See the note on 42 : 15. It is not likely that allusion to a "Schöp-
fungsmythus" (Gunkel, Marti) is to be found here.

תבאש. The verb (בָּאַשׁ) is here used with the meaning common
in Aramaic (and, indeed, more or less prominently present in all
the Semitic languages), 'to be badly off, in evil case,' etc. The
context seems to be decisive for this meaning here, and it is not
even necessary to suppose Aramaic influence, easy as that would
be. The use in the Hebrew Sirach, 3 : 26, affords a perfect parallel. The variant reading, תִּיבַשׁ, attested by the LXX, seems inferior.

The suffix in דגתם, masc. plural, is unobjectionable, abundantly
supported by the best classical Hebrew usage.

With this use of צמא cf. Ezek. 19 : 13; also Is. 44 : 3, and the
word צמאון.

50 : 3. קדרות. See on כריתות, above, verse 1. If the poet has
been alluding here to the Exodus, this is the 'Egyptian darkness.'

50 : 4. אדני יהוה. Of this combination Duhm says: "אדני
dient v. 4. 7. 9 nur zur Ausfüllung des ersten Hemistichs." On the
contrary, the unusual expression was chosen and employed all
through this paragraph with studied purpose; the poet was not
driven to any such straits for the means of 'filling out his hemistichs.' The added אדני, "Yahwè, my Lord," emphasizes the close
relation of the Servant to his God, his feeling of dependence on
him and confidence in his help; ideas which play a very prominent
part in this poem. It is not by accident that this same expression
is employed in 61 : 1, where it serves a similar purpose.

למודים in its first occurrence in the verse is the abstract noun,
"teaching, instruction," as in Sir. 51 : 28. So the Greek and Syriac
versions render, correctly. For the noun-form, see Ges.-Kautzsch,
124, d, f; and compare the similar forms in the preceding chapter,
verse 20; 43 : 28; 51 : 7; 63 : 4. "Pupils" or "disciples" would be
altogether out of place in this clause; pupils have ears, not tongues,
and the word is not qualified in any way.*

On the other hand, כלמדים at the end of this same verse is to be
translated "like pupils," the noun having here the same meaning

* It is probably this same abstract noun, למדים, which occurs in 8 : 16, a
passage which has caused much difficulty. The words צור תעודה חתום תורה בלמדי
must be translated in some such way as this: "The binding up of testimony,
the sealing of law, is in [or, through] my teaching."

as in 54 : 13. This repetition of a word *in two distinct meanings* is a characteristic and favorite device of this writer, as has been shown elsewhere in this treatise.

In לדעת לעות we have an obvious doublet, shown to be such also by the meter. לעות was the original. Grk., Syr., Lat., Targ., all had before them precisely the same text which we have. For the meaning of the infinitive לעות the context strongly favors "assist," or something of the kind; what the "fainting" man needs is *help*, primarily; instruction may be postponed. This is therefore the Aramaic עות, "aid, help" (occurring frequently in both Palmyrene and Nabatæan inscriptions; see Lidzbarski, *Handbuch*); a verb very much used in Arabic in this same sense. Aquila was right with his ὑποστηρίσαι, and Jerome with his *sustentare*. This is merely another of the many cases in which the Second Isaiah borrows words or constructions from the Aramaic. דבר is of course adverbial accusative; Ges.-Kautzsch, § 118, m.

The massoretic division of this verse is wrong, and very misleading. The clause "to give the fainting a word of help" is not to be connected with what precedes, but with the verb immediately following.

יעיר (first) means "he awakens *me*"; the object being omitted, as so often elsewhere, because it can be inferred from the context.

50 : 5. On the general meaning of this and the following verses, see the introduction to 52 : 13–53 : 12, and the chapter on the Servant.

50 : 6. *Cf.* 53 : 3 ff. The plural form כלמות may have been chosen in order to give the idea of repetition, or it may be simply the abstract plural, as so often in this writer.

For the phrase כלמה ורק *cf.* 61 : 7, emended as suggested in the note there.

50 : 8. As the context shows, מצדיקי means here especially "He who will prove that I am in the right." *Cf.* verse 10 and 44 : 26; and especially 53 : 11 (as emended).

בעל משפט is the exact equivalent of the Aramaic בעל דין; *cf.*, *e. g.*, the Syriac of Matt. 5 : 25, Luke 12 : 58; 18 : 3.

50 : 10, 11. These concluding verses are eminently characteristic. The prophet was not dealing with weaklings, nor was he a weakling himself. For the attitude of stern rebuke, *cf.* especially 46 : 8–13; 48 : 1–11; 57 : 1–13; 58 : 1–18, and the first three verses of this chapter. This dramatic way of bringing the short poem to an end is very effective. See also the introduction to the chapter.

50 : 10. "Who is there among you?" Yahwè's final warning to the obdurate children of Israel, summoning them to hear and obey. *Cf.* especially 42 : 23.

The construction of שמע is the same as that of ירא: "Who is there . . . that fears . . . that hearkens?" The Servant is *a teacher*. As such he was expressly introduced at the outset in this chapter, it is to be observed. He is the one gifted by God with the "tongue of instruction," the patient learner whom the Spirit arouses early to proclaim his message of help. One would suppose that the purpose of the poet in repeating this leading idea in the closing paragraph was sufficiently obvious, but Duhm remarks: "עבדו mag er als sing. geschrieben haben, aber versteht es gewiss als Kollektiv." He then explains that the poet (or rather, 'the editor'; he would not give him the rank of a poet) had in mind the Prophets, who were for him the teachers of "the Law."

"He [*i. e.*, the Servant] who walked in darkness," etc. This is not only the translation most naturally suggested by the Hebrew text, it is also the one best suited to its surroundings. Yahwè is represented as drawing the contrast between his Servant, who walked in darkness, trusting in his God, and the stiff-necked people, walking indeed in their own "light," but doomed to perish in the flames they have kindled. Thus rendered, the whole passage gains decidedly in power, and is given its intended connection with the preceding division of the poem. Yahwè speaks of himself in the third person here, just as he does in 51 : 3; 42 : 21 ff., and many other places.

"Walked through the darkness." *Cf.* Ps. 23 : 4: "though I walk through the valley of deep darkness." For this construction, direct object with the verb הלך, *cf.* 33 : 15; 48 : 21 (see note); 57 : 2; Lam. 3 : 2; and the frequent use of הלך דרך in Second Isaiah.

"Trusting in the name of Yahwè, leaning on his God." The obvious counterpart of this is found in verse 7.

50 : 11. "Ye *all*"; it is a mistake to limit the word to any class or company. The prophet has in mind the people as a whole, without the distinction between unfaithful and faithful which he might make elsewhere. Yahwè himself is the speaker, and in his sight every son of Israel merited the severest rebuke, as the prophet declares again and again. So, unmistakably, the first verses of this very chapter, where also Yahwè is the speaker; *cf.* further the words of Yahwè in 43 : 22; 48 : 1–9; 63 : 5; 65 : 1, 2, etc. See also the first chapter of Isaiah, 'The Great Arraignment,' which in every paragraph expresses the view of the Second Isaiah. The

prophet's conviction, when in this mood, was that of the psalmist: "There is none that doeth good, no, not one." See especially his powerful portrayal in chapter 59, verse 4: "Not one calleth in righteousness, not one pleadeth in truth"; verse 12: "Our transgressions are multiplied before thee, and our sins testify against us"; verse 14: "Truth is fallen in the street, and uprightness cannot enter." Also 48:8, 9: "For I know that thou (the 'House of Jacob,' verse 1) playest false, transgressor from birth thou art rightly called. *For my name's sake* I restrain mine anger; for the sake of *my praise* I spare thee, not cutting thee off!"

"Kindlers of fire." With this figure of the fire and the blazing brands *cf.* 47:14, and especially 42:25. The metaphor was chosen here simply for the sake of the contrast with the "darkness"—yet darkness with safety—of the preceding sentence. Repent now, before it is too late! is the warning of the passage. So in 42:25 it is said of Israel: "The fire scorched him round about, but he understood not; it burned him, but he would not comprehend."

For מאזרי, "girt with," read מאירי, "lighting," with the Syriac. The former reading has something in its favor, it is true, but the phrases which immediately follow render the emendation probable. The reading מאזרי was very likely occasioned by the external resemblance between זקות, "brands," and זקים, "fetters" (see Prov. 26:18).

למעצבה, "in misery." The noun is an abstract; the construction with ל exactly as in לחלי, "in sickness," 1:5. *Cf.* also לאמת, 42:3.

CHAPTER 51:1–16

A composition lofty in tone and splendidly eloquent. No translation could do it justice. Unlike the most of its fellows, it is addressed to *the faithful* in Israel, men who were both religious and thoughtful but needed the encouragement which a great teacher could give them. They are the "followers of righteousness," those who "carry Yahwè's law in their hearts" (verses 1, 7). But their faith is not strong enough. Each one of them has fear for his own safety (verse 12; *cf.* Ps. 118:6, which is its counterpart), and all are troubled for the future of Zion (verse 3). As usual, the prophet's encouragement is addressed to the reason of his hearers. His argument is precisely the same which has been reiterated so often in the preceding poems. Since Yahwè, the one omnipotent God, has chosen Abraham and every one of his seed, doubt and fear are inexcusable. The men of Israel need therefore to be reminded, first, that they are indeed the children of Abraham and Sarah; and then, that Yahwè is indeed omnipotent. The prophet adds, moreover, the assurance of his own faith that the day of triumph is close at hand.

The Second Isaiah wrote not only as a prophet but also as a poet, and this is one of the poems in which his pride in the literary dress of his productions is evident. It is filled with high-sounding phrases and striking figures of speech. The passage verses 9–11, with its bold apostrophe to the "arm of Yahwè," its skilful use of popular mythology, its refrainlike reminiscence of a preceding poem (verse 11), and its effective changes of rhythm and meter (see the notes on verses 9 and 11), is perhaps as good a single illustration as we possess of the resources at the command of a Hebrew poet of the classical period. Another example of a refrain-like repetition is seen at the end of verses 6 and 8, with the phrase slightly varied for rhetorical effect. Poetical forms (תחולל, מחצבת, כמו כן, the imperfect ending in *ūn*) and constructions (inverted order, the ellipses in verse 1, etc.) abound. We have examples of assonance in verses 3, 8, 9 f., 11, and of the favorite repetition of a word with changed meaning in 5 (זרוע) and 6 f. (התת). The diction throughout is bold and free, and has made trouble for those commentators who have treated the composition as though it were a sermon in prose. And finally, as an example of the poet's art in the construction of his poems, this one is worthy of study. There is the favorite division into two parts by means of a rhapsodical intermezzo, and the brief summarizing conclusion (verses 15 f.). See also the note on verse 9. Beyond doubt, each one of the several paragraphs was carefully constructed, and its relation to the whole taken into account.

Verse 16 formed the original close of the poem; an entirely distinct composition begins with verse 17; see the introduction there. That 51 : 1–16 belongs to the same period of the prophet's literary activity as chapters 41–48, and, indeed, followed close upon them, is made probable both by the way in which it reiterates the material of the 'Great Argument,' and also by its use of the formula שמעו אלי, which is peculiar to the three chapters 46, 48, and 51; see the introduction to 46. The manner in which certain principal themes of 49 and 50 are plainly alluded to in verse 16 (see the note there) is further evidence that these poems were written down by their author in the order in which we now have them.

The text of the poem appears to have suffered hardly any change

from its original form. In several places the massoretic division is
wrong, and must be corrected.

———

The meter is 3 | 3, except in verses 9, 10, which afford a fine
example of the change to 3 | 2 for the sake of the dramatic effect.

———

51 : 1. "Listen to me"; the formula which seems to give chapters 46, 48, and 51 a certain mutual connection. See also 55 : 2.
The speaker is Yahwè.

צדק is "righteousness," with the same meaning as δικαιοσύνη
in Matt. 5 : 6: "they that hunger and thirst after righteousness."
It is not to be identified with the צדק of verse 5, but rather with
that of verse 7.

The ellipsis in the last two clauses of the verse is characteristic.
Compare the first clause of 48 : 21.

There is no reason for supposing that בור is a gloss on מקבת
(Duhm). Neither word is superfluous, metrically or logically, and
מקבת could not possibly have been misunderstood.

51 : 2. Duhm completely misunderstands the meaning of this
command: "Look to Abraham, *your father*." The prophet is not
trying to encourage his fellow countrymen by pointing them to
the example of a successful man (!); he is repeating once more the
argument which has filled chapters 40–49: what it means to be
the people chosen of Yahwè. The election of Abraham was a historical fact, which no one doubted; but there were not many whose
faith and reason could comprehend the true significance of this
fact for the scattered and scattering race—the "remnant"—as it
existed in the Persian period. The prophet is saying the very
same thing here that he said in 41 : 2; 42 : 6; and 48 : 14 f. The
figure of the stones taken from the quarry was undoubtedly a
commonplace of Hebrew literature; it could hardly have been
otherwise, in view of the multitude of stone-quarries all about
Jerusalem.

"Sarah who bore you"; the only reference to Sarah in all the
O. T., after the Book of Genesis. The form תחוללכם is hardly
right; read the perfect tense חוללתכם, with Grätz and others. The
verb is, of course, the same which was used in 45 : 10.

The meaning of the emphatic אחד (= לבדו), "him *only*," has
been quite generally misunderstood. The Second Isaiah is not

trying to encourage his people by setting before them an arith-
metical proportion; he is rather calling to their attention the absolute uniqueness of Israel in the sight of Yahwè. The One God
did not choose the Egyptians, or the Phœnicians, or the Persians;
he did not elect Rameses II, or Hiram of Tyre, or Nebuchadrezzar; he chose *only* Abraham and Israel, out of all the world. *Cf.*
43:3 f., Amos 3:2, etc. The position of אחד is manifestly emphatic; the construction is adverbial accus. We have the same
use of the word, in a precisely similar context, in I Chron. 29:1:
"Solomon, my son, whom *alone* (אחד) God hath chosen." Very
similar is the use of יחד in Ezra 4:3: "We, only, will build."

"I called him, and blessed him"; almost the same words in
48:15, where the argument is precisely the same. The last two
verbs are imperf. consecutive.

51:3. Duhm, Cheyne, and Marti, proceeding on the mistaken
theory that the meter of the poem is 3 | 2, and using their pro-
crustean bed the "strophe," sadly mutilate a considerable proportion of the verses in the chapter.

The כי is emphatic. The perfect tense (with the imperf. consec.
וישם) has the same meaning here as in so many other passages in
these poems; see the note on 44:22, for example. It is the strongest way of putting a prediction in Hebrew.

"Like Eden"; one of the numerous indications that the prophet
had read the Book of Genesis.

"The wilderness and the desert," "joy and gladness"; the same
phrases which were used in 35:1, 2, 10, where the picture of the
Messianic age which is only hinted at here is sketched in some
detail.

51:4. *Cf.* 34:1; 41:1; 49:1. With the "law" and the "light
of the peoples" *cf.* 42:4, 6.

The best thing to do with ארגיע is to make it the first word of
verse 5 (so the Greek), regarding it as an adjective, to which קרוב
is a later gloss. We have no other evidence of such a *hiphil* as this
would be; while the testimony as to the existence of the adjective
is quite conclusive.

If verse 4 is made to end with the word עמים, as seems necessary,
it is not possible, metrically, to retain both ארגיע and קרוב; nor
does it seem likely, from the structure of the verse, that both
adjectives were in the original text. It is not certain that the
Greek translates both, and the Syriac renders only one. קרוב was
probably added later, to explain the difficult word.

51:5. The Greek trans. makes a bad piece of work of this

verse. The ὡς φῶς in the first clause may have been derived from
the preceding verse, but perhaps more likely from Hos. 6:5
(LXX). In any case, it is secondary. The confusion in the following clauses is due to a common scribal blunder, occasioned by the
twofold occurrence of the same word. Our Hebrew text is sound
throughout.

With this characteristic use of צדק and ישע, compare 45:8;
58:8; 59:17; 61:1, as well as verses 6 and 8 in this chapter. יצא
as in 45:23. For the gender of ישפטו, compare, e. g., 17:5. With
the last two clauses of the verse compare 60:9; 42:4; and 53:1.

Notice how זרוע is used with two distinct meanings in this
verse, after the favorite manner of this writer. The first time it
has the literal meaning "arm"; namely, the arm which *subdues
and governs* (as in verse 9 f.); the second time, it is "help," as in
33:2, Ps. 83:9. *Cf.* the note on תחת in verse 6.

51:6. The precise meaning of נמלח is unknown, as the verb
occurs only here. There is no reason to suspect the text.

It is a pity to introduce *gnats* into the verse, as most modern
scholars do. The comparison would be very weak, and the rhythm
will not permit any lengthening of the word כן. What valid objection can be urged against כמו כן = "likewise," "gleichfalls"?
Thus all the old versions, and the Jewish tradition with one voice.
The word כן refers to the certain destruction of heavens and
earth, just predicted, and the expression is both logically and
formally correct. It is neither a 'pregnant expression' nor accompanied by a gesture (Luther, Delitzsch); but simply a natural way
of saying that, as the heavens and the earth are perishable, *just
so* shall mankind die and disappear. Grammatically, it is just as
unobjectionable as the Greek ὡσαύτως, Modern Arabic *mitl hek,*
Ethiopic *kamahu,* etc. The reason for the unusual lengthened
form appears from the context: it is in order to give added solem-
nity to this clause, which is brought in unexpectedly.

The alteration of תחת into תחדל is quite uncalled for. The appeal to "the LXX" in support of this change (Oort, Duhm, Klostermann, Ryssel, Cheyne, Marti) is a curious blunder. The translation ἐκλίπῃ corresponds exactly to the ἐκλείψει which renders
the same form יחת in 7:8 (where the translation must be: "Ephra-
im shall cease [lit., be broken off] from being a people"). That
this is a natural meaning for a passive stem of חתת, as of other
verbs meaning to "break, cut," and the like, it is hardly necessary
to argue. *Cf.* נשבר, אתפסק, Arabic *inqata‘,* and many others. Re-

garding the manner in which this same verb is employed in a
different signification at the end of the next verse, see page 202.

51 : 7. "Ye who know righteousness"; see the note on verse 1.
With the latter part of the verse compare verse 12 f., and also
65 : 13 f.

Regarding תתת, see the note on תחת in verse 6. The meaning
of the verb is not the same in the two passages.

51 : 8. *Cf.* 50 : 9. This poet's extraordinary fondness for repeating words and phrases ,whose sound he likes is excellently
illustrated in this verse.

51 : 9. Verses 9 and 10 are in the 3 | 2 meter. The effect is
plainly studied. The poem (verses 1–16) as a whole is in the didactic vein, but this sudden outburst illuminates it all like a flash
of lightning, the change of meter adding greatly to the effect. The
way to this short rhapsody had been prepared by the "repeated
clause which forms the end of verses 6 and 8, the first division of
the poem being thus brought to a manifest close. Similarly, the
transition to the last division of the poem (in tone quite like the
first) is very skilfully managed. Verse 11—one of the most beautiful in the book—is taken over by the prophet from the close of one
of his former poems (35 : 10); it thus has here almost the character of a refrain. It is of the three-beat structure, but is very closely
connected in thought with the verse preceding. We are thus
brought back to the main current of the poem without any sense
of interruption. A very similar case is 57 : 14.

The reason for the change of accent in עורי (at first with
stressed ultima, then, in the second line, with stressed penult) is
obviously the rhythm of the words which follow in either case.
The massoretic tradition certainly corresponds here with the intent of the author himself. *Cf.* Judges 5 : 12, and see Moore's
note there.

A very interesting bit of old Semitic mythology is introduced
here, the conflict of the Great God with the sea-monster variously
known as Tiamat, Rahab, and the Dragon. The Babylonian form
of the myth is now especially well known to us; see Jastrow, *Religion of Babylonia and Assyria*, s. v. "Tiamat." Among the Hebrews this was a familiar and probably much-used literary allusion, employed especially in highly poetical descriptions of the
power of God over the sea; as is obvious from Ps. 89 : 9 f., Job
26 : 12 f., and the present passage. That the myth should have
been used by poets in illustrating the deliverance from Egypt is
most natural; for that was the one occasion on which the supreme

power of Yahwè over the sea had been manifested in such a wonderful manner. *Cf.* 43:14–17. Hence, also, it happened that "Rahab" came to be used as a symbol of Egypt (but not in the present passage). Here the prophet begins with the mythical allusion, and passes over into the historical fact; it was, of course, merely for the sake of the latter that the myth was introduced. The way in which such properties as these were employed by the best Hebrew writers shows that they were not merely religious essayists, but men who wrote with a distinctly literary aim, using the materials at their command in very much the same way as they would be used by modern writers.

המחצבת is certainly not to be "emended." The meaning of חצב, "hew, cleave" (Is. 10:15), suits admirably, and even if this were not the case, the paronomasia with המחרבת, in the parallel line, would be conclusive, in view of the constant habit of the Second Isaiah. It was undoubtedly for the sake of this play on words that the *hiphil* was used here.

51:10. The whole verse, not merely the second half (Duhm), refers to the miracle of the Red Sea. Its waters were, of course, a part of the "waters of the great abyss (תהום)." With the "drying up" *cf.* 42:15; 50:2; and with the path through the waters, 43:16. On the word גאולים see the note on 48:20.

51:11. See the note on verse 9. This is an example of the effective repetition of a fine verse—one of which its author had reason to be proud. See the note on 35:10, where it first occurs.

51:12. Read מנחמך; the final ם came in by accident from the following word.

In the phrase "how is it that thou fearest?" the מי is probably not the personal interrogative pronoun, but a form of מֶה, מָה, "how?" The idiom is one which has hardly received sufficient attention from Hebrew grammarians. The best example of its use is Ruth 3:16: מִי אַתְּ בִּתִּי: "How has it fared with you, my daughter?" * Another example is Judges 18:8, מֶה אַתֶּם. In Hag. 2:16, מהיותם (Greek τίνες ἦτε) should be הֱיִיתֶם (or מֶה) מִי: "How fared it with you?" For this idiom compare not only the use of מה to mean "how," "why," and the "how are you?" found in so many languages, but also the vulgar Arabic *išak*, literally: "What are you?" It may be that the change from מה to מי was not merely

---

* The English Revised Version still translates: "Who art thou, my daughter?" !

phonetic, but was due more or less to the influence of the personal pronoun which immediately followed in the phrase. מִי for מַה, "how?" occurs elsewhere occasionally, as in Amos 7 : 2, 5.

With the second half of the verse *cf.* verse 7*b*. The way in which the return is now made to the theme with which the first half of the poem closed is further evidence of the care with which the whole was planned.

51 : 13. With עֹשֶׂךְ, "thy maker," *cf.* 46 : 4; 54 : 5. The phrase תָּמִיד כָּל הַיּוֹם occurs again in 52 : 5.

"Who stretched the heavens and founded the earth." Here, as everywhere else, the prophet's aim is not to increase the awe of his hearers before God, or to give them instruction as to his attributes, so much as to remind them that this is the God who has promised *to help them.* The Second Isaiah's mind dwelt far more on the need of his people than on any other subject.

The clause כַּאֲשֶׁר כּוֹנֵן לְהַשְׁחִית not only presents no difficulty, but adds greatly to the force of the whole passage. The oppressor *is determined to destroy.* Nevertheless, he is but *human,* and his prey shall be taken from him (*cf.* 49 : 24 f., which is an excellent parallel). Why כַּאֲשֶׁר should be called "schwerfällig" (Duhm) it would be difficult for any one to explain.

51 : 14. The failure to understand the word צֹעֶה in this verse caused the ancient translators a good deal of trouble. The same word occurs in 63 : 1 (there the result of text-corruption!), where it is descriptive of a mighty personage in a stern mood—*i. e.,* exactly the opposite of what is plainly required here. All of the old versions seem to have had that passage in mind, and translate accordingly, or refuse to translate at all, in the present verse. The Syriac, Latin, and Targum all render by the same word which is used in 63 : 1. In the Syr. and Lat. it is the mighty oppressor who is referred to; in the Targ. it is God ("the avenger"). The Greek translator throws the Hebrew overboard bodily, and substitutes his own guess; a proceeding which is paralleled in numerous other places, and is characteristic of the somewhat hasty and irresponsible manner of this version. The root meaning of צָעָה, "to bow, bend down" (see Ges.-Buhl), is just what is required here. The use is figurative.

For נִפְתַּח, "to be released," compare Jer. 1 : 14, and the occasional use of the active stems to mean "liberate" (*qal,* Is. 14 : 17; *piel,* Jer. 40 : 4, Ps. 102 : 21; 105 : 20).

שַׁחַת for the "pit of death," as often; *cf.* especially Job 33 : 22, 24, 28, 30. For the pregnant construction, לֹא יָמוּת לַשַּׁחַת, "he shall not die [and go down] to the pit," *cf.* Ps. 74 : 7; 89 : 40; Cant. 7 : 13.

The conclusion of this verse is of course a climax: The "oppressor" (the term used in the most general way, as in the Psalms) will have no power to hurt the righteous who trust in God; they have no need to fear the violent death with which he threatens them, *nor will they even be brought to want* (*cf.* Ps. 34 : 11; 37 : 25).

51 : 15. It may be doubted whether the conjunction at the beginning of the verse is original. It is unnecessary, and ו is the last letter of the preceding word.

The latter part of the verse, from רגע on, is repeated in Jer. 31 : 35.

Yahwè speaks of himself in the third person, as in verse 1, and very often elsewhere.

51 : 15, 16. Duhm, Cheyne, and Kittel's *Biblia Hebraica* make sad work of the meter of these verses, printing them as though they were prose. For what reason? There is no passage in the book in which the metrical division is more regular or more obvious. Even the Massorites have marked it off correctly.

51 : 16. This is one of the passages that show most unequivocally what the prophet ordinarily had in mind when he wrote of 'the Servant.' It was the actual people, with all its imperfection and in spite of its humiliated condition. Hence the repetition here of phrases which had been used in the poems just preceding to describe the training of the Servant for his mission; see 49 : 2; 50 : 4, 10, and observe how the same thing is said again in 59 : 21. These two closing verses, 15 and 16, put in a nutshell the ground of Israel's confidence: *Yahwè, the omnipotent God, has chosen and trained this people to do a great work for him.*

Read לנטות (so the Syr.); *cf.* verse 13. The writing of ע in place of ת was a mere bit of carelessness. Duhm has a very curious explanation of the form. For the construction here, and the use of this infinitive with ל, which has been strangely misunderstood, see Ges.-Kautzsch, 114, *o*. It is the construction whose most familiar example is the omnipresent לאמר (also in this verse); and it should be observed that the intent of the clause (verse 16*b*) is to repeat with emphasis what has just been said in another form in verses 15, 16*a*. It is none other than Yahwè, the creator and ruler of the world, who has chosen Israel. *Cf.* 42 : 5, 6; 44 : 24, and the other passages where the 'founding of the world' and the call of Israel are put side by side.

The use of "Zion" for the people of Israel is to be observed.

CHAPTERS 51 : 17–52 : 12

This is a poem of singular beauty and great power. The poet writes in the tender strain which he always assumes when he is addressing personified Jerusalem. As in 40 : 2 he had said that she had already paid double for all her sins, so here he declares that she has drained to the dregs the cup of Yahwè's wrath, and need never drink it again. It is not so much that the holy city has suffered to the limit of her endurance, as that Yahwè himself can remain silent no longer, but must act for his own name's sake. The herald of freedom is close at hand; the shackles of sin and disgrace are soon to be stricken from her neck, and she will rise from the dust and sit in glory surpassing that of old. As the promise reaches its climax the poet suddenly, and in a most dramatic manner, strikes the old familiar note (52 : 11 f.): Remember the deliverance from Egypt! This way of bringing the poem to a close is so peculiarly the property of the Second Isaiah, and of such value as a specimen of his literary art, that it deserves close attention.

In manner, as in subject-matter, this poem is quite different from 51 : 1–16. From beginning to end it is an almost constant succession of figures of speech, in which the poet's restless and splendid imagination appears at its best. 51 : 1–16 was generally didactic and deliberative, but this poem is impetuous and impassioned throughout. On the other hand, the formal resemblance between 51 : 9 and 51 : 17; 52 : 1 may fairly be claimed as a bit of evidence (slight in itself, but not to be ignored) that the two poems were written at about the same time and probably in this same order. In all its leading ideas, moreover, this present composition is a piece cut from the very same cloth as its predecessors. Compare 51 : 17, 22; 52 : 1, 2 with 40 : 2; 52 : 7 with 40 : 9; 51 : 19–22 with 42 : 22 ff.; 43 : 28; 49 : 19; 52 : 3 with 45 : 13; 50 : 1; 52 : 5 with 43 : 25; 48 : 11; and 52 : 6 with 43 : 10 and the other similar passages which are characteristic of the "Great Argument." And finally, it is to be observed that 51 : 17–52 : 12 is in some respects the evident antithesis of chapter 47, as Duhm (on 52 : 1 f.) and others have noticed. All the indications point to the conclusion that the series of closely related poems which has been shown to include 40–51 : 16 included also 51 : 17–52 : 12.

Metrically the poem has some interesting features. The meter is uniformly 3 | 2 up to the last two verses, which are plainly 3 | 3.

See the note on 52 : 12, and the introductory remarks on the meter
of chapter 47. The proportion of three-member (3 | 2 | 3) lines
is noticeable; the examples are 51 : 22; 52 : 3, 6, 7. In the three
last-named cases the line in question forms the close of a paragraph or logical division of the poem; see page 158.

---

51 : 17. "Arouse thyself !" The same stem of the verb is again
used by the poet in 64 : 6. In both passages the idea of *a call to
duty* is present. Neither in this poem nor in any of the others of
the collection does it appear that the prophet has in mind chiefly
the material prosperity of Jerusalem. He is longing to see her
fit to be, in fact as well as in name, *the holy city*, the city of Yahwè.

"The cup of intoxication"; *cf.* סַף רַעַל, Zech. 12 : 2, and the
phrase "wine of intoxication" (only other occurrence of the Hebrew word) in Ps. 60 : 5.

For the meaning of the verse, *cf.* 50 : 2; 59 : 16; 63 : 5, and the
powerful arraignment of Israel in 59 : 1–15. "How is the faithful
city become a harlot !" 1 : 21.

As recent commentators have generally recognized, כּוֹס is a
gloss defining the rare word קֻבַּעַת. So also in verse 22.

"Thou hast drained it to the dregs"; *cf.* 40 : 2.

51 : 18. An excellent example of the dramatic imagination
which so often appears in these poems. Duhm's note on the verse
shows how completely he has misunderstood it in all particulars:
meaning, meter, relation to the context, and the intent of the
whole passage.

51 : 19. "These *two* ills," while *four* appear to be enumerated.
We have in reality two pairs, the former referring to ethical and
the latter to material conditions, as the comparison of this writer's
use of the same phrase שֹׁד וָשֶׁבֶר, "rapine and ruin," in 59 : 7 and
60 : 18 seems to make certain. "These two things," then, are:
first, moral decay, and, *second*, outward distress. As for the latter couplet, "famine and sword," it is of course not necessary to
suppose that Jerusalem was actually engaged in war, or suffering
from famine at that very time—though this may well have been
the case; such standing phrases are freely used in imaginative
poetry. In שֹׁד וָשֶׁבֶר we have the usual paronomasia.

The participle קְרֹאתַיִךְ is of course not to be translated by a
single past tense. Render either "have been [constantly] coming
upon thee," or, better (*cf.* verse 20), "are [now] upon thee." In
any case, the prophet has primarily in view present conditions,

and is speaking of the Jerusalem of his own day. There is no other natural interpretation. That the 'Babylonian exile' is altogether out of view here is sufficiently obvious.

Read at the end of the verse ינחמך. There is no grammatical difficulty in the massoretic text, for מי might be the adverb "how?"; see the note on 51 : 12; but the first person is very unlikely here, and all of the old versions render the third person. It seems probable that our text gives us a double reading, occasioned perhaps by 66 : 13.

51 : 20. "They are fallen down fainting"; compare Amos 8 : 13. Duhm (followed by Cheyne and Marti) is certainly right in regarding "at the head of all the streets" as a later addition derived from Lam. 2 : 19; 4 : 1.

The figure is a forcible one, and the text quite unobjectionable after the excision of the clause just mentioned. Here, again, as in the preceding verse, the conditions are present, not past.

With the latter half of the verse *cf.* 66 : 15*b*.

51 : 21. The impossible and hitherto unexplained pointing of וּשְׁכֻרַת is the result of combining two readings. One manuscript tradition had וְשִׁכְרָה וְגו׳; the other (probably the original) had the reading וּשְׁכֻרַת לֹא מִיָּיִן; the terse form of expression for the sake of the meter. This wider use of the construct state is perfectly idiomatic, *cf.* 14 : 6; 28 : 9, etc. A remarkably close parallel from the Syriac is the phrase "born without connection" cited by Nöldeke in his *Grammar*, § 206.

51 : 22. Observe how the writer, in repeating the expressions "cup of wrath" and "cup of intoxication" from verse 17, changes their form. For other examples of this rhetorical device, see verses 6, 8, in this chapter, 46 : 2, etc.

The second כוס is a gloss, as in verse 17; see the note there. The text of the verse is otherwise sound, and the metrical division altogether regular.

51 : 23. The first clause is a good example of the 'isolated' three-beat line in a 3 | 2 poem. The Greek has a double translation of מוגיך; one of many similar cases in this version.

In לנפשך the word נפש seems to be used simply for the sake of the meter.

With the whole verse *cf.* 53 : 3, and what was said of the Servant in 50 : 6.

52 : 1. There is no break here. The poem goes on without in-

terruption, in the same strain. On the chapter division at this
point see the introduction to 42.

עוּרִי; on the accent see the note on 51 : 9. We should have
expected to see also קוּמִי in 51 : 17 accented on the last syllable.

"There shall no longer enter thee the uncircumcised and the
unclean"; the promise so often made by the later prophets and
psalmists. *Cf.* 35 : 8, and Joel 3 : 17, Ob. 17. This means simply:
Jerusalem will be pure and holy, the abode of upright and God-
fearing men; not foul and wicked, as it is at present. (Obviously
our poet is addressing a city that is builded and peopled, not a
heap of ruins.) The sentence has in it no hatred of Gentiles, nor
does it express a wish that Jerusalem may be reserved for the
Jews only; see on the contrary 60 : 11 and the many similar passages. J. H. Michaelis and his fellows were right in interpreting
עָרֵל here as *præputiatus corde.*

52 : 2. Read שְׁבִיָּה in the first line, as in the second. It does not
seem possible to explain שְׁבִי as an intentional variation of the
form. It is, on the contrary, the result of incorporating *a variant
MS. reading.*

The "captivity" of Jerusalem is figurative. The "bonds on
her neck" are all those things which keep her from her rightful
place: her moral and spiritual degradation, the humiliation of the
Jews in the world, and the contempt and ill-treatment which they
receive at the hands of all their neighbors (verse 5, etc.). There
are passages in which the prophet's use of figurative language (the
road through the desert; streams in the wilderness; return of the
faithful to Jerusalem; and so on) might easily be misunderstood;
here, however, it might well seem to be absolutely unmistakable.
But no, the theory of 'the prophet of the Babylonian exile' has
such a hold that some commentators see here allusions to literal
captivity. Duhm, for example, finds the expression "captive
Jerusalem" difficult, "weil Zion eigentlich nicht exiliert ist," and
finally concludes that we have here "eine kühne poetische Erset-
zung des Volkes durch die Stadt."

52 : 3. "Ye were sold for naught, and ye shall be redeemed
without money"; the same expressions, used with just the same
meaning, in 50 : 1 and 45 : 13.

Here is another example of the 3 | 2 | 3 line. In this case it
stands at the close of a section, as often elsewhere.

52 : 4. This verse is a gloss, the purpose of which was to interpret "for nought" in verse 3. It is prosaic in both matter and
form, besides interrupting the connection of thought. Notice

especially the word "Asshur," for the Babylonians; *cf.* Ezra 6:22, etc. There is certainly reason to doubt whether even this glossator had ever heard the Chronicler's theory of the "exile." Had he done so (and believed it) he could hardly have expressed himself in this way.

52:5, 6. A fine passage, in the prophet's most vigorous style. 42:22–24 is a good parallel.

52:5. It is obvious that the *second* "saith the Lord" is not original. No metrical division of the verse is possible while it remains in the text; without it everything is in order.

"And now, what do I here?" a characteristic turn. "Here" (פֹה), that is, in the present situation. "Their rulers"; compare especially 49:7 and 42:22. All the nations of the earth had trodden them under foot.

The word יְהֵילִילוּ, "howl, wail," is of course out of place here. Notice, however, that the Targum (משתבחין) and probably Aquila read the word in the form יהללו.* It is, in fact, to be read יְהַלֵּלוּ, a verb used to describe the insolent folly of godless men. *Cf.* Ps. 10:3, observing how in this latter passage also the verb is used in parallelism with נִאֵץ יהוה. The *piel* is stronger than the *qal*, which occurs in Ps. 5:6; 73:3; 75:5. The form in our massoretic text is the result of intentional alteration, brought about by the fact that the *piel* הלל is used in the O. T. almost exclusively of praising God. See the notes on 41:21; 45:16; 48:5; and *cf.* especially the similar twist given by the Massorites in 14:12 (Gray's *Commentary*, p. 257, middle). The fact that the word was thus disfigured affords the best of evidence that it was from the first written and pronounced as a *piel*.

With the phrase תמיד כל היום *cf.* 51:13. At the end of the verse we should probably point מְנֹאָץ, comparing 60:14. The massoretic punctuation apparently intends a ת— reflexive stem: "permits itself to be profaned."

52:6. The לכן, "therefore, because of this very thing," is strongly emphatic, and its repetition was deliberate. The fact that the old versions render it but once does not deserve to be given any weight.

"That I am he"; *cf.* 41:4; 43:25; one of the prophet's favorite phrases.

Here, again, we have the 3 | 2 | 3 line; and this time also (as in verse 3) it forms the close of a section.

* See Field, *Origenis Hexapl.*, ii, p. 531, note 13.

For the meaning of this verse, *cf.* 42 : 24 f.; 43 : 26 ff.; and 48 : 10.
How could I suffer my people to be oppressed? It was in order
that they might know me better! A fine passage, worthy of this
poet.

52 : 7. The first part of the verse is borrowed by the writer of
Nah. 2 : 1, who probably cited it from memory. Compare with
this picture the similar ones in 40 : 3, 9.

52 : 8. With the "watchmen" compare especially 62 : 6, but
also 56 : 10.

צִיּוֹן, at the end of the verse, is the direct object of שׁוּב (*cf.*
Ps. 85 : 5, etc.), not the limit of motion. The idea of a return of
Yahwè to Zion is altogether foreign to the writer's thought, here
and elsewhere.

52 : 10. It is possible that the word "Yahwè" is secondary
here.

"In the sight of all the nations," the idea so essential to the
prophet's argument, and which he repeats so often.

52 : 11, 12. This sudden and dramatic outburst, which forms
the *coda* of the poem, is as characteristic of the Second Isaiah's
art as anything in the book. Compare especially 48 : 20 f.; also
57 : 14; 62 : 10; 51 : 9, and the many similar passages.

Although the whole poem, up to this point, has been in the
3 | 2 meter, we plainly have in these verses four 3 | 3 couplets.
This is accordingly an interesting example of the poet's manner
of combining the two metric forms. See the note on the meter
of chapter 47.

It has been customary, because of the Cyrus interpolations and
the thereby necessitated theory of the 'exilic prophecy,' to regard
this passage as summoning the Jews in Babylon to escape. It is
on the contrary one of the poet's flash-light pictures of *the flight
from Egypt*—exactly like 48 : 20; see the note there, and the evidence adduced below.

52 : 11. There is the same room for doubt here as in 48 : 20
whether the address is to the prophet's own hearers or to the
imaginary audience, the Hebrews escaping from Egypt. Here, also,
the former alternative seems more likely. מִשָּׁם, "thence," really
means "from this *modern* Egyptian bondage," the favorite comparison which appears again and again in these poems. See the
notes on 43 : 16; 48 : 20 f.; 51 : 10. The word שָׁם shows that the
writer is looking away, in imagination, to Egypt, and all that follows indicates plainly the same thing. The injunction "Touch
naught unclean!" contains an allusion to the symbolism of the

unleavened bread (leaven = corruption) eaten by the Israelites before their departure, as well as to the fact that they were going out *to worship Yahwè*, whence the mention of the cultus utensils in the next clause. See Ex. 12 : 15, 19; 13 : 3, 7. The phrase צאו מתוך is taken from the story of the Exodus (Ex. 12 : 31), and חפזון, verse 12, is from the same chapter (Ex. 12: 11). The allusion to Egypt is so constantly present in the poet's mind, and he could so certainly count on his hearers to understand it, that he simply uses a suffix in בתוכה.

It has long been customary to interpret the כלי יהוה as the temple vessels carried away to Babylon by Nebuchadrezzar, and (according to the Chronicler) restored by Cyrus. But Duhm interprets here correctly, explaining כלי יהוה as "die zum Opferdienst nötigen Gegenstände," and saying that the prophet is expressing himself "nach Analogie des mosaischen Zuges."

52 : 12. "The God of Israel is your rear-guard"; see Ex. 14 : 19. The comparison of 58 : 8 is interesting, both as showing in what a figurative manner all this 'Messianic' restoration was conceived and as an example of this poet's habit of dwelling on his own words.

CHAPTERS 52 : 13–53 : 12

This is a composition which no thoughtful student of history can read without a feeling of awe. It is the most wonderful bit of religious poetry in all literature. The ideas out of which it is built—so broad and high, and filled with a spirit which is at once fervid and catholic—are such as no other ancient religious philosophy ever equalled. Written in the age of Plato and Aristotle, and appearing in the middle of a civilization which may already have been somewhat influenced by that of Greece, though in most respects inferior to it, it is truly Israelite in its atmosphere and yet universal in its tone, written with deep sympathy for the whole human brotherhood. It is the prophet's conception of the plan through which the God of all the world designs to reclaim his erring children of every race and region. With all its originality, it is the legitimate fruit of that marvellous religious development which produced the Hebrew scriptures.

The Second Isaiah does not 'surpass himself' in this effort, he merely presents a feature of his theological scheme which happens not to appear elsewhere; a most noble feature, *Israel's atonement for the Gentiles*. Though in perfect harmony with all that he has

written, it stands in a manner by itself, and could not have been
inferred if he had left it unexpressed. No one could have dared
even to suggest it as probable. That it is once clearly stated is
thus a piece of good fortune for which the world is incalculably
richer. Now we know with certainty what heights this Hebrew
theologian and philosopher had reached in his thinking.

The prophet is here looking into the future, as usual, and his
prediction is in the main the same with which we are so familiar.
It is new, nevertheless, as will appear from the following statement
of its underlying thought. The nation will not be done with toil
and suffering even when it has atoned for its own grievous sin,
but will continue to be afflicted, this time not for its own sake but
for the sake of others. Understanding at last Yahwè's plan for
the Gentiles, it will voluntarily take upon itself the punishment
which they have merited. When this has been done, the "Salvation of God" (always conceived as the salvation of *both* Jews and
Gentiles) can be realized. The nations will understand and acknowledge what Israel has done for them, and will turn to Yahwè.
The faithful people will be exalted in proportion as it had been
humbled.

During a considerable part of the poem this work of atonement
is spoken of as though it had already taken place. But this is
merely due to the literary dress. The prophet follows his usual
custom in taking his stand, in imagination, at the point when the
redemption of the world is an accomplished fact. The speakers
whom he introduces in the passage 53 : 1–9 are represented as
looking back from the time of Israel's final triumph to the time
when it was still afflicted. In the other parts of the poem, where
Yahwè is the speaker, the atoning work is represented as yet to
be done.

This is all set forth in abundant and striking imagery. The figure of the 'Servant of Yahwè' is again introduced, and it is he who
dominates the whole poem, which is really a portrait. Literature
can show no other bit of imaginative painting equal to this majestic picture of a suffering redeemer, standing alone in the world,
patiently enduring chastisement for the sake of his fellows. The
personification is startlingly real; nevertheless, the Servant in this
case is not the imaginary *representative* of Israel, the Messiah, but
rather the nation itself, as it is to be. In other words, it is the
Servant of chapter 50, rather than of 45 : 1, 4 and 49 : 5, that we
meet here. See further the Chapter on the Servant and the Messiah.

As often happens in these poems, the principal theme is given out at once, in the opening verses. The comparison with 42:1 is interesting. There the announcement was: "Behold my Servant, *on whom I rely*," and the sequel described the Servant's mission and the work he was to do for Yahwè. Here it is: "Behold my Servant, *who shall be lifted up*," and the theme is, the Servant's patient endurance of toil and suffering, and its reward. Chapter 42 was entitled "The Great Contrast," and the same title would be suitable here, though the contrast is an altogether different one. There it was the contrast between the glorious task and the wretchedly inadequate performance of it by Israel; here the contrast is between the despised, downtrodden people, chastised by God, and the Israel who has "turned to Yahwè" (44:22) and thus at last been enabled to fulfil his great mission.

The formal statement of this theme occupies the first three verses (52:13-15). The main body of the poem, which is conceived in somewhat dramatic form, as usual, begins with 53:1. In 52:14, 15 the prophet had indicated both the depth of the misery and the height of the exaltation of Israel by describing their effect on the Gentile beholders. So now he develops this idea at length, in a most effective manner. The heathen potentates (52:15) are introduced as the speakers, and themselves tell how little they had regarded this weak and stricken people, and how they have now seen and "understood" (*ibid.*) its exaltation to the leadership of the world. They now recognize in all this "the arm of Yahwè," and testify that it was his plan, from first to last. This is a picture which the prophet has painted before (45:14, where also the heathen are introduced as the speakers, and say much the same thing; *cf.* 49:23), and to which he returns again (60:9-14; 66:20 ff.). In the present case, however, the side which is presented and the details which are dwelt on are such as to render the scene and its effect quite unique. Here the Gentile rulers are made to describe at length the distress and humiliation of Israel, and his apparent inferiority to all his fellows. Obviously, no other witness of these things could describe them in so striking a way. Israel was insignificant and despised, he was afflicted beyond all others (verses 2, 3). Even his god seemed to have nothing but chastisement for him (4*b*). What little authority and prosperity he had once acquired was plucked away from him, and his day seemed to be over; he was as one cut off from the land of the living (8). Men watched for his death, and were ready to bury him ignobly, along with common criminals (9*a*). Nevertheless, even his enemies were impressed, all along, with his fortitude and his uprightness. They saw with wonder how patiently he bore his distresses, the maltreatment of men and the punishment of God (7). And this testimony of the Gentiles closes with the unreserved confession, that "he had done no violence, nor was any deceit in his mouth" (9*b*).

There is one other feature of this Gentile tribute, and that the most important feature of all, which remains to be noticed, namely, its remarkable utterances concerning the relation which the sufferings of the Servant bear to his mission. The woes are not merely disciplinary, they are *efficacious for the salvation of the foreign peoples*. This idea is reiterated with emphasis not only in the speech of the heathen rulers (verses 5, 6, 8), but also in the closing section (verses 10, 11, 12) where Yahwè is the speaker. Taken together with its counterpart, the promised reward, it forms the true subject of the poem.

The purified nation is to "bear the sufferings and carry the sorrows" of its fellows (verse 4). This does not mean merely that Israel will be "purified in the furnace of affliction" (48:10), and thus made fit to accomplish the great work assigned to it; nor does it mean simply that the nation, by patiently enduring its own well-deserved punishment, enables Yahwè to carry out his plan for the world; the prophet says plainly and emphatically that the Servant is to endure chastisement *in the stead* of the Gentiles, the punishment of *their* sin against Yahwè. It is a truly vicarious suffering that is intended; there is no other natural way of understanding the words. "He was wounded for our transgressions" (verse 5); "Yahwè . . . required of him the guilt of us all" (6); "For the sin of each one of us, smitten was he" (8); "His life shall be made an offering for sin" (10). This of course involves no contradiction with the idea, so prominent elsewhere in Second Isaiah, that Israel's sufferings have been, and are still, the punishment of its own sin. It is of something quite different that the prophet is thinking here. The passages just cited plainly imply a chastisement which is over and above that which the nation's own guilt has merited. This is also the case in 53:12: "He was numbered with the transgressors"; and again: "Because he poured out his life . . . and made intercession for the transgressors," where the implication is that the work of atonement was voluntarily assumed. Israel need not have submitted to this plan, but might have renounced Yahwè and thrown in its lot with the surrounding peoples. But it chose to remain faithful and to bear the load; compare especially 50:5–7. See further the notes below.

That which brings the Gentiles to Yahwè is not the moral effect of Israel's behavior, strong though that ultimately is. There is true substitution. They are healed with his stripes, and his chastisement makes them whole (verse 5). When at last Israel triumphs, and the Servant "dashes mountains in pieces," tramples on kingdoms, and forces all the Gentile world to submission (41 : 2, 15; 45 : 1; 50 : 9, etc.), the erstwhile enemies of the chosen people will see and acknowledge the one true God and turn to him (52 : 15; 49 : 7; 45 : 6, 14; 59 : 19; 60 : 14; 66 : 21, 23). He will accept them, for their penance has been accomplished, and they will share in the blessings of the Messianic age.

As was remarked above, nearly all of the features of this scheme of the redemption of the world are repeated over and over again in Second Isaiah; only the vicarious atonement is unique. Several passages approach the idea very nearly; especially 50 : 5–7, where it is probable that the writer had in mind the very same picture which he portrays in chapter 53. Observe how in 50 : 5 f. the Servant says that when Yahwè revealed to him his plan, he did not refuse to comply (*as he might have done*), but gave his back to the smiters.

The limits of the poem are certain; 52 : 13 was the original beginning, and 53 : 12 the end. The poem is complete, and there is no reason to doubt that every line is in its original place. Nevertheless, the reading presents unusual difficulties; so great, in fact, that many scholars have pronounced the text of certain verses incurably corrupt. In 53 : 8–11, especially, the most of the phrases have an 'improbable' sound, and it is easy to conclude that accidents of transmission have considerably altered the Hebrew. But the justice of this judgment is more than questionable. There are two facts to be borne in mind. The first is, that a small obstruction may cause great disturbance in such a text as this. The other is, that in any extended passage in regard to whose textual soundness the confidence of scholars has once been shaken, words and constructions seem improbable which under other circumstances would cause little or no difficulty. A few passages here must be emended, it is true, but the changes necessary are slight and obvious. When they have been made, we have before us a text which, though not without its difficulties, is by no means improbable. Metrically, it is to be observed, there is the utmost regularity. Every line is well marked and musical, and this very part of the poem consists of an unbroken series of divisions of four lines each. Nor does any line or clause, so far as its meaning is obvious, contain anything incongruous; on the contrary, the ideas are all in

place and in their natural order. It is only the mode of expression
that is troublesome. The language sounds obscure, and' the
phrases are not such as are ordinarily used. But by what right
do we limit such a man and such a poem to phrases which are
ordinarily used? Why not accord to him the freedom, and postulate for him the methods, of other great writers? In both ancient
and modern times poets conscious of writing upon lofty and unusual themes have chosen language to correspond, not the phraseology of ordinary narrative and conversation. The text as here
emended contains no form or construction which goes contrary to
even our limited knowledge of Hebrew grammar, while no one
with an ear for poetry will deny that it is high-sounding throughout. And it must be remembered that we are dealing with the
most original, and the most untrammelled, of all the Hebrew
writers; one who had at his command all the resources of the
language, and loved to go his own way. For my own part, I believe that the text which I have translated differs but very slightly,
if at all, from that which was originally written.

The poem is not strophic, that is, made up of a regular series of
stanzas each containing a given number of metric lines. It is
necessary to say this with some emphasis because of the prevailing
custom of dividing this and most other Hebrew poems into stanzas
of four lines.

There could be no more effective rebuke of this vicious proceeding than is furnished by Is. 53. The two principal divisions in the
poem are at 53:1 and 12, marking off the introduction and the
conclusion, respectively, from the body of the composition. In
the former case there is even a very striking dramatic transition,
introducing new speakers and an altogether unexpected scene.
The heathen nations come upon the stage, and with the exclamation "Who had believed what we report?" begin their amazing
testimony. In either case, the paragraph-division is concealed, in
some of the most widely read modern translations, in the middle
of one of the manufactured "stanzas," with great detriment to
the poem as a result.

The meter of the poem is 3 | 3. The rhythm is unusually smooth
and regular, leaving often the impression of a truly syllabic meter.
A certain strophic symmetry in the body of the poem also witnesses to the care with which it was constructed. In 53:2–11 we
have a continuous series of four-line stanzas; more or less uncon-

sciously formed, no doubt (see page 178). The frequent use of rhyme in this poem has been noticed in the Chapter on Metric Forms. The examples are: 1 and 2*a*; 2*b* (emending the punctuation); 5*a*; 6*a*; 6*b* (emended); 9*a* (?); 12, middle. The Massorites have in several places divided wrongly.

---

52 : 13.   A *verb* יַשְׂכִּיל is impossible here. The main thought of this opening verse, which is at the same time the key-note of the poem which follows, is: *Behold, my Servant shall be exalted,* הִנֵּה עַבְדִּי יָרוּם; and if any other idea is substituted or inserted, the introduction is ruined. The testimony to יַשְׂכִּיל is flawless; all the ancient versions render it. To omit the word, as Duhm does, without attempting to explain it, is anything but a critical procedure. To pronounce it a corruption of יִשְׂרָאֵל (Budde, Marti) is to adopt a most improbable conjecture. יַשְׂכִּיל might easily be corrupted into יִשְׂרָאֵל, but not *vice versa*.

It is a proper name, *Yaskil*, The Wise One, which is intended here, in all probability. This is one of the prophet's own poetical designations of Israel, the Servant; similar to *Meshullam*, the Perfected One, 42 : 19 (see the note there), and *Yeshurun*, 44 : 2. Like the latter, it was chosen partly because of its resemblance to the name יִשְׂרָאֵל; see the note on 44 : 2.

יָרוּם *belongs to the first member of the verse, not to the second.* The collocation of three synonymous verbs in one half-verse would be clumsy; and parallelism is to be expected, especially in the opening couplet of such a masterpiece of poetry as this. The Greek translator follows his usual custom in not attempting to render all of the synonymous words.

52 : 14.   "At thee" is evidently the result of a copyist's error. Read עָלָיו, with Syr. and many scholars. With the phrase "were dismayed at him" *cf.* Ezek. 28 : 19.

We must restore כִּי, "for, because," in place of כֵּן. The latter reading arose through a very natural mistake, the scribe expecting it at once, whereas it really should not appear until verse 15. Observe now the perfect correspondence of verses 14 and 15, the main clauses introduced by כַּאֲשֶׁר and כֵּן, and the subordinate clauses (giving the reason for the emotion) by כִּי.

The curious vocalization of the word מִשְׁחַת (!) certainly was intended by the Massorites, as in a multitude of similar instances all through the Old Testament (very few in the Pentateuch, how-

ever), to call attention to evidence of *variant readings*. It may be
conjectured that in this case the readings intended to be kept in
sight were (1) the *nif'al* participle, נִשְׁחָת, and (2) the *hof'al* participle, מָשְׁחָת. The former, from its use elsewhere, seems more likely
to have been the original reading. The following word, מֵאִישׁ, is
quite correct as it stands (*cf.* Prov. 30 : 2).

52 : 15. The difficulties of the first clause are well known. The
most thorough discussion of the passage is that by Moore, in the
Journal of Bibl. Lit., 1890, pp. 216–222, whose conjecture יִרְגְּזוּ
(Jer. 33 : 9) I have adopted. The difficulty is hardly solved, however, by simply substituting ירגזו for יזה. The noun גוים is not
required here, and the parallelism would be more satisfactory
without it. The original reading was probably כן ירגזו רבים עליו,
the meaning of רַבִּים being "mighty ones," the "great" among
men, as in 53 : 12 (in this same poem), Job 35 : 9, Jer. 41 : 1, etc.
If we suppose a scribe to have made the easy mistake of writing
יורגו, the further corruption of this meaningless group of letters
into יזה גוים would not be difficult to understand. In the double
use of רבים ("many" in verse 14, "great ones" in verse 15) we
have the favorite literary habit. עליו belongs of course to the
first clause of the verse, not to the second.

The signification of the second half of the verse is twofold:
first, that the foreign princes and peoples saw with their own
eyes this marvellous transformation of Israel's condition; and
again, that they had been in no wise prepared for it. This was a
thing the like of which they had never been told, such as they
had never heard. If it had been predicted to them, they would
not have believed it, as is implied in 53 : 1: "Who would have
believed what we (now) report?"

With the whole verse compare especially 49 : 7.

53 : 1. The poet, always thoroughly dramatic, begins a new
division of his poem here. With this verse the speaker changes
and the whole scene shifts; from this point on, through verse 9, the
Servant is described by the nations, who had been looking on in
wonder (as the preceding verse has just said). The conception is
a fine one, and altogether characteristic. Only heroic devotion to
a theory—in this case the theory of 'strophes of four lines'—could
lead any one to make a single 'stanza' by plastering together 53 : 1
and 52 : 15*b*, as Cheyne has done. The effect is most painful.

The perfect tense הֶאֱמִין expresses the supposed result of an un-
fulfilled condition: Who *would have* believed? An exactly similar

case is Gen. 21 : 7, ‏מי מלל‎: "Who would have said?" There is no need to carry on the construction to ‏נגלתה‎, which is better regarded as expressing simple past time.

‏שמועה‎ means the trustworthy "report" of things ascertained, as often elsewhere. Its meaning here is fully explained by 52 : 15b.

53 : 2. For ‏לפניו‎ we must read ‏לפנינו‎, which many scholars have preferred.

Marti writes: "Mit Bertholet ist ‏ולא הדר‎, *das sich durch das Fehlen des* ‏לו‎ *als Erklärung zu* ‏לא תאר‎ *ausweist, zu tilgen.*" Thus Hebrew grammar and style are made to count for nothing. The italics are mine.

The word ‏ונראהו‎ is not to be joined to the following clause (massoretic punctuation, and most translations), but to the preceding (with Symmachus). So parallelism, rhythm, and grammatical construction decide. To omit it (Duhm, Cheyne) is quite unjustifiable. The line, with this word included, is by no means unusually long.

53 : 3. There is no need to insert ‏הוא‎ at the beginning of the verse; why not let the prophet write in his own style? Even in prose the omission of the pronominal subject in a participial clause is permissible. *Cf.* the last clause of this same verse, and see Ges.-Kautzsch, § 116, *s.*

There is no real difficulty in the words ‏חדל אישים‎. This plural form occurs elsewhere (Ps. 141 : 4, Prov. 8 : 4), and the meaning of the phrase is assured by the context. Some commentators have thought ‏אישים‎ improbable here because ‏איש‎ follows immediately; but that is precisely the reason why the prophet chose this form, following his strong preference for such assonances and direct repetitions. In Ges.-Buhl, s. v. ‏חָדֵל‎, the expression is rendered: "auf menschliche Gesellschaft Verzicht leistend," but this rendering is quite out of the question; not even a second-rate poet would have written such a weak phrase. This ‏חֲדַל‎ is the construct state of a verbal adjective with *passive* signification, "left alone." The form is quite regular—in fact, the only possible one—inasmuch as ‏חדל‎ is an originally stative verb (‏חָדֵל‎). Just as in the second member of the couplet ‏איש מכאבות‎ is synonymous with ‏ידוע חלי‎, so in this first member ‏נבזה‎ and ‏חדל אישים‎ are equivalent in meaning.

‏ידוע‎, "*acquainted* with," is an example of a passive participle with active signification (a thing very common in Aramaic). See Barth, *Nominalbildung*, § 124 *b*; Davidson, *Syntax*, § 100, rem. 7.

מֻסְתָּר. The case is exactly like that of מִשְׁחַת in 52 : 14; see the note there. This time also the choice is between two participles, the *nif'al* and the *hof'al*. The word as pointed in our text is impossible, and was intended by the Massorites to be so.

"We esteemed him not, made no account of him"; *cf.* the use of חשׁב in 13 : 17; 33 : 8.

53 : 4. With אָכֵן compare 49 : 4, where it has the same meaning.

נגוע means simply "smitten"; there is not the least indication nor likelihood, anywhere in the poem, that the figure of a *leprous* person occurred to the author.

53 : 5. "The chastisement which made us whole"; the idea expressed in the fewest possible words. There is no poem in the collection which contains more pregnant phrases—sometimes almost obscurely condensed—than this one. See the introduction.

53 : 6. This stanza, like the most of its fellows, is made up of short and strongly marked lines, very musical, and with hardly any superfluous syllables. It is evident that verse *b*, . . . ויהוה כלנו, cannot be treated as a single line. On the other hand, it is equally certain that the half-clause את עון כלנו cannot have formed a line by itself, as Duhm (doubtfully; see his note) and Cheyne have made it. Furthermore, there is difficulty with the beginning of verse 7. The phrase נגש והוא נענה sounds very improbable. The usual meaning of נענה is "afflicted," *cf.* 58 : 10, but if it is thus rendered, the pronoun is superfluous. Grätz, Cheyne, Marti, and others transpose the conjunction, while Klostermann makes עון the subject of נגש! A circumstantial clause is out of place here, however it is rendered. Duhm's "Gequält wurde er, doch war er demütig," would not have been written thus in Hebrew. Moreover, this use of נגש is suspicious; it does not elsewhere have the shade of meaning which is required here. And finally, the meter in the beginning of verse 7 is overloaded, since ולא יפתח פיו is insufficient to form a three-beat line by itself.

To remove all these difficulties, transpose נגש ו from the beginning of verse 7 to the end of verse 6, pointing נִגְּשׂוֹ. This verb is used with two accusatives, in the sense 'to compel one to pay what is due,' etc.; see II Kings 23 : 35: נגש את הכסף ואת הזהב את עם הארץ, "He compelled the people of the land to pay the silver and gold." The verb is used in this very same signification, "to exact," in 58 : 3. The stanza then reads:

כלנו כצאן תעינו | איש לדרכו פנינו
ויהוה הפגיע בו | את עון כלנו נגשו

and the next line proceeds: הוא נענה ולא יפתח פיו. The phrase
הפגיע בו is to be understood as elliptical, the direct object being
omitted: "He brought *it* (*i. e.*, the blow, or the punishment) upon
him." The idiom would be a very natural one even if the word
"chastisement" had not just occurred in the preceding verse.

53 : 7. A stanza of four parts, so arranged that the correspondence is between the first and fourth, and the second and third,
respectively.

With the (emended) beginning of the verse, הוא נענה, pronoun
and participle, compare the beginning of verse 5, הוא מחלל. With
נענה, "afflicted," compare 58 : 10.

The word נאלמה must be read נֶאְלָם, or better נֶאֱלָם, participle,
and connected with the following. So the meter, the grammatical
connection (ולא), and especially the sense, demand. The Syriac
translator, it should be observed, read it in this way. Some scribe,
writing hastily, made the not unnatural mistake.

ולא יפתח פיו could not form a complete line by itself, as Duhm
and Cheyne have made it. With the line as emended compare
the closing line of verse 3.

53 : 8. Cheyne's translation, "through an oppressive doom,"
does not do justice to the Hebrew. The difficulty of the passage
lies in the uncertainty as to the meaning of עצר. The words ממשפט
לקח can only mean, it seems to me, "he was taken away from
[exercising] judgment," that is, from the seat of rule and authority. This is not only the natural translation of these two words
taken by themselves, but is what the whole context suggests. The
prophet thinks of the glory of David and Solomon, and of the
most powerful of their successors. The whole force of the figure
which he is employing lies in this, that humiliation and distress
had not always been the lot of the Servant; when they were
brought upon him, the nations believed that the 'stripes' were
God's judgment upon him. 'He had once held an honorable place,
but he was brought down from it; who would make any account
of his line? for he was cut off from the land of the living.' If this
is the meaning of the verse, then עצר must be interpreted in accordance with I Sam. 9 : 17, II Chron. 14 : 10, Judg. 18 : 7 (?), and the
עֹצֵר, "ruler," of the Mishna.

In the following clause דורו must be the direct object of the

verb; any other construction is intolerable. It is quite natural
that שׁוּחַה should be used transitively, and we have here the best
of evidence that this writer did thus use it. The verb should not
be translated by a simple past tense, as is so often done. It should
be rendered as potential (Gesenius-Kautzsch, § 107, *t*), 'how was
any one to think it worthy of notice?' *Cf.* Gen. 43 : 7, which is a
perfect parallel. For the meaning of דּוֹרוֹ, 'his race, his line' (so,
e. g., Kimchi), *cf.* Ps. 73 : 15; 112 : 2; Deut. 32 : 20 (*cf.* verse 19),
etc.

There is no sufficient reason for emending the last clause of the
verse. עַמִּי is the idiom found in I Sam. 5 : 10; 30 : 22, etc. (Gesenius-Kautzsch, § 145, *m*), as Ibn Ezra explained it. The heathen
potentates do not cease speaking with the end of verse 6; on the
contrary, their testimony continues through verse 9. By making
each one of them speak for himself here (עַמִּי, "*my* people") the
vividness and force of the passage were perceptibly increased. No
one would find this mode of expression strange in a modern poet.
It is certainly far more effective than any of the substitutes which
have been proposed.

The correction נֻגַּע לָמָוֶת (Greek, ἤχθη εἰς θάνατον) is tempting,
but the reading of our Hebrew seems to me more probable. לָמוֹ
= לוֹ, as is certainly the case in 44 : 15, to say nothing of other
passages which are more or less doubtful. See the note on 44 : 15.
It is possible that we should point נֻגַּע, *nif'al*, the construction
being like that in verse 5, II Sam. 17 : 16, Lam. 5 : 5. But the
noun can be retained as it is. The meter of the line is best satisfied
by the form of words in our text.

53 : 9. The subject of וַיִּתֵּן is indefinite,* and the meaning of
the verb is "appoint."

עָשִׁיר cannot be right; what is required is an expression parallel
to רְשָׁעִים. Read עֹשֵׂי רָע, with Böttcher and others. This gives the
desired sense, and the only emendation necessary is the insertion
of a single letter.

בָּמֹתוֹ is a more likely reading than בָּמֹתָיו, in spite of Ezek.
28 : 10. To the word itself I can see no objection.

It is certain that where "death" is spoken of in these verses, it
is either in hyperbole or else (as in the present case) in the description of what the onlooking Gentiles *expected*. They did not
dig his grave; they "assigned" it, "designated" it; a signification

---

* Marti calls this rather common construction "schwierig." See note on
65 : 8, *e. g.*

of the verb used here which is very common. They were all ready
to bury him with the criminals, as soon as the last spark of life
should be gone. He was "as good as dead." But of course the
whole significance of the poem rests on the fact that the Servant
did *not* die, but lived to be brought to triumph. 52 : 13–15 and
especially 53 : 12 are entirely conclusive on this point.

The second half of the verse is merely an expression of the feeling of the Gentiles toward Israel, when they understood what he
had done for them. He was far better than those for whom he
suffered. See further the note on verse 11.

53 : 10. The Gentile rulers have ceased speaking, and now
Yahwè takes the word. He speaks of himself in the third person
—side by side with the first person—as so often elsewhere.

We should point הֶחֱלִי; the noun (so also Symmachus regards it)
is cognate accusative, the direct object of דכא: "Yahwè saw fit to
afflict him *with the suffering*" (the same word which was used in
verse 3).

There is nothing in the prophet's words, anywhere in the poem,
to show that he thought of this plan of the salvation of the Gentiles, through the suffering of Israel, as the *only* one possible.
Very possibly he did so regard it, under the existing circumstances,
for how should the chosen people be needlessly afflicted? At all
events, this was the way which Yahwè chose as the best, and the
Servant submitted.

The subject of תשים is נפשו. אשם is the payment for a wrong, or
that which atones for guilt; see especially I Sam. 6 : 3. שום אשם
would be a natural idiom for "make atonement." It would be
possible to read תּוּשַׂם, understanding אשם as "sin-offering"; but
the active construction is decidedly preferable. The subject is
characteristically transposed for the sake of the assonance, תשים
אשם.

In this four-line stanza also, as in verse 7, the first member corresponds with the fourth, while the second is closely joined with
the third.

"He will see his seed." Just the sort of promise we should expect, after verse 8: "Who could make any account *of his line?*"
The Servant not only escapes the death which came so near, but
sees the sure promise of long life and a blessed posterity. This
assurance he gains at the time when he offers his life as a sin-
offering. The next verse carries on this same idea.

53 : 11. A single scribal error, the accidental transposition of
צדיק with יצדיק, has made the whole verse incomprehensible and

brought about a false division of the first half. The second line
should read:

יִשְׂבַּע בדתו צדיק

and the third line:

יצדיק עבדי לרבים

The Servant's reward is twofold; not only the "portion with
the great" (verse 12), but also the earlier reward of knowing and
understanding the great work accomplished. He will see some of
the fruit of his toil and anguish, in the turning of many of the
Gentiles to the true way, and will at last be satisfied with the full
assurance that he had been *right* (צדיק). He had often been
tempted to doubt whether his God were really the only God, and
the Lord of the Gentiles as well as of the Jews; but now he sees
redemption brought to all nations through his own faithfulness,
and knows that he will be vindicated in the eyes of the world. *Cf.*
especially 50 : 8, which should by no means be overlooked in the
study of 53 : 11.

On the use of מן in מעמל, "He will see *some of* the fruit of his
toil," see Ges.-Kautzsch, § 119 *w*, note 1. This is a construction
which is especially familiar in Aramaic. The phrase עֲמַל נֶפֶשׁ means
a struggle in which the very 'life' is at stake; I have rendered it
"mortal travail."

ישבע must be connected with בדעתו; so Aquila, Symmachus,
Theodotion, and a few modern scholars. *The suffix pronoun in the
latter word is reflexive;* on this usage see Ges.-Kautzsch, § 135, 3;
Davidson, *Syntax,* § 11 (*b*). ידע with two accusatives, as usual.
As remarked above, צדיק and יצדק must be transposed: "He will
be satisfied with the knowledge that he is right." The massoretic
punctuation is altogether wrong here.

This sentence of course involves no contradiction of such passages as 42 : 19–25; 48 : 1–11, and 59 : 1–14. The Israel of the past
had indeed sinned so grievously and persistently that it deserved
to be "cut off" (48 : 9); but the prophet is here speaking of something altogether different; see the introduction to the poem. This
use of צדיק, moreover, belongs to a phraseology which is very
characteristic of the Second Isaiah. The adjective means "*reli-
giously* right," used of one who is "right" *in his relation to God.*
The abstract nouns צֶדֶק and צְדָקָה are used to designate this right
relation. As they are used over and over again in these poems
side by side with ישע and ישועה, in speaking of the coming triumph,

they mean restored "religious harmony." So also the *hif'il* of the verb (the next word in this verse) means "to bring [others] into the right relation with God," to turn them into the right religious way. The participle מצדיקים appears to have this same meaning in Dan. 12 : 3: "they who turn many to the right way."

The ל in לרבים is the (Aramaic) preposition used to introduce the direct object; Ges.-Kautzsch, § 117, *n.* We have the same construction in 56 : 8; 61 : 1, and 65 : 15 (as emended). In the passage in Daniel, just cited, the accusative is used.

With the last clause of the verse compare Lam. 5 : 7—where the meaning of the phrase is very different, however.

53 : 12. A grand close to the poem. According to the poet's favorite custom, this final paragraph gives a summary of what has preceded.

The phrase "unto death," which has been much misunderstood, is the very same hyperbole which appears in the English "tired *to death,* frightened *to death,*" etc.; the meaning being "utterly, *to the very last degree.*" We have the best of evidence that this idiom was fixed in Jewish usage, in Jonah 4 : 9 and Mark 14 : 34 (Matt. 26 : 38). See also Judg. 16 : 16, II Kings 20 : 1, Ps. 18 : 5 f. Excellent examples in Syriac literature: Bedjan's *Acta Martyrum et Sanctorum,* IV, 615 mid., 637 below; Hoffmann's *Julianos,* 25, line 6. The same idiom also in Arabic. It is strange that this familiar Semitic mode of speech should have been unrecognized here.

The metric line is not overloaded, even if we do not read *lĕmā-weth,* which is of course permissible.

"Poured out his life," or "emptied himself"; compare the similar phrase in 58 : 10, where the idea is that of giving up oneself entirely, for the sake of another.

With יפגיע compare 47 : 3 (as emended) and 59 : 16.

CHAPTER 54

A poem of consolation, addressed to personified Jerusalem. She who has been forsaken for a short season is to be received into endless favor. There is close resemblance to 49 : 14–21; 50 : 1–3, and 51 : 17–52 : 12 on the one side, and to 60 and 62 on the other.

This is one of the poems in which it is especially evident that no 'prophet of the Babylonian exile' is writing. Jerusalem is exhorted to expand on all sides, adding new territory to her former extent, in confidence of increasing prosperity (verses 2 f.). These words would be a pitiful mockery if they were addressed to a city actually in ruins. On the contrary, it is plain from the poet's language that Jerusalem is already enjoying a considerable measure of material well-being.

In verse 9 the mention of the flood in the days of Noah, and especially the reminder of the solemn covenant which God gave to mankind at that time, is the most interesting of the numerous allusions in Second Isaiah to the scriptures contained in the Pentateuch. The reference is obviously to Gen. 9 : 8–17, a passage in the Priestly document, not paralleled elsewhere. This is not the only place where our prophet shows acquaintance with this document. We have in the Samaritan text the best of evidence that the final redaction of the Pentateuch was completed before the Samaritan schism (latter half of the fourth century), and it is not at all unlikely that it lay before the prophet in the same form which we now possess.

Duhm, in his comment on the first verse, remarks that this poem 'takes not the slightest notice of its predecessor' (52 : 13–53 : 12). Is there any reason why we should expect it to do so?

The meter is 3 | 3 except in verse 6, which is 3 | 2. The momentary introduction of the 3 | 2 verse is to be compared with the similar instances in 44 : 25; 48 : 12 f.; 60 : 14; 65 : 13; 66 : 11. There are several 3 | 3 | 3 verses, as often.

---

54 : 1. With the contrasted adjectives "desolate" and "wedded," cf. 62 : 4.

54 : 3. It is better to read ירשו, plural. It is possible that the massoretic vocalization was intended to indicate the fact of variant readings.

54 : 5. The form bo'alaik is not an example of pluralis maiestatis (Kautzsch, § 124, k), but is employed merely for the sake of assonance with 'ōsaik, which is singular number. There are numerous characteristic examples of paronomasia in the chapter. The next verse begins with one; so also does verse 8. Verses 9 and 10 contain examples, and in 11–13 there is evident play on banim and abanim.

54 : 8. Whatever the first word in this verse may mean (but the usual explanation, making it a paronomastic variation of šeṭef, is fully satisfactory), we can be sure that it is correctly transmitted. The assonance with the following word is too characteristic to be

doubted. It may well have been a familiar coinage, not original
with Second Isaiah. Phonetic doublets of just this nature are
common in any popular speech. In Arabic, for instance, the examples are very numerous.

54 : 9. The first two words in the verse should be brought together into a single word, כִּימֵי, "*as in the days of* Noah." Very
likely the use of the *maqqeph* by the Massorites was intended to
indicate this as an alternative. *Cf.*, for example, 51 : 9, "as in the
days of old." The poet's characteristic play on words misled some
readers.

On the allusion here to the passage in Genesis (Priestly document!) see the introduction to the chapter.

54 : 10. The original reading of the Greek at the end of this
verse was evidently εἶπεν ὁ ἐλεῶν σε, κύριος.

54 : 11. The beginning of the second half-verse, הנה אנכי,
which is much too heavy for the meter, has suffered contamination
from the beginning of verse 16; the original reading was certainly
הֵן אָנִי.

The one thing certain about the word פוּךְ in this passage is that
the poet intended here a precious stone. The monosyllable sounds
distinctly better in the verse than נֹּפֶךְ, which LXX and Syr. apparently had in mind, and it is better not to emend. Jerome, in
spite of the 'antimony' of the Targum, renders *per ordinem*. We
must of course read אֲדָנַיִךְ, "thy foundations." With the array
of precious stones compare 60 : 13, 17, and similar passages. The
poet is noticeably fond of such enumerations.

54 : 13. It is possible that we should read "thy daughters" instead of "thy sons" at the end of the verse.

54 : 15. This verse is absolutely hopeless unless the prophet's
fondness for playing upon words is taken into account. As soon
as the fact is recognized that we have here another instance of his
own favorite device, the juxtaposition of words identical in sound
but distinct in meaning (see Chapter XI), there is no more difficulty. The verb גור in the first half-verse means "act as an enemy, make an attack," as in Ps. 59 : 4. In the second half-verse it
means "sojourn, dwell as a stranger or guest." חן is for הנה, as
in verse 16. It is better to point גָּר (participle) rather than גֵּר,
גוּר, both because of the assonance with גָּר in the second half-
verse, and because the grammatical construction is smoother.
יגוּר is then a relative verb, "the foe *who shall* attack." אפס must

be pointed as the participle, אָפֵס, "shall perish at my hand." Observe that this verb occurs in the same verse with גוּר in 16 : 4; perhaps a mere coincidence. With מֵאוֹתִי cf. Ps. 22 : 26, Hos. 8 : 4, etc., and the *qere* in 44 : 24. The meaning of גָּר אִתְּךָ, in the second half-verse, is beyond all question; cf. Ex. 12 : 48, Lev. 19 : 33. The prophet is speaking the very same word of encouragement here as in 56 : 7 f.: Not only will Israel be restored safe and sound, but recruits will also be added in multitude from the nations round about (cf. 56 : 8). This is the regular use of the idiom נָפַל עַל: pass over from one party or army to another. The verse is perfectly suited to its context.

The old versions, not recognizing the double use of גוּר, made very awkward work of the translation. It appears that the Greek (cf. Lev. 26 : 25) and Syriac (here, as often, dependent on the Greek) read אָסַף in place of אָפֵס.

54 : 16. The הֵן in these verses, 11 (as emended), 15, 16, is the equivalent of הִנֵּה. The Massorites record here two readings, in their usual manner. The shorter form is the original in each of these instances.

The word לַחְבֹּל is an interpretative addition, and was probably intended to be connected *with the following words*, the beginning of verse 17.

54 : 17. The word לְמִשְׁפָּט seems also to be an interpretative gloss, giving the true sense, but unnecessary, and metrically superfluous. The Greek version has a curious variant rendering of this clause.

CHAPTERS 55 : 1–56 : 8

A noble utterance, conceived in a truly catholic spirit. The direct address is to all mankind, except in the dramatic interlude, verses 4 f., where Yahwè turns to address the Davidic Messiah. Throughout the poem the prophet has in mind God's children of all the races on earth, without distinction. It may be that in verses 8 f., where the God of all the world speaks of his own thoughts and purposes as greater and loftier than those of his hearers, he has especially in mind the narrow view of his work of salvation traditionally held by many, perhaps the great majority, in Israel. Compare especially the very striking passage 45 : 9–12, where the chosen people are sternly warned against this conception of their God as the 'father' of only the one race. There are other points of close resemblance between this poem and the latter half of chapter 45. Thus, verse 11 reminds of 45 : 23; the express inclusion of foreign nations in the blessings to be enjoyed by Israel, in 55 : 4 f., 56 : 7 f., is paralleled by 45 : 22; and the utterance "my house shall be called a house of prayer for all nations" (56 : 7) is the same thing which was said in 45 : 23b. It is perhaps needless to say that "my house," "my holy mountain," and the "sacrifices on my altar" are typical phrases necessarily employed and not to be taken too literally.

The opening verse, with its invitation to "*all* those who thirst," has its fitting counterpart in the closing words of the poem declaring that the Lord, who is to restore the exiles of Israel, is also making ready to gather into the fold other sheep of his flock. The picture of a joyful 'return,' *the home-coming of the Gentiles*, is drawn here in a way that takes us back to the first half of chapter 49, which is closely parallel. Like the former poem, this also is truly Messianic.

The passage verses 3–5 is one of the most important in the whole collection of poems. This is the only mention of David in Second Isaiah, and the express identification of the individual 'Servant' with the leader long expected by the people is most welcome. See further the Chapter on the Servant and the Messiah.

I have set aside 56 : 2–6 as an insertion by a later hand. On the sole ground of incongruity with its surroundings there would not be sufficient justification for rejecting the passage. Even a very great poet may have his lapses. The prophet may conceivably have had a personal interest in some eunuch, and also in certain Jewish proselytes; and as for the Sabbath, we cannot doubt that he honored it as a divine institution of high importance, though "made for man" (Mark 2 : 27). It cannot be called inconceivable that he should have written a brief poem such as 56 : 1–8, commonplace in diction and on a low plane of ideas—except in verses 7 and 8! That which decides the matter is the obvious relation of this passage to 58 : 13 f. The latter is generally recognized as an addition by a later hand, also out of keeping with its surroundings; see the introduction to chapter 58. It is quite evident that the two passages were written by the same hand, each in metric form and with some imitation of the diction of the Second Isaiah (*cf.* especially 56 : 5b with 55 : 13b), and each intended for the precise place which it now occupies.

The broad humanity of 56 : 7 f., which is so impressive when it is recognized as the immediate sequel of 55 : 13 and the close of a

poem conceived throughout in the same spirit, is not quite obscured even by the interpolation (see the standard commentaries),
but its effect is sadly impaired; and this result was doubtless intended. There are other briefer interpolations, to be noticed in
some of the following poems, made by an editor, or editors, who
could not stand on quite the same plane of liberality as the prophet,
but felt that the special prerogatives of the chosen people should
be given more emphasis. The passages to which I refer have already been recognized, by other commentators, as interpolated.

The meter is 3 | 3 throughout.

55 : 1. The massoretic division of the verse is wrong, and the
text has suffered conflation. The principal division should follow
the word לכו. The words ולכו שברו, which are wanting in the
Greek and Syriac versions and plainly had their origin in a transcriber's error, must be omitted.

55 : 4. This verse contains one of the poet's favorite word-
plays. The first *le'ummīm* is plural of *le'ōm*, the second contains
the preposition and the plural of *'ummah*. The plural of the latter
word is masculine in form in Biblical Aramaic (regularly); in O. T.
Hebrew it is found also in Ps. 117 : 1. (The evidence of the present
passage—with the poet's known literary habit—appears sufficient
to overcome the doubt expressed by Nöldeke, *Beiträge zur semi-
tischen Sprachwissenschaft*, p. 57.) The Hebrew learned tradition
seems to have preserved the distinction here; compare the pointing of the word in its first occurrence with the form in 51 : 4; and
observe the alternative reading at the end, where the purpose of
the massoretic note is to record another reading (*the better reading*), ומצוה.

The original reading is "I have made *thee* the witness of the
peoples," the verb having the suffix of the *second* person, as in the
Syriac version. The dramatic passage, with the sudden change of
address, begins at verse 4, not with the following verse. See the
introduction to the chapter. It is easy to see how the mistaken
alteration of the suffix came about.

55 : 5. The word "nation" is virtually plural, in each occurrence, as more than once elsewhere in these poems. *Cf.* 42 : 6;
49 : 7; Ps. 22 : 7, etc.

55 : 8 f. On the interpretation of these two verses see the in-

troduction to the chapter. Verse 9 is a good example of a triad, 3 | 3 | 3. Duhm and Marti, not recognizing this frequent metric form, suppose something to be missing.

55 : 11. The relative pronoun in the first clause, which is unnecessary and seems to overload the meter, is probably secondary.

55 : 12 f. Compare especially chapter 35 and 49 : 9–11, the parallel pictures of the 'home-coming' of Yahwè's children of all the nations and races of the earth.

55 : 13. With the enumeration of trees in this verse compare 41 : 19; 60 : 13, and the picture in 35 : 7.

Observe the alternative reading noted by the Massorites (the prefixed conjunction) at the beginning of the second clause.

56 : 2–6. *This is an interpolated passage, not a new poem; see the introduction.*

56 : 7. Before the word לרצון it is probable that יעלו originally stood, and was omitted by accident. *Cf.* 60 : 7, where the form of words is slightly different. Either form might be used, and there is no good reason for conforming the one passage to the other.

56 : 8. The context seems to make it clear that the last word in the verse should be written לְנִקְבָּצָי, with the suffix of the first person. The preposition ל indicates the *direct* object, as usually in Aramaic and often in the later Hebrew, also in 53 : 11; 61 : 1, and 65 : 15 (as emended).

CHAPTERS 56 : 9–57 : 21

This remarkable poem is in some respects the most interesting in the collection. It is a composition of great vigor and directness. Whoever has read it, or heard it, returns to it again and again in his thought. Its most striking feature is a burst of invective, 57 : 3 ff., so passionate and seemingly personal as to be fairly startling. Those who are attacked are the faithless of Israel, the apostates of the prophet's own countrymen; the same whom he assails fiercely, for a moment, in 46 : 9, 12; 48 : 8; 50 : 11 (!); 65 : 11 f., and somewhat more mildly in numerous other passages. The fact that the denunciation comes from one whom we know to be the embodiment of magnanimity is what makes it so impressive.

The prophet's invective is not confined to the passage just mentioned. The whole poem consists chiefly of rebuke, unsparing in its force and intensely dramatic in its form. Exordium and conclusion are equally sententious, the latter returning, after a pas-

sage in milder vein, to the note struck at the outset. The poem
begins with a cry to the beasts of prey, in a single 3 | 3 line. The
ending, 57 : 20 f., is a brief and forcible simile, the restless misery
of sin, followed by the isolated phrase, "No peace for the wicked!"
which was employed at the end of the very similar poem, chapter
48.

As has already been indicated, however, there is a secondary
theme, a note of hope. This also was present in implication even
at the very beginning, for the threatened flock is innocent and not
wholly doomed, even though its keepers are worthless. As chapter
48 issued in a call to repentance, with a momentary picture of the
'return home,' so in the present instance the necessity of the contrite heart is set forth (57 : 15), and in verse 14 (cf. 48 : 20; 52 : 11;
62 : 10) the sound of triumph rings out for a moment.

The construction of the poem is carefully planned, as usual.
The brief exordium is followed by a sarcastic passage of some
length, 56 : 10–57 : 2, conceived in the manner already familiar
from the descriptions of idol-worship and especially from chapter
47. The prophet is now writing in deep indignation, and his sarcasm is sharper than in any of the former passages. Then, suddenly, comes the *sheṣef qeṣef*, as though his wrath could be kept
within bounds no longer. It certainly overflows in verses 3–5.
The manner of effecting the transition from this outburst to the
strongly contrasted 'second theme' mentioned above is worthy of
notice. The invective is continued in verses 6–8, but is now addressed to a collective personification in the second person singular feminine, the Israelite people being represented by the familiar
figure of a faithless wife. The tone then drops in 9 f. to irony strikingly reminiscent of that in chapter 47. This is followed by a passage in which Yahwè reasons with the culprit (the feminine singular being retained), the tone at length becoming wistful. The way
is now prepared for the favorite lyric interlude (verse 14), after
which the second subject is treated in verses 15–19.

The whole poem is a most effective composition. When its special features are also taken into account; the passion displayed
and the manner of its expression, the cutting sarcasm, the succession of lively pictures drawn with this poet's extraordinary power
of imagination, the unusual interest of some of the subjects touched
upon; it may well be pronounced unique in its field.

There are several reminiscences of chapter 54, of such a nature
as to make the supposition probable that the one poem was written soon after the other. 57 : 16 and 17 reproduce 54 : 7–9. The

figure of 'carrying in the arms' in 57 : 13 (see the note) seems to refer directly to 54 : 7.

In 57 : 12 there is a very significant return to the substance and the phraseology of the 'great argument' which occupied such a prominent place in chapters 41–48. Chapter 46, for example, might be regarded as an expansion of the teaching of this verse. The resemblance to 43 : 12 is also very striking, especially when the context is taken into account.

The allusion in verses 9 f., however understood, is of great interest. To what distant "king" were ambassadors sent with a present of oil, when there seemed to be an opportunity to "revive the power" of the Jewish province? Many modern scholars have found here a reference to the adoption or renewal of a foreign cult; namely, that of Milcom, the god of the Ammonites; others, with the older interpreters generally, suppose a Gentile ruler to be intended. The former of these two interpretations appears to be based on a misunderstanding; the latter is supported by parallel passages, the immediately following context, and especially by the evidence contained in the passage itself.

The Melek ('Moloch') to whose idolatrous cult numerous O. T. passages refer was not in any way connected with the Ammonite Milcom. The worship of Melek was Canaanite, specifically Phœnician, in its origin, and seems to have been transferred to Yahwè under this name ('King'). See the article "Molech, Moloch" by G. F. Moore in the *Encyclopædia Biblica*, especially col. 3187 f. Again, the passage speaking of a 'descent to Sheol' (end of verse 9) has been supposed to refer to necromancy or the worship of some god of the nether world. With this understanding the whole passage becomes disjointed and confused; the beginning of verse 10, in particular, is made meaningless or miserably weak. On the contrary, the parenthetical "and thou wast brought down to Sheol!" is one of the poet's characteristic 'asides'; observe how it occupies an *extra* three-beat member in the verse. The whole passage, from the last two words of verse 8 (see the note) to the end of verse 10, refers to a single definite event.

It is perhaps useless to inquire to what recent embassy the prophet refers. A possibility that readily suggests itself, however, is that when Egypt threw off the Persian yoke, in 407 B. C., the Jewish province (always far more closely connected with Egypt than with Babylonia) saw the opportunity to make a new alliance. The comparison of Hos. 12 : 2, "They make a covenant with Assyria, and *oil is carried into Egypt*," would seem to be significant.

As for the 'long, long way' (57 : 10), compare 30 : 6, where, after denouncing the 'rebellious children, who trust in the shadow of Egypt and *send their ambassadors* to Hanes,' the writer continues, describing the perilous journey through the intervening desert: "Through the land of trouble and anguish, from whence come the lioness and the lion, the viper and fiery flying serpent, they carry their riches upon the shoulders of young asses, and their treasures upon the humps of camels, to a people that will not profit them." The next verse in our passage, 57 : 11, begins with the question: "Now whom hast thou dreaded and feared, that thou hast proved faithless?" The resemblance of these and the immediately following words to 51 : 12 f., where the connection of thought is the same and the allusion to *human oppressors* is certain, is so close as to be decisive; the prophet is speaking of human allies and tormentors in 57 : 9 ff. The aspect of the situation which interested him was religious, not political, but in those days the one necessarily involved the other.

In several places the text of the poem seems to have been expanded by the incorporation of clauses which had their origin in marginal variant readings. See the notes on 56 : 11 (last clause of the first half-verse); 57 : 6 (end); 19 (end).

The meter is 3 | 3 in the exordium, 56 : 9; then 3 | 2 in the main body of the poem, up to 57 : 14, the lyric intermezzo, which, with the remainder of the poem, is 3 | 3.

---

56 : 9. The verse must be divided as 3 | 3. The attempt to make it 3 | 2 has a very unpleasing result, the first member of the verse being then overloaded and the second member weak. The poet's purpose to hold this exclamatory introduction separate from the description which follows is obvious.

56 : 10. The word חֹזִים is one that should not be tampered with. It certainly receives support from the Arabic *hadhā*, Syriac *hadā*, meaning 'wander' in mind or speech, 'talk in one's sleep' (Dozy, *Supplément*), etc.

56 : 11. The second clause of the verse, "and they are shepherds who know not how to discern," is quite impossible. Where it stands it is very disturbing, and there is no other place where it could be of use. It is difficult to take seriously Duhm's suggestion that the words הֵמָּה רֹעִים are a gloss (!) to the צֹפוּ of the preceding

verse. Even glossators must be supposed to have some reason
for their proceedings.

It seems probable that the superfluous clause originated in marginal variant readings of the first clause of verse 10. One variant
was רעים, for עורים, and beside it stood לא ידעו הבין. We know
already the fact of this latter variant, because of the testimony of
the Greek, οὐκ ἔγνωσαν φρονῆσαι. Some one combined the two
in a clause and inserted it in verse 11. For evidence of a similar
proceeding in other parts of this poem see the notes on verses
6 and 19.

The verse ends with לבצעו. The next word was originally the
beginning of verse 12, and the correct reading is מֵהָקִיצוֹ, "as soon
as he wakes." Cf. especially Prov. 23 : 35.

57 : 1.   הֵן should probably be supplied at the beginning: "Lo,
the righteous man disappears." The testimony of the Greek,
ἴδετε ὡς ὁ δίκαιος ἀπώλετο, would be all but worthless if it were
unsupported; but the Syriac also has ha, and the rhetorical form
of the verse, as well as the meter, is improved when the interjec-
tion is prefixed.

The כִּי seems to be secondary, introduced because of misunderstanding of the way in which מבין is here used, without an expressed object. The new verse (57 : 2) should begin at this point.
That יבוא שלום and הלך נכחו (better pointed הֹלֵך) mean the
same thing is made probable both by the parallelism of the clauses
and also by the context. The writer is not speaking of death. The
upright man leaves Jerusalem, without looking behind him, because he would feel more at home somewhere else. Cf. Ps. 12 : 2,
Wisd. 2 : 10–20, James 5 : 6. The subject of ינוחו is provided
by the preceding lines; it is the multitude who 'do not care.'

57 : 3.   Read מְנָאֶפֶת וַזֹּנָה at the end of the (massoretic) verse,
with Klostermann and others. The traditional verse-division at
this point is wrong, being in the middle of a 3 | 2 line.

57 : 5.   With the אלים cf. 1 : 29. The second תחת is the result
of an early transcriber's error. Read וְסָעִיפֵי, for there is no need of
repeating the preposition ב. The Greek, translating freely, replaces
this noun by ἀνὰ μέσον; the old versions were often in doubt as
to the exact meaning of סעיף; see Moore on Judg. 15 : 8.

57 : 6.   The consonant text of the first clause is quite unassailable; the word חלקי, however, is, and will probably remain, more
or less of a riddle. The preceding context argues very strongly in

favor of a word signifying some natural object, or conformation
of the ground; and it is hardly too much to say that no use of חלק
found (or even suggested) elsewhere in the Old Testament would
be permissible here. The fact of the play upon words increases the
precariousness of every conjecture; besides, we know next to nothing of the rites, the terminology, and the current phrases connected
with the varieties of heathen worship described in these chapters.
It may be doubted whether any actual cultus object is described
or intended by the word חלקי. The whole verse is strongly ironical, and it may be that the prophet merely intended to say: 'Your
sacrifices are offered to rocks and valleys, and from these you
must expect help.' Those who wish to understand a cultus object
can hardly do better than to be content with the traditional guess,
"smooth stones." * Otherwise the meaning "hollows" might be
conjectured; Arabic ḥalīqa = pit, hollow, or cavity in a mountain-
side. Duhm's attempt to obtain the meaning "Betrug," etc.,
from the word is quite futile; חָלָק does not mean "trügerisch"
either in Ezek. 12 : 24 or in Is. 30 : 10, except in so far as this idea
is supplied by the context; here it would be far-fetched.

The pronouns הם, להם, may refer either to the חלקים or (possibly) to the heathen deities implied, but not named, in the pre-
ceding; cf. the use of הם in 43 : 9; 48 : 14, etc.|

The last clause of the verse in our Hebrew text is another instance of conflation by the insertion of a marginal reading. The
clause is merely a variant of the preceding, the form perhaps suggested by 64 : 11. Compare the notes on 56 : 11 and 57 : 19. I find
I have been anticipated in this conjecture by Duhm and others.

57 : 7. The last clause is a single verse-member of three beats.
It is too short to be made into a 3 | 2 line.

57 : 8. The last two words of the massoretic verse, יד חזית,
obviously belong to verse 9. Both meter and sense (cf. חית ידך in
verse 10) make this certain.

57 : 9. The connection between the verb וַתָּשֻׁרִי, "thou didst
bring a present," and the noun תְּשׁוּרָה, a present brought to a superior, should be sufficiently established by I Sam. 9 : 7 and the context of the present passage. The verb as used here is very probably merely denominative.

For the meaning of the parenthetical "And thou wast brought
down to the pit !" (a typical use of the hifil stem) see the introduc-

* Perhaps suggested originally by I Sam. 17 : 40: חלקי אבנים מן הנחל.

tion to the poem. Suing for the favor of the foreign king involved participation in the foreign cult.

57 : 11. מַחֲשָׂה. A favorite verb with this writer. The signification of the *hifil*, used here and in 42 : 14, seems to be identical with that of the *qal*, used in 62 : 1, 6; 64 : 11; 65 : 6.

It is better to point וּמֵעֹלָם, with LXX, Lat.; so most modern commentators. *Cf.* 1 : 15 and 58 : 7, as well as the closer parallels Ps. 10 : 1, etc. The pointing of our M. T. was occasioned by 42 : 14. In Cheyne's emended text עֵינִי is also added, with the diacritical mark indicating that it is inserted on the authority of an old version; what version is intended I have been unable to learn.

We must read תִּרְאִי (from רָאָה) instead of תִּירְאִי at the end of the verse. So the Latin, *et mei oblita es.* A phrase parallel to לֹא זָכַרְתְּ and לֹא שַׂמְתְּ עַל לִבֵּךְ is what is needed. The choice of this verb was probably occasioned by the use of the outwardly identical וְתִירְאִי in the first line of the stanza. Another instance of the writer's constant habit.

57 : 12. Instead of וְאֶת מַעֲשַׂיִךְ we must certainly read וַאֲנִי מוֹשִׁיעֵךְ. Compare especially 43 : 12, noticing the context; also such passages as 49 : 26 and 60 : 16. This is the ever-present collocation of צדק and ישׁע.

The conjunction in וְלֹא is wanting in Grk., Syr., and Lat., and should be omitted. The massoretic division of the verses is again incorrect.

57 : 13. The word קִבּוּצַיִךְ is a massoretic creation based on שִׁקּוּץ, "abomination." The original reading was מְקַבְּצַיִךְ, "those who carry thee" (in their arms); *cf.* especially 54 : 7, which the writer seems to have had in mind, but also the passage 46 : 3–7, "those who carry you cannot save you!" which in its context corresponds exactly to this verse. See the introduction to the poem.

57 : 14. We have here a fine example of the brief outburst, half lyric, half dramatic, with which this poet so often makes the division between the two principal parts of his poem. *Cf.* 45 : 8; 49 : 13; 66 : 6 ff., as well as 48 : 20; 62 : 10, and such interludes as 42 : 10–12.

The reading of our text, וְאָמַר, with indefinite subject, "and the word will be, the cry will be raised," is the true reading. Grk. and Syr. render well, by using the plural. Our poet is very fond of this indefinite third person singular. So in 40 : 6; 45 : 24; 63 : 11;

65 : 8, and elsewhere. The word might well stand outside the meter, but is here evidently to be included.

57 : 16. The meaning of the verb יַעֲטוֹף was correctly understood by the ancient versions. The Grk. is exactly right with its ἐξελεύσεται, Syr. with its *nafqa*, Lat. with its *egredietur*. The Targum, which has a very free rendering, as usual, translates by "return." Compare the Syriac root, which means "return, turn away." The use of the verb (unexampled elsewhere in the Hebrew which we have, and perhaps an Aramaism) is intended to represent God as the direct source of each and every human life. The soul turns from him to dwell in man, and at last returns to him (Eccles. 12 : 7). 'I made the souls of men.' *Cf.* 42 : 5; 45 : 12, 18.

57 : 17 The first two words are wrong as they stand. The word בֶּצַע has its etymological meaning, "bit, *morceau, Bisschen.*" The prophet of course does not mean to say, "for his momentary sin I was angry," but "for his sin I was angry for a moment." The original reading was בְּעוֹנוֹ בֶּצַע, the word used precisely like רֶגַע. The Greek translator's βραχύ τι was not a mere guess, though he may have had our massoretic text before him.

וָאֶקְצֹף is a double reading, and the verb in the first person is secondary and inferior. The Greek translator had before him the correct form, וְקָצֹף, originally intended as *infinitive absolute.*

57 : 18. The "mourners," those who share Israel's distress at his condition, are the people of the foreign nations who begin to see the meaning of his punishment.

57 : 19. For the construction of בָּרָא with double object compare 65 : 18. Lat., *creavi fructum labiorum pacem.* Some commentators have aptly compared the Koran passages 19 : 63; 33 : 43; in paradise they shall hear only "Peace."

The last clause of the verse (three words) is still another instance of the expansion of this poem, by some editor, through the inclusion of marginal readings; see the notes on 56 : 11 and 57 : 6. The אָמַר יְהֹוָה was intended by some one (very naturally) for the end of verse 18, preparing the way for verse 19. וּרְפָאתִיו was a variant to וְאֶרְפָּאֵהוּ. The manner in which the two were combined is precisely that described above, in the note on 56 : 11.

57 : 20. The verb is probably נִדָּשׁ, not נִגְרָשׁ, both here and in Amos 8 : 8. The former root is suitable, the latter not.

CHAPTER 58

This is indeed a "trumpet-cry" (verse 1), a demand for the warm heart and the helping hand, a sharp rebuke of sin in its broadest aspect; namely, *selfishness, lack of human sympathy.* The prophet is not speaking to mankind in general, but to those whom he personally knows, whom he sees day by day.

What is the essence of true religion? In what service performed by his children does Yahwè find pleasure? Of how great relative importance is the faithful observance of a ritual? The prophet, taking the subject of *fasting* as typical, plainly implies, by his indignation, that his hearers ought to know the answer to these questions. And with good reason. They, of all the peoples of the earth, might be expected to know what many of the gentile nations found it not difficult to learn.

Those who have not taken into account the Second Isaiah's tendency to introduce irony into his rebuke, and his fondness for carrying on an imaginary dialogue with those whom he is addressing, have failed to understand the second verse of the chapter; and misunderstanding here ruins the whole poem. The prophet is here arraigning the outwardly 'faithful' but inwardly selfish; those who 'tithed mint and anise and cummin, but left undone the weightier matters of the law, *justice and mercy*' (Matt. 23:23). He has had occasion to touch upon this subject once before, in 43:22–24. It is interesting to see that the manner of approach to the rebuke is precisely the same in the two passages: the self-righteous worshippers, confident in their observance of the outward forms, are represented as complaining that they have not been justly treated, and their imagined words are quoted in irony.

The prophet's answer, in both instances given as Yahwè's reply to the complainers, is, in effect, that the ritual is relatively of very small consequence. It is not worth considering at all if the worshipper is not right at heart. One after another of the Hebrew prophets had said this, and now the Second Isaiah adds his weighty word, with especial clearness and emphasis. His definition of true religion is precisely that of Mic. 6:8: 'To do justly, to love mercy, and to walk humbly before God.' He takes his stand beside the author of Ps. 51:18 f.

The poem ends with verse 12. There follows a curious appendix, verses 13 f., by another hand; utterly unsuited to this place, and yet written to occupy it. See the note.

———

The meter of the poem is 3 | 3. The appendix also is in this meter.   ———

58:1. With the charge "refrain not!" compare the same words in 54:2. The speaker is the God of Israel; the command is given, as often elsewhere, to every one who is able to understand and obey it.

58 : 2. The words of these 'legally righteous' complainers are quoted ironically not only in verse 3 but also in verse 2—where the prophet's own indignant exclamation is interjected. Compare the similarly imagined quotations in 40 : 27; 41 : 6 f.; 42 : 22; 43 : 23 f. (a very close parallel to the present passage); 44 : 19; 47 : 7 f., 10; 48 : 1 f.; 49 : 4, 14, 20 f., etc.

The meaning of קִרְבַת אֱלֹהִים in this verse is not the same as in Ps. 73 : 28. On the contrary, it is to be compared with the use of קרב in 41 : 1, 21, Deut. 1 : 17. The following verse makes this certain.

58 : 3. The הֵן here and in the following verse is the Aramaic conditional particle, "if." Its use gives evidence of strong Aramaic influence, inasmuch as the Hebrew אִם would have suited the metrical and rhetorical requirements as well.

For the use of תִּנְגֹּשׂוּ, "require, exact in full," cf. 53 : 6 f., as emended.

58 : 4. With מַצָּה, a rare word, cf. the use of an equivalent derivative of this root in 41 : 12.

58 : 5. The word תִקְרָא (second person singular, logically inadmissible here) is one of the 'alternative readings' of the Massorites. Either יִקְרָא, conforming to the verb immediately preceding, or (better) תִּקְרָאוּ, plural, as in the Greek and Syriac.

58 : 6. With רְצוּצִים compare 42 : 3 f. It is possible that there is a play on words in the double use of מוֹטָה. We have not the means of determining this, however.

58 : 7. The word מְרוּדִים seems to be a *qal* passive participle from a *secondary root* מרד derived (like many similar Semitic formations) from רדד. The meaning then is "the downtrodden."

When the prophet uses the words "from thine own flesh" in the latter part of this verse, he means *all mankind*.

58 : 8. There are reminiscences here of several poems in the earlier part of the collection. Compare especially 42 : 9; 43 : 19; 52 : 12. The last example is a very characteristic repetition.

58 : 9. In this verse the pointing מוֹטָה is incorrect. We must read מֻטֶּה, "false dealing" (see Ezek. 9 : 9), as many scholars have seen. With the last words of the (massoretic) verse compare James 1 : 26: "If any man thinketh himself to be religious, while he bridleth not his tongue, this man's religion is vain."

58 : 11.   The word צחצחות must be explained by the Arabic root *ṣaḥ*, "good, sound, healthful," etc.   There is no place here for a "desert," nor for any derivative of the root which means "to shine" (Jerome has here *splendoribus*).   Targum and Syr. render correctly with their "delicacies."   The Grk. merely guesses.

58 : 12.   The phrase ממך חרבות, meaning simply "thy ruins," is an example of a construction very common in Arabic, especially in poetry; we have no need to object to it in Hebrew.   Thus, *minka nafsan*, 'thyself,' Aghani VIII, 119 below; *minka 'ḍ-ḍulū'u*, 'thy ribs,' *ibid.*, XX, 155, 16.   It would be easy to collect a hundred examples of the kind; there are five, for instance, in the *mu'allaqa* of Imrulqais.   Yet all the commentators propose to alter the Hebrew text here.

Instead of נתיבות, "paths," we certainly must read נתצות, "ruined places, ruins."   This passive participle is used as an adjective in Jer. 33 : 4.   From usage in general we should expect the substantive to be feminine; compare סללות, "walls," in this same verse of Jeremiah.   The graphic resemblance of יב to צ is likely to be very close in the Hebrew-Aramaic script.

58 : 13 f.   These two verses, which in the amount of emphasis which they put upon the observance of the sabbath are out of keeping with the preceding poem and with the teaching of the prophet in general, are recognized as a later addition.   In all probability the reason for their position here is to be found in the accidental corruption in the text of verse 12, as noted above.   People do not "*dwell*" in "*paths*."   The close of the verse seems to have been interpreted thus: "Restorer of paths leading to (the observance of) *the sabbath*."   In order to make this sure, and emphasize it, the addition was made.   Its author is plainly the very same who made the similar insertion in the poem 55 : 1–56 : 8; namely, the passage 56 : 2–6, also utterly out of keeping with its surroundings, but written to occupy that place.   See the introduction to the poem.   Both passages are prosaic, but in fair metric form, and were probably added at a very early date.

CHAPTER 59

This great poem *de profundis* stands alone in the collection as a picture of sin and misery.   The prevailing impression, through the most of its extent, is of *darkness*.   Sin has separated the people from their God (verse 2), his face is hidden from them.   Thus the

light is gone; they have become as blind men, staggering in the
dark, groping for support, stumbling at noon as in twilight.

It is likely that the figure thus developed by the poet was suggested by a verse in the preceding poem. 58 : 10 had made the
conditional promise:

> Then thy light shall shine forth in the darkness, | thy gloom
>   shall become as the noonday.

The comparison of this with 59 : 9 is very striking. In view of
the indications, slight, but constantly appearing, that the poems
in our collection were written in the order in which we now find
them and put forth in a single 'book,' we are justified in the conjecture that when the poet had finished 58, he proceeded to elaborate in the two following poems, 59 and 60, the contrasted pictures suggested in 58 : 10. It is hardly possible to doubt that the
two were intended to stand side by side; see the introduction to
chapter 60 for further evidence of this, and also for a more general
view of the relation between the two poems, with a comparison of
the poet's similar proceeding in other instances.

The gloom of the poem is not unrelieved. The Second Isaiah
could never have written *of his own people* in this strain without
the relief of an overtone of hope. The 'second theme' is suggested
in the very first verse of the chapter: "Is the Lord's hand power-
less to save? Is he deaf, so that he cannot hear?" As verse 20
declares, there is still hope of 'glory' *for those who repent.* The
transition to this second subject, with the treatment of which the
poem concludes, is made by the use of a sort of refrain, verses 15*b*,
16, also employed, in varied form, in 41 : 28 and 63 : 5, *cf.* 50 : 2.

The poem 56 : 9–57 : 21 was addressed mainly to the unfaithful,
in part to the renegades; 58 was spoken to those in Israel who
were at least outwardly faithful; 59 is addressed to the whole
community. Such a portrayal of guilt and distress bordering on
despair is hardly to be found elsewhere. It is confession as well as
accusation; from verse 9 onward the prophet speaks in the first
person plural.

The meter is 3 | 3, closing with two triads, verse 21 consisting of
two 3 | 3 | 3 lines.

---

59 : 1. The proper name, Yahwè, is probably secondary, as in
so many other places, the original reading here being יָדוֹ. This

greatly improves not only the meter but also the assonance of the two half-verses.

59 : 2. The word היו is theological retouching for the benefit of later readers, seemingly justified not only by the perfect tense in the second half-verse but also by the promise in verse 21. It overloads the line, and puts the emphasis in the wrong place; "sin" and "separation" are the emphatic words. The Greek would have rendered the word if it had been present; in fact, it renders only the present participle.

"Between" is expressed in this way only here in the O. T. It is common in the Palestinian Aramaic; see Dalman, *Grammatik*, 2d ed., p. 231.

59 : 2. פנים with poetical ellipsis of the suffix pronoun. Job 34 : 29 is a precisely similar case.

59 : 3. In נגאלו one of the massoretic double readings is to be seen. Either *puʻal* or *nifʻal*. So also Lam. 4 : 14.

59 : 4. The meaning of עמל is "trouble, mischief." *Cf.* Ps. 7 : 15, Job 15 : 35.

59 : 5. הזורה seems to be another double reading; one was certainly חַזּוּרָה (the original), the other perhaps הַזְרְרָה (*cf.* Is. 1 : 6). This verse contains allusions to Hebrew folk-lore which were obvious to contemporaries of the prophet, but which we can hardly hope to understand.

59 : 6. In the first half of this verse we can see unmistakably the author of 47 : 14*b*! See also the mention of this passage in Chapter XI.

59 : 8. With the "crooked, uneven" path compare 40 : 4; 42 : 16. The form בָּהּ is correct, "Whoever treads one of them." The versions of course render by the plural, but they probably had our text before them.

59 : 9. The prophet's introduction of himself, even in the first person plural, along with the rest of his people, is so unusual as to be noteworthy.

59 : 10. The meaning of the verb נשש seems here to be "strike against" rather than simply "feel" or "touch." Compare the frequent use in late Hebrew and Aramaic, and consider the writer's fondness for repeating a word in varied meaning. The direct object is then understood, as so often.

The last clause of the verse contains a word, *ashmannim*, which is otherwise unknown and is seemingly impossible in this connection, for the following word, "like dying men," is certainly cor-

rectly transmitted. The emendation מָאֲשִׁים נְעִים may be ventured;
cf. Deut. 28 : 29 and Job 5 : 14, which seem to be closely parallel.
The form of the participle, from מָשַׁשׁ, would then be an Aramaism.
"Groping, reeling, like dying men." The reading of our present
text would then be accounted for by the frequent graphic confusion of ב and מ, here rendered especially easy by the construction
in the preceding clause.

59 : 13. Instead of עֹשֶׁק we must read עָקֵשׁ, with Lagarde and
others. The word וְהֹגוֹ is secondary and must be expunged. The
vowel-pointing of הֹרוֹ embraces two readings, both infin. absolute
but from different verbs: הָרֹו *qal*, as in verse 4, and הֹרֵה *hif'il* of
ירה; "teaching," a very natural variant. It seems likely that from
the latter (marginal?) reading, combined with הֹגה in verse 11. our
text was obtained.

59 : 15a. The last word in this sentence is the result of some
mistake, as the commentators generally agree. By reading הַשְׂכֵּל,
"piety," the sense is restored and the parallelism perfect (observe
that the Greek translator read just these consonants). The writer's
meaning is the same as in 57 : 1. For the rendering "piety," as
contrasted with "wickedness," *cf.* especially Dan. 11 : 32 f.; 12 : 3,
10; also Is. 44 : 18, Ps. 14 : 2, Job 22 : 2, Prov. 15 : 24. Our present
text is the result of a misunderstanding of סָר מֵרָע, which ordinarily
means '*turning away from evil*.'

The massoretic division of the verses is obviously incorrect and
disturbing here. It doubtless was occasioned by the misunderstanding just mentioned.

59 : 15 f. Compare 41 : 28; 63 : 5, as well as the similar transition
in 42 : 13 and elsewhere. Notice also in this connection the קִנְאָה
in verse 17, compared with 42 : 13 and 63 : 15.

59 : 18. This verse affords a remarkable illustration of the
prophet's favorite manner of playing upon words. The first *kě'al*
is the particle of comparison combined with the preposition. The
same word-form in its second occurrence is the temporal adverb
"now," *kě'an* (properly Aramaic) having the phonetic variation
kě'al, whence the Syriac *kēl* (*kēn* in the Mandæan dialect). In
like manner the parallel form *kě'eneth, kě'eth,* becomes in Syriac
kēth—and eventually *kē, kai.*

Again, the word *gěmūl* (or *gěmūla*) is capable of two different
meanings, "deed" and "requital." It is used in the former sense
at the beginning of the verse, but in the latter sense in the immediate sequel.

59 : 19. It appears that there is a play on words here, between the meanings "fear" and "see." The former applies only to the *name*, the latter to the *glory*. See Chapter XI.

The form צָר seems impossible in this context. Should we not read צָרָר? Observe that the next word begins with the letter *resh*.

59 : 20. The words "saith Yahwè," at the end of the verse in our text, are shown to be a later addition—by the meter combined with the fact of their absence in the Greek. So Duhm, Cheyne, Marti.

59 : 21. The first clause certainly was suggested by Gen. 9 : 9; 17 : 4, etc.; another instance of allusion to the *Priestly* document in the Pentateuch. See the note on 54 : 9.

CHAPTER 60

A poem with a single theme: the glory of Jerusalem in the Messianic age, which is at hand. From the first verse to the last it is one blaze of light. *Light*, in fact, is the idea which is given the leading place, and the most varied and striking expression, in the poem; see verses 1–3, 5, 11, 19 f. This is in evident contrast with the almost unrelieved gloom of chapter 59, in which the wickedness of the chosen people is so unsparingly set forth, the prophet declaring in anguish that the Jerusalem of his own day is plunged in the *darkness* of guilt (verses 9, 10; *cf.* also 58 : 8*a*, 10*b*). We remember that in other places in the *divan* of the Second Isaiah an outburst of especial severity is immediately followed by a poem in which the faith and hope of the poet carry him away completely. Thus, after the horror of 34 comes, as its companion piece, the glory of 35; 44, the sharp rebuke of idolatry, is followed by the great Messianic chapter 45; 48, equal to 59 in its vehement denunciation, beginning with the stern assertion that the "children of Israel" have no right to the name, and ending with the cry, "No peace for the wicked!" has for its sequel the splendid prediction and surpassing tenderness of 49. The probability that here also the collocation is deliberate, the partial picture given in 59 being corrected and completed by 60, is made almost certainty by the way in which certain phrases of the former chapter are alluded to in the latter. In 59 : 6 f. it is said that "violence (חמס) is in their hands," and that "rapine and ruin (שד ושבר) are in their paths." In 60 : 18, on the contrary, it is predicted: "Naught more

shall be heard of violence (חמס) in thy land, rapine and ruin (שׂד
ושבר) in thy borders." It is noticeable, moreover, how the concluding verses of 59 prepare the way for 60: redemption is promised for
those in Israel *who repent* (59 : 20); Yahwè's covenant with them
will never be abandoned (verse 21); his glory will come like a
mighty stream; the farthest countries will see and acknowledge it
(verse 19).

The subject of the poem, the New Jerusalem, purified and glorious, the centre of the world and the joy of all nations, is one upon
which the Second Isaiah has often touched in the preceding poems
of the collection. See 35 : 10; 45 : 14; 46 : 13; 49 : 14–26; 51 : 3, 11;
52 : 1, 8 ff.; 54 : 11–14; 55 : 12 f. Now, however, he develops the
theme in full detail, with the imagery and the literary art which
are so striking and so unlike those of any other Old Testament
writer. One picture follows another in rapid succession, the language being nearly everywhere figurative.

The home-gathering of scattered Israel, from all corners of the
earth, is a feature which is made prominent here, as in so many
chapters from 43 onward. Some details of the scene, as well as
the manner of treatment, remind us strongly of chapter 49. The
foreign peoples and their kings come to the holy city, bringing
with them all the "exiled" members of the chosen race; the Gentiles are represented as nurses and attendants, and the Israelites
as little children borne in their arms. Compare verses 3 f., 8 f.,
16, with 49 : 18, 22 f. The words of 4*a* are repeated, in the author's
characteristic manner, from 49 : 18*a*. There they referred only to
the children of Israel; here they are applied primarily to the foreign peoples. The startled soliloquy of Zion in 49 : 21 has its interesting counterpart in 60 : 5*a*, though the form is altogether different. The pathetic motive which is developed so eloquently in
49, the distress and despair of downtrodden Zion, is barely touched
upon in 60, in verses 14 f. (see below, on the meter), with the
slightest allusion in one or two other passages (verses 17, 20).
Still another point of close contact between the two chapters is
the repetition of 49 : 26*b* in 60 : 16*b*.

A point of especial interest is *the share of the Gentiles in the blessings of the Messianic age.* The prophet has in his mind's eye a
definite picture, a typical scene, which he repeats in several of
his poems. After the final crash, in which the foes of Yahwè, both
Jew and Gentile, are utterly overthrown, all peoples acknowledge
and serve the one true God, and Israel and Jerusalem enjoy the
triumph for which they have waited so many weary centuries; a

triumph which is theirs not merely by virtue of an arbitrary promise in the remote past, but one which has been more than earned
by their achievement of salvation for all the world (49 : 6; 53 : 5 f.).
Then the poet sees in imagination a vast throng, from all parts of
the earth, seeking the holy land and entering the holy city. The
foreign nations, led by their kings, bring home the Israelites who
had been dwelling among them, and do glad homage to the chosen
people of Yahwè (now the God of them all), bowing down to the
ground in true Oriental fashion and giving their formal testimony
that the despised and tormented race was right, and that through
it alone light and life have come to the peoples of the world. This
picture was drawn first in 45 : 14, a verse which is a perfect minia-
ture of 60 : 3–16. It next appears in 49 : 22 f., a passage whose
intimate relationship with chapter 60 has already been pointed
out. Finally, the scene returns once more in 66 : 12–14, 18–21,
with all the familiar imagery. The ships and caravans of the
Gentiles throng to the New Jerusalem; the infant children of Israel
nurse at the breast of the nations, who bring them home with
rejoicing; some of these foreigners will even be chosen by Yahwè
to be his priests and Levites. All these passages are written from
precisely the same point of view, and are plainly the product of
one imagination and one great soul. Here in chapter 60 *the participation of the Gentiles,* in one way or another, is kept in sight all
the way from verse 3 to the end of verse 16. Verse 12 is a later
interpolation, as many have recognized; it is altogether foreign to
the spirit in which the poem was written. The interpolation of
the word בַּזּקִים in the similar passage 45 : 14 is an instructive
parallel; see the note there.

The meter of the poem is 3 | 3, except verse 14*a*, which is obvi-
ously 3 | 2. The reason for the momentary change was no doubt
chiefly dramatic, since this is the most striking and significant
single episode in the great pageant, and the point at which the
"pathetic note" mentioned above is momentarily sounded. Perhaps the poet was moved also by his recollection of the parallel
45 : 14, and the strongly contrasted passage 51 : 23, in both of
which the 3 | 2 verse was employed. Other examples of the ap-
pearance of a single 3 | 2 couplet in a 3 | 3 context, in this collec-
tion, are 44 : 25; 54 : 6; and 66 : 11; *cf.* also 65 : 13.
The text of the poem is generally sound, but in a few verses

(16, 19, 21) the combination of external and internal (metrical) evidence gives ground for slight emendation.

---

60 : 1.   In the first clause we have the usual paronomasia. The אוֹרִי אוֹרִי rendered by the Greek is an inferior reading.

The prophet's conception of "darkness" and "light," here as elsewhere, is primarily ethical. Light is the presence of God; verses 1–3, 19 f. Sin means separation from him, and through sin Israel is in darkness; 50 : 1; 54 : 8; 59 : 9. They are groping like blind men; 42 : 16, 19; 59 : 10. Only the return to God, in righteousness of life, can bring back the light of day; 58 : 8, 10. The Gentiles will come to the knowledge of the true God, that is, unto the light. *Cf.* 25 : 7 f.

60 : 2.   The article in הַחֹשֶׁךְ is probably the result of dittography.

60 : 4.   This verse excellently illustrates the poet's characteristic habit of repeating striking phrases which he has used in previous poems. The first half of the verse is word for word as in 49 : 18, and the second half is slightly varied from 49 : 22. *Cf.* also 66 : 12*b*. This was a picture to which his mind kept returning. It is better to point יָבִיאוּ, *hiph'il*, rather than יָבֹאוּ, since it is a constant feature of this scene that the Gentiles "bring home" the Jews, who are represented as little children, the children of Zion, borne in arms; see verse 9; 49 : 22; 66 : 20. Duhm fails, as usual, to see that all this is figurative.

60 : 5.   The assonance in פָּחַד וְרָחַב is obviously intentional. The meaning of פחד, *joyful* excitement, ecstasy, is best paralleled in Jer. 33 : 9; with the use of רחב, to signify the "widening" of the understanding, *cf.* especially I Kings 5 : 9, רֹחַב לֵב, also Ps. 119 : 32. In the first clause of the verse the verb נהרת (probably an Aramaism) signifies the same thing, "enlightenment"; *cf.* the figurative use in Syriac, and the phrase מנהיר עיני חכמים, "He who enlightens the eyes of the wise," quoted in Levy, *Neuhebr. Wörterbuch*. The parallelism of the verse is thus complete.

The words המון (late in this sense) and חיל include all the resources of the great Western lands: men, arts and industries, commerce, wealth of every kind. Jerusalem shall be no longer an insignificant city, but in very truth "the joy of the whole earth." The M. T. reading יָבֹאוּ is probably a combination of the two readings יבוא (preferable also metrically) and יָבֹאוּ (suggested by verse 11; *cf.* also the Targ.).

The current exegesis of this and the following verses is gro-
tesquely perverted and unfair. Having postulated that the
prophet is neither a good poet (see Duhm's introd. to the chapter,
echoed by Marti, and his notes on verses 2 and 13) nor a man of
high ethical ideals, our interpreters proceed to explain that the
mainspring of the enthusiasm of this poem, and the chief cause of
Zion's ecstasy at the dawn of the new age (see Duhm and Marti
on verse 5 especially), is the thought that the Jews are to get possession of the riches of the Gentiles! The foreign nations, now in
subjection to Israel, bring tribute; and, in addition, the returning
"exiles" despoil the peoples with whom they have been dwelling
(see the same commentators, on verses 6, 9, 10). Not a word of
all this is to be found in the text, if the prophet is allowed to interpret himself, and it is utterly foreign to the spirit of this poem
and the others in the collection.

60 : 6. With the first clause cf. Ezek. 26 : 10. The resemblance
seems too close to be accidental, and Second Isaiah is certainly
not the borrower. Cf. also שֶׁפַע יַמִּים, Deut. 33 : 19.

Some one might raise the question why the prophet does not
mention in the following passage the steeds of Mesopotamia, the
chariots of Egypt, the merchandise of Aram and Phœnicia. The
obvious answer is that he is speaking in the mood and terms of a
poet, with his thought far removed from anything like realism.
He uses the popular, half-proverbial phrases commonly employed
in allusions to the peoples and products of the ends of the earth;
very much as our forefathers spoke of "the wealth of Ormus," the
"jewels of Golconda," and "the treasures of the Incas." Whom
shall he mention as typical Gentiles? A true poet, he turns away
from whatever could suggest the present turmoil and misery, and
sings of the wide, free spaces of the earth—the desert and the
ocean; the nomads and the sailors. In a precisely similar way in
42 : 10 f. and 45 : 14 he had sung of the wilderness, the seas, and
the isles as acknowledging Yahwè; mentioning the Bedouins of
Kedar, the dwellers in the mountain cliffs, the merchants of Ethiopia, the giant Sabeans—whatever was picturesque and far away.
But our commentators labor at these passages without ever suspecting that they have poetry before them.

The gold and frankincense are typical, and a detail of the picture. Whoever finds evidence of greed here could find it also in
Matt. 2 : 11.

The last clause of the verse, "*proclaiming the praise of the Lord,*"
is the important one; in fact, it strikes the key-note of the whole

chapter. In other passages the prophet has given us typical words spoken by the Gentiles on this occasion; see especially 45 : 14 (end) and chapter 53.

60 : 7. This is a very characteristic verse. Here we have again the writer of 43 : 20 and 34 : 14 ff.; see the notes on those passages, and *cf.* also 65 : 25. The participation of the dumb animals, in one way or another, gives added life to the picture.

ישרתונך "shall serve thee," *i. e.*, shall be at thy disposal, stand ready for thy service. The verb means precisely the same in verse 10. Some commentators have been misled by the Greek translator's free rendering, since he employs παραστήσονται, "will be at hand," in verse 10, but writes ἥξουσιν, "will come," in this verse—obviously in order to avoid the collocation of *four* verbs ending in –ησονται or –ησεται.

The reading על רצון is correct. The reason why a few MSS. have לרצון על is the proximity of 57 : 7, combined with the fact that לר׳ is the usual idiom. But the use of על is very natural. The equivalent phrase, *'alā riḍwān,* "acceptable," is regular in Arabic. It is not a good plan to "emend" away such idioms as these. There is no evidence that any ancient version had here a text differing from our M. T. The translators render, of course, by their own idioms, just as the English R. V. has: "they shall come up with acceptance *on* mine altar."

With this use of תפארתי *cf.* 63 : 15 and 64 : 10. The reading of the Greek, obtained from 56 : 7, is worthless.

We should perhaps hardly expect the verb in the first person, אפאר, "*I will* beautify." But Second Isaiah is fond of giving just this turn to the sentence, where the first person has already appeared in the preceding context. We have an example in verse 13: "To adorn my sanctuary, and the place where I tread *I will* glorify." 45 : 1: "To trample nations before him, and the loins of Kings *I will* loosen." 49 : 5 (as emended): "To restore Jacob to him, and Israel *I will* gather."

60 : 8. The same picture which the poet had before his eyes in 43 : 5-7, 14 (as emended); 49 : 18, 21 f. In עב—עוף we have the usual paronomasia. Another example at the beginning of verse 10.

60 : 9. The reading איים would be better than ציים on its own merits, even if it were not attested by all the existing evidence. "Isles" (meaning the most remote lands, the outskirts of the inhabited world) is the most important word in the verse; *cf.* also the parallel passage 66 : 19. "Ships" is not needed, as a reply to

the rhetorical question in the preceding verse,* when we are told
that these white-winged messengers came from the Isles.

The pointing of the word יְקַוּוּ ought not to be in doubt, but
there is ground for debate as to the meaning. The versions all
render "wait," as in 51 : 5; and this meaning is not only possible
but suitab'e if the words are regarded as a definite allusion to the
former passage (this being the first great manifestation of what
was there predicated of the far countries), or if we can suppose
that the verb has the meaning "wait upon," "present oneself in
expectancy," Lat. *praestolari*. But it seems to me far more probable that the meaning is "*gather, collect*." No active stem of this
verb קוה happens to occur in the O. T., but such were of course in
use, and in view of the verbal noun קִוּוּי, "collection," preserved
in late Hebrew, it cannot be doubted that the *pi'el* was one of
them. The use of the word here is then a striking illustration of
the peculiar habit of this writer which is described and illustrated
often in this volume, namely the repetition of a word with altered
meaning—since the reminiscence of 51 : 5 is too obvious to be accidental.

The attempt to refer the suffix in כספם וזהבם to the Gentiles (!)
is as indefensible stylistically as it is from every other point of
view. See the note on verse 5. The New Jerusalem, the holy city
of the coming Messianic age, was indeed to be the centre of all
splendor and magnificence, just as it is pictured in the New Testament in Rev. 21 : 10–27, where the description is in part derived
from this very poem. The foreign nations, led by their kings, were
to bring thither their abundance and their treasures, but of their
own free will and in fulfilment of their chief desire, with enthusiastic affection for the city and the people through whom light and
life had come to them. Rev. 21 : 24 interprets correctly, paraphrasing verse 3 of this chapter: "The nations shall walk in its
light, and the kings of the earth bring their glory into it"; and
verses 26 and 27 also reproduce exactly the thought of the great
prophet: All that is choicest in the world shall come to the holy
city; none that are unclean or false; only those (including the
Gentiles) who are written in the book of life. As for the prophet's
thought of the Jews of the Dispersion, see Chapter IV. The Jerusalem and Palestine of his own day, though measurably prosperous,
were poor and unattractive enough in comparison with the riches
and comfort of the outside world. Should not the Jewish wealth,

* Moreover, the use of the particle כִּי implies that the answer to the question has already been given mentally.

as well as the Gentile wealth, of the foreign lands be brought in with joy to beautify the renewed city? This is what the prophet predicts.

The last clause of the verse is repeated from 55:5, in characteristic manner.

60:10. The city walls imagined by the poet are doubtless like those pictured in Rev. 21:12–21, such walls as never were seen on earth. They are thought of as an ornament, not as a protection; see the next verse. Jerusalem is the pride of all men, and the Gentiles are hardly less eager than the Jews to contribute to her glory; their kings are gladly "at her service" (see the note on verse 7). Nevertheless, the question remains: Does not this prediction indicate that the walls of Jerusalem were in fact lying in ruins in the prophet's day? The question is answered affirmatively in the standard commentaries, with good reason. And why the mention of the walls at just this point? The thought with which the writer is busied is the participation of the Gentiles in the coming glory of Jerusalem, and he has in mind the promise which he is about to make in verse 11: "Thy gates shall be open continually." This could only remind his hearers of the present forlorn condition of the city, without gates or walls; hence, evidently, the insertion of verse 10, to prepare the way. The first impression gained from the reading is correct, the devastation wrought by the Chaldeans had not yet been repaired. Compare also 58:12. A discussion of the date of Nehemiah's work is therefore necessary, since according to the prevailing view (which I believe I can show to be erroneous) it was accomplished many years before the date here assigned to Second Isaiah. The matter is fully treated in the note on 62:6.

With the second half of the verse cf. especially 54:7 f. and 57:17 f.

The whole verse gives good illustration of the inclination of Second Isaiah to make use of rhyme.

60:11. The pointing of וּפִתְּחוּ, intrans. pi'el, is correct; see the note on 48:8.

The phrase חֵיל גּוֹיִם has here a meaning different from that in verse 5; another example of the favorite literary mannerism of this writer. Here חֵיל means "train, host, throng," exactly as in I Kings 10:2, where the arrival in Jerusalem of the "train" of the Queen of Sheba is narrated. Here again the equally large-hearted prophet of Rev. 21:24–26 gives us the true interpretation of his ancient Hebrew predecessor. The gates of the city will stand open eternally (תָּמִיד) in order that the nations and peoples of all the

world may throng to the sanctuary of their God without cessation.
Cf. 2 : 2–4: the stream of foreign nations flowing like a great river
to Jerusalem, seeking the teaching and help of the God of Israel;
and see especially 49 : 6, 8–12, and the notes on the latter passage;
also such utterances as Jer. 3 : 17.

Further reason for giving to the word חֵיל in this passage the
meaning "host" is found in the following clause, וּמַלְכֵיהֶם נְהוּגִים,
which is decidedly in place after mention of great processions of
foreign nations, but not at all natural (see our commentators) in
continuation of words telling of the heaping up of *riches*. As for
the meaning of the clause, it is one of the characteristic specimens
of the poet's dry humor; less grim than 47 : 14*b*, and not continued
into details as in 41 : 5–7; 44 : 12–17, but the product of the same
irrepressible spirit. The word נְהוּגִים means no more—and no less
—than this, that the kings of Persia, Egypt, Syria, etc., will not
be in charge of affairs, on the occasion of this great pageant. They
will be 'personally conducted' by their proud benefactors. Bear in
mind that the ordinary meaning of חֵיל, as applied to the גוים, is
army. Jerusalem had had more than enough experience of foreign
armies, and there was terror in the thought of Gentile kings entering the city. Just as the prophet had said in 47 : 14, in a brief
parenthesis, "This 'fire' is not one to sit beside!" so here, by this
one good-humored touch, he says in effect: "*This* 'host of the
Gentiles,' with their kings, is not of the kind we have known!"
Cheyne's Comm. (1889) speaks of "their reluctant chiefs." Not
so; see verse 3. All the reluctant have perished in the great catastrophe, this is a renovated world. No unwilling spirit, whether
Gentile or Jew, will enter the holy city.

60 : 12. This verse is an addition by a later hand, an exegetical
appendage to נְהוּגִים (misunderstood). The interpolator is far
away from the spirit of the poem, just as he, or his fellow, was in
45 : 14 with the interpolation בַּזִּקִּים; see the note there. 61 : 5 is a
similar case.

60 : 13. This is a good example of the poet's habit of repeating
favorite phrases from his former poems. The first clause is slightly
changed from 35 : 2; the second clause is from 41 : 19. The word
יַחְדָּו, however, is not a part of the poet's own repetition, but came
in later from 41 : 19, as the meter shows. Precisely the same thing
happened in verse 16 of this chapter (the word יהוה, see below),
also in 49 : 8 (וְאֶצָּרְךָ repeated from 42 : 6); see the note on the
former passage.

As in 41 : 19; 35 : 1 f.; 55 : 12 f., the trees are mentioned merely in order to complete the picture of beauty. Cheyne (1889): "The barren hills of Jerusalem shall henceforth be decked with the most beautiful forest-trees." Yes, though the picture in the poet's mind was perhaps more inclusive and less definite than this; all the glories of field and forest will contribute to the splendor of the holy city, within and without.

With the last clause of the verse *cf.* the end of verse 7, and see the note there. מְקוֹם רַגְלַי, "my place of abode," includes the whole city, as does the phrase "place of my sanctuary" just preceding.

60 : 14. The correct pointing is שְׁחוֹחַ. The Massorites presumably intended by the anomalous vocalization to call attention to a variant reading; perhaps לִשְׁחוֹחַ?

60 : 15. The meaning of the phrase אֵין עוֹבֵר can be seen from 34 : 10; Jer. 9 : 9, 11; Ezek. 14 : 15; 33 : 28; Zeph. 3 : 6. From such phrases as this—characteristic Oriental exaggeration—arose the fiction of a Jerusalem uninhabited for forty years!

We must read לִמְשׂוֹשׂ, repeating, as usual, the construction with the preposition. The meter also shows this to be necessary.

60 : 16. The proper name Yahwè is probably secondary here, as so often elsewhere. The verse reads much more smoothly without it. It was probably derived from the closely parallel passage 49 : 26; observe the similar connection there.

60 : 19. At the end of the first half-verse לַיְלָה must be restored, as in the LXX. It is needed for both meter and parallelism. The best place for it is just before לֹא.

60 : 21*b*. The Massorites have here combined *two* readings in characteristic manner: (1) "the sprout of *his* planting, the work of *his* hands," as in 61 : 3 and LXX; (2) "the sprout of *my* planting, the work of *my* hands," as in Syr., Lat., and Targ. In verses 19 f. Yahwè had spoken of himself in the third person, as often elsewhere in these poems (*cf.* also Ex. 19 : 24, Jer. 29 : 7, and many other passages).

CHAPTER 61

A 'Servant' poem, with the figure of the Servant Messianically conceived, as in chapter 42 (first part), 45, and 49. The soliloquy is in the manner of 49 : 1–6 and 50 : 4–9 especially. The picture of the sympathetic and magnanimous helper of the distressed, the world over, takes us back to 42 : 1–7, and the beauty of the present description surpasses that of its predecessor.

A phrase from the preceding poem, chapter 60, seems to have lingered in the mind of the poet. Verse 3*b* introduces a figure not suggested by the context, but repeated from 60 : 21. This seems to be another of the many indications of the close sequence of the poems in time and the preservation of their original order.

The Hebrew text has suffered slight accidental corruption in a few places. Verse 5 is an interpolation, a product of the same narrow spirit which caused the insertion of verse 12 in chapter 60. The interpolation here necessitated slight alterations in the immediately following context; see the notes.

The meter is 3 | 3.

61 : 1. "My Lord, Yahwè." *Cf.* the use of this phrase in 50 : 4–9. The resemblance to 42 : 1 in these opening words is equally noticeable; the more so, as there is no direct quotation.

The employment of the verb "anoint" is not accidental, nor insignificant. The Servant, who is the speaker, is *The Messiah.* The noun itself, with this meaning, appears in 45 : 1.

"To bind up the broken-hearted." With the use of the preposition ל with *direct* object *cf.* 53 : 12; 56 : 8.

Instead of אסורים, "prisoners," the Grk. read עורים, "blind." I believe this to be the original reading; not only because of 42 : 7, and the evident possibility that "prisoners" were expected here by some transcriber because of the "captives" in the preceding clause and the recollection of 49 : 9, but especially because of the closing word of the verse. The root פקח is used specifically of the "opening" *of eyes;* and the various tropical uses, in Hebrew, Aramaic, and Arabic, are all taken directly from this signification. The use of the root for the opening of *doors,* etc., is otherwise unexampled.

61 : 2. The "year of favor" is the same as the "time of favor" of 49 : 8; namely, the dawn of the Messianic age.

"Vengeance" is not an adequate rendering of נקם, either here or in 35 : 4; 63 : 4, and other similar passages. Notice the parallel words in the Hebrew text, and the renderings of the ancient translators.

61 : 3. After the first word in this verse the word לֵב, "heart, courage," fell out by accident. A direct object is required for the verb, and the love of this writer for paronomasia points out the monosyllable that was lost. The accidental omission was easy because of the resemblance to the first letters of the following word.

The proposal to transpose the words מַעֲטֵה and אֵבֶל (Bickell, Cheyne, Oort, Duhm, Kittel, Marti) is surprising in view of verse 10 of this chapter. Just why the "mantle of righteousness," or "clothing of deliverance," could not also be a "garment of praise," I am unable to see. The text as it stands is better in every way than the proposed emendation. The effect, so characteristic of the poet, gained by the rhythmical *and assonant* parallel — תַּחַת עָפָר, תַּחַת אֵבֶל—should not be disturbed. It is not necessary, moreover, that מַעֲטֵה תְהִלָה should be parallel with רוּחַ כֵּהָה.

61 : 4. With the "cities" of this passage *cf.* 43 : 28, as emended.

61 : 5. This verse is shown to be a later interpolation (see the introduction to the chapter) not only by its narrow spirit, but also by the way in which it breaks the grammatical connection. Verses 4 and 7 are in the third person, except for a telltale *second person* at the beginning of 7. Verse 6, as originally written, was certainly in the third person. Along with the alteration to the second person was made the necessary addition of וְאַתֶּם, "But ye," at the beginning of the verse.

61 : 6. Cancel the first word (see the preceding note), and emend the verbs of the verse to the third person.

The last word in the verse is a riddle. The reading of the Greek, θαυμασθήσεσθε, seems to show that the translator saw (or conjectured) תִּתְאַדְּמָרוּ. The original was probably תִּתְיַמְּרוּ, since in the Aramaic script of the fifth and fourth centuries B. C. the characters מ and ק are often nearly or quite identical in form. *Cf.* especially the Targum to 43 : 4.

61 : 7. Read בָּשְׁתָם (see above) and וְרֹק in place of יָרֹנּוּ, following Klostermann's excellent emendation on the basis of 50 : 6.

61 : 8. The בְּעוֹלָה is absolutely impossible. The original reading was מֵעוֹלָם, "false dealing I hate *from eternity*." The Grk. translator's ἐξ ἀδικίας shows that he read the first letter of the word in this way. It is the גֵּזֶל מִשְׁפָּט that is meant; *cf.* 10 : 2 and Eccles. 5 : 7. Yahwè says: 'I deal justly, and will give my people all their due.'

61 : 10 f. Compare especially 42 : 10 ff. Also 62 : 1 and 63 : 7.

The massoretic יעטני is the usual 'alternative' combination, some MSS. reading the perfect tense, others the imperfect.

For every reason, read יְכוֹנֵן here instead of the utterly improbable יכהן.

The 'coda' of the poem, verses 10 and 11, sums up the two principal themes: the exalted mission of the Servant (verses 1–3), and the restoration of Israel, in the eyes of the nations (verses 4–9).

CHAPTER 62

This poem, which is another monologue by the Servant (the Messiah), is closely related to its predecessor. It is conceived in a lyric mood throughout, reminding perhaps especially of 52 : 7–12.

The remarkable passage, verses 6 f., brings before us the Anointed One in the time of his preparation, *before* the arrival of the great 'year of favor.' So also 45 : 4 f.; 49 : 4.

In verse 10 we have another of the brief and picturesque outbursts which are so eminently the peculiar property of this poet. The language here is strongly reminiscent of 49 : 22 and 57 : 14. Verse 11*b* repeats the words of 40 : 10, in a manner very frequently illustrated in these poems.

_____

The Hebrew text is generally well preserved. The meter is 3 | 3 in the introductory paragraph, verses 1 f.; 3 | 2 in the remainder of the poem.

_____

62 : 4. The words "shall not again be called" *in their second occurrence* are probably a later expansion of the text, as the meter seems to show.

62 : 5. At the beginning of this verse two readings seem to have been combined, though the evidence is not very clear. Either כִּי בָעַל or כְּבָעֹל (thus the LXX) would make good sense (practically the same sense). The reading of our text is hardly permissible.

At the end of the first half-verse the original reading must have been יִבְעָלֵךְ בֹּנֵךְ, as many scholars have seen. The present reading is nonsense.

62 : 6. This is the last of the three passages in which mention is made of the *walls* of Jerusalem; see 49 : 16 and 60 : 10, and com-

pare also 58 : 12. The question whether the rebuilding of the
walls of the city, as narrated in the Book of Nehemiah, had already been accomplished at the time when these poems were written is one of considerable importance, in view of the fortunate cir-
cumstance that we are able to date the prophet's work.

In 49 : 16 the poet is speaking of an ideal city, as all interpreters
agree. This passage may therefore be left out of account. In the
present passage, 62 : 6, we are certainly dealing with a figure of
speech, and yet it seems probable here that the "walls" mentioned
are thought of as actually existing. The natural interpretation is
that which is given in the standard commentaries: the "watchmen" are imagined as standing on the shattered remnants of wall
and towers and calling upon the God of Israel to restore the city
and make it once more "a praise in the earth." Thus Duhm,
Cheyne, Marti, and many others. The passage which has generally been regarded as conclusive is 60 : 10. Here the prophet promises that in the day of triumph, pictured as close at hand, the foreigners who are now hostile to Jerusalem "shall build up her
walls." It would be claiming too much to say of this that it leaves
no room for doubt, but the argument derived from it will not be
overthrown without very strong and unequivocal evidence to the
contrary. The view which holds the field is certainly this, that
when chapter 60 was written the walls which had been razed by
the Babylonian army had not yet been rebuilt.

In Chapter VI, after arguing for the date of about 400 B. C. for
the prophecy of Second Isaiah, I mentioned the bearing of these
conclusions upon the disputed date of Nehemiah's work, and reserved the discussion of the question for this place. Was Nehemiah's patron Artaxerxes I Longimanus, or Artaxerxes II Mnemon? The former view has been commonly held, chiefly because
of a misunderstanding of the chronological scheme furnished by
the Chronicler; the latter view is maintained by Marquart, *Fun-
damente isr. und jüd. Geschichte*, 31, and by Henry Preserved Smith,
Old Testament History, 382, 395. In my *Ezra Studies* I demonstrated, and emphasized in many places, the perfectly certain fact
that *the Jewish tradition*, represented by the Chronicler and reappearing in the Book of Daniel, placed Darius Hystaspis before
Cyrus, thus assigning the completion of the temple to the reign of
Darius II; and also, that in this pseudo-history the patron of Ezra
and Nehemiah can be no other than Artaxerxes Mnemon; see pp.
38 ff., 135 f., 140, 249, 334 f.

The Elephantine papyri have given us very important information on this point, which, however, has not yet been fully utilized in combination with the Biblical and other evidence. I touched upon this matter in my *Ezra Studies*, 334 f., but left it only half considered. We know from the petition to the governor of Judea that a Sanballat was governor of Samaria under Artaxerxes I, and the conclusion has been drawn, very naturally but too hastily, that he is the Sanballat of the Book of Nehemiah. It must not be forgotten that we have documentary evidence of *another* Sanballat, governor of Samaria, who lived two generations later. Josephus, *Antt.* xi, 7, 2; 8, 2, tells how, in the time of this latter personage, in the reign of Darius III, the Samaritan schism took place.

The account in Josephus cannot simply be waved aside as incomprehensible. Nor can it possibly be made to suit another historical background; it is far too extensive, detailed, and self-consistent to permit any such adaptation. Josephus certainly did not invent the story, though he doubtless embellished and exaggerated it in his usual fashion; we may see his hand in the characterization of the Samaritans and their adherents, the incidents in which Alexander the Great plays a part, the statement that this Sanballat was "a Cuthean" (the favorite name for the Samaritans) who had been "sent into the land by Darius," and so on. I have conjectured (*op. cit.*, 331 f.) that he obtained this account from the same source—unknown to us, but evidently well informed—from which he derived the narrative of the high priest Johanan, his brother Jeshua, and the Persian governor Bagoas (Bagoses), which in Josephus's history immediately precedes the narrative of the Samaritan schism. The historical setting and principal details of this latter event could not possibly have been forgotten in Jerusalem—no tradition in all Jewish history would have been more certain to be preserved—and there could not fail to be historians to record and describe the occurrence. What is more, it is precisely this historical situation, in the time of Darius III Codomannus, which best agrees with the other data which we possess.

The petition of the Jews at Elephantine shows that the two sons of the Sanballat there mentioned, named Delaiah and Shelemiah, were in charge of affairs at Samaria in the year 408. This clearly implies that the Persian king had permitted the office of governor to remain in that family; and also that Sanballat was still living, though incapacitated, and was to be succeeded at his death by the elder of the two sons. According to a very wide-spread custom, the oldest grandson was likely to be given the name of the grandfather; it would therefore follow that in the ordinary course of

events the successor of Delaiah or Shelemiah as governor of the
province of Samaria would be another Sanballat. Our evidence is
quite sufficient to show that this was actually the case, and by
this supposition every document is explained and every chronological difficulty removed. "At the time when Alexander the Great
arrived in Syria the governor of Samaria was in fact Sanballat II." *

We could have been certain, in any case, that the Samaritan
schism did not take place in the time of Artaxerxes I. We might
indeed believe, as would be necessary under that supposition, that
the Pentateuch had already received its final redaction and its
latest accretion by the middle of the fifth century B. C., though
this has not been the prevailing opinion.† But the petition of
Jedoniah and his fellows shows us plainly that as late as the year
408 there had been no breach between Jews and Samaritans, nor,
apparently, any open hostility. To quote from Cowley, *Aramaic
Papyri of the Fifth Century B. C.*, p. 110: "The fact that the Jews
of Elephantine applied also to Delaiah and Shelemiah at Samaria,
and mention this to the authorities at Jerusalem, shows that (at
any rate as far as they knew) no religious schism had as yet taken
place." The Egyptian Jews cannot possibly have remained long
in ignorance of important happenings in Palestine. Moreover,
from what we know of the long-existing rivalry between the community in Shechem and that in Jerusalem, and the intensely bitter
feeling after the feud had once broken out, it seems utterly improbable that the Sanballat whose sons are appealed to in the
Elephantine letter should have been the same man whose determined enmity is described in Neh. 2–6; who was formally cursed
by the Jewish leader; the one whose son-in-law was "chased" out
of Jerusalem. No, the father of Delaiah and Shelemiah was not
"Sanballat the Horonite," ‡ but his grandfather. The account of
the schism given by Josephus is substantially true, and in its proper
setting. The first outbreak of open hostility, as narrated in the
Book of Nehemiah, was in the time of Artaxerxes II (the Jewish
tradition was right as to this); the date of the rebuilding of the city

---

* *Ezra Studies*, p. 330. This conclusion was accepted and utilized by W. F.
Albright in the *Journal of Biblical Literature*, vol. XL (1921), p. 122.

† It is obvious, and beyond question, that no addition made *after* the schism
by either party would be accepted by the other; it would, on the contrary, be
made the ground of a charge of falsification. The agreement of the Samaritan
Pentateuch with the massoretic Hebrew is conclusive evidence that the Five
Books were in their final form before the departure of Manasseh from Jerusalem.

‡ As to the origin of this nickname, we shall probably continue to be in the
dark.

wall was 384;* the expulsion of the renegade Manasseh took place
in the time of Darius III.

It is easy to show that the hypothesis of *two* Sanballats, grandfather and grandson, works out perfectly in point of chronology as
well as in every other way. If we suppose Sanballat I to have
been seventy-five years of age at the time of the Elephantine letter (408 B. C.), this would give 483 as the year of his birth. Reck-
oning thirty-five years to the generation, we could then assume
413 as the natal year of Sanballat II. The latter would thus have
been twenty-nine years of age at the time (384 B. C.) when Nehemiah repaired the wall, and eighty-one in the year 332, when
Alexander came to Palestine. This agrees with Josephus's statement (*Antt.* xi, 8, 2) that he was an old man and that he died in
this same year.

It remains to notice the curious item, half narrated, half concealed, which the Chronicler brings before us momentarily in
Neh. 13:28 f.† He represents Nehemiah as saying that a son of
Joiada the high priest (*cf.* 12:10 f., 22) married a daughter of
Sanballat "the Horonite," wherefore (says Nehemiah) "I drove
him away from me." This is not an allusion to the circumstances
of the Samaritan schism. Nehemiah was *not* the chief actor on that
occasion, nor was he even living in Jerusalem when the priestly
renegades were expelled; if he had been, the fact would infallibly
have been preserved in Jewish tradition, *kept alive by this written
record* (Neh. 13:28) of the great leader himself. It is plain from
the account in Josephus that Nehemiah was not associated in any
way with the great event, nor with any incident connected with it.
On the other hand, the natural interpretation of verse 29 sees in it
a veiled allusion to the happenings described by Josephus in *Antt.*
xi, 8, 2. Those unnamed persons who "defiled the covenant of the
priesthood and of the Levites" are presumably the priests and
Levites who revolted to Manasseh and entered the service of the
Samaritan sanctuary. As I have maintained for more than thirty
years, the Chronicler is here dealing a characteristic thrust at the
Samaritans through the medium of Nehemiah.

It is to be remarked that there is no anachronism or other im-

* It is very easy to believe that permission for this undertaking was given
by the utterly weak and incompetent Artaxerxes Mnemon, after the Persian
power had lost its hold in the West. Longimanus would have been quite
likely to do what the Jewish popular narrator of the third century B. C. asserts
him to have done, in Ezra 4:8–23.

† For the evidence that the Chronicler, not Nehemiah, is the writer see *Ezra
Studies*, 248 f.

possibility in the incident of verse 28. A son of the high priest Joiada might well have married a daughter of the same Sanballat who opposed Nehemiah in 384, and whose still younger daughter was espoused by Manasseh in 333. The decision as to the historical probability of the incident should depend on the estimate of the Chronicler's trustworthiness as a historian.

The way in which the conclusions here reached explain difficulties hitherto felt, and confirm results already obtained from other lines of evidence, must not be overlooked. The date (*c.* 400) conjectured for Second Isaiah; the necessity of supposing the Samaritan schism to have been a comparatively late occurrence; and, also, of supposing the expulsion of Sanballat's son-in-law from Jerusalem to have been immediately connected with the founding of the rival church on Mt. Gerizim and not separated from that event by a hundred years; the absence of any hostility on the part of Sanballat (I) and his sons at the time of the Elephantine letter; the confirmation, in its main features, of the account of the schism given by Josephus; the striking unanimity with which the Jewish traditional chronology in the writings of the O. T. brings the activities of Ezra and Nehemiah into the reign of Artaxerxes II Mnemon;* and, finally, the agreement with the implication of Is. 60:10 that in the time of Second Isaiah the walls of the city had not yet been rebuilt—among all these details there is perfect harmony, and every document known to us gives its support. As for the present passage in II Isaiah, the current exegesis is undoubtedly correct.

62:7. The principal pause in the verse must follow the word יכונן.

62:8. Compare 65:21 f.: "They shall plant vineyards, and eat their fruit; . . . they shall not plant, and another eat."

62:10. See the note on 57:14, and also on 35:8. The poet still sees in imagination the same 'highway through the desert' which he had described in the latter passage and then immediately afterward in chapter 40; the road of the fugitives from Egyptian bondage, the way by which the 'ransomed' of all nations return home. In this poem, to be sure, it is the restoration of Israel that the poet has in mind.

---

* Thus the Aramaic Document in Ezra, the Chronicler, the two authors of the Book of Daniel, and the consonant text of the massoretic tradition, as I have shown in detail elsewhere.

Chapters 63 : 1–64 : 11

This poem shows the Second Isaiah at the summit of his power and in full consciousness of it. It is among his greatest compositions, unsurpassed for dramatic vigor and for intensity of emotion. Its subject is contained in the question with which it closes: "May not the great day come *soon ?*"

The opening passage, in which the *dies iræ* is described in a dramatic dialogue, is perhaps the most impressive scene which the poet's imagination has created. The terror of the description is at once relieved by the tender lyric chant, verses 7 ff., uttered in the first person. It is not at once obvious who is the speaker. If the poet, then the passage stands alone, for in no other place does the Second Isaiah use the first person singular of himself, and he habitually keeps himself out of sight. If the Servant, which seems far more probable (see the Chapter on the Servant), there will perhaps be difference of opinion as to the extent of the passage in which he is the speaker. He might, indeed, retain the word to the end of the poem. It is much more likely, however, that his voice ceases with verse 14, and that the poet resumes in verse 15, *where the meter changes*. The Servant's soliloquy, in which he describes Yahwè's miraculous guidance of Israel in the return from Egypt, is all in the 3 | 2 mode; the remainder of the poem, both before and after this homogeneous passage, is 3 | 3.

The main body of the poem is a prayer, of singular fervor and power, uttered in the name of the whole Israelite people. Beginning with verse 15, it continues without interruption to the end. The utterance in verse 16 is especially noteworthy:

> Refrain not, for thou art our father;
> Though Abraham know us no longer,
> And Israel acknowledge us not!
> Thou, Yahwè, art our father.

The prophet had indeed said elsewhere, what in effect he says here, that the children of the One God are in all lands, and that his affection is not confined to any one race. The use of the first person plural, throughout this long passage, has its counterpart in chapter 59.

At first sight the structure of the poem seems unlike that of any other in the group. It may be interesting to compare it in this regard with one of the earlier poems, chapter 42, showing a striking correspondence in the number and order of subjects treated, and also in the metric scheme. (1) A picture of the time of deliverance: 42 : 1–9 and 63 : 1–6. There is a dramatic scene, and a dialogue, in which Yahwè takes part. In the one poem the first words are "Behold my Servant!"; in the other "Who is this?" (2) A lyric passage, a Psalmlike meditation uttered by the Servant: 42 : 10–13 and 63 : 7–10. (3) A passage referring to the flight from Egypt. Yahwè must rescue his people, as in the escape through the Red Sea, leading them so that even the blind will not stumble: 42 : 14–17, corresponding to 63 : 11–14. (4) There is but one God, but his chosen people have been blind and deaf: 42 : 17–22, and thus in substance 63 : 15–64 : 6. (5) Yahwè himself has chastised them severely, allowing them to be despoiled and their cities to be laid waste: 42 : 23–25 and 64 : 7–10. (6) But the rescue must come at last: 43 : 1–7, the same implied in 64 : 11.

As for the metric resemblance: both poems are in the 3 | 3 meter, with a 3 | 2 interlude.

All this tells a plain story. It obviously does not show that the one composition was modelled on the other, nor that the poet had the earlier in mind while he was writing the later; it simply shows how the same mind tends to work in the same way at different times. It may be added that no other Old Testament writer could have produced either poem.

The chapter-division (!) in the middle of the composition, and at a point where not even a slight pause can be tolerated, is one of the most unfortunate of the many performances of the sort. The Hebrew text has suffered an unusual amount of corruption through faulty transcription, but it seems possible to restore the original reading in nearly every case. As the poem left its author's hands, it was certainly one of the supreme achievements of Hebrew literature.

The meter, as has already been said, is 3 | 3, excepting the middle section, 63 : 7–14, which is 3 | 2.

63: 1. What the prophet means by "Edom" is concisely expressed in 1 : 28, where it is prophesied that "the rebellious and wicked and those who forsake Yahwè" shall be utterly destroyed. So also the "Edom" of chapter 34.

Read צֹעֵד, "marching, striding," with Vulg. and the majority of modern scholars. We must also read רָב, participle, and restore עַמִּי

(omitted by a natural haplography) at the end of the verse. For the former compare Jerome's *propugnator* and the parallel passage 34 : 8.

63 : 3-6.   Compare 42 : 13 ff. and 59 : 15*b*-17.

63 : 6.   As shown elsewhere, the word נצחם has a very different meaning here from that in verse 3. The Greek translator, not understanding the poet's play on words, is misled. Not so Syr. and Lat. *Cf.* Ps. 7 : 6*b*.

63 : 7.   The poet loves to introduce an imagined speaker, in this case the Servant of Yahwè. *Cf.* 61 : 10, and see the introduction to chapter 61, as well as that to the present chapter. The *third* "Yahwè" in the verse is probably a later insertion.

63 : 9.   The false verse-division between verses 8 and 9 was incident to the *double reading*, which has long been recognized here, and which the Massorites booked with their usual faithfulness and ingenuity.

Instead of *ṣār* the Greek translator certainly read *ṣîr* (Duhm and others); but this simply means that he had before him our officially manipulated text, recognized the allusion to Ex. 33 : 14, and tried to make good sense. But "envoy" is hardly suitable here. Comparison of other Biblical passages makes it almost certain that the original reading was *zār;* see especially 43 : 12 and Deut. 32 : 12, 16; also Is. 17 : 10; Jer. 2 : 25; 3 : 13; Ps. 44 : 21; 81 : 10. The initial consonant was altered, as the only way of preserving the other current reading: "In all their affliction *He* was afflicted." With *pānîm*, "person," compare not only Ex. 33 : 14, the passage to which the poet directly refers, but also Deut. 4 : 37; II Sam. 17 : 11.

63 : 11-14.   It is perfectly obvious here, as indeed it is elsewhere, that the writer *knew of no 'restoration' from Babylonia.*

63 : 11.   The first word may illustrate the writer's frequent use of the indefinite third person singular, "Then one recalled"; otherwise, we must read ויזכרו מעולם, "Then they remembered, from the olden time," comparing 46 : 9 and Ps. 119 : 52.

Instead of "Moses, his people," the original reading was certainly "the savior (משיע) of his people." What they 'remembered,' as the following verses show in detail, was *the One who rescued them.*

המעלם is the usual combination of alternative readings. Omitting the article: "The one who brought *them* up from the sea *along with* the shepherds of his flock"; evidently the inferior reading.

It is better to retain the plural, "shepherds" (Ps. 77:21), and in the following clause to render "put in *their* midst," the suffix referring to the people.

63:13. The last two words in the verse are shown by the meter to be an exegetical addition (correct, but not necessary).

63:14. Read תְּנַחֵנוּ, with Ewald and many others. "Guidance," not "rest," is what the poet is describing. Duhm's objection to the *gender* of the suffix is not supported by Hebrew usage. The prophet's characteristic fondness for dumb animals, appears here once more.

63:15 f. Verse 15 must end with the words "thy pity and mercy." Verse 16 then begins: אַל תִּתְאַפָּק, "Refrain not!" *Cf.* 64:11 and 42:14. This is so obvious that many readers have made the emendation (or a similar one) independently, as I did.*

In the two verbs of 16a alternative readings are combined: either two perfect tenses, *yĕda'ānū* and *hikkīrānū*, or else imperfect, *yēda'ēnū* and *yakkīrēnū*. The former alternative is the better, and doubtless originally intended, for the particle *kī* is conditional, as frequently elsewhere. The rhyme is probably intentional, also in the following verse; see Chapter XI.

63:17. The "Yahwè" is probably secondary, as in so many other places. The verse reads better without it.

63:18. Read לָמֶה צָעֲרוּ רְשָׁעִים קָדְשֶׁךָ: "Why did evil men desecrate thy sanctuary?" I had myself made this emendation before noticing that it had been made by Marti. The verb here conjectured is known in late Hebrew and Aramaic and is especially common in Syriac. The prophet refers here, in the usual manner, to the destruction of Solomon's temple. "Profanation" exactly as in Ezek. 25:3. See also 64:9 f.

63:19. The four words ירדת מפניך הרים נזלו occur both here and in 64:2. ירדת is required in both passages (in this former instance וירדת, *with the conjunction*, is necessary), the other three words are possible only in 64:2. A mistake in copying, caused by the double occurrence of the verb, in the two very similar contexts, wrought the mischief. The ירדת *without the conjunction*, in 63:19, shows with certainty that the transcriber at this point had his eye on 64:2, and therefore proceeded to add the following words. Instances of the kind are very familiar in the O. T. One

---

* The verb always has this same meaning. In I Sam. 13:12, where the lexicons, translations, and commentaries find a different signification, a *question* is intended: "Could I refrain?"

of the best examples, closely similar to the above, is in II Sam.
6 : 3 f.

The resulting disturbance of the connection between 63 : 19 and
the following verse was presumably what occasioned the false
chapter-division.

64 : 1. A word is evidently missing just before מִים; a noun or
infinitive to correspond to the word at the beginning of the verse,
and governed by the same particle (understood). The metric line,
also, is too short. The most probable conjecture seems to be הֲמוֹן,
not only because this word could easily drop out by accident after
המסים, but still more because the same phrase, "roar of waters"
(meaning the heavenly deeps), is used elsewhere in a passage describing the portents which announce Yahwè's presence. Jer.
10 : 13 (= 51 : 16) tells how the voice of God is heard in the thun-
der-storm: "When he utters his voice, there is *a roar of waters in
the heavens;* he causes the vapors to ascend from the ends of the
earth; he makes lightnings for the rain, and brings forth the wind
out of his treasuries." In our passage the "fire" which causes the
celestial seas to boil is the lightning; they then "thunder" like the
waves of the ocean. This sounds like a bit of genuine folk-lore.

64 : 2. 'In the days of old, when thou didst work thy wonders
for us, we did not have to wait, thou didst *come down!*' There
was doubtless vehemence in the imagined utterance of the last
Hebrew word, as the poet wrote it down.

64 : 3. Here there is a change of tone, and the writer brings
into view another side of the picture. 'And yet,' he says, 'it is
true that we are deaf and blind! There is no other God who thus
cares for his people and rewards those who do right. We have
sinned, and have deserved all our punishment. Nevertheless, *thou
art our father;* pardon us, and restore us to favor!' (verses 7 ff.).

The original reading of the second clause of verse 3 was, obviously, אֵין אֱלֹהִים זוּלָתֶךָ. Under the influence of the preceding
clause עַיִן was written, and the rest followed of necessity. The
"eye hath not seen" is quite impossible here.

The anomalous pointing of יַעֲשֶׂה calls attention, as usual, to
variant readings; in this case, the imperfect tense and the participle. The verb is used absolutely here, as occasionally elsewhere with this preposition, with the meaning "do well by"
(some one).

64 : 4. The first clause should read: פָּגַע אֶת שָׂשׂוֹן עֹשֵׂי צֶדֶק, "Thou
bringest rejoicing to those who do right." *Cf.* especially the Syriac

version. The corrupt reading שֵׁשׁ caused the alteration to עשׂה
(singular number). Notice the succession of sibilants in the line.
The word at the middle of the (massoretic) verse was originally
יִדְלֹכוּן.

The last clause of the verse is also badly corrupt; it should read:
בָּגֹד מֵעוֹלָם וּפִשֹׁעַ, with the poet's favorite use of the infinitive absolute. The graphic variation is very slight.

64 : 5. The punctuation וַנֹּבֶל (impossible here) calls attention
to variant readings. What was originally written was presumably
וַנִּבֹּל, "we have withered away." Jerome's text had וַנִּפֹּל, cecidi-
mus, and וַנָּבֶל (from בלה), "we have wasted away" is also a possible reading.

At the end of the verse יִשָּׂאֵנוּ (probably the original) and נִשָּׂאֵנוּ
are combined.

64 : 6b. וַתְּסַגְּרֵנוּ is perhaps the most likely reading for the last
verb; otherwise, a form from the root מגר.

64 : 9. It is the destruction of Jerusalem by the armies of
Nebuchadrezzar that he has in mind. Cf. Neh. 1 : 3.

At the end of the verse read, with LXX, לִקְלָלָה (so Duhm,
Cheyne, Marti). In the preceding clause we should then probably
read שְׁמָמָה in place of מדבר (cf. the Grk. in 62 : 4). Cf. 43 : 28 especially.

CHAPTER 65

The two poems 65 and 66 are companion pieces, as has always
been recognized. They have in common striking features not appearing elsewhere in the same way. On the other hand, they are
unmistakably of one piece with the preceding poems; written in
the same spirit, presenting the same literary features, developing
the same ideas. Both are so evidently Palestinian in origin that
they came under suspicion of constituting a later accretion to the
'book' as soon as the theory of a 'Second Isaiah' was developed.
No 'prophet of the exile' could have written them.

The question has often been raised whether the initial utterance
of chapter 65 is not a reply to the question with which chapter 64
concluded. This has generally been denied in recent years, because
the true intent of neither poem has been understood. It is only
necessary to point to the superscription, "Threatenings against the

Samaritans" (!), which Cheyne prefixes to his translation of
chapter 65 in the *Polychrome Bible*. To me the fact of the reply
seems quite certain. Here again, as in almost every other part of
the collection, we have clear evidence of the immediate succession
of the poems as they were composed by their author. 65:1 unquestionably begins a new poem; it could not possibly be regarded
as belonging to the preceding. On the other hand, the ending of
such a poem as 63:1–64:11 *with a question* is too significant to
be put aside. The poet, when he wrote the concluding verse, had
already in mind the poem which was to follow. And, in fact, chapter 65 taken as a whole is an answer, a true and satisfying reply,
to the deeply felt interrogation which is the climax of the preceding prayer. Instead of the tirade of a small partisan, we have the
clear vision and fearless exposition of a great theologian. He has
repeatedly answered the same question before, in the preceding
poems of the group, and always in the same way.

The text of the poem, as it has come down to us, is often faulty,
and the restoration sometimes difficult. The meter is generally
3 | 3; the 3 | 2 mode is employed in verses 13 (three lines) and
17–19.

65:1–3. These verses have a close parallel in the first chapter
of Isaiah—a chapter which in style, tone, and underlying conceptions constantly reminds of the work of the Second Isaiah. Compare 1:2–4 with 65:1 f.; 1:29 with 65:3.

65:1. It is better to read שְׁאֵלוּנִי, with Lowth, Grätz, Cheyne,
Marti, and others. The נ, followed by the same letter in the next
word, fell out by accident. Notice the rhyme.

The two verbs in the *nif'al* stem are not to be rendered by the
passive voice. The reference is to the chosen people, Israel, not to
the Gentiles, as in Paul's Epistle to the Romans, 10:20, 21 (where
the LXX rendering is followed).

"To a nation *not called by my name*." The pointing of the Massorites, קֹרָא, passive, gives a much stronger and more characteristic
reading than the active voice קָרָא, rendered by the old versions,
and preferred by many commentators. 48:1 f. (making the correct division of the verses, and observing the irony in verse 1) is
as good a parallel as could be wished.

65 : 2. That a word has fallen out after סורר is evident both
from the rhythmical incompleteness of the line, and from the
LXX, which adds καὶ ἀντιλέγοντα. It is not so evident, at first
sight, *what* Hebrew word has fallen out. But from the Greek
trans. of 50 : 5 (where it is to be observed that both the Greek
and the Syr. translators found the last two clauses transposed),
aided by the comparison of Deut. 21 : 18, 20; Ps. 78 : 8, it is practically certain that the word to be supplied is וּמוֹרֶה (so Duhm,
Klostermann, Cheyne, Marti).

65 : 4. Because of the paronomasia the *kethîv* is to be preferred
to the variant preserved in the *qerē*. Before the last word of the
verse we should expect a preposition; either "in" or "from."

65 : 5. On the construction "I am taboo *for* thee," the suffix
really signifying an *indirect* object, see *Am. Journ. of Sem. Langs.*,
xxxiv (1918), p. 197. The text is correctly transmitted.

65 : 6. There is really a double use of שׁלמתי here. It is first
used absolutely (just as in Jer. 50 : 29, Ps. 62 : 13), then with
direct object.

The verse-division (!) between verses 6 and 7 is an amusing
instance of its kind. One MS. tradition had suffixes of the *third*
person plural in the two successive clauses at this point, the other
(inferior) had the *second* person. When the two were combined in
the customary way, so that neither should be lost, the resulting
disturbance of the sense seemed to make it necessary to make a
full stop between them! We must read the third person in all
three cases, and make verse 6 end with the word "together." The
words "saith the Lord," which follow this, are shown by the meter
to be a later addition.

65 : 7. See the preceding note. The ראשׁנה על at the end of this
verse is a very interesting example of the introduction of a text-
critical note into the text itself. The clause in which it stands
had already been written, in slightly different form, in verse 6. In
the former instance the preposition used was על; in verse 7, on the
contrary, it was אֶל (see the *qerē*). A marginal note opposite the
word אֶל in verse 7 was intended to confirm the traditional reading,
saying ראשׁנה על, *i. e.*, "on the *first* occurrence it was על." This
note found its way into the text, as did similar notes in numerous
other passages in the O. T.* We must read אֶל in verse 7 and omit
ראשׁנה (which, it should be observed, is wanting in the Greek).

* See George Dahl, "The Materials for the History of Dor," in the *Transactions of the Conn. Acad. of Arts and Sciences*, vol. XX (1915), pp. 50 f. *Cf.*
also the marginal note in the Rabbinical Bibles at Lev. 20 : 20 f.

65 : 8. "And one says"; another example of the poet's frequently used indefinite third person singular. *Cf.* 40 : 6; 57 : 14. With the last clause of the verse, "not destroying the whole," *cf.* especially 48 : 9.

65 : 9. I suspect the clause "and my chosen shall inherit her" (*i. e.*, Jerusalem) of being a later addition to the text, as the verse would be better off without it, and the usage which it illustrates is late. There is no ground for verbal emendation.

65 : 11. With the form of the denunciation here compare 57 : 3. There is the same dramatic treatment (but with no such *blaze* of wrath as in the former instance), and again a very noticeable sarcastic play on words.

65 : 14. The form תְּיֵלִילוּ is probably artificial combination of a reading as *piʻel* (as in late Hebrew) with one containing the more common *hifʻil*, in order to preserve both. So in the other cases where this peculiar form occurs.

The division of the verses here is improved by including three more words in verse 14.

65 : 15. "Ye shall leave your name for a curse." *Cf.* Jer. 29 : 22, Ps. 101 : 8, Enoch 5 : 6.

The text of the second clause of the verse is impossible, as the attempted explanations sufficiently show. The first word, originally preceded by the conjunction ו, has been given a false connection with the preceding clause. The main cause of all the trouble seems to have been the accidental corruption of אמר to אדני; compare 47 : 3, where almost exactly the same accident took place and wrought corresponding mischief. For the verb form originally used, אֶתְמֹךְ is suggested both by the word now present in the text and also by the context. The direct object of the verb has the preposition ל here, as in 56 : 8 and 61 : 1. "But *my chosen* I will uphold, saith the Lord." The contrast is now clear, and the following sentences are fully comprehensible. As the apostates (verses 11–14) are to be an execration, so the 'chosen' will be the subject of a formula of blessing.

In the last clause of the verse *two* readings, first person and third person, have been combined. The former is the original: "and *my* servants will *be* called (point the verb as *nifʻal*) by another name."

65 : 16. Again a double reading. The choice is between the relative pronoun *with the imperfect tense* (the form of the text which lay before the Greek translator) and the participle *without*

the relative pronoun, the construction employed in the parallel clause just below.

The "new name" promised at the close of verse 15 is now given; it is אָמֵן, "true, faithful, dependable." * This, the original signification of the old Semitic adjective, has been completely usurped in Hebrew by other adjectives, except in the single use, both liturgical and popular, as a response, "True!" It may have been for that very reason that the prophet chose it for use in this striking passage. The article omitted, as so often in poetry with adjectives used in this general way; compare, *e. g.*, יָשָׁר in Ps. 11:7, Job 23:7, צַדִּיק in Is. 26:7; and similar cases are very numerous.

65:18. Read of course עָרֵי עַד, "eternal cities." *Cf.* especially 40:9; 61:4; 64:9. The dramatic apostrophe to the cities is very characteristic; a fine literary touch.

The אֵת in this verse seems superfluous syntactically, as it certainly is metrically.

65:20. This whole verse is a later addition to the text, perhaps by the same hand that gave us 60:12 and 61:5. It is unmetrical, unpoetical, and altogether unlike the author of these poems. The text of the verse seems to be correct, except that in place of יָמִים in the first clause, יְמוֹת must be read.

65:23 (end). The reading "with them" seems a little weak. אֲתַם, "*I will perfect*," is more probable as the original. The transition to the first person in just this way is frequent in these poems.

65:25. The relation of this to 11:7–9 has yet to be made clear. My own view for many years past has been that the Messianic passages in the earlier part of the book were written under the influence of Second Isaiah. In the present instance of certain literary dependence it seems quite plain to me that the author of chapter 11 was the borrower from 65:25 (expanded by him), not vice versa.

The parenthetical allusion to the serpent's food (!) is another example of the writer's sly humor, which is likely to appear suddenly at any time. His thought often turns to the dumb animals and their fortunes, whether he is imagining heaven or hell (recollect 34:11, 14 ff.). As he thinks here of the improved diet of once dangerous beasts, Gen. 3:14 comes into his mind, and he adds the reflection,

---

* Students of Mohammedan affairs will remember how, according to the popular tradition, the young man Mohammed in Mecca was given the name *al-Amin* ("the trustworthy").

'No change for the old serpent!' Compare the grim parenthesis
in 47 : 14 and 59 : 6. This remark about the serpent undoubtedly
suggested to the author of chapter 11 *verse 8* in that chapter; observe how it stands between the two directly quoted passages.

CHAPTER 66

See the introduction to the preceding. If our 'chapter 66' was
originally the concluding poem of the prophet's sheaf, as is very
likely, we may agree that it was worthy to occupy this position.
It is a poem of which every part is conceived on a large scale, from
the impressive declaration regarding places of worship, with which
it opens, to the everlasting fire at the close. In many respects it
bears a close resemblance to chapter 49, which was said above to
hold the central place, in thought as well as in actual position, in
the great collection.

In speaking of the Day of Judgment, the return home of the
saved, and the future worship of the One God throughout the renovated world, the prophet repeats the phrase "*all mankind.*" One
utterance, in particular, goes beyond any prediction previously
made, when it is said, in verse 21, that even the *priesthood* is not
to be confined to Israel. It must not be supposed that the prophet
thinks here of the Israelitish forms of worship as prescribed also
for the renovated world of the Gentiles. It is quite plain that this
is not the case; see Chapter VII. He says in 43 : 23 that the Hebrew ritual is not essential, and in the first verses of this chapter
that there is no preferred place of worship; preferred, that is, by
the God of Israel and of all the earth. The express teaching of
these passages is in line with all his other utterances. The children
of Israel will retain their ritual, as their own special distinction—
and even here his liberality admits exceptions. The nations will
delight to visit Jerusalem, as modern devotees journey thither, or
to Rome, or to Mecca, while knowing that their worship is acceptable in every other place.

The poet's characteristic 'intermezzo,' verses 6–9, is in this instance a splendid picture of the universal fatherhood of God, with
a definitely Messianic detail. It recalls the scene in 49 : 21, but is
really to be contrasted with it, for there the "children" were the
scattered of Israel; here the prophet has in view the sons of God
from all the races of the world. The passage which is truly parallel
is 45 : 9–12. The "male child" who is brought forth (verse 7) is
the Messiah (Targum, "The King"), whose advent ushers in the

New Age. Thus also the passage is interpreted in the New Testament, Rev. 12 : 5. Can all these 'children' of the Gentile world be born into the family without travail? Can lands and nations be adopted at once (verse 8a)? And this, although Zion bore *her* children only after enduring the birth-pangs (8b)? *Cf*. Matt. 20 : 12. Yahwè's answer, verse 9, is precisely that which he had given in 45 : 11, there also in a definitely Messianic context. He will accomplish his eternal purpose. The Messiah, and through him his brethren of the greater family, are produced in one brief measure of time, '*without* the pains of childbirth' (verse 7).

The text of the poem has suffered damage in numerous places, most of all in verses 17 f.

The meter is generally 3 | 3. The two passages in the 3 | 2 mode are verses 6–9 and verse 11; the meter varied in both cases because of the subject-matter.

---

66 : 1. The *place* of worship is a relatively unimportant matter. Temples (including the temple at Jerusalem) are useful but not essential. A noble utterance, companion to those in 43 : 23 f. and 58 : 1 ff. Compare also 40 : 12, 16.

I suspect the name "Yahwè," in the opening clause, of being a later insertion. The last two words in the verse should be in the construct relation.

66 : 2. After ויהיו the word לי has fallen out by accident. The Greek seems to have read it. *Cf*. 40 : 26. With the second half of the verse *cf*. 57 : 15.

66 : 3. The prophet seems here to have in mind a considerable body of his fellow countrymen, dwellers in Jerusalem and Judea. *Cf*. 59 : 2 ff. especially; also 43 : 22 ff., and the first chapter of the Book of Isaiah, which is in the spirit and tone of Second Isaiah. These renegades still bring the customary offerings to Yahwè (among other gods), but in his eyes it is as though they were performing the most abominable rites.

66 : 5. A very important verse. There is evidence here that the 'enemies of Yahwè' in Israel really had the upper hand at this time. See the note on verse 3.

I suspect that the text in the last clause of the verse has suffered accidental corruption. As it stands, it seems weak. And what is the "word of Yahwè" which the faithful are asked to hear? Cer-

tainly not the two words which now end the verse! Nor, on the
other hand, is the following passage, verses 6 ff., this "word,"
for it is a new division of the poem, with nothing said regarding
either the pious or their wicked brethren. I would conjecture
וְשִׂמַּחְתְּכֶם in place of בשמחתכם. 'Who and where is this Yahwè
of yours, about whose "glory" we have heard so much? Let him
be glorious* for once, so that we may behold.' *But I will make
you rejoice; and they shall be put to shame!* This is a forcible continuation, and quite sufficient as the "word" which was announced.

66 : 7. Omit the conjunction before the last verb in the verse.
It is wanting in Grk. and Lat., and is out of place here. As to the
"male child" (the Messiah) see the introduction to this chapter.
This prediction is expanded by a later writer in 9 : 5 (see also the
note on 65 : 25).

66 : 8. The verb יוּלַד should be pointed as *hof'al*, not *nif'al*.
The meter of the line and the assonance with יָחִל combine to indicate this. With the latter verb *cf.* 51 : 2.

66 : 10. *Cf.* 40 : 1. The subject of the plural imperative, there
left indefinite, is here expressed. In the following verses the
prophet repeats, in varied form, phrases previously used by him
in chapters 49, 51, 58, and 60.

66 : 14. Last clause. We must of course read וְזָעְמוֹ.

66 : 16. The ideas contained in this verse are developed in
some detail in 34 : 2–10, which is a picture of the same great day.

66 : 17 f. The disorder of the text is greater here than at any
other place in Second Isaiah, but a plausible restoration can be
made, as far as the main ideas and their connection are concerned.
Some details will remain obscure.

The three words which now stand at the beginning of verse 18
originally formed the beginning of verse 17. Instead of ומחשבתיהם,
however, the reading was simply חָשַׁבְתִּי, "I have reckoned, taken
into account." The two letters which now form the close of the
word came from the beginning of המתקדשים, the initial מ from the
preceding word; all this because of some transcriber's impression
that "deeds and thoughts" were to be mentioned. But it is too
late to speak of *thoughts* here! The clause, after it had been thus
corrupted, doubtless seemed less disturbing after the "saith

---

* The *qal* stem is much more effective, in its sarcasm, than the *nif'al*, which
many scholars have wished to substitute.

Yahwè" at the end of verse 17 than in its former place, where it appeared to break the connection of thought.

The whole parenthetical passage, including verse 17 and the present beginning of 18, is a striking instance of the way in which the prophet's strong feeling is sometimes manifested. He had intended, we may conjecture, to pass on from verse 16 directly to verse 18 (as emended below); but as he spoke of "the slain of the Lord" he thought of those arch-enemies of God, the renegades who had been false to their birthright, who were even then working such havoc in Israel; and his wrath at them burst out again for a moment, as it had been poured upon them in 57:3 ff. The outburst is by no means foreign to the poem, for it attaches to one of the principal motives, introduced in verses 3 f.

The original beginning of verse 18 has been lost. The connection and the feminine participle באה show with certainty what *noun* originally stood here. My own conjecture, made some twenty years ago, is that the verse began with the words כִּי הָעֵת. This suits the meter perfectly.

I believe that the participle "purifying themselves" (verse 17a) is secondary, a variant reading. The pause in the line should follow the word "gardens." The immediately succeeding phrase is certainly very obscure, and perhaps not correctly transmitted. There seems to be no sufficient ground for changing it.

There is, however, another possibility which should be taken into account. The *qerē*, with its strange *aḥath*(!), seems to give warning of another reading known to the Massorites, though not to us. The Syriac *ḥadh bāthar ḥadh bamĕṣaʻthā*, "one after another (in the midst)," supported by the *alter post alterum* attributed to Symmachus and Theodotion (see Field's *Hexapla*) and the "troop after troop" of the Targum, suggests a reading which originally did not contain "in the midst." If we suppose that the Hebrew clause was אֶחָד אַחַר אֶחָד, *eḥādh aḥar eḥādh*, "one after another," and recollect that the characters ד and ר were precisely identical in the script then employed, it is easy to see that a marginal gloss, אַחַר בְּתוֹך, which could only mean, "The word in the middle is *aḥar*," might produce the text which we now have.

Instead of שׁקֶץ we should doubtless read שֶׁרֶץ, with the Syriac and most commentators.

66:19. "I will put *my* sign"; add the suffix to the noun. It probably fell out by accident occasioned by the letter immediately following. *Cf.* especially 49:22 and 62:10.

We must also read the proper name *Put* instead of *Pul;* and also *Meshech* (the "bow" is an erroneous addition which probably came in under the influence of Jer. 46 : 9, etc.). The list of names is certainly original, quite in the manner of this writer.

66 : 20. "To *me*" instead of "to *Yahwè*" is better suited to context and meter. "Jerusalem" is certainly a gloss, and so also is "the children of Israel" in the second half-verse.

66 : 21. Read "*and* Levites."

66 : 23. Compare 45 : 23 and 56 : 7*b*. The temple *at Jerusalem* is merely figuratively representative, as in all the similar passages. The Gentiles can appear "before Yahwè" at any and every place. The beginning of the verse may be understood thus: "As long as there shall be new moon in its month, and sabbath in its week," that is, forever.

66 : 24. The close of the whole with a picture of the everlasting fire (*cf.* 34 : 9 f.; 47 : 14; 50 : 11; 66 : 16) is as characteristic as the ending of the truly representative poems, chapters 48 and 57. In spite of the prophet's joy in wonderful scenes of restoration, his principal duty was *to warn*, and it is with this note that he begins and ends his great work. The scene here is of course purely figurative, conceived in the same way as Luke 16 : 23–26, where Abraham and Lazarus, looking across the "great gulf," see the rich egotist in torment. The sight brings only horror; and with it recognit on of the justice and mercy of God. Duhm, in his commentary, echoed by Marti, sees here an "Augenweide für die Frommen," and laments the ending of the book with such a "dämonischen Missklang." The fiendish dissonance, however, is the exclusive property of the commentator and his followers; there is no trace nor hint of it in the text.

INDEX

I. Alternative Readings (variant manuscript readings ingeniously combined by the Massorites; see pages 206 f.).

34:6; 35:2, 4 (twice); 40:10; 41:2; 42:15, 20, 22, 24; 43:8 f. (twice), 28; 44:21, 24; 45:2, 8, 24; 46:1; 47:13 (twice); 48:6 (twice), 15; 49:5, 13; 51:19, 21; 52:2, 5, 14; 53:3; 54:3, 9, 16; 55:4, 13; 57:17; 58:5; 59:3, 5, 13; 60:5, 14, 21; 61:10; 63:9, 11, 16; 64:3, 5 (twice); 65:6, 14, 15, 16; 66:17.

II. Aramaic Words (listed in the order of the Hebrew alphabet). The added (K) refers to Kautzsch's *Aramäismen im Alten Testament*.

'*āšaš* (*hithp.*), 46:8.
'*āthā*, 41:25 *al.*
'*att*, 64:4.
bā'aš (?), 50:2.
bāhar (K), 48:10.
gāšaš (?), 59:10.
dāmā, 40:18 *al.*
dā'ak, 43:17.
hēn, "if" (K), 58:3.
zūl (?) (*cf.* Egyptian Aramaic), 46:6.
hātam, 48:9.
hōrīm (K), 34:12.
tippah (?), 48:13.
yāqar (*hithp.*), 61:6 (?).
kĕ'al, 59:18.
kĕrīthūth, 50:1.
maṣṣūth, 41:12.
mā'ăśīm, 59:10 (?).

māthah, 40:22.
nāhar, 60:5.
nāṭal (?), 40:15; 63:9.
nāphaq (*tappīq ?*), 58:10.
sāgadh, sagēdh (K), 44:15 *al.*
sūph (K), 66:17.
sikkēl, 44:25.
'*ūth*, 50:4.
'*āṭaph*, 57:16.
ṣā'ar (*pi'el*), 63:18.
qadrūlh, 50:3.
qippōdh, 34:11, 15.
sālaq, salēq (K), 44:15.
šārābh (?), 35:7; 49:10.

Observe also the preposition *li* introducing the direct object in 53:11; 56:8; 61:1; and 65:15 (as emended).